The Java™ Language Specification

The Java™ Series

Lisa Friendly, Series Editor
Bill Joy, Technical Advisor

The Java™ Programming Language
Ken Arnold and James Gosling
ISBN 0-201-63455-4

The Java™ Language Specification
James Gosling, Bill Joy, and Guy Steele
ISBN 0-201-63451-1

The Java™ Virtual Machine Specification
Tim Lindholm and Frank Yellin
ISBN 0-201-63452-X

The Java™ Application Programming Interface, Volume 1: Core Packages
James Gosling, Frank Yellin, and the Java Team
ISBN 0-201-63453-8

The Java™ Application Programming Interface, Volume 2: Window Toolkit and Applets
James Gosling, Frank Yellin, and the Java Team
ISBN 0-201-63459-7

The Java™ Tutorial: Object-Oriented Programming for the Internet
Mary Campione and Kathy Walrath
ISBN 0-201-63454-6

The Java™ Class Libraries: An Annotated Reference
Patrick Chan and Rosanna Lee
ISBN 0-201-63458-9

The Java™ FAQ: Frequently Asked Questions
Jonni Kanerva
ISBN 0-201-63456-2

The Java™ Language Specification

James Gosling
Bill Joy
Guy Steele

ADDISON-WESLEY
An imprint of Addison Wesley Longman, Inc.

Reading, Massachusetts • Harlow, England • Menlo Park, California
Berkeley, California • Don Mills, Ontario • Sydney
Bonn • Amsterdam • Tokyo • Mexico City

Credits and permissions for quoted material appear in a separate section on page 823.

Text printed on recycled and acid-free paper

ISBN 0-201-63451-1
1 2 3 4 5 6 7 8 9-MA-99989796
First printing, August 1996

"When *I* use a word," Humpty Dumpty said, in rather a scornful tone, "it means just what I choose it to mean—neither more nor less."

"The question is," said Alice, "whether you *can* make words mean so many different things."

"The question is," said Humpty Dumpty, "which is to be master—that's all."

—Lewis Carroll, *Through the Looking Glass*

Table of Contents

Series Foreword

THE Java Series books provide definitive reference documentation for Java programmers and end users. They are written by members of the Java team and published under the auspices of JavaSoft, a Sun Microsystems business. The World-Wide-Web allows Java documentation to be made available over the Internet, either by downloading or as hypertext. Nevertheless, the world-wide interest in Java technology led us to write and publish these books to supplement all of the documentation at our Web site

To learn the latest about the Java Platform and Environment or download the latest Java release, visit our World Wide Web site at `http://java.sun.com`. For updated information about the Java Series, including sample code, errata, and previews of forthcoming books, visit `http://java.sun.com/Series`.

We would like to thank the Corporate and Professional Publishing Group at Addison-Wesley for their partnership in putting together the Series. Our editor Mike Hendrickson and his team have done a superb job of navigating us through the world of publishing. Within Sun Microsystems, the support of James Gosling, Jon Kannegaard, and Bill Joy ensured that this series would have the resources it needed to be successful. In addition to the tremendous effort by individual authors, many members of the JavaSoft team have contributed behind the scenes to bring the highest level of quality and engineering to the books in the Series. A personal note of thanks to my children Christopher and James for putting a positive spin on the many trips to my office during the development of the Series.

Lisa Friendly
Series Editor

Preface

JAVA was originally called Oak, and designed for use in embedded consumer-electronic applications by James Gosling. After several years of experience with the language, and significant contributions by Ed Frank, Patrick Naughton, Jonathan Payne, and Chris Warth it was retargeted to the Internet, renamed Java, and substantially revised to be the language specified here. The final form of the language was defined by James Gosling, Bill Joy, Guy Steele, Richard Tuck, Frank Yellin, and Arthur van Hoff, with help from Graham Hamilton, Tim Lindholm, and many other friends and colleagues.

Java is a general-purpose concurrent class-based object-oriented programming language, specifically designed to have as few implementation dependencies as possible. Java allows application developers to write a program once and then be able to run it everywhere on the Internet.

This book attempts a complete specification of the syntax and semantics of the Java language and the core packages `java.lang`, `java.io`, and `java.util` of its Application Programming Interface. We intend that the behavior of every language construct is specified here, so that all implementations of Java will accept the same programs. Except for timing dependencies or other non-determinisms and given sufficient time and sufficient memory space, a Java program should compute the same result on all machines and in all implementations.

We believe that Java is a mature language, ready for widespread use. Nevertheless, we expect some evolution of the language in the years to come. We intend to manage this evolution in a way that is completely compatible with existing applications. To do this, we intend to make relatively few new versions of the language, and to distinguish each new version with a different filename extension. Java compilers and systems will be able to support the several versions simultannously, with complete compatibility.

Much research and experimentation with Java is already underway. We encourage this work, and will continue to cooperate with external groups to explore improvements to Java. For example, we have already received several interesting proposals for parameterized types. In technically difficult areas, near the state of the art, this kind of research collaboration is essential.

We acknowledge and thank the many people who have contributed to this book through their excellent feedback, assistance and encouragement:

Particularly thorough, careful, and thoughtful reviews of drafts were provided by Tom Cargill, Peter Deutsch, Paul Hilfinger, Masayuki Ida, David Moon, Steven Muchnick, Charles L. Perkins, Chris Van Wyk, Steve Vinoski, Philip Wadler, Daniel Weinreb, and Kenneth Zadeck. We are very grateful for their extraordinary volunteer efforts.

We are also grateful for reviews, questions, comments, and suggestions from Stephen Adams, Bowen Alpern, Glenn Ammons, Leonid Arbuzov, Kim Bruce, Edwin Chan, David Chase, Pavel Curtis, Drew Dean, William Dietz, David Dill, Patrick Dussud, Ed Felten, John Giannandrea, John Gilmore, Charles Gust, Warren Harris, Lee Hasiuk, Mike Hendrickson, Mark Hill, Urs Hoelzle, Roger Hoover, Susan Flynn Hummel, Christopher Jang, Mick Jordan, Mukesh Kacker, Peter Kessler, James Larus, Derek Lieber, Bill McKeeman, Steve Naroff, Evi Nemeth, Robert O'Callahan, Dave Papay, Craig Partridge, Scott Pfeffer, Eric Raymond, Jim Roskind, Jim Russell, William Scherlis, Edith Schonberg, Anthony Scian, Matthew Self, Janice Shepherd, Kathy Stark, Barbara Steele, Rob Strom, William Waite, Greg Weeks, and Bob Wilson. (This list was generated semi-automatically from our E-mail records. We apologize if we have omitted anyone.)

The feedback from all these reviewers was invaluable to us in improving the definition of the Java language as well as the form of the presentation in this book. We thank them for their diligence. Any remaining errors in this book—we hope they are few—are our responsibility and not theirs.

We thank Francesca Freedman and Doug Kramer for assistance with matters of typography and layout. We thank Dan Mills of Adobe Systems Incorporated for assistance in exploring possible choices of typefaces.

Many of our colleagues at Sun Microsystems have helped us in one way or another. Lisa Friendly, our series editor, managed our relationship with Addison-Wesley. Susan Stambaugh managed the distribution of many hundreds of copies of drafts to reviewers. We received valuable assistance and technical advice from Ben Adida, Ole Agesen, Ken Arnold, Rick Cattell, Asmus Freytag, Norm Hardy, Steve Heller, David Hough, Doug Kramer, Nancy Lee, Marianne Mueller, Akira Tanaka, Greg Tarsy, David Ungar, Jim Waldo, Ann Wollrath, Geoff Wyant, and Derek White. We thank Alan Baratz, David Bowen, Mike Clary, John Doerr, Jon Kannegaard, Eric Schmidt, Bob Sproull, Bert Sutherland, and Scott McNealy for leadership and encouragement.

The on-line Bartleby Library of Columbia University, at URL:

`http://www.cc.columbia.edu/acis/bartleby/`

was invaluable to us during the process of researching and verifying many of the quotations that are scattered throughout this book. Here is one example:

They lard their lean books with the fat of others' works.
—Robert Burton (1576–1640)

We are grateful to those who have toiled on Project Bartleby, for saving us a great deal of effort and reawakening our appreciation for the works of Walt Whitman.

We are thankful for the tools and services we had at our disposal in writing this book: telephones, overnight delivery, desktop workstations, laser printers, photocopiers, text formatting and page layout software, fonts, electronic mail, the World Wide Web, and, of course, the Internet. We live in three different states, scattered across a continent, but collaboration with each other and with our reviewers has seemed almost effortless. Kudos to the thousands of people who have worked over the years to make these excellent tools and services work quickly and reliably.

Mike Hendrickson, Katie Duffy, Simone Payment, and Rosa Aimée González of Addison-Wesley were very helpful, encouraging, and patient during the long process of bringing this book to print. We also thank the copy editors.

Rosemary Simpson worked hard, on a very tight schedule, to create the index. We got into the act at the last minute, however; blame us and not her for any jokes you may find hidden therein.

Finally, we are grateful to our families and friends for their love and support during this last, crazy, year.

In their book *The C Programming Language*, Brian Kernighan and Dennis Ritchie said that they felt that the C language "wears well as one's experience with it grows." If you like C, we think you will like Java. We hope that Java, too, wears well for you.

James Gosling
Cupertino, California

Bill Joy
Aspen, Colorado

Guy Steele
Chelmsford, Massachusetts

July, 1996

CHAPTER 1

Introduction

If I have seen further it is by standing upon the shoulders of Giants.
—Sir Isaac Newton

JAVA is a general-purpose, concurrent, class-based, object-oriented language. It is designed to be simple enough that many programmers can achieve fluency in the language. Java is related to C and C++ but is organized rather differently, with a number of aspects of C and C++ omitted and a few ideas from other languages included. Java is intended to be a production language, not a research language, and so, as C. A. R. Hoare suggested in his classic paper on language design, the design of Java has avoided including new and untested features.

Java is strongly typed. This specification clearly distinguishes between the *compile-time errors* that can and must be detected at compile time, and those that occur at run time. Compile time normally consists of translating Java programs into a machine-independent byte-code representation. Run-time activities include loading and linking of the classes needed to execute a program, optional machine code generation and dynamic optimization of the program, and actual program execution.

Java is a relatively high-level language, in that details of the machine representation are not available through the language. It includes automatic storage management, typically using a garbage collector, to avoid the safety problems of explicit deallocation (as in C's `free` or C++'s `delete`). High-performance garbage-collected implementations of Java can have bounded pauses to support systems programming and real-time applications. Java does not include any unsafe constructs, such as array accesses without index checking, since such unsafe constructs would cause a program to behave in an unspecified way.

Java is normally compiled to a bytecoded instruction set and binary format defined in *The Java Virtual Machine Specification* (Addison-Wesley, 1996). Most implementations of Java for general-purpose programming will support the additional packages defined in the series of books under the general title *The Java Application Programming Interface* (Addison-Wesley).

This Java Language Specification is organized as follows:

Chapter 2 describes grammars and the notation used to present the lexical and syntactic grammars for Java.

Chapter 3 describes the lexical structure of Java, which is based on C and C++. Java is written in the Unicode character set. Java supports the writing of Unicode characters on systems that support only ASCII.

Chapter 4 describes Java's types, values, and variables. Java's types are the primitive types and reference types.

The primitive types are defined to be the same on all machines and in all implementations, and are various sizes of two's-complement integers, single- and double-precision IEEE 754 standard floating-point numbers, a `boolean` type, and a Unicode character `char` type. Values of the primitive types do not share state.

Java's reference types are the class types, the interface types, and the array types. The reference types are implemented by dynamically created objects that are either instances of classes or arrays. Many references to each object can exist. All objects (including arrays) support the methods of the standard class `Object`, which is the (single) root of the class hierarchy. A predefined `String` class supports Unicode character strings. Standard classes exist for wrapping primitive values inside of objects.

Variables are typed storage locations. A variable of a primitive type holds a value of that exact primitive type. A variable of a class type can hold a null reference or a reference to an object whose type is that class type or any subclass of that class type. A variable of an interface type can hold a null reference or a reference to an instance of any class that implements the interface. A variable of an array type can hold a null reference or a reference to an array. A variable of class type `Object` can hold a null reference or a reference to any object, whether class instance or array.

Chapter 5 describes Java's conversions and numeric promotions. Conversions change the compile-time type and, sometimes, the value of an expression. Numeric promotions are used to convert the operands of a numeric operator to a common type where an operation can be performed. There are no loopholes in the language; casts on reference types are checked at run time to ensure type safety.

Chapter 6 describes declarations and names, and how to determine what names mean (denote). Java does not require types or their members to be declared before they are used. Declaration order is significant only for local variables and the order of initializers of fields in a class or interface.

Java provides control over the scope of names and supports limitations on external access to members of packages, classes, and interfaces. This helps in writing large programs by distinguishing the implementation of a type from its users and those who extend it. Standard naming conventions that make for more readable programs are described here.

Chapter 7 describes the structure of a Java program, which is organized into packages similar to the modules of Modula. The members of a package are compilation units and subpackages. Compilation units contain type declarations and can import types from other packages to give them short names. Packages have names in a hierarchical namespace, and the Internet domain name system can be used to form unique package names.

Chapter 8 describes Java's classes. The members of classes are fields (variables) and methods. Class variables exist once per class. Class methods operate without reference to a specific object. Instance variables are dynamically created in objects that are instances of classes. Instance methods are invoked on instances of classes; such instances become the current object `this` during their execution, supporting the object-oriented programming style.

Classes support single implementation inheritance, in which the implementation of each class is derived from that of a single superclass, and ultimately from the class `Object`. Variables of a class type can reference an instance of that class or of any subclass of that class, allowing new types to be used with existing methods, polymorphically.

Classes support concurrent programming with `synchronized` methods. Methods declare the checked exceptions that can arise from their execution, which allows compile-time checking to ensure that exceptional conditions are handled. Objects can declare a `finalize` method that will be invoked before the objects are discarded by the garbage collector, allowing the objects to clean up their state.

For simplicity, Java has neither declaration "headers" separate from the implementation of a class nor separate type and class hierarchies.

Although Java does not include parameterized classes, the semantics of arrays are those of a parameterized class with some syntactic sugar. Like the programming language Beta, Java uses a run-time type check when storing references in arrays to ensure complete type safety.

Chapter 9 describes Java's interface types, which declare a set of abstract methods and constants. Classes that are otherwise unrelated can implement the same interface type. A variable of an interface type can contain a reference to any object that implements the interface. Multiple interface inheritance is supported.

Chapter 10 describes Java arrays. Array accesses include bounds checking. Arrays are dynamically created objects and may be assigned to variables of type `Object`. Java supports arrays of arrays, rather than multidimensional arrays.

Chapter 11 describes Java's exceptions, which are nonresuming and fully integrated with the language semantics and concurrency mechanisms. There are three kinds of exceptions: checked exceptions, run-time exceptions, and errors. The compiler ensures that checked exceptions are properly handled by requiring that a method or constructor can result in a checked exception only if it declares it. This provides compile-time checking that exception handlers exist, and aids programming in the large. Most user-defined exceptions should be checked exceptions. Invalid operations in the program detected by the Java Virtual Machine result in run-time exceptions, such as `NullPointerException`. Errors result from failures detected by the virtual machine, such as `OutOfMemoryError`. Most simple programs do not try to handle errors.

Chapter 12 describes activities that occur during execution of a Java program. A Java program is normally stored as binary files representing compiled classes and interfaces. These binary files can be loaded into a Java Virtual Machine, linked to other classes and interfaces, and initialized.

After initialization, class methods and class variables may be used. Some classes may be instantiated to create new objects of the class type. Objects that are class instances also contain an instance of each superclass of the class, and object creation involves recursive creation of these superclass instances.

When an object is no longer referenced, it may be reclaimed by the garbage collector. If an object declares a finalizer, the finalizer is executed before the object is reclaimed to give the object a last chance to clean up resources that would not otherwise be released. When a class is no longer needed, it may be unloaded; if a class finalizer is declared, it is given a chance to clean up first. Objects and classes may be finalized on exit of the Java Virtual Machine.

Chapter 13 describes binary compatibility, specifying the impact of changes to types on other types that use the changed types but have not been recompiled. These considerations are of interest to developers of types that are to be widely distributed, in a continuing series of versions, often through the Internet. Good program development environments automatically recompile dependent code whenever a type is changed, so most programmers need not be concerned about these details.

Chapter 14 describes Java's blocks and statements, which are based on C and C++. Java has no `goto`, but includes labeled `break` and `continue` statements. Unlike C, Java requires `boolean` expressions in control-flow statements, and does not convert types to `boolean` implicitly, in the hope of catching more errors at compile time. A `synchronized` statement provides basic object-level monitor locking. A `try` statement can include `catch` and `finally` clauses to protect against non-local control transfers.

Chapter 15 describes Java's expressions. Java fully specifies the (apparent) order of evaluation of expressions, for increased determinism and portability. Overloaded methods and constructors are resolved at compile time by picking the most specific method or constructor from those which are applicable. Java chooses which method or constructor by using the same basic algorithm used in languages with richer dispatching, such as Lisp's CLOS and Dylan, for the future.

Chapter 16 describes the precise way in which Java ensures that local variables are definitely set before use. While all other variables are automatically initialized to a default value, Java does not automatically initialize local variables in order to avoid masking programming errors.

Chapter 17 describes the semantics of Java threads and locks, which are based on the monitor-based concurrency originally introduced with the Mesa programming language. Java specifies a memory model for shared-memory multiprocessors that supports high-performance implementations.

Chapter 18 describes the facilities for automatically generating documentation from special comments in Java source code.

Chapter 19 presents a LALR(1) syntactic grammar for Java, and describes the differences between this grammar and the expository grammar used in the body of the language specification that precedes it.

Chapters 20 through 22 are the reference manual for the core of the standard Java Application Programming Interface. These packages must be included in all general purpose Java systems.

Chapter 20 describes the package `java.lang`. The types defined in `java.lang` are automatically imported to be available without qualification in all Java programs. They include the primordial class `Object`, which is a superclass of all other classes; classes such as `Integer` and `Float`, which wrap the primitive types inside objects; exceptions and errors defined by the language and the Java Virtual Machine; `Thread` support; metalinguistic classes such as `Class` and `ClassLoader`; and the class `System`, which abstracts the host system.

Chapter 21 describes the package `java.util`, which defines a few basic utility classes, such as a hashtable class and a pseudo-random number generator.

Chapter 22 describes the package `java.io`, which defines basic input/output facilities, including random access files and streams of values of primitive types.

The book concludes with an index, credits for quotations used in the book, and a colophon describing how the book was created.

1.1 Example Programs

Most of the example programs given in the text are ready to be executed by a Java system and are similar in form to:

```
class Test {
    public static void main(String[] args) {
        for (int i = 0; i < args.length; i++)
            System.out.print(i == 0 ? args[i] : " " + args[i]);
        System.out.println();
    }
}
```

On a Sun workstation, this class, stored in the file `Test.java`, can be compiled and executed by giving the commands:

```
javac Test.java
java Test Hello, world.
```

producing the output:

```
Hello, world.
```

1.2 References

Apple Computer. *Dylan™ Reference Manual.* Apple Computer Inc., Cupertino, California. September 29, 1995. See also `http://www.cambridge.apple.com`.

Bobrow, Daniel G., Linda G. DeMichiel, Richard P. Gabriel, Sonya E. Keene, Gregor Kiczales, and David A. Moon. *Common Lisp Object System Specification*, X3J13 Document 88-002R, June 1988; appears as Chapter 28 of Steele, Guy. *Common Lisp: The Language*, 2nd ed. Digital Press, 1990, ISBN 1-55558-041-6, 770–864.

Ellis, Margaret A., and Bjarne Stroustrup. *The Annotated C++ Reference Manual.* Addison-Wesley, Reading, Massachusetts, 1990, reprinted with corrections October 1992, ISBN 0-201-51459-1.

Harbison, Samuel. *Modula-3.* Prentice Hall, Englewood Cliffs, New Jersey, 1992, ISBN 0-13-596396.

Hoare, C. A. R. *Hints on Programming Language Design.* Stanford University Computer Science Department Technical Report No. CS-73-403, December 1973. Reprinted in SIGACT/SIGPLAN Symposium on Principles of Programming Languages. Association for Computing Machinery, New York, October 1973.

IEEE Standard for Binary Floating-Point Arithmetic. ANSI/IEEE Std. 754-1985. Available from Global Engineering Documents, 15 Inverness Way East, Englewood, Colorado 80112-5704 USA; 800-854-7179.

Kernighan, Brian W., and Dennis M. Ritchie. *The C Programming Language,* 2nd ed. Prentice Hall, Englewood Cliffs, New Jersey, 1988, ISBN 0-13-110362-8.

Madsen, Ole Lehrmann, Birger Møller-Pedersen, and Kristen Nygaard. *Object-Oriented Programming in the Beta Programming Language.* Addison-Wesley, Reading, Massachusetts, 1993, ISBN 0-201-62430-3.

Mitchell, James G., William Maybury, and Richard Sweet. *The Mesa Programming Language*, Version 5.0. Xerox PARC, Palo Alto, California, CSL 79-3, April 1979.

Stroustrup, Bjarne. *The C++ Progamming Language,* 2nd ed. Addison-Wesley, Reading, Massachusetts, 1991, reprinted with corrections January 1994, ISBN 0-201-53992-6.

Unicode Consortium, The. *The Unicode Standard: Worldwide Character Encoding, Version 1.0.* Addison-Wesley, Reading, Massachusetts, Volume 1, 1991, ISBN 0-201-56788-1, and Volume 2, 1992, ISBN 0-201-60845-6. (Version 2, forthcoming, 1996.)

CHAPTER 2

Grammars

Grammar, which knows how to control even kings . . .
—Molière, *Les Femmes Savantes* (1672), Act II, scene vi

THIS chapter describes the context-free grammars used in this specification to define the lexical and syntactic structure of a Java program.

2.1 Context-Free Grammars

A *context-free grammar* consists of a number of *productions*. Each production has an abstract symbol called a *nonterminal* as its *left-hand side*, and a sequence of one or more nonterminal and *terminal* symbols as its *right-hand side*. For each grammar, the terminal symbols are drawn from a specified *alphabet*.

Starting from a sentence consisting of a single distinguished nonterminal, called the *goal symbol*, a given context-free grammar specifies a *language*, namely, the infinite set of possible sequences of terminal symbols that can result from repeatedly replacing any nonterminal in the sequence with a right-hand side of a production for which the nonterminal is the left-hand side.

2.2 The Lexical Grammar

A *lexical grammar* for Java is given in §3. This grammar has as its terminal symbols the characters of the Unicode character set. It defines a set of productions, starting from the goal symbol *Input* (§3.5), that describe how sequences of Unicode characters (§3.1) are translated into a sequence of input elements (§3.5).

These input elements, with white space (§3.6) and comments (§3.7) discarded, form the terminal symbols for the syntactic grammar for Java and are called Java *tokens* (§3.5). These tokens are the identifiers (§3.8), keywords (§3.9), literals (§3.10), separators (§3.11), and operators (§3.11) of the Java language.

2.3 The Syntactic Grammar

The *syntactic grammar* for Java is given in Chapters 4, 6–10, 14, and 15. This grammar has Java tokens defined by the lexical grammar as its terminal symbols. It defines a set of productions, starting from the goal symbol *CompilationUnit* (§7.3), that describe how sequences of tokens can form syntactically correct Java programs.

A LALR(1) version of the syntactic grammar is presented in Chapter 19. The grammar in the body of this specification is very similar to the LALR(1) grammar but more readable.

2.4 Grammar Notation

Terminal symbols are shown in `fixed width` font in the productions of the lexical and syntactic grammars, and throughout this specification whenever the text is directly referring to such a terminal symbol. These are to appear in a program exactly as written.

Nonterminal symbols are shown in *italic* type. The definition of a nonterminal is introduced by the name of the nonterminal being defined followed by a colon. One or more alternative right-hand sides for the nonterminal then follow on succeeding lines. For example, the syntactic definition:

IfThenStatement:
    `if (` *Expression* `)` *Statement*

states that the nonterminal *IfThenStatement* represents the token `if`, followed by a left parenthesis token, followed by an *Expression*, followed by a right parenthesis token, followed by a *Statement*. As another example, the syntactic definition:

ArgumentList:
    Argument
    ArgumentList `,` *Argument*

states that an *ArgumentList* may represent either a single *Argument* or an *ArgumentList*, followed by a comma, followed by an *Argument*. This definition of *ArgumentList* is *recursive*, that is to say, it is defined in terms of itself. The result is that an *ArgumentList* may contain any positive number of arguments. Such recursive definitions of nonterminals are common.

The subscripted suffix "*opt*", which may appear after a terminal or nonterminal, indicates an *optional symbol*. The alternative containing the optional symbol actually specifies two right-hand sides, one that omits the optional element and one that includes it. This means that:

BreakStatement:
    `break` *Identifier*$_{opt}$ `;`

is a convenient abbreviation for:

BreakStatement:
    `break ;`
    `break` *Identifier* `;`

and that:

ForStatement:
    `for (` *ForInit*$_{opt}$ `;` *Expression*$_{opt}$ `;` *ForUpdate*$_{opt}$ `)` *Statement*

is a convenient abbreviation for:

ForStatement:
    `for ( ;` *Expression*$_{opt}$ `;` *ForUpdate*$_{opt}$ `)` *Statement*
    `for (` *ForInit* `;` *Expression*$_{opt}$ `;` *ForUpdate*$_{opt}$ `)` *Statement*

which in turn is an abbreviation for:

ForStatement:
    `for ( ; ;` *ForUpdate*$_{opt}$ `)` *Statement*
    `for ( ;` *Expression* `;` *ForUpdate*$_{opt}$ `)` *Statement*
    `for (` *ForInit* `; ;` *ForUpdate*$_{opt}$ `)` *Statement*
    `for (` *ForInit* `;` *Expression* `;` *ForUpdate*$_{opt}$ `)` *Statement*

which in turn is an abbreviation for:

ForStatement:
    `for ( ; ; )` *Statement*
    `for ( ; ;` *ForUpdate* `)` *Statement*
    `for ( ;` *Expression* `; )` *Statement*
    `for ( ;` *Expression* `;` *ForUpdate* `)` *Statement*
    `for (` *ForInit* `; ; )` *Statement*
    `for (` *ForInit* `; ;` *ForUpdate* `)` *Statement*
    `for (` *ForInit* `;` *Expression* `; )` *Statement*
    `for (` *ForInit* `;` *Expression* `;` *ForUpdate* `)` *Statement*

so the nonterminal *ForStatement* actually has eight alternative right-hand sides.

A very long right-hand side may be continued on a second line by substantially indenting this second line, as in:

ConstructorDeclaration:
    ConstructorModifiers$_{opt}$ *ConstructorDeclarator*
                                        Throws$_{opt}$ *ConstructorBody*

which defines one right-hand side for the nonterminal *ConstructorDeclaration*. (This right-hand side is an abbreviation for four alternative right-hand sides, because of the two occurrences of "$_{opt}$".)

When the words "one of" follow the colon in a grammar definition, they signify that each of the terminal symbols on the following line or lines is an alternative definition. For example, the lexical grammar for Java contains the production:

ZeroToThree: one of
```
    0 1 2 3
```

which is merely a convenient abbreviation for:

ZeroToThree:
```
    0
    1
    2
    3
```

When an alternative in a lexical production appears to be a token, it represents the sequence of characters that would make up such a token. Thus, the definition:

BooleanLiteral: one of
```
    true  false
```

in a lexical grammar production is shorthand for:

BooleanLiteral:
```
    t r u e
    f a l s e
```

The right-hand side of a lexical production may specify that certain expansions are not permitted by using the phrase "but not" and then indicating the expansions to be excluded, as in the productions for *InputCharacter* (§3.4) and *Identifier* (§3.8):

InputCharacter:
  UnicodeInputCharacter but not CR or LF

Identifier:
  IdentifierName but not a *Keyword* or *BooleanLiteral* or *NullLiteral*

Finally, a few nonterminal symbols are described by a descriptive phrase in roman type in cases where it would be impractical to list all the alternatives:

RawInputCharacter:
  any Unicode character

CHAPTER 3

Lexical Structure

Lexicographer: A writer of dictionaries, a harmless drudge.
—Samuel Johnson, *Dictionary* (1755)

THIS chapter specifies the lexical structure of Java.

Java programs are written in Unicode (§3.1), but lexical translations are provided (§3.2) so that Unicode escapes (§3.3) can be used to include any Unicode character using only ASCII characters. Line terminators are defined (§3.4) to support the different conventions of existing host systems while maintaining consistent line numbers.

The Unicode characters resulting from the lexical translations are reduced to a sequence of input elements (§3.5), which are white space (§3.6), comments (§3.7), and tokens. The tokens are the identifiers (§3.8), keywords (§3.9), literals (§3.10), separators (§3.11), and operators (§3.12) of the Java syntactic grammar.

3.1 Unicode

Java programs are written using the Unicode character set, version 2.0. Information about this encoding may be found at:

`http://www.unicode.org` and `ftp://unicode.org`

Versions of Java prior to 1.1 used Unicode version 1.1.5 (see *The Unicode Standard: Worldwide Character Encoding* (§1.2) and updates). See §20.5 for a discussion of the differences between Unicode version 1.1.5 and Unicode version 2.0.

Except for comments (§3.7), identifiers, and the contents of character and string literals (§3.10.4, §3.10.5), all input elements (§3.5) in a Java program are formed only from ASCII characters (or Unicode escapes (§3.3) which result in ASCII characters). ASCII (ANSI X3.4) is the American Standard Code for Information Interchange. The first 128 characters of the Unicode character encoding are the ASCII characters.

3.2 Lexical Translations

A raw Unicode character stream is translated into a sequence of Java tokens, using the following three lexical translation steps, which are applied in turn:

1. A translation of Unicode escapes (§3.3) in the raw stream of Unicode characters to the corresponding Unicode character. A Unicode escape of the form `\uxxxx`, where *xxxx* is a hexadecimal value, represents the Unicode character whose encoding is *xxxx*. This translation step allows any Java program to be expressed using only ASCII characters.
2. A translation of the Unicode stream resulting from step 1 into a stream of input characters and line terminators (§3.4).
3. A translation of the stream of input characters and line terminators resulting from step 2 into a sequence of Java input elements (§3.5) which, after white space (§3.6) and comments (§3.7) are discarded, comprise the tokens (§3.5) that are the terminal symbols of the syntactic grammar (§2.3) for Java.

Java always uses the longest possible translation at each step, even if the result does not ultimately make a correct Java program, while another lexical translation would. Thus the input characters `a--b` are tokenized (§3.5) as `a`, `--`, `b`, which is not part of any grammatically correct Java program, even though the tokenization `a`, `-`, `-`, `b` could be part of a grammatically correct Java program.

3.3 Unicode Escapes

Java implementations first recognize *Unicode escapes* in their input, translating the ASCII characters `\u` followed by four hexadecimal digits to the Unicode character with the indicated hexadecimal value, and passing all other characters unchanged. This translation step results in a sequence of Unicode input characters:

UnicodeInputCharacter:
    UnicodeEscape
    RawInputCharacter

UnicodeEscape:
    `\` *UnicodeMarker HexDigit HexDigit HexDigit HexDigit*

UnicodeMarker:
    `u`
    UnicodeMarker `u`

RawInputCharacter:
any Unicode character

HexDigit: one of
`0 1 2 3 4 5 6 7 8 9 a b c d e f A B C D E F`

The \, u, and hexadecimal digits here are all ASCII characters.

In addition to the processing implied by the grammar, for each raw input character that is a backslash \, input processing must consider how many other \ characters contiguously precede it, separating it from a non-\ character or the start of the input stream. If this number is even, then the \ is eligible to begin a Unicode escape; if the number is odd, then the \ is not eligible to begin a Unicode escape. For example, the raw input "\\u2297=\u2297" results in the eleven characters " \ \ u 2 2 9 7 = ⊗ " (\u2297 is the Unicode encoding of the character "⊗").

If an eligible \ is not followed by u, then it is treated as a *RawInputCharacter* and remains part of the escaped Unicode stream. If an eligible \ is followed by u, or more than one u, and the last u is not followed by four hexadecimal digits, then a compile-time error occurs.

The character produced by a Unicode escape does not participate in further Unicode escapes. For example, the raw input \u005cu005a results in the six characters \ u 0 0 5 a, because 005c is the Unicode value for \. It does not result in the character Z, which is Unicode character 005a, because the \ that resulted from the \u005c is not interpreted as the start of a further Unicode escape.

Java specifies a standard way of transforming a Unicode Java program into ASCII that changes a Java program into a form that can be processed by ASCII-based tools. The transformation involves converting any Unicode escapes in the source text of the program to ASCII by adding an extra u—for example, \uxxxx becomes \uuxxxx—while simultaneously converting non-ASCII characters in the source text to a \uxxxx escape containing a single u. This transformed version is equally acceptable to a Java compiler and represents the exact same program. The exact Unicode source can later be restored from this ASCII form by converting each escape sequence where multiple u's are present to a sequence of Unicode characters with one fewer u, while simultaneously converting each escape sequence with a single u to the corresponding single Unicode character.

Java systems should use the \uxxxx notation as an output format to display Unicode characters when a suitable font is not available.

3.4 Line Terminators

Java implementations next divide the sequence of Unicode input characters into lines by recognizing *line terminators*. This definition of lines determines the line numbers produced by a Java compiler or other Java system component. It also specifies the termination of the // form of a comment (§3.7).

LineTerminator:
  the ASCII LF character, also known as "newline"
  the ASCII CR character, also known as "return"
  the ASCII CR character followed by the ASCII LF character

InputCharacter:
  UnicodeInputCharacter but not CR or LF

Lines are terminated by the ASCII characters CR, or LF, or CR LF. The two characters CR immediately followed by LF are counted as one line terminator, not two. The result is a sequence of line terminators and input characters, which are the terminal symbols for the third step in the tokenization process.

3.5 Input Elements and Tokens

The input characters and line terminators that result from escape processing (§3.3) and then input line recognition (§3.4) are reduced to a sequence of *input elements*. Those input elements that are not white space (§3.6) or comments (§3.7) are *tokens*. The tokens are the terminal symbols of the Java syntactic grammar (§2.3).

This process is specified by the following productions:

Input:
  $InputElements_{opt}\ Sub_{opt}$

InputElements:
  InputElement
  InputElements InputElement

InputElement:
  WhiteSpace
  Comment
  Token

Token:
  Identifier
  Keyword
  Literal
  Separator
  Operator

Sub:
the ASCII SUB character, also known as “control-Z”

White space (§3.6) and comments (§3.7) can serve to separate tokens that, if adjacent, might be tokenized in another manner. For example, the ASCII characters `-` and `=` in the input can form the operator token `-=` (§3.12) only if there is no intervening white space or comment.

As a special concession for compatibility with certain operating systems, the ASCII SUB character (`\u001a`, or control-Z) is ignored if it is the last character in the escaped input stream.

Consider two tokens `x` and `y` in the resulting input stream. If `x` precedes `y`, then we say that `x` is *to the left of* `y` and that `y` is *to the right of* `x`. For example, in this simple piece of Java code:

```
class Empty {
}
```

we say that the `}` token is to the right of the `{` token, even though it appears, in this two-dimensional representation on paper, downward and to the left of the `{` token. This convention about the use of the words left and right allows us to speak, for example, of the right-hand operand of a binary operator or of the left-hand side of an assignment.

3.6 White Space

White space is defined as the ASCII space, horizontal tab, and form feed characters, as well as line terminators (§3.4).

WhiteSpace:
the ASCII SP character, also known as “space”
the ASCII HT character, also known as “horizontal tab”
the ASCII FF character, also known as “form feed”
LineTerminator

3.7 Comments

Java defines three kinds of *comments*:

`/*` *text* `*/` A *traditional comment*: all the text from the ASCII characters `/*` to the ASCII characters `*/` is ignored (as in C and C++).

`//` *text*	A *single-line comment*: all the text from the ASCII characters `//` to the end of the line is ignored (as in C++).
`/**` *documentation* `*/`	A *documentation comment*: the text enclosed by the ASCII characters `/**` and `*/` can be processed by a separate tool to prepare automatically generated documentation of the following class, interface, constructor, or member (method or field) declaration. See §18 for a full description of how the supplied *documentation* is processed.

These comments are formally specified by the following productions:

Comment:
    TraditionalComment
    EndOfLineComment
    DocumentationComment

TraditionalComment:
    `/ *` *NotStar CommentTail*

EndOfLineComment:
    `/ /` *CharactersInLine*$_{opt}$ *LineTerminator*

DocumentationComment:
    `/ * *` *CommentTailStar*

CommentTail:
    `*` *CommentTailStar*
    NotStar CommentTail

CommentTailStar:
    `/`
    `*` *CommentTailStar*
    NotStarNotSlash CommentTail

NotStar:
    InputCharacter but not `*`
    LineTerminator

NotStarNotSlash:
    InputCharacter but not `*` or `/`
    LineTerminator

CharactersInLine:
  InputCharacter
  CharactersInLine InputCharacter

These productions imply all of the following properties:

- Comments do not nest.
- `/*` and `*/` have no special meaning in comments that begin with `//`.
- `//` has no special meaning in comments that begin with `/*` or `/**`.

As a result, the text:

```
/* this comment /* // /** ends here: */
```

is a single complete comment.

The lexical grammar implies that comments do not occur within character literals (§3.10.4) or string literals (§3.10.5).

Note that `/**/` is considered to be a documentation comment, while `/* */` (with a space between the asterisks) is a traditional comment.

3.8 Identifiers

An *identifier* is an unlimited-length sequence of *Java letters* and *Java digits*, the first of which must be a Java letter. An identifier cannot have the same spelling (Unicode character sequence) as a keyword (§3.9), Boolean literal (§3.10.3), or the null literal (§3.10.7).

Identifier:
  IdentifierChars but not a *Keyword* or *BooleanLiteral* or *NullLiteral*

IdentifierChars:
  JavaLetter
  IdentifierChars JavaLetterOrDigit

JavaLetter:
  any Unicode character that is a Java letter (see below)

JavaLetterOrDigit:
  any Unicode character that is a Java letter-or-digit (see below)

Letters and digits may be drawn from the entire Unicode character set, which supports most writing scripts in use in the world today, including the large sets for Chinese, Japanese, and Korean. This allows Java programmers to use identifiers in their programs that are written in their native languages.

A Java letter is a character for which the method `Character.isJavaLetter` (§20.5.17) returns `true`. A Java letter-or-digit is a character for which the method `Character.isJavaLetterOrDigit` (§20.5.18) returns `true`.

The Java letters include uppercase and lowercase ASCII Latin letters `A–Z` (`\u0041–\u005a`), and `a–z` (`\u0061–\u007a`), and, for historical reasons, the ASCII underscore (`_`, or `\u005f`) and dollar sign (`$`, or `\u0024`). The `$` character should be used only in mechanically generated Java code or, rarely, to access preexisting names on legacy systems.

The Java digits include the ASCII digits `0-9` (`\u0030–\u0039`).

Two identifiers are the same only if they are identical, that is, have the same Unicode character for each letter or digit.

Identifiers that have the same external appearance may yet be different. For example, the identifiers consisting of the single letters LATIN CAPITAL LETTER A (`A`, `\u0041`), LATIN SMALL LETTER A (`a`, `\u0061`), GREEK CAPITAL LETTER ALPHA (`A`, `\u0391`), and CYRILLIC SMALL LETTER A (`a`, `\u0430`) are all different.

Unicode composite characters are different from the decomposed characters. For example, a LATIN CAPITAL LETTER A ACUTE (`Á`, `\u00c1`) could be considered to be the same as a LATIN CAPITAL LETTER A (`A`, `\u0041`) immediately followed by a NON-SPACING ACUTE (`´`, `\u0301`) when sorting, but these are different in Java identifiers. See *The Unicode Standard*, Volume 1, pages 412ff for details about decomposition, and see pages 626–627 of that work for details about sorting.

Examples of identifiers are:

```
String    i3    αρετη    MAX_VALUE    isLetterOrDigit
```

3.9 Keywords

The following character sequences, formed from ASCII letters, are reserved for use as *keywords* and cannot be used as identifiers (§3.8):

Keyword: one of

```
abstract    default    if            private       throw
boolean     do         implements    protected     throws
break       double     import        public        transient
byte        else       instanceof    return        try
case        extends    int           short         void
catch       final      interface     static        volatile
char        finally    long          super         while
class       float      native        switch
const       for        new           synchronized
continue    goto       package       this
```

The keywords `const` and `goto` are reserved by Java, even though they are not currently used in Java. This may allow a Java compiler to produce better error messages if these C++ keywords incorrectly appear in Java programs.

While `true` and `false` might appear to be keywords, they are technically Boolean literals (§3.10.3). Similarly, while `null` might appear to be a keyword, it is technically the null literal (§3.10.7).

3.10 Literals

A *literal* is the source code representation of a value of a primitive type (§4.2), the `String` type (§4.3.3, §20.12), or the null type (§4.1):

Literal:
    IntegerLiteral
    FloatingPointLiteral
    BooleanLiteral
    CharacterLiteral
    StringLiteral
    NullLiteral

3.10.1 Integer Literals

See §4.2.1 for a general discussion of the integer types and values.

An *integer literal* may be expressed in decimal (base 10), hexadecimal (base 16), or octal (base 8):

IntegerLiteral:
    DecimalIntegerLiteral
    HexIntegerLiteral
    OctalIntegerLiteral

DecimalIntegerLiteral:
    DecimalNumeral IntegerTypeSuffix$_{opt}$

HexIntegerLiteral:
    HexNumeral IntegerTypeSuffix$_{opt}$

OctalIntegerLiteral:
    OctalNumeral IntegerTypeSuffix$_{opt}$

IntegerTypeSuffix: one of
    `l L`

An integer literal is of type `long` if it is suffixed with an ASCII letter `L` or `l` (ell); otherwise it is of type `int` (§4.2.1). The suffix `L` is preferred, because the letter `l` (ell) is often hard to distinguish from the digit `1` (one).

A decimal numeral is either the single ASCII character `0`, representing the integer zero, or consists of an ASCII digit from `1` to `9`, optionally followed by one or more ASCII digits from `0` to `9`, representing a positive integer:

DecimalNumeral:
  `0`
  NonZeroDigit Digits$_{opt}$

Digits:
  Digit
  Digits Digit

Digit:
  `0`
  NonZeroDigit

NonZeroDigit: one of
  `1 2 3 4 5 6 7 8 9`

A hexadecimal numeral consists of the leading ASCII characters `0x` or `0X` followed by one or more ASCII hexadecimal digits and can represent a positive, zero, or negative integer. Hexadecimal digits with values 10 through 15 are represented by the ASCII letters `a` through `f` or `A` through `F`, respectively; each letter used as a hexadecimal digit may be uppercase or lowercase.

HexNumeral:
  `0 x` *HexDigit*
  `0 X` *HexDigit*
  HexNumeral HexDigit

The following production from §3.3 is repeated here for clarity:

HexDigit: one of
  `0 1 2 3 4 5 6 7 8 9 a b c d e f A B C D E F`

An octal numeral consists of an ASCII digit `0` followed by one or more of the ASCII digits `0` through `7` and can represent a positive, zero, or negative integer.

OctalNumeral:
  `0` *OctalDigit*
  OctalNumeral OctalDigit

OctalDigit: one of
  `0 1 2 3 4 5 6 7`

Note that octal numerals are always consist of two or more digits; `0` is always considered to be a decimal numeral—not that it matters much in practice, for the numerals `0`, `00`, and `0x0` all represent exactly the same integer value.

The largest decimal literal of type `int` is `2147483648` (2^{31}). All decimal literals from `0` to `2147483647` may appear anywhere an `int` literal may appear, but the literal `2147483648` may appear only as the operand of the unary negation operator `-`.

The largest positive hexadecimal and octal literals of type `int` are `0x7fffffff` and `017777777777`, respectively, which equal `2147483647` ($2^{31}-1$). The most negative hexadecimal and octal literals of type `int` are `0x80000000` and `020000000000`, respectively, each of which represents the decimal value `-2147483648` (-2^{31}). The hexadecimal and octal literals `0xffffffff` and `037777777777`, respectively, represent the decimal value `-1`.

See also `Integer.MIN_VALUE` (§20.7.1) and `Integer.MAX_VALUE` (§20.7.2).

A compile-time error occurs if a decimal literal of type `int` is larger than `2147483648` (2^{31}), or if the literal `2147483648` appears anywhere other than as the operand of the unary `-` operator, or if a hexadecimal or octal `int` literal does not fit in 32 bits.

Examples of `int` literals:

```
0     2     0372     0xDadaCafe     1996   0x00FF00FF
```

The largest decimal literal of type `long` is `9223372036854775808L` (2^{63}). All decimal literals from `0L` to `9223372036854775807L` may appear anywhere a `long` literal may appear, but the literal `9223372036854775808L` may appear only as the operand of the unary negation operator `-`.

The largest positive hexadecimal and octal literals of type `long` are `0x7fffffffffffffffL` and `0777777777777777777777L`, respectively, which equal `9223372036854775807L` ($2^{63}-1$). The literals `0x8000000000000000L` and `01000000000000000000000L` are the most negative `long` hexadecimal and octal literals, respectively. Each has the decimal value `-9223372036854775808L` (-2^{63}). The hexadecimal and octal literals `0xffffffffffffffffL` and `01777777777777777777777L`, respectively, represent the decimal value `-1L`.

See also `Long.MIN_VALUE` (§20.8.1) and `Long.MAX_VALUE` (§20.8.2).

A compile-time error occurs if a decimal literal of type `long` is larger than `9223372036854775808L` (2^{63}), or if the literal `9223372036854775808L` appears anywhere other than as the operand of the unary `-` operator, or if a hexadecimal or octal `long` literal does not fit in 64 bits.

Examples of `long` literals:

```
0l     0777L     0x100000000L     2147483648L     0xC0B0L
```

3.10.2 Floating-Point Literals

See §4.2.3 for a general discussion of the floating-point types and values.

A *floating-point literal* has the following parts: a whole-number part, a decimal point (represented by an ASCII period character), a fractional part, an exponent, and a type suffix. The exponent, if present, is indicated by the ASCII letter `e` or `E` followed by an optionally signed integer.

At least one digit, in either the whole number or the fraction part, and either a decimal point, an exponent, or a float type suffix are required. All other parts are optional.

A floating-point literal is of type `float` if it is suffixed with an ASCII letter `F` or `f`; otherwise its type is `double` and it can optionally be suffixed with an ASCII letter `D` or `d`.

FloatingPointLiteral:
  Digits `.` $Digits_{opt}$ $ExponentPart_{opt}$ $FloatTypeSuffix_{opt}$
  `.` *Digits* $ExponentPart_{opt}$ $FloatTypeSuffix_{opt}$
  Digits ExponentPart $FloatTypeSuffix_{opt}$
  Digits $ExponentPart_{opt}$ *FloatTypeSuffix*

ExponentPart:
  ExponentIndicator SignedInteger

ExponentIndicator: one of
  `e E`

SignedInteger:
  $Sign_{opt}$ *Digits*

Sign: one of
  `+ -`

FloatTypeSuffix: one of
  `f F d D`

The Java types `float` and `double` are IEEE 754 32-bit single-precision and 64-bit double-precision binary floating-point values, respectively.

The details of proper input conversion from a Unicode string representation of a floating-point number to the internal IEEE 754 binary floating-point representation are described for the methods `valueOf` of class `Float` (§20.9.17) and class `Double` (§20.10.16) of the package `java.lang`.

The largest positive finite `float` literal is `3.40282347e+38f`. The smallest positive finite nonzero literal of type `float` is `1.40239846e-45f`. The largest positive finite `double` literal is `1.79769313486231570e+308`. The smallest positive finite nonzero literal of type `double` is `4.94065645841246544e-324`.

See `Float.MIN_VALUE` (§20.9.1) and `Float.MAX_VALUE` (§20.9.2); see also `Double.MIN_VALUE` (§20.10.1) and `Double.MAX_VALUE` (§20.10.2).

A compile-time error occurs if a nonzero floating-point literal is too large, so that on rounded conversion to its internal representation it becomes an IEEE 754 infinity. A Java program can represent infinities without producing a compile-time error by using constant expressions such as `1f/0f` or `-1d/0d` or by using the predefined constants `POSITIVE_INFINITY` and `NEGATIVE_INFINITY` of the classes `Float` (§20.9) and `Double` (§20.10).

A compile-time error occurs if a nonzero floating-point literal is too small, so that, on rounded conversion to its internal representation, it becomes a zero. A compile-time error does not occur if a nonzero floating-point literal has a small value that, on rounded conversion to its internal representation, becomes a non-zero denormalized number.

Predefined constants representing Not-a-Number values are defined in the classes `Float` and `Double` as `Float.NaN` (§20.9.5) and `Double.NaN` (§20.10.5).

Examples of `float` literals:

```
1e1f    2.f    .3f   0f   3.14f    6.022137e+23f
```

Examples of `double` literals:

```
1e1     2.     .3    0.0  3.14     1e-9d    1e137
```

There is no provision for expressing floating-point literals in other than decimal radix. However, method `intBitsToFloat` (§20.9.23) of class `Float` and method `longBitsToDouble` (§20.10.22) of class `Double` provide a way to express floating-point values in terms of hexadecimal or octal integer literals. For example, the value of:

```
Double.longBitsToDouble(0x400921FB54442D18L)
```

is equal to the value of `Math.PI` (§20.11.2).

3.10.3 Boolean Literals

The `boolean` type has two values, represented by the literals `true` and `false`, formed from ASCII letters.

A *boolean literal* is always of type `boolean`.

BooleanLiteral: one of
```
    true false
```

3.10.4 Character Literals

A *character literal* is expressed as a character or an escape sequence, enclosed in ASCII single quotes. (The single-quote, or apostrophe, character is `\u0027`.)

A character literal is always of type `char`.

CharacterLiteral:
  `'` *SingleCharacter* `'`
  `'` *EscapeSequence* `'`

SingleCharacter:
  InputCharacter but not `'` or `\`

The escape sequences are described in §3.10.6.

As specified in §3.4, the characters CR and LF are never an *InputCharacter*; they are recognized as constituting a *LineTerminator.*

It is a compile-time error for the character following the *SingleCharacter* or *EscapeSequence* to be other than a `'`.

It is a compile-time error for a line terminator to appear after the opening `'` and before the closing `'`.

The following are examples of `char` literals:

```
'a'
'%'
'\t'
'\\'
'\''
'\u03a9'
'\uFFFF'
'\177'
'Ω'
'⊗'
```

Because Unicode escapes are processed very early, it is not correct to write `'\u000a'` for a character literal whose value is linefeed (LF); the Unicode escape `\u000a` is transformed into an actual linefeed in translation step 1 (§3.3) and the linefeed becomes a *LineTerminator* in step 2 (§3.4), and so the character literal is not valid in step 3. Instead, one should use the escape sequence `'\n'` (§3.10.6). Similarly, it is not correct to write `'\u000d'` for a character literal whose value is carriage return (CR). Instead, use `'\r'`.

In C and C++, a character literal may contain representations of more than one character, but the value of such a character literal is implementation-defined. In Java, a character literal always represents exactly one character.

3.10.5 String Literals

A *string literal* consists of zero or more characters enclosed in double quotes. Each character may be represented by an escape sequence.

A string literal is always of type `String` (§4.3.3, §20.12). A string literal always refers to the same instance (§4.3.1) of class `String`.

StringLiteral:
    " *StringCharacters*$_{opt}$ "

StringCharacters:
    StringCharacter
    StringCharacters StringCharacter

StringCharacter:
    InputCharacter but not " or \
    EscapeSequence

The escape sequences are described in §3.10.6.

As specified in §3.4, neither of the characters CR and LF is ever considered to be an *InputCharacter*; each is recognized as constituting a *LineTerminator.*

It is a compile-time error for a line terminator to appear after the opening " and before the closing matching ". A long string literal can always be broken up into shorter pieces and written as a (possibly parenthesized) expression using the string concatenation operator + (§15.17.1).

The following are examples of string literals:

```
""                      // the empty string
"\""                    // a string containing " alone
"This is a string"      // a string containing 16 characters

"This is a " +          // actually a string-valued constant expression,
   "two-line string"    //       formed from two string literals
```

Because Unicode escapes are processed very early, it is not correct to write `"\u000a"` for a string literal containing a single linefeed (LF); the Unicode escape `\u000a` is transformed into an actual linefeed in translation step 1 (§3.3) and the linefeed becomes a *LineTerminator* in step 2 (§3.4), and so the string literal is not valid in step 3. Instead, one should write `"\n"` (§3.10.6). Similarly, it is not correct to write `"\u000d"` for a string literal containing a single carriage return (CR). Instead use `"\r"`.

Each string literal is a reference (§4.3) to an instance (§4.3.1, §12.5) of class `String` (§4.3.3, §20.12). `String` objects have a constant value. String literals—or, more generally, strings that are the values of constant expressions (§15.27)—are “interned” so as to share unique instances, using the method `String.intern` (§20.12.47).

Thus, the test program consisting of the compilation unit (§7.3):

```
package testPackage;

class Test {
    public static void main(String[] args) {
        String hello = "Hello", lo = "lo";
        System.out.print((hello == "Hello") + " ");
        System.out.print((Other.hello == hello) + " ");
        System.out.print((other.Other.hello == hello) + " ");
        System.out.print((hello == ("Hel"+"lo")) + " ");
        System.out.print((hello == ("Hel"+lo)) + " ");
        System.out.println(hello == ("Hel"+lo).intern());
    }
}

class Other { static String hello = "Hello"; }
```

and the compilation unit:

```
package other;

public class Other { static String hello = "Hello"; }
```

produces the output:

```
true true true true false true
```

This example illustrates six points:

- Literal strings within the same class (§8) in the same package (§7) represent references to the same `String` object (§4.3.1).
- Literal strings within different classes in the same package represent references to the same `String` object.
- Literal strings within different classes in different packages likewise represent references to the same `String` object.
- Strings computed by constant expressions (§15.27) are computed at compile time and then treated as if they were literals.
- Strings computed at run time are newly created and therefore distinct.
- The result of explicitly interning a computed string is the same string as any pre-existing literal string with the same contents.

3.10.6 Escape Sequences for Character and String Literals

The character and string *escape sequences* allow for the representation of some nongraphic characters as well as the single quote, double quote, and backslash characters in character literals (§3.10.4) and string literals (§3.10.5).

EscapeSequence:
```
\ b            /* \u0008: backspace BS */
\ t            /* \u0009: horizontal tab HT */
\ n            /* \u000a: linefeed LF */
\ f            /* \u000c: form feed FF */
\ r            /* \u000d: carriage return CR */
\ "            /* \u0022: double quote "  */
\ '            /* \u0027: single quote '  */
\ \            /* \u005c: backslash \ */
OctalEscape    /* \u0000 to \u00ff: from octal value */
```

OctalEscape:
 \ *OctalDigit*
 \ *OctalDigit OctalDigit*
 \ *ZeroToThree OctalDigit OctalDigit*

OctalDigit: one of
 `0 1 2 3 4 5 6 7`

ZeroToThree: one of
 `0 1 2 3`

It is a compile-time error if the character following a backslash in an escape is not an ASCII `b`, `t`, `n`, `f`, `r`, `"`, `'`, `\`, `0`, `1`, `2`, `3`, `4`, `5`, `6`, or `7`. The Unicode escape `\u` is processed earlier (§3.3). (Octal escapes are provided for compatibility with C, but can express only Unicode values `\u0000` through `\u00FF`, so Unicode escapes are usually preferred.)

3.10.7 The Null Literal

The null type has one value, the null reference, represented by the literal `null`, which is formed from ASCII characters. A *null literal* is always of the null type.

NullLiteral:
 `null`

3.11 Separators

The following nine ASCII characters are the Java *separators* (punctuators):

Separator: one of
```
(    )    {    }    [    ]    ;    ,    .
```

3.12 Operators

The following 37 tokens are the Java *operators*, formed from ASCII characters:

Operator: one of

```
=    >    <    !    ~    ?    :
==   <=   >=   !=   &&   ||   ++   --
+    -    *    /    &    |    ^    %    <<   >>   >>>
+=   -=   *=   /=   &=   |=   ^=   %=   <<=  >>=  >>>=
```

Give her no token but stones; for she's as hard as steel.
—William Shakespeare, *Two Gentlemen of Verona*, Act I, scene i

These lords are visited; you are not free;
For the Lord's tokens on you do I see.
—William Shakespeare, *Love's Labour's Lost*, Act V, scene ii

Thou, thou, Lysander, thou hast given her rhymes,
And interchanged love-tokens with my child.
—William Shakespeare, *A Midsummer Night's Dream*, Act I, scene i

Here is a letter from Queen Hecuba,
A token from her daughter . . .
—William Shakespeare, *Troilus and Cressida*, Act V, scene i

Are there no other tokens . . . ?
—William Shakespeare, *Measure for Measure*, Act IV, scene i

Hush, my darling, don't fear, my darling, the lion sleeps tonight.
—Luigi Creatore, George David Weiss, and Hugo E. Peretti

CHAPTER 4

Types, Values, and Variables

I send no agent or medium,
offer no representative of value,
but offer the value itself.
—Walt Whitman, *Carol of Occupations* (1855),
in *Leaves of Grass*

JAVA is a *strongly typed* language, which means that every variable and every expression has a type that is known at compile time. Types limit the values that a variable (§4.5) can hold or that an expression can produce, limit the operations supported on those values, and determine the meaning of the operations. Strong typing helps detect errors at compile time.

The types of the Java language are divided into two categories: primitive types and reference types. The primitive types (§4.2) are the `boolean` type and the numeric types. The numeric types are the integral types `byte`, `short`, `int`, `long`, and `char`, and the floating-point types `float` and `double`. The reference types (§4.3) are class types, interface types, and array types. There is also a special null type. An object (§4.3.1) in Java is a dynamically created instance of a class type or a dynamically created array. The values of a reference type are references to objects. All objects, including arrays, support the methods of class `Object` (§4.3.2). String literals are represented by `String` objects (§4.3.3).

Types are the same (§4.3.4) if they have the same fully qualified names and are loaded by the same class loader. Names of types are used (§4.4) in declarations, in casts, in class instance creation expressions, in array creation expressions, and in `instanceof` operator expressions.

A variable (§4.5) is a storage location. A variable of a primitive type always holds a value of that exact type. A variable of a class type *T* can hold a null reference or a reference to an instance of class *T* or of any class that is a subclass of *T*. A variable of an interface type can hold a null reference or a reference to any instance of any class that implements the interface. If *T* is a primitive type, then a variable of type "array of *T*" can hold a null reference or a reference to any array of type "array of `T`"; if `T` is a reference type, then a variable of type "array of `T`" can hold a null reference or a reference to any array of type "array of `S`" such that type `S` is assignable (§5.2) to type `T`. A variable of type `Object` can hold a null reference or a reference to any object, whether class instance or array.

4.1 The Kinds of Types and Values

There are two kinds of *types* in Java: primitive types (§4.2) and reference types (§4.3). There are, correspondingly, two kinds of data values that can be stored in variables, passed as arguments, returned by methods, and operated on: primitive values (§4.2) and reference values (§4.3).

Type:
    PrimitiveType
    ReferenceType

There is also a special *null type*, the type of the expression `null`, which has no name. Because the null type has no name, it is impossible to declare a variable of the null type or to cast to the null type. The null reference is the only possible value of an expression of null type. The null reference can always be cast to any reference type. In practice, the Java programmer can ignore the null type and just pretend that `null` is merely a special literal that can be of any reference type.

4.2 Primitive Types and Values

A *primitive type* is predefined by the Java language and named by its reserved keyword (§3.9):

PrimitiveType:
    NumericType
    `boolean`

NumericType:
    IntegralType
    FloatingPointType

IntegralType: one of
    `byte short int long char`

FloatingPointType: one of
    `float double`

Primitive values do not share state with other primitive values. A variable whose type is a primitive type always holds a primitive value of that same type. The value of a variable of primitive type can be changed only by assignment operations on that variable.

The *numeric types* are the integral types and the floating-point types.

The *integral types* are `byte`, `short`, `int`, and `long`, whose values are 8-bit, 16-bit, 32-bit and 64-bit signed two's-complement integers, respectively, and `char`, whose values are 16-bit unsigned integers representing Unicode characters.

The *floating-point types* are `float`, whose values are 32-bit IEEE 754 floating-point numbers, and `double`, whose values are 64-bit IEEE 754 floating-point numbers.

The `boolean` type has exactly two values: `true` and `false`.

4.2.1 Integral Types and Values

The values of the integral types are integers in the following ranges:

- For `byte`, from –128 to 127, inclusive
- For `short`, from –32768 to 32767, inclusive
- For `int`, from –2147483648 to 2147483647, inclusive
- For `long`, from –9223372036854775808 to 9223372036854775807, inclusive
- For `char`, from `'\u0000'` to `'\uffff'` inclusive, that is, from 0 to 65535

4.2.2 Integer Operations

Java provides a number of operators that act on integral values:

- The comparison operators, which result in a value of type `boolean`:
  - The numerical comparison operators <, <=, >, and >= (§15.19.1)
  - The numerical equality operators == and `!=` (§15.20.1)
- The numerical operators, which result in a value of type `int` or `long`:
  - The unary plus and minus operators `+` and `-` (§15.14.3, §15.14.4)
  - The multiplicative operators `*`, `/`, and `%` (§15.16)
  - The additive operators `+` and `-` (§15.17.2)
  - The increment operator `++`, both prefix (§15.14.1) and postfix (§15.13.2)
  - The decrement operator `--`, both prefix (§15.14.2) and postfix (§15.13.3)

  - The signed and unsigned shift operators <<, >>, and >>> (§15.18)
  - The bitwise complement operator ~ (§15.14.5)
  - The integer bitwise operators &, |, and ^ (§15.21.1)
- The conditional operator ? : (§15.24)
- The cast operator, which can convert from an integral value to a value of any specified numeric type (§5.4, §15.15)
- The string concatenation operator + (§15.17.1), which, when given a `String` operand and an integral operand, will convert the integral operand to a `String` representing its value in decimal form, and then produce a newly created `String` that is the concatenation of the two strings

Other useful constructors, methods, and constants are predefined in the classes `Integer` (§20.7), `Long` (§20.8), and `Character` (§20.5).

If an integer operator other than a shift operator has at least one operand of type `long`, then the operation is carried out using 64-bit precision, and the result of the numerical operator is of type `long`. If the other operand is not `long`, it is first widened (§5.1.2) to type `long` by numeric promotion (§5.6). Otherwise, the operation is carried out using 32-bit precision, and the result of the numerical operator is of type `int`. If either operand is not an `int`, it is first widened to type `int` by numeric promotion.

The built-in integer operators do not indicate overflow or underflow in any way. The only numeric operators that can throw an exception (§11) are the integer divide operator `/` (§15.16.2) and the integer remainder operator `%` (§15.16.3), which throw an `ArithmeticException` if the right-hand operand is zero.

The example:

```
class Test {
    public static void main(String[] args) {
        int i = 1000000;
        System.out.println(i * i);
        long l = i;
        System.out.println(l * l);
        System.out.println(20296 / (l - i));
    }
}
```

produces the output:

```
-727379968
1000000000000
```

and then encounters an `ArithmeticException` in the division by `l - i`, because `l - i` is zero. The first multiplication is performed in 32-bit precision, whereas the second multiplication is a `long` multiplication. The value `-727379968` is the decimal value of the low 32 bits of the mathematical result, `1000000000000`, which is a value too large for type `int`.

Any value of any integral type may be cast to or from any numeric type. There are no casts between integral types and the type `boolean`.

4.2.3 Floating-Point Types and Values

The floating-point types are `float` and `double`, representing the single-precision 32-bit and double-precision 64-bit format IEEE 754 values and operations as specified in *IEEE Standard for Binary Floating-Point Arithmetic*, ANSI/IEEE Standard 754-1985 (IEEE, New York).

The IEEE 754 standard includes not only positive and negative sign-magnitude numbers, but also positive and negative zeros, positive and negative *infinities*, and a special *Not-a-Number* (hereafter abbreviated NaN). The NaN value is used to represent the result of certain operations such as dividing zero by zero. NaN constants of both `float` and `double` type are predefined as `Float.NaN` (§20.9.5) and `Double.NaN` (§20.10.5).

The finite nonzero values of type `float` are of the form $s \cdot m \cdot 2^e$, where s is +1 or –1, m is a positive integer less than 2^{24}, and e is an integer between –149 and 104, inclusive. Values of that form such that m is positive but less than 2^{23} and e is equal to –149 are said to be *denormalized.*

The finite nonzero values of type `double` are of the form $s \cdot m \cdot 2^e$, where s is +1 or –1, m is a positive integer less than 2^{53}, and e is an integer between –1075 and 970, inclusive. Values of that form such that m is positive but less than 2^{52} and e is equal to –1075 are said to be *denormalized.*

Except for NaN, floating-point values are *ordered*; arranged from smallest to largest, they are negative infinity, negative finite nonzero values, negative zero, positive zero, positive finite nonzero values, and positive infinity.

Positive zero and negative zero compare equal; thus the result of the expression `0.0==-0.0` is `true` and the result of `0.0>-0.0` is `false`. But other operations can distinguish positive and negative zero; for example, `1.0/0.0` has the value positive infinity, while the value of `1.0/-0.0` is negative infinity. The operations `Math.min` and `Math.max` also distinguish positive zero and negative zero.

NaN is *unordered*, so the numerical comparison operators `<`, `<=`, `>`, and `>=` return `false` if either or both operands are NaN (§15.19.1). The equality operator `==` returns `false` if either operand is NaN, and the inequality operator `!=` returns `true` if either operand is NaN (§15.20.1). In particular, `x!=x` is `true` if and only if `x` is NaN, and `(x<y) == !(x>=y)` will be `false` if `x` or `y` is NaN.

Any value of a floating-point type may be cast to or from any numeric type. There are no casts between floating-point types and the type `boolean`.

4.2.4 Floating-Point Operations

Java provides a number of operators that act on floating-point values:

- The comparison operators, which result in a value of type `boolean`:
  - The numerical comparison operators `<`, `<=`, `>`, and `>=` (§15.19.1)
  - The numerical equality operators `==` and `!=` (§15.20.1)
- The numerical operators, which result in a value of type `float` or `double`:
  - The unary plus and minus operators `+` and `-` (§15.14.3, §15.14.4)
  - The multiplicative operators `*`, `/`, and `%` (§15.16)
  - The additive operators `+` and `-` (§15.17.2)
  - The increment operator `++`, both prefix (§15.14.1) and postfix (§15.13.2)
  - The decrement operator `--`, both prefix (§15.14.2) and postfix (§15.13.3)
- The conditional operator `? :` (§15.24)
- The cast operator, which can convert from a floating-point value to a value of any specified numeric type (§5.4, §15.15)
- The string concatenation operator `+` (§15.17.1), which, when given a `String` operand and a floating-point operand, will convert the floating-point operand to a `String` representing its value in decimal form (without information loss), and then produce a newly created `String` by concatenating the two strings

Other useful constructors, methods, and constants are predefined in the classes `Float` (§20.9), `Double` (§20.10), and `Math` (§20.11).

If at least one of the operands to a binary operator is of floating-point type, then the operation is a floating-point operation, even if the other is integral.

If at least one of the operands to a numerical operator is of type `double`, then the operation is carried out using 64-bit floating-point arithmetic, and the result of the numerical operator is a value of type `double`. (If the other operand is not a `double`, it is first widened to type `double` by numeric promotion (§5.6).) Otherwise, the operation is carried out using 32-bit floating-point arithmetic, and the result of the numerical operator is a value of type `float`. If the other operand is not a `float`, it is first widened to type `float` by numeric promotion.

Operators on floating-point numbers behave exactly as specified by IEEE 754. In particular, Java requires support of IEEE 754 *denormalized* floating-point numbers and *gradual underflow*, which make it easier to prove desirable properties of particular numerical algorithms. Floating-point operations in Java do not "flush to zero" if the calculated result is a denormalized number.

Java requires that floating-point arithmetic behave as if every floating-point operator rounded its floating-point result to the result precision. *Inexact* results must be rounded to the representable value nearest to the infinitely precise result; if the two nearest representable values are equally near, the one with its least significant bit zero is chosen. This is the IEEE 754 standard's default rounding mode known as *round to nearest*.

Java uses *round toward zero* when converting a floating value to an integer (§5.1.3), which acts, in this case, as though the number were truncated, discarding the mantissa bits. Rounding toward zero chooses at its result the format's value closest to and no greater in magnitude than the infinitely precise result.

Java floating-point operators produce no exceptions (§11). An operation that overflows produces a signed infinity, an operation that underflows produces a signed zero, and an operation that has no mathematically definite result produces NaN. All numeric operations with NaN as an operand produce NaN as a result. As has already been described, NaN is unordered, so a numeric comparison operation involving one or two NaNs returns `false` and any `!=` comparison involving NaN returns `true`, including `x!=x` when `x` is NaN.

The example program:

```
class Test {
    public static void main(String[] args) {
        // An example of overflow:
        double d = 1e308;
        System.out.print("overflow produces infinity: ");
        System.out.println(d + "*10==" + d*10);

        // An example of gradual underflow:
        d = 1e-305 * Math.PI;
        System.out.print("gradual underflow: " + d + "\n     ");
        for (int i = 0; i < 4; i++)
            System.out.print(" " + (d /= 100000));
        System.out.println();

        // An example of NaN:
        System.out.print("0.0/0.0 is Not-a-Number: ");
        d = 0.0/0.0;
        System.out.println(d);

        // An example of inexact results and rounding:
        System.out.print("inexact results with float:");
        for (int i = 0; i < 100; i++) {
            float z = 1.0f / i;
            if (z * i != 1.0f)
                System.out.print(" " + i);
        }
        System.out.println();
```

```
            // Another example of inexact results and rounding:
            System.out.print("inexact results with double:");
            for (int i = 0; i < 100; i++) {
                double z = 1.0 / i;
                if (z * i != 1.0)
                    System.out.print(" " + i);
            }
            System.out.println();

            // An example of cast to integer rounding:
            System.out.print("cast to int rounds toward 0: ");
            d = 12345.6;
            System.out.println((int)d + " " + (int)(-d));
        }
    }
```

produces the output:

```
overflow produces infinity: 1.0e+308*10==Infinity
gradual underflow: 3.141592653589793E-305
    3.1415926535898E-310 3.141592653E-315 3.142E-320 0.0
0.0/0.0 is Not-a-Number: NaN
inexact results with float: 0 41 47 55 61 82 83 94 97
inexact results with double: 0 49 98
cast to int rounds toward 0: 12345 -12345
```

This example demonstrates, among other things, that gradual underflow can result in a gradual loss of precision.

The inexact results when `i` is `0` involve division by zero, so that `z` becomes positive infinity, and `z * 0` is NaN, which is not equal to `1.0`.

4.2.5 The `boolean` Type and `boolean` Values

The `boolean` type represents a logical quantity with two possible values, indicated by the literals `true` and `false` (§3.10.3). The boolean operators are:

- The relational operators `==` and `!=` (§15.20.2)
- The logical-complement operator `!` (§15.14.6)
- The logical operators `&`, `^`, and `|` (§15.21.2)
- The conditional-and and conditional-or operators `&&` (§15.22) and `||` (§15.23)
- The conditional operator `? :` (§15.24)
- The string concatenation operator `+` (§15.17.1), which, when given a `String` operand and a boolean operand, will convert the boolean operand to a `String` (either `"true"` or `"false"`), and then produce a newly created `String` that is the concatenation of the two strings

Boolean expressions determine the control flow in several kinds of statements:

- The `if` statement (§14.8)
- The `while` statement (§14.10)
- The `do` statement (§14.11)
- The `for` statement (§14.12)

A `boolean` expression also determines which subexpression is evaluated in the conditional `? :` operator (§15.24).

Only `boolean` expressions can be used in control flow statements and as the first operand of the conditional operator `? :`. An integer `x` can be converted to a `boolean`, following the C language convention that any nonzero value is `true`, by the expression `x!=0`. An object reference `obj` can be converted to a `boolean`, following the C language convention that any reference other than `null` is `true`, by the expression `obj!=null`.

A cast of a `boolean` value to type `boolean` is allowed (§5.1.1); no other casts on type `boolean` are allowed. A `boolean` can be converted to a string by string conversion (§5.4).

4.3 Reference Types and Values

There are three kinds of *reference types*: class types (§8), interface types (§9), and array types (§10).

ReferenceType:
    ClassOrInterfaceType
    ArrayType

ClassOrInterfaceType:
    ClassType
    InterfaceType

ClassType:
    TypeName

InterfaceType:
    TypeName

ArrayType:
    Type `[ ]`

Names are described in §6; type names in §6.5 and, specifically, §6.5.4.

The sample code:

```
class Point { int[] metrics; }
interface Move { void move(int deltax, int deltay); }
```

declares a class type `Point`, an interface type `Move`, and uses an array type `int[]` (an array of `int`) to declare the field `metrics` of the class `Point`.

4.3.1 Objects

An *object* is a *class instance* or an array.

The reference values (often just *references*) are *pointers* to these objects, and a special null reference, which refers to no object.

A class instance is explicitly created by a class instance creation expression (§15.8), or by invoking the `newInstance` method of class `Class` (§20.3.8). An array is explicitly created by an array creation expression (§15.8).

A new class instance is implicitly created when the string concatenation operator + (§15.17.1) is used in an expression, resulting in a new object of type `String` (§4.3.3, §20.12). A new array object is implicitly created when an array initializer expression (§10.6) is evaluated; this can occur when a class or interface is initialized (§12.4), when a new instance of a class is created (§15.8), or when a local variable declaration statement is executed (§14.3).

Many of these cases are illustrated in the following example:

```
class Point {
    int x, y;
    Point() { System.out.println("default"); }
    Point(int x, int y) { this.x = x; this.y = y; }

    // A Point instance is explicitly created at class initialization time:
    static Point origin = new Point(0,0);

    // A String can be implicitly created by a + operator:
    public String toString() {
        return "(" + x + "," + y + ")";
    }
}

class Test {
    public static void main(String[] args) {
        // A Point is explicitly created using newInstance:
        Point p = null;
        try {
            p = (Point)Class.forName("Point").newInstance();
        } catch (Exception e) {
            System.out.println(e);
        }
```

```
        // An array is implicitly created by an array constructor:
        Point a[] = { new Point(0,0), new Point(1,1) };

        // Strings are implicitly created by + operators:
        System.out.println("p: " + p);
        System.out.println("a: { " + a[0] + ", "
                                   + a[1] + " }");

        // An array is explicitly created by an array creation expression:
        String sa[] = new String[2];
        sa[0] = "he"; sa[1] = "llo";
        System.out.println(sa[0] + sa[1]);
    }
}
```

which produces the output:

```
default
p: (0,0)
a: { (0,0), (1,1) }
hello
```

The operators on references to objects are:

- Field access, using either a qualified name (§6.6) or a field access expression (§15.10)
- Method invocation (§15.11)
- The cast operator (§5.4, §15.15)
- The string concatenation operator + (§15.17.1), which, when given a `String` operand and a reference, will convert the reference to a `String` by invoking the `toString` method (§20.1.2) of the referenced object (using `"null"` if either the reference or the result of `toString` is a null reference), and then will produce a newly created `String` that is the concatenation of the two strings
- The `instanceof` operator (§15.19.2)
- The reference equality operators `==` and `!=` (§15.20.3)
- The conditional operator `? :` (§15.24).

There may be many references to the same object. Most objects have state, stored in the fields of objects that are instances of classes or in the variables that are the components of an array object. If two variables contain references to the same object, the state of the object can be modified using one variable's reference to the object, and then the altered state can be observed through the reference in the other variable.

The example program:

```
class Value { int val; }

class Test {
    public static void main(String[] args) {
        int i1 = 3;
        int i2 = i1;
        i2 = 4;
        System.out.print("i1==" + i1);
        System.out.println(" but i2==" + i2);
        Value v1 = new Value();
        v1.val = 5;
        Value v2 = v1;
        v2.val = 6;
        System.out.print("v1.val==" + v1.val);
        System.out.println(" and v2.val==" + v2.val);
    }
}
```

produces the output:

```
i1==3 but i2==4
v1.val==6 and v2.val==6
```

because `v1.val` and `v2.val` reference the same instance variable (§4.5.3) in the one `Value` object created by the only `new` expression, while `i1` and `i2` are different variables.

See §10 and §15.9 for examples of the creation and use of arrays.

Each object has an associated lock (§17.13), which is used by `synchronized` methods (§8.4.3) and the `synchronized` statement (§14.17) to provide control over concurrent access to state by multiple threads (§17.12, §20.20).

4.3.2 The Class `Object`

The standard class `Object` is a superclass (§8.1) of all other classes. A variable of type `Object` can hold a reference to any object, whether it is an instance of a class or an array (§10). All class and array types inherit the methods of class `Object`, which are summarized here and completely specified in §20.1:

```
package java.lang;

public class Object {
    public final Class getClass() { . . . }
    public String toString() { . . . }
    public boolean equals(Object obj) { . . . }
    public int hashCode() { . . . }
    protected Object clone()
        throws CloneNotSupportedException { . . . }
```

```
    public final void wait()
        throws IllegalMonitorStateException,
            InterruptedException { ... }
    public final void wait(long millis)
        throws IllegalMonitorStateException,
            InterruptedException { ... }
    public final void wait(long millis, int nanos) { ... }
        throws IllegalMonitorStateException,
            InterruptedException { ... }
    public final void notify() { ... }
        throws IllegalMonitorStateException
    public final void notifyAll() { ... }
        throws IllegalMonitorStateException
    protected void finalize()
        throws Throwable { ... }
}
```

The members of `Object` are as follows:

- The method `getClass` returns the `Class` (§20.3) object that represents the class of the object. A `Class` object exists for each reference type. It can be used, for example, to discover the fully qualified name of a class, its members, its immediate superclass, and any interfaces that it implements. A class method that is declared `synchronized` (§8.4.3.5) synchronizes on the lock associated with the `Class` object of the class.
- The method `toString` returns a `String` representation of the object.
- The methods `equals` and `hashCode` are declared for the benefit of hashtables such as `java.util.Hashtable` (§21.7). The method `equals` defines a notion of object equality, which is based on value, not reference, comparison.
- The method `clone` is used to make a duplicate of an object.
- The methods `wait`, `notify`, and `notifyAll` are used in concurrent programming using threads, as described in §17.
- The method `finalize` is run just before an object is destroyed and is described in §12.6.

4.3.3 The Class `String`

Instances of class `String` (§20.12) represent sequences of Unicode characters. A `String` object has a constant (unchanging) value. String literals (§3.10.5) are references to instances of class `String`.

The string concatenation operator + (§15.17.1) implicitly creates a new `String` object.

4.3.4 When Reference Types Are the Same

Two reference types the *same type* if:

- They are both class or both interface types, are loaded by the same class loader, and have the same fully-qualified name (§6.6), in which case they are sometimes said to be the *same class* or the *same interface*.
- They are both array types, and have the same component type (§10).

4.4 Where Types Are Used

Types are used when they appear in declarations or in certain expressions.

The following code fragment contains one or more instances of each kind of usage of a type:

```
import java.util.Random;

class MiscMath {

    int divisor;

    MiscMath(int divisor) {
        this.divisor = divisor;
    }

    float ratio(long l) {
        try {
            l /= divisor;
        } catch (Exception e) {
            if (e instanceof ArithmeticException)
                l = Long.MAX_VALUE;
            else
                l = 0;
        }
        return (float)l;
    }

    double gausser() {
        Random r = new Random();
        double[] val = new double[2];
        val[0] = r.nextGaussian();
        val[1] = r.nextGaussian();
        return (val[0] + val[1]) / 2;
    }

}
```

In this example, types are used in declarations of the following:

- Imported types (§7.5); here the type `Random`, imported from the type `java.util.Random` of the package `java.util`, is declared
- Fields, which are the class variables and instance variables of classes (§8.3), and constants of interfaces (§9.3); here the field `divisor` in the class `MiscMath` is declared to be of type `int`
- Method parameters (§8.4.1); here the parameter `l` of the method `ratio` is declared to be of type `long`
- Method results (§8.4); here the result of the method `ratio` is declared to be of type `float`, and the result of the method `gausser` is declared to be of type `double`
- Constructor parameters (§8.6.1); here the parameter of the constructor for `MiscMath` is declared to be of type `int`
- Local variables (§14.3, §14.12); the local variables `r` and `val` of the method `gausser` are declared to be of types `Random` and `double[]` (array of `double`)
- Exception handler parameters (§14.18); here the exception handler parameter `e` of the `catch` clause is declared to be of type `Exception`

and in expressions of the following kinds:

- Class instance creations (§15.8); here a local variable `r` of method `gausser` is initialized by a class instance creation expression that uses the type `Random`
- Array creations (§15.9); here the local variable `val` of method `gausser` is initialized by an array creation expression that creates an array of `double` with size 2
- Casts (§15.15); here the `return` statement of the method `ratio` uses the `float` type in a cast
- The `instanceof` operator (§15.19.2); here the `instanceof` operator tests whether `e` is assignment compatible with the type `ArithmeticException`

4.5 Variables

A variable is a storage location and has an associated type, sometimes called its *compile-time type*, that is either a primitive type (§4.2) or a reference type (§4.3). A variable always contains a value that is assignment compatible (§5.2) with its type. A variable's value is changed by an assignment (§15.25) or by a prefix or postfix `++` (increment) or `--` (decrement) operator (§15.13.2, §15.13.3, §15.14.1, §15.14.2).

Compatibility of the value of a variable with its type is guaranteed by the design of the Java language. Default values are compatible (§4.5.4) and all assignments to a variable are checked for assignment compatibility (§5.2), usually at compile time, but, in a single case involving arrays, a run-time check is made (§10.10).

4.5.1 Variables of Primitive Type

A variable of a primitive type always holds a value of that exact primitive type.

4.5.2 Variables of Reference Type

A variable of reference type can hold either of the following:

- A null reference
- A reference to any object (§4.3) whose class (§4.5.5) is assignment compatible (§5.2) with the type of the variable

4.5.3 Kinds of Variables

There are seven kinds of variables:

1. A *class variable* is a field declared using the keyword `static` within a class declaration (§8.3.1.1), or with or without the keyword `static` within an interface declaration (§9.3). A class variable is created when its class or interface is loaded (§12.2) and is initialized to a default value (§4.5.4). The class variable effectively ceases to exist when its class or interface is unloaded (§12.8), after any necessary finalization of the class or interface (§12.6) has been completed.
2. An *instance variable* is a field declared within a class declaration without using the keyword `static` (§8.3.1.1). If a class *T* has a field *a* that is an instance variable, then a new instance variable *a* is created and initialized to a default value (§4.5.4) as part of each newly created object of class *T* or of any class that is a subclass of *T* (§8.1.3). The instance variable effectively ceases to exist when the object of which it is a field is no longer referenced, after any necessary finalization of the object (§12.6) has been completed.
3. *Array components* are unnamed variables that are created and initialized to default values (§4.5.4) whenever a new object that is an array is created (§15.9). The array components effectively cease to exist when the array is no longer referenced. See §10 for a description of arrays.

4. *Method parameters* (§8.4.1) name argument values passed to a method. For every parameter declared in a method declaration, a new parameter variable is created each time that method is invoked (§15.11). The new variable is initialized with the corresponding argument value from the method invocation. The method parameter effectively ceases to exist when the execution of the body of the method is complete.

5. *Constructor parameters* (§8.6.1) name argument values passed to a constructor. For every parameter declared in a constructor declaration, a new parameter variable is created each time a class instance creation expression (§15.8) or explicit constructor invocation (§8.6.5) invokes that constructor. The new variable is initialized with the corresponding argument value from the creation expression or constructor invocation. The constructor parameter effectively ceases to exist when the execution of the body of the constructor is complete.

6. An *exception-handler parameter* is created each time an exception is caught by a `catch` clause of a `try` statement (§14.18). The new variable is initialized with the actual object associated with the exception (§11.3, §14.16). The exception-handler parameter effectively ceases to exist when execution of the block associated with the `catch` clause is complete.

7. *Local variables* are declared by local variable declaration statements (§14.3). Whenever the flow of control enters a block (§14.2) or `for` statement (§14.12), a new variable is created for each local variable declared in a local variable declaration statement immediately contained within that block or `for` statement. A local variable declaration statement may contain an expression which initializes the variable. The local variable with an initializing expression is not initialized, however, until the local variable declaration statement that declares it is executed. (The rules of definite assignment (§16) prevent the value of a local variable from being used before it has been initialized or otherwise assigned a value.) The local variable effectively ceases to exist when the execution of the block or `for` statement is complete.

   Were it not for one exceptional situation, a local variable could always be regarded as being created when its local variable declaration statement is executed. The exceptional situation involves the `switch` statement (§14.9), where it is possible for control to enter a block but bypass execution of a local variable declaration statement. Because of the restrictions imposed by the rules of definite assignment (§16), however, the local variable declared by such a bypassed local variable declaration statement cannot be used before it has been definitely assigned a value by an assignment expression (§15.25).

The following example contains several different kinds of variables:

```
class Point {
    static int numPoints;        // numPoints is a class variable
    int x, y;                    // x and y are instance variables
    int[] w = new int[10];       // w[0] is an array component
    int setX(int x) {            // x is a method parameter
        int oldx = this.x;       // oldx is a local variable
        this.x = x;
        return oldx;
    }
}
```

4.5.4 Initial Values of Variables

Every variable in a Java program must have a value before its value is used:

- Each class variable, instance variable, or array component is initialized with a *default value* when it is created (§15.8, §15.9, §20.3.6):
    - For type `byte`, the default value is zero, that is, the value of `(byte)0`.
    - For type `short`, the default value is zero, that is, the value of `(short)0`.
    - For type `int`, the default value is zero, that is, `0`.
    - For type `long`, the default value is zero, that is, `0L`.
    - For type `float`, the default value is positive zero, that is, `0.0f`.
    - For type `double`, the default value is positive zero, that is, `0.0d`.
    - For type `char`, the default value is the null character, that is, `'\u0000'`.
    - For type `boolean`, the default value is `false`.
    - For all reference types (§4.3), the default value is `null`.
- Each method parameter (§8.4.1) is initialized to the corresponding argument value provided by the invoker of the method (§15.11).
- Each constructor parameter (§8.6.1) is initialized to the corresponding argument value provided by a class instance creation expression (§15.8) or explicit constructor invocation (§8.6.5).
- An exception-handler parameter (§14.18) is initialized to the thrown object representing the exception (§11.3, §14.16).
- A local variable (§14.3, §14.12) must be explicitly given a value before it is used, by either initialization (§14.3) or assignment (§15.25), in a way that can be verified by the compiler using the rules for definite assignment (§16).

The example program:

```
class Point {
    static int npoints;
    int x, y;
    Point root;
}

class Test {
    public static void main(String[] args) {
        System.out.println("npoints=" + Point.npoints);
        Point p = new Point();
        System.out.println("p.x=" + p.x + ", p.y=" + p.y);
        System.out.println("p.root=" + p.root);
    }
}
```

prints:

```
npoints=0
p.x=0, p.y=0
p.root=null
```

illustrating the default initialization of `npoints`, which occurs when the class `Point` is prepared (§12.3.2), and the default initialization of `x`, `y`, and `root`, which occurs when a new `Point` is instantiated. See §12 for a full description of all aspects of loading, linking, and initialization of classes and interfaces, plus a description of the instantiation of classes to make new class instances.

4.5.5 Variables Have Types, Objects Have Classes

Every object belongs to some particular class: the class that was mentioned in the creation expression that produced the object, the class whose class object was used to invoke the `newInstance` method (§20.3.6) to produce the object, or the `String` class for objects implicitly created by the string concatenation operator + (§15.17.1). This class is called the *class of the object*. (Arrays also have a class, as described at the end of this section.) An object is said to be an instance of its class and of all superclasses of its class.

(Sometimes a variable or expression is said to have a "run-time type" but that is an abuse of terminology; it refers to the class of the object referred to by the value of the variable or expression at run time, assuming that the value is not `null`. Properly speaking, type is a compile-time notion. A variable or expression has a type; an object or array has no type, but belongs to a class.)

The type of a variable is always declared, and the type of an expression can be deduced at compile time. The type limits the possible values that the variable can hold or the expression can produce at run time. If a run-time value is a reference that is not `null`, it refers to an object or array that has a class (not a type), and that class will necessarily be compatible with the compile-time type.

Even though a variable or expression may have a compile-time type that is an interface type, there are no instances of interfaces. A variable or expression whose type is an interface type can reference any object whose class implements (§8.1.4) that interface.

Here is an example of creating new objects and of the distinction between the type of a variable and the class of an object:

```
public interface Colorable {
    void setColor(byte r, byte g, byte b);
}

class Point { int x, y; }

class ColoredPoint extends Point implements Colorable {

    byte r, g, b;

    public void setColor(byte rv, byte gv, byte bv) {
        r = rv; g = gv; b = bv;
    }

}

class Test {
    public static void main(String[] args) {
        Point p = new Point();
        ColoredPoint cp = new ColoredPoint();
        p = cp;
        Colorable c = cp;
    }
}
```

In this example:

- The local variable `p` of the method `main` of class `Test` has type `Point` and is initially assigned a reference to a new instance of class `Point`.
- The local variable `cp` similarly has as its type `ColoredPoint`, and is initially assigned a reference to a new instance of class `ColoredPoint`.
- The assignment of the value of `cp` to the variable `p` causes `p` to hold a reference to a `ColoredPoint` object. This is permitted because `ColoredPoint` is a subclass of `Point`, so the class `ColoredPoint` is assignment compatible (§5.2) with the type `Point`. A `ColoredPoint` object includes support for all the methods of a `Point`. In addition to its particular fields `r`, `g`, and `b`, it has the fields of class `Point`, namely `x` and `y`.

- The local variable `c` has as its type the interface type `Colorable`, so it can hold a reference to any object whose class implements `Colorable`; specifically, it can hold a reference to a `ColoredPoint`.
- Note that an expression such as "`new Colorable()`" is not valid because it is not possible to create an instance of an interface, only of a class.

Every array also has a class; the method `getClass` (§20.1.1), when invoked for an array object, will return a class object (of class `Class`) that represents the class of the array. The classes for arrays have strange names that are not valid Java identifiers; for example, the class for an array of `int` components has the name "`[I`" and so the value of the expression:

```
new int[10].getClass().getName()
```

is the string `"[I"`; see §20.1.1 for details.

Oft on the dappled turf at ease
I sit, and play with similes,
Loose types of things through all degrees.
—William Wordsworth, *To the Same Flower*

CHAPTER 5

Conversions and Promotions

Thou art not for the fashion of these times,
Where none will sweat but for promotion.
—William Shakespeare, *As You Like It*, Act II, scene iii

EVERY Java expression has a type that can be deduced from the structure of the expression and the types of the literals, variables, and methods mentioned in the expression. It is possible, however, to write an expression in a context where the type of the expression is not appropriate. In some cases, this leads to an error at compile time; for example, if the expression in an `if` statement (§14.8) has any type other than `boolean`, a compile-time error occurs. In other cases, the context may be able to accept a type that is related to the type of the expression; as a convenience, rather than requiring the programmer to indicate a type conversion explicitly, the Java language performs an implicit *conversion* from the type of the expression to a type acceptable for its surrounding context.

A specific conversion from type *S* to type *T* allows an expression of type *S* to be treated at compile time as if it had type *T* instead. In some cases this will require a corresponding action at run time to check the validity of the conversion or to translate the run-time value of the expression into a form appropriate for the new type *T*. For example:

- A conversion from type `Object` (§20.1) to type `Thread` (§20.20) requires a run-time check to make sure that the run-time value is actually an instance of class `Thread` or one of its subclasses; if it is not, an exception is thrown.
- A conversion from type `Thread` to type `Object` requires no run-time action; `Thread` is a subclass of `Object`, so any reference produced by an expression of type `Thread` is a valid reference value of type `Object`.
- A conversion from type `int` to type `long` requires run-time sign-extension of a 32-bit integer value to the 64-bit `long` representation. No information is lost.

- A conversion from type `double` to type `long` requires a nontrivial translation from a 64-bit floating-point value to the 64-bit integer representation. Depending on the actual run-time value, information may be lost.

In every conversion context, only certain specific conversions are permitted. The specific conversions that are possible in Java are grouped for convenience of description into several broad categories:

- Identity conversions
- Widening primitive conversions
- Narrowing primitive conversions
- Widening reference conversions
- Narrowing reference conversions
- String conversions

There are five *conversion contexts* in which conversion of Java expressions may occur. Each context allows conversions in some of the categories named above but not others. The term "conversion" is also used to describe the process of choosing a specific conversion for such a context. For example, we say that an expression that is an actual argument in a method invocation is subject to "method invocation conversion," meaning that a specific conversion will be implicitly chosen for that expression according to the rules for the method invocation argument context.

One conversion context is the operand of a numeric operator such as + or *. The conversion process for such operands is called *numeric promotion*. Promotion is special in that, in the case of binary operators, the conversion chosen for one operand may depend in part on the type of the other operand expression.

This chapter first describes the six categories of conversions (§5.1), including the special conversions to `String` allowed for the string concatenation operator +. Then the five conversion contexts are described:

- Assignment conversion (§5.2, §15.25) converts the type of an expression to the type of a specified variable. The conversions permitted for assignment are limited in such a way that assignment conversion never causes an exception.
- Method invocation conversion (§5.3, §15.8, §15.11) is applied to each argument in a method or constructor invocation and, except in one case, performs the same conversions that assignment conversion does. Method invocation conversion never causes an exception.

- Casting conversion (§5.4) converts the type of an expression to a type explicitly specified by a cast operator (§15.15). It is more inclusive than assignment or method invocation conversion, allowing any specific conversion other than a string conversion, but certain casts to a reference type may cause an exception at run time.
- String conversion (§5.4, §15.17.1) allows any type to be converted to type `String`.
- Numeric promotion (§5.6) brings the operands of a numeric operator to a common type so that an operation can be performed.

Here are some examples of the various contexts for conversion:

```
class Test {
    public static void main(String[] args) {
        // Casting conversion (§5.4) of a float literal to
        // type int. Without the cast operator, this would
        // be a compile-time error, because this is a
        // narrowing conversion (§5.1.3):
        int i = (int)12.5f;

        // String conversion (§5.4) of i's int value:
        System.out.println("(int)12.5f==" + i);

        // Assignment conversion (§5.2) of i's value to type
        // float. This is a widening conversion (§5.1.2):
        float f = i;

        // String conversion of f's float value:
        System.out.println("after float widening: " + f);

        // Numeric promotion (§5.6) of i's value to type
        // float. This is a binary numeric promotion.
        // After promotion, the operation is float*float:
        System.out.print(f);
        f = f * i;

        // Two string conversions of i and f:
        System.out.println("*" + i + "==" + f);

        // Method invocation conversion (§5.3) of f's value
        // to type double, needed because the method Math.sin
        // accepts only a double argument:
        double d = Math.sin(f);

        // Two string conversions of f and d:
        System.out.println("Math.sin(" + f + ")==" + d);
    }
}
```

which produces the output:

```
(int)12.5f==12
after float widening: 12.0
12.0*12==144.0
Math.sin(144.0)==-0.49102159389846934
```

5.1 Kinds of Conversion

Specific type conversions in Java are divided into six categories.

5.1.1 Identity Conversions

A conversion from a type to that same type is permitted for any type. This may seem trivial, but it has two practical consequences. First, it is always permitted for an expression to have the desired type to begin with, thus allowing the simply stated rule that every expression is subject to conversion, if only a trivial identity conversion. Second, it implies that it is permitted for a program to include redundant cast operators for the sake of clarity.

The only permitted conversion that involves the type `boolean` is the identity conversion from `boolean` to `boolean`.

5.1.2 Widening Primitive Conversions

The following 19 specific conversions on primitive types are called the *widening primitive conversions*:

- `byte` to `short`, `int`, `long`, `float`, or `double`
- `short` to `int`, `long`, `float`, or `double`
- `char` to `int`, `long`, `float`, or `double`
- `int` to `long`, `float`, or `double`
- `long` to `float` or `double`
- `float` to `double`

Widening primitive conversions do not lose information about the overall magnitude of a numeric value. Indeed, conversions widening from an integral type to another integral type and from `float` to `double` do not lose any information at all; the numeric value is preserved exactly. Conversion of an `int` or a `long` value to `float`, or of a `long` value to `double`, may result in *loss of precision*—that is, the result may lose some of the least significant bits of the value. In this case, the resulting floating-point value will be a correctly rounded version of the integer value, using IEEE 754 round-to-nearest mode (§4.2.4).

A widening conversion of a signed integer value to an integral type *T* simply sign-extends the two's-complement representation of the integer value to fill the wider format. A widening conversion of a character to an integral type *T* zero-extends the representation of the character value to fill the wider format.

Despite the fact that loss of precision may occur, widening conversions among primitive types never result in a run-time exception (§11).

Here is an example of a widening conversion that loses precision:

```
class Test {
    public static void main(String[] args) {
        int big = 1234567890;
        float approx = big;
        System.out.println(big - (int)approx);
    }
}
```

which prints:

```
-46
```

thus indicating that information was lost during the conversion from type `int` to type `float` because values of type `float` are not precise to nine significant digits.

5.1.3 Narrowing Primitive Conversions

The following 23 specific conversions on primitive types are called the *narrowing primitive conversions*:

- `byte` to `char`
- `short` to `byte` or `char`
- `char` to `byte` or `short`
- `int` to `byte`, `short`, or `char`
- `long` to `byte`, `short`, `char`, or `int`
- `float` to `byte`, `short`, `char`, `int`, or `long`
- `double` to `byte`, `short`, `char`, `int`, `long`, or `float`

Narrowing conversions may lose information about the overall magnitude of a numeric value and may also lose precision.

A narrowing conversion of a signed integer to an integral type *T* simply discards all but the *n* lowest order bits, where *n* is the number of bits used to represent type *T*. In addition to a possible loss of information about the magnitude of the numeric value, this may cause the sign of the resulting value to differ from the sign of the input value.

A narrowing conversion of a character to an integral type *T* likewise simply discards all but the *n* lowest order bits, where *n* is the number of bits used to represent type *T*. In addition to a possible loss of information about the magnitude of the numeric value, this may cause the resulting value to be a negative number, even though characters represent 16-bit unsigned integer values.

A narrowing conversion of a floating-point number to an integral type *T* takes two steps:

1. In the first step, the floating-point number is converted either to a `long`, if *T* is `long`, or to an `int`, if *T* is `byte`, `short`, `char`, or `int`, as follows:

   - If the floating-point number is NaN (§4.2.3), the result of the first step of the conversion is an `int` or `long` `0`.

   - Otherwise, if the floating-point number is not an infinity, the floating-point value is rounded to an integer value *V*, rounding toward zero using IEEE 754 round-toward-zero mode (§4.2.3). Then there are two cases:

     - If *T* is `long`, and this integer value can be represented as a `long`, then the result of the first step is the `long` value *V*.

     - Otherwise, if this integer value can be represented as an `int`, then the result of the first step is the `int` value *V*.

   - Otherwise, one of the following two cases must be true:

     - The value must be too small (a negative value of large magnitude or negative infinity), and the result of the first step is the smallest representable value of type `int` or `long`.

     - The value must be too large (a positive value of large magnitude or positive infinity), and the result of the first step is the largest representable value of type `int` or `long`.

2. In the second step:

   - If *T* is `int` or `long`, the result of the conversion is the result of the first step.

   - If *T* is `byte`, `char`, or `short`, the result of the conversion is the result of a narrowing conversion to type *T* (§5.1.3) of the result of the first step.

The example:

```
class Test {
    public static void main(String[] args) {
        float fmin = Float.NEGATIVE_INFINITY;
        float fmax = Float.POSITIVE_INFINITY;
        System.out.println("long: " + (long)fmin +
                           ".." + (long)fmax);
        System.out.println("int: " + (int)fmin +
                           ".." + (int)fmax);
        System.out.println("short: " + (short)fmin +
                           ".." + (short)fmax);
        System.out.println("char: " + (int)(char)fmin +
                           ".." + (int)(char)fmax);
        System.out.println("byte: " + (byte)fmin +
                           ".." + (byte)fmax);
    }
}
```

produces the output:

```
long: -9223372036854775808..9223372036854775807
int: -2147483648..2147483647
short: 0..-1
char: 0..65535
byte: 0..-1
```

The results for `char`, `int`, and `long` are unsurprising, producing the minimum and maximum representable values of the type.

The results for `byte` and `short` lose information about the sign and magnitude of the numeric values and also lose precision. The results can be understood by examining the low order bits of the minimum and maximum `int`. The minimum `int` is, in hexadecimal, `0x80000000`, and the maximum `int` is `0x7fffffff`. This explains the `short` results, which are the low 16 bits of these values, namely, `0x0000` and `0xffff`; it explains the `char` results, which also are the low 16 bits of these values, namely, `'\u0000'` and `'\uffff'`; and it explains the `byte` results, which are the low 8 bits of these values, namely, `0x00` and `0xff`.

A narrowing conversion from `double` to `float` behaves in accordance with IEEE 754. The result is correctly rounded using IEEE 754 round-to-nearest mode. A value too small to be represented as a `float` is converted to positive or negative zero; a value too large to be represented as a `float` is converted to a (positive or negative) infinity. A `double` NaN is always converted to a `float` NaN.

Despite the fact that overflow, underflow, or other loss of information may occur, narrowing conversions among primitive types never result in a run-time exception (§11).

Here is a small test program that demonstrates a number of narrowing conversions that lose information:

```
class Test {
    public static void main(String[] args) {
        // A narrowing of int to short loses high bits:
        System.out.println("(short)0x12345678==0x" +
                    Integer.toHexString((short)0x12345678));
        // A int value not fitting in byte changes sign and magnitude:
        System.out.println("(byte)255==" + (byte)255);
        // A float value too big to fit gives largest int value:
        System.out.println("(int)1e20f==" + (int)1e20f);
        // A NaN converted to int yields zero:
        System.out.println("(int)NaN==" + (int)Float.NaN);
        // A double value too large for float yields infinity:
        System.out.println("(float)-1e100==" + (float)-1e100);
        // A double value too small for float underflows to zero:
        System.out.println("(float)1e-50==" + (float)1e-50);
    }
}
```

This test program produces the following output:

```
(short)0x12345678==0x5678
(byte)255==-1
(int)1e20f==2147483647
(int)NaN==0
(float)-1e100==-Infinity
(float)1e-50==0.0
```

5.1.4 Widening Reference Conversions

The following conversions are called the *widening reference conversions*:

- From any class type *S* to any class type *T*, provided that *S* is a subclass of *T*. (An important special case is that there is a widening conversion to the class type `Object` from any other class type.)
- From any class type *S* to any interface type *K*, provided that *S* implements *K*.
- From the null type to any class type, interface type, or array type.
- From any interface type *J* to any interface type *K*, provided that *J* is a subinterface of *K*.

- From any interface type to type `Object`.
- From any array type to type `Object`.
- From any array type to type `Cloneable`.
- From any array type *SC*`[]` to any array type *TC*`[]`, provided that *SC* and *TC* are reference types and there is a widening conversion from *SC* to *TC*.

Such conversions never require a special action at run time and therefore never throw an exception at run time. They consist simply in regarding a reference as having some other type in a manner that can be proved correct at compile time.

See §8 for the detailed specifications for classes, §9 for interfaces, and §10 for arrays.

5.1.5 Narrowing Reference Conversions

The following conversions are called the *narrowing reference conversions*:

- From any class type *S* to any class type *T*, provided that *S* is a superclass of *T*. (An important special case is that there is a narrowing conversion from the class type `Object` to any other class type.)
- From any class type *S* to any interface type *K*, provided that *S* is not final and does not implement *K*. (An important special case is that there is a narrowing conversion from the class type `Object` to any interface type.)
- From type `Object` to any array type.
- From type `Object` to any interface type.
- From any interface type *J* to any class type *T* that is not `final`.
- From any interface type *J* to any class type *T* that is `final`, provided that *T* implements *J*.
- From any interface type *J* to any interface type *K*, provided that *J* is not a subinterface of *K* and there is no method name *m* such that *J* and *K* both declare a method named *m* with the same signature but different return types.
- From any array type *SC*`[]` to any array type *TC*`[]`, provided that *SC* and *TC* are reference types and there is a narrowing conversion from *SC* to *TC*.

Such conversions require a test at run time to find out whether the actual reference value is a legitimate value of the new type. If not, then a `ClassCastException` is thrown.

5.1.6 String Conversions

There is a string conversion to type `String` from every other type, including the null type.

5.1.7 Forbidden Conversions

- There is no permitted conversion from any reference type to any primitive type.
- Except for the string conversions, there is no permitted conversion from any primitive type to any reference type.
- There is no permitted conversion from the null type to any primitive type.
- There is no permitted conversion to the null type other than the identity conversion.
- There is no permitted conversion to the type `boolean` other than the identity conversion.
- There is no permitted conversion from the type `boolean` other than the identity conversion and string conversion.
- There is no permitted conversion other than string conversion from class type *S* to a different class type *T* if *S* is not a subclass of *T* and *T* is not a subclass of *S*.
- There is no permitted conversion from class type *S* to interface type *K* if *S* is `final` and does not implement *K*.
- There is no permitted conversion from class type *S* to any array type if *S* is not `Object`.
- There is no permitted conversion other than string conversion from interface type *J* to class type *T* if *T* is `final` and does not implement *J*.
- There is no permitted conversion from interface type *J* to interface type *K* if *J* and *K* declare methods with the same signature but different return types.
- There is no permitted conversion from any array type to any class type other than `Object` or `String`.
- There is no permitted conversion from any array type to any interface type, except to the interface type `Cloneable`, which is implemented by all arrays.
- There is no permitted conversion from array type *SC*`[]` to array type *TC*`[]` if there is no permitted conversion other than a string conversion from *SC* to *TC*.

5.2 Assignment Conversion

Assignment conversion occurs when the value of an expression is assigned (§15.25) to a variable: the type of the expression must be converted to the type of the variable. Assignment contexts allow the use of an identity conversion (§5.1.1), a widening primitive conversion (§5.1.2), or a widening reference conversion (§5.1.4). In addition, a narrowing primitive conversion may be used if all of the following conditions are satisfied:

- The expression is a constant expression of type `int`.
- The type of the variable is `byte`, `short`, or `char`.
- The value of the expression (which is known at compile time, because it is a constant expression) is representable in the type of the variable.

If the type of the expression cannot be converted to the type of the variable by a conversion permitted in an assignment context, then a compile-time error occurs.

If the type of an expression can be converted to the type a variable by assignment conversion, we say the expression (or its value) is *assignable to* the variable or, equivalently, that the type of the expression is *assignment compatible with* the type of the variable.

An assignment conversion never causes an exception. (Note, however, that an assignment may result in an exception in a special case involving array elements —see §10.10 and §15.25.1.)

The compile-time narrowing of constants means that code such as:

```
byte theAnswer = 42;
```

is allowed. Without the narrowing, the fact that the integer literal `42` has type `int` would mean that a cast to `byte` would be required:

```
byte theAnswer = (byte)42;     // cast is permitted but not required
```

A value of primitive type must not be assigned to a variable of reference type; an attempt to do so will result in a compile-time error. A value of type `boolean` can be assigned only to a variable of type `boolean`.

The following test program contains examples of assignment conversion of primitive values:

```
class Test {
    public static void main(String[] args) {
        short s = 12;           // narrow 12 to short
        float f = s;            // widen short to float
        System.out.println("f=" + f);
```

```
        char c = '\u0123';
        long l = c;                    // widen char to long
        System.out.println("l=0x" + Long.toString(l,16));

        f = 1.23f;
        double d = f;                  // widen float to double
        System.out.println("d=" + d);
    }
}
```

It produces the following output:

```
f=12.0
i=0x123
d=1.2300000190734863
```

The following test, however, produces compile-time errors:

```
class Test {
    public static void main(String[] args) {
        short s = 123;
        char c = s;                    // error: would require cast
        s = c;                         // error: would require cast
    }
}
```

because not all `short` values are `char` values, and neither are all `char` values `short` values.

A value of reference type must not be assigned to a variable of primitive type; an attempt to do so will result in a compile-time error.

A value of the null type (the null reference is the only such value) may be assigned to any reference type, resulting in a null reference of that type.

Here is a sample program illustrating assignments of references:

```
public class Point { int x, y; }

public class Point3D extends Point { int z; }

public interface Colorable {
    void setColor(int color);
}

public class ColoredPoint extends Point implements Colorable
{
    int color;
    public void setColor(int color) { this.color = color; }
}
```

```
class Test {
    public static void main(String[] args) {
        // Assignments to variables of class type:
        Point p = new Point();
        p = new Point3D();      // ok: because Point3d is a
                                // subclass of Point

        Point3D p3d = p;        // error: will require a cast because a
                                // Point might not be a Point3D
                                // (even though it is, dynamically,
                                // in this example.)
        // Assignments to variables of type Object:
        Object o = p;           // ok: any object to Object
        int[] a = new int[3];
        Object o2 = a;          // ok: an array to Object
        // Assignments to variables of interface type:
        ColoredPoint cp = new ColoredPoint();
        Colorable c = cp;       // ok: ColoredPoint implements
                                // Colorable
        // Assignments to variables of array type:
        byte[] b = new byte[4];
        a = b;                  // error: these are not arrays
                                // of the same primitive type
        Point3D[] p3da = new Point3D[3];
        Point[] pa = p3da;      // ok: since we can assign a
                                // Point3D to a Point
        p3da = pa;              // error: (cast needed) since a Point
                                // can't be assigned to a Point3D
    }
}
```

Assignment of a value of compile-time reference type *S* (source) to a variable of compile-time reference type *T* (target) is checked as follows:

- If *S* is a class type:
    - If *T* is a class type, then *S* must either be the same class as *T*, or *S* must be a subclass of *T*, or a compile-time error occurs.
    - If *T* is an interface type, then *S* must implement interface *T*, or a compile-time error occurs.
    - If *T* is an array type, then a compile-time error occurs.

- If *S* is an interface type:
  - If *T* is a class type, then *T* must be `Object`, or a compile-time error occurs.
  - If *T* is an interface type, then *T* must be either the same interface as *S* or a superinterface of *S*, or a compile-time error occurs.
  - If *T* is an array type, then a compile-time error occurs.
- If *S* is an array type *SC*`[]`, that is, an array of components of type *SC*:
  - If *T* is a class type, then *T* must be `Object`, or a compile-time error occurs.
  - If *T* is an interface type, then a compile-time error occurs unless *T* is the interface type `Cloneable`, the only interface implemented by arrays.
  - If *T* is an array type *TC*`[]`, that is, an array of components of type *TC*, then a compile-time error occurs unless one of the following is true:
    - *TC* and *SC* are the same primitive type.
    - *TC* and *SC* are both reference types and type *SC* is assignable to *TC*, as determined by a recursive application of these compile-time rules for assignability.

See §8 for the detailed specifications of classes, §9 for interfaces, and §10 for arrays.

The following test program illustrates assignment conversions on reference values, but fails to compile because it violates the preceding rules, as described in its comments. This example should be compared to the preceding one.

```
public class Point { int x, y; }
public interface Colorable { void setColor(int color); }
public class ColoredPoint extends Point implements Colorable
{
	int color;
	public void setColor(int color) { this.color = color; }
}
class Test {
	public static void main(String[] args) {
		Point p = new Point();
		ColoredPoint cp = new ColoredPoint();
		// Okay because ColoredPoint is a subclass of Point:
		p = cp;
		// Okay because ColoredPoint implements Colorable:
		Colorable c = cp;
```

```
            // The following cause compile-time errors because
            // we cannot be sure they will succeed, depending on
            // the run-time type of p; a run-time check will be
            // necessary for the needed narrowing conversion and
            // must be indicated by including a cast:
            cp = p;         // p might be neither a ColoredPoint
                            // nor a subclass of ColoredPoint
            c = p;          // p might not implement Colorable
        }
    }
```

Here is another example involving assignment of array objects:

```
class Point { int x, y; }

class ColoredPoint extends Point { int color; }

class Test {
    public static void main(String[] args) {
        long[] veclong = new long[100];
        Object o = veclong;             // okay
        Long l = veclong;               // compile-time error
        short[] vecshort = veclong;     // compile-time error
        Point[] pvec = new Point[100];
        ColoredPoint[] cpvec = new ColoredPoint[100];
        pvec = cpvec;                   // okay
        pvec[0] = new Point();          // okay at compile time,
                                        // but would throw an
                                        // exception at run time
        cpvec = pvec;                   // compile-time error
    }
}
```

In this example:

- The value of `veclong` cannot be assigned to a `Long` variable, because `Long` is a class type (§20.8) other than `Object`. An array can be assigned only to a variable of a compatible array type, or to a variable of type `Object`.
- The value of `veclong` cannot be assigned to `vecshort`, because they are arrays of primitive type, and `short` and `long` are not the same primitive type.
- The value of `cpvec` can be assigned to `pvec`, because any reference that could be the value of an expression of type `ColoredPoint` can be the value of a variable of type `Point`. The subsequent assignment of the new `Point` to a component of `pvec` then would throw an `ArrayStoreException` (if the program were otherwise corrected so that it could be compiled), because a `ColoredPoint` array can't have an instance of `Point` as the value of a component.

- The value of `pvec` cannot be assigned to `cpvec`, because not every reference that could be the value of an expression of type `ColoredPoint` can correctly be the value of a variable of type `Point`. If the value of `pvec` at run time were a reference to an instance of `Point[]`, and the assignment to `cpvec` were allowed, a simple reference to a component of `cpvec`, say, `cpvec[0]`, could return a `Point`, and a `Point` is not a `ColoredPoint`. Thus to allow such an assignment would allow a violation of the type system. A cast may be used (§5.4, §15.15) to ensure that `pvec` references a `ColoredPoint[]`:

```
cpvec = (ColoredPoint[])pvec;     // okay, but may throw an
                                  // exception at run time
```

5.3 Method Invocation Conversion

Method invocation conversion is applied to each argument value in a method or constructor invocation (§15.8, §15.11): the type of the argument expression must be converted to the type of the corresponding parameter. Method invocation contexts allow the use of an identity conversion (§5.1.1), a widening primitive conversion (§5.1.2), or a widening reference conversion (§5.1.4).

Method invocation conversions specifically do not include the implicit narrowing of integer constants which is part of assignment conversion (§5.2). The Java designers felt that including these implicit narrowing conversions would add additional complexity to the overloaded method matching resolution process (§15.11.2). Thus, the example:

```
class Test {
    static int m(byte a, int b) { return a+b; }
    static int m(short a, short b) { return a-b; }
    public static void main(String[] args) {
        System.out.println(m(12, 2));    // compile-time error
    }
}
```

causes a compile-time error because the integer literals `12` and `2` have type `int`, so neither method `m` matches under the rules of (§15.11.2). A language that included implicit narrowing of integer constants would need additional rules to resolve cases like this example.

5.4 String Conversion

String conversion applies only to the operands of the binary + operator when one of the arguments is a `String`. In this single special case, the other argument to the + is converted to a `String`, and a new `String` which is the concatenation of the two strings is the result of the +. String conversion is specified in detail within the description of the string concatenation + operator (§15.17.1).

5.5 Casting Conversion

Sing away sorrow, cast away care.
—Miguel de Cervantes (1547–1616),
Don Quixote (Lockhart's translation), Chapter viii

Casting conversion is applied to the operand of a cast operator (§15.15): the type of the operand expression must be converted to the type explicitly named by the cast operator. Casting contexts allow the use of an identity conversion (§5.1.1), a widening primitive conversion (§5.1.2), a narrowing primitive conversion (§5.1.3), a widening reference conversion (§5.1.4), or a narrowing reference conversion (§5.1.5). Thus casting conversions are more inclusive than assignment or method invocation conversions: a cast can do any permitted conversion other than a string conversion.

Some casts can be proven incorrect at compile time; such casts result in a compile-time error.

A value of a primitive type can be cast to another primitive type by identity conversion, if the types are the same, or by a widening primitive conversion or a narrowing primitive conversion.

A value of a primitive type cannot be cast to a reference type by casting conversion, nor can a value of a reference type be cast to a primitive type.

The remaining cases involve conversion between reference types. The detailed rules for compile-time correctness checking of a casting conversion of a value of compile-time reference type *S* (source) to a compile-time reference type *T* (target) are as follows:

- If *S* is a class type:
  - If *T* is a class type, then *S* and *T* must be related classes—that is, *S* and *T* must be the same class, or *S* a subclass of *T*, or *T* a subclass of *S*; otherwise a compile-time error occurs.
  - If *T* is an interface type:
    - If *S* is not a `final` class (§8.1.2), then the cast is always correct at compile time (because even if *S* does not implement *T*, a subclass of *S* might).
    - If *S* is a `final` class (§8.1.2), then *S* must implement *T*, or a compile-time error occurs.
  - If *T* is an array type, then *S* must be the class `Object`, or a compile-time error occurs.
- If *S* is an interface type:
  - If *T* is a class type that is not `final` (§8.1.2), then the cast is always correct at compile time (because even if *T* does not implement *S*, a subclass of *T* might).
  - If *T* is a class type that is `final` (§8.1.2), then *T* must implement *S*, or a compile-time error occurs.
  - If *T* is an interface type and if *T* and *S* contain methods with the same signature (§8.4.2) but different return types, then a compile-time error occurs.
- If *S* is an array type *SC*`[]`, that is, an array of components of type *SC*:
  - If *T* is a class type, then if *T* is not `Object`, then a compile-time error occurs (because `Object` is the only class type to which arrays can be assigned).
  - If *T* is an interface type, then a compile-time error occurs unless *T* is the interface type `Cloneable`, the only interface implemented by arrays.
  - If *T* is an array type *TC*`[]`, that is, an array of components of type *TC*, then a compile-time error occurs unless one of the following is true:
    - *TC* and *SC* are the same primitive type.
    - *TC* and *SC* are reference types and type *SC* can be cast to *TC* by a recursive application of these compile-time rules for casting.

See §8 for the detailed specifications of classes, §9 for interfaces, and §10 for arrays.

If a cast to a reference type is not a compile-time error, there are two cases:

- The cast can be determined to be correct at compile time. A cast from the compile-time type *S* to compile-time type *T* is correct at compile time if and only if *S* can be converted to *T* by assignment conversion (§5.2).
- The cast requires a run-time validity check. If the value at run time is `null`, then the cast is allowed. Otherwise, let *R* be the class of the object referred to by the run-time reference value, and let *T* be the type named in the cast operator. A cast conversion must check, at run time, that the class *R* is assignment compatible with the type *T*, using the algorithm specified in §5.2 but using the class *R* instead of the compile-time type *S* as specified there. (Note that *R* cannot be an interface when these rules are first applied for any given cast, but *R* may be an interface if the rules are applied recursively because the run-time reference value refers to an array whose element type is an interface type.) This modified algorithm is shown here:
  - If *R* is an ordinary class (not an array class):
    - If *T* is a class type, then *R* must be either the same class (§4.3.4) as *T* or a subclass of *T*, or a run-time exception is thrown.
    - If *T* is an interface type, then *R* must implement (§8.1.4) interface *T*, or a run-time exception is thrown.
    - If *T* is an array type, then a run-time exception is thrown.
  - If *R* is an interface:
    - If *T* is a class type, then *T* must be `Object` (§4.3.2, §20.1), or a run-time exception is thrown.
    - If *T* is an interface type, then *R* must be either the same interface as *T* or a subinterface of *T*, or a run-time exception is thrown.
    - If *T* is an array type, then a run-time exception is thrown.
  - If *R* is a class representing an array type *RC*`[]`—that is, an array of components of type *RC:*
    - If *T* is a class type, then *T* must be `Object` (§4.3.2, §20.1), or a run-time exception is thrown.
    - If *T* is an interface type, then a run-time exception is thrown unless *T* is the interface type `Cloneable`, the only interface implemented by arrays (this case could slip past the compile-time checking if, for example, a reference to an array were stored in a variable of type `Object`).

- If *T* is an array type *TC*[], that is, an array of components of type *TC*, then a run-time exception is thrown unless one of the following is true:
  - *TC* and *RC* are the same primitive type.
  - *TC* and *RC* are reference types and type *RC* can be cast to *TC* by a recursive application of these run-time rules for casting.

If a run-time exception is thrown, it is a `ClassCastException` (§11.5.1.1, §20.22).

Here are some examples of casting conversions of reference types, similar to the example in §5.2:

```
public class Point { int x, y; }

public interface Colorable { void setColor(int color); }

public class ColoredPoint extends Point implements Colorable
{
    int color;
    public void setColor(int color) { this.color = color; }
}

final class EndPoint extends Point { }

class Test {

    public static void main(String[] args) {
        Point p = new Point();
        ColoredPoint cp = new ColoredPoint();
        Colorable c;

        // The following may cause errors at run time because
        // we cannot be sure they will succeed; this possibility
        // is suggested by the casts:
        cp = (ColoredPoint)p;  // p might not reference an
                               // object which is a ColoredPoint
                               // or a subclass of ColoredPoint
        c = (Colorable)p;      // p might not be Colorable

        // The following are incorrect at compile time because
        // they can never succeed as explained in the text:
        Long l = (Long)p;      // compile-time error #1
        EndPoint e = new EndPoint();
        c = (Colorable)e;      // compile-time error #2

    }

}
```

Here the first compile-time error occurs because the class types `Long` and `Point` are unrelated (that is, they are not the same, and neither is a subclass of the other), so a cast between them will always fail.

The second compile-time error occurs because a variable of type `EndPoint` can never reference a value that implements the interface `Colorable`. This is because `EndPoint` is a `final` type, and a variable of a `final` type always holds a value of the same run-time type as its compile-time type. Therefore, the run-time type of variable `e` must be exactly the type `EndPoint`, and type `EndPoint` does not implement `Colorable`.

Here is an example involving arrays (§10):

```
class Point {
    int x, y;
    Point(int x, int y) { this.x = x; this.y = y; }
    public String toString() { return "("+x+","+y+")"; }
}
public interface Colorable { void setColor(int color); }
public class ColoredPoint extends Point implements Colorable
{
    int color;
    ColoredPoint(int x, int y, int color) {
        super(x, y); setColor(color);
    }
    public void setColor(int color) { this.color = color; }
    public String toString() {
        return super.toString() + "@" + color;
    }
}
class Test {
    public static void main(String[] args) {
        Point[] pa = new ColoredPoint[4];
        pa[0] = new ColoredPoint(2, 2, 12);
        pa[1] = new ColoredPoint(4, 5, 24);
        ColoredPoint[] cpa = (ColoredPoint[])pa;
        System.out.print("cpa: {");
        for (int i = 0; i < cpa.length; i++)
            System.out.print((i == 0 ? " " : ", ") + cpa[i]);
        System.out.println(" }");
    }
}
```

This example compiles without errors and produces the output:

```
cpa: { (2,2)@12, (4,5)@24, null, null }
```

The following example uses casts to compile, but it throws exceptions at run time, because the types are incompatible:

```
public class Point { int x, y; }
public interface Colorable { void setColor(int color); }
public class ColoredPoint extends Point implements Colorable
{
    int color;
    public void setColor(int color) { this.color = color; }
}
class Test {
    public static void main(String[] args) {
        Point[] pa = new Point[100];
        // The following line will throw a ClassCastException:
        ColoredPoint[] cpa = (ColoredPoint[])pa;
        System.out.println(cpa[0]);
        int[] shortvec = new int[2];
        Object o = shortvec;
        // The following line will throw a ClassCastException:
        Colorable c = (Colorable)o;
        c.setColor(0);
    }
}
```

5.6 Numeric Promotions

Numeric promotion is applied to the operands of an arithmetic operator. Numeric promotion contexts allow the use of an identity conversion (§5.1.1) or a widening primitive conversion (§5.1.2).

Numeric promotions are used to convert the operands of a numeric operator to a common type so that an operation can be performed. The two kinds of numeric promotion are unary numeric promotion (§5.6.1) and binary numeric promotion (§5.6.2). The analogous conversions in C are called "the usual unary conversions" and "the usual binary conversions."

Numeric promotion is not a general feature of Java, but rather a property of the specific definitions of the built-in operations.

5.6.1 Unary Numeric Promotion

Some operators apply *unary numeric promotion* to a single operand, which must produce a value of a numeric type:

- If the operand is of compile-time type `byte`, `short`, or `char`, unary numeric promotion promotes it to a value of type `int` by a widening conversion (§5.1.2).
- Otherwise, a unary numeric operand remains as is and is not converted.

Unary numeric promotion is performed on expressions in the following situations:

- The dimension expression in array creations (§15.9)
- The index expression in array access expressions (§15.12)
- Operands of the unary operators plus + (§15.14.3) and minus - (§15.14.4)
- The operand of the bitwise complement operator ~ (§15.14.5)
- Each operand, separately, of the shift operators >>, >>>, and << (§15.18), so that a `long` shift distance (right operand) does not promote the value being shifted (left operand) to `long`

Here is a test program that includes examples of unary numeric promotion:

```
class Test {
    public static void main(String[] args) {
        byte b = 2;
        int a[] = new int[b];  // dimension expression promotion
        char c = '\u0001';
        a[c] = 1;              // index expression promotion
        a[0] = -c;             // unary - promotion
        System.out.println("a: " + a[0] + "," + a[1]);

        b = -1;
        int i = ~b;            // bitwise complement promotion
        System.out.println("~0x" + Integer.toHexString(b)
                        + "==0x" + Integer.toHexString(i));

        i = b << 4L;           // shift promotion (left operand)
        System.out.println("0x" + Integer.toHexString(b)
                    + "<<4L==0x" + Integer.toHexString(i));
    }
}
```

This test program produces the output:

```
a: -1,1
~0xffffffff==0x0
0xffffffff<<4L==0xfffffff0
```

5.6.2 Binary Numeric Promotion

When an operator applies *binary numeric promotion* to a pair of operands, each of which must denote a value of a numeric type, the following rules apply, in order, using widening conversion (§5.1.2) to convert operands as necessary:

- If either operand is of type `double`, the other is converted to `double`.
- Otherwise, if either operand is of type `float`, the other is converted to `float`.
- Otherwise, if either operand is of type `long`, the other is converted to `long`.
- Otherwise, both operands are converted to type `int`.

Binary numeric promotion is performed on the operands of certain operators:

- The multiplicative operators `*`, `/` and `%` (§15.16)
- The addition and subtraction operators for numeric types `+` and `-` (§15.17.2)
- The numerical comparison operators `<`, `<=`, `>`, and `>=` (§15.19.1)
- The numerical equality operators `==` and `!=` (§15.20.1)
- The integer bitwise operators `&`, `^`, and `|` (§15.21.1)
- In certain cases, the conditional operator `? :` (§15.24)

An example of binary numeric promotion appears above in §5.1. Here is another:

```
class Test {
    public static void main(String[] args) {
        int i = 0;
        float f = 1.0f;
        double d = 2.0;

        // First i*f promoted to float*float, then
        // float==double is promoted to double==double:
        if (i * f == d)
            System.out.println("oops");

        // A char&byte is promoted to int&int:
        byte b = 0x1f;
        char c = 'G';
        int control = c & b;
        System.out.println(Integer.toHexString(control));

        // A int:float promoted to float:float:
        f = (b==0) ? f : 4.0f;
        System.out.println(1.0/f);
    }
}
```

which produces the output:

```
7
0.25
```

The example converts the ASCII character `G` to the ASCII control-G (BEL), by masking off all but the low 5 bits of the character. The `7` is the numeric value of this control character.

O suns! O grass of graves! O perpetual transfers and promotions!
—Walt Whitman, *Walt Whitman* (1855),
in *Leaves of Grass*

CHAPTER 6

Names

The Tao that can be told is not the eternal Tao;
The name that can be named is not the eternal name.
The Nameless is the origin of Heaven and Earth;
The Named is the mother of all things.
—Lao-Tsu (c. 6th century BC)

NAMES are used to refer to entities declared in a Java program. A declared entity (§6.1) is a package, class type, interface type, member (field or method) of a reference type, parameter (to a method, constructor, or exception handler), or local variable.

Names in Java programs are either simple, consisting of a single identifier, or qualified, consisting of a sequence of identifiers separated by "`.`" tokens (§6.2).

Every name introduced by a declaration has a *scope* (§6.3), which is the part of the Java program text within which the declared entity can be referred to by a simple name.

Packages and reference types (that is, class types, interface types, and array types) have members (§6.4). A member can be referred to using a qualified name `N.x`, where `N` is a simple or qualified name and `x` is an identifier. If `N` names a package, then `x` is a member of that package, which is either a class or interface type or a subpackage. If `N` names a reference type or a variable of a reference type, then `x` names a member of that type, which is either a field or a method.

In determining the meaning of a name (§6.5), Java uses the context of the occurrence to disambiguate among packages, types, variables, and methods with the same name.

Access control (§6.6) can be specified in a class, interface, method, or field declaration to control when *access* to a member is allowed. Access is a different concept from scope; access specifies the part of the Java program text within which the declared entity can be referred to by a qualified name, a field access expression (§15.10), or a method invocation expression (§15.11) in which the method is not specified by a simple name. The default access is that a member can be accessed anywhere within the package that contains its declaration; other possibilities are `public`, `protected`, and `private`.

Fully qualified names (§6.7) and naming conventions (§6.8) are also discussed in this chapter.

The name of a field, parameter, or local variable may be used as an expression (§15.13.1). The name of a method may appear in an expression only as part of a method invocation expression (§15.11). The name of a class or interface type may appear in an expression only as part of a class instance creation expression (§15.8), an array creation expression (§15.9), a cast expression (§15.15), or an `instanceof` expression (§15.19.2), or as part of a qualified name for a field or method. The name of a package may appear in an expression only as part of a qualified name for a class or interface type.

6.1 Declarations

A *declaration* introduces an entity into a Java program and includes an identifier (§3.8) that can be used in a name to refer to this entity. A declared entity is one of the following:

- A package, declared in a `package` declaration (§7.4)
- An imported type, declared in a single-type-import declaration (§7.5.1) or a type-import-on-demand declaration (§7.5.2)
- A class, declared in a class type declaration (§8.1)
- An interface, declared in an interface type declaration (§9.1)
- A member of a reference type (§8.2, §9.2, §10.7), one of the following:
  - A field, one of the following:
    - A field declared in a class type (§8.3)
    - A constant field declared in an interface type (§9.3)
    - The field `length`, which is implicitly a member of every array type (§10.7)
  - A method, one of the following:
    - A method (`abstract` or otherwise) declared in a class type (§8.4)
    - A method (always `abstract`) declared in an interface type (§9.4)

- A parameter, one of the following:
  - A parameter of a method or constructor of a class (§8.4.1, §8.6.1)
  - A parameter of an `abstract` method of an interface (§9.4)
  - A parameter of an exception handler declared in a `catch` clause of a `try` statement (§14.18)
- A local variable, one of the following:
  - A local variable declared in a block (§14.3)
  - A local variable declared in a `for` statement (§14.12)

Constructors (§8.6) are also introduced by declarations, but use the name of the class in which they are declared rather than introducing a new name.

6.2 Names and Identifiers

A *name* is used to refer to an entity declared in a Java program.

There are two forms of names: simple names and qualified names. A *simple name* is a single identifier. A *qualified name* consists of a name, a "`.`" token, and an identifier.

In determining the meaning of a name (§6.5), the Java language takes into account the context in which the name appears. It distinguishes among contexts where a name must denote (refer to) a package (§6.5.3), a type (§6.5.4), a variable or value in an expression (§6.5.5), or a method (§6.5.6).

Not all identifiers in Java programs are a part of a name. Identifiers are also used in the following situations:

- In declarations (§6.1), where an identifier may occur to specify the name by which the declared entity will be known
- In field access expressions (§15.10), where an identifier occurs after a "`.`" token to indicate a member of an object that is the value of an expression or the keyword `super` that appears before the "`.`" token
- In some method invocation expressions (§15.11), where an identifier may occur after a "`.`" token and before a "`(`" token to indicate a method to be invoked for an object that is the value of an expression or the keyword `super` that appears before the "`.`" token
- As labels in labeled statements (§14.6) and in `break` (§14.13) and `continue` (§14.14) statements that refer to statement labels

In the example:

```
class Test {
   public static void main(String[] args) {
      Class c = System.out.getClass();
      System.out.println(c.toString().length() +
                              args[0].length() + args.length);
   }
}
```

the identifiers Test, main, and the first occurrences of args and c are not names; rather, they are used in declarations to specify the names of the declared entities. The names String, Class, System.out.getClass, System.out.println, c.toString, args, and args.length appear in the example. The first occurrence of length is not a name, but rather an identifier appearing in a method invocation expression (§15.11). The second occurrence of length is not a name, but rather an identifier appearing in a method invocation expression (§15.11).

The identifiers used in labeled statements and their associated break and continue statements are completely separate from those used in declarations. Thus, the following code is valid:

```
class TestString {

   char[] value;

   int offset, count;

   int indexOf(TestString str, int fromIndex) {
      char[] v1 = value, v2 = str.value;
      int max = offset + (count - str.count);
      int start = offset + ((fromIndex < 0) ? 0 : fromIndex);
   i:
      for (int i = start; i <= max; i++)
      {
         int n = str.count, j = i, k = str.offset;
         while (n-- != 0) {
            if (v1[j++] != v2[k++])
               continue i;
         }
         return i - offset;
      }
      return -1;
   }
}
```

This code was taken from a version of the class String and its method indexOf (§20.12.26), where the label was originally called test. Changing the label to have the same name as the local variable i does not hide the label in the scope of the declaration of i. The identifier max could also have been used as the statement label; the label would not hide the local variable max within the labeled statement.

6.3 Scope of a Simple Name

The *scope* of a declaration is the region of the program within which the entity declared by the declaration can be referred to using a simple name:

- The scope of a package, as introduced by a `package` declaration, is determined by the host system (§7.4.3). All Java code is within the scope of the standard package named `java`, so the package `java` can always be referred to by Java code.
- The scope of a type imported by a single-type-import declaration (§7.5.1) or type-import-on-demand declaration (§7.5.2) is all the class and interface type declarations (§7.6) in the compilation unit in which the import declaration appears.
- The scope of a type introduced by a class type declaration (§8.1.1) or interface type declaration (§9.1.1) is the declarations of all class and interface types in all the compilation units (§7.3) of the package in which it is declared.
- The scope of a member declared in or inherited by a class type (§8.2) or interface type (§9.2) is the entire declaration of the class or interface type. The declaration of a member needs to appear before it is used only when the use is in a field initialization expression (§8.3.2, §12.4.2, §12.5). This means that a compile-time error results from the test program:

  ```
  class Test {
      int i = j;    // compile-time error: incorrect forward reference
      int j = 1;
  }
  ```

  whereas the following example compiles without error:

  ```
  class Test {
      Test() { k = 2; }
      int j = 1;
      int i = j;
      int k;
  }
  ```

  even though the constructor (§8.6) for `Test` refers to the field `k` that is declared three lines later.
- The scope of a parameter of a method (§8.4.1) is the entire body of the method.

- The scope of a parameter of a constructor (§8.6.1) is the entire body of the constructor.
- The scope of a local variable declaration in a block (§14.3.2) is the rest of the block in which the declaration appears, starting with its own initializer (§14.3) and including any further declarators to the right in the local variable declaration statement.
- The scope of a local variable declared in the *ForInit* part of a `for` statement (§14.12) includes all of the following:
  - Its own initializer
  - Any further declarators to the right in the *ForInit* part of the `for` statement
  - The *Expression* and *ForUpdate* parts of the `for` statement
  - The contained *Statement*
- The scope of a parameter of an exception handler that is declared in a `catch` clause of a `try` statement (§14.18) is the entire block associated with the `catch`.

These rules imply that declarations of class and interface types need not appear before uses of the types.

In the example:

```
package points;

class Point {
    int x, y;
    PointList list;
    Point next;
}

class PointList {
    Point first;
}
```

the use of `PointList` in class `Point` is correct, because the scope of the class type name `PointList` includes both class `Point` and class `PointList`, as well as any other type declarations in other compilation units of package `points`.

6.3.1 Hiding Names

Some declarations may be hidden (§6.3.1) in part of their scope by another declaration of the same name, in which case a simple name cannot be used to refer to the declared entity.

The example:

```
class Test {
    static int x = 1;
    public static void main(String[] args) {
        int x = 0;
        System.out.print("x=" + x);
        System.out.println(", Test.x=" + Test.x);
    }
}
```

produces the output:

```
x=0, Test.x=1
```

This example declares:

- a class `Test`
- a class (`static`) variable `x` that is a member of the class `Test`
- a class method `main` that is a member of the class `Test`
- a parameter `args` of the `main` method
- a local variable `x` of the `main` method

Since the scope of a class variable includes the entire body of the class (§8.2) the class variable `x` would normally be available throughout the entire body of the method `main`. In this example, however, the class variable `x` is hidden within the body of the method `main` by the declaration of the local variable `x`.

A local variable has as its scope the rest of the block in which it is declared (§14.3.2); in this case this is the rest of the body of the `main` method, namely its initializer "`0`" and the invocations of `print` and `println`.

This means that:

- The expression "`x`" in the invocation of `print` refers to (denotes) the value of the local variable `x`.
- The invocation of `println` uses a qualified name (§6.6) `Test.x`, which uses the class type name `Test` to access the class variable `x`, because the declaration of `Test.x` is hidden at this point and cannot be referred to by its simple name.

If the standard naming conventions (§6.8) are followed, then hiding that would make the identification of separate naming contexts matter should be rare. The following contrived example involves hiding because it does not follow the standard naming conventions:

```
class Point { int x, y; }

class Test {

    static Point Point(int x, int y) {
        Point p = new Point();
        p.x = x; p.y = y;
        return p;
    }

    public static void main(String[] args) {
        int Point;
        Point[] pa = new Point[2];
        for (Point = 0; Point < 2; Point++) {
            pa[Point] = new Point();
            pa[Point].x = Point;
            pa[Point].y = Point;
        }
        System.out.println(pa[0].x + "," + pa[0].y);
        System.out.println(pa[1].x + "," + pa[1].y);
        Point p = Point(3, 4);
        System.out.println(p.x + "," + p.y);
    }

}
```

This compiles without error and executes to produce the output:

```
0,0
1,1
3,4
```

Within the body of `main`, the lookups of `Point` find different declarations depending on the context of the use:

- In the expression "`new Point[2]`", the two occurrences of the class instance creation expression "`new Point()`", and at the start of three different local variable declaration statements, the `Point` is a *TypeName* (§6.5.4) and denotes the class type `Point` in each case.
- In the method invocation expression "`Point(3, 4)`" the occurrence of `Point` is a *MethodName* (§6.5.6) and denotes the class (`static`) method `Point`.
- All other names are *ExpressionNames* (§6.5.5) and refer to the local variable `Point`.

The example:

```
import java.util.*;

class Vector {
    int val[] = { 1 , 2 };
}

class Test {
    public static void main(String[] args) {
        Vector v = new Vector();
        System.out.println(v.val[0]);
    }
}
```

compiles and prints:

```
1
```

using the class `Vector` declared here in preference to class `java.util.Vector` that might be imported on demand.

6.4 Members and Inheritance

Packages and reference types have *members*. The members of a package (§7) are subpackages (§7.1) and all the class (§8) and interface (§9) types declared in all the compilation units (§7.3) of the package. The members of a reference type (§4.3) are fields (§8.3, §9.3, §10.7) and methods (§8.4, §9.4). Members are either declared in the type, or *inherited* because they are accessible members of a superclass or superinterface which are neither hidden nor overridden (§8.4.6).

This section provides an overview of the members of packages and reference types here, as background for the discussion of qualified names and the determination of the meaning of names. For a complete description of membership, see §7.1, §8.2, §9.2, and §10.7.

6.4.1 The Members of a Package

A member of a package (§7) is a subpackage (§7.1), or a class (§8) or interface (§9) type declared in a compilation unit (§7.3) of the package.

In general, the subpackages of a package are determined by the host system (§7.2). However, the standard package `java` always includes the subpackages `lang`, `util`, `io`, and `net` and may include other subpackages. No two distinct members of the same package may have the same simple name (§7.1), but members of different packages may have the same simple name. For example, it is possible to declare a package:

```
package vector;

public class Vector { Object[] vec; }
```

that has as a member a `public` class named `Vector`, even though the standard package `java.util` also declares a class named `Vector`. These two class types are different, reflected by the fact that they have different fully qualified names (§6.7). The fully qualified name of this example `Vector` is `vector.Vector`, whereas `java.util.Vector` is the fully qualified name of the standard `Vector` class. Because the package `vector` contains a class named `Vector`, it cannot also have a subpackage named `Vector`.

6.4.2 The Members of a Class Type

The members of a class type (§8.2) are fields and methods. The members of a class type are all of the following:

- Members inherited from its direct superclass (§8.1.3), if it has one (the class `Object` has no direct superclass)
- Members inherited from any direct superinterfaces (§8.1.4)
- Members declared in the body of the class (§8.1.5)

Constructors (§8.6) are not members.

There is no restriction against a field and a method of a class type having the same simple name.

A class may have two or more fields with the same simple name if they are declared in different interfaces and inherited. An attempt to refer to any of the fields by its simple name results in a compile-time error (§6.5.6.2, §8.2).

In the example:

```
interface Colors {
    int WHITE = 0, BLACK = 1;
}

interface Separates {
    int CYAN = 0, MAGENTA = 1, YELLOW = 2, BLACK = 3;
}

class Test implements Colors, Separates {
    public static void main(String[] args) {
        System.out.println(BLACK); // compile-time error: ambiguous
    }
}
```

the name `BLACK` in the method `main` is ambiguous, because class `Test` has two members named `BLACK`, one inherited from `Colors` and one from `Separates`.

A class type may have two or more methods with the same simple name if the methods have different signatures (§8.4.2), that is, if they have different numbers of parameters or different parameter types in at least one parameter position. Such a method member name is said to be *overloaded.*

A class type may contain a declaration for a method with the same name and the same signature as a method that would otherwise be inherited from a superclass or superinterface. In this case, the method of the superclass or superinterface is not inherited. If the method not inherited is `abstract`, then the new declaration is said to *implement* it; if the method not inherited is not `abstract`, then the new declaration is said to *override* it.

In the example:

```
class Point {
    float x, y;
    void move(int dx, int dy) { x += dx; y += dy; }
    void move(float dx, float dy) { x += dx; y += dy; }
    public String toString() { return "("+x+","+y+")"; }
}
```

the class `Point` has two members that are methods with the same name, `move`. The overloaded `move` method of class `Point` chosen for any particular method invocation is determined at compile time by the overloading resolution procedure given in §15.11.

In this example, the members of the class `Point` are the `float` instance variables `x` and `y` declared in `Point`, the two declared `move` methods, the declared `toString` method, and the members that `Point` inherits from its implicit direct superclass `Object` (§4.3.2), such as the method `hashCode` (§20.1.4). Note that `Point` does not inherit the `toString` method (§20.1.2) of class `Object` because that method is overridden by the declaration of the `toString` method in class `Point`.

6.4.3 The Members of an Interface Type

The members of an interface type (§9.2) are fields and methods. The members of an interface are all of the following:

- Members inherited from any direct superinterfaces (§9.1.3)
- Members declared in the body of the interface (§9.1.4)

An interface may have two or more fields with the same simple name if they are declared in different interfaces and inherited. An attempt to refer to any such field by its simple name results in a compile-time error (§6.5.5.1, §9.2).

In the example:

```
interface Colors {
    int WHITE = 0, BLACK = 1;
}

interface Separates {
    int CYAN = 0, MAGENTA = 1, YELLOW = 2, BLACK = 3;
}

interface ColorsAndSeparates extends Colors, Separates {
    int DEFAULT = BLACK;          // compile-time error: ambiguous
}
```

the members of the interface `ColorsAndSeparates` include those members inherited from `Colors` and those inherited from `Separates`, namely `WHITE`, `BLACK` (first of two), `CYAN`, `MAGENTA`, `YELLOW`, and `BLACK` (second of two). The member name `BLACK` is ambiguous in the interface `ColorsAndSeparates`.

6.4.4 The Members of an Array Type

The members of an array type (§10.7) are all of the following:

- Members inherited from its implicit superclass `Object` (§4.3.2, §20.1)
- The field `length`, which is a constant (`final`) field of every array; its type is `int` and it contains the number of components of the array

The example:

```
class Test {
    public static void main(String[] args) {
        int[] ia = new int[3];
        int[] ib = new int[6];
        System.out.println(ia.getClass() == ib.getClass());
        System.out.println("ia has length=" + ia.length);
    }
}
```

produces the output:

```
true
ia has length=3
```

This example uses the method `getClass` inherited from class `Object` and the field `length`. The result of the comparison of the `Class` objects in the second `println` demonstrates that all arrays whose components are of type `int` are instances of the same array type, which is `int[]`.

6.5 Determining the Meaning of a Name

The meaning of a name in Java depends on the context in which it is used. The determination of the meaning of a name requires three steps. First, context causes a name syntactically to fall into one of five categories: *PackageName*, *TypeName*, *ExpressionName*, *MethodName*, or *AmbiguousName*. Second, a name that is initially classified by its context as an *AmbiguousName* is then reclassified by certain scoping rules to be a *PackageName*, *TypeName*, or *ExpressionName*. Third, the resulting category then dictates the final determination of the meaning of the name (or a compilation error if the name has no meaning).

PackageName:
  Identifier
  PackageName . *Identifier*

TypeName:
  Identifier
  PackageName . *Identifier*

ExpressionName:
  Identifier
  AmbiguousName . *Identifier*

MethodName:
  Identifier
  AmbiguousName . *Identifier*

AmbiguousName:
  Identifier
  AmbiguousName . *Identifier*

Java's use of context helps to minimize name conflicts between entities of different kinds. Such conflicts will be rare if the naming conventions described in §6.8 are followed. Nevertheless, conflicts may arise unintentionally as types developed by different programmers or different organizations evolve. For example, types, methods, and fields may have the same name. Java never has trouble distinguishing between a method and a field with the same name, since the context of a use always tells whether a method or a field is intended.

6.5.1 Syntactic Classification of a Name According to Context

A name is syntactically classified as a *PackageName* in these contexts:

- In a package declaration (§7.4)
- In a type-import-on-demand declaration (§7.5.2)
- To the left of the "`.`" in a qualified *PackageName*
- To the left of the "`.`" in a qualified *TypeName*

A name is syntactically classified as a *TypeName* in these contexts:

- In a single-type-import declaration (§7.5.1)
- In an `extends` clause in a class declaration (§8.1.3)
- In an `implements` clause in a class declaration (§8.1.4)
- In an `extends` clause in an interface declaration (§9.1.3)
- As a *Type* (or the part of a *Type* that remains after all brackets are deleted) in any of the following contexts:
  - In a field declaration (§8.3, §9.3)
  - As the result type of a method (§8.4, §9.4)
  - As the type of a formal parameter of a method or constructor (§8.4.1, §8.6.1, §9.4)
  - As the type of an exception that can be thrown by a method or constructor (§8.4.4, §8.6.4, §9.4)
  - As the type of a local variable (§14.3)
  - As the type of an exception parameter in a `catch` clause of a `try` statement (§14.18)
  - As the class type of an instance that is to be created in a class instance creation expression (§15.8)
  - As the element type of an array to be created in an array creation expression (§15.9)
  - As the type mentioned in the cast operator of a cast expression (§15.15)
  - As the type that follows the `instanceof` relational operator (§15.19.2)

A name is syntactically classified as an *ExpressionName* in these contexts:

- As the array reference expression in an array access expression (§15.12)
- As a *PostfixExpression* (§15.13)
- As the left-hand operand of an assignment operator (§15.25)

A name is syntactically classified as a *MethodName* in this context:

- Before the "(" in a method invocation expression (§15.11)

A name is syntactically classified as an *AmbiguousName* in these contexts:

- To the left of the "." in a qualified *ExpressionName*
- To the left of the "." in a qualified *MethodName*
- To the left of the "." in a qualified *AmbiguousName*

6.5.2 Reclassification of Contextually Ambiguous Names

An *AmbiguousName* is then reclassified as follows:

- If the *AmbiguousName* is a simple name, consisting of a single *Identifier*:
  - If the *Identifier* appears within the scope (§6.3) of a local variable declaration (§14.3) or parameter declaration (§8.4.1, §8.6.1, §14.18) with that name, then the *AmbiguousName* is reclassified as an *ExpressionName*.
  - Otherwise, consider the class or interface `C` within whose declaration the *Identifier* occurs. If `C` has one or more fields with that name, which may be either declared within it or inherited, then the *AmbiguousName* is reclassified as an *ExpressionName*.
  - Otherwise, if a type of that name is declared in the compilation unit (§7.3) containing the *Identifier*, either by a single-type-import declaration (§7.5.1) or by a class or interface type declaration (§7.6), then the *AmbiguousName* is reclassified as a *TypeName*.
  - Otherwise, if a type of that name is declared in another compilation unit (§7.3) of the package (§7.1) of the compilation unit containing the *Identifier*, then the *AmbiguousName* is reclassified as a *TypeName*.
  - Otherwise, if a type of that name is declared by exactly one type-import-on-demand declaration (§7.5.2) of the compilation unit containing the *Identifier*, then the *AmbiguousName* is reclassified as a *TypeName*.

- Otherwise, if a type of that name is declared by more than one type-import-on-demand declaration of the compilation unit containing the *Identifier*, then a compile-time error results.
- Otherwise, the *AmbiguousName* is reclassified as a *PackageName*. A later step determines whether or not a package of that name actually exists.

* If the *AmbiguousName* is a qualified name, consisting of a name, a "`.`", and an *Identifier*, then the name to the left of the "`.`" is first reclassified, for it is itself an *AmbiguousName*. There is then a choice:
  - If the name to the left of the "`.`" is reclassified as a *PackageName*, then there is a further choice:
    - If there is a package whose name is the name to the left of the "`.`" and that package contains a declaration of a type whose name is the same as the *Identifier*, then this *AmbiguousName* is reclassified as a *TypeName*.
    - Otherwise, this *AmbiguousName* is reclassified as a *PackageName*. A later step determines whether or not a package of that name actually exists.
  - If the name to the left of the "`.`" is reclassified as a *TypeName*, then this *AmbiguousName* is reclassified as an *ExpressionName*.
  - If the name to the left of the "`.`" is reclassified as an *ExpressionName*, then this *AmbiguousName* is reclassified as an *ExpressionName*.

As an example, consider the following contrived "library code":

```
package ORG.rpgpoet;

import java.util.Random;

interface Music { Random[] wizards = new Random[4]; }
```

and then consider this example code in another package:

```
package bazola;

class Gabriel {
	static int n = ORG.rpgpoet.Music.wizards.length;
}
```

First of all, the name `ORG.rpgpoet.Music.wizards.length` is classified as an *ExpressionName* because it functions as a *PostfixExpression*. Therefore, each of the names:

```
ORG.rpgpoet.Music.wizards
ORG.rpgpoet.Music
```

```
ORG.rpgpoet
ORG
```

is initially classified as an *AmbiguousName*. These are then reclassified:

- Assuming that there is no class or interface named `ORG` in any other compilation unit of package `bazola`, then the simple name `ORG` is reclassified as a *PackageName*.
- Next, assuming that there is no class or interface named `rpgpoet` in any compilation unit of package `ORG` (and we know that there is no such class or interface because package `ORG` has a subpackage named `rpgpoet`), the qualified name `ORG.rpgpoet` is reclassified as a *PackageName*.
- Next, because package `ORG.rpgpoet` has an interface type named `Music`, the qualified name `ORG.rpgpoet.Music` is reclassified as a *TypeName*.
- Finally, because the name `ORG.rpgpoet.Music` is a *TypeName*, the qualified name `ORG.rpgpoet.Music.wizards` is reclassified as an *ExpressionName*.

6.5.3 Meaning of Package Names

The meaning of a name classified as a *PackageName* is determined as follows.

6.5.3.1 *Simple Package Names*

If a package name consists of a single *Identifier*, then this identifier denotes a top-level package named by that identifier. If no package of that name is accessible, as determined by the host system (§7.4.3), then a compile-time error occurs.

6.5.3.2 *Qualified Package Names*

If a package name is of the form *`Q.Id`*, then *`Q`* must also be a package name. The package name *`Q.Id`* names a package that is the member named *`Id`* within the package named by *`Q`*. If *`Q`* does not name an accessible package or *`Id`* does not name an accessible subpackage of that package, then a compile-time error occurs.

6.5.4 Meaning of Type Names

The meaning of a name classified as a *TypeName* is determined as follows.

6.5.4.1 *Simple Type Names*

If a type name consists of a single *Identifier*, then the identifier must occur in the scope of a declaration of a type with this name, or a compile-time error occurs. It is possible that the identifier occurs within the scope of more than one type with that name, in which case the type denoted by the name is determined as follows:

- If a type with that name is declared in the current compilation unit (§7.3), either by a single-type-import declaration (§7.5.1) or by a declaration of a class or interface type (§7.6), then the simple type name denotes that type.
- Otherwise, if a type with that name is declared in another compilation unit (§7.3) of the package (§7.1) containing the identifier, then the identifier denotes that type. Note that, in systems that store compilation units in a file system, such a compilation unit must have a file name that is the name of the type (§7.6).
- Otherwise, if a type of that name is declared by exactly one type-import-on-demand declaration (§7.5.2) of the compilation unit containing the identifier, then the simple type name denotes that type.
- Otherwise, if a type of that name is declared by more than one type-import-on-demand declaration of the compilation unit, then the name is ambiguous as a type name; a compile-time error occurs.
- Otherwise, the name is undefined as a type name; a compile-time error occurs.

This order for considering type declarations is designed to choose the most explicit of two or more applicable type declarations.

6.5.4.2 *Qualified Type Names*

If a type name is of the form `Q.Id`, then `Q` must be a package name. The type name `Q.Id` names a type that is the member named `Id` within the package named by `Q`. If `Q` does not name an accessible package, or `Id` does not name a type within that package, or the type named `Id` within that package is not accessible (§6.6), then a compile-time error occurs.

The example:

```
package wnj.test;

class Test {
    public static void main(String[] args) {
        java.util.Date date =
            new java.util.Date(System.currentTimeMillis());
        System.out.println(date.toLocaleString());
    }
}
```

produced the following output the first time it was run:

```
Sun Jan 21 22:56:29 1996
```

In this example:

- The name `wnj.test` must name a package on the host system. It is resolved by first looking for the package `wnj`, using the procedure described in §6.5.3.1, and then making sure that the subpackage `test` of this package is accessible.
- The name `java.util.Date` (§21.3) must denote a type, so we first use the procedure recursively to determine if `java.util` is an accessible package, which it is, and then look to see if the type `Date` is accessible in this package.

6.5.5 Meaning of Expression Names

The meaning of a name classified as an *ExpressionName* is determined as follows.

6.5.5.1 *Simple Expression Names*

If an expression name consists of a single *Identifier*, then:

- If the *Identifier* appears within the scope (§6.3) of a local variable declaration (§14.3) or parameter declaration (§8.4.1, §8.6.1, §14.18) with that name, then the expression name denotes a variable, that is, that local variable or parameter. Local variables and parameters are never hidden (§6.3, §6.3.1, §14.3), so there is necessarily at most one such local variable or parameter. The type of the expression name is the declared type of the local variable or parameter.
- Otherwise, if the *Identifier* appears within a class declaration (§8):
  - If there is not exactly one member of that class (§8.2) that is a field with that name, then a compile-time error results.
  - Otherwise, if the single member field with that name is declared `final` (§8.3.1.2), then the expression name denotes the value of the field. The type of the expression name is the declared type of the field. If the *Identifier* appears in a context that requires a variable and not a value, then a compile-time error occurs.
  - Otherwise, the expression name denotes a variable, the single member field with that name. The type of the expression name is the field's declared type.

  If the field is an instance variable (§8.3.1.1), the expression name must appear within the declaration of an instance method (§8.4), constructor (§8.6), or instance variable initializer (§8.3.2.2). If it appears within a `static` method (§8.4.3.2), static initializer (§8.5), or initializer for a `static` variable (§8.3.1.1, §12.4.2), then a compile-time error occurs.

- Otherwise, the identifier appears within an interface declaration (§9):
  - If there is not exactly one member of that interface (§9.2) that is a field with that name, then a compile-time error results.
  - Otherwise, the expression name denotes the value of the single member field of that name. The type of the expression name is the declared type of the field. If the *Identifier* appears in a context that requires a variable and not a value, then a compile-time error occurs.

In the example:

```
class Test {
    static int v;

    static final int f = 3;

    public static void main(String[] args) {
        int i;
        i = 1;
        v = 2;
        f = 33;                         // compile-time error
        System.out.println(i + " " + v + " " + f);
    }
}
```

the names used as the left-hand-sides in the assignments to `i`, `v`, and `f` denote the local variable `i`, the field `v`, and the value of `f` (not the variable `f`, because `f` is a `final` variable). The example therefore produces an error at compile time because the last assignment does not have a variable as its left-hand side. If the erroneous assignment is removed, the modified code can be compiled and it will produce the output:

```
1 2 3
```

6.5.5.2 *Qualified Expression Names*

If an expression name is of the form *`Q.Id`*, then *`Q`* has already been classified as a package name, a type name, or an expression name:

- If *`Q`* is a package name, then a compile-time error occurs.
- If *`Q`* is a type name that names a class type (§8), then:
  - If there is not exactly one accessible (§6.6) member of the class type that is a field named *`Id`*, then a compile-time error occurs.
  - Otherwise, if the single accessible member field is not a class variable (that is, it is not declared `static`), then a compile-time error occurs.

- Otherwise, if the class variable is declared `final`, then *`Q.Id`* denotes the value of the class variable. The type of the expression *`Q.Id`* is the declared type of the class variable. If *`Q.Id`* appears in a context that requires a variable and not a value, then a compile-time error occurs.
- Otherwise, *`Q.Id`* denotes the class variable. The type of the expression *`Q.Id`* is the declared type of the class variable.

- If *Q* is a type name that names an interface type (§9), then:
  - If there is not exactly one accessible (§6.6) member of the interface type that is a field named *Id*, then a compile-time error occurs.
  - Otherwise, *`Q.Id`* denotes the value of the field. The type of the expression *`Q.Id`* is the declared type of the field. If *`Q.Id`* appears in a context that requires a variable and not a value, then a compile-time error occurs.
- If *Q* is an expression name, let *T* be the type of the expression *Q*:
  - If *T* is not a reference type, a compile-time error occurs.
  - If there is not exactly one accessible (§6.6) member of the type *T* that is a field named *Id*, then a compile-time error occurs.
  - Otherwise, if this field is any of the following:
    - A field of an interface type
    - A `final` field of a class type (which may be either a class variable or an instance variable)
    - The `final` field `length` of an array type

    then *`Q.Id`* denotes the value of the field. The type of the expression *`Q.Id`* is the declared type of the field. If *`Q.Id`* appears in a context that requires a variable and not a value, then a compile-time error occurs.
  - Otherwise, *`Q.Id`* denotes a variable, the field *Id* of class *T*, which may be either a class variable or an instance variable. The type of the expression *`Q.Id`* is the declared type of the field

The example:

```
class Point {
    int x, y;
    static int nPoints;
}

class Test {
    public static void main(String[] args) {
        int i = 0;
        i.x++;                      // compile-time error
        Point p = new Point();
        p.nPoints();                // compile-time error
    }
}
```

encounters two compile-time errors, because the `int` variable `i` has no members, and because `nPoints` is not a method of class `Point`.

6.5.6 Meaning of Method Names

A *MethodName* can appear only in a method invocation expression (§15.11). The meaning of a name classified as a *MethodName* is determined as follows.

6.5.6.1 *Simple Method Names*

If a method name consists of a single *Identifier*, then *Identifier* is the method name to be used for method invocation. The *Identifier* must name at least one method of the class or interface within whose declaration the *Identifier* appears. See §15.11 for further discussion of the interpretation of simple method names in method invocation expressions.

6.5.6.2 *Qualified Method Names*

If a method name is of the form *Q.Id*, then *Q* has already been classified as a package name, a type name, or an expression name. If *Q* is a package name, then a compile-time error occurs. Otherwise, *Id* is the method name to be used for method invocation. If *Q* is a type name, then *Id* must name at least one `static` method of the type *Q*. If *Q* is an expression name, then let *T* be the type of the expression *Q*; *Id* must name at least one method of the type *T*. See §15.11 for further discussion of the interpretation of qualified method names in method invocation expressions.

6.6 Qualified Names and Access Control

Qualified names are a means of access to members of packages and reference types; related means of access include field access expressions (§15.10) and method invocation expressions (§15.11). All three are syntactically similar in that a "`.`" token appears, preceded by some indication of a package, type, or expression having a type and followed by an *Identifier* that names a member of the package or type. These are collectively known as constructs for *qualified access*.

Java provides mechanisms for *access control*, to prevent the users of a package or class from depending on unnecessary details of the implementation of that package or class. Access control applies to qualified access and to the invocation of constructors by class instance creation expressions (§15.8), explicit constructor invocations (§8.6.5), and the method `newInstance` of class `Class` (§20.3.6).

If access is permitted, then the accessed entity is said to be *accessible*.

6.6.1 Determining Accessibility

- Whether a package is accessible is determined by the host system (§7.2).
- If a class or interface type is declared `public`, then it may be accessed by any Java code that can access the package in which it is declared. If a class or interface type is not declared `public`, then it may be accessed only from within the package in which it is declared.
- A member (field or method) of a reference (class, interface, or array) type or a constructor of a class type is accessible only if the type is accessible and the member or constructor is declared to permit access:
  - If the member or constructor is declared `public`, then access is permitted. All members of interfaces are implicitly `public`.
  - Otherwise, if the member or constructor is declared `protected`, then access is permitted only when one of the following is true:
    - Access to the member or constructor occurs from within the package containing the class in which the `protected` member is declared.
    - Access occurs within a subclass of the class in which the `protected` member is declared, and the access is correct as described in §6.6.2.
  - Otherwise, if the member or constructor is declared `private`, then access is permitted only when it occurs from within the class in which it is declared.
  - Otherwise, we say there is default access, which is permitted only when the access occurs from within the package in which the type is declared.

6.6.2 Details on `protected` Access

A `protected` member or constructor of an object may be accessed from outside the package in which it is declared only by code that is responsible for the implementation of that object. Let *C* be the class in which a `protected` member or constructor is declared and let *S* be the subclass of *C* in whose declaration the use of the `protected` member or constructor occurs. Then:

- If an access is of a `protected` member (field or method), let *Id* be its name. Consider then the means of qualified access:
  - If the access is by a field access expression of the form `super.`*Id*, then the access is permitted.
  - If the access is by a qualified name *Q*`.`*Id*, where *Q* is a *TypeName*, then the access is permitted if and only if *Q* is *S* or a subclass of *S*.
  - If the access is by a qualified name *Q*`.`*Id*, where *Q* is an *ExpressionName*, then the access is permitted if and only if the type of the expression *Q* is *S* or a subclass of *S*.
  - If the access is by a field access expression *E*`.`*Id*, where *E* is a *Primary* expression, or by a method invocation expression *E*`.`*Id*`(...)`, where *E* is a *Primary* expression, then the access is permitted if and only if the type of *E* is *S* or a subclass of *S*.
- Otherwise, if an access is of a `protected` constructor:
  - If the access is by a superclass constructor invocation `super(...)`, then the access is permitted.
  - If the access is by a class instance creation expression `new` *T*`(...)`, then the access is not permitted. (A `protected` constructor can be accessed by a class instance creation expression only from within the package in which it is defined.)
  - If the access is by an invocation of the method `newInstance` of class `Class` (§20.3.6), then the access is not permitted.

6.6.3 An Example of Access Control

For examples of access control, consider the two compilation units:

```
package points;
class PointVec { Point[] vec; }
```

and:

```
package points;

public class Point {
    protected int x, y;
    public void move(int dx, int dy) { x += dx; y += dy; }
    public int getX() { return x; }
    public int getY() { return y; }
}
```

which declare two class types in the package `points`:

- The class type `PointVec` is not `public` and not part of the `public` interface of the package `points`, but rather can be used only by other classes in the package.
- The class type `Point` is declared `public` and is available to other packages. It is part of the `public` interface of the package `points`.
- The methods `move`, `getX`, and `getY` of the class `Point` are declared `public` and so are available to any Java code that uses an object of type `Point`.
- The fields `x` and `y` are declared `protected` and are accessible outside the package `points` only in subclasses of class `Point`, and only when they are fields of objects that are being implemented by the code that is accessing them.

See §6.6.7 for an example of how the `protected` access modifier limits access.

6.6.4 Example: Access to public and Non-public Classes

If a class lacks the `public` modifier, access to the class declaration is limited to the package in which it is declared (§6.6). In the example:

```
package points;

public class Point {
    public int x, y;
    public void move(int dx, int dy) { x += dx; y += dy; }
}

class PointList {
    Point next, prev;
}
```

two classes are declared in the compilation unit. The class `Point` is available outside the package `points`, while the class `PointList` is available for access only within the package. Thus a compilation unit in another package can access `points.Point`, either by using its fully qualified name:

```
package pointsUser;

class Test {
    public static void main(String[] args) {
        points.Point p = new points.Point();
        System.out.println(p.x + " " + p.y);
    }
}
```

or by using a single-type-import declaration (§7.5.1) that mentions the fully qualfied name, so that the simple name may be used thereafter:

```
package pointsUser;

import points.Point;

class Test {
    public static void main(String[] args) {
        Point p = new Point();
        System.out.println(p.x + " " + p.y);
    }
}
```

However, this compilation unit cannot use or import `points.PointList`, which is not declared `public` and is therefore inaccessible outside package `points`.

6.6.5 Example: Default-Access Fields, Methods, and Constructors

If none of the access modifiers `public`, `protected`, or `private` are specified, a class member or constructor is accessible throughout the package that contains the declaration of the class in which the class member is declared, but the class member or constructor is not accessible in any other package. If a `public` class has a method or constructor with default access, then this method or constructor is not accessible to or inherited by a subclass declared outside this package.

For example, if we have:

```
package points;

public class Point {
    public int x, y;
    void move(int dx, int dy) { x += dx; y += dy; }
    public void moveAlso(int dx, int dy) { move(dx, dy); }
}
```

then a subclass in another package may declare an unrelated `move` method, with the same signature (§8.4.2) and return type. Because the original `move` method is not accessible from package `morepoints`, `super` may not be used:

```
package morepoints;

public class PlusPoint extends points.Point {
    public void move(int dx, int dy) {
        super.move(dx, dy);         // compile-time error
        moveAlso(dx, dy);
    }
}
```

Because move of `Point` is not overridden by `move` in `PlusPoint`, the method `moveAlso` in `Point` never calls the method move in `PlusPoint`.

Thus if you delete the `super.move` call from `PlusPoint` and execute the test program:

```
import points.Point;

import morepoints.PlusPoint;

class Test {

    public static void main(String[] args) {
        PlusPoint pp = new PlusPoint();
        pp.move(1, 1);
    }

}
```

it terminates normally. If move of `Point` were overridden by `move` in `PlusPoint`, then this program would recurse infinitely, until a `StackoverflowError` occurred.

6.6.6 Example: `public` Fields, Methods, and Constructors

A `public` class member or constructor is accessible throughout the package where it is declared and from any other package that has access to the package in which it is declared (§7.4.4). For example, in the compilation unit:

```
package points;

public class Point {

    int x, y;

    public void move(int dx, int dy) {
        x += dx; y += dy;
        moves++;
    }

    public static int moves = 0;

}
```

the public class Point has as public members the move method and the moves field. These public members are accessible to any other package that has access to package points. The fields x and y are not public and therefore are accessible only from within the package points.

6.6.7 Example: protected Fields, Methods, and Constructors

Consider this example, where the point package declares:

```
package points;
public class Point {
    protected int x, y;
    void warp(threePoint.Point3d a) {
        if (a.z > 0)        // compile-time error: cannot access a.z
            a.delta(this);
    }
}
```

and the threePoint package declares:

```
package threePoint;
import points.Point;
public class Point3d extends Point {
    protected int z;
    public void delta(Point p) {
        p.x += this.x;      // compile-time error: cannot access p.x
        p.y += this.y;      // compile-time error: cannot access p.y
    }
    public void delta3d(Point3d q) {
        q.x += this.x;
        q.y += this.y;
        q.z += this.z;
    }
}
```

which defines a class Point3d. A compile-time error occurs in the method delta here: it cannot access the protected members x and y of its parameter p, because while Point3d (the class in which the references to fields x and y occur) is a subclass of Point (the class in which x and y are declared), it is not involved in the implementation of a Point (the type of the parameter p). The method delta3d can access the protected members of its parameter q, because the class Point3d is a subclass of Point and is involved in the implementation of a Point3d.

The method delta could try to cast (§5.4, §15.15) its parameter to be a Point3d, but this cast would fail, causing an exception, if the class of p at run time were not Point3d.

A compile-time error also occurs in the method warp: it cannot access the protected member z of its parameter a, because while the class Point (the class in which the reference to field z occurs) is involved in the implementation of a Point (the type of the parameter a), it is not a subclass of Point (the class in which z is declared).

6.6.8 Example: private Fields, Methods, and Constructors

A private class member or constructor is accessible only within the class body in which the member is declared and is not inherited by subclasses. In the example:

```
class Point {
    Point() { setMasterID(); }

    int x, y;
    private int ID;
    private static int masterID = 0;

    private void setMasterID() { ID = masterID++; }
}
```

the private members ID, masterID, and setMasterID may be used only within the body of class Point. They may not be accessed by qualified names, field access expressions, or method invocation expressions outside the body of the declaration of Point.

See §8.6.8 for an example that uses a private constructor.

6.7 Fully Qualified Names

Every package, class, interface, array type, and primitive type has a fully qualified name. It follows that every type except the null type has a fully qualified name.

- The fully qualified name of a primitive type is the keyword for that primitive type, namely boolean, char, byte, short, int, long, float, or double.
- The fully qualified name of a named package that is not a subpackage of a named package is its simple name.
- The fully qualified name of a named package that is a subpackage of another named package consists of the fully qualified name of the containing package, followed by ".", followed by the simple (member) name of the subpackage.

- The fully qualified name of a class or interface that is declared in an unnamed package is the simple name of the class or interface.
- The fully qualified name of a class or interface that is declared in a named package consists of the fully qualified name of the package, followed by "`.`", followed by the simple name of the class or interface.
- The fully qualified name of an array type consists of the fully qualified name of the component type of the array type followed by "`[]`".

Examples:

- The fully qualified name of the type `long` is "`long`".
- The fully qualified name of the standard package `java.lang` is "`java.lang`" because it is subpackage `lang` of package `java`.
- The fully qualified name of the class `Object`, which is defined in the package `java.lang`, is "`java.lang.Object`".
- The fully qualified name of the interface `Enumeration`, which is defined in the package `java.util`, is "`java.util.Enumeration`".
- The fully qualified name of the type "array of `double`" is "`double[]`".
- The fully qualified name of the type "array of array of array of array of `String`" is "`java.lang.String[][][][]`".

In the example:

```
package points;

class Point { int x, y; }

class PointVec {
    Point[] vec;
}
```

the fully qualified name of the type `Point` is "`points.Point`"; the fully qualified name of the type `PointVec` is "`points.PointVec`"; and the fully qualified name of the type of the field `vec` of class `PointVec` is "`points.Point[]`".

6.8 Naming Conventions

The Java system and standard classes attempt to use, whenever possible, names chosen according to the conventions presented here. These conventions help to make code more readable and avoid certain kinds of name conflicts.

We recommend these conventions for use in all Java programs. However, these conventions should not be followed slavishly if long-held conventional usage dictates otherwise. So, for example, the `sin` and `cos` methods of the class `java.lang.Math` have mathematically conventional names, even though these method names flout Java convention because they are short and are not verbs.

6.8.1 Package Names

Names of packages that are to be made widely available should be formed as described in §7.7. Such names are always qualified names whose first identifier consists of two or three uppercase letters that name an Internet domain, such as `COM`, `EDU`, `GOV`, `MIL`, `NET`, `ORG`, or a two-letter ISO country code such as `UK` or `JP`. Here are examples of hypothetical unique names that might be formed under this convention:

```
COM.JavaSoft.jag.Oak
ORG.NPR.pledge.driver
UK.ac.city.rugby.game
```

Names of packages intended only for local use should have a first identifier that begins with a lowercase letter, but that first identifier specifically should not be the identifier `java`; package names that start with the identifier `java` are reserved to JavaSoft for naming standard Java packages.

When package names occur in expressions:

- If a package name is hidden by a field declaration, then `import` declarations (§7.5) can usually be used to make available the type names declared in that package.
- If a package name is hidden by a declaration of a parameter or local variable, then the name of the parameter or local variable can be changed without affecting other Java code.
- The first component of a package name is normally not easily mistaken for a type name, as a type name normally begins with a single uppercase letter. (The Java language does not actually rely on case distinctions to determine whether a name is a package name or a type name. It is not possible for a type name to hide a package name.)

6.8.2 Class and Interface Type Names

Names of class types should be descriptive nouns or noun phrases, not overly long, in mixed case with the first letter of each word capitalized. For example:

```
ClassLoader
SecurityManager
Thread
Dictionary
BufferedInputStream
```

Likewise, names of interface types should be short and descriptive, not overly long, in mixed case with the first letter of each word capitalized. The name may be a descriptive noun or noun phrase, which is appropriate when an interface is used as if it were an abstract superclass, such as interfaces `java.io.DataInput` and `java.io.DataOutput`; or it may be an adjective describing a behavior, as for the interfaces `java.lang.Runnable` and `java.lang.Cloneable`.

Hiding involving class and interface type names is rare. Names of fields, parameters, and local variables normally do not hide type names because they conventionally begin with a lowercase letter whereas type names conventionally begin with an uppercase letter.

6.8.3 Method Names

Method names should be verbs or verb phrases, in mixed case, with the first letter lowercase and the first letter of any subsequent words capitalized. Here are some additional specific conventions for method names:

- Methods to `get` and `set` an attribute that might be thought of as a variable *V* should be named `get`*V* and `set`*V*. An example is the methods `getPriority` (§20.20.22) and `setPriority` (§20.20.23) of class `java.lang.Thread`.

- A method that returns the length of something should be named `length`, as in class `java.lang.String` (§20.12.11).

- A method that tests a `boolean` condition *V* about an object should be named `is`*V*. An example is the method `isInterrupted` of class `java.lang.Thread` (§20.20.32).

- A method that converts its object to a particular format *F* should be named `to`*F*. Examples are the method `toString` of class `java.lang.Object` (§20.1.2) and the methods `toLocaleString` (§21.3.27) and `toGMTString` (§21.3.28) of class `java.util.Date`.

Whenever possible and appropriate, basing the names of methods in a new class on names in an existing class that is similar, especially a class from the standard Java Application Programming Interface classes, will make it easier to use.

Method names cannot hide or be hidden by other names (§6.5.6).

6.8.4 Field Names

Names of fields that are not `final` should be in mixed case with a lowercase first letter and the first letters of subsequent words capitalized. Note that well-designed Java classes have very few `public` or `protected` fields, except for fields that are constants (`final static` fields) (§6.8.5).

Fields should have names that are nouns, noun phrases, or abbreviations for nouns. Examples of this convention are the fields `buf`, `pos`, and `count` of the class `java.io.ByteArrayInputStream` (§22.6) and the field `bytesTransferred` of the class `java.io.InterruptedIOException` (§22.30.1).

Hiding involving field names is rare.

- If a field name hides a package name, then an `import` declaration (§7.5) can usually be used to make available the type names declared in that package.
- If a field name hides a type name, then a fully qualified name for the type can be used.
- Field names cannot hide method names.
- If a field name is hidden by a declaration of a parameter or local variable, then the name of the parameter or local variable can be changed without affecting other Java code.

6.8.5 Constant Names

The names of constants in interface types should be, and `final` variables of class types may conventionally be, a sequence of one or more words, acronyms, or abbreviations, all uppercase, with components separated by underscore "_" characters. Constant names should be descriptive and not unnecessarily abbreviated. Conventionally they may be any appropriate part of speech. Examples of names for constants include `MIN_VALUE`, `MAX_VALUE`, `MIN_RADIX`, and `MAX_RADIX` of the class `java.lang.Character`.

A group of constants that represent alternative values of a set, or, less frequently, masking bits in an integer value, are sometimes usefully specified with a common acronym as a name prefix, as in:

```
interface ProcessStates {
    int PS_RUNNING = 0;
    int PS_SUSPENDED = 1;
}
```

Hiding involving constant names is rare:

- Constant names should be longer than three letters, so that they do not hide the initial component of a unique package name.
- Constant names normally have no lowercase letters, so they will not normally hide names of packages, types, or fields, whose names normally contain at least one lowercase letter.
- Constant names cannot hide method names, because they are distinguished syntactically.

6.8.6 Local Variable and Parameter Names

Local variable and parameter names should be short, yet meaningful. They are often short sequences of lowercase letters that are not words. For example:

- Acronyms, that is the first letter of a series of words, as in `cp` for a variable holding a reference to a `ColoredPoint`
- Abbreviations, as in `buf` holding a pointer to a `buffer` of some kind
- Mnemonic terms, organized in some way to aid memory and understanding, typically by using a set of local variables with conventional names patterned after the names of parameters to widely used classes. For example:
  - `in` and `out`, whenever some kind of input and output are involved, patterned after the fields of `java.lang.System`
  - `off` and `len`, whenever an offset and length are involved, patterned after the parameters to the `read` and `write` methods of the interfaces `DataInput` and `DataOutput` of `java.io`

One-character local variable or parameter names should be avoided, except for temporary and looping variables, or where a variable holds an undistinguished value of a type. Conventional one-character names are:

- `b` for a `byte`
- `c` for a `char`
- `d` for a `double`
- `e` for an `Exception`

- `f` for a `float`
- `i`, `j`, and `k` for integers
- `l` for a `long`
- `o` for an `Object`
- `s` for a `String`
- `v` for an arbitrary value of some type

Local variable or parameter names that consist of only two or three uppercase letters should be avoided to avoid potential conflicts with the initial country codes and domain names that are the first component of unique package names (§7.7).

What's in a name? That which we call a rose
By any other name would smell as sweet.
—William Shakespeare, *Romeo and Juliet* (c. 1594), Act II, scene ii

Rose is a rose is a rose is a rose.
—Gertrude Stein, *Sacred Emily* (1913), in *Geographies and Plays*

. . . stat rosa pristina nomine, nomina nuda tenemus.
—Bernard of Morlay, *De contemptu mundi* (12th century),
quoted in Umberto Eco, *The Name of the Rose* (1980)

Rose, Rose, bo-Bose,
Banana-fana fo-Fose,
Fee, fie, mo-Mose—
—Rose!
—Lincoln Chase and Shirley Elliston, *The Name Game*
(#3 pop single in the U.S., January 1965),
as applied to the name "Rose"

CHAPTER 7

Packages

Good things come in small packages.
—Traditional proverb

JAVA programs are organized as sets of packages. Each package has its own set of names for types, which helps to prevent name conflicts. A type is accessible (§6.6) outside the package that declares it only if the type is declared `public`.

The naming structure for packages is hierarchical (§7.1). The members of a package are class and interface types (§7.6), which are declared in compilation units of the package, and subpackages, which may contain compilation units and subpackages of their own.

A package can be stored in a file system (§7.2.1) or in a database (§7.2.2). Packages that are stored in a file system have certain constraints on the organization of their compilation units to allow a simple implementation to find classes easily. In either case, the set of packages available to a Java program is determined by the host system, but must always include at least the three standard packages `java.lang`, `java.util`, and `java.io` as specified in Chapters 20, 21, and 22. In most host environments, the standard packages `java.applet`, `java.awt`, and `java.net`, which are not described in this specification, are also available to Java programs.

A package consists of a number of compilation units (§7.3). A compilation unit automatically has access to all types declared in its package and also automatically imports each of the types declared in the predefined package `java.lang`.

A compilation unit has three parts, each of which is optional:

- A `package` declaration (§7.4), giving the fully qualified name (§6.7) of the package to which the compilation unit belongs
- `import` declarations (§7.5) that allow types from other packages to be referred to using their simple names
- Type declarations (§7.6) of class and interface types

For small programs and casual development, a package can be unnamed (§7.4.2) or have a simple name, but if Java code is to be widely distributed, unique package names should be chosen (§7.7). This can prevent the conflicts that would otherwise occur if two development groups happened to pick the same package name and these packages were later to be used in a single program.

7.1 Package Members

A *package* can have members of either or both of the following kinds:

- Subpackages of the package
- Types declared in the compilation units (§7.3) of the package

For example, in the standard Java Application Programming Interface:

- The package `java` has subpackages `awt`, `applet`, `io`, `lang`, `net`, and `util`, but no compilation units.
- The package `java.awt` has a subpackage named `image`, as well as a number of compilation units containing declarations of class and interface types.

If the fully qualified name (§6.7) of a package is *P*, and *Q* is a subpackage of *P*, then *P*.*Q* is the fully qualified name of the subpackage.

The subpackages of package `java` named `lang`, `util`, and `io` (whose fully qualified package names are therefore `java.lang`, `java.util`, and `java.io`) are a standard part of every Java implementation and are specified in Chapters 20, 21, and 22. Many Java implementations will include the entire set of `java` packages defined in the series of books *The Java Application Programming Interface*.

A package may not contain a type declaration and a subpackage of the same name, or a compile-time error results. Here are some examples:

- Because the package `java.awt` has a subpackage `image`, it cannot (and does not) contain a declaration of a class or interface type named `image`.
- If there is a package named `mouse` and a type `Button` in that package (which then might be referred to as `mouse.Button`), then there cannot be any package with the fully qualified name `mouse.Button` or `mouse.Button.Click`.
- If `COM.Sun.java.jag` is the fully qualified name of a type, then there cannot be any package whose fully qualified name is either `COM.Sun.java.jag` or `COM.Sun.java.jag.scrabble`.

The hierarchical naming structure for packages is intended to be convenient for organizing related packages in a conventional manner, but has no significance in the Java language itself other than the prohibition against a package having a subpackage with the same simple name as a type declared in that package. There is no special access relationship in the Java language between a package named `oliver` and another package named `oliver.twist`, or between packages named `evelyn.wood` and `evelyn.Waugh`. For example, the code in a package named `oliver.twist` has no better access to the types declared within package `oliver` than code in any other package.

7.2 Host Support for Packages

Each Java host determines how packages, compilation units, and subpackages are created and stored; which top-level package names are in scope in a particular compilation; and which packages are accessible.

The packages may be stored in a local file system in simple implementations of Java. Other implementations may use a distributed file system or some form of database to store Java source and/or binary code.

7.2.1 Storing Packages in a File System

As an extremely simple example, all the Java packages and source and binary code on a system might be stored in a single directory and its subdirectories. Each immediate subdirectory of this directory would represent a top-level package, that is, one whose fully qualified name consists of a single simple name. The directory might contain the following immediate subdirectories:

```
COM
gls
jag
java
wnj
```

where directory `java` would contain the standard Java Application Programming Interface packages that are part of every standard Java system; the directories `jag`, `gls`, and `wnj` might contain packages that the three authors of this specification created for their personal use and to share with each other within this small group; and the directory `COM` would contain packages procured from companies that used the conventions described in §7.7 to generate unique names for their packages.

Continuing the example, the directory `java` would probably contain at least the following subdirectories:

```
applet
awt
io
lang
net
util
```

corresponding to the standard packages `java.applet`, `java.awt`, `java.io`, `java.lang`, `java.net`, and `java.util` that are defined as part of the standard Java Application Programming Interface.

Still continuing the example, if we were to look inside the directory `util`, we might see the following files:

```
BitSet.java                        Observable.java
BitSet.class                       Observable.class
Date.java                          Observer.java
Date.class                         Observer.class
Dictionary.java                    Properties.java
Dictionary.class                   Properties.class
EmptyStackException.java           Random.java
EmptyStackException.class          Random.class
Enumeration.java                   Stack.java
Enumeration.class                  Stack.class
Hashtable.java                     StringTokenizer.java
Hashtable.class                    StringTokenizer.class
NoSuchElementException.java        Vector.java
NoSuchElementException.class       Vector.class
```

where each of the `.java` files contains the source for a compilation unit (§7.3) that contains the definition of a class or interface whose binary compiled form is contained in the corresponding `.class` file.

Under this simple organization of packages, an implementation of Java would transform a package name into a pathname by concatenating the components of the package name, placing a file name separator (directory indicator) between adjacent components. For example, if this simple organization were used on a UNIX system, where the file name separator is `/`, the package name:

```
jag.scrabble.board
```

would be transformed into the directory name:

```
jag/scrabble/board
```

and:

```
COM.Sun.sunsoft.DOE
```

would be transformed to the directory name:

```
COM/Sun/sunsoft/DOE
```

In fact, the standard JavaSoft Java Developer's Kit on UNIX differs from the very simple discipline described here only in that it provides a `CLASSPATH` environment variable that specifies a set of directories, each of which is treated like the single directory described here. These directories are searched in order for definitions of named packages and types.

A package name component or class name might contain a character that cannot correctly appear in a host file system's ordinary directory name, such as a Unicode character on a system that allows only ASCII characters in file names. As a convention, the character can be escaped by using, say, the `@` character followed by four hexadecimal digits giving the numeric value of the character, as in the `\uxxxx` escape (§3.3), so that the package name:

```
children.activities.crafts.papierM\u00e2ch\u00e9
```

which can also be written using full Unicode as:

```
children.activities.crafts.papierMâché
```

might be mapped to the directory name:

```
children/activities/crafts/papierM@00e2ch@00e9
```

If the `@` character is not a valid character in a file name for some given host file system, then some other character that is not valid in a Java identifier could be used instead.

7.2.2 Storing Packages in a Database

A host system may store packages and their compilation units and subpackages in a database.

Java allows such a database to relax the restrictions (§7.6) on compilation units in file-based implementations. For example, a system that uses a database to store packages need not enforce a maximum of one `public` class or interface per compilation unit. Systems that use a database must, however, provide an option to convert a Java program to a form that obeys the restrictions, for purposes of export to file-based implementations.

7.3 Compilation Units

CompilationUnit is the goal symbol (§2.1) for the syntactic grammar (§2.3) of Java programs. It is defined by the following productions:

CompilationUnit:
  PackageDeclaration$_{opt}$ *ImportDeclarations*$_{opt}$ *TypeDeclarations*$_{opt}$

ImportDeclarations:
  ImportDeclaration
  ImportDeclarations ImportDeclaration

TypeDeclarations:
  TypeDeclaration
  TypeDeclarations TypeDeclaration

Types declared in different compilation units can depend on each other, circularly. A Java compiler must arrange to compile all such types at the same time.

A *compilation unit* consists of three parts, each of which is optional:

- A `package` declaration (§7.4), giving the fully qualified name (§6.7) of the package to which the compilation unit belongs
- `import` declarations (§7.5) that allow types from other packages to be referred to using their simple names
- Type declarations (§7.6) of class and interface types

Every compilation unit automatically and implicitly imports every `public` type name declared in the predefined package `java.lang`, so that the names of all those types are available as simple names, as described in §7.5.3.

7.4 Package Declarations

A package declaration appears within a compilation unit to indicate the package to which the compilation unit belongs. A compilation unit that has no package declaration is part of an unnamed package.

7.4.1 Named Packages

A *package declaration* in a compilation unit specifies the name (§6.2) of the package to which the compilation unit belongs.

PackageDeclaration:
  `package` *PackageName* `;`

The package name mentioned in a package declaration must be the fully qualified name (§6.7) of the package.

If a type named *T* is declared in a compilation unit of a package whose fully qualified name is *P*, then the fully qualified name of the type is *P*.*T*; thus in the example:

```
package wnj.points;

class Point { int x, y; }
```

the fully qualified name of class `Point` is `wnj.points.Point`.

7.4.2 Unnamed Packages

A compilation unit that has no package declaration is part of an unnamed package. As an example, the compilation unit:

```
class FirstCall {
    public static void main(String[] args) {
        System.out.println("Mr. Watson, come here. "
                                    + "I want you.");
    }
}
```

defines a very simple compilation unit as part of an unnamed package.

A Java system must support at least one unnamed package; it may support more than one unnamed package but is not required to do so. Which compilation units are in each unnamed package is determined by the host system.

In Java systems that use a hierarchical file system for storing packages, one typical strategy is to associate an unnamed package with each directory; only one unnamed package is available at a time, namely the one that is associated with the "current working directory." The precise meaning of "current working directory" depends on the host system.

Unnamed packages are provided by Java principally for convenience when developing small or temporary applications or when just beginning development.

Caution must be taken when using unnamed packages. It is possible for a compilation unit in a named package to import a type from an unnamed package, but the compiled version of this compilation unit will likely then work only when that particular unnamed package is "current." For this reason, it is strongly recommended that compilation units of named packages never import types from unnamed packages. It is also recommended that any type declared in an unnamed package not be declared `public`, to keep them from accidentally being imported by a named package.

It is recommended that a Java system provide safeguards against unintended consequences in situations where compilation units of named packages import types from unnamed packages. One strategy is to provide a way to associate with each named package at most one unnamed package, and then to detect and warn about situations in which a named package is used by more than one unnamed package. It is specifically not required—indeed, it is strongly discouraged—for an implementation to support use of a named package by more than one unnamed package by maintaining multiple compiled versions of the named package.

7.4.3 Scope and Hiding of a Package Name

Which top-level package names are in scope (§6.3, §6.5) is determined by conventions of the host system.

Package names never hide other names.

7.4.4 Access to Members of a Package

Whether access to members of a package is allowed is determined by the host system. The package `java` should always be accessible, and its standard subpackages `lang`, `io`, and `util` should always be accessible.

It is strongly recommended that the protections of a file system or database used to store Java programs be set to make all compilation units of a package available whenever any of the compilation units is available.

7.5 Import Declarations

An *import declaration* allows a type declared in another package to be referred to by a simple name (§6.2) that consists of a single identifier. Without the use of an appropriate `import` declaration, the only way to refer to a type declared in another package is to use its fully qualified name (§6.7).

ImportDeclaration:
  SingleTypeImportDeclaration
  TypeImportOnDemandDeclaration

A single-type-import declaration (§7.5.1) imports a single type, by mentioning its fully qualified name. A type-import-on-demand declaration (§7.5.2) imports all the `public` types of a named package as needed.

An `import` declaration makes types available by their simple names only within the compilation unit that actually contains the `import` declaration. The scope of the name(s) it introduces specifically does not include the `package` statement, other `import` statements in the current compilation unit, or other compilation units in the same package. Please see §7.5.4 for an illustrative example.

7.5.1 Single-Type-Import Declaration

A *single-type-import declaration* imports a single type by giving its fully qualified name, making it available under a simple name in the class and interface declarations of its compilation unit.

SingleTypeImportDeclaration:
  `import` *TypeName* `;`

The *TypeName* must be the fully qualified name of a class or interface type; a compile-time error occurs if the named type does not exist. If the named type is not in the current package, then it must be accessible (§6.6)—in an accessible package and declared `public` (§8.1.2, §9.1.2)—or a compile-time error occurs.

The example:

```
import java.util.Vector;
```

causes the simple name `Vector` to be available within the class and interface declarations in a compilation unit. Thus, the simple name `Vector` refers to the type `Vector` in the package `java.util` in all places where it is not hidden (§6.3) by a declaration of a field, parameter, or local variable with the same name.

If two single-type-import declarations in the same compilation unit attempt to import types with the same simple name, then a compile-time error occurs, unless the two types are the same type, in which case the duplicate declaration is ignored. If another type with the same name is otherwise declared in the current compilation unit except by a type-import-on-demand declaration (§7.5.2), then a compile-time error occurs.

So the sample program:

```
import java.util.Vector;
class Vector { Object[] vec; }
```

causes a compile-time error because of the duplicate declaration of `Vector`, as does:

```
import java.util.Vector;
import myVector.Vector;
```

where `myVector` is a package containing the compilation unit:

```
package myVector;
public class Vector { Object[] vec; }
```

The compiler keeps track of types by their fully qualified names (§6.7). Simple names and fully qualified names may be used interchangeably whenever they are both available.

Note that an import statement cannot import a subpackage, only a type. For example, it does not work to try to import `java.util` and then use the name `util.Random` to refer to the type `java.util.Random`:

```
import java.util;                    // incorrect: compile-time error
class Test { util.Random generator; }
```

7.5.2 Type-Import-on-Demand Declaration

A *type-import-on-demand declaration* allows all `public` types declared in the package named by a fully qualified name to be imported as needed.

TypeImportOnDemandDeclaration:
  `import` *PackageName* `. * ;`

It is a compile-time error for a type-import-on-demand declaration to name a package that is not accessible (§6.6), as determined by the host system (§7.2). Two or more type-import-on-demand declarations in the same compilation unit may name the same package; the effect is as if there were exactly one such declaration. It is not a compile-time error to name the current package or `java.lang` in a type-import-on-demand declaration, even though they are already imported; the duplicate type-import-on-demand declaration is ignored.

The example:

```
import java.util.*;
```

causes the simple names of all `public` types declared in the package `java.util` to be available within the class and interface declarations of the compilation unit. Thus, the simple name `Vector` refers to the type `Vector` in the package `java.util` in all places where it is not hidden (§6.3) by a single-type-import declaration of a type whose simple name is `Vector`; by a type named `Vector` and declared in the package to which the compilation unit belongs; or by a declaration of a field, parameter, or local variable named `Vector`. (It would be unusual for any of these conditions to occur.)

7.5.3 Automatic Imports

Each compilation unit automatically imports each of the `public` type names declared in the predefined package `java.lang`, as if the declaration:

```
import java.lang.*;
```

appeared at the beginning of each compilation unit, immediately following any `package` statement.

The full specification of `java.lang` is given in Chapter 20. The following `public` types are defined in `java.lang`:

```
AbstractMethodError
ArithmeticException
ArrayStoreException
Boolean
Character
Class
ClassCastException
ClassCircularityError
ClassFormatError
ClassLoader
ClassNotFoundException
CloneNotSupportedException
Cloneable
Compiler
Double
Error
Exception
ExceptionInInitializerError
Float
IllegalAccessError
IllegalAccessException
IllegalArgumentException
IllegalMonitorStateException
IllegalThreadStateException
IncompatibleClassChangeError
IndexOutOfBoundsException
InstantiationError
InstantiationException
Integer
InternalError
InterruptedException
LinkageError
Long
Math
NegativeArraySizeException
NoClassDefFoundError
NoSuchFieldError
NoSuchMethodError
NullPointerException
Number
NumberFormatException
Object
OutOfMemoryError
Process
Runnable
Runtime
RuntimeException
SecurityException
SecurityManager
StackOverflowError
String
StringBuffer
System
Thread
ThreadDeath
ThreadGroup
Throwable
UnknownError
UnsatisfiedLinkError
VerifyError
VirtualMachineError
```

7.5.4 A Strange Example

Package names and type names are usually different under the naming conventions described in §6.8. Nevertheless, in a contrived example where there is an unconventionally-named package `Vector`, which declares a `public` class named `Mosquito`:

```
package Vector;

public class Mosquito { int capacity; }
```

and then the compilation unit:

```
package strange.example;

import java.util.Vector;
```

```
import Vector.Mosquito;

class Test {
   public static void main(String[] args) {
      System.out.println(new Vector().getClass());
      System.out.println(new Mosquito().getClass());
   }
}
```

the single-type-import declaration (§7.5.1) importing class `Vector` from package `java.util` does not prevent the package name `Vector` from appearing and being correctly recognized in subsequent `import` declarations. The example compiles and produces the output:

```
class java.util.Vector
class Vector.Mosquito
```

7.6 Type Declarations

A type declaration declares a class type (§8) or an interface type (§9):

TypeDeclaration:
  ClassDeclaration
  InterfaceDeclaration
  ;

A Java compiler must ignore extra "`;`" tokens appearing at the level of type declarations. Stray semicolons are permitted in Java solely as a concession to C++ programmers who are used to writing:

```
class date { int month, day, year; };
```

(In C++, but not in Java, one can provide a comma-separated list of identifiers in order to declare variables between the "`}`" and the "`;`".) Extra semicolons should not be used in new Java code. Software that reformats Java code can delete them.

By default, the types declared in a package are accessible only within the compilation units of that package, but a type may be declared to be `public` to grant access to the type from code in other packages (§6.6, §8.1.2, §9.1.2).

A Java implementation must keep track of types within packages by their fully qualified names (§6.7). Multiple ways of naming a type must be expanded to fully qualified names to make sure that such names are understood as referring to the same type. For example, if a compilation unit contains the single-type-import declaration (§7.5.1):

```
import java.util.Vector;
```

then within that compilation unit the simple name `Vector` and the fully qualified name `java.util.Vector` refer to the same type.

When Java packages are stored in a file system (§7.2.1), the host system may choose to enforce the restriction that it is a compile-time error if a type is not found in a file under a name composed of the type name plus an extension (such as `.java` or `.jav`) if either of the following is true:

- The type is referred to by code in other compilation units of the package in which the type is declared.
- The type is declared `public` (and therefore is potentially accessible from code in other packages).

This restriction implies that there must be at most one such type per compilation unit. This restriction makes it easy for a Java compiler and Java Virtual Machine to find a named class within a package; for example, the source code for a `public` type `wet.sprocket.Toad` would be found in a file `Toad.java` in the directory `wet/sprocket`, and the corresponding object code would be found in the file `Toad.class` in the same directory.

When Java packages are stored in a database (§7.2.2), the host system need not enforce such restrictions.

In practice, many Java programmers choose to put each class or interface type in its own compilation unit, whether or not it is `public` or is referred to by code in other compilation units.

7.7 Unique Package Names

Did I ever tell you that Mrs. McCave
Had twenty-three sons and she named them all "Dave"?
Well, she did. And that wasn't a smart thing to do. . . .
—Dr. Seuss (Theodore Geisel), *Too Many Daves* (1961)

Developers should take steps to avoid the possibility of two published packages having the same name by choosing *unique package names* for packages that are widely distributed. This allows packages to be easily and automatically installed and catalogued. This section specifies a standard convention, not enforced by a Java compiler, for generating such unique package names. Java systems are encouraged to provide automatic support for converting a set of packages from local and casual package names to the unique name format described here.

If unique package names are not used, then package name conflicts may arise far from the point of creation of either of the conflicting packages. This may create a situation that is difficult or impossible for the user or programmer to resolve. The class `ClassLoader` (§20.14) of the standard Java Virtual Machine environment can be used to isolate packages with the same name from each other in those cases where the packages will have constrained interactions, but not in a way that is transparent to a naïve Java program.

You form a unique package name by first having (or belonging to an organization that has) an Internet domain name, such as `Sun.COM`. You then reverse this name, component by component, to obtain, in this example, `COM.Sun`, and use this as a prefix for your package names, using a convention developed within your organization to further administer package names.

Such a convention might specify that certain directory name components be division, department, project, machine, or login names. Some possible examples:

```
COM.Sun.sunsoft.DOE
COM.Sun.java.jag.scrabble
COM.Apple.quicktime.v2
EDU.cmu.cs.bovik.cheese
GOV.whitehouse.socks.mousefinder
```

The first component of a unique package name is always written in all-uppercase ASCII letters and should be one of the top-level domain names, currently `COM`, `EDU`, `GOV`, `MIL`, `NET`, `ORG`, or one of the English two-letter codes identifying countries as specified in ISO Standard 3166, 1981. For more information, refer to the documents stored at `ftp://rs.internic.net/rfc`, for example, `rfc920.txt` and `rfc1032.txt`.

The name of a package is not meant to imply anything about where the package is stored within the Internet; for example, a package named `EDU.cmu.cs.bovik.cheese` is not necessarily obtainable from Internet address `cmu.EDU` or from `cs.cmu.EDU` or from `bovik.cs.cmu.EDU`. The Java convention for generating unique package names is merely a way to piggyback a package naming convention on top of an existing, widely known unique name registry instead of having to create a separate registry for Java package names.

If you need to get a new Internet domain name, you can get an application form from `ftp://ftp.internic.net` and submit the complete forms by E-mail to `domreg@internic.net`. To find out what the currently registered domain names are, you can `telnet` to `rs.internic.net` and use the `whois` facility.

Brown paper packages tied up with strings,
These are a few of my favorite things.
—Oscar Hammerstein II, *My Favorite Things* (1959)

CHAPTER 8

Classes

class 1. The noun *class* derives from
Medieval French and French *classe* from Latin *classis*,
probably originally a summons,
hence a summoned collection of persons,
a group liable to be summoned:
perhaps for *callassis* from *calare*,
to call, hence to summon.
—Eric Partridge
Origins: A Short Etymological Dictionary of Modern English

CLASS declarations define new reference types and describe how they are implemented (§8.1).

The name of a class has as its scope all type declarations in the package in which the class is declared (§8.1.1). A class may be declared `abstract` (§8.1.2.1) and must be declared `abstract` if it is incompletely implemented; such a class cannot be instantiated, but can be extended by subclasses. A class may be declared `final` (§8.1.2.2), in which case it cannot have subclasses. If a class is declared `public`, then it can be referred to from other packages.

Each class except `Object` is an extension of (that is, a subclass of) a single existing class (§8.1.3) and may implement interfaces (§8.1.4).

The body of a class declares members (fields and methods), static initializers, and constructors (§8.1.5). The scope of the name of a member is the entire declaration of the class to which the member belongs. Field, method, and constructor declarations may include the access modifiers (§6.6) `public`, `protected`, or `private`. The members of a class include both declared and inherited members (§8.2). Newly declared fields can hide fields declared in a superclass or superinterface. Newly declared methods can hide, implement, or override methods declared in a superclass or superinterface.

Field declarations (§8.3) describe class variables, which are incarnated once, and instance variables, which are freshly incarnated for each instance of the class.

A field may be declared `final` (§8.3.1.2), in which case it cannot be assigned to except as part of its declaration. Any field declaration may include an initializer; the declaration of a `final` field must include an initializer.

Method declarations (§8.4) describe code that may be invoked by method invocation expressions (§15.11). A class method is invoked relative to the class type; an instance method is invoked with respect to some particular object that is an instance of the class type. A method whose declaration does not indicate how it is implemented must be declared `abstract`. A method may be declared `final` (§8.4.3.3), in which case it cannot be hidden or overridden. A method may be implemented by platform-dependent `native` code (§8.4.3.4). A `synchronized` method (§8.4.3.5) automatically locks an object before executing its body and automatically unlocks the object on return, as if by use of a `synchronized` statement (§14.17), thus allowing its activities to be synchronized with those of other threads (§17).

Method names may be overloaded (§8.4.7).

Static initializers (§8.5) are blocks of executable code that may be used to help initialize a class when it is first loaded (§12.4).

Constructors (§8.6) are similar to methods, but cannot be invoked directly by a method call; they are used to initialize new class instances. Like methods, they may be overloaded (§8.6.6).

8.1 Class Declaration

A *class declaration* specifies a new reference type:

ClassDeclaration:
  ClassModifiers$_{opt}$ `class` *Identifier Super*$_{opt}$ *Interfaces*$_{opt}$ *ClassBody*

If a class is declared in a named package (§7.4.1) with fully qualified name `P` (§6.7), then the class has the fully qualified name `P.`*Identifier*. If the class is in an unnamed package (§7.4.2), then the class has the fully qualified name *Identifier*. In the example:

```
class Point { int x, y; }
```

the class `Point` is declared in a compilation unit with no `package` statement, and thus `Point` is its fully qualified name, whereas in the example:

```
package vista;
class Point { int x, y; }
```

the fully qualified name of the class `Point` is `vista.Point`. (The package name `vista` is suitable for local or personal use; if the package were intended to be widely distributed, it would be better to give it a unique package name (§7.7).)

A compile-time error occurs if the *Identifier* naming a class appears as the name of any other class type or interface type declared in the same package (§7.6).

A compile-time error occurs if the *Identifier* naming a class is also declared as a type by a single-type-import declaration (§7.5.1) in the compilation unit (§7.3) containing the class declaration.

In the example:

```
package test;

import java.util.Vector;

class Point {
    int x, y;
}

interface Point {                    // compile-time error #1
    int getR();
    int getTheta();
}

class Vector { Point[] pts; }        // compile-time error #2
```

the first compile-time error is caused by the duplicate declaration of the name `Point` as both a `class` and an `interface` in the same package. A second error detected at compile time is the attempt to declare the name `Vector` both by a class type declaration and by a single-type-import declaration.

Note, however, that it is not an error for the *Identifier* that names a class also to name a type that otherwise might be imported by a type-import-on-demand declaration (§7.5.2) in the compilation unit (§7.3) containing the class declaration. In the example:

```
package test;

import java.util.*;

class Vector { Point[] pts; }        // not a compile-time error
```

the declaration of the class `Vector` is permitted even though there is also a class `java.util.Vector`. Within this compilation unit, the simple name `Vector` refers to the class `test.Vector`, not to `java.util.Vector` (which can still be referred to by code within the compilation unit, but only by its fully qualified name).

8.1.1 Scope of a Class Type Name

The *Identifier* in a class declaration specifies the name of the class. This class name has as its scope (§6.3) the entire package in which the class is declared. As an example, the compilation unit:

```
package points;

class Point {
    int x, y;                        // coordinates
    PointColor color;                // color of this point
    Point next;                      // next point with this color
    static int nPoints;
}

class PointColor {
    Point first;                     // first point with this color
    PointColor(int color) {
        this.color = color;
    }
    private int color;               // color components
}
```

defines two classes that use each other in the declarations of their class members. Because the class type names `Point` and `PointColor` have the entire package `points`, including the entire current compilation unit, as their scope, this example compiles correctly—that is, forward reference is not a problem.

8.1.2 Class Modifiers

A class declaration may include *class modifiers*.

ClassModifiers:
  ClassModifier
  ClassModifiers ClassModifier

ClassModifier: one of
  `public  abstract  final`

The access modifier `public` is discussed in §6.6. A compile-time error occurs if the same modifier appears more than once in a class declaration. If two or more class modifiers appear in a class declaration, then it is customary, though not required, that they appear in the order consistent with that shown above in the production for *ClassModifier*.

8.1.2.1 abstract *Classes*

An abstract class is a class that is incomplete, or to be considered incomplete. Only abstract classes may have abstract methods (§8.4.3.1, §9.4), that is, methods that are declared but not yet implemented. If a class that is not abstract contains an abstract method, then a compile-time error occurs. A class has abstract methods if any of the following is true:

- It explicitly contains a declaration of an abstract method (§8.4.3).
- It inherits an abstract method from its direct superclass (§8.1.3).
- A direct superinterface (§8.1.4) of the class declares or inherits a method (which is therefore necessarily abstract) and the class neither declares nor inherits a method that implements it.

In the example:

```
abstract class Point {
    int x = 1, y = 1;
    void move(int dx, int dy) {
        x += dx;
        y += dy;
        alert();
    }
    abstract void alert();
}

abstract class ColoredPoint extends Point {
    int color;
}

class SimplePoint extends Point {
    void alert() { }
}
```

a class Point is declared that must be declared abstract, because it contains a declaration of an abstract method named alert. The subclass of Point named ColoredPoint inherits the abstract method alert, so it must also be declared abstract. On the other hand, the subclass of Point named SimplePoint provides an implementation of alert, so it need not be abstract.

A compile-time error occurs if an attempt is made to create an instance of an abstract class using a class instance creation expression (§15.8). An attempt to instantiate an abstract class using the newInstance method of class Class (§20.3.6) will cause an InstantiationException (§11.5.1) to be thrown. Thus, continuing the example just shown, the statement:

```
Point p = new Point();
```

would result in a compile-time error; the class `Point` cannot be instantiated because it is `abstract`. However, a `Point` variable could correctly be initialized with a reference to any subclass of `Point`, and the class `SimplePoint` is not `abstract`, so the statement:

```
Point p = new SimplePoint();
```

would be correct.

A subclass of an `abstract` class that is not itself `abstract` may be instantiated, resulting in the execution of a constructor for the `abstract` class and, therefore, the execution of the field initializers for instance variables of that class. Thus, in the example just given, instantiation of a `SimplePoint` causes the default constructor and field initializers for `x` and `y` of `Point` to be executed.

It is a compile-time error to declare an `abstract` class type such that it is not possible to create a subclass that implements all of its `abstract` methods. This situation can occur if the class would have as members two `abstract` methods that have the same method signature (§8.4.2) but different return types. As an example, the declarations:

```
interface Colorable { void setColor(int color); }

abstract class Colored implements Colorable {
    abstract int setColor(int color);
}
```

result in a compile-time error: it would be impossible for any subclass of class `Colored` to provide an implementation of a method named `setColor`, taking one argument of type `int`, that can satisfy both `abstract` method specifications, because the one in interface `Colorable` requires the same method to return no value, while the one in class `Colored` requires the same method to return a value of type `int` (§8.4).

A class type should be declared `abstract` only if the intent is that subclasses can be created to complete the implementation. If the intent is simply to prevent instantiation of a class, the proper way to express this is to declare a constructor (§8.6.8) of no arguments, make it `private`, never invoke it, and declare no other constructors. A class of this form usually contains class methods and variables. The class `java.lang.Math` is an example of a class that cannot be instantiated; its declaration looks like this:

```
public final class Math {

    private Math() { }        // never instantiate this class

    . . . declarations of class variables and methods . . .

}
```

8.1.2.2 `final` *Classes*

A class can be declared `final` if its definition is complete and no subclasses are desired or required. A compile-time error occurs if the name of a `final` class appears in the `extends` clause (§8.1.3) of another `class` declaration; this implies that a `final` class cannot have any subclasses. A compile-time error occurs if a class is declared both `final` and `abstract`, because the implementation of such a class could never be completed (§8.1.2.1).

Because a `final` class never has any subclasses, the methods of a `final` class are never overridden (§8.4.6.1).

8.1.3 Superclasses and Subclasses

The optional `extends` clause in a class declaration specifies the *direct superclass* of the current class. A class is said to be a *direct subclass* of the class it extends. The direct superclass is the class from whose implementation the implementation of the current class is derived. The `extends` clause must not appear in the definition of the class `java.lang.Object` (§20.1), because it is the primordial class and has no direct superclass. If the class declaration for any other class has no `extends` clause, then the class has the class `java.lang.Object` as its implicit direct superclass.

Super:
 `extends` *ClassType*

The following is repeated from §4.3 to make the presentation here clearer:

ClassType:
 TypeName

The *ClassType* must name an accessible (§6.6) class type, or a compile-time error occurs. All classes in the current package are accessible. Classes in other packages are accessible if the host system permits access to the package (§7.2) and the class is declared `public`. If the specified *ClassType* names a class that is `final` (§8.1.2.2), then a compile-time error occurs; `final` classes are not allowed to have subclasses.

In the example:

```
class Point { int x, y; }
final class ColoredPoint extends Point { int color; }
class Colored3DPoint extends ColoredPoint { int z; } // error
```

the relationships are as follows:

- The class `Point` is a direct subclass of `java.lang.Object`.
- The class `java.lang.Object` is the direct superclass of the class `Point`.
- The class `ColoredPoint` is a direct subclass of class `Point`.
- The class `Point` is the direct superclass of class `ColoredPoint`.

The declaration of class `Colored3dPoint` causes a compile-time error because it attempts to extend the `final` class `ColoredPoint`.

The *subclass* relationship is the transitive closure of the direct subclass relationship. A class *A* is a subclass of class *C* if either of the following is true:

- *A* is the direct subclass of *C*.
- There exists a class *B* such that *A* is a subclass of *B*, and *B* is a subclass of *C*, applying this definition recursively.

Class *C* is said to be a *superclass* of class *A* whenever *A* is a subclass of *C*.

In the example:

```
class Point { int x, y; }
class ColoredPoint extends Point { int color; }
final class Colored3dPoint extends ColoredPoint { int z; }
```

the relationships are as follows:

- The class `Point` is a superclass of class `ColoredPoint`.
- The class `Point` is a superclass of class `Colored3dPoint`.
- The class `ColoredPoint` is a subclass of class `Point`.
- The class `ColoredPoint` is a superclass of class `Colored3dPoint`.
- The class `Colored3dPoint` is a subclass of class `ColoredPoint`.
- The class `Colored3dPoint` is a subclass of class `Point`.

A compile-time error occurs if a class is declared to be a subclass of itself. For example:

```
class Point extends ColoredPoint { int x, y; }
class ColoredPoint extends Point { int color; }
```

causes a compile-time error. If circularly declared classes are detected at run time, as classes are loaded (§12.2), then a `ClassCircularityError` is thrown.

8.1.4 Superinterfaces

The optional `implements` clause in a class declaration lists the names of interfaces that are *direct superinterfaces* of the class being declared:

Interfaces:
    `implements` *InterfaceTypeList*

InterfaceTypeList:
    InterfaceType
    InterfaceTypeList , *InterfaceType*

The following is repeated from §4.3 to make the presentation here clearer:

InterfaceType:
    TypeName

Each *InterfaceType* must name an accessible (§6.6) interface type, or a compile-time error occurs. All interfaces in the current package are accessible. Interfaces in other packages are accessible if the host system permits access to the package (§7.4.4) and the interface is declared `public`.

A compile-time error occurs if the same interface is mentioned two or more times in a single `implements` clause, even if the interface is named in different ways; for example, the code:

```
class Redundant implements java.lang.Cloneable, Cloneable {
    int x;
}
```

results in a compile-time error because the names `java.lang.Cloneable` and `Cloneable` refer to the same interface.

An interface type `I` is a *superinterface* of class type `C` if any of the following is true:

- `I` is a direct superinterface of `C`.
- `C` has some direct superinterface `J` for which `I` is a superinterface, using the definition of "superinterface of an interface" given in §9.1.3.
- `I` is a superinterface of the direct superclass of `C`, using this definition recursively.

A class is said to *implement* all its superinterfaces.

In the example:

```
public interface Colorable {
   void setColor(int color);
   int getColor();
}

public interface Paintable extends Colorable {
   int MATTE = 0, GLOSSY = 1;
   void setFinish(int finish);
   int getFinish();
}

class Point { int x, y; }

class ColoredPoint extends Point implements Colorable {
   int color;
   public void setColor(int color) { this.color = color; }
   public int getColor() { return color; }
}

class PaintedPoint extends ColoredPoint implements Paintable
{
   int finish;
   public void setFinish(int finish) {
      this.finish = finish;
   }
   public int getFinish() { return finish; }
}
```

the relationships are as follows:

- The interface `Paintable` is a superinterface of class `PaintedPoint`.
- The interface `Colorable` is a superinterface of class `ColoredPoint` and of class `PaintedPoint`.
- The interface `Paintable` is a subinterface of the interface `Colorable`, and `Colorable` is a superinterface of `Paintable`, as defined in §9.1.3.

A class can have a superinterface in more than one way. In this example, the class `PaintedPoint` has `Colorable` as a superinterface both because it is a superinterface of `ColoredPoint` and because it is a superinterface of `Paintable`.

Unless the class being declared is `abstract`, the declarations of the methods defined in each direct superinterface must be implemented either by a declaration in this class or by an existing method declaration inherited from the direct superclass, because a class that is not `abstract` is not permitted to have `abstract` methods (§8.1.2.1).

Thus, the example:

```
interface Colorable {
    void setColor(int color);
    int getColor();
}

class Point { int x, y; };

class ColoredPoint extends Point implements Colorable {
    int color;
}
```

causes a compile-time error, because ColoredPoint is not an abstract class but it fails to provide an implementation of methods setColor and getColor of the interface Colorable.

It is permitted for a single method declaration in a class to implement methods of more than one superinterface. For example, in the code:

```
interface Fish { int getNumberOfScales(); }

interface Piano { int getNumberOfScales(); }

class Tuna implements Fish, Piano {
    // You can tune a piano, but can you tuna fish?
    int getNumberOfScales() { return 91; }
}
```

the method getNumberOfScales in class Tuna has a name, signature, and return type that matches the method declared in interface Fish and also matches the method declared in interface Piano; it is considered to implement both.

On the other hand, in a situation such as this:

```
interface Fish { int getNumberOfScales(); }

interface StringBass { double getNumberOfScales(); }

class Bass implements Fish, StringBass {
    // This declaration cannot be correct, no matter what type is used.
    public ??? getNumberOfScales() { return 91; }
}
```

it is impossible to declare a method named getNumberOfScales with the same signature and return type as those of both the methods declared in interface Fish and in interface StringBass, because a class can have only one method with a given signature (§8.4). Therefore, it is impossible for a single class to implement both interface Fish and interface StringBass (§8.4.6).

8.1.5 Class Body and Member Declarations

A *class body* may contain declarations of members of the class, that is, fields (§8.3) and methods (§8.4). A class body may also contain static initializers (§8.5) and declarations of constructors (§8.6) for the class.

ClassBody:
    { *ClassBodyDeclarations$_{opt}$* }

ClassBodyDeclarations:
    ClassBodyDeclaration
    ClassBodyDeclarations ClassBodyDeclaration

ClassBodyDeclaration:
    ClassMemberDeclaration
    StaticInitializer
    ConstructorDeclaration

ClassMemberDeclaration:
    FieldDeclaration
    MethodDeclaration

The scope of the name of a member declared in or inherited by a class type is the entire body of the class type declaration.

8.2 Class Members

I wouldn't want to belong to any club that would accept me as a member.
—Groucho Marx

The members of a class type are all of the following:

- Members inherited from its direct superclass (§8.1.3), except in class `Object`, which has no direct superclass
- Members inherited from any direct superinterfaces (§8.1.4)
- Members declared in the body of the class (§8.1.5)

Members of a class that are declared `private` are not inherited by subclasses of that class. Only members of a class that are declared `protected` or `public` are inherited by subclasses declared in a package other than the one in which the class is declared.

Constructors and static initializers are not members and therefore are not inherited.

The example:

```
class Point {
    int x, y;
    private Point() { reset(); }
    Point(int x, int y) { this.x = x; this.y = y; }
    private void reset() { this.x = 0; this.y = 0; }
}
class ColoredPoint extends Point {
    int color;
    void clear() { reset(); }                       // error
}
class Test {
    public static void main(String[] args) {
        ColoredPoint c = new ColoredPoint(0, 0);    // error
        c.reset();                                  // error
    }
}
```

causes four compile-time errors:

- An error occurs because `ColoredPoint` has no constructor declared with two integer parameters, as requested by the use in `main`. This illustrates the fact that `ColoredPoint` does not inherit the constructors of its superclass `Point`.
- Another error occurs because `ColoredPoint` declares no constructors, and therefore a default constructor for it is automatically created (§8.6.7), and this default constructor is equivalent to:

  ```
  ColoredPoint() { super(); }
  ```

  which invokes the constructor, with no arguments, for the direct superclass of the class `ColoredPoint`. The error is that the constructor for `Point` that takes no arguments is `private`, and therefore is not accessible outside the class `Point`, even through a superclass constructor invocation (§8.6.5).
- Two more errors occur because the method `reset` of class `Point` is `private`, and therefore is not inherited by class `ColoredPoint`. The method invocations in method `clear` of class `ColoredPoint` and in method `main` of class `Test` are therefore not correct.

8.2.1 Examples of Inheritance

This section illustrates inheritance of class members through several examples.

8.2.1.1 *Example: Inheritance with Default Access*

Consider the example where the `points` package declares two compilation units:

```
package points;

public class Point {
    int x, y;
    public void move(int dx, int dy) { x += dx; y += dy; }
}
```

and:

```
package points;

public class Point3d extends Point {
    int z;
    public void move(int dx, int dy, int dz) {
        x += dx; y += dy; z += dz;
    }
}
```

and a third compilation unit, in another package, is:

```
import points.Point3d;

class Point4d extends Point3d {
    int w;
    public void move(int dx, int dy, int dz, int dw) {
        x += dx; y += dy; z += dz; w += dw; // compile-time errors
    }
}
```

Here both classes in the `points` package compile. The class `Point3d` inherits the fields `x` and `y` of class `Point`, because it is in the same package as `Point`. The class `Point4d`, which is in a different package, does not inherit the fields `x` and `y` of class `Point` or the field `z` of class `Point3d`, and so fails to compile.

A better way to write the third compilation unit would be:

```
import points.Point3d;

class Point4d extends Point3d {
    int w;
    public void move(int dx, int dy, int dz, int dw) {
        super.move(dx, dy, dz); w += dw;
    }
}
```

using the `move` method of the superclass `Point3d` to process `dx`, `dy`, and `dz`. If `Point4d` is written in this way it will compile without errors.

8.2.1.2 *Inheritance with* `public` *and* `protected`

Given the class `Point`:

```
package points;
public class Point {
    public int x, y;
    protected int useCount = 0;
    static protected int totalUseCount = 0;
    public void move(int dx, int dy) {
        x += dx; y += dy; useCount++; totalUseCount++;
    }
}
```

the `public` and `protected` fields `x`, `y`, `useCount` and `totalUseCount` are inherited in all subclasses of `Point`. Therefore, this test program, in another package, can be compiled successfully:

```
class Test extends points.Point {
    public void moveBack(int dx, int dy) {
        x -= dx; y -= dy; useCount++; totalUseCount++;
    }
}
```

8.2.1.3 *Inheritance with* `private`

In the example:

```
class Point {
    int x, y;
    void move(int dx, int dy) {
        x += dx; y += dy; totalMoves++;
    }
    private static int totalMoves;
    void printMoves() { System.out.println(totalMoves); }
}
class Point3d extends Point {
    int z;
    void move(int dx, int dy, int dz) {
        super.move(dx, dy); z += dz; totalMoves++;
    }
}
```

the class variable `totalMoves` can be used only within the class `Point`; it is not inherited by the subclass `Point3d`. A compile-time error occurs at the point where method `move` of class `Point3d` tries to increment `totalMoves`.

8.2.1.4 *Accessing Members of Inaccessible Classes*

Even though a class might not be declared `public`, instances of the class might be available at run time to code outside the package in which it is declared if it has a `public` superclass or superinterface. An instance of the class can be assigned to a variable of such a `public` type. An invocation of a `public` method of the object referred to by such a variable may invoke a method of the class if it implements or overrides a method of the `public` superclass or superinterface. (In this situation, the method is necessarily declared `public`, even though it is declared in a class that is not `public`.)

Consider the compilation unit:

```
package points;

public class Point {
    public int x, y;
    public void move(int dx, int dy) {
        x += dx; y += dy;
    }
}
```

and another compilation unit of another package:

```
package morePoints;

class Point3d extends points.Point {
    public int z;
    public void move(int dx, int dy, int dz) {
        super.move(dx, dy); z += dz;
    }
}

public class OnePoint {
    static points.Point getOne() { return new Point3d(); }
}
```

An invocation `morePoints.OnePoint.getOne()` in yet a third package would return a `Point3d` that can be used as a `Point`, even though the type `Point3d` is not available outside the package `morePoints`. The method `move` could then be invoked for that object, which is permissible because method `move` of `Point3d` is `public` (as it must be, for any method that overrides a `public` method must itself be `public`, precisely so that situations such as this will work out correctly). The fields `x` and `y` of that object could also be accessed from such a third package.

While the field `z` of class `Point3d` is `public`, it is not possible to access this field from code outside the package `morePoints`, given only a reference to an instance of class `Point3d` in a variable `p` of type `Point`. This is because the expression `p.z` is not correct, as `p` has type `Point` and class `Point` has no field named `z`; also, the expression `((Point3d)p).z` is not correct, because the class type `Point3d` cannot be referred to outside package `morePoints`. The declaration of the field `z` as `public` is not useless, however. If there were to be, in package `morePoints`, a `public` subclass `Point4d` of the class `Point3d`:

```
package morePoints;

public class Point4d extends Point3d {
    public int w;
    public void move(int dx, int dy, int dz, int dw) {
        super.move(dx, dy, dz); w += dw;
    }
}
```

then class `Point4d` would inherit the field `z`, which, being `public`, could then be accessed by code in packages other than `morePoints`, through variables and expressions of the `public` type `Point4d`.

8.3 Field Declarations

Poetic fields encompass me around,
And still I seem to tread on classic ground.
—Joseph Addison (1672–1719), *A Letter from Italy*

The variables of a class type are introduced by *field declarations*:

FieldDeclaration:
    FieldModifiers$_{opt}$ *Type VariableDeclarators* `;`

VariableDeclarators:
    VariableDeclarator
    VariableDeclarators `,` *VariableDeclarator*

VariableDeclarator:
    VariableDeclaratorId
    VariableDeclaratorId `=` *VariableInitializer*

VariableDeclaratorId:
    Identifier
    VariableDeclaratorId `[ ]`

VariableInitializer:
  Expression
  ArrayInitializer

The *FieldModifiers* are described in §8.3.1. The *Identifier* in a *FieldDeclarator* may be used in a name to refer to the field. The name of a field has as its scope (§6.3) the entire body of the class declaration in which it is declared. More than one field may be declared in a single field declaration by using more than one declarator; the *FieldModifiers* and *Type* apply to all the declarators in the declaration. Variable declarations involving array types are discussed in §10.2.

It is a compile-time error for the body of a class declaration to contain declarations of two fields with the same name. Methods and fields may have the same name, since they are used in different contexts and are disambiguated by the different lookup procedures (§6.5).

If the class declares a field with a certain name, then the declaration of that field is said to *hide* (§6.3.1) any and all accessible declarations of fields with the same name in the superclasses and superinterfaces of the class.

If a field declaration hides the declaration of another field, the two fields need not have the same type.

A class inherits from its direct superclass and direct superinterfaces all the fields of the superclass and superinterfaces that are both accessible to code in the class and not hidden by a declaration in the class.

It is possible for a class to inherit more than one field with the same name (§8.3.3.3). Such a situation does not in itself cause a compile-time error. However, any attempt within the body of the class to refer to any such field by its simple name will result in a compile-time error, because such a reference is ambiguous.

There might be several paths by which the same field declaration might be inherited from an interface. In such a situation, the field is considered to be inherited only once, and it may be referred to by its simple name without ambiguity.

A hidden field can be accessed by using a qualified name (if it is `static`) or by using a field access expression (§15.10) that contains the keyword `super` or a cast to a superclass type. See §15.10.2 for discussion and an example.

8.3.1 Field Modifiers

FieldModifiers:
  FieldModifier
  FieldModifiers FieldModifier

FieldModifier: one of
```
public protected private
final static transient volatile
```

The access modifiers `public`, `protected`, and `private` are discussed in §6.6. A compile-time error occurs if the same modifier appears more than once in a field declaration, or if a field declaration has more than one of the access modifiers `public`, `protected`, and `private`. If two or more (distinct) field modifiers appear in a field declaration, it is customary, though not required, that they appear in the order consistent with that shown above in the production for *FieldModifier*.

8.3.1.1 `static` *Fields*

If a field is declared `static`, there exists exactly one incarnation of the field, no matter how many instances (possibly zero) of the class may eventually be created. A `static` field, sometimes called a *class variable*, is incarnated when the class is initialized (§12.4).

A field that is not declared `static` (sometimes called a non-`static` field) is called an *instance variable*. Whenever a new instance of a class is created, a new variable associated with that instance is created for every instance variable declared in that class or any of its superclasses.

The example program:

```
class Point {
    int x, y, useCount;
    Point(int x, int y) { this.x = x; this.y = y; }
    final static Point origin = new Point(0, 0);
}

class Test {
    public static void main(String[] args) {
        Point p = new Point(1,1);
        Point q = new Point(2,2);
        p.x = 3; p.y = 3; p.useCount++; p.origin.useCount++;
        System.out.println("(" + q.x + "," + q.y + ")");
        System.out.println(q.useCount);
        System.out.println(q.origin == Point.origin);
        System.out.println(q.origin.useCount);
    }
}
```

prints:

```
(2,2)
0
true
1
```

showing that changing the fields `x`, `y`, and `useCount` of `p` does not affect the fields of `q`, because these fields are instance variables in distinct objects. In this example, the class variable `origin` of the class `Point` is referenced both using the class name as a qualifier, in `Point.origin`, and using variables of the class type in field access expressions (§15.10), as in `p.origin` and `q.origin`. These two ways of accessing the `origin` class variable access the same object, evidenced by the fact that the value of the reference equality expression (§15.20.3):

```
q.origin==Point.origin
```

is `true`. Further evidence is that the incrementation:

```
p.origin.useCount++;
```

causes the value of `q.origin.useCount` to be `1`; this is so because `p.origin` and `q.origin` refer to the same variable.

8.3.1.2 `final` *Fields*

A field can be declared `final`, in which case its declarator must include a variable initializer or a compile-time error occurs. Both class and instance variables (`static` and non-`static` fields) may be declared `final`.

Any attempt to assign to a `final` field results in a compile-time error. Therefore, once a `final` field has been initialized, it always contains the same value. If a `final` field holds a reference to an object, then the state of the object may be changed by operations on the object, but the field will always refer to the same object. This applies also to arrays, because arrays are objects; if a `final` field holds a reference to an array, then the components of the array may be changed by operations on the array, but the field will always refer to the same array.

Declaring a field `final` can serve as useful documentation that its value will not change, can help to avoid programming errors, and can make it easier for a compiler to generate efficient code.

In the example:

```
class Point {
    int x, y;
    int useCount;
    Point(int x, int y) { this.x = x; this.y = y; }
    final static Point origin = new Point(0, 0);
}
```

the class `Point` declares a `final` class variable `origin`. The `origin` variable holds a reference to an object that is an instance of class `Point` whose coordinates are (0, 0). The value of the variable `Point.origin` can never change, so it always refers to the same `Point` object, the one created by its initializer. However, an operation on this `Point` object might change its state—for example, modifying its `useCount` or even, misleadingly, its `x` or `y` coordinate.

8.3.1.3 `transient` *Fields*

Variables may be marked `transient` to indicate that they are not part of the persistent state of an object. If an instance of the class `Point`:

```
class Point {
    int x, y;
    transient float rho, theta;
}
```

were saved to persistent storage by a system service, then only the fields `x` and `y` would be saved. This specification does not yet specify details of such services; we intend to provide them in a future version of this specification.

8.3.1.4 `volatile` *Fields*

As described in §17, the Java language allows threads that access shared variables to keep private working copies of the variables; this allows a more efficient implementation of multiple threads. These working copies need be reconciled with the master copies in the shared main memory only at prescribed synchronization points, namely when objects are locked or unlocked. As a rule, to ensure that shared variables are consistently and reliably updated, a thread should ensure that it has exclusive use of such variables by obtaining a lock that, conventionally, enforces mutual exclusion for those shared variables.

Java provides a second mechanism that is more convenient for some purposes: a field may be declared `volatile`, in which case a thread must reconcile its working copy of the field with the master copy every time it accesses the variable. Moreover, operations on the master copies of one or more volatile variables on behalf of a thread are performed by the main memory in exactly the order that the thread requested.

If, in the following example, one thread repeatedly calls the method `one` (but no more than `Integer.MAX_VALUE` (§20.7.2) times in all), and another thread repeatedly calls the method `two`:

```
class Test {
    static int i = 0, j = 0;
    static void one() { i++; j++; }
    static void two() {
        System.out.println("i=" + i + " j=" + j);
    }
}
```

then method two could occasionally print a value for j that is greater than the value of i, because the example includes no synchronization and, under the rules explained in §17, the shared values of i and j might be updated out of order.

One way to prevent this out-or-order behavior would be to declare methods one and two to be synchronized (§8.4.3.5):

```
class Test {
    static int i = 0, j = 0;
    static synchronized void one() { i++; j++; }
    static synchronized void two() {
        System.out.println("i=" + i + " j=" + j);
    }
}
```

This prevents method one and method two from being executed concurrently, and furthermore guarantees that the shared values of i and j are both updated before method one returns. Therefore method two never observes a value for j greater than that for i; indeed, it always observes the same value for i and j.

Another approach would be to declare i and j to be volatile:

```
class Test {
    static volatile int i = 0, j = 0;
    static void one() { i++; j++; }
    static void two() {
        System.out.println("i=" + i + " j=" + j);
    }
}
```

This allows method one and method two to be executed concurrently, but guarantees that accesses to the shared values for i and j occur exactly as many times, and in exactly the same order, as they appear to occur during execution of the program text by each thread. Therefore, method two never observes a value for j greater than that for i, because each update to i must be reflected in the shared value for i before the update to j occurs. It is possible, however, that any given invocation of method two might observe a value for j that is much greater than the value observed for i, because method one might be executed many times between the moment when method two fetches the value of i and the moment when method two fetches the value of j.

See §17 for more discussion and examples.

A compile-time error occurs if a final variable is also declared volatile.

8.3.2 Initialization of Fields

If a field declarator contains a *variable initializer*, then it has the semantics of an assignment (§15.25) to the declared variable, and:

- If the declarator is for a class variable (that is, a `static` field), then the variable initializer is evaluated and the assignment performed exactly once, when the class is initialized (§12.4).
- If the declarator is for an instance variable (that is, a field that is not `static`), then the variable initializer is evaluated and the assignment performed each time an instance of the class is created (§12.5).

The example:

```
class Point {
    int x = 1, y = 5;
}
class Test {
    public static void main(String[] args) {
        Point p = new Point();
        System.out.println(p.x + ", " + p.y);
    }
}
```

produces the output:

```
1, 5
```

because the assignments to `x` and `y` occur whenever a new `Point` is created.

Variable initializers are also used in local variable declaration statements (§14.3), where the initializer is evaluated and the assignment performed each time the local variable declaration statement is executed.

It is a compile-time error if the evaluation of a variable initializer for a field of a class (or interface) can complete abruptly with a checked exception (§11.2).

8.3.2.1 *Initializers for Class Variables*

A compile-time error occurs if an initialization expression for a class variable contains a use by a simple name of that class variable or of another class variable whose declaration occurs to its right (that is, textually later) in the same class. Thus:

```
class Test {
    static float f = j;     // compile-time error: forward reference
    static int j = 1;
    static int k = k+1;     // compile-time error: forward reference
}
```

causes two compile-time errors, because `j` is referred to in the initialization of `f` before `j` is declared and because the initialization of `k` refers to `k` itself.

If a reference by simple name to any instance variable occurs in an initialization expression for a class variable, then a compile-time error occurs.

If the keyword `this` (§15.7.2) or the keyword `super` (§15.10.2, §15.11) occurs in an initialization expression for a class variable, then a compile-time error occurs.

(One subtlety here is that, at run time, `static` variables that are `final` and that are initialized with compile-time constant values are initialized first. This also applies to such fields in interfaces (§9.3.1). These variables are "constants" that will never be observed to have their default initial values (§4.5.4), even by devious programs. See §12.4.2 and §13.4.8 for more discussion.)

8.3.2.2 *Initializers for Instance Variables*

A compile-time error occurs if an initialization expression for an instance variable contains a use by a simple name of that instance variable or of another instance variable whose declaration occurs to its right (that is, textually later) in the same class. Thus:

```
class Test {
    float f = j;
    int j = 1;
    int k = k+1;
}
```

causes two compile-time errors, because `j` is referred to in the initialization of `f` before `j` is declared and because the initialization of `k` refers to `k` itself.

Initialization expressions for instance variables may use the simple name of any `static` variable declared in or inherited by the class, even one whose declaration occurs textually later. Thus the example:

```
class Test {
    float f = j;
    static int j = 1;
}
```

compiles without error; it initializes `j` to `1` when class `Test` is initialized, and initializes `f` to the current value of `j` every time an instance of class `Test` is created.

Initialization expressions for instance variables are permitted to refer to the current object `this` (§15.7.2) and to use the keyword `super` (§15.10.2, §15.11).

8.3.3 Examples of Field Declarations

The following examples illustrate some (possibly subtle) points about field declarations.

8.3.3.1 *Example: Hiding of Class Variables*

The example:

```
class Point {
    static int x = 2;
}

class Test extends Point {
    static double x = 4.7;
    public static void main(String[] args) {
        new Test().printX();
    }
    void printX() {
        System.out.println(x + " " + super.x);
    }
}
```

produces the output:

```
4.7 2
```

because the declaration of x in class Test hides the definition of x in class Point, so class Test does not inherit the field x from its superclass Point. Within the declaration of class Test, the simple name x refers to the field declared within class Test. Code in class Test may refer to the field x of class Point as super.x (or, because x is static, as Point.x). If the declaration of Test.x is deleted:

```
class Point {
    static int x = 2;
}

class Test extends Point {
    public static void main(String[] args) {
        new Test().printX();
    }
    void printX() {
        System.out.println(x + " " + super.x);
    }
}
```

then the field x of class Point is no longer hidden within class Test; instead, the simple name x now refers to the field Point.x. Code in class Test may still refer to that same field as super.x. Therefore, the output from this variant program is:

```
2 2
```

8.3.3.2 *Example: Hiding of Instance Variables*

This example is similar to that in the previous section, but uses instance variables rather than static variables. The code:

```
class Point {
    int x = 2;
}

class Test extends Point {
    double x = 4.7;
    void printBoth() {
        System.out.println(x + " " + super.x);
    }
    public static void main(String[] args) {
        Test sample = new Test();
        sample.printBoth();
        System.out.println(sample.x + " " +
                                        ((Point)sample).x);
    }
}
```

produces the output:

```
4.7 2
4.7 2
```

because the declaration of `x` in class `Test` hides the definition of `x` in class `Point`, so class `Test` does not inherit the field `x` from its superclass `Point`. It must be noted, however, that while the field `x` of class `Point` is not *inherited* by class `Test`, it is nevertheless *implemented* by instances of class `Test`. In other words, every instance of class `Test` contains two fields, one of type `int` and one of type `float`. Both fields bear the name `x`, but within the declaration of class `Test`, the simple name `x` always refers to the field declared within class `Test`. Code in instance methods of class `Test` may refer to the instance variable `x` of class `Point` as `super.x`.

Code that uses a field access expression to access field `x` will access the field named `x` in the class indicated by the type of reference expression. Thus, the expression `sample.x` accesses a `float` value, the instance variable declared in class `Test`, because the type of the variable sample is `Test`, but the expression `((Point)sample).x` accesses an `int` value, the instance variable declared in class `Point`, because of the cast to type `Point`.

If the declaration of `x` is deleted from class `Test`, as in the program:

```
class Point {
    static int x = 2;
}
```

```
class Test extends Point {
   void printBoth() {
      System.out.println(x + " " + super.x);
   }
   public static void main(String[] args) {
      Test sample = new Test();
      sample.printBoth();
      System.out.println(sample.x + " " +
                                    ((Point)sample).x);
   }
}
```

then the field x of class Point is no longer hidden within class Test. Within instance methods in the declaration of class Test, the simple name x now refers to the field declared within class Point. Code in class Test may still refer to that same field as super.x. The expression sample.x still refers to the field x within type Test, but that field is now an inherited field, and so refers to the field x declared in class Point. The output from this variant program is:

```
2 2
2 2
```

8.3.3.3 *Example: Multiply Inherited Fields*

A class may inherit two or more fields with the same name, either from two interfaces or from its superclass and an interface. A compile-time error occurs on any attempt to refer to any ambiguously inherited field by its simple name. A qualified name or a field access expression that contains the keyword super (§15.10.2) may be used to access such fields unambiguously. In the example:

```
interface Frob { float v = 2.0f; }

class SuperTest { int v = 3; }

class Test extends SuperTest implements Frob {
   public static void main(String[] args) {
      new Test().printV();
   }
   void printV() { System.out.println(v); }
}
```

the class Test inherits two fields named v, one from its superclass SuperTest and one from its superinterface Frob. This in itself is permitted, but a compile-time error occurs because of the use of the simple name v in method printV: it cannot be determined which v is intended.

The following variation uses the field access expression super.v to refer to the field named v declared in class SuperTest and uses the qualified name Frob.v to refer to the field named v declared in interface Frob:

```
interface Frob { float v = 2.0f; }

class SuperTest { int v = 3; }

class Test extends SuperTest implements Frob {
    public static void main(String[] args) {
        new Test().printV();
    }
    void printV() {
        System.out.println((super.v + Frob.v)/2);
    }
}
```

It compiles and prints:

```
2.5
```

Even if two distinct inherited fields have the same type, the same value, and are both `final`, any reference to either field by simple name is considered ambiguous and results in a compile-time error. In the example:

```
interface Color { int RED=0, GREEN=1, BLUE=2; }

interface TrafficLight { int RED=0, YELLOW=1, GREEN=2; }

class Test implements Color, TrafficLight {
    public static void main(String[] args) {
        System.out.println(GREEN);      // compile-time error
        System.out.println(RED);        // compile-time error
    }
}
```

it is not astonishing that the reference to `GREEN` should be considered ambiguous, because class `Test` inherits two different declarations for `GREEN` with different values. The point of this example is that the reference to `RED` is also considered ambiguous, because two distinct declarations are inherited. The fact that the two fields named `RED` happen to have the same type and the same unchanging value does not affect this judgment.

8.3.3.4 *Example: Re-inheritance of Fields*

If the same field declaration is inherited from an interface by multiple paths, the field is considered to be inherited only once. It may be referred to by its simple name without ambiguity. For example, in the code:

```
public interface Colorable {
    int RED = 0xff0000, GREEN = 0x00ff00, BLUE = 0x0000ff;
}
```

```
public interface Paintable extends Colorable {
    int MATTE = 0, GLOSSY = 1;
}
class Point { int x, y; }
class ColoredPoint extends Point implements Colorable {
    ...
}
class PaintedPoint extends ColoredPoint implements Paintable
{
    ... RED ...
}
```

the fields `RED`, `GREEN`, and `BLUE` are inherited by the class `PaintedPoint` both through its direct superclass `ColoredPoint` and through its direct superinterface `Paintable`. The simple names `RED`, `GREEN`, and `BLUE` may nevertheless be used without ambiguity within the class `PaintedPoint` to refer to the fields declared in interface `Colorable`.

8.4 Method Declarations

The diversity of physical arguments and opinions embraces all sorts of methods.
—Michael de Montaigne (1533–1592), *Of Experience*

A *method* declares executable code that can be invoked, passing a fixed number of values as arguments.

MethodDeclaration:
  MethodHeader MethodBody

MethodHeader:
  MethodModifiers$_{opt}$ *ResultType MethodDeclarator Throws*$_{opt}$

ResultType:
  Type
  `void`

MethodDeclarator:
  Identifer `(` *FormalParameterList*$_{opt}$ `)`

The *MethodModifiers* are described in §8.4.3, the *Throws* clause in §8.4.4, and the *MethodBody* in §8.4.5. A method declaration either specifies the type of value that the method returns or uses the keyword `void` to indicate that the method does not return a value.

The *Identifier* in a *MethodDeclarator* may be used in a name to refer to the method. A class can declare a method with the same name as the class or a field of the class.

For compatibility with older versions of Java, a declaration form for a method that returns an array is allowed to place (some or all of) the empty bracket pairs that form the declaration of the array type after the parameter list. This is supported by the obsolescent production:

MethodDeclarator:
 MethodDeclarator `[ ]`

but should not be used in new Java code.

It is a compile-time error for the body of a class to have as members two methods with the same signature (§8.4.2) (name, number of parameters, and types of any parameters). Methods and fields may have the same name, since they are used in different contexts and are disambiguated by the different lookup procedures (§6.5).

8.4.1 Formal Parameters

The *formal parameters* of a method, if any, are specified by a list of comma-separated parameter specifiers. Each parameter specifier consists of a type and an identifier (optionally followed by brackets) that specifies the name of the parameter:

FormalParameterList:
 FormalParameter
 FormalParameterList `,` *FormalParameter*

FormalParameter:
 Type VariableDeclaratorId

The following is repeated from §8.3 to make the presentation here clearer:

VariableDeclaratorId:
 Identifier
 VariableDeclaratorId `[ ]`

If a method has no parameters, only an empty pair of parentheses appears in the method's declaration.

If two formal parameters are declared to have the same name (that is, their declarations mention the same *Identifier*), then a compile-time error occurs.

When the method is invoked (§15.11), the values of the actual argument expressions initialize newly created parameter variables, each of the declared *Type,* before execution of the body of the method. The *Identifier* that appears in the *DeclaratorId* may be used as a simple name in the body of the method to refer to the formal parameter.

The scope of formal parameter names is the entire body of the method. These parameter names may not be redeclared as local variables or exception parameters within the method; that is, hiding the name of a parameter is not permitted.

Formal parameters are referred to only using simple names, never by using qualified names (§6.6).

8.4.2 Method Signature

The *signature* of a method consists of the name of the method and the number and types of formal parameters to the method. A class may not declare two methods with the same signature, or a compile-time error occurs. The example:

```
class Point implements Move {
    int x, y;
    abstract void move(int dx, int dy);
    void move(int dx, int dy) { x += dx; y += dy; }
}
```

causes a compile-time error because it declares two `move` methods with the same signature. This is an error even though one of the declarations is `abstract`.

8.4.3 Method Modifiers

MethodModifiers:
  MethodModifier
  MethodModifiers MethodModifier

MethodModifier: one of
  `public protected private`
  `abstract static final synchronized native`

The access modifiers `public`, `protected`, and `private` are discussed in §6.6. A compile-time error occurs if the same modifier appears more than once in a method declaration, or if a method declaration has more than one of the access modifiers `public`, `protected`, and `private`. A compile-time error occurs if a method declaration that contains the keyword `abstract` also contains any one of the keywords `private`, `static`, `final`, `native`, or `synchronized`.

If two or more method modifiers appear in a method declaration, it is customary, though not required, that they appear in the order consistent with that shown above in the production for *MethodModifier*.

8.4.3.1 `abstract` *Methods*

An `abstract` method declaration introduces the method as a member, providing its signature (name and number and type of parameters), return type, and `throws` clause (if any), but does not provide an implementation. The declaration of an `abstract` method *m* must appear within an `abstract` class (call it *A*); otherwise a compile-time error results. Every subclass of *A* that is not `abstract` must provide an implementation for *m*, or a compile-time error occurs. More precisely, for every subclass *C* of the `abstract` class *A*, if *C* is not `abstract`, then there must be some class *B* such that all of the following are true:

- *B* is a superclass of *C* or is *C* itself.
- *B* is a subclass of *A*.
- *B* provides a declaration of the method *m* that is not `abstract`, and this declaration is inherited by *C*, thereby providing an implementation of method *m* that is visible to *C*.

If there is no such class *B*, then a compile-time error occurs.

It is a compile-time error for a `private` method to be declared `abstract`. It would be impossible for a subclass to implement a `private abstract` method, because `private` methods are not visible to subclasses; therefore such a method could never be used.

It is a compile-time error for a `static` method to be declared `abstract`.

It is a compile-time error for a `final` method to be declared `abstract`.

An `abstract` class can override an `abstract` method by providing another `abstract` method declaration. This can provide a place to put a documentation comment (§18), or to declare that the set of checked exceptions (§11.2) that can be thrown by that method, when it is implemented by its subclasses, is to be more limited. For example, consider this code:

```
class BufferEmpty extends Exception {
	BufferEmpty() { super(); }
	BufferEmpty(String s) { super(s); }
}

class BufferError extends Exception {
	BufferError() { super(); }
	BufferError(String s) { super(s); }
}

public interface Buffer {
	char get() throws BufferEmpty, BufferError;
}
```

```
public abstract class InfiniteBuffer implements Buffer {
    abstract char get() throws BufferError;
}
```

The overriding declaration of method `get` in class `InfiniteBuffer` states that method `get` in any subclass of `InfiniteBuffer` never throws a `BufferEmpty` exception, putatively because it generates the data in the buffer, and thus can never run out of data.

An instance method that is not `abstract` can be overridden by an `abstract` method. For example, we can declare an `abstract` class `Point` that requires its subclasses to implement `toString` if they are to be complete, instantiable classes:

```
abstract class Point {
    int x, y;
    public abstract String toString();
}
```

This `abstract` declaration of `toString` overrides the non-`abstract` `toString` method of class `Object` (§20.1.2). (Class `Object` is the implicit direct superclass of class `Point`.) Adding the code:

```
class ColoredPoint extends Point {
    int color;
    public String toString() {
        return super.toString() + ": color " + color; // error
    }
}
```

results in a compile-time error because the invocation `super.toString()` refers to method `toString` in class `Point`, which is `abstract` and therefore cannot be invoked. Method `toString` of class `Object` can be made available to class `ColoredPoint` only if class `Point` explicitly makes it available through some other method, as in:

```
abstract class Point {
    int x, y;
    public abstract String toString();
    protected String objString() { return super.toString(); }
}

class ColoredPoint extends Point {
    int color;
    public String toString() {
        return objString() + ": color " + color;    // correct
    }
}
```

8.4.3.2 `static` *Methods*

A method that is declared `static` is called a *class method*. A class method is always invoked without reference to a particular object. An attempt to reference the current object using the keyword `this` or the keyword `super` in the body of a class method results in a compile time error. It is a compile-time error for a `static` method to be declared `abstract`.

A method that is not declared `static` is called an *instance method,* and sometimes called a non-`static` method). An instance method is always invoked with respect to an object, which becomes the current object to which the keywords `this` and `super` refer during execution of the method body.

8.4.3.3 `final` *Methods*

A method can be declared `final` to prevent subclasses from overriding or hiding it. It is a compile-time error to attempt to override or hide a `final` method.

A `private` method and all methods declared in a `final` class (§8.1.2.2) are implicitly `final`, because it is impossible to override them. It is permitted but not required for the declarations of such methods to redundantly include the `final` keyword.

It is a compile-time error for a `final` method to be declared `abstract`.

At run-time, a machine-code generator or optimizer can easily and safely "inline" the body of a `final` method, replacing an invocation of the method with the code in its body, as in the example:

```
final class Point {
    int x, y;
    void move(int dx, int dy) { x += dx; y += dy; }
}
class Test {
    public static void main(String[] args) {
        Point[] p = new Point[100];
        for (int i = 0; i < p.length; i++) {
            p[i] = new Point();
            p[i].move(i, p.length-1-i);
        }
    }
}
```

Here, inlining the method `move` of class `Point` in method `main` would transform the `for` loop to the form:

```
for (int i = 0; i < p.length; i++) {
    p[i] = new Point();
    Point pi = p[i];
    pi.x += i;
    pi.y += p.length-1-i;
}
```

The loop might then be subject to further optimizations.

Such inlining cannot be done at compile time unless it can be guaranteed that `Test` and `Point` will always be recompiled together, so that whenever `Point`—and specifically its `move` method—changes, the code for `Test.main` will also be updated.

8.4.3.4 `native` *Methods*

A method that is `native` is implemented in platform-dependent code, typically written in another programming language such as C, C++, FORTRAN, or assembly language. The body of a `native` method is given as a semicolon only, indicating that the implementation is omitted, instead of a block.

A compile-time error occurs if a `native` method is declared `abstract`.

For example, the class `RandomAccessFile` of the standard package `java.io` might declare the following `native` methods:

```
package java.io;

public class RandomAccessFile
    implements DataOutput, DataInput
{   ...
    public native void open(String name, boolean writeable)
        throws IOException;
    public native int readBytes(byte[] b, int off, int len)
        throws IOException;
    public native void writeBytes(byte[] b, int off, int len)
        throws IOException;
    public native long getFilePointer() throws IOException;
    public native void seek(long pos) throws IOException;
    public native long length() throws IOException;
    public native void close() throws IOException;
}
```

8.4.3.5 `synchronized` *Methods*

A `synchronized` method acquires a lock (§17.1) before it executes. For a class (`static`) method, the lock associated with the `Class` object (§20.3) for the method's class is used. For an instance method, the lock associated with `this` (the object for which the method was invoked) is used. These are the same locks that can be used by the `synchronized` statement (§14.17); thus, the code:

```
class Test {
   int count;
   synchronized void bump() { count++; }
   static int classCount;
   static synchronized void classBump() {
      classCount++;
   }
}
```

has exactly the same effect as:

```
class BumpTest {
   int count;
   void bump() {
      synchronized (this) {
         count++;
      }
   }
   static int classCount;
   static void classBump() {
      try {
         synchronized (Class.forName("BumpTest")) {
            classCount++;
         }
      } catch (ClassNotFoundException e) {
            ...
      }
   }
}
```

The more elaborate example:

```
public class Box {

   private Object boxContents;

   public synchronized Object get() {
      Object contents = boxContents;
      boxContents = null;
      return contents;
   }

   public synchronized boolean put(Object contents) {
      if (boxContents != null)
         return false;
      boxContents = contents;
      return true;
   }

}
```

defines a class which is designed for concurrent use. Each instance of the class `Box` has an instance variable `contents` that can hold a reference to any object.

You can put an object in a `Box` by invoking `put`, which returns `false` if the box is already full. You can get something out of a `Box` by invoking `get`, which returns a null reference if the `box` is empty.

If `put` and `get` were not `synchronized`, and two threads were executing methods for the same instance of `Box` at the same time, then the code could misbehave. It might, for example, lose track of an object because two invocations to `put` occurred at the same time.

See §17 for more discussion of threads and locks.

8.4.4 Method Throws

A *throws clause* is used to declare any checked exceptions (§11.2) that can result from the execution of a method or constructor:

Throws:
  `throws` *ClassTypeList*

ClassTypeList:
  ClassType
  ClassTypeList `,` *ClassType*

A compile-time error occurs if any *ClassType* mentioned in a `throws` clause is not the class `Throwable` (§20.22) or a subclass of `Throwable`. It is permitted but not required to mention other (unchecked) exceptions in a `throws` clause.

For each checked exception that can result from execution of the body of a method or constructor, a compile-time error occurs unless that exception type or a superclass of that exception type is mentioned in a `throws` clause in the declaration of the method or constructor.

The requirement to declare checked exceptions allows the compiler to ensure that code for handling such error conditions has been included. Methods or constructors that fail to handle exceptional conditions thrown as checked exceptions will normally result in a compile-time error because of the lack of a proper exception type in a `throws` clause. Java thus encourages a programming style where rare and otherwise truly exceptional conditions are documented in this way.

The predefined exceptions that are not checked in this way are those for which declaring every possible occurrence would be unimaginably inconvenient:

- Exceptions that are represented by the subclasses of class `Error`, for example `OutOfMemoryError`, are thrown due to a failure in or of the virtual machine. Many of these are the result of linkage failures and can occur at unpredictable points in the execution of a Java program. Sophisticated programs may yet wish to catch and attempt to recover from some of these conditions.

- The exceptions that are represented by the subclasses of the class `RuntimeException`, for example `NullPointerException`, result from runtime integrity checks and are thrown either directly from the Java program or in library routines. It is beyond the scope of the Java language, and perhaps beyond the state of the art, to include sufficient information in the program to reduce to a manageable number the places where these can be proven not to occur.

A method that overrides or hides another method (§8.4.6), including methods that implement `abstract` methods defined in interfaces, may not be declared to throw more checked exceptions than the overridden or hidden method.

More precisely, suppose that *B* is a class or interface, and *A* is a superclass or superinterface of *B*, and a method declaration *n* in *B* overrides or hides a method declaration *m* in *A*. If *n* has a `throws` clause that mentions any checked exception types, then *m* must have a `throws` clause, and for every checked exception type listed in the `throws` clause of *n*, that same exception class or one of its superclasses must occur in the `throws` clause of *m*; otherwise, a compile-time error occurs.

See §11 for more information about exceptions and a large example.

8.4.5 Method Body

A *method body* is either a block of code that implements the method or simply a semicolon, indicating the lack of an implementation. The body of a method must be a semicolon if and only if the method is either `abstract` (§8.4.3.1) or `native` (§8.4.3.4).

MethodBody:
    Block
    ;

A compile-time error occurs if a method declaration is either `abstract` or `native` and has a block for its body. A compile-time error occurs if a method declaration is neither `abstract` nor `native` and has a semicolon for its body.

If an implementation is to be provided for a method but the implementation requires no executable code, the method body should be written as a block that contains no statements: "`{ }`".

If a method is declared `void`, then its body must not contain any `return` statement (§14.15) that has an *Expression*.

If a method is declared to have a return type, then every `return` statement (§14.15) in its body must have an *Expression*. A compile-time error occurs if the body of the method can complete normally (§14.1). In other words, a method with a return type must return only by using a return statement that provides a value return; it is not allowed to "drop off the end of its body."

Note that it is possible for a method to have a declared return type and yet contain no return statements. Here is one example:

```
class DizzyDean {
    int pitch() { throw new RuntimeException("90 mph?!"); }
}
```

8.4.6 Inheritance, Overriding, and Hiding

A class *inherits* from its direct superclass and direct superinterfaces all the methods (whether `abstract` or not) of the superclass and superinterfaces that are accessible to code in the class and are neither overridden (§8.4.6.1) nor hidden (§8.4.6.2) by a declaration in the class.

8.4.6.1 *Overriding (By Instance Methods)*

If a class declares an instance method, then the declaration of that method is said to *override* any and all methods with the same signature in the superclasses and superinterfaces of the class that would otherwise be accessible to code in the class. Moreover, if the method declared in the class is not `abstract`, then the declaration of that method is said to *implement* any and all declarations of `abstract` methods with the same signature in the superclasses and superinterfaces of the class that would otherwise be accessible to code in the class.

A compile-time error occurs if an instance method overrides a `static` method. In this respect, overriding of methods differs from hiding of fields (§8.3), for it is permissible for an instance variable to hide a `static` variable.

An overridden method can be accessed by using a method invocation expression (§15.11) that contains the keyword `super`. Note that a qualified name or a cast to a superclass type is not effective in attempting to access an overridden method; in this respect, overriding of methods differs from hiding of fields. See §15.11.4.10 for discussion and examples of this point.

8.4.6.2 *Hiding (By Class Methods)*

If a class declares a `static` method, then the declaration of that method is said to *hide* any and all methods with the same signature in the superclasses and superinterfaces of the class that would otherwise be accessible to code in the class. A compile-time error occurs if a `static` method hides an instance method. In this respect, hiding of methods differs from hiding of fields (§8.3), for it is permissible for a `static` variable to hide an instance variable.

A hidden method can be accessed by using a qualified name or by using a method invocation expression (§15.11) that contains the keyword `super` or a cast to a superclass type. In this respect, hiding of methods is similar to hiding of fields.

8.4.6.3 *Requirements in Overriding and Hiding*

If a method declaration overrides or hides the declaration of another method, then a compile-time error occurs if they have different return types or if one has a return type and the other is `void`. Moreover, a method declaration must not have a `throws` clause that conflicts (§8.4.4) with that of any method that it overrides or hides; otherwise, a compile-time error occurs. In these respects, overriding of methods differs from hiding of fields (§8.3), for it is permissible for a field to hide a field of another type.

The access modifier (§6.6) of an overriding or hiding method must provide at least as much access as the overridden or hidden method, or a compile-time error occurs. In more detail:

- If the overridden or hidden method is `public`, then the overriding or hiding method must be `public`; otherwise, a compile-time error occurs.
- If the overridden or hidden method is `protected`, then the overriding or hiding method must be `protected` or `public`; otherwise, a compile-time error occurs.
- If the overridden or hidden method has default (package) access, then the overriding or hiding method must not be `private`; otherwise, a compile-time error occurs.

Note that a `private` method is never accessible to subclasses and so cannot be hidden or overridden in the technical sense of those terms. This means that a subclass can declare a method with the same signature as a `private` method in one of its superclasses, and there is no requirement that the return type or `throws` clause of such a method bear any relationship to those of the `private` method in the superclass.

8.4.6.4 *Inheriting Methods with the Same Signature*

It is possible for a class to inherit more than one method with the same signature (§8.4.6.4). Such a situation does not in itself cause a compile-time error. There are then two possible cases:

- If one of the inherited methods is not `abstract`, then there are two subcases:
  - If the method that is not `abstract` is `static`, a compile-time error occurs.
  - Otherwise, the method that is not `abstract` is considered to override, and therefore to implement, all the other methods on behalf of the class that inherits it. A compile-time error occurs if, comparing the method that is not `abstract` with each of the other of the inherited methods, for any such pair, either they have different return types or one has a return type and the other is `void`. Moreover, a compile-time error occurs if the inherited method that is not `abstract` has a `throws` clause that conflicts (§8.4.4) with that of any other of the inherited methods.
- If none of the inherited methods is not `abstract`, then the class is necessarily an `abstract` class and is considered to inherit all the `abstract` methods. A compile-time error occurs if, for any two such inherited methods, either they have different return types or one has a return type and the other is `void`. (The `throws` clauses do not cause errors in this case.)

It is not possible for two or more inherited methods with the same signature not to be `abstract`, because methods that are not `abstract` are inherited only from the direct superclass, not from superinterfaces.

There might be several paths by which the same method declaration might be inherited from an interface. This fact causes no difficulty and never, of itself, results in a compile-time error.

8.4.7 Overloading

If two methods of a class (whether both declared in the same class, or both inherited by a class, or one declared and one inherited) have the same name but different signatures, then the method name is said to be *overloaded*. This fact causes no difficulty and never of itself results in a compile-time error. There is no required relationship between the return types or between the `throws` clauses of two methods with the same name but different signatures.

Methods are overridden on a signature-by-signature basis. If, for example, a class declares two `public` methods with the same name, and a subclass overrides one of them, the subclass still inherits the other method. In this respect, Java differs from C++.

When a method is invoked (§15.11), the number of actual arguments and the compile-time types of the arguments are used, at compile time, to determine the signature of the method that will be invoked (§15.11.2). If the method that is to be invoked is an instance method, the actual method to be invoked will be determined at run time, using dynamic method lookup (§15.11.4).

8.4.8 Examples of Method Declarations

The following examples illustrate some (possibly subtle) points about method declarations.

8.4.8.1 *Example: Overriding*

In the example:

```
class Point {
    int x = 0, y = 0;
    void move(int dx, int dy) { x += dx; y += dy; }
}
class SlowPoint extends Point {
    int xLimit, yLimit;
    void move(int dx, int dy) {
        super.move(limit(dx, xLimit), limit(dy, yLimit));
    }
    static int limit(int d, int limit) {
        return d > limit ? limit : d < -limit ? -limit : d;
    }
}
```

the class `SlowPoint` overrides the declarations of method `move` of class `Point` with its own `move` method, which limits the distance that the point can move on each invocation of the method. When the `move` method is invoked for an instance of class `SlowPoint`, the overriding definition in class `SlowPoint` will always be called, even if the reference to the `SlowPoint` object is taken from a variable whose type is `Point`.

8.4.8.2 *Example: Overloading, Overriding, and Hiding*

In the example:

```
class Point {
    int x = 0, y = 0;
    void move(int dx, int dy) { x += dx; y += dy; }
    int color;
}
class RealPoint extends Point {
    float x = 0.0f, y = 0.0f;
```

```
        void move(int dx, int dy) { move((float)dx, (float)dy); }
        void move(float dx, float dy) { x += dx; y += dy; }
}
```

the class RealPoint hides the declarations of the int instance variables x and y of class Point with its own float instance variables x and y, and overrides the method move of class Point with its own move method. It also overloads the name move with another method with a different signature (§8.4.2).

In this example, the members of the class RealPoint include the instance variable color inherited from the class Point, the float instance variables x and y declared in RealPoint, and the two move methods declared in RealPoint.

Which of these overloaded move methods of class RealPoint will be chosen for any particular method invocation will be determined at compile time by the overloading resolution procedure described in §15.11.

8.4.8.3 *Example: Incorrect Overriding*

This example is an extended variation of that in the preceding section:

```
class Point {
    int x = 0, y = 0, color;
    void move(int dx, int dy) { x += dx; y += dy; }
    int getX() { return x; }
    int getY() { return y; }
}
class RealPoint extends Point {
    float x = 0.0f, y = 0.0f;
    void move(int dx, int dy) { move((float)dx, (float)dy); }
    void move(float dx, float dy) { x += dx; y += dy; }
    float getX() { return x; }
    float getY() { return y; }
}
```

Here the class Point provides methods getX and getY that return the values of its fields x and y; the class RealPoint then overrides these methods by declaring methods with the same signature. The result is two errors at compile time, one for each method, because the return types do not match; the methods in class Point return values of type int, but the wanna-be overriding methods in class RealPoint return values of type float.

8.4.8.4 *Example: Overriding versus Hiding*

This example corrects the errors of the example in the preceding section:

```
class Point {
    int x = 0, y = 0;
    void move(int dx, int dy) { x += dx; y += dy; }
    int getX() { return x; }
    int getY() { return y; }
    int color;
}
class RealPoint extends Point {
    float x = 0.0f, y = 0.0f;
    void move(int dx, int dy) { move((float)dx, (float)dy); }
    void move(float dx, float dy) { x += dx; y += dy; }
    int getX() { return (int)Math.floor(x); }
    int getY() { return (int)Math.floor(y); }
}
```

Here the overriding methods `getX` and `getY` in class `RealPoint` have the same return types as the methods of class `Point` that they override, so this code can be successfully compiled.

Consider, then, this test program:

```
class Test {
    public static void main(String[] args) {
        RealPoint rp = new RealPoint();
        Point p = rp;
        rp.move(1.71828f, 4.14159f);
        p.move(1, -1);
        show(p.x, p.y);
        show(rp.x, rp.y);
        show(p.getX(), p.getY());
        show(rp.getX(), rp.getY());
    }
    static void show(int x, int y) {
        System.out.println("(" + x + ", " + y + ")");
    }
```

```
    static void show(float x, float y) {
        System.out.println("(" + x + ", " + y + ")");
    }
}
```

The output from this program is:

```
(0, 0)
(2.7182798, 3.14159)
(2, 3)
(2, 3)
```

The first line of output illustrates the fact that an instance of `RealPoint` actually contains the two integer fields declared in class `Point`; it is just that their names are hidden from code that occurs within the declaration of class `RealPoint` (and those of any subclasses it might have). When a reference to an instance of class `RealPoint` in a variable of type `Point` is used to access the field `x`, the integer field `x` declared in class `Point` is accessed. The fact that its value is zero indicates that the method invocation `p.move(1, -1)` did not invoke the method `move` of class `Point`; instead, it invoked the overriding method `move` of class `RealPoint`.

The second line of output shows that the field access `rp.x` refers to the field `x` declared in class `RealPoint`. This field is of type `float`, and this second line of output accordingly displays floating-point values. Incidentally, this also illustrates the fact that the method name `show` is overloaded; the types of the arguments in the method invocation dictate which of the two definitions will be invoked.

The last two lines of output show that the method invocations `p.getX()` and `rp.getX()` each invoke the `getX` method declared in class `RealPoint`. Indeed, there is no way to invoke the `getX` method of class `Point` for an instance of class `RealPoint` from outside the body of `RealPoint`, no matter what the type of the variable we may use to hold the reference to the object. Thus, we see that fields and methods behave differently: hiding is different from overriding.

8.4.8.5 *Example: Invocation of Hidden Class Methods*

A hidden class (`static`) method can be invoked by using a reference whose type is the class that actually contains the declaration of the method. In this respect, hiding of static methods is different from overriding of instance methods. The example:

```
class Super {
   static String greeting() { return "Goodnight"; }
   String name() { return "Richard"; }
}
class Sub extends Super {
   static String greeting() { return "Hello"; }
   String name() { return "Dick"; }
}
class Test {
   public static void main(String[] args) {
      Super s = new Sub();
      System.out.println(s.greeting() + ", " + s.name());
   }
}
```

produces the output:

```
Goodnight, Dick
```

because the invocation of `greeting` uses the type of `s`, namely `Super`, to figure out, at compile time, which class method to invoke, whereas the invocation of `name` uses the class of `s`, namely `Sub`, to figure out, at run time, which instance method to invoke.

8.4.8.6 *Large Example of Overriding*

Overriding makes it easy for subclasses to extend the behavior of an existing class, as shown in this example:

```
import java.io.OutputStream;
import java.io.IOException;
class BufferOutput {
   private OutputStream o;
   BufferOutput(OutputStream o) { this.o = o; }
   protected byte[] buf = new byte[512];
   protected int pos = 0;
   public void putchar(char c) throws IOException {
      if (pos == buf.length)
         flush();
      buf[pos++] = (byte)c;
   }
```

```
    public void putstr(String s) throws IOException {
        for (int i = 0; i < s.length(); i++)
            putchar(s.charAt(i));
    }

    public void flush() throws IOException {
        o.write(buf, 0, pos);
        pos = 0;
    }
}

class LineBufferOutput extends BufferOutput {

    LineBufferOutput(OutputStream o) { super(o); }

    public void putchar(char c) throws IOException {
        super.putchar(c);
        if (c == '\n')
            flush();
    }
}

class Test {
    public static void main(String[] args)
        throws IOException
    {
        LineBufferOutput lbo =
            new LineBufferOutput(System.out);
        lbo.putstr("lbo\nlbo");
        System.out.print("print\n");
        lbo.putstr("\n");
    }
}
```

This example produces the output:

```
lbo
print
lbo
```

The class `BufferOutput` implements a very simple buffered version of an `OutputStream`, flushing the output when the buffer is full or `flush` is invoked. The subclass `LineBufferOutput` declares only a constructor and a single method `putchar`, which overrides the method `putchar` of `BufferOutput`. It inherits the methods `putstr` and `flush` from class `Buffer`.

In the `putchar` method of a `LineBufferOutput` object, if the character argument is a newline, then it invokes the `flush` method. The critical point about overriding in this example is that the method `putstr`, which is declared in class `BufferOutput`, invokes the `putchar` method defined by the current object `this`, which is not necessarily the `putchar` method declared in class `BufferOutput`.

Thus, when putstr is invoked in main using the LineBufferOutput object lbo, the invocation of putchar in the body of the putstr method is an invocation of the putchar of the object lbo, the overriding declaration of putchar that checks for a newline. This allows a subclass of BufferOutput to change the behavior of the putstr method without redefining it.

Documentation for a class such as BufferOutput, which is designed to be extended, should clearly indicate what is the contract between the class and its subclasses, and should clearly indicate that subclasses may override the putchar method in this way. The implementor of the BufferOutput class would not, therefore, want to change the implementation of putstr in a future implementation of BufferOutput not to use the method putchar, because this would break the preexisting contract with subclasses. See the further discussion of binary compatibility in §13, especially §13.2.

8.4.8.7 *Example: Incorrect Overriding because of Throws*

This example uses the usual and conventional form for declaring a new exception type, in its declaration of the class BadPointException:

```
class BadPointException extends Exception {
    BadPointException() { super(); }
    BadPointException(String s) { super(s); }
}

class Point {
    int x, y;
    void move(int dx, int dy) { x += dx; y += dy; }
}

class CheckedPoint extends Point {
    void move(int dx, int dy) throws BadPointException {
        if ((x + dx) < 0 || (y + dy) < 0)
            throw new BadPointException();
        x += dx; y += dy;
    }
}
```

This example results in a compile-time error, because the override of method move in class CheckedPoint declares that it will throw a checked exception that the move in class Point has not declared. If this were not considered an error, an invoker of the method move on a reference of type Point could find the contract between it and Point broken if this exception were thrown.

Removing the throws clause does not help:

```
class CheckedPoint extends Point {
    void move(int dx, int dy) {
        if ((x + dx) < 0 || (y + dy) < 0)
            throw new BadPointException();
        x += dx; y += dy;
    }
}
```

A different compile-time error now occurs, because the body of the method `move` cannot throw a checked exception, namely `BadPointException`, that does not appear in the `throws` clause for `move`.

8.5 Static Initializers

Any *static initializers* declared in a class are executed when the class is initialized and, together with any field initializers (§8.3.2) for class variables, may be used to initialize the class variables of the class (§12.4).

StaticInitializer:
    `static` *Block*

It is a compile-time error for a static initializer to be able to complete abruptly (§14.1, §15.5) with a checked exception (§11.2).

The static initializers and class variable initializers are executed in textual order and may not refer to class variables declared in the class whose declarations appear textually after the use, even though these class variables are in scope. This restriction is designed to catch, at compile time, circular or otherwise malformed initializations. Thus, both:

```
class Z {
    static int i = j + 2;
    static int j = 4;
}
```

and:

```
class Z {
    static { i = j + 2; }
    static int i, j;
    static { j = 4; }
}
```

result in compile-time errors.

Accesses to class variables by methods are not checked in this way, so:

```
class Z {
   static int peek() { return j; }
   static int i = peek();
   static int j = 1;
}

class Test {
   public static void main(String[] args) {
      System.out.println(Z.i);
   }
}
```

produces the output:

```
0
```

because the variable initializer for `i` uses the class method `peek` to access the value of the variable `j` before `j` has been initialized by its variable initializer, at which point it still has its default value (§4.5.4).

If a `return` statement (§14.15) appears anywhere within a static initializer, then a compile-time error occurs.

If the keyword `this` (§15.7.2) or the keyword `super` (§15.10, §15.11) appears anywhere within a static initializer, then a compile-time error occurs.

8.6 Constructor Declarations

The constructor of wharves, bridges, piers, bulk-heads,
floats, stays against the sea . . .
—Walt Whitman, *Song of the Broad-Axe* (1856)

A *constructor* is used in the creation of an object that is an instance of a class:

ConstructorDeclaration:
  ConstructorModifiers$_{opt}$ *ConstructorDeclarator*
    Throws$_{opt}$ *ConstructorBody*

ConstructorDeclarator:
  SimpleTypeName `(` *FormalParameterList*$_{opt}$ `)`

The *SimpleTypeName* in the *ConstructorDeclarator* must be the simple name of the class that contains the constructor declaration; otherwise a compile-time error occurs. In all other respects, the constructor declaration looks just like a method declaration that has no result type.

Here is a simple example:

```
class Point {
    int x, y;
    Point(int x, int y) { this.x = x; this.y = y; }
}
```

Constructors are invoked by class instance creation expressions (§15.8), by the `newInstance` method of class `Class` (§20.3), by the conversions and concatenations caused by the string concatenation operator + (§15.17.1), and by explicit constructor invocations from other constructors (§8.6.5). Constructors are never invoked by method invocation expressions (§15.11).

Access to constructors is governed by access modifiers (§6.6). This is useful, for example, in preventing instantiation by declaring an inaccessible constructor (§8.6.8).

Constructor declarations are not members. They are never inherited and therefore are not subject to hiding or overriding.

8.6.1 Formal Parameters

The formal parameters of a constructor are identical in structure and behavior to the formal parameters of a method (§8.4.1).

8.6.2 Constructor Signature

The signature of a constructor is identical in structure and behavior to the signature of a method (§8.4.2).

8.6.3 Constructor Modifiers

ConstructorModifiers:
    ConstructorModifier
    ConstructorModifiers ConstructorModifier

ConstructorModifier: one of
    `public protected private`

The access modifiers `public`, `protected`, and `private` are discussed in §6.6. A compile-time error occurs if the same modifier appears more than once in a constructor declaration, or if a constructor declaration has more than one of the access modifiers `public`, `protected`, and `private`.

Unlike methods, a constructor cannot be `abstract`, `static`, `final`, `native`, or `synchronized`. A constructor is not inherited, so there is no need to declare it `final` and an `abstract` constructor could never be implemented. A constructor is always invoked with respect to an object, so it makes no sense for a constructor to be `static`. There is no practical need for a constructor to be `synchronized`, because it would lock the object under construction, which is normally not made available to other threads until all constructors for the object have completed their work. The lack of `native` constructors is an arbitrary language design choice that makes it easy for an implementation of the Java Virtual Machine to verify that superclass constructors are always properly invoked during object creation.

8.6.4 Constructor Throws

The `throws` clause for a constructor is identical in structure and behavior to the `throws` clause for a method (§8.4.4).

8.6.5 Constructor Body

The first statement of a constructor body may be an explicit invocation of another constructor of the same class, written as `this` followed by a parenthesized argument list, or an explicit invocation of a constructor of the direct superclass, written as `super` followed by a parenthesized argument list.

ConstructorBody:
`{` *ExplicitConstructorInvocation$_{opt}$* *BlockStatements$_{opt}$* `}`

ExplicitConstructorInvocation:
`this (` *ArgumentList$_{opt}$* `) ;`
`super (` *ArgumentList$_{opt}$* `) ;`

It is a compile-time error for a constructor to directly or indirectly invoke itself through a series of one or more explicit constructor invocations involving `this`.

If a constructor body does not begin with an explicit constructor invocation and the constructor being declared is not part of the primordial class `Object`, then the constructor body is implicitly assumed by the compiler to begin with a superclass constructor invocation "`super();`", an invocation of the constructor of its direct superclass that takes no arguments.

Except for the possibility of explicit constructor invocations, the body of a constructor is like the body of a method (§8.4.5). A `return` statement (§14.15) may be used in the body of a constructor if it does not include an expression.

In the example:

```
class Point {
    int x, y;
    Point(int x, int y) { this.x = x; this.y = y; }
}
class ColoredPoint extends Point {
    static final int WHITE = 0, BLACK = 1;
    int color;
    ColoredPoint(int x, int y) {
        this(x, y, WHITE);
    }
    ColoredPoint(int x, int y, int color) {
        super(x, y);
        this.color = color;
    }
}
```

the first constructor of `ColoredPoint` invokes the second, providing an additional argument; the second constructor of `ColoredPoint` invokes the constructor of its superclass `Point`, passing along the coordinates.

An explicit constructor invocation statement may not refer to any instance variables or instance methods declared in this class or any superclass, or use `this` or `super` in any expression; otherwise, a compile-time error occurs. For example, if the first constructor of `ColoredPoint` in the example above were changed to:

```
ColoredPoint(int x, int y) {
    this(x, y, color);
}
```

then a compile-time error would occur, because an instance variable cannot be used within a superclass constructor invocation.

An invocation of the constructor of the direct superclass, whether it actually appears as an explicit constructor invocation statement or is provided automatically (§8.6.7), performs an additional implicit action after a normal return of control from the constructor: all instance variables that have initializers are initialized at that time, in the textual order in which they appear in the class declaration. An invocation of another constructor in the same class using the keyword `this` does not perform this additional implicit action.

§12.5 describes the creation and initialization of new class instances.

8.6.6 Constructor Overloading

Overloading of constructors is identical in behavior to overloading of methods. The overloading is resolved at compile time by each class instance creation expression (§15.8).

8.6.7 Default Constructor

If a class contains no constructor declarations, then a *default constructor* that takes no parameters is automatically provided:

- If the class being declared is the primordial class `Object`, then the default constructor has an empty body.
- Otherwise, the default constructor takes no parameters and simply invokes the superclass constructor with no arguments.

A compile-time error occurs if a default constructor is provided by the compiler but the superclass does not have a constructor that takes no arguments.

If the class is declared `public`, then the default constructor is implicitly given the access modifier `public` (§6.6); otherwise, the default constructor has the default access implied by no access modifier. Thus, the example:

```
public class Point {
    int x, y;
}
```

is equivalent to the declaration:

```
public class Point {
    int x, y;
    public Point() { super(); }
}
```

where the default constructor is `public` because the class `Point` is `public`.

8.6.8 Preventing Instantiation of a Class

A class can be designed to prevent code outside the class declaration from creating instances of the class by declaring at least one constructor, to prevent the creation of an implicit constructor, and declaring all constructors to be `private`. A `public` class can likewise prevent the creation of instances outside its package by declaring at least one constructor, to prevent creation of a default constructor with `public` access, and declaring no constructor that is `public`.

Thus, in the example:

```
class ClassOnly {
   private ClassOnly() { }
   static String just = "only the lonely";
}
```

the class `ClassOnly` cannot be instantiated, while in the example:

```
package just;

public class PackageOnly {
   PackageOnly() { }
   String[] justDesserts = { "cheesecake", "ice cream" };
}
```

the class `PackageOnly` can be instantiated only within the package `just`, in which it is declared.

Bow, bow, ye lower middle classes!
Bow, bow, ye tradesmen, bow, ye masses!
Blow the trumpets, bang the brasses!
Tantantara! Tzing! Boom!
—W. S. Gilbert, *Iolanthe*

CHAPTER 9

Interfaces

My apple trees will never get across
And eat the cones under his pines, I tell him.
He only says "Good Fences Make Good Neighbors."
—Robert Frost, *Mending Wall* (1914)

AN interface declaration introduces a new reference type whose members are constants and abstract methods. This type has no implementation, but otherwise unrelated classes can implement it by providing implementations for its abstract methods.

Java programs can use interfaces to make it unnecessary for related classes to share a common abstract superclass or to add methods to `Object`.

An interface may be declared to be an *direct extension* of one or more other interfaces, meaning that it implicitly specifies all the abstract methods and constants of the interfaces it extends, except for any constants that it may hide.

A class may be declared to *directly implement* one or more interfaces, meaning that any instance of the class implements all the abstract methods specified by the interface or interfaces. A class necessarily implements all the interfaces that its direct superclasses and direct superinterfaces do. This (multiple) interface inheritance allows objects to support (multiple) common behaviors without sharing any implementation.

A variable whose declared type is an interface type may have as its value a reference to any object that is an instance of a class declared to implement the specified interface. It is not sufficient that the class happen to implement all the abstract methods of the interface; the class or one of its superclasses must actually be declared to implement the interface, or else the class is not considered to implement the interface.

9.1 Interface Declarations

An interface declaration specifies a new reference type:

InterfaceDeclaration:
  InterfaceModifiers$_{opt}$ `interface` *Identifier*
    ExtendsInterfaces$_{opt}$ *InterfaceBody*

A compile-time error occurs if the *Identifier* naming an interface appears as the name of any other class or interface in the same package. A compile-time error also occurs if the *Identifier* naming an interface appears as the name by which a class or interface is to be known via a single-type-import declaration (§7.5.1) in the compilation unit containing the interface declaration. In the example:

```
class Point { int x, y; }
interface Point { void move(int dx, int dy); }
```

a compile-time error occurs because a `class` and an `interface` in the same package cannot have the same name.

9.1.1 Scope of an Interface Type Name

The *Identifier* specifies the name of the interface and has as its scope the entire package in which it is declared. This is the same scoping rule as for class type names; see §8.1.1 for an example involving classes.

9.1.2 Interface Modifiers

An interface declaration may be preceded by *interface modifiers*:

InterfaceModifiers:
  InterfaceModifier
  InterfaceModifiers InterfaceModifier

InterfaceModifier: one of
  `public abstract`

The access modifier `public` is discussed in §6.6. A compile-time error occurs if the same modifier appears more than once in an interface declaration.

9.1.2.1 `abstract` *Interfaces*

Every interface is implicitly `abstract`. This modifier is obsolete and should not be used in new Java programs.

9.1.3 Superinterfaces

If an `extends` clause is provided, then the interface being declared extends each of the other named interfaces and therefore inherits the methods and constants of each of the other named interfaces. These other named interfaces are the *direct superinterfaces* of the interface being declared. Any class that `implements` the declared interface is also considered to implement all the interfaces that this interface `extends` and that are accessible to the class.

ExtendsInterfaces:
  `extends` *InterfaceType*
  ExtendsInterfaces `,` *InterfaceType*

The following is repeated from §4.3 to make the presentation here clearer:

InterfaceType:
  TypeName

Each *InterfaceType* in the `extends` clause of an interface declaration must name an accessible interface type; otherwise a compile-time error occurs.

A compile-time error occurs if there is a circularity such that an interface directly or indirectly extends itself.

There is no analogue of the class `Object` for interfaces; that is, while every class is an extension of class `Object`, there is no single interface of which all interfaces are extensions.

The *superinterface* relationship is the transitive closure of the direct superinterface relationship. An interface `K` is a superinterface of interface `I` if either of the following is true:

- `K` is a direct superinterface of `I`.
- There exists an interface `J` such that `K` is a superinterface of `J`, and `J` is a superinterface of `I`, applying this definition recursively.

Interface `I` is said to be a *subinterface* of interface `K` whenever `K` is a superinterface of `I`.

9.1.4 Interface Body and Member Declarations

The body of an interface may declare members of the interface:

InterfaceBody:
  `{` *InterfaceMemberDeclarations$_{opt}$* `}`

InterfaceMemberDeclarations:
  InterfaceMemberDeclaration
  InterfaceMemberDeclarations InterfaceMemberDeclaration

InterfaceMemberDeclaration:
  ConstantDeclaration
  AbstractMethodDeclaration

The scope of the name of a member declared in an interface type is the entire body of the interface type declaration.

9.1.5 Access to Interface Member Names

All interface members are implicitly `public`. They are accessible outside the package where the interface is declared if the interface is also declared `public` and the package containing the interface is accessible as described in §7.1.

9.2 Interface Members

The members of an interface are those members inherited from direct superinterfaces and those members declared in the interface.

The interface inherits, from the interfaces it extends, all members of those interfaces, except for fields that it hides and methods that it overrides.

9.3 Field (Constant) Declarations

The materials of action are variable,
but the use we make of them should be constant.
—Epictetus (circa 60 A.D.),
translated by Thomas Wentworth Higginson

ConstantDeclaration:
  ConstantModifiers Type VariableDeclarator

ConstantModifiers: one of
  `public static final`

Every field declaration in the body of an interface is implicitly `public`, `static`, and `final`. It is permitted, but strongly discouraged as a matter of style, to redundantly specify any or all of these modifiers for such fields.

A constant declaration in an interface must not include any of the modifiers `synchronized`, `transient`, or `volatile`, or a compile-time error occurs.

It is possible for an interface to inherit more than one field with the same name (§8.3.3.3). Such a situation does not in itself cause a compile-time error. However, any attempt within the body of the interface to refer to either field by its simple name will result in a compile-time error, because such a reference is ambiguous.

There might be several paths by which the same field declaration might be inherited from an interface. In such a situation, the field is considered to be inherited only once, and it may be referred to by its simple name without ambiguity.

9.3.1 Initialization of Fields in Interfaces

Every field in the body of an interface must have an initialization expression, which need not be a constant expression. The variable initializer is evaluated and the assignment performed exactly once, when the interface is initialized (§12.4).

A compile-time error occurs if an initialization expression for an interface field contains a reference by simple name to the same field or to another field whose declaration occurs textually later in the same interface. Thus:

```
interface Test {
    float f = j;
    int j = 1;
    int k = k+1;
}
```

causes two compile-time errors, because `j` is referred to in the initialization of `f` before `j` is declared and because the initialization of `k` refers to `k` itself.

(One subtlety here is that, at run time, `fields` that are initialized with compile-time constant values are initialized first. This applies also to `static final` fields in classes (§8.3.2.1). This means, in particular, that these fields will never be observed to have their default initial values (§4.5.4), even by devious programs. See §12.4.2 and §13.4.8 for more discussion.)

If the keyword `this` (§15.7.2) or the keyword `super` (15.10.2, 15.11) occurs in an initialization expression for a field of an interface, then a compile-time error occurs.

9.3.2 Examples of Field Declarations

The following example illustrates some (possibly subtle) points about field declarations.

9.3.2.1 *Ambiguous Inherited Fields*

If two fields with the same name are inherited by an interface because, for example, two of its direct superinterfaces declare fields with that name, then a single *ambiguous member* results. Any use of this ambiguous member will result in a compile-time error. Thus in the example:

```
interface BaseColors {
    int RED = 1, GREEN = 2, BLUE = 4;
}
interface RainbowColors extends BaseColors {
    int YELLOW = 3, ORANGE = 5, INDIGO = 6, VIOLET = 7;
}
interface PrintColors extends BaseColors {
    int YELLOW = 8, CYAN = 16, MAGENTA = 32;
}
interface LotsOfColors extends RainbowColors, PrintColors {
    int FUCHSIA = 17, VERMILION = 43, CHARTREUSE = RED+90;
}
```

the interface `LotsOfColors` inherits two fields named `YELLOW`. This is all right as long as the interface does not contain any reference by simple name to the field `YELLOW`. (Such a reference could occur within a variable initializer for a field.)

Even if interface `PrintColors` were to give the value `3` to `YELLOW` rather than the value `8`, a reference to field `YELLOW` within interface `LotsOfColors` would still be considered ambiguous.

9.3.2.2 *Multiply Inherited Fields*

If a single field is inherited multiple times from the same interface because, for example, both this interface and one of this interface's direct superinterfaces extend the interface that declares the field, then only a single member results. This situation does not in itself cause a compile-time error.

In the example in the previous section, the fields `RED`, `GREEN`, and `BLUE` are inherited by interface `LotsOfColors` in more than one way, through interface `RainbowColors` and also through interface `PrintColors`, but the reference to field `RED` in interface `LotsOfColors` is not considered ambiguous because only one actual declaration of the field `RED` is involved.

9.4 Abstract Method Declarations

AbstractMethodDeclaration:
  AbstractMethodModifiers$_{opt}$ *ResultType MethodDeclarator Throws*$_{opt}$;

AbstractMethodModifiers:
  AbstractMethodModifier
  AbstractMethodModifiers AbstractMethodModifier

AbstractMethodModifier: one of
  `public abstract`

The access modifier `public` is discussed in §6.6. A compile-time error occurs if the same modifier appears more than once in an abstract method declaration.

Every method declaration in the body of an interface is implicitly `abstract`, so its body is always represented by a semicolon, not a block. For compatibility with older versions of Java, it is permitted but discouraged, as a matter of style, to redundantly specify the `abstract` modifier for methods declared in interfaces.

Every method declaration in the body of an interface is implicitly `public`. It is permitted, but strongly discouraged as a matter of style, to redundantly specify the `public` modifier for interface methods.

Note that a method declared in an interface must not be declared `static`, or a compile-time error occurs, because in Java `static` methods cannot be `abstract`.

Note that a method declared in an interface must not be declared `native` or `synchronized`, or a compile-time error occurs, because those keywords describe implementation properties rather than interface properties. However, a method declared in an interface may be implemented by a method that is declared `native` or `synchronized` in a class that implements the interface.

Note that a method declared in an interface must not be declared `final` or a compile-time error occurs. However, a method declared in an interface may be implemented by a method that is declared `final` in a class that implements the interface.

9.4.1 Inheritance and Overriding

If the interface declares a method, then the declaration of that method is said to *override* any and all methods with the same signature in the superinterfaces of the interface that would otherwise be accessible to code in this interface.

If a method declaration in an interface overrides the declaration of a method in another interface, a compile-time error occurs if the methods have different return types or if one has a return type and the other is `void`. Moreover, a method declaration must not have a `throws` clause that conflicts (§8.4.4) with that of any method that it overrides; otherwise, a compile-time error occurs.

Methods are overridden on a signature-by-signature basis. If, for example, an interface declares two `public` methods with the same name, and a subinterface overrides one of them, the subinterface still inherits the other method.

An interface inherits from its direct superinterfaces all methods of the superinterfaces that are not overridden by a declaration in the interface.

It is possible for an interface to inherit more than one method with the same signature (§8.4.2). Such a situation does not in itself cause a compile-time error. The interface is considered to inherit all the methods. However, a compile-time error occurs if, for any two such inherited methods, either they have different return types or one has a return type and the other is `void`. (The `throws` clauses do not cause errors in this case.)

There might be several paths by which the same method declaration is inherited from an interface. This fact causes no difficulty and never of itself results in a compile-time error.

9.4.2 Overloading

If two methods of an interface (whether both declared in the same interface, or both inherited by a interface, or one declared and one inherited) have the same name but different signatures, then the method name is said to be *overloaded*. This fact causes no difficulty and never of itself results in a compile-time error. There is no required relationship between the return types or between the `throws` clauses of two methods with the same name but different signatures.

9.4.3 Examples of Abstract Method Declarations

The following examples illustrate some (possibly subtle) points about abstract method declarations.

9.4.3.1 *Example: Overriding*

Methods declared in interfaces are `abstract` and thus contain no implementation. About all that can be accomplished by an overriding method declaration, other than to affirm a method signature, is to restrict the exceptions that might be thrown by an implementation of the method. Here is a variation of the example shown in §8.4.3.1:

```
class BufferEmpty extends Exception {
   BufferEmpty() { super(); }
   BufferEmpty(String s) { super(s); }
}

class BufferError extends Exception {
   BufferError() { super(); }
   BufferError(String s) { super(s); }
}

public interface Buffer {
   char get() throws BufferEmpty, BufferError;
}

public interface InfiniteBuffer extends Buffer {
    char get() throws BufferError;        // override
}
```

9.4.3.2 *Example: Overloading*

In the example code:

```
interface PointInterface {
   void move(int dx, int dy);
}

interface RealPointInterface extends PointInterface {
   void move(float dx, float dy);
   void move(double dx, double dy);
}
```

the method name `move` is overloaded in interface `RealPointInterface` with three different signatures, two of them declared and one inherited. Any class that implements interface `RealPointInterface` must provide implementations of all three method signatures.

Death, life, and sleep, reality and thought,
Assist me, God, their boundaries to know . . .
—William Wordsworth, *Maternal Grief*

CHAPTER 10

Arrays

Even Solomon in all his glory was not arrayed like one of these.
—Matthew 6:29

JAVA *arrays* are objects (§4.3.1), are dynamically created, and may be assigned to variables of type `Object` (§4.3.2). All methods of class `Object` may be invoked on an array.

An array object contains a number of variables. The number of variables may be zero, in which case the array is said to be *empty*. The variables contained in an array have no names; instead they are referenced by array access expressions that use nonnegative integer index values. These variables are called the *components* of the array. If an array has n components, we say n is the *length* of the array; the components of the array are referenced using integer indices from 0 to $n-1$, inclusive.

All the components of an array have the same type, called the *component type* of the array. If the component type of an array is *T*, then the type of the array itself is written *T*`[]`.

The component type of an array may itself be an array type. The components of such an array may contain references to subarrays. If, starting from any array type, one considers its component type, and then (if that is also an array type) the component type of that type, and so on, eventually one must reach a component type that is not an array type; this is called the *element type* of the original array, and the components at this level of the data structure are called the *elements* of the original array.

There is one situation in which an element of an array can be an array: if the element type is `Object`, then some or all of the elements may be arrays, because any array object can be assigned to any variable of type `Object`.

10.1 Array Types

An array type is written as the name of an element type followed by some number of empty pairs of square brackets `[]`. The number of bracket pairs indicates the depth of array nesting. An array's length is not part of its type.

The element type of an array may be any type, whether primitive or reference. In particular:

- Arrays with an interface type as the component type are allowed. The elements of such an array may have as their value a null reference or instances of any class type that implements the interface.
- Arrays with an `abstract` class type as the component type are allowed. The elements of such an array may have as their value a null reference or instances of any subclass of the `abstract` class that is not itself `abstract`.

Array types are used in declarations and in cast expressions (§15.15).

10.2 Array Variables

A variable of array type holds a reference to an object. Declaring a variable of array type does not create an array object or allocate any space for array components. It creates only the variable itself, which can contain a reference to an array. However, the initializer part of a declarator (§8.3) may create an array, a reference to which then becomes the initial value of the variable.

Because an array's length is not part of its type, a single variable of array type may contain references to arrays of different lengths.

Here are examples of declarations of array variables that do not create arrays:

```
int[] ai;               // array of int
short[][] as;           // array of array of short
Object[]  ao,           // array of Object
          otherAo;      // array of Object
short s,                // scalar short
      aas[][];          // array of array of short
```

Here are some examples of declarations of array variables that create array objects:

```
Exception ae[] = new Exception[3];
Object aao[][] = new Exception[2][3];
int[] factorial = { 1, 1, 2, 6, 24, 120, 720, 5040 };
char ac[] = { 'n', 'o', 't', ' ', 'a', ' ',
              'S', 't', 'r', 'i', 'n', 'g' };
String[] aas = { "array", "of", "String", };
```

The [] may appear as part of the type at the beginning of the declaration, or as part of the declarator for a particular variable, or both, as in this example:

```
byte[] rowvector, colvector, matrix[];
```

This declaration is equivalent to:

```
byte rowvector[], colvector[], matrix[][];
```

Once an array object is created, its length never changes. To make an array variable refer to an array of different length, a reference to a different array must be assigned to the variable.

If an array variable `v` has type `A[]`, where `A` is a reference type, then `v` can hold a reference to an instance of any array type `B[]`, provided `B` can be assigned to `A`. This may result in a run-time exception on a later assignment; see §10.10 for a discussion.

10.3 Array Creation

An array is created by an array creation expression (§15.9) or an array initializer (§10.6).

An array creation expression specifies the element type, the number of levels of nested arrays, and the length of the array for at least one of the levels of nesting. The array's length is available as a final instance variable `length`.

An array initializer creates an array and provides initial values for all its components. (Contrast this with C and C++, where it is possible for an array initializer to specify initial values for some but not all of the components of an array.)

10.4 Array Access

A component of an array is accessed by an array access expression (§15.12) that consists of an expression whose value is an array reference followed by an indexing expression enclosed by `[` and `]`, as in `A[i]`. All arrays are `0`-origin. An array with length `n` can be indexed by the integers `0` to `n-1`.

Arrays must be indexed by `int` values; `short`, `byte`, or `char` values may also be used as index values because they are subjected to unary numeric promotion (§5.6.1) and become `int` values. An attempt to access an array component with a `long` index value results in a compile-time error.

All array accesses are checked at run time; an attempt to use an index that is less than zero or greater than or equal to the length of the array causes an `IndexOutOfBoundsException` to be thrown.

10.5 Arrays: A Simple Example

The example:

```
class Gauss {
    public static void main(String[] args) {
        int[] ia = new int[101];
        for (int i = 0; i < ia.length; i++)
            ia[i] = i;
        int sum = 0;
        for (int i = 0; i < ia.length; i++)
            sum += ia[i];
        System.out.println(sum);
    }
}
```

that produces output:

```
5050
```

declares a variable `ia` that has type array of `int`, that is, `int[]`. The variable `ia` is initialized to reference a newly created array object, created by an array creation expression (§15.9). The array creation expression specifies that the array should have `101` components. The length of the array is available using the field `length`, as shown.

The example program fills the array with the integers from `0` to `100`, sums these integers, and prints the result.

10.6 Arrays Initializers

An *array initializer* may be specified in a declaration, creating an array and providing some initial values:

ArrayInitializer:
  { *VariableInitializers*$_{opt}$,$_{opt}$ }

VariableInitializers:
  VariableInitializer
  VariableInitializers , *VariableInitializer*

The following is repeated from §8.3 to make the presentation here clearer:

VariableInitializer:
  Expression
  ArrayInitializer

An array initializer is written as a comma-separated list of expressions, enclosed by braces "{" and "}".

The length of the constructed array will equal the number of expressions.

Each expression specifies a value for one array component. Each expression must be assignment-compatible (§5.2) with the array's component type, or a compile-time error results.

If the component type is itself an array type, then the expression specifying a component may itself be an array initializer; that is, array initializers may be nested.

A trailing comma may appear after the last expression in an array initializer and is ignored.

As an example:

```
class Test {
    public static void main(String[] args) {
        int ia[][] = { {1, 2}, null };
        for (int i = 0; i < 2; i++)
            for (int j = 0; j < 2; j++)
                System.out.println(ia[i][j]);
    }
}
```

prints:

```
1
2
```

before causing a `NullPointerException` in trying to index the second component of the array `ia`, which is a null reference.

10.7 Array Members

The members of an array type are all of the following:

- The `public final` field `length`, which contains the number of components of the array (`length` may be positive or zero)
- The `public` method `clone`, which overrides the method of the same name in class `Object` and throws no checked exceptions
- All the members inherited from class `Object`; the only method of `Object` that is not inherited is its `clone` method

An array thus has the same methods as the following class:

```
class A implements Cloneable {
    public final int length = X;
    public Object clone() {
        try {
            return super.clone();
        } catch (CloneNotSupportedException e) {
            throw new InternalError(e.getMessage());
        }
    }
}
```

Every array implements interface `Cloneable`. That arrays are cloneable is shown by the test program:

```
class Test {
    public static void main(String[] args) {
        int ia1[] = { 1, 2 };
        int ia2[] = (int[])ia1.clone();
        System.out.print((ia1 == ia2) + " ");
        ia1[1]++;
        System.out.println(ia2[1]);
    }
}
```

which prints:

```
false 2
```

showing that the components of the arrays referenced by `ia1` and `ia2` are different variables. (In some early implementations of Java this example failed to compile because the compiler incorrectly believed that the clone method for an array could throw a `CloneNotSupportedException`.)

A `clone` of a multidimensional array is shallow, which is to say that it creates only a single new array. Subarrays are shared, as shown by the example program:

```
class Test {
    public static void main(String[] args) throws Throwable {
        int ia[][] = { { 1 , 2}, null };
        int ja[][] = (int[][])ia.clone();
        System.out.print((ia == ja) + " ");
        System.out.println(ia[0] == ja[0] && ia[1] == ja[1]);
    }
}
```

which prints:

```
false true
```

showing that the `int[]` array that is `ia[0]` and the `int[]` array that is `ja[0]` are the same array.

10.8 Class Objects for Arrays

Every array has an associated Class object, shared with all other arrays with the same component type. The superclass of an array type is considered to be Object, as shown by the following example code:

```
class Test {
    public static void main(String[] args) {
        int[] ia = new int[3];
        System.out.println(ia.getClass());
        System.out.println(ia.getClass().getSuperclass());
    }
}
```

which prints:

```
class [I
class java.lang.Object
```

where the string "[I" is the run-time type signature for the class object "array with component type int" (§20.1.1).

10.9 An Array of Characters is Not a String

In Java, unlike C, an array of char is not a String (§20.12), and neither a String nor an array of char is terminated by '\u0000' (the NUL character).

A Java String object is immutable, that is, its contents never change, while an array of char has mutable elements. The method toCharArray in class String returns an array of characters containing the same character sequence as a String. The class StringBuffer implements useful methods on mutable arrays of characters (§20.13).

10.10 Array Store Exception

If an array variable *v* has type *A*[], where *A* is a reference type, then *v* can hold a reference to an instance of any array type *B*[], provided *B* can be assigned to *A*.

Thus, the example:

```
class Point { int x, y; }

class ColoredPoint extends Point { int color; }
```

```
class Test {
    public static void main(String[] args) {
        ColoredPoint[] cpa = new ColoredPoint[10];
        Point[] pa = cpa;
        System.out.println(pa[1] == null);
        try {
            pa[0] = new Point();
        } catch (ArrayStoreException e) {
            System.out.println(e);
        }
    }
}
```

produces the output:

```
true
java.lang.ArrayStoreException
```

Here the variable `pa` has type `Point[]` and the variable `cpa` has as its value a reference to an object of type `ColoredPoint[]`. A `ColoredPoint` can be assigned to a `Point`; therefore, the value of `cpa` can be assigned to `pa`.

A reference to this array `pa`, for example, testing whether `pa[1]` is `null`, will not result in a run-time type error. This is because the element of the array of type `ColoredPoint[]` is a `ColoredPoint`, and every `ColoredPoint` can stand in for a `Point`, since `Point` is the superclass of `ColoredPoint`.

On the other hand, an assignment to the array `pa` can result in a run-time error. At compile time, an assignment to an element of `pa` is checked to make sure that the value assigned is a `Point`. But since `pa` holds a reference to an array of `ColoredPoint`, the assignment is valid only if the type of the value assigned at run-time is, more specifically, a `ColoredPoint`.

Java checks for such a situation at run-time to ensure that the assignment is valid; if not, an `ArrayStoreException` is thrown. More formally: an assignment to an element of an array whose type is *`A`*`[]`, where *`A`* is a reference type, is checked at run-time to ensure that the value assigned can be assigned to the actual element type of the array, where the actual element type may be any reference type that is assignable to *`A`*.

At length burst in the argent revelry,
With plume, tiara, and all rich array . . .
—John Keats, *The Eve of St. Agnes* (1819)

CHAPTER 11

Exceptions

If anything can go wrong, it will.
—Finagle's Law
(often incorrectly attributed to Murphy, whose law is rather different—which only goes to show that Finagle was right)

WHEN a Java program violates the semantic constraints of the Java language, a Java Virtual Machine signals this error to the program as an *exception*. An example of such a violation is an attempt to index outside the bounds of an array. Some programming languages and their implementations react to such errors by peremptorily terminating the program; other programming languages allow an implementation to react in an arbitrary or unpredictable way. Neither of these approaches is compatible with the design goals of Java: to provide portability and robustness. Instead, Java specifies that an exception will be thrown when semantic constraints are violated and will cause a non-local transfer of control from the point where the exception occurred to a point that can be specified by the programmer. An exception is said to be *thrown* from the point where it occurred and is said to be *caught* at the point to which control is transferred.

Java programs can also throw exceptions explicitly, using `throw` statements (§14.16). This provides an alternative to the old-fashioned style of handling error conditions by returning funny values, such as the integer value `-1` where a negative value would not normally be expected. Experience shows that too often such funny values are ignored or not checked for by callers, leading to programs that are not robust, exhibit undesirable behavior, or both.

Every exception is represented by an instance of the class `Throwable` or one of its subclasses; such an object can be used to carry information from the point at which an exception occurs to the handler that catches it. Handlers are established by `catch` clauses of `try` statements (§14.18). During the process of throwing an exception, a Java Virtual Machine abruptly completes, one by one, any expressions, statements, method and constructor invocations, static initializers, and field initialization expressions that have begun but not completed execution in the current thread. This process continues until a handler is found that indicates that it handles that particular exception by naming the class of the exception or a superclass of the class of the exception. If no such handler is found, then the method `uncaughtException` (§20.21.31) is invoked for the `ThreadGroup` that is the parent of the current thread—thus every effort is made to avoid letting an exception go unhandled.

The Java exception mechanism is integrated with the Java synchronization model (§17), so that locks are released as `synchronized` statements (§14.17) and invocations of `synchronized` methods (§8.4.3.5, §15.11) complete abruptly.

This chapter describes the different causes of exceptions (§11.1). It details how exceptions are checked at compile time (§11.2) and processed at run time (§11.3). A detailed example (§11.4) is then followed by an explanation of the exception hierarchy and the standard exception classes (§11.5).

11.1 The Causes of Exceptions

If we do not succeed, then we run the risk of failure.
—J. Danforth Quayle (1990)

An exception is thrown for one of three *reasons*:

- An abnormal execution condition was synchronously detected by a Java Virtual Machine. Such conditions arise because:
  - evaluation of an expression violates the normal semantics of the Java language, such as an integer divide by zero, as summarized in §15.5
  - an error occurs in loading or linking part of the Java program (§12.2, §12.3)
  - some limitation a resource is exceeded, such as using too much memory

  These exceptions are not thrown at an arbitrary point in the program, but rather at a point where they are specified as a possible result of an expression evaluation or statement execution.
- A `throw` statement (§14.16) was executed in Java code.
- An asynchronous exception occurred either because:
  - the method `stop` of class `Thread` (§20.20.16) was invoked
  - an internal error has occurred in the virtual machine (§11.5.2.2)

Exceptions are represented by instances of the class `Throwable` and instances of its subclasses. These classes are, collectively, the *exception classes*.

11.2 Compile-Time Checking of Exceptions

The Java language checks, at compile time, that a Java program contains handlers for *checked exceptions*, by analyzing which checked exceptions can result from execution of a method or constructor. For each checked exception which is a possible result, the `throws` clause for the method (§8.4.4) or constructor (§8.6.4) must mention the class of that exception or one of the superclasses of the class of that exception. This compile-time checking for the presence of exception handlers is designed to reduce the number of exceptions which are not properly handled.

The *unchecked exceptions classes* are the class `RuntimeException` and its subclasses, and the class `Error` and its subclasses. All other exception classes are *checked exception classes*. The standard Java API defines a number of exception classes, both checked and unchecked. Additional exception classes, both checked and unchecked, may be declared by Java programmers. See §11.5 for a description of the Java exception class hierarchy and the exception classes defined by the standard Java API and Java Virtual Machine.

The checked exception classes named in the `throws` clause are part of the contract between the implementor and user of the method or constructor. The `throws` clause of an overriding method may not specify that this method will result in throwing any checked exception which the overridden method is not permitted, by its `throws` clause, to throw. When interfaces are involved, more than one method declaration may be overridden by a single overriding declaration. In this case, the overriding declaration must have a `throws` clause that is compatible with *all* the overridden declarations (§9.4).

Variable initializers for fields (§8.3.2) and static initializers (§8.5) must not result in a checked exception; if one does, a compile-time error occurs.

11.2.1 Why Errors are Not Checked

Those unchecked exception classes which are the *error classes* (`Error` and its subclasses) are exempted from compile-time checking because they can occur at many points in the program and recovery from them is difficult or impossible. A Java program declaring such exceptions would be cluttered, pointlessly.

11.2.2 Why Runtime Exceptions are Not Checked

The *runtime exception classes* (`RuntimeException` and its subclasses) are exempted from compile-time checking because, in the judgment of the designers of Java, having to declare such exceptions would not aid significantly in establishing the correctness of Java programs. Many of the operations and constructs of the

Java language can result in runtime exceptions. The information available to a Java compiler, and the level of analysis the compiler performs, are usually not sufficient to establish that such runtime exceptions cannot occur, even though this may be obvious to the Java programmer. Requiring such exception classes to be declared would simply be an irritation to Java programmers.

For example, certain code might implement a circular data structure that, by construction, can never involve `null` references; the programmer can then be certain that a `NullPointerException` cannot occur, but it would be difficult for a compiler to prove it. The theorem-proving technology that is needed to establish such global properties of data structures is beyond the scope of this Java Language Specification.

11.3 Handling of an Exception

When an exception is thrown, control is transferred from the code that caused the exception to the nearest dynamically-enclosing `catch` clause of a `try` statement (§14.18) that handles the exception.

A statement or expression is *dynamically enclosed* by a `catch` clause if it appears within the `try` block of the `try` statement of which the `catch` clause is a part, or if the caller of the statement or expression is dynamically enclosed by the `catch` clause.

The *caller* of a statement or expression depends on where it occurs:

- If within a method, then the caller is the method invocation expression (§15.11) that was executed to cause the method to be invoked.
- If within a constructor or the initializer for an instance variable, then the caller is the class instance creation expression (§15.8) or the method invocation of `newInstance` that was executed to cause an object to be created.
- If within a static initializer or an initializer for a `static` variable, then the caller is the expression that used the class or interface so as to cause it to be initialized.

Whether a particular `catch` clause *handles* an exception is determined by comparing the class of the object that was thrown to the declared type of the parameter of the `catch` clause. The `catch` clause handles the exception if the type of its parameter is the class of the exception or a superclass of the class of the exception. Equivalently, a `catch` clause will catch any exception object that is an `instanceof` (§15.19.2) the declared parameter type.

The control transfer that occurs when an exception is thrown causes abrupt completion of expressions (§15.5) and statements (§14.1) until a `catch` clause is encountered that can handle the exception; execution then continues by executing the block of that `catch` clause. The code that caused the exception is never resumed.

If no `catch` clause handling an exception can be found, then the current thread (the thread that encountered the exception) is terminated, but only after all `finally` clauses have been executed and the method `uncaughtException` (§20.21.31) has been invoked for the `ThreadGroup` that is the parent of the current thread.

In situations where it is desirable to ensure that one block of code is always executed after another, even if that other block of code completes abruptly, a `try` statement with a `finally` clause (§14.18.2) may be used. If a `try` or `catch` block in a `try–finally` or `try–catch–finally` statement completes abruptly, then the `finally` clause is executed during propagation of the exception, even if no matching `catch` clause is ultimately found. If a `finally` clause is executed because of abrupt completion of a `try` block and the `finally` clause itself completes abruptly, then the reason for the abrupt completion of the `try` block is discarded and the new reason for abrupt completion is propagated from there.

The exact rules for abrupt completion and for the catching of exceptions are specified in detail with the specification of each statement in §14 and for expressions in §15 (especially §15.5).

11.3.1 Exceptions are Precise

Exceptions in Java are *precise*: when the transfer of control takes place, all effects of the statements executed and expressions evaluated before the point from which the exception is thrown must appear to have taken place. No expressions, statements, or parts thereof that occur after the point from which the exception is thrown may appear to have been evaluated. If optimized code has speculatively executed some of the expressions or statements which follow the point at which the exception occurs, such code must be prepared to hide this speculative execution from the user-visible state of the Java program.

11.3.2 Handling Asynchronous Exceptions

Most exceptions in Java occur synchronously as a result of an action by the thread in which they occur, and at a point in the Java program that is specified to possibly result in such an exception. An asynchronous exception is, by contrast, an exception that can potentially occur at any point in the execution of a Java program.

Proper understanding of the semantics of asynchronous exceptions is necessary if high-quality machine code is to be generated.

Asynchronous exceptions are rare in Java. They occur only as a result of:

- An invocation of the `stop` methods of class `Thread` (§20.20.15, §20.20.16) or `ThreadGroup` (§20.21.8, §20.21.9)
- An `InternalError` (§11.5.2.2) in the Java Virtual Machine

The `stop` methods may be invoked by one thread to affect another thread or all the threads in a specified thread group. They are asynchronous because they may occur at any point in the execution of the other thread or threads. An `InternalError` is considered asynchronous so that it may be handled using the same mechanism that handles the `stop` method, as will now be described.

Java permits a small but bounded amount of execution to occur before an asynchronous exception is thrown. This delay is permitted to allow optimized code to detect and throw these exceptions at points where it is practical to handle them while obeying the semantics of the Java language.

A simple implementation might poll for asynchronous exceptions at the point of each control transfer instruction. Since a Java program has a finite size, this provides a bound on the total delay in detecting an asynchronous exception. Since no asynchronous exception will occur between control transfers, the code generator has some flexibility to reorder computation between control transfers for greater performance.

The paper *Polling Efficiently on Stock Hardware* by Mark Feeley, *Proc. 1993 Conference on Functional Programming and Computer Architecture*, Copenhagen, Denmark, pp. 179–187, is recommended as further reading.

Like all exceptions, asynchronous exceptions are precise (§11.3.1).

11.4 An Example of Exceptions

Consider the following example:

```
class TestException extends Exception {
    TestException() { super(); }
    TestException(String s) { super(s); }
}

class Test {
    public static void main(String[] args) {
        for (int i = 0; i < args.length; i++) {
```

```
            try {
                thrower(args[i]);
                System.out.println("Test \"" + args[i] +
                    "\" didn't throw an exception");
            } catch (Exception e) {
                System.out.println("Test \"" + args[i] +
                    "\" threw a " + e.getClass() +
                    "\n    with message: " + e.getMessage());
            }
        }
    }

    static int thrower(String s) throws TestException {
        try {
            if (s.equals("divide")) {
                int i = 0;
                return i/i;
            }
            if (s.equals("null")) {
                s = null;
                return s.length();
            }
            if (s.equals("test"))
                throw new TestException("Test message");
            return 0;
        } finally {
            System.out.println("[thrower(\"" + s +
                    "\") done]");
        }
    }
}
```

If we execute the test program, passing it the arguments:

```
divide null not test
```

it produces the output:

```
[thrower("divide") done]
Test "divide" threw a class java.lang.ArithmeticException
    with message: / by zero
[thrower("null") done]
Test "null" threw a class java.lang.NullPointerException
    with message: null
[thrower("not") done]
Test "not" didn't throw an exception
[thrower("test") done]
Test "test" threw a class TestException
    with message: Test message
```

This example declares an exception class `TestException`. The `main` method of class `Test` invokes the `thrower` method four times, causing exceptions to be thrown three of the four times. The `try` statement in method `main` catches each exception that the `thrower` throws. Whether the invocation of `thrower` completes normally or abruptly, a message is printed describing what happened.

The declaration of the method `thrower` must have a `throws` clause because it can throw instances of `TestException`, which is a checked exception class (§11.2). A compile-time error would occur if the `throws` clause were omitted.

Notice that the `finally` clause is executed on every invocation of `thrower`, whether or not an exception occurs, as shown by the "`[thrower(...) done]`" output that occurs for each invocation

11.5 The Exception Hierarchy

The possible exceptions in a Java program are organized in a hierarchy of classes, rooted at class `Throwable` (§11.5, §20.22), a direct subclass of `Object`. The classes `Exception` and `Error` are direct subclasses of `Throwable`. The class `RuntimeException` is a direct subclass of `Exception`.

The exception classes declared by the standard packages `java.lang`, `java.util`, `java.io` and `java.net` are called the *standard exception classes*.

Java programs can use the pre-existing exception classes in `throw` statements, or define additional exception classes, as subclasses of `Throwable` or of any of its subclasses, as appropriate. To take advantage of Java's compile-time checking for exception handlers, it is typical to define most new exception classes as checked exception classes, specifically as subclasses of `Exception` that are not subclasses of `RuntimeException`.

11.5.1 The Classes `Exception` and `RuntimeException`

The class `Exception` is the superclass of all the exceptions that ordinary programs may wish to recover from.

11.5.1.1 *Standard Runtime Exceptions*

The class `RuntimeException` is a subclass of class `Exception`. The subclasses of `RuntimeException` are unchecked exception classes.

Package `java.lang` defines the following standard unchecked runtime exceptions, which, like all other classes in package `java.lang`, are implicitly imported and therefore may be referred to by their simple names:

- `ArithmeticException`: An exceptional arithmetic situation has arisen, such as an integer division (§15.16.2) operation with a zero divisor.
- `ArrayStoreException`: An attempt has been made to store into an array component a value whose class is not assignment compatible with the component type of the array (§10.10, §15.25.1).
- `ClassCastException`: An attempt has been made to cast (§5.4, §15.15) a reference to an object to an inappropriate type.
- `IllegalArgumentException`: A method was passed an invalid or inappropriate argument or invoked on an inappropriate object. Subclasses of this class include:
  - `IllegalThreadStateException`: A thread was not in an appropriate state for a requested operation.
  - `NumberFormatException`: An attempt was made to convert a `String` to a value of a numeric type, but the `String` did not have an appropriate format.
- `IllegalMonitorStateException`: A thread has attempted to wait on (§20.1.6, §20.1.7, §20.1.8) or notify (§20.1.9, §20.1.10) other threads waiting on an object that it has not locked.
- `IndexOutOfBoundsException`: Either an index of some sort (such as to an array, a string, or a vector) or a subrange, specified either by two index values or by an index and a length, was out of range.
- `NegativeArraySizeException`: An attempt was made to create an array with a negative length (§15.9).
- `NullPointerException`: An attempt was made to use a null reference in a case where an object reference was required.
- `SecurityException`: A security violation was detected (§20.17).

Package `java.util` defines the following additional standard unchecked runtime exceptions:

- `java.util.EmptyStackException`: An attempt was made to access an element of an empty stack.
- `java.util.NoSuchElementException`: An attempt was made to access an element of an empty vector.

11.5.1.2 *Standard Checked Exceptions*

The standard subclasses of `Exception` other than `RuntimeException` are all checked exception classes.

Package `java.lang` defines the following standard exceptions, which, like all other classes in package `java.lang`, are implicitly imported and therefore may be referred to by their simple names:

- `ClassNotFoundException`: A class or interface with a specified name could not be found (§20.3.8).
- `CloneNotSupportedException`: The `clone` method (§20.1.5) of class `Object` has been invoked to clone an object, but the class of that object does not implement the `Cloneable` interface.
- `IllegalAccessException`: An attempt has been made to load a class using a string giving its fully qualified name, but the currently executing method does not have access to the definition of the specified class because the class is not `public` and is in another package.
- `InstantiationException`: An attempt was made to create an instance of a class using the `newInstance` method in class `Class`, but the specified class object cannot be instantiated because it is an interface, is `abstract`, or is an array.
- `InterruptedException`: The current thread was waiting, and another thread has interrupted the current thread, using the `interrupt` method of class `Thread` (§20.20.31).

Package `java.io` defines the following additional standard exceptions:

- `java.io.IOException`: A requested I/O operation could not be completed normally. Subclasses of this class include:
  - `java.io.EOFException`: End of file has been encountered before normal completion of an input operation.
  - `java.io.FileNotFoundException`: A file with the name specified by a file name string or path was not found within the file system.
  - `java.io.InterruptedIOException`: The current thread was waiting for completion of an I/O operation, and another thread has interrupted the current thread, using the `interrupt` method of class `Thread` (§20.20.31).
  - `java.io.UTFDataFormatException`: A requested conversion of a string to or from Java modified UTF-8 format could not be completed (§22.1.15,

§22.2.14) because the string was too long or because the purported UTF-8 data was not the result of encoding a Unicode string into UTF-8.

The standard package `java.net` defines the following additional subclasses of `java.io.IOException`:

- `java.net.MalformedURLException`: A string that was provided as a URL, or as part of a URL, had an inappropriate format or specified an unknown protocol.
- `java.net.ProtocolException`: Some aspect of a network protocol was not correctly carried out.
- `java.net.SocketException`: An operation involving a socket could not be completed normally.
- `java.net.UnknownHostException`: The name of a network host could not be resolved to a network address.
- `java.net.UnknownServiceException`: The network connection cannot support the requested service.

11.5.2 The Class `Error`

The class `Error` and its standard subclasses are exceptions from which ordinary programs are not ordinarily expected to recover. The class `Error` is a separate subclass of `Throwable`, distinct from `Exception` in the class hierarchy, to allow programs to use the idiom:

```
} catch (Exception e) {
```

to catch all exceptions from which recovery may be possible without catching errors from which recovery is typically not possible.

Package `java.lang` defines all the error classes described here. These classes, like all other classes in package `java.lang`, are implicitly imported and therefore may be referred to by their simple names.

11.5.2.1 *Loading and Linkage Errors*

A Java Virtual Machine throws an object that is an instance of a subclass of `LinkageError` when a loading, linkage, preparation, verification or initialization error occurs:

- The loading process is described in §12.2. The errors `ClassFormatError`, `ClassCircularityError`, and `NoClassDefFoundError` are described there.
- The linking process is described in §12.3. The linking errors are described there. These errors include `IllegalAccessError`, `InstantiationError`, `NoSuchFieldError`, and `NoSuchMethodError`, all of which are subclasses of `IncompatibleClassChangeError`, and, also, `UnsatisfiedLinkError`.
- The class verification process is described in §12.3.1. The verification failure error `VerifyError` is described there.
- The class preparation process is described in §12.3.2. The preparation error described there is `AbstractMethodError`.
- The class initialization process is described in §12.4. A virtual machine will throw the error `ExceptionInInitializerError` if execution of a static initializer or of an initializer for a `static` field results in an exception that is not an `Error` or a subclass of `Error`.

11.5.2.2 *Virtual Machine Errors*

A Java Virtual Machine throws an object that is an instance of a subclass of the class `VirtualMachineError` when an internal error or resource limitation prevents it from implementing the semantics of the Java Language. This language specification and the Java Virtual Machine Specification define the following virtual machine errors:

- `InternalError`: An internal error has occurred in a Java Virtual Machine, because of a fault in the software implementing the virtual machine, a fault in the underlying host system software, or a fault in the hardware. This error is delivered asynchronously when it is detected, and may occur at any point in a Java program.
- `OutOfMemoryError`: A Java Virtual Machine has run out of either virtual or physical memory, and the automatic storage manager wasn't able to reclaim enough memory to satisfy an object creation request.
- `StackOverflowError`: A Java Virtual Machine has run out of stack space for a thread, typically because the thread is doing an unbounded number of recursive invocations due to a fault in the executing program.
- `UnknownError`: An exception or error has occurred but, for some reason, a Java Virtual Machine is unable to report the actual exception or error.

A sophisticated Java program may be designed to handle `OutOfMemoryError` and attempt to recover from it, perhaps by carefully dropping references to objects.

We are exploring enhancements to Java to simplify handling of out-of-memory conditions. One possibility would be to support automatic suspension of a thread which encounters an `OutOfMemoryError` and allow another thread to handle the `error` situation. Such a technique might also permit a Java program to recover from a `StackOverflowError` if this overflow does not result from a non-terminating recursion. Suggestions for other approaches are welcomed.

No rule is so general, which admits not some exception.
—Robert Burton (1576–1640)

I never forget a face—but in your case I'll be glad to make an exception.

—Groucho Marx

CHAPTER 12

Execution

We must all hang together, or assuredly we shall all hang separately.
—Benjamin Franklin (July 4, 1776)

THIS chapter specifies activities that occur during execution of a Java program. It is organized around the life cycle of a Java Virtual Machine and of the classes, interfaces, and objects that form a Java program.

A Java Virtual Machine starts up by loading a specified class and then invoking the method `main` in this specified class. Section §12.1 outlines the loading, linking, and initialization steps involved in executing `main`, as an introduction to the concepts in this chapter. Further sections specify the details of loading (§12.2), linking (§12.3), and initialization (§12.4).

The chapter continues with a specification of the procedures for creation of new class instances (§12.5); finalization of class instances (§12.6); and finalization of classes (§12.7). It concludes by describing the unloading of classes (§12.8) and the procedure followed when a virtual machine exits (§12.9).

12.1 Virtual Machine Start-Up

A Java Virtual Machine starts execution by invoking the method `main` of some specified class, passing it a single argument, which is an array of strings. In the examples in this specification, this first class is typically called `Test`.

The manner in which the initial class is specified to the Java Virtual Machine is beyond the scope of this specification, but it is typical, in host environments that use command lines, for the fully-qualified name of the class to be specified as a command-line argument and for following command-line arguments to be used as strings to be provided as the argument to the method `main`. For example, in a UNIX implementation, the command line:

```
java Test reboot Bob Dot Enzo
```

will typically start a Java Virtual Machine by invoking method `main` of class `Test` (a class in an unnamed package), passing it an array containing the four strings `"reboot"`, `"Bob"`, `"Dot"`, and `"Enzo"`.

We now outline the steps the virtual machine may take to execute `Test`, as an example of the loading, linking, and initialization processes that are described further in later sections.

12.1.1 Load the Class `Test`

The initial attempt to execute the method `main` of class `Test` discovers that the class `Test` is not loaded—that is, that the virtual machine does not currently contain a binary representation for this class. The virtual machine then uses a class loader (§20.14) to attempt to find such a binary representation. If this process fails, then an error is thrown. This loading process is described further in §12.2.

12.1.2 Link `Test`: Verify, Prepare, (Optionally) Resolve

After `Test` is loaded, it must be initialized before `main` can be invoked. And `Test`, like all (class or interface) types, must be linked before it is initialized. Linking involves verification, preparation and (optionally) resolution. Linking is described further in §12.3.

Verification checks that the loaded representation of `Test` is well-formed, with a proper symbol table. Verification also checks that the code that implements `Test` obeys the semantic requirements of Java and the Java Virtual Machine. If a problem is detected during verification, then an error is thrown. Verification is described further in §12.3.1.

Preparation involves allocation of static storage and any data structures that are used internally by the virtual machine, such as method tables. If a problem is detected during preparation, then an error is thrown. Preparation is described further in §12.3.2.

Resolution is the process of checking symbolic references from `Test` to other classes and interfaces, by loading the other classes and interfaces that are mentioned and checking that the references are correct.

The resolution step is optional at the time of initial linkage. An implementation may resolve symbolic references from a class or interface that is being linked very early, even to the point of resolving all symbolic references from the classes and interfaces that are further referenced, recursively. (This resolution may result in errors from these further loading and linking steps.) This implementation choice represents one extreme and is similar to the kind of "static" linkage that has been done for many years in simple implementations of the C language. (In these implementations, a compiled program is typically represented as an "`a.out`" file that contains a fully-linked version of the program, including completely resolved links to library routines used by the program. Copies of these library routines are included in the "`a.out`" file.)

An implementation may instead choose to resolve a symbolic reference only when it is actively used; consistent use of this strategy for all symbolic references would represent the "laziest" form of resolution. In this case, if `Test` had several symbolic references to another class, then the references might be resolved one at a time, as they are used, or perhaps not at all, if these references were never used during execution of the program.

The only requirement on when resolution is performed is that any errors detected during resolution must be thrown at a point in the program where some action is taken by the program that might, directly or indirectly, require linkage to the class or interface involved in the error. Using the "static" example implementation choice described above, loading and linkage errors could occur before the program is executed if they involved a class or interface mentioned in the class `Test` or any of the further, recursively referenced, classes and interfaces. In a system that implemented the "laziest" resolution, these errors would be thrown only when an incorrect symbolic reference is actively used.

The resolution process is described further in §12.3.3.

12.1.3 Initialize `Test`: Execute Initializers

In our continuing example, the virtual machine is still trying to execute the method `main` of class `Test`. This is an attempted active use (§12.4.1) of the class, which is permitted only if the class has been initialized.

Initialization consists of execution of any class variable initializers and static initializers of the class `Test`, in textual order. But before `Test` can be initialized, its direct superclass must be initialized, as well as the direct superclass of its direct superclass, and so on, recursively. In the simplest case, `Test` has `Object` as its implicit direct superclass; if class `Object` has not yet been initialized, then it must be initialized before `Test` is initialized. Class `Object` has no superclass, so the recursion terminates here.

If class `Test` has another class `Super` as its superclass, then `Super` must be initialized before `Test`. This requires loading, verifying, and preparing `Super` if this has not already been done and, depending on the implementation, may also involve resolving the symbolic references from `Super` and so on, recursively.

Initialization may thus cause loading, linking, and initialization errors, including such errors involving other types.

The initialization process is described further in §12.4.

12.1.4 Invoke `Test.main`

Finally, after completion of the initialization for class `Test` (during which other consequential loading, linking, and initializing may have occurred), the method `main` of `Test` is invoked.

The method `main` must be declared `public`, `static`, and `void`. It must accept a single argument that is an array of strings.

12.2 Loading of Classes and Interfaces

Loading refers to the process of finding the binary form of a class or interface type with a particular name, perhaps by computing it on the fly, but more typically by retrieving a binary representation previously computed from source code by a compiler, and constructing, from that binary form, a `Class` object to represent the class or interface.

The binary format of a class or interface is normally the `class` file format described in *The Java Virtual Machine*, but other formats are possible, provided they meet the requirements specified in §13.1. The method `defineClass` (§20.14.3) of class `ClassLoader` may be used to construct `Class` objects from binary representations in the `class` file format.

A Java Virtual Machine system should maintain an internal table of classes and interfaces that have been loaded for the sake of resolving symbolic references. Each entry in the table should consist of a fully qualified class name (as a string), a class loader, and a `Class` object. Whenever a symbolic reference to a class or interface is to be resolved, a class loader is identified that is responsible for loading the class or interface, if necessary. The table should be consulted first, however; if it already contains an entry for that class name and class loader, then the class object in that entry should be used and no method of the class loader should be invoked. If the table contains no such entry, then the method `loadClass` (§20.14.2) of the class loader should be invoked, giving it the name of the class or interface. If and when it returns, the class object that it returns should be used to make a new entry in the table for that class name and class loader.

The purpose of this internal table is to allow the verification process (§12.3.1) to assume, for its purposes, that two classes or interfaces are the same if they have the same name and the same class loader. This property allows a class to be verified without loading all the classes and interfaces that it uses, whether actively or passively. Well-behaved class loaders do maintain this property: given the same name twice, a good class loader should return the same class object each time. But without the internal table, a malicious class loader could violate this property and undermine the security of the Java type system. A basic principle of the design of the Java language is that the type system cannot be subverted by code written in Java, not even by implementations of such otherwise sensitive system classes as `ClassLoader` (§20.14) and `SecurityManager` (§20.17).

An entry may be deleted from the internal table only after unloading (§12.8) the class or interface represented by the class object in the entry.

12.2.1 The Loading Process

The loading process is implemented by the class `ClassLoader` (§20.14) and its subclasses. Different subclasses of `ClassLoader` may implement different loading policies. In particular, a class loader may cache binary representations of classes and interfaces, prefetch them based on expected usage, or load a group of related classes together. These activities may not be completely transparent to a running Java application if, for example, a newly compiled version of a class is not found because an older version is cached by a class loader. It is the responsibility of a class loader, however, to reflect loading errors only at points in the program they could have arisen without prefetching or group loading.

If an error occurs during class loading, then an instance of one of the following subclasses of class `LinkageError` will be thrown at any point in the Java program that (directly or indirectly) uses the type:

- `ClassCircularityError`: A class or interface could not be loaded because it would be its own superclass or superinterface (§13.4.4).
- `ClassFormatError`: The binary data that purports to specify a requested compiled class or interface is malformed.
- `NoClassDefFoundError`: No definition for a requested class or interface could be found by the relevant class loader.

Because loading involves the allocation of new data structures, it may fail with an `OutOfMemoryError`.

12.2.2 Loading: Implications for Code Generation

A cooperating class loader can enable a code generator to generate code for a group of class and interface types—perhaps an entire package—by loading the binary code for these types as a group. A format can be designed that allows all the internal symbolic references in such a group to be resolved, before the group is loaded. Such a strategy may also allow the generated code to be optimized before loading based on the known concrete types in the group. This approach may be useful in specific cases, but is discouraged as a general technique, since such a class file format is unlikely to be widely understood.

12.3 Linking of Classes and Interfaces

Linking is the process of taking a binary form of a class or interface type and combining it into the runtime state of the Java Virtual Machine, so that it can be executed. A class or interface type is always loaded before it is linked. Three different activities are involved in linking: verification, preparation, and resolution of symbolic references.

Java allows an implementation flexibility as to when linking activities (and, because of recursion, loading) take place, provided that the semantics of the language are respected, that a class or interface is completely verified and prepared before it is initialized, and that errors detected during linkage are thrown at a point in the program where some action is taken by the program that might require linkage to the class or interface involved in the error.

For example, an implementation may choose to resolve each symbolic reference in a class or interface individually, only when it is used (lazy or late resolution), or to resolve them all at once while the class is being verified (static resolution). This means that the resolution process may continue, in some implementations, after a class or interface has been initialized.

Because linking involves the allocation of new data structures, it may fail with an `OutOfMemoryError`.

12.3.1 Verification of the Binary Representation

Verification ensures that the binary representation of a class or interface is structurally correct. For example, it checks that every instruction has a valid operation code; that every branch instruction branches to the start of some other instruction, rather than into the middle of an instruction; that every method is provided with a structurally correct signature; and that every instruction obeys the type discipline of the Java language.

For a more detailed description of the verification process, see the separate volume of this series, *The Java Virtual Machine Specification*.

If an error occurs during verification, then an instance of the following subclass of class `LinkageError` will be thrown at the point in the Java program that caused the class to be verified:

- `VerifyError`: The binary definition for a class or interface failed to pass a set of required checks to verify that it obeys the semantics of the Java language and that it cannot violate the integrity of the Java Virtual Machine. (See §13.4.2, §13.4.4, §13.4.8, and §13.4.16 for some examples.)

12.3.2 Preparation of a Class or Interface Type

Preparation involves creating the `static` fields (class variables and constants) for a class or interface and initializing such fields to the standard default values (§4.5.4). This does not require the execution of any Java code; explicit initializers for `static` fields are executed as part of initialization (§12.4), not preparation.

Java implementations must detect the following error during preparation:

- `AbstractMethodError`: A class that is not declared to be `abstract` has an `abstract` method. This can occur, for example, if a method that is originally not `abstract` is changed to be `abstract` after another class that inherits the now `abstract` method declaration has been compiled (§13.4.15).

If such an error is detected, then an instance of `AbstractMethodError` should be thrown at the point in the Java program that caused the class to be prepared.

Implementations of the Java Virtual Machine may precompute additional data structures at preparation time in order to make later operations on a class or interface more efficient. One particularly useful data structure is a "method table" or other data structure that allows any method to be invoked on instances of a class without requiring a search of superclasses at invocation time.

12.3.3 Resolution of Symbolic References

A Java binary file references other classes and interfaces and their fields, methods, and constructors symbolically, using the fully-qualified names of the other classes and interfaces (§13.1). For fields and methods, these symbolic references include the name of the class or interface type that declares the field or method as well as the name of the field or method itself, together with appropriate type information.

Before a symbolic reference can be used it must be undergo *resolution*, wherein a symbolic reference is checked to be correct and, typically, replaced with a direct reference that can be more efficiently processed if the reference is used repeatedly.

If an error occurs during resolution, then an error will be thrown. Most typically, this will be an instance of one of the following subclasses of the class `IncompatibleClassChangeError`, but it may also be an instance of some other subclass of `IncompatibleClassChangeError` or even an instance of the class `IncompatibleClassChangeError` itself. This error may be thrown at any point in the program that uses a symbolic reference to the type, directly or indirectly:

- `IllegalAccessError`: A symbolic reference has been encountered that specifies a use or assignment of a field, or invocation of a method, or creation of an instance of a class, to which the code containing the reference does not have access because the field or method was declared `private`, `protected`, or default access (not `public`), or because the class was not declared `public`. This can occur, for example, if a field that is originally declared `public` is changed to be `private` after another class that refers to the field has been compiled (§13.4.6).

- `InstantiationError`: A symbolic reference has been encountered that is used in a class instance creation expression, but an instance cannot be created because the reference turns out to refer to an interface or to an `abstract` class. This can occur, for example, if a class that is originally not `abstract` is changed to be `abstract` after another class that refers to the class in question has been compiled (§13.4.1).
- `NoSuchFieldError`: A symbolic reference has been encountered that refers to a specific field of a specific class or interface, but the class or interface does not declare a field of that name (it is specifically not sufficient for it simply to be an inherited field of that class or interface). This can occur, for example, if a field declaration was deleted from a class after another class that refers to the field was compiled (§13.4.7).
- `NoSuchMethodError`: A symbolic reference has been encountered that refers to a specific method of a specific class or interface, but the class or interface does not declare a method of that signature (it is specifically not sufficient for it simply to be an inherited method of that class or interface). This can occur, for example, if a method declaration was deleted from a class after another class that refers to the method was compiled (§13.4.12).

Additionally, an `UnsatisfiedLinkError` (a subclass of `LinkageError`) may be thrown if a class declares a `native` method for which no implementation can be found. The error will occur if the method is used, or earlier depending on what kind of resolution strategy is being used by the virtual machine (§12.3).

12.3.4 Linking: Implications for Code Generation

The symbolic references within a group of types may be resolved even before the group is loaded (§12.2.2), in an implementation that uses a special (non-standard) binary format (§13.1). This corresponds to the traditional practice of "linkage editing." Even if this is not done, a Java implementation has a lot of flexibility. It may resolve all symbolic references from a type at the point of the first linkage activity on the type, or defer the resolution of each symbolic reference to the first use of that reference.

We note that the flexibility accorded the Java implementation in the linkage process does not affect correctly formed Java programs, which should never encounter linkage errors.

12.4 Initialization of Classes and Interfaces

Initialization of a class consists of executing its static initializers and the initializers for `static` fields (class variables) declared in the class. Initialization of an interface consists of executing the initializers for fields (constants) declared there.

Before a class is initialized, its superclass must be initialized, but interfaces implemented by the class need not be initialized. Similarly, the superinterfaces of an interface need not be initialized before the interface is initialized.

12.4.1 When Initialization Occurs

A class or interface type *T* will be *initialized* at its first *active use*, which occurs if:

- *T* is a class and a method actually declared in *T* (rather than inherited from a superclass) is invoked.
- *T* is a class and a constructor for class *T* is invoked, or *U* is an array with element type *T*, and an array of type *U* is created.
- A non-constant field declared in *T* (rather than inherited from a superclass or superinterface) is used or assigned. A *constant field* is one that is (explicitly or implicitly) both `final` and `static`, and that is initialized with the value of a compile-time constant expression (§15.27). Java specifies that a reference to a constant field must be resolved at compile time to a copy of the compile-time constant value, so uses of such a field are never active uses. See §13.4.8 for a further discussion.

All other uses of a type are *passive uses*.

The intent here is that a class or interface type has a set of initializers that put it in a consistent state, and that this state is the first state that is observed by other classes. The static initializers and class variable initializers are executed in textual order, and may not refer to class variables declared in the class whose declarations appear textually after the use, even though these class variables are in scope (§8.5). This restriction is designed to detect, at compile time, most circular or otherwise malformed initializations.

As shown in an example in §8.5, the fact that initialization code is unrestricted allows examples to be constructed where the value of a class variable can be observed when it still has its initial default value, before its initializing expression is evaluated, but such examples are rare in practice. (Such examples can be also constructed for instance variable initialization; see the example at the end of §12.5). Java provides the full power of the language in these initializers; programmers must exercise some care. This power places an extra burden on code generators, but this burden would arise in any case because Java is concurrent (§12.4.3).

Before a class is initialized, its superclasses are initialized, if they have not previously been initialized.

Thus, the test program:

```
class Super {
    static { System.out.print("Super "); }
}

class One {
    static { System.out.print("One "); }
}

class Two extends Super {
    static { System.out.print("Two "); }
}

class Test {
    public static void main(String[] args) {
        One o = null;
        Two t = new Two();
        System.out.println((Object)o == (Object)t);
    }
}
```

prints:

```
Super Two false
```

The class `One` is never initialized, because it not used actively and therefore is never linked to. The class `Two` is initialized only after its superclass `Super` has been initialized.

A reference to a field is an active use of only the class or interface that actually declares it, even though it might be referred to through the name of a subclass, a subinterface, or a class that implements an interface. The test program:

```
class Super { static int taxi = 1729; }

class Sub extends Super {
    static { System.out.print("Sub "); }
}

class Test {
    public static void main(String[] args) {
        System.out.println(Sub.taxi);
    }
}
```

prints only:

```
1729
```

because the class Sub is never initialized; the reference to Sub.taxi is a reference to a field actually declared in class Super and is not an active use of the class Sub.

Initialization of an interface does not, of itself, require initialization of any of its superinterfaces. Thus, the test program:

```
interface I {
    int i = 1, ii = Test.out("ii", 2);
}

interface J extends I {
    int j = Test.out("j", 3), jj = Test.out("jj", 4);
}

interface K extends J {
    int k = Test.out("k", 5);
}

class Test {

    public static void main(String[] args) {
        System.out.println(J.i);
        System.out.println(K.j);
    }

    static int out(String s, int i) {
        System.out.println(s + "=" + i);
        return i;
    }

}
```

produces the output:

```
1
j=3
jj=4
3
```

The reference to J.i is to a field that is a compile-time constant; therefore, it does not cause I to be initialized. The reference to K.j is a reference to a field actually declared in interface J that is not a compile-time constant; this causes initialization of the fields of interface J, but not those of its superinterface I, nor those of interface K. Despite the fact that the name K is used to refer to field j of interface J, interface K is not actively used.

12.4.2 Detailed Initialization Procedure

Because Java is multithreaded, initialization of a class or interface requires careful synchronization, since some other thread may be trying to initialize the same class or interface at the same time. There is also the possibility that initialization of a class or interface may be requested recursively as part of the initialization of that class or interface; for example, a variable initializer in class `A` might invoke a method of an unrelated class `B`, which might in turn invoke a method of class `A`. The implementation of the Java Virtual Machine is responsible for taking care of synchronization and recursive initialization by using the following procedure. It assumes that the `Class` object has already been verified and prepared, and that the `Class` object contains state that indicates one of four situations:

- This `Class` object is verified and prepared but not initialized.
- This `Class` object is being initialized by some particular thread `T`.
- This `Class` object is fully initialized and ready for use.
- This `Class` object is in an erroneous state, perhaps because the verification or preparation step failed, or because initialization was attempted and failed.

The procedure for initializing a class or interface is then as follows:

1. Synchronize (§14.17) on the `Class` object that represents the class or interface to be initialized. This involves waiting until the current thread can obtain the lock for that object (§17.13).
2. If initialization is in progress for the class or interface by some other thread, then `wait` (§20.1.6) on this `Class` object (which temporarily releases the lock). When the current thread awakens from the `wait`, repeat this step.
3. If initialization is in progress for the class or interface by the current thread, then this must be a recursive request for initialization. Release the lock on the `Class` object and complete normally.
4. If the class or interface has already been initialized, then no further action is required. Release the lock on the `Class` object and complete normally.
5. If the `Class` object is in an erroneous state, then initialization is not possible. Release the lock on the `Class` object and throw a `NoClassDefFoundError`.
6. Otherwise, record the fact that initialization of the `Class` object is now in progress by the current thread and release the lock on the `Class` object.
7. Next, if the `Class` object represents a class rather than an interface, and the superclass of this class has not yet been initialized, then recursively perform this entire procedure for the superclass. If necessary, verify and prepare the superclass first. If the initialization of the superclass completes abruptly because of a thrown exception, then lock this `Class` object, label it erroneous, notify all waiting threads (§20.1.10), release the lock, and complete abruptly, throwing the same exception that resulted from initializing the superclass.

8. Next, execute either the class variable initializers and static initializers of the class, or the field initializers of the interface, in textual order, as though they were a single block, except that `final` class variables and fields of interfaces whose values are compile-time constants are initialized first (§8.3.2.1, §9.3.1, §13.4.8).
9. If the execution of the initializers completes normally, then lock this `Class` object, label it fully initialized, notify all waiting threads (§20.1.10), release the lock, and complete this procedure normally.
10. Otherwise, the initializers must have completed abruptly by throwing some exception *E*. If the class of *E* is not `Error` or one of its subclasses, then create a new instance of the class `ExceptionInInitializerError`, with *E* as the argument, and use this object in place of *E* in the following step. But if a new instance of `ExceptionInInitializerError` cannot be created because an `OutOfMemoryError` occurs, then instead use an `OutOfMemoryError` object in place of *E* in the following step.
11. Lock the `Class` object, label it erroneous, notify all waiting threads (§20.1.10), release the lock, and complete this procedure abruptly with reason *E* or its replacement as determined in the previous step.

(Due to a flaw in some early implementations of Java, a exception during class initialization was ignored, rather than causing an `ExceptionInInitializerError` as described here.)

12.4.3 Initialization: Implications for Code Generation

Code generators need to preserve the points of possible initialization of a class or interface, inserting an invocation of the initialization procedure just described. If this initialization procedure completes normally and the `Class` object is fully initialized and ready for use, then the invocation of the initialization procedure is no longer necessary and it may be eliminated from the code—for example, by patching it out or otherwise regenerating the code.

Compile-time analysis may, in some cases, be able to eliminate many of the checks that a type has been initialized from the generated code, if an initialization order for a group of related types can be determined. Such analysis must, however, fully account for the fact that Java is concurrent and that initialization code is unrestricted.

12.5 Creation of New Class Instances

A new class instance is explicitly created when one of the following situations occurs:

- Evaluation of a class instance creation expression (§15.8) creates a new instance of the class whose name appears in the expression.
- Invocation of the `newInstance` method (§20.3.6) of class `Class` creates a new instance of the class represented by the `Class` object for which the method was invoked.

A new class instance may be implicitly created in the following situations:

- Loading of a class or interface that contains a `String` literal (§3.10.5) may create a new `String` object (§20.12) to represent that literal. (This might not occur if the same `String` has previously been interned (§3.10.5).)
- Execution of a string concatenation operator (§15.17.1) that is not part of a constant expression sometimes creates a new `String` object to represent the result. String concatenation operators may also create temporary wrapper objects for a value of a primitive type.

Each of these situations identifies a particular constructor to be called with specified arguments (possibly none) as part of the class instance creation process.

Whenever a new class instance is created, memory space is allocated for it with room for all the instance variables declared in the class type and all the instance variables declared in each superclass of the class type, including all the instance variables that may be hidden. If there is not sufficient space available to allocate memory for the object, then creation of the class instance completes abruptly with an `OutOfMemoryError`. Otherwise, all the instance variables in the new object, including those declared in superclasses, are initialized to their default values (§4.5.4). Just before a reference to the newly created object is returned as the result, the indicated constructor is processed to initialize the new object using the following procedure:

1. Assign the arguments for the constructor to newly created parameter variables for this constructor invocation.
2. If this constructor begins with an explicit constructor invocation of another constructor in the same class (using `this`), then evaluate the arguments and process that constructor invocation recursively using these same five steps. If that constructor invocation completes abruptly, then this procedure completes abruptly for the same reason; otherwise, continue with step 5.

3. This constructor does not begin with an explicit constructor invocation of another constructor in the same class (using `this`). If this constructor is for a class other than `Object`, then this constructor will begin with a explicit or implicit invocation of a superclass constructor (using `super`). Evaluate the arguments and process that superclass constructor invocation recursively using these same five steps. If that constructor invocation completes abruptly, then this procedure completes abruptly for the same reason. Otherwise, continue with step 4.

4. Execute the instance variable initializers for this class, assigning their values to the corresponding instance variables, in the left-to-right order in which they appear textually in the source code for the class. If execution of any of these initializers results in an exception, then no further initializers are processed and this procedure completes abruptly with that same exception. Otherwise, continue with step 5. (In some early Java implementations, the compiler incorrectly omitted the code to initialize a field if the field initializer expression was a constant expression whose value was equal to the default initialization value for its type.)

5. Execute the rest of the body of this constructor. If that execution completes abruptly, then this procedure completes abruptly for the same reason. Otherwise, this procedure completes normally.

In the example:

```
class Point {
    int x, y;
    Point() { x = 1; y = 1; }
}

class ColoredPoint extends Point {
    int color = 0xFF00FF;
}

class Test {
    public static void main(String[] args) {
        ColoredPoint cp = new ColoredPoint();
        System.out.println(cp.color);
    }
}
```

a new instance of `ColoredPoint` is created. First, space is allocated for the new `ColoredPoint`, to hold the fields `x`, `y`, and `color`. All these fields are then initialized to their default values (in this case, `0` for each field). Next, the `ColoredPoint` constructor with no arguments is first invoked. Since `ColoredPoint` declares no constructors, a default constructor of the form:

```
ColoredPoint() { super(); }
```

is provided for it automatically by the Java compiler.

This constructor then invokes the Point constructor with no arguments. The Point constructor does not begin with an invocation of a constructor, so the compiler provides an implicit invocation of its superclass constructor of no arguments, as though it had been written:

```
Point() { super(); x = 1; y = 1; }
```

Therefore, the constructor for Object which takes no arguments is invoked.

The class Object has no superclass, so the recursion terminates here. Next, any instance variable initializers and static initializers of Object are invoked. Next, the body of the constructor of Object that takes no arguments is executed. No such constructor is declared in Object, so the compiler supplies a default one, which in this special case is:

```
Object() { }
```

This constructor executes without effect and returns.

Next, all initializers for the instance variables of class Point are executed. As it happens, the declarations of x and y do not provide any initialization expressions, so no action is required for this step of the example. Then the body of the Point constructor is executed, setting x to 1 and y to 1.

Next, the initializers for the instance variables of class ColoredPoint are executed. This step assigns the value 0xFF00FF to color. Finally, the rest of the body of the ColoredPoint constructor is executed (the part after the invocation of super); there happen to be no statements in the rest of the body, so no further action is required and initialization is complete.

Unlike C++, the Java language does not specify altered rules for method dispatch during the creation of a new class instance. If methods are invoked that are overridden in subclasses in the object being initialized, then these overriding methods are used, even before the new object is completely initialized. Thus, compiling and running the example:

```
class Super {
    Super() { printThree(); }
    void printThree() { System.out.println("three"); }
}
```

```
class Test extends Super {
    int indiana = (int)Math.PI;                    // That is, 3

    public static void main(String[] args) {
        Test t = new Test();
        t.printThree();
    }

    void printThree() { System.out.println(indiana); }
}
```

produces the output:

```
0
3
```

This shows that the invocation of `printThree` in the constructor for class `Super` does not invoke the definition of `printThree` in class `Super`, but rather invokes the overriding definition of `printThree` in class `Test`. This method therefore runs before the field initializers of `Test` have been executed, which is why the first value output is `0`, the default value to which the field `three` of `Test` is initialized. The later invocation of `printThree` in method `main` invokes the same definition of `printThree`, but by that point the initializer for instance variable `three` has been executed, and so the value `3` is printed.

See §8.6 for more details on constructor declarations.

12.6 Finalization of Class Instances

The class `Object` has a `protected` method called `finalize` (§20.1.11); this method can be overridden by other classes. The particular definition of `finalize` that can be invoked for an object is called the *finalizer* of that object. Before the storage for an object is reclaimed by the garbage collector, the Java Virtual Machine will invoke the finalizer of that object.

Finalizers provide a chance to free up resources (such as file descriptors or operating system graphics contexts) that cannot be freed automatically by an automatic storage manager. In such situations, simply reclaiming the memory used by an object would not guarantee that the resources it held would be reclaimed.

The Java language does not specify how soon a finalizer will be invoked, except to say that it will happen before the storage for the object is reused. Also, the Java language does not specify which thread will invoke the finalizer for any given object. If an uncaught exception is thrown during the finalization, the exception is ignored and finalization of that object terminates.

The `finalize` method declared in class `Object` takes no action. However, the fact that class `Object` declares a `finalize` method means that the `finalize` method for any class can always invoke the `finalize` method for its superclass, which is usually good practice. (Unlike constructors, finalizers do not automatically invoke the finalizer for the superclass; such an invocation must be coded explicitly.)

For efficiency, an implementation may keep track of classes that do not override the `finalize` method of class `Object`, or override it in a trivial way, such as:

```
protected void finalize() throws Throwable {
    super.finalize();
}
```

We encourage implementations to treat such objects as having a finalizer that is not overridden, and to finalize them more efficiently, as described in §12.6.1.

A finalizer may be invoked explicitly, just like any other method.

12.6.1 Implementing Finalization

Every object can be characterized by two attributes: it may be *reachable*, *finalizer-reachable*, or *unreachable*, and it may also be *unfinalized*, *finalizable*, or *finalized*.

A *reachable* object is any object that can be accessed in any potential continuing computation from any live thread. Optimizing transformations of a program can be designed that reduce the number of objects that are reachable to be less than those which would naively be considered reachable. For example, a compiler or code generator may choose, explicitly or implicitly, to set a variable or parameter that will no longer be used to `null` to cause the storage for such an object to be potentially reclaimable sooner. A *finalizer-reachable* object can be reached from some finalizable object through some chain of references, but not from any live thread. An *unreachable* object cannot be reached by either means.

An *unfinalized* object has never had its finalizer automatically invoked; a *finalized* object has had its finalizer automatically invoked. A *finalizable* object has never had its finalizer automatically invoked, but the Java Virtual Machine may eventually automatically invoke its finalizer.

The life cycle of an object obeys the following transition diagram, where we abbreviate "finalizer-reachable" as "f-reachable":

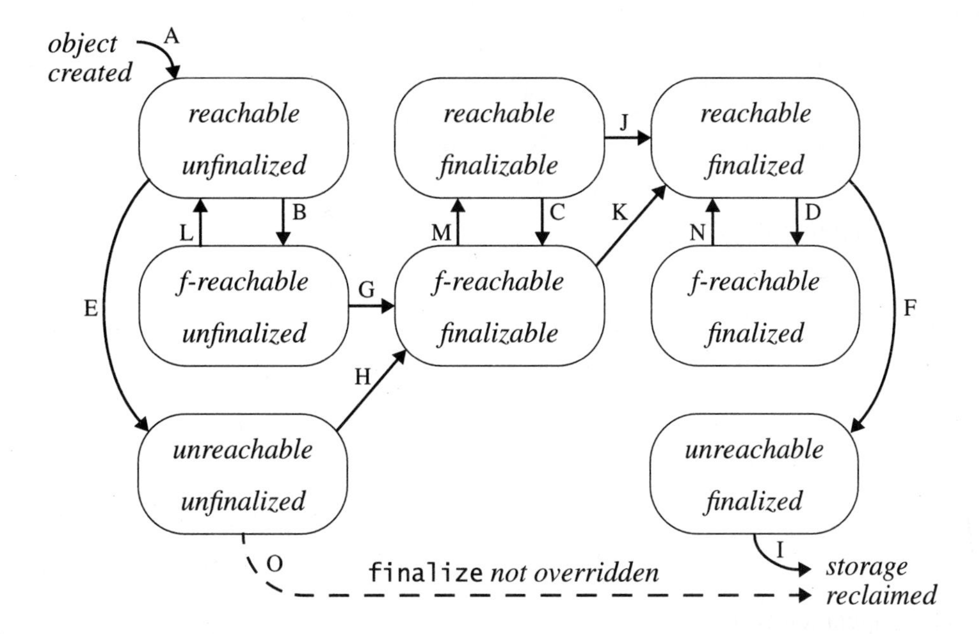

When an object is first created (A), it is reachable and unfinalized.

As references to an object are discarded during program execution, an object that was reachable may become finalizer-reachable (B, C, D) or unreachable (E, F). (Note that a finalizer-reachable object never becomes unreachable directly; it becomes reachable when the finalizer from which it can be reached is invoked, as explained below.)

If the Java Virtual Machine detects that an unfinalized object has become finalizer-reachable or unreachable, it may label the object finalizable (G, H); moreover, if the object was unreachable, it becomes finalizer-reachable (H).

If the Java Virtual Machine detects that a finalized object has become unreachable, it may reclaim the storage occupied by the object because the object will never again become reachable (I).

At any time, a Java Virtual Machine may take any finalizable object, label it finalized, and then invoke its `finalize` method in some thread. This causes the object to become finalized and reachable (J, K), and it also may cause other objects that were finalizer-reachable to become reachable again (L, M, N).

A finalizable object cannot also be unreachable; it can be reached because its finalizer may eventually be invoked, whereupon the thread running the finalizer will have access to the object, as `this` (§15.7.2). Thus, there are actually only eight possible states for an object.

After an object has been finalized, no further action is taken until the automatic storage management determines that it is unreachable. Because of the way that an object progresses from the *unfinalized* state through the *finalizable* state to the *finalized* state, the `finalize` method is never automatically invoked more than once by a Java Virtual Machine for each object, even if the object is again made reachable after it has been finalized.

Explicit invocation of a finalizer ignores the current state of the object and does not change the state of the object from unfinalized or finalizable to finalized.

If a class does not override method `finalize` of class `Object` (or overrides it in only a trivial way, as described above), then if instances of such as class become unreachable, they may be discarded immediately rather than made to await a second determination that they have become unreachable. This strategy is indicated by the dashed arrow (O) in the transition diagram.

Java programmers should also be aware that a finalizer can be automatically invoked, even though it is reachable, during finalization-on-exit (§12.9); moreover, a finalizer can also be invoked explicitly as an ordinary method. Therefore, we recommend that the design of `finalize` methods be kept simple and that they be programmed defensively, so that they will work in all cases.

12.6.2 Finalizer Invocations are Not Ordered

Java imposes no ordering on finalize method calls. Finalizers may be called in any order, or even concurrently.

As an example, if a circularly linked group of unfinalized objects becomes unreachable (or finalizer-reachable), then all the objects may become finalizable together. Eventually, the finalizers for these objects may be invoked, in any order, or even concurrently using multiple threads. If the automatic storage manager later finds that the objects are unreachable, then their storage can be reclaimed.

It is straightforward to implement a Java class that will cause a set of finalizer-like methods to be invoked in a specified order for a set of objects when all the objects become unreachable. Defining such a class is left as an exercise for the reader.

12.7 Finalization of Classes

If a class declares a class method `classFinalize` that takes no arguments and returns no result:

```
static void classFinalize() throws Throwable { ... }
```

then this method will be invoked before the class is unloaded (§12.8). Like the `finalize` method for objects, this method will be automatically invoked only once. This method may optionally be declared `private`, `protected`, or `public`.

12.8 Unloading of Classes and Interfaces

A Java Virtual Machine may provide mechanisms whereby classes are *unloaded*. The details of such mechanisms are not specified in this version of the Java Language Specification. In general, groups of related class and interface types will be unloaded together. This can be used, for example, to unload a group of related types that have been loaded using a particular class loader. Such a group might consist of all the classes implementing a single applet in a Java-based browser such as HotJava, for example.

A class may not be unloaded while any instance of it is still reachable (§12.6). A class or interface may not be unloaded while the `Class` object that represents it is still reachable.

Classes that declare class finalizers (§12.7) will have these finalizers run before they are unloaded.

12.9 Virtual Machine Exit

A Java Virtual Machine terminates all its activity and *exits* when one of two things happens:

- All the threads that are not daemon threads (§20.20.24) terminate.
- Some thread invokes the `exit` method (§20.16.2) of class `Runtime` or class `System` and the exit operation is not forbidden by the security manager (§20.17.13).

A Java program can specify that the finalizers of all objects that have finalizers, and all classes that have class finalizers, that have not yet been automatically invoked are to be run before the virtual machine exits. This is done by invoking the method `runFinalizersOnExit` of class `System` with the argument `true`. The default is to not run finalizers on exit, and this behavior may be restored by invoking `runFinalizersOnExit` with the argument `false`. An invocation of the `runFinalizersOnExit` method is permitted only if the caller is allowed to `exit`, and is otherwise rejected by the `SecurityManager` (§20.17).

. . . Farewell!
The day frowns more and more. Thou'rt like to have
A lullaby too rough: I never saw
The heavens so dim by day: A savage clamour!
Well may I get aboard! This is the chase.
I am gone for ever!

[Exit, pursued by a bear]

—William Shakespeare, *The Winter's Tale*, Act III, scene iii

CHAPTER 13

Binary Compatibility

Despite all of its promise, software reuse in object-oriented programming has yet to reach its full potential. A major impediment to reuse is the inability to evolve a compiled class library without abandoning the support for already compiled applications. . . . [A]n object-oriented model must be carefully designed so that class-library transformations that should not break already compiled applications, indeed, do not break such applications.

—Ira Forman, Michael Conner, Scott Danforth, and Larry Raper, *Release-to-Release Binary Compatibility in SOM* (1995)

JAVA development tools should support automatic recompilation as necessary whenever source code is available. Particular implementations of Java may also store the source and binary of types in a versioning database and implement a `ClassLoader` (§20.14) that uses integrity mechanisms of the database to prevent linkage errors by providing binary-compatible versions of types to clients.

Developers of packages and classes that are to be widely distributed face a different set of problems. In the Internet, which is our favorite example of a widely distributed system, it is often impractical or impossible to automatically recompile the pre-existing binaries that directly or indirectly depend on a type that is to be changed. Instead, Java defines a set of changes that developers are permitted to make to a package or to a class or interface type while preserving (not breaking) compatibility with existing binaries.

The paper quoted above appears in *Proceedings of OOPSLA '95*, published as *ACM SIGPLAN Notices*, Volume 30, Number 10, October 1995, pages 426–438. Within the framework of that paper, Java binaries are binary (release-to-release) compatible under all relevant transformations that the authors identify. Using their scheme, here is a list of some important binary compatible changes that Java supports:

- Reimplementing existing methods, constructors, and initializers to improve performance.
- Changing methods or constructors to return values on inputs for which they previously either threw exceptions that normally should not occur or failed by going into an infinite loop or causing a deadlock.
- Adding new fields, methods, or constructors to an existing class or interface.
- Deleting `private` fields, methods, or constructors of a class or interface.
- When an entire package is updated, deleting default (package-only) access fields, methods, or constructors of classes and interfaces in the package.
- Reordering the fields, methods, or constructors in an existing type declaration.
- Moving a method upward in the class hierarchy, provided a forwarding method is left in its place.
- Reordering the list of direct superinterfaces of a class or interface.
- Inserting new class or interface types in the type hierarchy.

This chapter specifies minimum standards for binary compatibility guaranteed by all Java implementations. Java guarantees compatibility when binaries of classes and interfaces are mixed that are not known to be from compatible sources, but whose sources have been modified in the compatible ways described here.

We encourage Java development systems to provide facilities that alert developers to the impact of changes on pre-existing binaries that cannot be recompiled.

This chapter first specifies some properties that any Java binary format must have (§13.1). It next defines binary compatibility, explaining what it is and what it is not (§13.2). It finally enumerates a large set of possible changes to packages (§13.3), classes (§13.4) and interfaces (§13.5), specifying which changes are guaranteed to preserve binary compatibility and which are not.

13.1 The Form of a Java Binary

While many Java binary files are likely to be in exactly the `class` file format specified by the *The Java Virtual Machine Specification*, this specification does not mandate the use of any specific binary file format. Rather, it specifies properties that any binary format for compiled types must obey. A number of these properties are specifically chosen to support source code transformations that preserve binary compatibility.

The requirements are:

- Binary formats for Java programs must be defined and processed to respect the specifications of loading (§12.2), linking (§12.3) and initialization (§12.4) of class and interface types.
- A reference to another class or interface type must be symbolic, using the fully qualified name of the type as determined at compile time.
- A reference to a field of another class or interface must be resolved at compile time to a symbolic reference to the class or interface in which the field is declared, plus the simple name of the field. (Including the exact class or interface in which the field is declared makes the binaries more robust, since adding another field with the same name, even in a subclass, cannot cause confusion at link time. This rule does mean, however, that moving a field to a superclass is not a binary compatible change; see §13.4.5 for a discussion.) The reference must also include a symbolic reference to the declared type of the field so that the verifier can check that the type is as expected. References to fields that are `static`, `final`, and initialized with compile-time constant expressions are resolved at compile time to the constant value that is denoted. No reference to such a constant field should be present in the code in a binary file (except in the class or interface containing the constant field, which will have code to initialize it), and such constant fields must always appear to have been initialized; the default initial value for the type of such a field must never be observed. See §13.4.8 for a discussion.
- A reference to a method or constructor must be resolved at compile time to a symbolic reference to the class or interface in which the denoted method or constructor is declared, plus the signature of the method or constructor. (As for fields, this makes the binaries more robust, with the caveat that such a method cannot be moved to a superclass without leaving a forwarding method behind; see §13.4.5 for a discussion.) A reference to a method must also include either a symbolic reference to the return type of the denoted method or an indication that the denoted method is declared `void` and does not return a value. The signature of a method must include all of the following:
  - The simple name of the method
  - The number of parameters to the method
  - A symbolic reference to the type of each parameter

The signature of a constructor must include both:

- The number of parameters to the constructor
- A symbolic reference to the type of each parameter

A Java binary representation for a class or interface must also contain all of the following:

- If it is a class and is not class `java.lang.Object`, then a symbolic reference to the direct superclass of this class
- A symbolic reference to each direct superinterface, if any
- A specification of each field that is not `private` declared in the class or interface, given as the simple name of the field and a symbolic reference to the type of the field
- If it is a class, then the signature of each constructor, as described above
- For each method that is not `private` declared in the class or interface, its signature and return type, as described above
- The code needed to implement the class or interface:
  - For an interface, code for the field initializers
  - For a class, code for the field initializers, the static initializers, and the implementation of each method or constructor that is not declared `private`

If a Java system defines a binary format that represents a group of classes and interfaces comprised by an entire package, then this binary format need not expose information about fields, methods, or constructors that are declared with default (package) access.

The following sections specify the changes that may be made to class and interface type declarations without breaking compatibility with pre-existing binaries. The Java Virtual Machine and its standard `class` file format support these changes; other Java binary formats are required to support these changes as well.

13.2 What Binary Compatibility Is and Is Not

A change to a type is *binary compatible with* (equivalently, does not *break binary compatibility* with) preexisting binaries if preexisting binaries that previously linked without error will continue to link without error.

As described in §13.1, symbolic references to methods and fields name the exact class or interface in which the method or field is declared. This means that binaries are compiled to rely on the accessible members and constructors of other classes and interfaces. To preserve binary compatibility, a class or interface should treat these accessible members and constructors, their existence and behavior, as a *contract* with users of the class or interface.

Java is designed to prevent additions to contracts and accidental name collisions from breaking binary compatibility; specifically:

- Introducing a new field with the same name as an existing field, in a subclass of the class containing the existing field declaration, does not break compatibility with preexisting binaries. See the example at the beginning of §13.4.5.
- Addition of more methods overloading a particular method name does not break compatibility with preexisting binaries. The method signature that the preexisting binary will use for method lookup is chosen by Java's method overload resolution algorithm at compile time (§15.11.2). (If Java had been designed so that the particular method to be executed was chosen at run time, then such an ambiguity might be detected at run time. Such a rule would imply that adding an additional overloaded method so as to make ambiguity possible at a call site became possible could break compatibility with an unknown number of preexisting binaries. See §13.4.22 for more discussion.)

Binary compatibility is not the same as source compatibility. In particular, the example in §13.4.5 shows that a set of compatible binaries can be produced from sources that will not compile all together. This example is typical: a new declaration is added, changing the meaning of a name in an unchanged part of the source code, while the preexisting binary for that unchanged part of the source code retains the fully-qualified, previous meaning of the name. Producing a consistent set of source code requires providing a qualified name or field access expression corresponding to the previous meaning.

We hope to make some improvements to future versions of Java to better support both source and binary compatible evolution of types. In particular, we are considering a mechanism to allow a class to implement two interfaces that have methods with the same signature but are to be considered different or have different return types. We welcome suggestions and proposals that would help us to make additional improvements, either in managing name and signature conflicts or other sources of incompatibility.

13.3 Evolution of Packages

A new class or interface type may be added to a package without breaking compatibility with pre-existing binaries, provided the new type does not reuse a name previously given to an unrelated type. If a new type reuses a name previously given to an unrelated type, then a conflict may result, since binaries for both types could not be loaded by the same class loader.

Changes in class and interface types that are not `public` and that are not a superclass or superinterface, respectively, of a `public` type, affect only types within the package in which they are declared. Such types may be deleted or otherwise changed, even if incompatibilities are otherwise described here, provided that the affected binaries of that package are updated together.

13.4 Evolution of Classes

This section describes the effects of changes to the declaration of a class and its members and constructors on pre-existing binaries.

13.4.1 `abstract` Classes

If a class that was not `abstract` is changed to be declared `abstract`, then pre-existing binaries that attempt to create new instances of that class will throw either an `InstantiationError` at link time, or an `InstantiationException` at run time (if the method `newInstance` (§20.3.6) of class `Class` is used); such a change is therefore not recommended for widely distributed classes.

Changing a class that was declared `abstract` to no longer be declared `abstract` does not break compatibility with pre-existing binaries.

13.4.2 `final` Classes

If a class that was not declared `final` is changed to be declared `final`, then a `VerifyError` is thrown if a binary of a pre-existing subclass of this class is loaded, because `final` classes can have no subclasses; such a change is not recommended for widely distributed classes.

Changing a class that was declared `final` to no longer be declared `final` does not break compatibility with pre-existing binaries.

13.4.3 `public` Classes

Changing a class that was not declared `public` to be declared `public` does not break compatibility with pre-existing binaries.

If a class that was declared `public` is changed to not be declared `public`, then an `IllegalAccessError` is thrown if a pre-existing binary is linked that needs but no longer has access to the class type; such a change is not recommended for widely distributed classes.

13.4.4 Superclasses and Superinterfaces

A `ClassCircularityError` is thrown at load time if a class would be a superclass of itself. Changes to the class hierarchy that could result in such a circularity when newly compiled binaries are loaded with pre-existing binaries are not recommended for widely distributed classes.

Changing the direct superclass or the set of direct superinterfaces of a class type will not break compatibility with pre-existing binaries, provided that the total set of superclasses or superinterfaces, respectively, of the class type loses no members.

Changes to the set of superclasses of a class will not break compatibility with pre-existing binaries simply because of uses of class variables and class methods. This is because uses of class variables and class methods are resolved at compile time to symbolic references to the name of the class that declares them. Such uses therefore depend only on the continuing existence of the class declaring the variable or method, not on the shape of the class hierarchy.

If a change to the direct superclass or the set of direct superinterfaces results in any class or interface no longer being a superclass or superinterface, respectively, then link-time errors may result if pre-existing binaries are loaded with the binary of the modified class. Such changes are not recommended for widely distributed classes. The resulting errors are detected by the verifier of the Java Virtual Machine when an operation that previously compiled would violate the type system. For example, suppose that the following test program:

```
class Hyper { char h = 'h'; }

class Super extends Hyper { char s = 's'; }

class Test extends Super {
    public static void main(String[] args) {
        Hyper h = new Super();
        System.out.println(h.h);
    }
}
```

is compiled and executed, producing the output:

```
h
```

Suppose that a new version of class `Super` is then compiled:

```
class Super { char s = 's'; }
```

This version of class `Super` is not a subclass of `Hyper`. If we then run the existing binaries of `Hyper` and `Test` with the new version of `Super`, then a `VerifyError` is thrown at link time. The verifier objects because the result of `new Super()` cannot be assigned to a variable of type `Hyper`, because `Super` is not a subclass of `Hyper`.

It is instructive to consider what might happen without the verification step: the program might run and print:

```
s
```

This demonstrates that without the verifier the type system could be defeated by linking inconsistent binary files, even though each was produced by a correct Java compiler.

As a further example, here is an implementation of a cast from a reference type to `int`, which could be made to run in certain implementations of Java if they failed to perform the verification process. Assume an implementation that uses method dispatch tables and whose linker assigns offsets into those tables in a sequential and straightforward manner. Then suppose that the following Java code is compiled:

```
class Hyper { int zero(Object o) { return 0; } }

class Super extends Hyper { int peek(int i) { return i; }  }

class Test extends Super {
    public static void main(String[] args) throws Throwable {
        Super as = new Super();
        System.out.println(as);
        System.out.println(Integer.toHexString(as.zero(as)));
    }
}
```

The assumed implementation determines that the class `Super` has two methods: the first is method `zero` inherited from class `Hyper`, and the second is the method `peek`. Any subclass of `Super` would also have these same two methods in the first two entries of its method table. (Actually, all these methods would be preceded in the method tables by all the methods inherited from class `Object` but, to simplify the discussion, we ignore that here.) For the method invocation `as.zero(as)`, the compiler specifies that the first method of the method table should be invoked; this is always correct if type safety is preserved.

If the compiled code is then executed, it prints something like:

```
Super@ee300858
0
```

which is the correct output. But if a new version of `Super` is compiled, which is the same except for the `extends` clause:

```
class Super { int peek(int i) { return i; } }
```

then the first method in the method table for `Super` will now be `peek`, not `zero`. Using the new binary code for `Super` with the old binary code for `Hyper` and `Test` will cause the method invocation `as.zero(as)` to dispatch to the method `peek` in `Super`, rather than the method `zero` in `Hyper`. This is a type violation, of course; the argument is of type `Super` but the parameter is of type `int`. With a few plausible assumptions about internal data representations and the consequences of the type violation, execution of this incorrect program might produce the output:

```
Super@ee300848
ee300848
```

A `poke` method, capable of altering any location in memory, could be concocted in a similar manner. This is left as an exercise for the reader.

The lesson is that a implementation of Java that lacks a verifier or fails to use it will not maintain type safety and is, therefore, not a valid Java implementation.

13.4.5 Class Body and Member Declarations

No incompatibility with pre-existing binaries is caused by adding a class member that has the same name (for fields) or same name, signature, and return type (for methods) as a member of a superclass or subclass. References to the original field or method were resolved at compile time to a symbolic reference containing the name of the class in which they were declared. This makes compiled Java code more robust against changes than it might otherwise be. No error occurs even if the set of classes being linked would encounter a compile-time error. As an example, if the program:

```
class Hyper { String h = "Hyper"; }

class Super extends Hyper { }

class Test extends Super {
    public static void main(String[] args) {
        String s = new Test().h;
        System.out.println(s);
    }
}
```

is compiled and executed, it produces the output:

```
Hyper
```

Suppose that a new version of class Super is then compiled:

```
class Super extends Hyper { char h = 'h'; }
```

If the resulting binary is used with the existing binaries for Hyper and Test, then the output is still:

```
Hyper
```

even though compiling the source for these binaries:

```
class Hyper { String h = "Hyper"; }

class Super extends Hyper { char h = 'h'; }

class Test extends Super {
   public static void main(String[] args) {
      String s = new Test().h;
      System.out.println(s);
   }
}
```

would result in a compile-time error, because the h in the source code for main would now be construed as referring to the char field declared in Super, and a char value can't be assigned to a String.

Deleting a class member or constructor that is not declared private may cause a linkage error if the member or constructor is used by a pre-existing binary, even if the member was an instance method that was overriding a superclass method. This is because, during resolution, the linker looks only in the class that was identified at compile time. Thus, if the program:

```
class Hyper {
   void hello() { System.out.println("hello from Hyper"); }
}

class Super extends Hyper {
   void hello() { System.out.println("hello from Super"); }
}

class Test {
   public static void main(String[] args) {
      new Super().hello();
   }
}
```

is compiled and executed, it produces the output:

```
hello from Super
```

Suppose that a new version of class Super is produced:

```
class Super extends Hyper { }
```

If Super and Hyper are recompiled but not Test, then a NoSuchMethodError will result at link time, because the method hello is no longer declared in class Super.

To preserve binary compatibility, methods should not be deleted; instead, "forwarding methods" should be used. In our example, replacing the declaration of Super with:

```
class Super extends Hyper {
    void hello() { super.hello(); }
}
```

then recompiling Super and Hyper and executing these new binaries with the original binary for Test, produces the output:

```
hello from Hyper
```

as might have naively been expected from the previous example.

The super keyword can be used to access a method declared in a superclass, bypassing any methods declared in the current class. The expression:

super.*Identifier*

is resolved, at compile time, to a method *M* declared in a particular superclass *S*. The method *M* must still be declared in that class at run time or a linkage error will result. If the method *M* is an instance method, then the method *MR* invoked at run time is the method with the same signature as *M* that is a member of the direct superclass of the class containing the expression involving super. Thus, if the program:

```
class Hyper {
    void hello() { System.out.println("hello from Hyper"); }
}

class Super extends Hyper { }

class Test extends Super {

    public static void main(String[] args) {
        new Test().hello();
    }

    void hello() {
        super.hello();
    }

}
```

is compiled and executed, it produces the output:

```
hello from Hyper
```

Suppose that a new version of class `Super` is produced:

```
class Super extends Hyper {
    void hello() { System.out.println("hello from Super"); }
}
```

If `Super` and `Hyper` are recompiled but not `Test`, then running the new binaries with the existing binary of `Test` produces the output:

```
hello from Super
```

as you might expect. (A flaw in some early versions of Java caused them to print:

```
hello from Hyper
```

incorrectly.)

13.4.6 Access to Members and Constructors

Changing the declared access of a member or constructor to permit less access may break compatibility with pre-existing binaries, causing a linkage error to be thrown when these binaries are resolved. Less access is permitted if the access modifier is changed from default access to `private` access; from `protected` access to default or `private` access; or from `public` access to `protected`, default, or `private` access. Changing a member or constructor to permit less access is therefore not recommended for widely distributed classes.

Perhaps surprisingly, Java is defined so that changing a member or constructor to be more accessible does not cause a linkage error when a subclass (already) defines a method to have less access. So, for example, if the package `points` defines the class `Point`:

```
package points;

public class Point {
    public int x, y;
    protected void print() {
        System.out.println("(" + x + "," + y + ")");
    }
}
```

used by the `Test` program:

```
class Test extends points.Point {

   protected void print() { System.out.println("Test"); }

   public static void main(String[] args) {
      Test t = new Test();
      t.print();
   }

}
```

then these classes compile and `Test` executes to produce the output:

```
Test
```

If the method `print` in class `Point` is changed to be `public`, and then only the `Point` class is recompiled, and then executed with the previously existing binary for `Test` then no linkage error occurs, even though it is improper, at compile time, for a `public` method to be overridden by a `protected` method (as shown by the fact that the class `Test` could not be recompiled using this new `Point` class unless print were changed to be `public`.)

Allowing superclasses to change `protected` methods to be `public` without breaking binaries of preexisting subclasses helps make Java binaries less fragile. The alternative, where such a change would cause a linkage error, would create additional binary incompatibilities with no apparent benefit.

13.4.7 Field Declarations

Adding a field to a class will not break compatibility with any pre-existing binaries that are not recompiled, even in the case where a class could no longer be recompiled because a field access previously referenced a field of a superclass with an incompatible type. The previously compiled class with such a reference will continue to reference the field declared in a superclass. Thus compiling and executing the code:

```
class Hyper { String h = "hyper"; }

class Super extends Hyper { String s = "super"; }

class Test {
   public static void main(String[] args) {
      System.out.println(new Super().h);
   }
}
```

produces the output:

```
hyper
```

Changing Super to be defined as:

```
class Super extends Hyper {
   String s = "super";
   int h = 0;
}
```

recompiling Hyper and Super, and executing the resulting new binaries with the old binary of Test produces the output:

```
hyper
```

The field h of Hyper is output by the original binary of main no matter what type field h is declared in Super. While this may seem surprising at first, it serves to reduce the number of incompatibilities that occur at run time. (In an ideal world, all source files that needed recompilation would be recompiled whenever any one of them changed, eliminating such surprises. But such a mass recompilation is often impractical or impossible, especially in the Internet. And, as was previously noted, such recompilation would sometimes require further changes to the source code.)

Deleting a field from a class will break compatibility with any pre-existing binaries that reference this field, and a NoSuchFieldError will be thrown when such a reference from a pre-existing binary is linked. Only private fields may be safely deleted from a widely distributed class.

13.4.8 final Fields and Constants

If a field that was not final is changed to be final, then it can break compatibility with pre-existing binaries that attempt to assign new values to the field. For example, if the program:

```
class Super { static char s; }

class Test extends Super {
   public static void main(String[] args) {
      s = 'a';
      System.out.println(s);
   }
}
```

is compiled and executed, it produces the output:

```
a
```

Suppose that a new version of class Super is produced:

```
class Super { static char s; }
```

If Super is recompiled but not Test, then running the new binary with the existing binary of Test results in a IncompatibleClassChangeError. (In certain early implementations of Java this example would run without error, because of a flaw in the implementation.)

We call a field that is static, final, and initialized with a compile-time constant expression a *primitive constant*. Note that all fields in interfaces are implicitly static and final, and they are often, but not always, constants.

If a field is not a primitive constant, then deleting the keyword final or changing the value to which the field is initialized does not break compatibility with existing binaries.

If a field is a primitive constant, then deleting the keyword final or changing its value will not break compatibility with pre-existing binaries by causing them not to run, but they will not see any new value for the constant unless they are recompiled. If the example:

```
class Flags { final static boolean debug = true; }

class Test {
    public static void main(String[] args) {
        if (Flags.debug)
            System.out.println("debug is true");
    }
}
```

is compiled and executed, it produces the output:

```
debug is true
```

Suppose that a new version of class Flags is produced:

```
class Flags { final static boolean debug = false; }
```

If Flags is recompiled but not Test, then running the new binary with the existing binary of Test produces the output:

```
debug is true
```

because the value of debug was a compile-time primitive constant, and could have been used in compiling Test without making a reference to the class Flags.

This result is a side-effect of the decision to support conditional compilation, as discussed at the end of §14.19.

This behavior would not change if Flags were changed to be an interface, as in the modified example:

```
interface Flags { boolean debug = true; }

class Test {
   public static void main(String[] args) {
      if (Flags.debug)
         System.out.println("debug is true");
   }
}
```

(One reason for requiring inlining of primitive constants is that Java switch statements require constants on each case, and no two such constant values may be the same. Java checks for duplicate constant values in a switch statement at compile time; the class file format does not do symbolic linkage of case values.)

The best way to avoid problems with "inconstant constants" in widely-distributed code is to declare as primitive constants only values which truly are unlikely ever to change. Many primitive constants in interfaces are small integer values replacing enumerated types, which Java does not support; these small values can be chosen arbitrarily, and should not need to be changed. Other than for true mathematical constants, we recommend that Java code make very sparing use of class variables that are declared static and final. If the read-only nature of final is required, a better choice is to declare a private static variable and a suitable accessor method to get its value. Thus we recommend:

```
private static int N;

public static int getN() { return N; }
```

rather than:

```
public static final int N = ...;
```

There is no problem with:

```
public static int N = ...;
```

if N need not be read-only. We also recommend, as a general rule, that only truly constant values be declared in interfaces. We note, but do not recommend, that if a field of primitive type of an interface may change, its value may be expressed idiomatically as in:

```
interface Flags {
   boolean debug = new Boolean(true).booleanValue();
}
```

insuring that this value is not a constant. Similar idioms exist for the other primitive types.

One other thing to note is that `static final` fields that have constant values (whether of primitive or `String` type) must never appear to have the default initial value for their type (§4.5.4). This means that all such fields appear to be initialized first during class initialization (§8.3.2.1, §9.3.1, §12.4.2).

13.4.9 `static` Fields

If a field that is not declared `private` was not declared `static` and is changed to be declared `static`, or vice versa, then a linkage time error, specifically an `IncompatibleClassChangeError`, will result if the field is used by a preexisting binary which expected a field of the other kind. Such changes are not recommended in code that has been widely distributed.

13.4.10 `transient` Fields

Adding or deleting a `transient` modifier of a field does not break compatibility with pre-existing binaries.

13.4.11 `volatile` Fields

If a field that is not declared `private` was not declared `volatile` and is changed to be declared `volatile`, or vice versa, then a linkage time error, specifically an `IncompatibleClassChangeError`, may result if the field is used by a preexisting binary that expected a field of the opposite volatility. Such changes are not recommended in code that has been widely distributed.

13.4.12 Method and Constructor Declarations

Adding a method or constructor declaration to a class will not break compatibility with any pre-existing binaries, even in the case where a type could no longer be recompiled because a method invocation previously referenced a method of a superclass with an incompatible type. The previously compiled class with such a reference will continue to reference the method declared in a superclass.

Deleting a method or constructor from a class will break compatibility with any pre-existing binary that referenced this method or constructor; a `NoSuchMethodError` will be thrown when such a reference from a pre-existing binary is linked. Only `private` methods or constructors may be safely deleted from a widely distributed class.

If the source code for a class contains no declared constructors, the Java compiler automatically supplies a constructor with no parameters. Adding one or more constructor declarations to the source code of such a class will prevent this default constructor from being supplied automatically, effectively deleting a constructor, unless one of the new constructors also has no parameters, thus replacing the default constructor. The automatically supplied constructor with no parameters is given the same access modifier as the class of its declaration, so any replacement should have as much or more access if compatibility with pre-existing binaries is to be preserved.

13.4.13 Method and Constructor Parameters

Changing the name of a formal parameter of a method or constructor does not impact pre-existing binaries. Changing the name of a method, the type of a formal parameter to a method or constructor, or adding a parameter to or deleting a parameter from a method or constructor declaration creates a method or constructor with a new signature, and has the combined effect of deleting the method or constructor with the old signature and adding a method or constructor with the new signature (see §13.4.12).

13.4.14 Method Result Type

Changing the result type of a method, replacing a result type with `void`, or replacing `void` with a result type has the combined effect of deleting the old method or constructor and adding a new method or constructor with the new result type or newly `void` result (see §13.4.12).

13.4.15 `abstract` Methods

Changing a method that is declared `abstract` to no longer be declared `abstract` does not break compatibility with pre-existing binaries.

Changing a method that is not declared `abstract` to be declared `abstract` will break compatibility with pre-existing binaries that previously invoked the method, causing an `AbstractMethodError`. If the example program:

```
class Super { void out() { System.out.println("Out"); } }

class Test extends Super {
    public static void main(String[] args) {
        Test t = new Test();
        System.out.println("Way ");
        t.out();
    }
}
```

is compiled and executed, it produces the output:

```
Way
Out
```

Suppose that a new version of class Super is produced:

```
abstract class Super {
    abstract void out();
}
```

If Super is recompiled but not Test, then running the new binary with the existing binary of Test results in a AbstractMethodError, because class Test has no implementation of the method out, and is therefore is (or should be) abstract. (An early version of Java incorrectly produced the output:

```
Way
```

before encountering an AbstractMethodError while invoking the method out, incorrectly allowing the class Test to be prepared even though it has an abstract method and is not declared abstract.)

13.4.16 final Methods

Changing an instance method that is not final to be final may break compatibility with existing binaries that depend on the ability to override the method. If the test program:

```
class Super { void out() { System.out.println("out"); } }

class Test extends Super {

    public static void main(String[] args) {
        Test t = new Test();
        t.out();
    }

    void out() { super.out(); }

}
```

is compiled and executed, it produces the output:

```
out
```

Suppose that a new version of class Super is produced:

```
class Super { final void out() { System.out.println("!"); } }
```

If Super is recompiled but not Test, then running the new binary with the existing binary of Test results in a VerifyError because the class Test improperly tries to override the instance method out.

Changing a class (`static`) method that is not `final` to be `final` does not break compatibility with existing binaries, because the class of the actual method to be invoked is resolved at compile time.

Removing the `final` modifier from a method does not break compatibility with pre-existing binaries.

13.4.17 `native` Methods

Adding or deleting a `native` modifier of a method does not break compatibility with pre-existing binaries.

The impact of changes to Java types on preexisting `native` methods that are not recompiled is beyond the scope of this specification and should be provided with the description of an implementation of Java. Implementations are encouraged, but not required, to implement `native` methods in a way that limits such impact.

13.4.18 `static` Methods

If a method that is not declared `private` was declared `static` (that is, a class method) and is changed to not be declared `static` (that is, to an instance method), or vice versa, then compatibility with pre-existing binaries may be broken, resulting in a linkage time error, namely an `IncompatibleClassChangeError`, if these methods are used by the pre-existing binaries. Such changes are not recommended in code that has been widely distributed.

13.4.19 `synchronized` Methods

Adding or deleting a `synchronized` modifier of a method does not break compatibility with existing binaries.

13.4.20 Method and Constructor Throws

Changes to the `throws` clause of methods or constructors do not break compatibility with existing binaries; these clauses are checked only at compile time.

We are considering whether a future version of the Java language should require more rigorous checking of `throws` clauses when classes are verified.

13.4.21 Method and Constructor Body

Changes to the body of a method or constructor do not break compatibility with pre-existing binaries.

We note that a compiler cannot inline expand a method at compile time unless, for example, either:

- the method is `private` to its class
- an entire package is guaranteed to be kept together and the method is accessible only within that package
- a set of Java code is being compiled to a special binary format where the specified method is available only within a binary or set of binaries which are being kept together.

The keyword `final` on a method does not mean that the method can be safely inlined; it only means that the method cannot be overridden. Unless the compiler has extraordinary knowledge, it is still possible that a new version of that method will be provided at link time.

In general we suggest that Java implementations use late-bound (run-time) code generation and optimization.

13.4.22 Method and Constructor Overloading

Adding new methods that overload existing method names does not break compatibility with pre-existing binaries. The method signature to be used for each method invocation was determined when these existing binaries were compiled; therefore newly added methods will not be used, even if their signatures are both applicable and more specific than the method signature originally chosen.

While adding a new overloaded method or constructor may cause a compile-time error the next time a class or interface is compiled because there is no method or constructor that is most specific (§15.11.2.2), no such error occurs when a Java program is executed, because no overload resolution is done at execution time.

If the example program:

```
class Super {
    static void out(float f) { System.out.println("float"); }
}

class Test {
    public static void main(String[] args) {
        Super.out(2);
    }
}
```

is compiled and executed, it produces the output:

```
float
```

Suppose that a new version of class Super is produced:

```
class Super {
    static void out(float f) { System.out.println("float"); }
    static void out(int i) { System.out.println("int"); }
}
```

If Super is recompiled but not Test, then running the new binary with the existing binary of Test still produces the output:

```
float
```

However, if Test is then recompiled, using this new Super, the output is then:

```
int
```

as might have been naively expected in the previous case.

13.4.23 Method Overriding

If an instance method is added to a subclass and it overrides a method in a superclass, then the subclass method will be found by method invocations in pre-existing binaries, and these binaries are not impacted. If a class method is added to a class, then this method will not be found, because the invocation of a class method is resolved at compile time to use the fully qualified name of the class where the method is declared. Thus if the example:

```
class Hyper {
    void hello() { System.out.print("Hello, "); }
    static void world() { System.out.println("world!"); }
}

class Super extends Hyper { }

class Test {
    public static void main(String[] args) {
        Super s = new Super();
        s.hello();
        s.world();
    }
}
```

is compiled and executed, it produces the output:

```
Hello, world!
```

Suppose that a new version of class Super is produced:

```
class Super extends Hyper {
   void hello() { System.out.print("Goodbye, cruel "); }
   static void world() { System.out.println("earth!"); }
}
```

If `Super` is recompiled but not `Hyper` or `Test`, then running the new binary with the existing binaries for `Hyper` and `Test` will produce the output:

```
Goodbye, cruel world!
```

This example demonstrates that the invocation in:

```
s.world();
```

in the method `main` is resolved, at compile time, to a symbolic reference to the class containing the class method `world`, as though it had been written:

```
Hyper.world();
```

This is why the `world` method of `Hyper` rather than `Super` is invoked in this example. Of course, recompiling all the classes to produce new binaries will allow the output:

```
Goodbye, cruel earth!
```

to be produced.

13.4.24 Static Initializers

Adding, deleting, or changing a static initializer (§8.5) of a class does not impact pre-existing binaries.

13.5 Evolution of Interfaces

This section describes the impact of changes to the declaration of an interface and its members on pre-existing binaries.

13.5.1 `public` Interfaces

Changing an interface that is not declared `public` to be declared `public` does not break compatibility with pre-existing binaries.

If an interface that is declared `public` is changed to not be declared `public`, then an `IllegalAccessError` is thrown if a pre-existing binary is linked that needs but no longer has access to the interface type, so such a change is not recommended for widely distributed interfaces.

13.5.2 Superinterfaces

Changes to the interface hierarchy cause errors in the same way that changes to the class hierarchy do, as described in §13.4.4. In particular, changes that result in any previous superinterface of a class no longer being a superinterface can break compatibility with pre-existing binaries, resulting in a `VerifyError`.

13.5.3 The Interface Members

Adding a member to an interface does not break compatibility with pre-existing binaries.

Deleting a member from an interface may cause linkage errors in pre-existing binaries. If the example program:

```
interface I { void hello(); }

class Test implements I {

    public static void main(String[] args) {
        I anI = new Test();
        anI.hello();
    }

    public void hello() { System.out.println("hello"); }

}
```

is compiled and executed, it produces the output:

```
hello
```

Suppose that a new version of interface `I` is compiled:

```
interface I { }
```

If `I` is recompiled but not `Test`, then running the new binary with the existing binary for `Test` will result in a `NoSuchMethodError`. (In some early implementations of Java this program still executed; the fact that the method `hello` no longer exists in interface `I` was not correctly detected.)

13.5.4 Field Declarations

The considerations for changing field declarations in interfaces are the same as those for `static final` fields in classes, as described in §13.4.7 and §13.4.8.

13.5.5 Abstract Method Declarations

The considerations for changing abstract method declarations in interfaces are the same as those for `abstract` methods in classes, as described in §13.4.13, §13.4.14, §13.4.20, and §13.4.22.

Lo! keen-eyed, towering Science! . . .
Yet again, lo! the Soul—above all science . . .
For it, the partial to the permanent flowing,
For it, the Real to the Ideal tends.
For it, the mystic evolution . . .

—Walt Whitman, *Song of the Universal* (1874)

CHAPTER 14

Blocks and Statements

He was not merely a chip of the old block, but the old block itself.
—Edmund Burke, *On Pitt's First Speech*

THE sequence of execution of a Java program is controlled by *statements*, which are executed for their effect and do not have values.

Some statements *contain* other statements as part of their structure; such other statements are substatements of the statement. We say that statement `S` *immediately contains* statement `U` if there is no statement `T` different from `S` and `U` such that `S` contains `T` and `T` contains `U`. In the same manner, some statements contain expressions (§15) as part of their structure.

The first section of this chapter discusses the distinction between normal and abrupt completion of statements (§14.1). Most of the remaining sections explain the various kinds of statements, describing in detail both their normal behavior and any special treatment of abrupt completion.

Blocks are explained first (§14.2), because they can appear in certain places where other kinds of statements are not allowed, and because one other kind of statement, a local variable declaration statement (§14.3), must be immediately contained within a block.

Next a grammatical maneuver is explained that sidesteps the familiar "dangling `else`" problem (§14.4).

Statements that will be familiar to C and C++ programmers are the empty (§14.5), labeled (§14.6), expression (§14.7), `if` (§14.8), `switch` (§14.9), `while` (§14.10), `do` (§14.11), `for` (§14.12), `break` (§14.13), `continue` (§14.14), and `return` (§14.15) statements.

Unlike C and C++, Java has no `goto` statement. However, the `break` and `continue` statements are extended in Java to allow them to mention statement labels.

The Java statements that are not in the C language are the `throw` (§14.16), `synchronized` (§14.17), and `try` (§14.18) statements.

The last section (§14.19) of this chapter addresses the requirement that every statement be *reachable* in a certain technical sense.

14.1 Normal and Abrupt Completion of Statements

Poirot's abrupt departure had intrigued us all greatly.
—Agatha Christie, *The Mysterious Affair at Styles* (1920), Chapter 12

Every statement has a normal mode of execution in which certain computational steps are carried out. The following sections describe the normal mode of execution for each kind of statement. If all the steps are carried out as described, with no indication of abrupt completion, the statement is said to *complete normally.* However, certain events may prevent a statement from completing normally:

- The `break` (§14.13), `continue` (§14.14), and `return` (§14.15) statements cause a transfer of control that may prevent normal completion of statements that contain them.
- Evaluation of certain Java expressions may throw exceptions from the Java Virtual Machine; these expressions are summarized in §15.5. An explicit `throw` (§14.16) statement also results in an exception. An exception causes a transfer of control that may prevent normal completion of statements.

If such an event occurs, then execution of one or more statements may be terminated before all steps of their normal mode of execution have completed; such statements are said to *complete abruptly.* An abrupt completion always has an associated *reason*, which is one of the following:

- A `break` with no label
- A `break` with a given label
- A `continue` with no label
- A `continue` with a given label
- A `return` with no value
- A `return` with a given value
- A `throw` with a given value, including exceptions thrown by the Java Virtual Machine

The terms "complete normally" and "complete abruptly" also apply to the evaluation of expressions (§15.5). The only reason an expression can complete abruptly is that an exception is thrown, because of either a `throw` with a given value (§14.16) or a run-time exception or error (§11, §15.5).

If a statement evaluates an expression, abrupt completion of the expression always causes the immediate abrupt completion of the statement, with the same reason. All succeeding steps in the normal mode of execution are not performed.

Unless otherwise specified in this chapter, abrupt completion of a substatement causes the immediate abrupt completion of the statement itself, with the same reason, and all succeeding steps in the normal mode of execution of the statement are not performed.

Unless otherwise specified, a statement completes normally if all expressions it evaluates and all substatements it executes complete normally.

14.2 Blocks

A *block* is a sequence of statements and local variable declaration statements within braces.

Block:
  { *BlockStatements*$_{opt}$ }

BlockStatements:
  BlockStatement
  BlockStatements BlockStatement

BlockStatement:
  LocalVariableDeclarationStatement
  Statement

A block is executed by executing each of the local variable declaration statements and other statements in order from first to last (left to right). If all of these block statements complete normally, then the block completes normally. If any of these block statements complete abruptly for any reason, then the block completes abruptly for the same reason.

14.3 Local Variable Declaration Statements

A *local variable declaration statement* declares one or more local variable names.

LocalVariableDeclarationStatement:
  LocalVariableDeclaration ;

LocalVariableDeclaration:
  Type VariableDeclarators

The following are repeated from §8.3 to make the presentation here clearer:

VariableDeclarators:
VariableDeclarator
VariableDeclarators , *VariableDeclarator*

VariableDeclarator:
VariableDeclaratorId
VariableDeclaratorId = *VariableInitializer*

VariableDeclaratorId:
Identifier
VariableDeclaratorId [ ]

VariableInitializer:
Expression
ArrayInitializer

Every local variable declaration statement is immediately contained by a block. Local variable declaration statements may be intermixed freely with other kinds of statements in the block.

A local variable declaration can also appear in the header of a `for` statement (§14.12). In this case it is executed in the same manner as if it were part of a local variable declaration statement.

14.3.1 Local Variable Declarators and Types

Each *declarator* in a local variable declaration declares one local variable, whose name is the *Identifier* that appears in the declarator.

The type of the variable is denoted by the *Type* that appears at the start of the local variable declaration, followed by any bracket pairs that follow the *Identifier* in the declarator. Thus, the local variable declaration:

```
int a, b[], c[][];
```

is equivalent to the series of declarations:

```
int a;
int[] b;
int[][] c;
```

Brackets are allowed in declarators as a nod to the tradition of C and C++. The general rule, however, also means that the local variable declaration:

```
float[][] f[][], g[][][], h[];                // Yechh!
```

is equivalent to the series of declarations:

```
float[][][][] f;
float[][][][][] g;
float[][][] h;
```

We do not recommend such "mixed notation" for array declarations.

14.3.2 Scope of Local Variable Declarations

The scope of a local variable declared in a block is the rest of the block, including its own initializer. The name of the local variable parameter may not be redeclared as a local variable or exception parameter within its scope, or a compile-time error occurs; that is, hiding the name of a local variable is not permitted.

A local variable cannot be referred to using a qualified name (§6.6), only a simple name.

The example:

```
class Test {
    static int x;
    public static void main(String[] args) {
        int x = x;
    }
}
```

causes a compile-time error because the initialization of x is within the scope of the declaration of x as a local variable, and the local x does not yet have a value and cannot be used.

The following program does compile:

```
class Test {
    static int x;
    public static void main(String[] args) {
        int x = (x=2)*2;
        System.out.println(x);
    }
}
```

because the local variable x is definitely assigned (§16) before it is used. It prints:

```
4
```

Here is another example:

```
class Test {
    public static void main(String[] args) {
        System.out.print("2+1=");
        int two = 2, three = two + 1;
        System.out.println(three);
    }
}
```

which compiles correctly and produces the output:

```
2+1=3
```

The initializer for `three` can correctly refer to the variable `two` declared in an earlier declarator, and the method invocation in the next line can correctly refer to the variable `three` declared earlier in the block.

The scope of a local variable declared in a `for` statement is the rest of the `for` statement, including its own initializer.

If a declaration of an identifier as a local variable appears within the scope of a parameter or local variable of the same name, a compile-time error occurs. Thus the following example does not compile:

```
class Test {
    public static void main(String[] args) {
        int i;
        for (int i = 0; i < 10; i++)
            System.out.println(i);
    }
}
```

This restriction helps to detect some otherwise very obscure bugs. (A similar restriction on hiding of members by local variables was judged impractical, because the addition of a member in a superclass could cause subclasses to have to rename local variables.)

On the other hand, local variables with the same name may be declared in two separate blocks or `for` statements neither of which contains the other. Thus:

```
class Test {
    public static void main(String[] args) {
        for (int i = 0; i < 10; i++)
            System.out.print(i + " ");
        for (int i = 10; i > 0; i--)
            System.out.print(i + " ");
        System.out.println();
    }
}
```

compiles without error and, when executed, produces the output:

```
0 1 2 3 4 5 6 7 8 9 10 9 8 7 6 5 4 3 2 1
```

14.3.3 Hiding of Names by Local Variables

If a name declared as a local variable is already declared as a field or type name, then that outer declaration is hidden throughout the scope of the local variable. The field or type name can almost always (§6.8) still be accessed using an appropriately qualified name. For example, the keyword `this` can be used to access a hidden field x, using the form this.x. Indeed, this idiom typically appears in constructors (§8.6):

```
class Pair {
   Object first, second;
   public Pair(Object first, Object second) {
      this.first = first;
      this.second = second;
   }
}
```

In this example, the constructor takes parameters having the same names as the fields to be initialized. This is simpler than having to invent different names for the parameters and is not too confusing in this stylized context. In general, however, it is considered poor style to have local variables with the same names as fields.

14.3.4 Execution of Local Variable Declarations

A local variable declaration statement is an executable statement. Every time it is executed, the declarators are processed in order from left to right. If a declarator has an initialization expression, the expression is evaluated and its value is assigned to the variable. If a declarator does not have an initialization expression, then a Java compiler must prove, using exactly the algorithm given in §16, that every reference to the variable is necessarily preceded by execution of an assignment to the variable. If this is not the case, then a compile-time error occurs.

Each initialization (except the first) is executed only if the evaluation of the preceding initialization expression completes normally. Execution of the local variable declaration completes normally only if evaluation of the last initialization expression completes normally; if the local variable declaration contains no initialization expressions, then executing it always completes normally.

14.4 Statements

There are many kinds of statements in the Java language. Most correspond to statements in the C and C++ languages, but some are unique to Java.

As in C and C++, the Java if statement suffers from the so-called "dangling else problem," illustrated by this misleadingly formatted example:

```
if (door.isOpen())
   if (resident.isVisible())
      resident.greet("Hello!");
else door.bell.ring();     // A "dangling else"
```

The problem is that both the outer `if` statement and the inner `if` statement might conceivably own the `else` clause. In this example, one might surmise that the programmer intended the `else` clause to belong to the outer `if` statement. The Java language, like C and C++ and many languages before them, arbitrarily decree that an `else` clause belongs to the innermost `if` to which it might possibly belong. This rule is captured by the following grammar:

- *Statement:*
  StatementWithoutTrailingSubstatement
  LabeledStatement
  IfThenStatement
  IfThenElseStatement
  WhileStatement
  ForStatement

- *StatementNoShortIf:*
  StatementWithoutTrailingSubstatement
  LabeledStatementNoShortIf
  IfThenElseStatementNoShortIf
  WhileStatementNoShortIf
  ForStatementNoShortIf

- *StatementWithoutTrailingSubstatement:*
  Block
  EmptyStatement
  ExpressionStatement
  SwitchStatement
  DoStatement
  BreakStatement
  ContinueStatement
  ReturnStatement
  SynchronizedStatement
  ThrowStatement
  TryStatement

The following are repeated from §14.8 to make the presentation here clearer:

IfThenStatement:
  `if (` *Expression* `)` *Statement*

IfThenElseStatement:
  `if (` *Expression* `)` *StatementNoShortIf* `else` *Statement*

IfThenElseStatementNoShortIf:
  `if (` *Expression* `)` *StatementNoShortIf* `else` *StatementNoShortIf*

Statements are thus grammatically divided into two categories: those that might end in an `if` statement that has no `else` clause (a "short `if` statement") and those that definitely do not. Only statements that definitely do not end in a short `if` statement may appear as an immediate substatement before the keyword `else` in an `if` statement that does have an `else` clause. This simple rule prevents the "dangling `else`" problem. The execution behavior of a statement with the "no short `if`" restriction is identical to the execution behavior of the same kind of statement without the "no short `if`" restriction; the distinction is drawn purely to resolve the syntactic difficulty.

14.5 The Empty Statement

An *empty statement* does nothing.

EmptyStatement:
    `;`

Execution of an empty statement always completes normally.

14.6 Labeled Statements

Statements may have *label* prefixes.

LabeledStatement:
    Identifier : *Statement*

LabeledStatementNoShortIf:
    Identifier : *StatementNoShortIf*

The *Identifier* is declared to be the label of the immediately contained *Statement*.

Unlike C and C++, the Java language has no `goto` statement; identifier statement labels are used with `break` (§14.13) or `continue` (§14.14) statements appearing anywhere within the labeled statement.

A statement labeled by an identifier must not appear anywhere within another statement labeled by the same identifier, or a compile-time error will occur. Two statements can be labeled by the same identifier only if neither statement contains the other.

There is no restriction against using the same identifier as a label and as the name of a package, class, interface, method, field, parameter, or local variable. Use of an identifier to label a statement does not hide a package, class, interface, method, field, parameter, or local variable with the same name. Use of an identifier as a local variable or as the parameter of an exception handler (§14.18) does not hide a statement label with the same name.

A labeled statement is executed by executing the immediately contained *Statement*. If the statement is labeled by an *Identifier* and the contained *Statement* completes abruptly because of a `break` with the same *Identifier*, then the labeled statement completes normally. In all other cases of abrupt completion of the *Statement*, the labeled statement completes abruptly for the same reason.

14.7 Expression Statements

Certain kinds of expressions may be used as statements by following them with semicolons:

ExpressionStatement:
    StatementExpression ;

StatementExpression:
    Assignment
    PreIncrementExpression
    PreDecrementExpression
    PostIncrementExpression
    PostDecrementExpression
    MethodInvocation
    ClassInstanceCreationExpression

An *expression statement* is executed by evaluating the expression; if the expression has a value, the value is discarded. Execution of the expression statement completes normally if and only if evaluation of the expression completes normally.

Unlike C and C++, the Java language allows only certain forms of expressions to be used as expression statements. Note that Java does not allow a "cast to `void`"—`void` is not a type in Java—so the traditional C trick of writing an expression statement such as:

```
(void) ... ;                    // This idiom belongs to C, not to Java!
```

does not work in Java. On the other hand, Java allows all the most useful kinds of expressions in expressions statements, and Java does not require a method invocation used as an expression statement to invoke a `void` method, so such a trick is almost never needed. If a trick is needed, either an assignment statement (§15.25) or a local variable declaration statement (§14.3) can be used instead.

14.8 The `if` Statement

The `if` statement allows conditional execution of a statement or a conditional choice of two statements, executing one or the other but not both.

IfThenStatement:
    `if (` *Expression* `)` *Statement*

IfThenElseStatement:
    `if (` *Expression* `)` *StatementNoShortIf* `else` *Statement*

IfThenElseStatementNoShortIf:
    `if (` *Expression* `)` *StatementNoShortIf* `else` *StatementNoShortIf*

The *Expression* must have type `boolean`, or a compile-time error occurs.

14.8.1 The `if–then` Statement

I took an early opportunity of testing that statement . . .
—Agatha Christie, *The Mysterious Affair at Styles* (1920), Chapter 12

An `if–then` statement is executed by first evaluating the *Expression*. If evaluation of the *Expression* completes abruptly for some reason, the `if–then` statement completes abruptly for the same reason. Otherwise, execution continues by making a choice based on the resulting value:

- If the value is `true`, then the contained *Statement* is executed; the `if–then` statement completes normally only if execution of the *Statement* completes normally.
- If the value is `false`, no further action is taken and the `if–then` statement completes normally.

14.8.2 The `if–then–else` Statement

Did you ever have to finally decide—
To say yes to one, and let the other one ride?
—John Sebastian, *Did You Ever Have to Make Up Your Mind?*

An `if–then–else` statement is executed by first evaluating the *Expression*. If evaluation of the *Expression* completes abruptly for some reason, then the `if–then–else` statement completes abruptly for the same reason. Otherwise, execution continues by making a choice based on the resulting value:

- If the value is `true`, then the first contained *Statement* (the one before the `else` keyword) is executed; the `if–then–else` statement completes normally only if execution of that statement completes normally.
- If the value is `false`, then the second contained *Statement* (the one after the `else` keyword) is executed; the `if–then–else` statement completes normally only if execution of that statement completes normally.

14.9 The `switch` Statement

The `switch` statement transfers control to one of several statements depending on the value of an expression.

SwitchStatement:
    `switch (` *Expression* `)` *SwitchBlock*

SwitchBlock:
    `{` *SwitchBlockStatementGroups*$_{opt}$ *SwitchLabels*$_{opt}$ `}`

SwitchBlockStatementGroups:
    SwitchBlockStatementGroup
    SwitchBlockStatementGroups SwitchBlockStatementGroup

SwitchBlockStatementGroup:
    SwitchLabels BlockStatements

SwitchLabels:
    SwitchLabel
    SwitchLabels SwitchLabel

SwitchLabel:
    `case` *ConstantExpression* `:`
    `default :`

The type of the *Expression* must be `char`, `byte`, `short`, or `int`, or a compile-time error occurs.

The body of a `switch` statement must be a block. Any statement immediately contained by the block may be labeled with one or more `case` or `default` labels. These labels are said to be *associated* with the `switch` statement, as are the values of the constant expressions (§15.27) in the `case` labels.

All of the following must be true, or a compile-time error will result:

- Every case constant expression associated with a switch statement must be assignable (§5.2) to the type of the switch *Expression*.
- No two of the case constant expressions associated with a switch statement may have the same value.
- At most one default label may be associated with the same switch statement.

In C and C++ the body of a switch statement can be a statement and statements with case labels do not have to be immediately contained by that statement. Consider the simple loop:

```
for (i = 0; i < n; ++i) foo();
```

where n is known to be positive. A trick known as *Duff's device* can be used in C or C++ to unroll the loop, but this is not valid Java code:

```
int q = (n+7)/8;
switch (n%8) {
case 0:   do {  foo();          // Great C hack, Tom,
case 7:         foo();          // but it's not valid in Java.
case 6:         foo();
case 5:         foo();
case 4:         foo();
case 3:         foo();
case 2:         foo();
case 1:         foo();
          } while (--q >= 0);
}
```

Fortunately, this trick does not seem to be widely known or used. Moreover, it is less needed nowadays; this sort of code transformation is properly in the province of state-of-the-art optimizing compilers.

When the switch statement is executed, first the *Expression* is evaluated. If evaluation of the *Expression* completes abruptly for some reason, the switch statement completes abruptly for the same reason. Otherwise, execution continues by comparing the value of the *Expression* with each case constant. Then there is a choice:

- If one of the case constants is equal to the value of the expression, then we say that the case matches, and all statements after the matching case label in the switch block, if any, are executed in sequence. If all these statements complete normally, or if there are no statements after the matching case label, then the entire switch statement completes normally.

- If no case matches but there is a default label, then all statements after the matching default label in the switch block, if any, are executed in sequence. If all these statements complete normally, or if there are no statements after the default label, then the entire switch statement completes normally.
- If no case matches and there is no default label, then no further action is taken and the switch statement completes normally.

If any statement immediately contained by the *Block* body of the switch statement completes abruptly, it is handled as follows:

- If execution of the *Statement* completes abruptly because of a break with no label, no further action is taken and the switch statement completes normally.
- If execution of the *Statement* completes abruptly for any other reason, the switch statement completes abruptly for the same reason. The case of abrupt completion because of a break with a label is handled by the general rule for labeled statements (§14.6).

As in C and C++, execution of statements in a switch block "falls through labels" in Java. For example, the program:

```
class Toomany {

    static void howMany(int k) {
        switch (k) {
        case 1:   System.out.print("one ");
        case 2:   System.out.print("too ");
        case 3:   System.out.println("many");
        }
    }

    public static void main(String[] args) {
        howMany(3);
        howMany(2);
        howMany(1);
    }
}
```

contains a switch block in which the code for each case falls through into the code for the next case. As a result, the program prints:

```
many
too many
one too many
```

If code is not to fall through case to case in this manner, then break statements should be used, as in this example:

```
class Twomany {

    static void howMany(int k) {
        switch (k) {
        case 1:   System.out.println("one");
                  break;           // exit the switch
        case 2:   System.out.println("two");
                  break;           // exit the switch
        case 3:   System.out.println("many");
                  break;           // not needed, but good style
        }
    }

    public static void main(String[] args) {
        howMany(1);
        howMany(2);
        howMany(3);
    }

}
```

This program prints:

```
one
two
many
```

14.10 The `while` Statement

The `while` statement executes an *Expression* and a *Statement* repeatedly until the value of the *Expression* is `false`.

WhileStatement:
  `while (` *Expression* `)` *Statement*

WhileStatementNoShortIf:
  `while (` *Expression* `)` *StatementNoShortIf*

The *Expression* must have type `boolean`, or a compile-time error occurs.

A `while` statement is executed by first evaluating the *Expression*. If evaluation of the *Expression* completes abruptly for some reason, the `while` statement completes abruptly for the same reason. Otherwise, execution continues by making a choice based on the resulting value:

- If the value is `true`, then the contained *Statement* is executed. Then there is a choice:
  - If execution of the *Statement* completes normally, then the entire `while` statement is executed again, beginning by re-evaluating the *Expression*.

- If execution of the *Statement* completes abruptly, see §14.10.1 below.

• If the value of the *Expression* is `false`, no further action is taken and the `while` statement completes normally.

If the value of the *Expression* is `false` the first time it is evaluated, then the *Statement* is not executed.

14.10.1 Abrupt Completion

Abrupt completion of the contained *Statement* is handled in the following manner:

• If execution of the *Statement* completes abruptly because of a `break` with no label, no further action is taken and the `while` statement completes normally.

- If execution of the *Statement* completes abruptly because of a `continue` with no label, then the entire `while` statement is executed again.
- If execution of the *Statement* completes abruptly because of a `continue` with label `L`, then there is a choice:
  - If the `while` statement has label `L`, then the entire `while` statement is executed again.
  - If the `while` statement does not have label `L`, the `while` statement completes abruptly because of a `continue` with label `L`.
- If execution of the *Statement* completes abruptly for any other reason, the `while` statement completes abruptly for the same reason. Note that the case of abrupt completion because of a `break` with a label is handled by the general rule for labeled statements (§14.6).

14.11 The do Statement

The `do` statement executes a *Statement* and an *Expression* repeatedly until the value of the *Expression* is `false`.

DoStatement:
  `do` *Statement* `while (` *Expression* `) ;`

The *Expression* must have type `boolean`, or a compile-time error occurs.

A `do` statement is executed by first executing the *Statement*. Then there is a choice:

• If execution of the *Statement* completes normally, then the *Expression* is evaluated. If evaluation of the *Expression* completes abruptly for some reason, the `do` statement completes abruptly for the same reason. Otherwise, there is a choice based on the resulting value:

- If the value is `true`, then the entire `do` statement is executed again.
- If the value is `false`, no further action is taken and the `do` statement completes normally.

- If execution of the *Statement* completes abruptly, see §14.11.1 below.

Executing a `do` statement always executes the contained *Statement* at least once.

14.11.1 Abrupt Completion

Abrupt completion of the contained *Statement* is handled in the following manner:

- If execution of the *Statement* completes abruptly because of a `break` with no label, then no further action is taken and the `do` statement completes normally.
- If execution of the *Statement* completes abruptly because of a `continue` with no label, then the *Expression* is evaluated. Then there is a choice based on the resulting value:
  - If the value is `true`, then the entire `do` statement is executed again.
  - If the value is `false`, no further action is taken and the `do` statement completes normally.
- If execution of the *Statement* completes abruptly because of a `continue` with label `L`, then there is a choice:
  - If the `do` statement has label `L`, then the *Expression* is evaluated. Then there is a choice:
    - If the value of the *Expression* is `true`, then the entire `do` statement is executed again.
    - If the value of the *Expression* is `false`, no further action is taken and the `do` statement completes normally.
  - If the `do` statement does not have label `L`, the `do` statement completes abruptly because of a `continue` with label `L`.
- If execution of the *Statement* completes abruptly for any other reason, the `do` statement completes abruptly for the same reason. The case of abrupt completion because of a `break` with a label is handled by the general rule (§14.6).

14.11.2 Example of do statement

The following code is one possible implementation of the `toHexString` method (§20.7.14) of class `Integer`:

```
public static String toHexString(int i) {
    StringBuffer buf = new StringBuffer(8);
    do {
        buf.append(Character.forDigit(i & 0xF, 16));
        i >>>= 4;
    } while (i != 0);
    return buf.reverse().toString();
}
```

Because at least one digit must be generated, the `do` statement is an appropriate control structure.

14.12 The for Statement

The `for` statement executes some initialization code, then executes an *Expression*, a *Statement*, and some update code repeatedly until the value of the *Expression* is `false`.

ForStatement:
    `for (` $ForInit_{opt}$ `;` $Expression_{opt}$ `;` $ForUpdate_{opt}$ `)`
        Statement

ForStatementNoShortIf:
    `for (` $ForInit_{opt}$ `;` $Expression_{opt}$ `;` $ForUpdate_{opt}$ `)`
        StatementNoShortIf

ForInit:
    StatementExpressionList
    LocalVariableDeclaration

ForUpdate:
    StatementExpressionList

StatementExpressionList:
    StatementExpression
    StatementExpressionList `,` *StatementExpression*

The *Expression* must have type `boolean`, or a compile-time error occurs.

14.12.1 Initialization of `for` statement

A `for` statement is executed by first executing the *ForInit* code:

- If the *ForInit* code is a list of statement expressions (§14.7), the expressions are evaluated in sequence from left to right; their values, if any, are discarded. If evaluation of any expression completes abruptly for some reason, the `for` statement completes abruptly for the same reason; any *ForInit* statement expressions to the right of the one that completed abruptly are not evaluated.
- If the *ForInit* code is a local variable declaration, it is executed as if it were a local variable declaration statement (§14.3) appearing in a block. In this case, the scope of a declared local variable is its own initializer and any further declarators in the *ForInit* part, plus the *Expression*, *ForUpdate*, and contained *Statement* of the `for` statement. If execution of the local variable declaration completes abruptly for any reason, the `for` statement completes abruptly for the same reason.
- If the *ForInit* part is not present, no action is taken.

14.12.2 Iteration of `for` statement

Next, a `for` iteration step is performed, as follows:

- If the *Expression* is present, it is evaluated, and if evaluation of the *Expression* completes abruptly, the `for` statement completes abruptly for the same reason. Otherwise, there is then a choice based on the presence or absence of the *Expression* and the resulting value if the *Expression* is present:
  - If the *Expression* is not present, or it is present and the value resulting from its evaluation is `true`, then the contained *Statement* is executed. Then there is a choice:
    - If execution of the *Statement* completes normally, then the following two steps are performed in sequence:
      - First, if the *ForUpdate* part is present, the expressions are evaluated in sequence from left to right; their values, if any, are discarded. If evaluation of any expression completes abruptly for some reason, the `for` statement completes abruptly for the same reason; any *ForUpdate* statement expressions to the right of the one that completed abruptly are not evaluated. If the *ForUpdate* part is not present, no action is taken.
      - Second, another `for` iteration step is performed.
    - If execution of the *Statement* completes abruptly, see §14.12.3 below.

- If the *Expression* is present and the value resulting from its evaluation is `false`, no further action is taken and the `for` statement completes normally.

If the value of the *Expression* is `false` the first time it is evaluated, then the *Statement* is not executed.

If the *Expression* is not present, then the only way a `for` statement can complete normally is by use of a `break` statement.

14.12.3 Abrupt Completion of `for` statement

Abrupt completion of the contained *Statement* is handled in the following manner:

- If execution of the *Statement* completes abruptly because of a `break` with no label, no further action is taken and the `for` statement completes normally.
- If execution of the *Statement* completes abruptly because of a `continue` with no label, then the following two steps are performed in sequence:
  - First, if the *ForUpdate* part is present, the expressions are evaluated in sequence from left to right; their values, if any, are discarded. If the *ForUpdate* part is not present, no action is taken.
  - Second, another `for` iteration step is performed.
- If execution of the *Statement* completes abruptly because of a `continue` with label `L`, then there is a choice:
  - If the `for` statement has label `L`, then the following two steps are performed in sequence:
    - First, if the *ForUpdate* part is present, the expressions are evaluated in sequence from left to right; their values, if any, are discarded. If the *ForUpdate* is not present, no action is taken.
    - Second, another `for` iteration step is performed.
  - If the `for` statement does not have label `L`, the `for` statement completes abruptly because of a `continue` with label `L`.
- If execution of the *Statement* completes abruptly for any other reason, the `for` statement completes abruptly for the same reason. Note that the case of abrupt completion because of a `break` with a label is handled by the general rule for labeled statements (§14.6).

14.13 The break Statement

A break statement transfers control out of an enclosing statement.

BreakStatement:
    `break` *Identifier*$_{opt}$ `;`

A `break` statement with no label attempts to transfer control to the innermost enclosing `switch`, `while`, `do`, or `for` statement; this statement, which is called the *break target*, then immediately completes normally. To be precise, a `break` statement with no label always completes abruptly, the reason being a `break` with no label. If no `switch`, `while`, `do`, or `for` statement encloses the `break` statement, a compile-time error occurs.

A `break` statement with label *Identifier* attempts to transfer control to the enclosing labeled statement (§14.6) that has the same *Identifier* as its label; this statement, which is called the *break target*, then immediately completes normally. In this case, the `break` target need not be a `while`, `do`, `for`, or `switch` statement. To be precise, a `break` statement with label *Identifier* always completes abruptly, the reason being a `break` with label *Identifier*. If no labeled statement with *Identifier* as its label encloses the `break` statement, a compile-time error occurs.

It can be seen, then, that a `break` statement always completes abruptly.

The preceding descriptions say "attempts to transfer control" rather than just "transfers control" because if there are any `try` statements (§14.18) within the break target whose `try` blocks contain the `break` statement, then any `finally` clauses of those `try` statements are executed, in order, innermost to outermost, before control is transferred to the break target. Abrupt completion of a `finally` clause can disrupt the transfer of control initiated by a `break` statement.

In the following example, a mathematical graph is represented by an array of arrays. A graph consists of a set of nodes and a set of edges; each edge is an arrow that points from some node to some other node, or from a node to itself. In this example it is assumed that there are no redundant edges; that is, for any two nodes `P` and `Q`, where `Q` may be the same as `P`, there is at most one edge from `P` to `Q`. Nodes are represented by integers, and there is an edge from node `i` to node `edges[i][j]` for every `i` and `j` for which the array reference `edges[i][j]` does not throw an `IndexOutOfBoundsException`.

The task of the method `loseEdges`, given integers `i` and `j`, is to construct a new graph by copying a given graph but omitting the edge from node `i` to node `j`, if any, and the edge from node `j` to node `i`, if any:

```
class Graph {
    int edges[][];

    public Graph(int[][] edges) { this.edges = edges; }

    public Graph loseEdges(int i, int j) {
        int n = edges.length;
        int[][] newedges = new int[n][];
        for (int k = 0; k < n; ++k) {

            edgelist: {
                int z;

                search: {
                    if (k == i) {
                        for (z = 0; z < edges[k].length; ++z)
                            if (edges[k][z] == j)
                                break search;
                    } else if (k == j) {
                        for (z = 0; z < edges[k].length; ++z)
                            if (edges[k][z] == i)
                                break search;
                    }
                    // No edge to be deleted; share this list.
                    newedges[k] = edges[k];
                    break edgelist;
                }//search

                // Copy the list, omitting the edge at position z.
                int m = edges[k].length - 1;
                int ne[] = new int[m];
                System.arraycopy(edges[k], 0, ne, 0, z);
                System.arraycopy(edges[k], z+1, ne, z, m-z);
                newedges[k] = ne;
            }//edgelist

        }
        return new Graph(newedges);
    }

}
```

Note the use of two statement labels, `edgelist` and `search`, and the use of `break` statements. This allows the code that copies a list, omitting one edge, to be shared between two separate tests, the test for an edge from node *i* to node *j*, and the test for an edge from node *j* to node *i*.

14.14 The `continue` Statement

A `continue` statement may occur only in a `while`, `do`, or `for` statement; statements of these three kinds are called *iteration statements*. Control passes to the loop-continuation point of an iteration statement.

ContinueStatement:
`continue` *Identifier*$_{opt}$ `;`

A `continue` statement with no label attempts to transfer control to the innermost enclosing `while`, `do`, or `for` statement; this statement, which is called the *continue target*, then immediately ends the current iteration and begins a new one. To be precise, such a `continue` statement always completes abruptly, the reason being a `continue` with no label. If no `while`, `do`, or `for` statement encloses the `continue` statement, a compile-time error occurs.

A `continue` statement with label *Identifier* attempts to transfer control to the enclosing labeled statement (§14.6) that has the same *Identifier* as its label; that statement, which is called the *continue target*, then immediately ends the current iteration and begins a new one. The continue target must be a `while`, `do`, or `for` statement or a compile-time error occurs. More precisely, a `continue` statement with label *Identifier* always completes abruptly, the reason being a `continue` with label *Identifier*. If no labeled statement with *Identifier* as its label contains the `continue` statement, a compile-time error occurs.

It can be seen, then, that a `continue` statement always completes abruptly.

See the descriptions of the `while` statement (§14.10), `do` statement (§14.11), and `for` statement (§14.12) for a discussion of the handling of abrupt termination because of `continue`.

The preceding descriptions say "attempts to transfer control" rather than just "transfers control" because if there are any `try` statements (§14.18) within the continue target whose `try` blocks contain the `continue` statement, then any `finally` clauses of those `try` statements are executed, in order, innermost to outermost, before control is transferred to the continue target. Abrupt completion of a `finally` clause can disrupt the transfer of control initiated by a `continue` statement.

In the `Graph` example in the preceding section, one of the `break` statements is used to finish execution of the entire body of the outermost `for` loop. This `break` can be replaced by a `continue` if the `for` loop itself is labeled:

```
class Graph {
    ...
    public Graph loseEdges(int i, int j) {
        int n = edges.length;
        int[][] newedges = new int[n][];

        edgelists: for (int k = 0; k < n; ++k) {
            int z;

            search: {
                if (k == i) {
                    ...
                } else if (k == j) {
                    ...
                }
                newedges[k] = edges[k];
                continue edgelists;
            }//search
            ...
        }//edgelists

        return new Graph(newedges);
    }
}
```

Which to use, if either, is largely a matter of programming style.

14.15 The return Statement

A `return` statement returns control to the invoker of a method (§8.4, §15.11) or constructor (§8.6, §15.8).

ReturnStatement:
    `return` *Expression*$_{opt}$ `;`

A `return` statement with no *Expression* must be contained in the body of a method that is declared, using the keyword `void`, not to return any value (§8.4), or in the body of a constructor (§8.6). A compile-time error occurs if a `return` statement appears within a static initializer (§8.5). A `return` statement with no *Expression* attempts to transfer control to the invoker of the method or constructor that contains it. To be precise, a `return` statement with no *Expression* always completes abruptly, the reason being a `return` with no value.

A `return` statement with an *Expression* must be contained in a method declaration that is declared to return a value (§8.4) or a compile-time error occurs. The *Expression* must denote a variable or value of some type `T`, or a compile-time error occurs. The type `T` must be assignable (§5.2) to the declared result type of the method, or a compile-time error occurs.

A `return` statement with an *Expression* attempts to transfer control to the invoker of the method that contains it; the value of the *Expression* becomes the value of the method invocation. More precisely, execution of such a `return` statement first evaluates the *Expression*. If the evaluation of the *Expression* completes abruptly for some reason, then the `return` statement completes abruptly for that reason. If evaluation of the *Expression* completes normally, producing a value *V*, then the `return` statement completes abruptly, the reason being a `return` with value *V*.

It can be seen, then, that a `return` statement always completes abruptly.

The preceding descriptions say "attempts to transfer control" rather than just "transfers control" because if there are any `try` statements (§14.18) within the method or constructor whose `try` blocks contain the `return` statement, then any `finally` clauses of those `try` statements will be executed, in order, innermost to outermost, before control is transferred to the invoker of the method or constructor. Abrupt completion of a `finally` clause can disrupt the transfer of control initiated by a `return` statement.

14.16 The `throw` Statement

A `throw` statement causes an exception (§11) to be thrown. The result is an immediate transfer of control (§11.3) that may exit multiple statements and multiple constructor, static and field initializer evaluations, and method invocations until a `try` statement (§14.18) is found that catches the thrown value. If no such `try` statement is found, then execution of the thread (§17, §20.20) that executed the `throw` is terminated (§11.3) after invocation of the `UncaughtException` method (§20.21.31) for the thread group to which the thread belongs.

ThrowStatement:
    `throw` *Expression* `;`

The *Expression* in a throw statement must denote a variable or value of a reference type which is assignable (§5.2) to the type `Throwable`, or a compile-time error occurs. Moreover, at least one of the following three conditions must be true, or a compile-time error occurs:

- The exception is not a checked exception (§11.2)—specifically, one of the following situations is true:
    - The type of the *Expression* is the class `RuntimeException` or a subclass of `RuntimeException`.
    - The type of the *Expression* is the class `Error` or a subclass of `Error`.

- The `throw` statement is contained in the `try` block of a `try` statement (§14.18) and the type of the *Expression* is assignable (§5.2) to the type of the parameter of at least one `catch` clause of the `try` statement. (In this case we say the thrown value is *caught* by the `try` statement.)
- The `throw` statement is contained in a method or constructor declaration and the type of the *Expression* is assignable (§5.2) to at least one type listed in the `throws` clause (§8.4.4, §8.6.4) of the declaration.

A `throw` statement first evaluates the *Expression*. If the evaluation of the *Expression* completes abruptly for some reason, then the `throw` completes abruptly for that reason. If evaluation of the *Expression* completes normally, producing a value *V*, then the `throw` statement completes abruptly, the reason being a `throw` with value *V*.

It can be seen, then, that a `throw` statement always completes abruptly.

If there are any enclosing `try` statements (§14.18) whose `try` blocks contain the `throw` statement, then any `finally` clauses of those `try` statements are executed as control is transferred outward, until the thrown value is caught. Note that abrupt completion of a `finally` clause can disrupt the transfer of control initiated by a `throw` statement.

If a `throw` statement is contained in a method declaration, but its value is not caught by some `try` statement that contains it, then the invocation of the method completes abruptly because of the `throw`.

If a `throw` statement is contained in a constructor declaration, but its value is not caught by some `try` statement that contains it, then the class instance creation expression (or the method invocation of method `newInstance` of class `Class`) that invoked the constructor will complete abruptly because of the `throw`.

If a `throw` statement is contained in a static initializer (§8.5), then a compile-time check ensures that either its value is always an unchecked exception or its value is always caught by some `try` statement that contains it. If, despite this check, the value is not caught by some `try` statement that contains the `throw` statement, then the value is rethrown if it is an instance of class `Error` or one of its subclasses; otherwise, it is wrapped in an `ExceptionInInitializerError` object, which is then thrown (§12.4.2).

By convention, user-declared throwable types should usually be declared to be subclasses of class `Exception`, which is a subclass of class `Throwable` (§11.5, §20.22).

14.17 The synchronized Statement

A synchronized statement acquires a mutual-exclusion lock (§17.13) on behalf of the executing thread, executes a block, then releases the lock. While the executing thread owns the lock, no other thread may acquire the lock.

SynchronizedStatement:
    synchronized (*Expression*) *Block*

The type of *Expression* must be a reference type, or a compile-time error occurs.

A synchronized statement is executed by first evaluating the *Expression*.

If evaluation of the *Expression* completes abruptly for some reason, then the synchronized statement completes abruptly for the same reason.

Otherwise, if the value of the *Expression* is null, a NullPointerException is thrown.

Otherwise, let the non-null value of the *Expression* be V. The executing thread locks the lock associated with V. Then the *Block* is executed. If execution of the *Block* completes normally, then the lock is unlocked and the synchronized statement completes normally. If execution of the *Block* completes abruptly for any reason, then the lock is unlocked and the synchronized statement then completes abruptly for the same reason.

Acquiring the lock associated with an object does not of itself prevent other threads from accessing fields of the object or invoking unsynchronized methods on the object. Other threads can also use synchronized methods or the synchronized statement in a conventional manner to achieve mutual exclusion.

The locks acquired by synchronized statements are the same as the locks that are acquired implicitly by synchronized methods; see §8.4.3.5. A single thread may hold a lock more than once. The example:

```
class Test {
    public static void main(String[] args) {
        Test t = new Test();
        synchronized(t) {
            synchronized(t) {
                System.out.println("made it!");
            }
        }
    }
}
```

prints:

```
made it!
```

This example would deadlock if a single thread were not permitted to lock a lock more than once.

14.18 The try statement

These are the times that try men's souls.
—Thomas Paine, *The American Crisis* (1780)

. . . and they all fell to playing the game of catch as catch can,
till the gunpowder ran out at the heels of their boots.
—Samuel Foote

A `try` statement executes a block. If a value is thrown and the `try` statement has one or more `catch` clauses that can catch it, then control will be transferred to the first such `catch` clause. If the `try` statement has a `finally` clause, then another block of code is executed, no matter whether the `try` block completes normally or abruptly, and no matter whether a `catch` clause is first given control.

TryStatement:
  `try` *Block Catches*
  `try` *Block* $Catches_{opt}$ *Finally*

Catches:
  CatchClause
  Catches CatchClause

CatchClause:
  `catch (` *FormalParameter* `)` *Block*

Finally:
  `finally` *Block*

The following is repeated from §8.4.1 to make the presentation here clearer:

FormalParameter:
  Type VariableDeclaratorId

The following is repeated from §8.3 to make the presentation here clearer:

VariableDeclaratorId:
  Identifier
  VariableDeclaratorId `[ ]`

The *Block* immediately after the keyword `try` is called the `try` block of the `try` statement. The *Block* immediately after the keyword `finally` is called the `finally` block of the `try` statement.

A `try` statement may have `catch` clauses (also called *exception handlers*). A `catch` clause must have exactly one parameter (which is called an *exception parameter*); the declared type of the exception parameter must be the class `Throwable` or a subclass of `Throwable`, or a compile-time error occurs. The scope of the parameter variable is the *Block* of the `catch` clause. An exception parameter must not have the same name as a local variable or parameter in whose scope it is declared, or a compile-time error occurs.

The scope of the name of an exception parameter is the *Block* of the `catch` clause. The name of the parameter may not be redeclared as a local variable or exception parameter within the *Block* of the `catch` clause; that is, hiding the name of an exception parameter is not permitted.

Exception parameters cannot be referred to using qualified names (§6.6), only by simple names.

Exception handlers are considered in left-to-right order: the earliest possible `catch` clause accepts the exception, receiving as its actual argument the thrown exception object.

A `finally` clause ensures that the `finally` block is executed after the `try` block and any `catch` block that might be executed, no matter how control leaves the `try` block or `catch` block.

Handling of the `finally` block is rather complex, so the two cases of a `try` statement with and without a `finally` block are described separately.

14.18.1 Execution of `try-catch`

Our supreme task is the resumption of our onward, normal way.
—Warren G. Harding, Inaugural Address (1921)

A `try` statement without a `finally` block is executed by first executing the `try` block. Then there is a choice:

- If execution of the `try` block completes normally, then no further action is taken and the `try` statement completes normally.
- If execution of the `try` block completes abruptly because of a `throw` of a value *V*, then there is a choice:
  - If the run-time type of *V* is assignable (§5.2) to the *Parameter* of any `catch` clause of the `try` statement, then the first (leftmost) such `catch` clause is selected. The value *V* is assigned to the parameter of the selected `catch` clause, and the *Block* of that `catch` clause is executed. If that block completes normally, then the `try` statement completes normally; if that block completes abruptly for any reason, then the `try` statement completes abruptly for the same reason.

- If the run-time type of *V* is not assignable to the parameter of any `catch` clause of the `try` statement, then the `try` statement completes abruptly because of a `throw` of the value *V*.

- If execution of the `try` block completes abruptly for any other reason, then the `try` statement completes abruptly for the same reason.

In the example:

```
class BlewIt extends Exception {
    BlewIt() { }
    BlewIt(String s) { super(s); }
}
class Test {
    static void blowUp() throws BlewIt { throw new BlewIt(); }
    public static void main(String[] args) {
        try {
            blowUp();
        } catch (RuntimeException r) {
            System.out.println("RuntimeException:" + r);
        } catch (BlewIt b) {
            System.out.println("BlewIt");
        }
    }
}
```

the exception `BlewIt` is thrown by the method `blowUp`. The `try`–`catch` statement in the body of `main` has two `catch` clauses. The run-time type of the exception is `BlewIt` which is not assignable to a variable of type `RuntimeException`, but is assignable to a variable of type `BlewIt`, so the output of the example is:

```
BlewIt
```

14.18.2 Execution of `try-catch-finally`

After the great captains and engineers have accomplish'd their work,
After the noble inventors—after the scientists, the chemist,
the geologist, ethnologist,
Finally shall come the Poet . . .
—Walt Whitman, *Passage to India* (1870)

A `try` statement with a `finally` block is executed by first executing the `try` block. Then there is a choice:

- If execution of the `try` block completes normally, then the `finally` block is executed, and then there is a choice:
  - If the `finally` block completes normally, then the `try` statement completes normally.
  - If the `finally` block completes abruptly for reason *S*, then the `try` statement completes abruptly for reason *S*.
- If execution of the `try` block completes abruptly because of a `throw` of a value *V*, then there is a choice:
  - If the run-time type of *V* is assignable to the parameter of any `catch` clause of the `try` statement, then the first (leftmost) such `catch` clause is selected. The value *V* is assigned to the parameter of the selected `catch` clause, and the *Block* of that `catch` clause is executed. Then there is a choice:
    - If the `catch` block completes normally, then the `finally` block is executed. Then there is a choice:
      - If the `finally` block completes normally, then the `try` statement completes normally.
      - If the `finally` block completes abruptly for any reason, then the `try` statement completes abruptly for the same reason.
    - If the `catch` block completes abruptly for reason *R*, then the `finally` block is executed. Then there is a choice:
      - If the `finally` block completes normally, then the `try` statement completes abruptly for reason *R*.
      - If the `finally` block completes abruptly for reason *S*, then the `try` statement completes abruptly for reason *S* (and reason *R* is discarded).
  - If the run-time type of *V* is not assignable to the parameter of any `catch` clause of the `try` statement, then the `finally` block is executed. Then there is a choice:
    - If the `finally` block completes normally, then the `try` statement completes abruptly because of a `throw` of the value *V*.
    - If the `finally` block completes abruptly for reason *S*, then the `try` statement completes abruptly for reason *S* (and the `throw` of value *V* is discarded and forgotten).

- If execution of the `try` block completes abruptly for any other reason *R*, then the `finally` block is executed. Then there is a choice:
  - If the `finally` block completes normally, then the `try` statement completes abruptly for reason *R*.
  - If the `finally` block completes abruptly for reason *S*, then the `try` statement completes abruptly for reason *S* (and reason *R* is discarded).

The example:

```
class BlewIt extends Exception {

    BlewIt() { }

    BlewIt(String s) { super(s); }

}

class Test {

    static void blowUp() throws BlewIt {
        throw new NullPointerException();
    }

    public static void main(String[] args) {
        try {
            blowUp();
        } catch (BlewIt b) {
            System.out.println("BlewIt");
        } finally {
            System.out.println("Uncaught Exception");
        }
    }

}
```

produces the output:

```
Uncaught Exception
java.lang.NullPointerException
    at Test.blowUp(Test.java:7)
    at Test.main(Test.java:11)
```

The `NullPointerException` (which is a kind of `RuntimeException`) that is thrown by method `blowUp` is not caught by the `try` statement in `main`, because a `NullPointerException` is not assignable to a variable of type `BlewIt`. This causes the `finally` clause to execute, after which the thread executing `main`, which is the only thread of the test program, terminates because of an uncaught exception (§20.21.31), which results in printing the exception name and a simple backtrace.

14.19 Unreachable Statements

That looks like a path.
Is that the way to reach the top from here?
—Robert Frost, *The Mountain* (1915)

It is a compile-time error if a statement cannot be executed because it is *unreachable*. Every Java compiler must carry out the conservative flow analysis specified here to make sure all statements are reachable.

This section is devoted to a precise explanation of the word "reachable." The idea is that there must be some possible execution path from the beginning of the constructor, method, or static initializer that contains the statement to the statement itself. The analysis takes into account the structure of statements. Except for the special treatment of `while`, `do`, and `for` statements whose condition expression has the constant value `true`, the values of expressions are not taken into account in the flow analysis. For example, a Java compiler will accept the code:

```
{
    int n = 5;
    while (n > 7) n = 2;
}
```

even though the value of `n` is known at compile time and in principle it can be known at compile time that the assignment to `k` can never be executed. A Java compiler must operate according to the rules laid out in this section.

The rules in this section define two technical terms:

- whether a statement is *reachable*
- whether a statement *can complete normally*

The definitions here allow a statement to complete normally only if it is reachable.

To shorten the description of the rules, the customary abbreviation "iff" is used to mean "if and only if."

The rules are as follows:

- The block that is the body of a constructor, method, or static initializer is reachable.
- An empty block that is not a switch block can complete normally iff it is reachable. A nonempty block that is not a switch block can complete normally iff the last statement in it can complete normally. The first statement in a nonempty block that is not a switch block is reachable iff the block is reachable. Every other statement *S* in a nonempty block that is not a switch block is reachable iff the statement preceding *S* can complete normally.

- A local variable declaration statement can complete normally iff it is reachable.
- An empty statement can complete normally iff it is reachable.
- A labeled statement can complete normally if at least one of the following is true:
  - The contained statement can complete normally.
  - There is a reachable `break` statement that exits the labeled statement.

  The contained statement is reachable iff the labeled statement is reachable.
- An expression statement can complete normally iff it is reachable.
- The `if` statement, whether or not it has an `else` part, is handled in an unusual manner. For this reason, it is discussed separately at the end of this section.
- A `switch` statement can complete normally iff at least one of the following is true:
  - The last statement in the switch block can complete normally.
  - The switch block is empty or contains only switch labels.
  - There is at least one switch label after the last switch block statement group.
  - There is a reachable `break` statement that exits the `switch` statement.
- A switch block is reachable iff its `switch` statement is reachable.
- A statement in a switch block is reachable iff its `switch` statement is reachable and at least one of the following is true:
  - It bears a `case` or `default` label.
  - There is a statement preceding it in the `switch` block and that preceding statement can complete normally.
- A `while` statement can complete normally iff at least one of the following is true:
  - The `while` statement is reachable and the condition expression is not a constant expression with value `true`.
  - There is a reachable `break` statement that exits the `while` statement.

  The contained statement is reachable iff the `while` statement is reachable and the condition expression is not a constant expression whose value is `false`.

- A `do` statement can complete normally iff at least one of the following is true:
  - The contained statement can complete normally and the condition expression is not a constant expression with value `true`.
  - There is a reachable `break` statement that exits the `do` statement.

  The contained statement is reachable iff the `do` statement is reachable.
- A `for` statement can complete normally iff at least one of the following is true:
  - The `for` statement is reachable, there is a condition expression, and the condition expression is not a constant expression with value `true`.
  - There is a reachable `break` statement that exits the `for` statement.

  The contained statement is reachable iff the `for` statement is reachable and the condition expression is not a constant expression whose value is `false`.
- A `break`, `continue`, `return`, or `throw` statement cannot complete normally.
- A `synchronized` statement can complete normally iff the contained statement can complete normally. The contained statement is reachable iff the `synchronized` statement is reachable.
- A `try` statement can complete normally iff both of the following are true:
  - The `try` block can complete normally or any `catch` block can complete `normally`.
  - If the `try` statement has a `finally` block, then the `finally` block can complete normally.
- The `try` block is reachable iff the `try` statement is reachable.
- A `catch` block *C* is reachable iff both of the following are true:
  - Some expression or `throw` statement in the `try` block is reachable and can throw an exception whose type is assignable to the parameter of the `catch` clause *C*. (An expression is considered reachable iff the innermost statement containing it is reachable.)
  - There is no earlier `catch` block *A* in the `try` statement such that the type of *C*'s parameter is the same as or a subclass of the type of *A*'s parameter.
- If a `finally` block is present, it is reachable iff the `try` statement is reachable.

One might expect the `if` statement to be handled in the following manner, but these are not the rules that Java actually uses:

- HYPOTHETICAL: An `if-then` statement can complete normally iff at least one of the following is `true`:
  - The `if–then` statement is reachable and the condition expression is not a constant expression whose value is `true`.
  - The `then`–statement can complete normally.

  The `then`–statement is reachable iff the `if–then` statement is reachable and the condition expression is not a constant expression whose value is `false`.

- HYPOTHETICAL: An `if–then–else` statement can complete normally iff the `then`–statement can complete normally or the `else`–statement can complete normally. The `then`-statement is reachable iff the `if–then–else` statement is reachable and the condition expression is not a constant expression whose value is `false`. The `else` statement is reachable iff the `if–then–else` statement is reachable and the condition expression is not a constant expression whose value is `true`.

This approach would be consistent with the treatment of other control structures in Java. However, in order to allow the if statement to be used conveniently for "conditional compilation" purposes, the actual rules are as follows:

- ACTUAL: An `if–then` statement can complete normally iff it is reachable. The `then`–statement is reachable iff the `if–then` statement is reachable.
- ACTUAL: An `if–then–else` statement can complete normally iff the `then`–statement can complete normally or the `else`–statement can complete normally. The `then`-statement is reachable iff the `if–then–else` statement is reachable. The `else`-statement is reachable iff the `if–then–else` statement is reachable.

As an example, the following statement results in a compile-time error:

```
while (false) { x=3; }
```

because the statement `x=3;` is not reachable; but the superficially similar case:

```
if (false) { x=3; }
```

does not result in a compile-time error. An optimizing compiler may realize that the statement `x=3;` will never be executed and may choose to omit the code for that statement from the generated `class` file, but the statement `x=3;` is not regarded as "unreachable" in the technical sense specified here.

The rationale for this differing treatment is to allow programmers to define "flag variables" such as:

```
static final boolean DEBUG = false;
```

and then write code such as:

```
if (DEBUG) { x=3; }
```

The idea is that it should be possible to change the value of `DEBUG` from `false` to `true` or from `true` to `false` and then compile the code correctly with no other changes to the program text.

This ability to "conditionally compile" has a significant impact on, and relationship to, binary compatibility (§13). If a set of classes that use such a "flag" variable are compiled and conditional code is omitted, it does not suffice later to distribute just a new version of the class or interface that contains the definition of the flag. A change to the value of a flag is, therefore, not binary compatible with preexisting binaries (§13.4.8). (There are other reasons for such incompatibility as well, such as the use of constants in `case` labels in `switch` statements; see §13.4.8.)

One ought not to be thrown into confusion
By a plain statement of relationship . . .
—Robert Frost, *The Generations of Men* (1914)

CHAPTER 15

Expressions

When you can measure what you are speaking about,
and express it in numbers, you know something about it;
but when you cannot measure it, when you cannot express it in numbers,
your knowledge of it is of a meager and unsatisfactory kind:
it may be the beginning of knowledge, but you have scarcely,
in your thoughts, advanced to the stage of science.
—William Thompson, Lord Kelvin

MUCH of the work in a Java program is done by evaluating *expressions*, either for their side effects, such as assignments to variables, or for their values, which can be used as arguments or operands in larger expressions, or to affect the execution sequence in statements, or both.

This chapter specifies the meanings of Java expressions and the rules for their evaluation.

15.1 Evaluation, Denotation, and Result

When an expression in a Java program is *evaluated* (*executed*), the *result* denotes one of three things:

- A variable (§4.5) (in C, this would be called an *lvalue*)
- A value (§4.2, §4.3)
- Nothing (the expression is said to be `void`)

Evaluation of an expression can also produce side effects, because expressions may contain embedded assignments, increment operators, decrement operators, and method invocations.

An expression denotes nothing if and only if it is a method invocation (§15.11) that invokes a method that does not return a value, that is, a method declared `void` (§8.4). Such an expression can be used only as an expression statement (§14.7), because every other context in which an expression can appear requires the expression to denote something. An expression statement that is a method invocation may also invoke a method that produces a result; in this case the value returned by the method is quietly discarded.

Each expression occurs in the declaration of some (class or interface) type that is being declared: in a field initializer, in a static initializer, in a constructor declaration, or in the code for a method.

15.2 Variables as Values

If an expression denotes a variable, and a value is required for use in further evaluation, then the value of that variable is used. In this context, if the expression denotes a variable or a value, we may speak simply of the *value* of the expression.

15.3 Type of an Expression

If an expression denotes a variable or a value, then the expression has a type known at compile time. The rules for determining the type of an expression are explained separately below for each kind of expression.

The value of an expression is always assignment compatible (§5.2) with the type of the expression, just as the value stored in a variable is always compatible with the type of the variable. In other words, the value of an expression whose type is *T* is always suitable for assignment to a variable of type *T*.

Note that an expression whose type is a class type *F* that is declared `final` is guaranteed to have a value that is either a null reference or an object whose class is *F* itself, because `final` types have no subclasses.

15.4 Expressions and Run-Time Checks

If the type of an expression is a primitive type, then the value of the expression is of that same primitive type. But if the type of an expression is a reference type, then the class of the referenced object, or even whether the value is a reference to an object rather than `null`, is not necessarily known at compile time. There are a few places in the Java language where the actual class of a referenced object affects program execution in a manner that cannot be deduced from the type of the expression. They are as follows:

- Method invocation (§15.11). The particular method used for an invocation `o.m(...)` is chosen based on the methods that are part of the class or interface that is the type of `o`. For instance methods, the class of the object referenced by the run-time value of `o` participates because a subclass may override a specific method already declared in a parent class so that this overriding method is invoked. (The overriding method may or may not choose to further invoke the original overridden `m` method.)
- The `instanceof` operator (§15.19.2). An expression whose type is a reference type may be tested using `instanceof` to find out whether the class of the object referenced by the run-time value of the expression is assignment compatible (§5.2) with some other reference type.
- Casting (§5.4, §15.15). The class of the object referenced by the run-time value of the operand expression might not be compatible with the type specified by the cast. For reference types, this may require a run-time check that throws an error if the class of the referenced object, as determined at run time, is not assignment compatible (§5.2) with the target type.
- Assignment to an array component of reference type (§10.10, §15.12, §15.25.1). The type-checking rules allow the array type *S*`[]` to be treated as a subtype of *T*`[]` if *S* is a subtype of *T*, but this requires a run-time check for assignment to an army component, similar to the check performed for a cast.
- Exception handling (§14.18). An exception is caught by a `catch` clause only if the class of the thrown exception object is an `instanceof` the type of the formal parameter of the `catch` clause.

The first two of the cases just listed ought never to result in detecting a type error. Thus, a Java run-time type error can occur only in these situations:

- In a cast, when the actual class of the object referenced by the value of the operand expression is not compatible with the target type specified by the cast operator (§5.4, §15.15); in this case a `ClassCastException` is thrown.
- In an assignment to an array component of reference type, when the actual class of the object referenced by the value to be assigned is not compatible with the actual run-time component type of the array (§10.10, §15.12, §15.25.1); in this case an `ArrayStoreException` is thrown.
- When an exception is not caught by any `catch` handler (§11.3); in this case the thread of control that encountered the exception first invokes the method `uncaughtException` (§20.21.31) for its thread group and then terminates.

15.5 Normal and Abrupt Completion of Evaluation

No more: the end is sudden and abrupt.
—William Wordsworth, *Apology for the Foregoing Poems* (1831)

Every expression has a normal mode of evaluation in which certain computational steps are carried out. The following sections describe the normal mode of evaluation for each kind of expression. If all the steps are carried out without an exception being thrown, the expression is said to *complete normally.*

If, however, evaluation of an expression throws an exception, then the expression is said to *complete abruptly.* An abrupt completion always has an associated *reason*, which is always a `throw` with a given value.

Run-time exceptions are thrown by the predefined operators as follows:

- A class instance creation expression (§15.8), array creation expression (§15.9), or string concatenation operatior expression (§15.17.1) throws an `OutOfMemoryError` if there is insufficient memory available.
- An array creation expression throws an `ArrayNegativeSizeException` if the value of any dimension expression is less than zero (§15.9).
- A field access (§15.10) throws a `NullPointerException` if the value of the object reference expression is `null`.
- A method invocation expression (§15.11) that invokes an instance method throws a `NullPointerException` if the target reference is `null`.
- An array access (§15.12) throws a `NullPointerException` if the value of the array reference expression is `null`.
- An array access (§15.12) throws an `IndexOutOfBoundsException` if the value of the array index expression is negative or greater than or equal to the `length` of the array.
- A cast (§15.15) throws a `ClassCastException` if a cast is found to be impermissible at run time.
- An integer division (§15.16.2) or integer remainder (§15.16.3) operator throws an `ArithmeticException` if the value of the right-hand operand expression is zero.
- An assignment to an array component of reference type (§15.25.1) throws an `ArrayStoreException` when the value to be assigned is not compatible with the component type of the array.

A method invocation expression can also result in an exception being thrown if an exception occurs that causes execution of the method body to complete abruptly. A class instance creation expression can also result in an exception being thrown if an exception occurs that causes execution of the constructor to complete abruptly. Various linkage and virtual machine errors may also occur during the evaluation of an expression. By their nature, such errors are difficult to predict and difficult to handle.

If an exception occurs, then evaluation of one or more expressions may be terminated before all steps of their normal mode of evaluation are complete; such expressions are said to complete abruptly. The terms "complete normally" and "complete abruptly" are also applied to the execution of statements (§14.1). A statement may complete abruptly for a variety of reasons, not just because an exception is thrown.

If evaluation of an expression requires evaluation of a subexpression, abrupt completion of the subexpression always causes the immediate abrupt completion of the expression itself, with the same reason, and all succeeding steps in the normal mode of evaluation are not performed.

15.6 Evaluation Order

Let all things be done decently and in order.
—I Corinthians 14:40

Java guarantees that the operands of operators appear to be evaluated in a specific *evaluation order*, namely, from left to right.

It is recommended that Java code not rely crucially on this specification. Code is usually clearer when each expression contains at most one side effect, as its outermost operation, and when code does not depend on exactly which exception arises as a consequence of the left-to-right evaluation of expressions.

15.6.1 Evaluate Left-Hand Operand First

The left-hand operand of a binary operator appears to be fully evaluated before any part of the right-hand operand is evaluated. For example, if the left-hand operand contains an assignment to a variable and the right-hand operand contains a reference to that same variable, then the value produced by the reference will reflect the fact that the assignment occurred first.

Thus:

```
class Test {
    public static void main(String[] args) {
        int i = 2;
        int j = (i=3) * i;
        System.out.println(j);
    }
}
```

prints:

```
9
```

It is not permitted for it to print 6 instead of 9.

If the operator is a compound-assignment operator (§15.25.2), then evaluation of the left-hand operand includes both remembering the variable that the left-hand operand denotes and fetching and saving that variable's value for use in the implied combining operation. So, for example, the test program:

```
class Test {
    public static void main(String[] args) {
        int a = 9;
        a += (a = 3);                    // first example
        System.out.println(a);
        int b = 9;
        b = b + (b = 3);                 // second example
        System.out.println(b);
    }
}
```

prints:

```
12
12
```

because the two assignment statements both fetch and remember the value of the left-hand operand, which is 9, before the right-hand operand of the addition is evaluated, thereby setting the variable to 3. It is not permitted for either example to produce the result 6. Note that both of these examples have unspecified behavior in C, according to the ANSI/ISO standard.

If evaluation of the left-hand operand of a binary operator completes abruptly, no part of the right-hand operand appears to have been evaluated.

Thus, the test program:

```
class Test {

    public static void main(String[] args) {

        int j = 1;

        try {
            int i = forgetIt() / (j = 2);
        } catch (Exception e) {
            System.out.println(e);
            System.out.println("Now j = " + j);
        }
    }

    static int forgetIt() throws Exception {
        throw new Exception("I'm outta here!");
    }

}
```

prints:

```
java.lang.Exception: I'm outta here!
Now j = 1
```

because the left-hand operand `forgetIt()` of the operator / throws an exception before the right-hand operand and its embedded assignment of 2 to `j` occurs.

15.6.2 Evaluate Operands before Operation

Java also guarantees that every operand of an operator (except the conditional operators &&, ||, and ? :) appears to be fully evaluated before any part of the operation itself is performed.

If the binary operator is an integer division / (§15.16.2) or integer remainder % (§15.16.3), then its execution may raise an `ArithmeticException`, but this exception is thrown only after both operands of the binary operator have been evaluated and only if these evaluations completed normally.

So, for example, the program:

```
class Test {

    public static void main(String[] args) {
        int divisor = 0;
        try {
            int i = 1 / (divisor * loseBig());
        } catch (Exception e) {
            System.out.println(e);
        }
    }
```

```
        static int loseBig() throws Exception {
            throw new Exception("Shuffle off to Buffalo!");
        }
    }
```

always prints:

```
java.lang.Exception: Shuffle off to Buffalo!
```

and not:

```
java.lang.ArithmeticException: / by zero
```

since no part of the division operation, including signaling of a divide-by-zero exception, may appear to occur before the invocation of `loseBig` completes, even though the implementation may be able to detect or infer that the division operation would certainly result in a divide-by-zero exception.

15.6.3 Evaluation Respects Parentheses and Precedence

That is too weighty a subject to be discussed parenthetically . . .
—John Stuart Mill, *On Liberty* (1869), Chapter IV

Java implementations must respect the order of evaluation as indicated explicitly by parentheses and implicitly by operator precedence. An implementation may not take advantage of algebraic identities such as the associative law to rewrite expressions into a more convenient computational order unless it can be proven that the replacement expression is equivalent in value and in its observable side effects, even in the presence of multiple threads of execution (using the thread execution model in §17), for all possible computational values that might be involved.

In the case of floating-point calculations, this rule applies also for infinity and not-a-number (NaN) values. For example, `!(x<y)` may not be rewritten as `x>=y`, because these expressions have different values if either `x` or `y` is NaN.

Specifically, floating-point calculations that appear to be mathematically associative are unlikely to be computationally associative. Such computations must not be naively reordered. For example, it is not correct for a Java compiler to rewrite `4.0*x*0.5` as `2.0*x`; while roundoff happens not to be an issue here, there are large values of `x` for which the first expression produces infinity (because of overflow) but the second expression produces a finite result.

So, for example, the test program:

```
class Test {

    public static void main(String[] args) {
        double d = 8e+307;
        System.out.println(4.0 * d * 0.5);
        System.out.println(2.0 * d);
    }
}
```

prints:

```
Infinity
1.6e+308
```

because the first expression overflows and the second does not.

In contrast, integer addition and multiplication *are* provably associative in Java; for example `a+b+c`, where `a`, `b`, and `c` are local variables (this simplifying assumption avoids issues involving multiple threads and `volatile` variables), will always produce the same answer whether evaluated as `(a+b)+c` or `a+(b+c)`; if the expression `b+c` occurs nearby in the code, a smart compiler may be able to use this common subexpression.

15.6.4 Argument Lists are Evaluated Left-to-Right

In a method or constructor invocation or class instance creation expression, argument expressions may appear within the parentheses, separated by commas. Each argument expression appears to be fully evaluated before any part of any argument expression to its right.

Thus:

```
class Test {

    public static void main(String[] args) {
        String s = "going, ";
        print3(s, s, s = "gone");
    }

    static void print3(String a, String b, String c) {
        System.out.println(a + b + c);
    }

}
```

always prints:

```
going, going, gone
```

because the assignment of the string `"gone"` to `s` occurs after the first two arguments to `print3` have been evaluated.

If evaluation of an argument expression completes abruptly, no part of any argument expression to its right appears to have been evaluated.

Thus, the example:

```
class Test {
    static int id;

    public static void main(String[] args) {
        try {
            test(id = 1, oops(), id = 3);
        } catch (Exception e) {
            System.out.println(e + ", id=" + id);
        }
    }

    static int oops() throws Exception {
        throw new Exception("oops");
    }

    static int test(int a, int b, int c) {
        return a + b + c;
    }
}
```

prints:

```
java.lang.Exception: oops, id=1
```

because the assignment of `3` to `id` is not executed.

15.6.5 Evaluation Order for Other Expressions

The order of evaluation for some expressions is not completely covered by these general rules, because these expressions may raise exceptional conditions at times that must be specified. See, specifically, the detailed explanations of evaluation order for the following kinds of expressions:

- class instance creation expressions (§15.8.1)
- array creation expressions (§15.9.1)
- method invocation expressions (§15.11.4)
- array access expressions (§15.12.1)
- assignments involving array components (§15.25)

15.7 Primary Expressions

Primary expressions include most of the simplest kinds of expressions, from which all others are constructed: literals, field accesses, method invocations, and array accesses. A parenthesized expression is also treated syntactically as a primary expression.

Primary:
  PrimaryNoNewArray
  ArrayCreationExpression

PrimaryNoNewArray:
  Literal
  `this`
  `(` *Expression* `)`
  ClassInstanceCreationExpression
  FieldAccess
  MethodInvocation
  ArrayAccess

As programming language grammars go, this part of the Java grammar is unusual, in two ways. First, one might expect simple names, such as names of local variables and method parameters, to be primary expressions. For technical reasons, names are lumped together with primary expressions a little later when postfix expressions are introduced (§15.13).

The technical reasons have to do with allowing left-to-right parsing of Java programs with only one-token lookahead. Consider the expressions `(z[3])` and `(z[])`. The first is a parenthesized array access (§15.12) and the second is the start of a cast (§15.15). At the point that the look-ahead symbol is `[`, a left-to-right parse will have reduced the `z` to the nonterminal *Name*. In the context of a cast we prefer not to have to reduce the name to a *Primary*, but if *Name* were one of the alternatives for *Primary*, then we could not tell whether to do the reduction (that is, we could not determine whether the current situation would turn out to be a parenthesized array access or a cast) without looking ahead two tokens, to the token following the `[`. The Java grammar presented here avoids the problem by keeping *Name* and *Primary* separate and allowing either in certain other syntax rules (those for *MethodInvocation*, *ArrayAccess*, *PostfixExpression*, but not for *FieldAccess,* because this is covered by *Name*). This strategy effectively defers the question of whether a *Name* should be treated as a *Primary* until more context can be examined. (Other problems remain with cast expressions; see §19.1.5.)

The second unusual feature avoids a potential grammatical ambiguity in the expression:

```
new int[3][3]
```

which in Java always means a single creation of a multidimensional array, but which, without appropriate grammatical finesse, might also be interpreted as meaning the same as:

```
(new int[3])[3]
```

This ambiguity is eliminated by splitting the expected definition of *Primary* into *Primary* and *PrimaryNoNewArray*. (This may be compared to the splitting of *Statement* into *Statement* and *StatementNoShortIf* (§14.4) to avoid the "dangling `else`" problem.)

15.7.1 Literals

A literal (§3.10) denotes a fixed, unchanging value.

The following production from §3.10 is repeated here for convenience:

Literal:
  IntegerLiteral
  FloatingPointLiteral
  BooleanLiteral
  CharacterLiteral
  StringLiteral
  NullLiteral

The type of a literal is determined as follows:

- The type of an integer literal that ends with `L` or `l` is `long`; the type of any other integer literal is `int`.
- The type of a floating-point literal that ends with `F` or `f` is `float`; the type of any other floating-point literal is `double`.
- The type of a boolean literal is `boolean`.
- The type of a character literal is `char`.
- The type of a string literal is `String`.
- The type of the null literal `null` is the null type; its value is the null reference.

Evaluation of a literal always completes normally.

15.7.2 `this`

The keyword `this` may be used only in the body of an instance method or constructor, or in the initializer of an instance variable of a class. If it appears anywhere else, a compile-time error occurs.

When used as a primary expression, the keyword `this` denotes a value, that is a reference to the object for which the instance method was invoked (§15.11), or to the object being constructed. The type of `this` is the class *C* within which the keyword `this` occurs. At run time, the class of the actual object referred to may be the class *C* or any subclass of *C*.

In the example:

```
class IntVector {
    int[] v;

    boolean equals(IntVector other) {
        if (this == other)
            return true;
        if (v.length != other.v.length)
            return false;
        for (int i = 0; i < v.length; i++)
            if (v[i] != other.v[i])
                return false;
        return true;
    }
}
```

the class `IntVector` implements a method `equals`, which compares two vectors. If the `other` vector is the same vector object as the one for which the `equals` method was invoked, then the check can skip the length and value comparisons. The `equals` method implements this check by comparing the reference to the `other` object to `this`.

The keyword `this` is also used in a special explicit constructor invocation statement, which can appear at the beginning of a constructor body (§8.6.5).

15.7.3 Parenthesized Expressions

A parenthesized expression is a primary expression whose type is the type of the contained expression and whose value at run time is the value of the contained expression.

15.8 Class Instance Creation Expressions

A class instance creation expression is used to create new objects that are instances of classes.

ClassInstanceCreationExpression:
    `new` *ClassType* `(` *ArgumentList*$_{opt}$ `)`

ArgumentList:
    Expression
    ArgumentList `,` *Expression*

In a class instance creation expression, the *ClassType* must name a class that is not `abstract`. This class type is the type of the creation expression.

The arguments in the argument list, if any, are used to select a constructor declared in the body of the named class type, using the same matching rules as for method invocations (§15.11). As in method invocations, a compile-time method matching error results if there is no unique constructor that is both applicable to the provided arguments and the most specific of all the applicable constructors.

15.8.1 Run-time Evaluation of Class Instance Creation Expressions

At run time, evaluation of a class instance creation expression is as follows.

First, space is allocated for the new class instance. If there is insufficient space to allocate the object, evaluation of the class instance creation expression completes abruptly by throwing an `OutOfMemoryError` (§15.8.2).

The new object contains new instances of all the fields declared in the specified class type and all its superclasses. As each new field instance is created, it is initialized to its standard default value (§4.5.4).

Next, the argument list is evaluated, left-to-right. If any of the argument evaluations completes abruptly, any argument expressions to its right are not evaluated, and the class instance creation expression completes abruptly for the same reason.

Next, the selected constructor of the specified class type is invoked. This results in invoking at least one constructor for each superclass of the class type. This process can be directed by explicit constructor invocation statements (§8.6) and is described in detail in §12.5.

The value of a class instance creation expression is a reference to the newly created object of the specified class. Every time the expression is evaluated, a fresh object is created.

15.8.2 Example: Evaluation Order and Out-of-Memory Detection

If evaluation of a class instance creation expression finds there is insufficient memory to perform the creation operation, then an `OutOfMemoryError` is thrown. This check occurs before any argument expressions are evaluated.

So, for example, the test program:

```
class List {
    int value;
    List next;
    static List head = new List(0);
    List(int n) { value = n; next = head; head = this; }
}

class Test {
    public static void main(String[] args) {
        int id = 0, oldid = 0;
        try {
            for (;;) {
                ++id;
                new List(oldid = id);
            }
        } catch (Error e) {
            System.out.println(e + ", " + (oldid==id));
        }
    }
}
```

prints:

```
java.lang.OutOfMemoryError: List, false
```

because the out-or-memory condition is detected before the argument expression `oldid = id` is evaluated.

Compare this to the treatment of array creation expressions (§15.9), for which the out-of-memory condition is detected after evaluation of the dimension expressions (§15.9.3).

15.9 Array Creation Expressions

An array instance creation expression is used to create new arrays (§10).

ArrayCreationExpression:
  `new` *PrimitiveType DimExprs* $Dims_{opt}$
  `new` *TypeName DimExprs* $Dims_{opt}$

DimExprs:
  DimExpr
  DimExprs DimExpr

DimExpr:
  `[` *Expression* `]`

Dims:
  `[ ]`
  Dims `[ ]`

An array creation expression creates an object that is a new array whose elements are of the type specified by the *PrimitiveType* or *TypeName*. The *TypeName* may name any reference type, even an `abstract` class type (§8.1.2.1) or an interface type (§9).

The type of the creation expression is an array type that can denoted by a copy of the creation expression from which the `new` keyword and every *DimExpr* expression have been deleted; for example, the type of the creation expression:

```
new double[3][3][]
```

is:

```
double[][][]
```

The type of each dimension expression *DimExpr* must be an integral type, or a compile-time error occurs. Each expression undergoes unary numeric promotion (§5.6.1). The promoted type must be `int`, or a compile-time error occurs; this means, specifically, that the type of a dimension expression must not be `long`.

15.9.1 Run-time Evaluation of Array Creation Expressions

At run time, evaluation of an array creation expression behaves as follows.

First, the dimension expressions are evaluated, left-to-right. If any of the expression evaluations completes abruptly, the expressions to the right of it are not evaluated.

Next, the values of the dimension expressions are checked. If the value of any *DimExpr* expression is less than zero, then an `NegativeArraySizeException` is thrown.

Next, space is allocated for the new array. If there is insufficient space to allocate the array, evaluation of the array creation expression completes abruptly by throwing an `OutOfMemoryError`.

Then, if a single *DimExpr* appears, a single-dimensional array is created of the specified length, and each component of the array is initialized to its standard default value (§4.5.4).

If an array creation expression contains *N DimExpr* expressions, then it effectively executes a set of nested loops of depth $N - 1$ to create the implied arrays of arrays. For example, the declaration:

```
float[][] matrix = new float[3][3];
```

is equivalent in behavior to:

```
float[][] matrix = new float[3][];
for (int d = 0; d < matrix.length; d++)
    matrix[d] = new float[3];
```

and:

```
Age[][][][][] Aquarius = new Age[6][10][8][12][];
```

is equivalent to:

```
Age[][][][][] Aquarius = new Age[6][][][][];
for (int d1 = 0; d1 < Aquarius.length; d1++) {
    Aquarius[d1] = new Age[8][][][];
    for (int d2 = 0; d2 < Aquarius[d1].length; d2++) {
        Aquarius[d1][d2] = new Age[10][][];
        for (int d3 = 0; d3 < Aquarius[d1][d2].length; d3++) {
            Aquarius[d1][d2][d3] = new Age[12][];
        }
    }
}
```

with `d`, `d1`, `d2` and `d3` replaced by names that are not already locally declared. Thus, a single `new` expression actually creates one array of length 6, 6 arrays of length 10, $6 \times 10 = 60$ arrays of length 8, and $6 \times 10 \times 8 = 480$ arrays of length 12. This example leaves the fifth dimension, which would be arrays containing the actual array elements (references to `Age` objects), initialized only to null references. These arrays can be filled in later by other code, such as:

```
Age[] Hair = { new Age("quartz"), new Age("topaz") };
Aquarius[1][9][6][9] = Hair;
```

A multidimensional array need not have arrays of the same length at each level; thus, a triangular matrix may be created by:

```
float triang[][] = new float[100][];
for (int i = 0; i < triang.length; i++)
    triang[i] = new float[i+1];
```

There is, however, no way to get this effect with a single creation expression.

15.9.2 Example: Array Creation Evaluation Order

In an array creation expression (§15.9), there may be one or more dimension expressions, each within brackets. Each dimension expression is fully evaluated before any part of any dimension expression to its right.

Thus:

```
class Test {
    public static void main(String[] args) {
        int i = 4;
        int ia[][] = new int[i][i=3];
        System.out.println(
            "[" + ia.length + "," + ia[0].length + "]");
    }
}
```

prints:

```
[4,3]
```

because the first dimension is calculated as 4 before the second dimension expression sets `i` to 3.

If evaluation of a dimension expression completes abruptly, no part of any dimension expression to its right will appear to have been evaluated. Thus, the example:

```
class Test {

    public static void main(String[] args) {
        int[][] a = { { 00, 01 }, { 10, 11 } };
        int i = 99;
        try {
            a[val()][i = 1]++;
        } catch (Exception e) {
            System.out.println(e + ", i=" + i);
        }
    }

    static int val() throws Exception {
        throw new Exception("unimplemented");
    }

}
```

prints:

```
java.lang.Exception: unimplemented, i=99
```

because the embedded assignment that sets `i` to `1` is never executed.

15.9.3 Example: Array Creation and Out-of-Memory Detection

If evaluation of an array creation expression finds there is insufficient memory to perform the creation operation, then an `OutOfMemoryError` is thrown. This check occurs only after evaluation of all dimension expressions has completed normally.

So, for example, the test program:

```
class Test {
    public static void main(String[] args) {
        int len = 0, oldlen = 0;
        Object[] a = new Object[0];
        try {
            for (;;) {
                ++len;
                Object[] temp = new Object[oldlen = len];
                temp[0] = a;
                a = temp;
            }
        } catch (Error e) {
            System.out.println(e + ", " + (oldlen==len));
        }
    }
}
```

prints:

```
java.lang.OutOfMemoryError, true
```

because the out-of-memory condition is detected after the argument expression `oldlen = len` is evaluated.

Compare this to class instance creation expressions (§15.8), which detect the out-of-memory condition before evaluating argument expressions (§15.8.2).

15.10 Field Access Expressions

A field access expression may access a field of an object or array, a reference to which is the value of either an expression or the special keyword `super`. (It is also possible to refer to a field of the current instance or current class by using a simple name; see §15.13.1.)

FieldAccess:
    Primary `.` *Identifier*
    `super .` *Identifier*

The meaning of a field access expression is determined using the same rules as for qualified names (§6.6), but limited by the fact that an expression cannot denote a package, class type, or interface type.

15.10.1 Field Access Using a Primary

The type of the *Primary* must be a reference type *T*, or a compile-time error occurs. The meaning of the field access expression is determined as follows:

- If the identifier names several accessible member fields of type *T*, then the field access is ambiguous and a compile-time error occurs.
- If the identifier does not name an accessible member field of type *T*, then the field access is undefined and a compile-time error occurs.
- Otherwise, the identifier names a single accessible member field of type *T* and the type of the field access expression is the declared type of the field. At run time, the result of the field access expression is computed as follows:
  - If the field is `static`:
    - If the field is `final`, then the result is the value of the specified class variable in the class or interface that is the type of the *Primary* expression.
    - If the field is not `final`, then the result is a variable, namely, the specified class variable in the class that is the type of the *Primary* expression.
  - If the field is not `static`:
    - If the value of the *Primary* is `null`, then a `NullPointerException` is thrown.
    - If the field is `final`, then the result is the value of the specified instance variable in the object referenced by the value of the *Primary*.
    - If the field is not `final`, then the result is a variable, namely, the specified instance variable in the object referenced by the value of the *Primary*.

Note, specifically, that only the type of the *Primary* expression, not the class of the actual object referred to at run time, is used in determining which field to use.

Thus, the example:

```
class S { int x = 0; }

class T extends S { int x = 1; }

class Test {

    public static void main(String[] args) {

        T t = new T();
        System.out.println("t.x=" + t.x + when("t", t));

        S s = new S();
        System.out.println("s.x=" + s.x + when("s", s));
```

```
        s = t;
        System.out.println("s.x=" + s.x + when("s", s));
    }
    static String when(String name, Object t) {
        return " when " + name + " holds a "
            + t.getClass() + " at run time.";
    }
}
```

produces the output:

```
t.x=1 when t holds a class T at run time.
s.x=0 when s holds a class S at run time.
s.x=0 when s holds a class T at run time.
```

The last line shows that, indeed, the field that is accessed does not depend on the run-time class of the referenced object; even if `s` holds a reference to an object of class `T`, the expression `s.x` refers to the `x` field of class `S`, because the type of the expression `s` is `S`. Objects of class `T` contain two fields named `x`, one for class `T` and one for its superclass `S`.

This lack of dynamic lookup for field accesses allows Java to run efficiently with straightforward implementations. The power of late binding and overriding is available in Java, but only when instance methods are used. Consider the same example using instance methods to access the fields:

```
class S { int x = 0; int z() { return x; } }

class T extends S { int x = 1; int z() { return x; } }

class Test {

    public static void main(String[] args) {
        T t = new T();
        System.out.println("t.z()=" + t.z() + when("t", t));
        S s = new S();
        System.out.println("s.z()=" + s.z() + when("s", s));
        s = t;
        System.out.println("s.z()=" + s.z() + when("s", s));
    }

    static String when(String name, Object t) {
        return " when " + name + " holds a "
            + t.getClass() + " at run time.";
    }

}
```

Now the output is:

```
t.z()=1 when t holds a class T at run time.
s.z()=0 when s holds a class S at run time.
s.z()=1 when s holds a class T at run time.
```

The last line shows that, indeed, the method that is accessed *does* depend on the run-time class of referenced object; when `s` holds a reference to an object of class `T`, the expression `s.z()` refers to the `z` method of class `T`, despite the fact that the type of the expression `s` is `S`. Method `z` of class `T` overrides method `z` of class `S`.

The following example demonstrates that a null reference may be used to access a class (`static`) variable without causing an exception:

```
class Test {

    static String mountain = "Chocorua";

    static Test favorite(){
        System.out.print("Mount ");
        return null;
    }

    public static void main(String[] args) {
        System.out.println(favorite().mountain);
    }

}
```

It compiles, executes, and prints:

```
Mount Chocorua
```

Even though the result of `favorite()` is `null`, a `NullPointerException` is *not* thrown. That "`Mount `" is printed demonstrates that the *Primary* expression is indeed fully evaluated at run time, despite the fact that only its type, not its value, is used to determine which field to access (because the field `mountain` is `static`).

15.10.2 Accessing Superclass Members using `super`

The special form using the keyword `super` is valid only in an instance method or constructor, or in the initializer of an instance variable of a class; these are exactly the same situations in which the keyword `this` may be used (§15.7.2). The form involving `super` may not be used anywhere in the class `Object`, since `Object` has no superclass; if `super` appears in class `Object`, then a compile-time error results.

Suppose that a field access expression `super.`*`name`* appears within class *`C`*, and the immediate superclass of *`C`* is class *`S`*. Then `super.`*`name`* is treated exactly as if it had been the expression `((`*`S`*`)this).`*`name`*; thus, it refers to the field named *`name`* of the current object, but with the current object viewed as an instance of the superclass. Thus it can access the field named *`name`* that is visible in class *S*, even if that field is hidden by a declaration of a field named *name* in class *C*.

The use of `super` is demonstrated by the following example:

```
interface I { int x = 0; }
class T1 implements I { int x = 1; }
class T2 extends T1 { int x = 2; }
class T3 extends T2 {
    int x = 3;
    void test() {
        System.out.println("x=\t\t"+x);
        System.out.println("super.x=\t\t"+super.x);
        System.out.println("((T2)this).x=\t"+((T2)this).x);
        System.out.println("((T1)this).x=\t"+((T1)this).x);
        System.out.println("((I)this).x=\t"+((I)this).x);
    }
}
class Test {
    public static void main(String[] args) {
        new T3().test();
    }
}
```

which produces the output:

```
x=              3
super.x=        2
((T2)this).x=   2
((T1)this).x=   1
((I)this).x=    0
```

Within class `T3`, the expression `super.x` is treated exactly as if it were:

```
((T2)this).x
```

15.11 Method Invocation Expressions

A method invocation expression is used to invoke a class or instance method.

MethodInvocation:
    MethodName (*ArgumentList*$_{opt}$)
    Primary . *Identifier* (*ArgumentList*$_{opt}$)
    `super` . *Identifier* (*ArgumentList*$_{opt}$)

The definition of *ArgumentList* from §15.8 is repeated here for convenience:

ArgumentList:
    Expression
    ArgumentList , *Expression*

Resolving a method name at compile time is more complicated than resolving a field name because of the possibility of method overloading. Invoking a method at run time is also more complicated than accessing a field because of the possibility of instance method overriding.

Determining the method that will be invoked by a method invocation expression involves several steps. The following three sections describe the compile-time processing of a method invocation; the determination of the type of the method invocation expression is described in §15.11.3.

15.11.1 Compile-Time Step 1: Determine Class or Interface to Search

The first step in processing a method invocation at compile time is to figure out the name of the method to be invoked and which class or interface to check for definitions of methods of that name. There are several cases to consider, depending on the form that precedes the left parenthesis, as follows:

- If the form is *MethodName*, then there are three subcases:
  - If it is a simple name, that is, just an *Identifier*, then the name of the method is the *Identifier* and the class or interface to search is the one whose declaration contains the method invocation.
  - If it is a qualified name of the form *TypeName* `.` *Identifier*, then the name of the method is the *Identifier* and the class to search is the one named by the *TypeName*. If *TypeName* is the name of an interface rather than a class, then a compile-time error occurs, because this form can invoke only `static` methods and interfaces have no `static` methods.
  - In all other cases, the qualified name has the form *FieldName* `.` *Identifier*; then the name of the method is the *Identifier* and the class or interface to search is the declared type of the field named by the *FieldName*.
- If the form is *Primary* `.` *Identifier*, then the name of the method is the *Identifier* and the class or interface to be searched is the type of the *Primary* expression.
- If the form is `super` `.` *Identifier*, then the name of the method is the *Identifier* and the class to be searched is the superclass of the class whose declaration contains the method invocation. A compile-time error occurs if such a method invocation occurs in an interface, or in the class `Object`, or in a `static` method, a static initializer, or the initializer for a `static` variable. It follows that a method invocation of this form may appear only in a class other than `Object`, and only in the body of an instance method, the body of a constructor, or an initializer for an instance variable.

15.11.2 Compile-Time Step 2: Determine Method Signature

The hand-writing experts were called upon for their opinion of the signature . . .
—Agatha Christie, *The Mysterious Affair at Styles* (1920), Chapter 11

The second step searches the class or interface determined in the previous step for method declarations. This step uses the name of the method and the types of the argument expressions to locate method declarations that are both *applicable* and *accessible*, that is, declarations that can be correctly invoked on the given arguments. There may be more than one such method declaration, in which case the *most specific* one is chosen. The descriptor (signature plus return type) of the most specific method declaration is one used at run time to do the method dispatch.

15.11.2.1 *Find Methods that are Applicable and Accessible*

A method declaration is *applicable* to a method invocation if and only if both of the following are true:

- The number of parameters in the method declaration equals the number of argument expressions in the method invocation.
- The type of each actual argument can be converted by method invocation conversion (§5.3) to the type of the corresponding parameter. Method invocation conversion is the same as assignment conversion (§5.2), except that constants of type `int` are never implicitly narrowed to `byte`, `short`, or `char`.

The class or interface determined by the process described in §15.11.1 is searched for all method declarations applicable to this method invocation; method definitions inherited from superclasses and superinterfaces are included in this search.

Whether a method declaration is *accessible* to a method invocation depends on the access modifier (`public`, none, `protected`, or `private`) in the method declaration and on where the method invocation appears.

If the class or interface has no method declaration that is both applicable and accessible, then a compile-time error occurs.

In the example program:

```
public class Doubler {
    static int two() { return two(1); }
    private static int two(int i) { return 2*i; }
}
```

```
class Test extends Doubler {

    public static long two(long j) {return j+j; }

    public static void main(String[] args) {
        System.out.println(two(3));
        System.out.println(Doubler.two(3)); // compile-time error
    }

}
```

for the method invocation `two(1)` within class `Doubler`, there are two accessible methods named `two`, but only the second one is applicable, and so that is the one invoked at run time. For the method invocation `two(3)` within class `Test`, there are two applicable methods, but only the one in class `Test` is accessible, and so that is the one to be invoked at run time (the argument `3` is converted to type `long`). For the method invocation `Doubler.two(3)`, the class `Doubler`, not class `Test`, is searched for methods named `two`; the only applicable method is not accessible, and so this method invocation causes a compile-time error.

Another example is:

```
class ColoredPoint {
    int x, y;
    byte color;
    void setColor(byte color) { this.color = color; }
}

class Test {
    public static void main(String[] args) {
        ColoredPoint cp = new ColoredPoint();
        byte color = 37;
        cp.setColor(color);
        cp.setColor(37);                        // compile-time error
    }
}
```

Here, a compile-time error occurs for the second invocation of `setColor`, because no applicable method can be found at compile time. The type of the literal `37` is `int`, and `int` cannot be converted to `byte` by method invocation conversion. Assignment conversion, which is used in the initialization of the variable `color`, performs an implicit conversion of the constant from type `int` to `byte`, which is permitted because the value `37` is small enough to be represented in type `byte`; but such a conversion is not allowed for method invocation conversion.

If the method `setColor` had, however, been declared to take an `int` instead of a `byte`, then both method invocations would be correct; the first invocation would be allowed because method invocation conversion does permit a widening conversion from `byte` to `int`. However, a narrowing cast would then be required in the body of `setColor`:

```
    void setColor(int color) { this.color = (byte)color; }
```

15.11.2.2 *Choose the Most Specific Method*

If more than one method is both accessible and applicable to a method invocation, it is necessary to choose one to provide the descriptor for the run-time method dispatch. Java uses the rule that the *most specific* method is chosen.

The informal intuition is that one method declaration is more specific than another if any invocation handled by the first method could be passed on to the other one without a compile-time type error.

The precise definition is as follows. Let `m` be a name and suppose that there are two declarations of methods named `m`, each having `n` parameters. Suppose that one declaration appears within a class or interface `T` and that the types of the parameters are `T1, ..., Tn`; suppose moreover that the other declaration appears within a class or interface `U` and that the types of the parameters are `U1, ..., Un`. Then the method `m` declared in `T` is *more specific* than the method `m` declared in `U` if and only if both of the following are true:

- `T` can be converted to `U` by method invocation conversion.
- `Tj` can be converted to `Uj` by method invocation conversion, for all `j` from `1` to `n`.

A method is said to be *maximally specific* for a method invocation if it is applicable and accessible and there is no other applicable and accessible method that is more specific.

If there is exactly one maximally specific method, then it is in fact *the most specific* method; it is necessarily more specific than any other method that is applicable and accessible. It is then subjected to some further compile-time checks as described in §15.11.3.

It is possible that no method is the most specific, because there are two or more maximally specific method declarations. In this case, we say that the method invocation is *ambiguous*, and a compile-time error occurs.

15.11.2.3 *Example: Overloading Ambiguity*

Consider the example:

```
class Point { int x, y; }

class ColoredPoint extends Point { int color; }
```

```
class Test {

    static void test(ColoredPoint p, Point q) {
        System.out.println("(ColoredPoint, Point)");
    }

    static void test(Point p, ColoredPoint q) {
        System.out.println("(Point, ColoredPoint)");
    }

    public static void main(String[] args) {
        ColoredPoint cp = new ColoredPoint();
        test(cp, cp);                           // compile-time error
    }

}
```

This example produces an error at compile time. The problem is that there are two declarations of `test` that are applicable and accessible, and neither is more specific than the other. Therefore, the method invocation is ambiguous.

If a third definition of `test` were added:

```
    static void test(ColoredPoint p, ColoredPoint q) {
        System.out.println("(ColoredPoint, ColoredPoint)");
    }
```

then it would be more specific than the other two, and the method invocation would no longer be ambiguous.

15.11.2.4 *Example: Return Type Not Considered*

As another example, consider:

```
class Point { int x, y; }

class ColoredPoint extends Point { int color; }

class Test {

    static int test(ColoredPoint p) {
        return color;
    }

    static String test(Point p) {
        return "Point";
    }

    public static void main(String[] args) {
        ColoredPoint cp = new ColoredPoint();
        String s = test(cp);                    // compile-time error
    }

}
```

Here the most specific declaration of method `test` is the one taking a parameter of type `ColoredPoint`. Because the result type of the method is `int`, a compile-time error occurs because an `int` cannot be converted to a `String` by assignment conversion. This example shows that, in Java, the result types of methods do not participate in resolving overloaded methods, so that the second `test` method, which returns a `String`, is not chosen, even though it has a result type that would allow the example program to compile without error.

15.11.2.5 *Example: Compile-Time Resolution*

The most applicable method is chosen at compile time; its descriptor determines what method is actually executed at run time. If a new method is added to a class, then Java code that was compiled with the old definition of the class might not use the new method, even if a recompilation would cause this method to be chosen.

So, for example, consider two compilation units, one for class `Point`:

```
package points;

public class Point {

    public int x, y;

    public Point(int x, int y) { this.x = x; this.y = y; }

    public String toString() { return toString(""); }

    public String toString(String s) {
        return "(" + x + "," + y + s + ")";
    }

}
```

and one for class `ColoredPoint`:

```
package points;

public class ColoredPoint extends Point {

    public static final int
        RED = 0, GREEN = 1, BLUE = 2;

    public static String[] COLORS =
        { "red", "green", "blue" };

    public byte color;

    public ColoredPoint(int x, int y, int color) {
        super(x, y); this.color = (byte)color;
    }
```

```
        /** Copy all relevant fields of the argument into
            this ColoredPoint object. */
        public void adopt(Point p) { x = p.x; y = p.y; }

        public String toString() {
            String s = "," + COLORS[color];
            return super.toString(s);
        }

    }
```

Now consider a third compilation unit that uses ColoredPoint:

```
    import points.*;

    class Test {
        public static void main(String[] args) {
            ColoredPoint cp =
                new ColoredPoint(6, 6, ColoredPoint.RED);
            ColoredPoint cp2 =
                new ColoredPoint(3, 3, ColoredPoint.GREEN);
            cp.adopt(cp2);
            System.out.println("cp: " + cp);
        }
    }
```

The output is:

```
    cp: (3,3,red)
```

The application programmer who coded class Test has expected to see the word green, because the actual argument, a ColoredPoint, has a color field, and color would seem to be a "relevant field" (of course, the documentation for the package Points ought to have been much more precise!).

Notice, by the way, that the most specific method (indeed, the only applicable method) for the method invocation of adopt has a signature that indicates a method of one parameter, and the parameter is of type Point. This signature becomes part of the binary representation of class Test produced by the compiler and is used by the method invocation at run time.

Suppose the programmer reported this software error and the maintainer of the points package decided, after due deliberation, to correct it by adding a method to class ColoredPoint:

```
    public void adopt(ColoredPoint p) {
        adopt((Point)p); color = p.color;
    }
```

If the application programmer then runs the old binary file for Test with the new binary file for ColoredPoint, the output is still:

```
cp: (3,3,red)
```

because the old binary file for Test still has the descriptor "one parameter, whose type is Point; void" associated with the method call cp.adopt(cp2). If the source code for Test is recompiled, the compiler will then discover that there are now two applicable adopt methods, and that the signature for the more specific one is "one parameter, whose type is ColoredPoint; void"; running the program will then produce the desired output:

```
cp: (3,3,green)
```

With forethought about such problems, the maintainer of the points package could fix the ColoredPoint class to work with both newly compiled and old code, by adding defensive code to the old adopt method for the sake of old code that still invokes it on ColoredPoint arguments:

```
public void adopt(Point p) {
    if (p instanceof ColoredPoint)
        color = ((ColoredPoint)p).color;
    x = p.x; y = p.y;
}
```

A similar consideration applies if a method is to be moved from a class to a superclass. In this case a forwarding method can be left behind for the sake of old code. The maintainer of the points package might choose to move the adopt method that takes a Point argument up to class Point, so that all Point objects may enjoy the adopt functionality. To avoid compatibility problems with old binary code, the maintainer should leave a forwarding method behind in class ColoredPoint:

```
public void adopt(Point p) {
    if (p instanceof ColoredPoint)
        color = ((ColoredPoint)p).color;
    super.adopt(p);
}
```

Ideally, Java code should be recompiled whenever code that it depends on is changed. However, in an environment where different Java classes are maintained by different organizations, this is not always feasible. Defensive programming with careful attention to the problems of class evolution can make upgraded code much more robust. See §13 for a detailed discussion of binary compatibility and type evolution.

15.11.3 Compile-Time Step 3: Is the Chosen Method Appropriate?

If there is a most specific method declaration for a method invocation, it is called the *compile-time declaration* for the method invocation. Two further checks must be made on the compile-time declaration:

- If the method invocation has, before the left parenthesis, a *MethodName* of the form *Identifier*, and the method invocation appears within a `static` method, a static initializer, or the initializer for a `static` variable, then the compile-time declaration must be `static`. If, instead, the compile-time declaration for the method invocation is for an instance method, then a compile-time error occurs. (The reason is that a method invocation of this form cannot be used to invoke an instance method in places where `this` (§15.7.2) is not defined.)
- If the method invocation has, before the left parenthesis, a *MethodName* of the form *TypeName* `.` *Identifier*, then the compile-time declaration should be `static`. If the compile-time declaration for the method invocation is for an instance method, then a compile-time error occurs. (The reason is that a method invocation of this form does not specify a reference to an object that can serve as `this` within the instance method.)
- If the compile-time declaration for the method invocation is `void`, then the method invocation must be a top-level expression, that is, the *Expression* in an expression statement (§14.7) or in the *ForInit* or *ForUpdate* part of a `for` statement (§14.12), or a compile-time error occurs. (The reason is that such a method invocation produces no value and so must be used only in a situation where a value is not needed.)

The following compile-time information is then associated with the method invocation for use at run time:

- The name of the method.
- The class or interface that contains the compile-time declaration.
- The number of parameters and the types of the parameters, in order.
- The result type, or `void`, as declared in the compile-time declaration.
- The invocation mode, computed as follows:
  - If the compile-time declaration has the `static` modifier, then the invocation mode is `static`.
  - Otherwise, if the compile-time declaration has the `private` modifier, then the invocation mode is `nonvirtual`.

- Otherwise, if the part of the method invocation before the left parenthesis is of the form `super . ` *Identifier*, then the invocation mode is `super`.
- Otherwise, if the compile-time declaration is in an interface, then the invocation mode is `interface`.
- Otherwise, the invocation mode is `virtual`.

If the compile-time declaration for the method invocation is not `void`, then the type of the method invocation expression is the result type specified in the compile-time declaration.

15.11.4 Runtime Evaluation of Method Invocation

At run time, method invocation requires five steps. First, a *target reference* may be computed. Second, the argument expressions are evaluated. Third, the accessibility of the method to be invoked is checked. Fourth, the actual code for the method to be executed is located. Fifth, a new activation frame is created, synchronization is performed if necessary, and control is transferred to the method code.

15.11.4.1 *Compute Target Reference (If Necessary)*

There are several cases to consider, depending on which of the three productions for *MethodInvocation* (§15.11) is involved:

- If the first production for *MethodInvocation*, which includes a *MethodName*, is involved, then there are three subcases:
  - If the *MethodName* is a simple name, that is, just an *Identifier*, then there are two subcases:
    - If the invocation mode is `static`, then there is no target reference.
    - Otherwise, the target reference is the value of `this`.
  - If the *MethodName* is a qualified name of the form *TypeName* `.` *Identifier*, then there is no target reference.
  - If the *MethodName* is a qualified name of the form *FieldName* `.` *Identifier*, then there are two subcases:
    - If the invocation mode is `static`, then there is no target reference.
    - Otherwise, the target reference is the value of the expression *FieldName*.

- If the second production for *MethodInvocation*, which includes a *Primary*, is involved, then there are two subcases:
  - If the invocation mode is `static`, then there is no target reference. The expression *Primary* is evaluated, but the result is then discarded.
  - Otherwise, the expression *Primary* is evaluated and the result is used as the target reference.

  In either case, if the evaluation of the *Primary* expression completes abruptly, then no part of any argument expression appears to have been evaluated, and the method invocation completes abruptly for the same reason.
- If the third production for *MethodInvocation*, which includes the keyword `super`, is involved, then the target reference is the value of `this`.

15.11.4.2 *Evaluate Arguments*

The argument expressions are evaluated in order, from left to right. If the evaluation of any argument expression completes abruptly, then no part of any argument expression to its right appears to have been evaluated, and the method invocation completes abruptly for the same reason.

15.11.4.3 *Check Accessibility of Type and Method*

Let *C* be the class containing the method invocation, and let *T* be the class or interface that contained the method being invoked, and *m* be the name of the method, as determined at compile time (§15.11.3).

A Java Virtual Machine must insure, as part of linkage, that the method *m* still exists in the type *T*. If this is not true, then a `NoSuchMethodError` (which is a subclass of `IncompatibleClassChangeError`) occurs. If the invocation mode is `interface`, then the virtual machine must also check that the target reference type still implements the specified interface. If the target reference type does not still implement the interface, then an `IncompatibleClassChangeError` occurs.

The virtual machine must also insure, during linkage, that the type *T* and the method *m* are accessible. For the type *T*:

- If *T* is in the same package as *C*, then *T* is accessible.
- If *T* is in a different package than *C*, and *T* is `public`, then *T* is accessible.

For the method *m*:

- If *m* is `public`, then *m* is accessible. (All members of interfaces are `public` (§9.2)).
- If *m* is `protected`, then *m* is accessible if and only if either *T* is in the same package as *C*, or *C* is *T* or a subclass of *T*.
- If *m* has default (package) access, then *m* is accessible if and only if *T* is in the same package as *C*.
- If *m* is `private`, then *m* is accessible if and only if and *C* is *T*.

If either *T* or *m* is not accessible, then an `IllegalAccessError` occurs (§12.3).

15.11.4.4 *Locate Method to Invoke*

Here inside my paper cup,
Everything is looking up.
—Jim Webb, *Paper Cup* (1967)

The strategy for method lookup depends on the invocation mode.

If the invocation mode is `static`, no target reference is needed and overriding is not allowed. Method *m* of class *T* is the one to be invoked.

Otherwise, an instance method is to be invoked and there is a target reference. If the target reference is `null`, a `NullPointerException` is thrown at this point. Otherwise, the target reference is said to refer to a *target object* and will be used as the value of the keyword `this` in the invoked method. The other four possibilities for the invocation mode are then considered.

If the invocation mode is `nonvirtual`, overriding is not allowed. Method *m* of class *T* is the one to be invoked.

Otherwise, the invocation mode is `interface`, `virtual`, or `super`, and overriding may occur. A *dynamic method lookup* is used. The dynamic lookup process starts from a class *S*, determined as follows:

- If the invocation mode is `interface` or `virtual`, then *S* is initially the actual run-time class *R* of the target object. If the target object is an array, *R* is the class `Object`. (Note that for invocation mode `interface`, *R* necessarily implements *T*; for invocation mode `virtual`, *R* is necessarily either *T* or a subclass of *T*.)
- If the invocation mode is `super`, then *S* is initially the superclass of the class *C* that contains the method invocation.

The dynamic method lookup uses the following procedure to search class *S*, and then the superclasses of class *S*, as necessary, for method *m*.

1. If class *S* contains a declaration for a method named *m* with the same descriptor (same number of parameters, the same parameter types, and the same return type) required by the method invocation as determined at compile time (§15.11.3), then this is the method to be invoked, and the procedure terminates. (We note that as part of the loading and linking process that the virtual machine checks that an overriding method is at least as accessible as the overridden method; an `IncompatibleClassChangeError` occurs if this is not the case.)

2. Otherwise, if *S* is not *T*, this same lookup procedure is performed using the superclass of *S*; whatever it comes up with is the result of this lookup.

This procedure will find a suitable method when it reaches class *T*, because otherwise an `IllegalAccessError` would have been thrown by the checks of the previous section §15.11.4.3.

We note that the dynamic lookup process, while described here explicitly, will often be implemented implicitly, for example as a side-effect of the construction and use of per-class method dispatch tables, or the construction of other per-class structures used for efficient dispatch.

15.11.4.5 *Create Frame, Synchronize, Transfer Control*

A method *m* in some class *S* has been identified as the one to be invoked.

Now a new *activation frame* is created, containing the target reference (if any) and the argument values (if any), as well as enough space for the local variables and stack for the method to be invoked and any other bookkeeping information that may be required by the implementation (stack pointer, program counter, reference to previous activation frame, and the like). If there is not sufficient memory available to create such an activation frame, an `OutOfMemoryError` is thrown.

The newly created activation frame becomes the current activation frame. The effect of this is to assign the argument values to corresponding freshly created parameter variables of the method, and to make the target reference available as `this`, if there is a target reference.

If the method *m* is a `native` method but the necessary native, implementation-dependent binary code has not been loaded (§20.16.15, §20.16.13) or otherwise cannot be dynamically linked, then an `UnsatisfiedLinkError` is thrown.

If the method *m* is not `synchronized`, control is transferred to the body of the method *m* to be invoked.

If the method *m* is `synchronized`, then an object must be locked before the transfer of control. No further progress can be made until the current thread can obtain the lock. If there is a target reference, then the target must be locked; otherwise the `Class` object for class *S*, the class of the method *m*, must be locked. Control is then transferred to the body of the method *m* to be invoked. The object is automatically unlocked when execution of the body of the method has completed, whether normally or abruptly. The locking and unlocking behavior is exactly as if the body of the method were embedded in a `synchronized` statement (§14.17).

15.11.4.6 *Implementation Note: Combining Frames*

In order to allow certain kinds of code optimization, implementations are permitted some freedom to combine activation frames. Suppose that a method invocation within class *C* is to invoke a method *m* within class *S*. Then the current activation frame may be used to provide space for *S* instead of creating a new activation frame only if one of the following conditions is true:

- Class *C* and class *S* have the same class loader (§20.14) and class *S* is not `SecurityManager` or a subclass of `SecurityManager`.
- Class *S* has no class loader (this fact indicates that it is a system class); class *S* is not `SecurityManager` or a subclass of `SecurityManager`; and method *m* is known not to call, directly or indirectly, any method of `SecurityManager` (§20.17) or any of its subclasses.

15.11.4.7 *Example: Target Reference and Static Methods*

When a target reference is computed and then discarded because the invocation mode is `static`, the reference is not examined to see whether it is `null`:

```
class Test {

    static void mountain() {
        System.out.println("Monadnock");
    }

    static Test favorite(){
        System.out.print("Mount ");
        return null;
    }

    public static void main(String[] args) {
        favorite().mountain();
    }

}
```

which prints:

```
Mount Monadnock
```

Here `favorite` returns `null`, yet no `NullPointerException` is thrown.

15.11.4.8 *Example: Evaluation Order*

As part of an instance method invocation (§15.11), there is an expression that denotes the object to be invoked. This expression appears to be fully evaluated before any part of any argument expression to the method invocation is evaluated.

So, for example, in:

```
class Test {
    public static void main(String[] args) {
        String s = "one";
        if (s.startsWith(s = "two"))
            System.out.println("oops");
    }
}
```

the occurrence of s before "`.startsWith`" is evaluated first, before the argument expression `s="two"`. Therefore, a reference to the string `"one"` is remembered as the target reference before the local variable s is changed to refer to the string `"two"`. As a result, the `startsWith` method (§20.12.20) is invoked for target object `"one"` with argument `"two"`, so the result of the invocation is `false`, as the string `"one"` does not start with `"two"`. It follows that the test program does not print "oops".

15.11.4.9 *Example: Overriding*

In the example:

```
class Point {

    final int EDGE = 20;
    int x, y;

    void move(int dx, int dy) {
        x += dx; y += dy;
        if (Math.abs(x) >= EDGE || Math.abs(y) >= EDGE)
            clear();
    }

    void clear() {
        System.out.println("\tPoint clear");
        x = 0; y = 0;
    }

}

class ColoredPoint extends Point {

    int color;
```

```
    void clear() {
        System.out.println("\tColoredPoint clear");
        super.clear();
        color = 0;
    }
}
```

the subclass `ColoredPoint` extends the `clear` abstraction defined by its superclass `Point`. It does so by overriding the `clear` method with its own method, which invokes the `clear` method of its superclass, using the form `super.clear`.

This method is then invoked whenever the target object for an invocation of `clear` is a `ColoredPoint`. Even the method `move` in `Point` invokes the `clear` method of class `ColoredPoint` when the class of `this` is `ColoredPoint`, as shown by the output of this test program:

```
class Test {
    public static void main(String[] args) {
        Point p = new Point();
        System.out.println("p.move(20,20):");
        p.move(20, 20);
        ColoredPoint cp = new ColoredPoint();
        System.out.println("cp.move(20,20):");
        cp.move(20, 20);
        p = new ColoredPoint();
        System.out.println("p.move(20,20), p colored:");
        p.move(20, 20);
    }
}
```

which is:

```
p.move(20,20):
    Point clear
cp.move(20,20):
    ColoredPoint clear
    Point clear
p.move(20,20), p colored:
    ColoredPoint clear
    Point clear
```

Overriding is sometimes called "late-bound self-reference"; in this example it means that the reference to `clear` in the body of `Point.move` (which is really syntactic shorthand for `this.clear`) invokes a method chosen "late" (at run time, based on the run-time class of the object referenced by `this`) rather than a method chosen "early" (at compile time, based only on the type of `this`). This provides the Java programmer a powerful way of extending abstractions and is a key idea in object-oriented programming.

15.11.4.10 *Example: Method Invocation using* `super`

An overridden instance method of a superclass may be accessed by using the keyword `super` to access the members of the immediate superclass, bypassing any overriding declaration in the class that contains the method invocation.

When accessing an instance variable, `super` means the same as a cast of `this` (§15.10.2), but this equivalence does not hold true for method invocation. This is demonstrated by the example:

```
class T1 {
    String s() { return "1"; }
}

class T2 extends T1 {
    String s() { return "2"; }
}

class T3 extends T2 {

    String s() { return "3"; }

    void test() {
        System.out.println("s()=\t\t"+s());
        System.out.println("super.s()=\t"+super.s());
        System.out.print("((T2)this).s()=\t");
            System.out.println(((T2)this).s());
        System.out.print("((T1)this).s()=\t");
            System.out.println(((T1)this).s());
    }

}

class Test {
    public static void main(String[] args) {
        T3 t3 = new T3();
        t3.test();
    }
}
```

which produces the output:

```
s()=            3
super.s()=      2
((T2)this).s()= 3
((T1)this).s()= 3
```

The casts to types `T1` and `T2` do not change the method that is invoked, because the instance method to be invoked is chosen according to the run-time class of the object referred to be `this`. A cast does not change the class of an object; it only checks that the class is compatible with the specified type.

15.12 Array Access Expressions

An array access expression refers to a variable that is a component of an array.

ArrayAccess:
  ExpressionName `[` *Expression* `]`
  PrimaryNoNewArray `[` *Expression* `]`

An array access expression contains two subexpressions, the *array reference expression* (before the left bracket) and the *index expression* (within the brackets). Note that the array reference expression may be a name or any primary expression that is not an array creation expression (§15.9).

The type of the array reference expression must be an array type (call it `T[]`, an array whose components are of type `T`) or a compile-time error results. Then the type of the array access expression is `T`.

The index expression undergoes unary numeric promotion (§5.6.1); the promoted type must be `int`.

The result of an array reference is a variable of type `T`, namely the variable within the array selected by the value of the index expression. This resulting variable, which is a component of the array, is never considered `final`, even if the array reference was obtained from a `final` variable.

15.12.1 Runtime Evaluation of Array Access

An array access expression is evaluated using the following procedure:

- First, the array reference expression is evaluated. If this evaluation completes abruptly, then the array access completes abruptly for the same reason and the index expression is not evaluated.
- Otherwise, the index expression is evaluated. If this evaluation completes abruptly, then the array access completes abruptly for the same reason.
- Otherwise, if the value of the array reference expression is `null`, then a `NullPointerException` is thrown.
- Otherwise, the value of the array reference expression indeed refers to an array. If the value of the index expression is less than zero, or greater than or equal to the array's length, then an `IndexOutOfBoundsException` is thrown.
- Otherwise, the result of the array reference is the variable of type `T`, within the array, selected by the value of the index expression. (Note that this resulting variable, which is a component of the array, is never considered `final`, even if the array reference expression is a `final` variable.)

15.12.2 Examples: Array Access Evaluation Order

In an array access, the expression to the left of the brackets appears to be fully evaluated before any part of the expression within the brackets is evaluated. For example, in the (admittedly monstrous) expression `a[(a=b)[3]]`, the expression `a` is fully evaluated before the expression `(a=b)[3]`; this means that the original value of `a` is fetched and remembered while the expression `(a=b)[3]` is evaluated. This array referenced by the original value of `a` is then subscripted by a value that is element `3` of another array (possibly the same array) that was referenced by `b` and is now also referenced by `a`.

Thus, the example:

```
class Test {
    public static void main(String[] args) {
        int[] a = { 11, 12, 13, 14 };
        int[] b = { 0, 1, 2, 3 };
        System.out.println(a[(a=b)[3]]);
    }
}
```

prints:

```
14
```

because the monstrous expression's value is equivalent to `a[b[3]]` or `a[3]` or `14`.

If evaluation of the expression to the left of the brackets completes abruptly, no part of the expression within the brackets will appear to have been evaluated. Thus, the example:

```
class Test {
    public static void main(String[] args) {
        int index = 1;
        try {
            skedaddle()[index=2]++;
        } catch (Exception e) {
            System.out.println(e + ", index=" + index);
        }
    }
    static int[] skedaddle() throws Exception {
        throw new Exception("Ciao");
    }
}
```

prints:

```
java.lang.Exception: Ciao, index=1
```

because the embedded assignment of `2` to `index` never occurs.

If the array reference expression produces `null` instead of a reference to an array, then a `NullPointerException` is thrown at run time, but only after all parts of the array reference expression have been evaluated and only if these evaluations completed normally. Thus, the example:

```
class Test {

    public static void main(String[] args) {
        int index = 1;
        try {
            nada()[index=2]++;
        } catch (Exception e) {
            System.out.println(e + ", index=" + index);
        }
    }

    static int[] nada() { return null; }

}
```

prints:

```
java.lang.NullPointerException, index=2
```

because the embedded assignment of 2 to `index` occurs before the check for a null pointer. As a related example, the program:

```
class Test {

    public static void main(String[] args) {
        int[] a = null;
        try {
            int i = a[vamoose()];
            System.out.println(i);
        } catch (Exception e) {
            System.out.println(e);
        }
    }

    static int vamoose() throws Exception {
        throw new Exception("Twenty-three skidoo!");
    }

}
```

always prints:

```
java.lang.Exception: Twenty-three skidoo!
```

A `NullPointerException` never occurs, because the index expression must be completely evaluated before any part of the indexing operation occurs, and that includes the check as to whether the value of the left-hand operand is `null`.

15.13 Postfix Expressions

Postfix expressions include uses of the postfix `++` and `--` operators. Also, as discussed in §15.7, names are not considered to be primary expressions, but are handled separately in the grammar to avoid certain ambiguities. They become interchangeable only here, at the level of precedence of postfix expressions.

PostfixExpression:
    Primary
    ExpressionName
    PostIncrementExpression
    PostDecrementExpression

15.13.1 Names

A name occurring in an expression may be, syntactically, an *ExpressionName* (§6.5). The meaning of such an *ExpressionName* depends on its form:

- If it is a simple name, that is, just an *Identifier*, then there are two cases:
  - If the *Identifier* occurs within the scope of a parameter or local variable named by that same *Identifier*, then the type of the *ExpressionName* is the declared type of the parameter or local variable; moreover, the value of the *ExpressionName* is a variable, namely, the parameter or local variable itself.
  - Otherwise, the *ExpressionName* is treated exactly as if it had been the field access expression (§15.10):

    `this.`*Identifier*

    containing the keyword `this` (§15.7.2).
- Otherwise, if it is a qualified name of the form *PackageName* `.` *Identifier*, then a compile-time error occurs.
- Otherwise, if it is a qualified name of the form *TypeName* `.` *Identifier*, then it is refers to a `static` field of the class or interface named by the *TypeName*. A compile-time error occurs if *TypeName* does not name a class or interface. A compile-time error occurs if the class or interface named by *TypeName* does not contain an accessible static field named by the *Identifier*. The type of the *ExpressionName* is the declared type of the `static` field. The value of the *ExpressionName* is a variable, namely, the `static` field itself.

- Otherwise, it is a qualified name of the form *Ename* . *Identifier*, where *Ename* is itself an *ExpressionName*, and the *ExpressionName* is treated exactly as if it had been the field access expression (§15.10):

  (*Ename*).*Identifier*

  containing a parenthesized expression (§15.7.3).

15.13.2 Postfix Increment Operator ++

PostIncrementExpression:
  PostfixExpression ++

A postfix expression followed by a ++ operator is a postfix increment expression. The result of the postfix expression must be a variable of a numeric type, or a compile-time error occurs. The type of the postfix increment expression is the type of the variable. The result of the postfix increment expression is not a variable, but a value.

At run time, if evaluation of the operand expression completes abruptly, then the postfix increment expression completes abruptly for the same reason and no incrementation occurs. Otherwise, the value `1` is added to the value of the variable and the sum is stored back into the variable. Before the addition, binary numeric promotion (§5.6.2) is performed on the value `1` and the value of the variable. If necessary, the sum is narrowed by a narrowing primitive conversion (§5.1.3) to the type of the variable before it is stored. The value of the postfix increment expression is the value of the variable *before* the new value is stored.

A variable that is declared `final` cannot be incremented, because when an access of a `final` variable is used as an expression, the result is a value, not a variable. Thus, it cannot be used as the operand of a postfix increment operator.

15.13.3 Postfix Decrement Operator --

PostDecrementExpression:
  PostfixExpression --

A postfix expression followed by a -- operator is a postfix decrement expression. The result of the postfix expression must be a variable of a numeric type, or a compile-time error occurs. The type of the postfix decrement expression is the type of the variable. The result of the postfix decrement expression is not a variable, but a value.

At run time, if evaluation of the operand expression completes abruptly, then the postfix decrement expression completes abruptly for the same reason and no decrementation occurs. Otherwise, the value `1` is subtracted from the value of the variable and the difference is stored back into the variable. Before the subtraction, binary numeric promotion (§5.6.2) is performed on the value `1` and the value of the variable. If necessary, the difference is narrowed by a narrowing primitive conversion (§5.1.3) to the type of the variable before it is stored. The value of the postfix decrement expression is the value of the variable *before* the new value is stored.

A variable that is declared `final` cannot be decremented, because when an access of a `final` variable is used as an expression, the result is a value, not a variable. Thus, it cannot be used as the operand of a postfix decrement operator.

15.14 Unary Operators

The *unary operators* include `+`, `-`, `++`, `--`, `~`, `!`, and cast operators. Expressions with unary operators group right-to-left, so that `-~x` means the same as `-(~x)`.

UnaryExpression:
- *PreIncrementExpression*
- *PreDecrementExpression*
- `+` *UnaryExpression*
- `-` *UnaryExpression*
- *UnaryExpressionNotPlusMinus*

PreIncrementExpression:
- `++` *UnaryExpression*

PreDecrementExpression:
- `--` *UnaryExpression*

UnaryExpressionNotPlusMinus:
- *PostfixExpression*
- `~` *UnaryExpression*
- `!` *UnaryExpression*
- *CastExpression*

The following productions from §15.15 are repeated here for convenience:

CastExpression:
- `(` *PrimitiveType* `)` *UnaryExpression*
- `(` *ReferenceType* `)` *UnaryExpressionNotPlusMinus*

This portion of the Java grammar contains some tricks to avoid two potential syntactic ambiguities.

The first potential ambiguity would arise in expressions such as `(p)+q`, which looks, to a C or C++ programmer, as though it could be either be a cast to type `p` of a unary + operating on q, or a binary addition of two quantities p and q. In C and C++, the parser handles this problem by performing a limited amount of semantic analysis as it parses, so that it knows whether p is the name of a type or the name of a variable.

Java takes a different approach. The result of the + operator must be numeric, and all type names involved in casts on numeric values are known keywords. Thus, if p is a keyword naming a primitive type, then (p)+q can make sense only as a cast of a unary expression. However, if p is not a keyword naming a primitive type, then (p)+q can make sense only as a binary arithmetic operation. Similar remarks apply to the - operator. The grammar shown above splits *CastExpression* into two cases to make this distinction. The nonterminal *UnaryExpression* includes all unary operator, but the nonterminal *UnaryExpressionNotPlusMinus* excludes uses of all unary operators that could also be binary operators, which in Java are + and -.

The second potential ambiguity is that the expression (p)++ could, to a C or C++ programmer, appear to be either a postfix increment of a parenthesized expression or the beginning of a cast, for example, in (p)++q. As before, parsers for C and C++ know whether p is the name of a type or the name of a variable. But a parser using only one-token lookahead and no semantic analysis during the parse would not be able to tell, when ++ is the lookahead token, whether (p) should be considered a *Primary* expression or left alone for later consideration as part of a *CastExpression*.

In Java, the result of the ++ operator must be numeric, and all type names involved in casts on numeric values are known keywords. Thus, if p is a keyword naming a primitive type, then (p)++ can make sense only as a cast of a prefix increment expression, and there had better be an operand such as q following the ++. However, if p is not a keyword naming a primitive type, then (p)++ can make sense only as a postfix increment of p. Similar remarks apply to the -- operator. The nonterminal *UnaryExpressionNotPlusMinus* therefore also excludes uses of the prefix operators ++ and --.

15.14.1 Prefix Increment Operator ++

A unary expression preceded by a ++ operator is a prefix increment expression. The result of the unary expression must be a variable of a numeric type, or a compile-time error occurs. The type of the prefix increment expression is the type of the variable. The result of the prefix increment expression is not a variable, but a value.

At run time, if evaluation of the operand expression completes abruptly, then the prefix increment expression completes abruptly for the same reason and no incrementation occurs. Otherwise, the value 1 is added to the value of the variable and the sum is stored back into the variable. Before the addition, binary numeric promotion (§5.6.2) is performed on the value `1` and the value of the variable. If necessary, the sum is narrowed by a narrowing primitive conversion (§5.1.3) to the type of the variable before it is stored. The value of the prefix increment expression is the value of the variable *after* the new value is stored.

A variable that is declared `final` cannot be incremented, because when an access of a `final` variable is used as an expression, the result is a value, not a variable. Thus, it cannot be used as the operand of a prefix increment operator.

15.14.2 Prefix Decrement Operator --

He must increase, but I must decrease.
—John 3:30

A unary expression preceded by a `--` operator is a prefix decrement expression. The result of the unary expression must be a variable of a numeric type, or a compile-time error occurs. The type of the prefix decrement expression is the type of the variable. The result of the prefix decrement expression is not a variable, but a value.

At run time, if evaluation of the operand expression completes abruptly, then the prefix decrement expression completes abruptly for the same reason and no decrementation occurs. Otherwise, the value `1` is subtracted from the value of the variable and the difference is stored back into the variable. Before the subtraction, binary numeric promotion (§5.6.2) is performed on the value `1` and the value of the variable. If necessary, the difference is narrowed by a narrowing primitive conversion (§5.1.3) to the type of the variable before it is stored. The value of the prefix decrement expression is the value of the variable *after* the new value is stored.

A variable that is declared `final` cannot be decremented, because when an access of a `final` variable is used as an expression, the result is a value, not a variable. Thus, it cannot be used as the operand of a prefix decrement operator.

15.14.3 Unary Plus Operator +

The type of the operand expression of the unary `+` operator must be a primitive numeric type, or a compile-time error occurs. Unary numeric promotion (§5.6.1) is performed on the operand. The type of the unary plus expression is the promoted type of the operand. The result of the unary plus expression is not a variable, but a value, even if the result of the operand expression is a variable.

At run time, the value of the unary plus expression is the promoted value of the operand.

15.14.4 Unary Minus Operator -

It is so very agreeable to hear a voice and to see all the signs of that expression.
—Gertrude Stein, *Rooms* (1914), in *Tender Buttons*

The type of the operand expression of the unary - operator must be a primitive numeric type, or a compile-time error occurs. Unary numeric promotion (§5.6.1) is performed on the operand. The type of the unary minus expression is the promoted type of the operand.

At run time, the value of the unary plus expression is the arithmetic negation of the promoted value of the operand.

For integer values, negation is the same as subtraction from zero. Java uses two's-complement representation for integers, and the range of two's-complement values is not symmetric, so negation of the maximum negative `int` or `long` results in that same maximum negative number. Overflow occurs in this case, but no exception is thrown. For all integer values `x`, `-x` equals `(~x)+1`.

For floating-point values, negation is not the same as subtraction from zero, because if `x` is `+0.0`, then `0.0-x` equals `+0.0`, but `-x` equals `-0.0`. Unary minus merely inverts the sign of a floating-point number. Special cases of interest:

- If the operand is NaN, the result is NaN (recall that NaN has no sign).
- If the operand is an infinity, the result is the infinity of opposite sign.
- If the operand is a zero, the result is the zero of opposite sign.

15.14.5 Bitwise Complement Operator ~

The type of the operand expression of the unary ~ operator must be a primitive integral type, or a compile-time error occurs. Unary numeric promotion (§5.6.1) is performed on the operand. The type of the unary bitwise complement expression is the promoted type of the operand.

At run time, the value of the unary bitwise complement expression is the bitwise complement of the promoted value of the operand; note that, in all cases, `~x` equals `(-x)-1`.

15.14.6 Logical Complement Operator !

The type of the operand expression of the unary ! operator must be `boolean`, or a compile-time error occurs. The type of the unary logical complement expression is `boolean`.

At run time, the value of the unary logical complement expression is `true` if the operand value is `false` and `false` if the operand value is `true`.

15.15 Cast Expressions

My days among the dead are passed;
Around me I behold,
Where'er these casual eyes are cast,
The mighty minds of old . . .
—Robert Southey (1774–1843),
Occasional Pieces, xviii

A cast expression converts, at run time, a value of one numeric type to a similar value of another numeric type; or confirms, at compile time, that the type of an expression is `boolean`; or checks, at run time, that a reference value refers to an object whose class is compatible with a specified reference type.

CastExpression:
(*PrimitiveType* $Dims_{opt}$) *UnaryExpression*
(*ReferenceType*) *UnaryExpressionNotPlusMinus*

See §15.14 for a discussion of the distinction between *UnaryExpression* and *UnaryExpressionNotPlusMinus*.

The type of a cast expression is the type whose name appears within the parentheses. (The parentheses and the type they contain are sometimes called the *cast operator*.) The result of a cast expression is not a variable, but a value, even if the result of the operand expression is a variable.

At run time, the operand value is converted by casting conversion (§5.4) to the type specified by the cast operator.

Not all casts are permitted by the Java language. Some casts result in an error at compile time. For example, a primitive value may not be cast to a reference type. Some casts can be proven, at compile time, always to be correct at run time. For example, it is always correct to convert a value of a class type to the type of its superclass; such a cast should require no special action at run time. Finally, some casts cannot be proven to be either always correct or always incorrect at compile time. Such casts require a test at run time. A `ClassCastException` is thrown if a cast is found at run time to be impermissible.

15.16 Multiplicative Operators

The operators `*`, `/`, and `%` are called the *multiplicative operators*. They have the same precedence and are syntactically left-associative (they group left-to-right).

MultiplicativeExpression:
  UnaryExpression
  MultiplicativeExpression `*` *UnaryExpression*
  MultiplicativeExpression `/` *UnaryExpression*
  MultiplicativeExpression `%` *UnaryExpression*

The type of each of the operands of a multiplicative operator must be a primitive numeric type, or a compile-time error occurs. Binary numeric promotion is performed on the operands (§5.6.2). The type of a multiplicative expression is the promoted type of its operands. If this promoted type is `int` or `long`, then integer arithmetic is performed; if this promoted type is `float` or `double`, then floating-point arithmetic is performed.

15.16.1 Multiplication Operator *

Entia non sunt multiplicanda praeter necessitatem.
—William of Occam (c. 1320)

The binary `*` operator performs multiplication, producing the product of its operands. Multiplication is a commutative operation if the operand expressions have no side effects. While integer multiplication is associative when the operands are all of the same type, floating-point multiplication is not associative.

If an integer multiplication overflows, then the result is the low-order bits of the mathematical product as represented in some sufficiently large two's-complement format. As a result, if overflow occurs, then the sign of the result may not be the same as the sign of the mathematical product of the two operand values.

The result of a floating-point multiplication is governed by the rules of IEEE 754 arithmetic:

- If either operand is NaN, the result is NaN.
- If the result is not NaN, the sign of the result is positive if both operands have the same sign, and negative if the operands have different signs.
- Multiplication of an infinity by a zero results in NaN.
- Multiplication of an infinity by a finite value results in a signed infinity. The sign is determined by the rule stated above.

- In the remaining cases, where neither an infinity or NaN is involved, the product is computed. If the magnitude of the product is too large to represent, we say the operation overflows. The result is then an infinity of appropriate sign. If the magnitude is too small to represent, we say the operation underflows; the result is then a zero of appropriate sign. Otherwise, the product is rounded to the nearest representable value using IEEE 754 round-to-nearest mode. The Java language requires support of gradual underflow as defined by IEEE 754 (§4.2.4).

Despite the fact that overflow, underflow, or loss of information may occur, evaluation of a multiplication operator `*` never throws a run-time exception.

15.16.2 Division Operator /

Gallia est omnis divisa in partes tres.
—Julius Caesar, *Commentaries on the Gallic Wars* (58 B.C.)

The binary `/` operator performs division, producing the quotient of its operands. The left-hand operand is the dividend and the right-hand operand is the divisor.

Integer division rounds toward `0`. That is, the quotient produced for operands n and d that are integers after binary numeric promotion (§5.6.2) is an integer value q whose magnitude is as large as possible while satisfying $|d \cdot q| \leq |n|$; moreover, q is positive when $|n| \geq |d|$ and n and d have the same sign, but q is negative when $|n| \geq |d|$ and n and d have opposite signs. There is one special case that does not satisfy this rule: if the dividend is the negative integer of largest possible magnitude for its type, and the divisor is `-1`, then integer overflow occurs and the result is equal to the dividend. Despite the overflow, no exception is thrown in this case. On the other hand, if the value of the divisor in an integer division is `0`, then an `ArithmeticException` is thrown.

The result of a floating-point division is determined by the specification of IEEE arithmetic:

- If either operand is NaN, the result is NaN.
- If the result is not NaN, the sign of the result is positive if both operands have the same sign, negative if the operands have different signs.
- Division of an infinity by an infinity results in NaN.
- Division of an infinity by a finite value results in a signed infinity. The sign is determined by the rule stated above.
- Division of a finite value by an infinity results in a signed zero. The sign is determined by the rule stated above.

- Division of a zero by a zero results in NaN; division of zero by any other finite value results in a signed zero. The sign is determined by the rule stated above.
- Division of a nonzero finite value by a zero results in a signed infinity. The sign is determined by the rule stated above.
- In the remaining cases, where neither an infinity, nor a zero, nor NaN is involved, the quotient is computed. If the magnitude of the quotient is too large to represent, we say the operation overflows; the result is then an infinity of appropriate sign. If the magnitude is too small to represent, we say the operation underflows and the result is then a zero of appropriate sign. Otherwise, the quotient is rounded to the nearest representable value using IEEE 754 round-to-nearest mode. The Java language requires support of gradual underflow as defined by IEEE 754 (§4.2.4).

Despite the fact that overflow, underflow, division by zero, or loss of information may occur, evaluation of a floating-point division operator `/` never throws a run-time exception.

15.16.3 Remainder Operator `%`

And on the pedestal these words appear:
"My name is Ozymandias, king of kings:
Look on my works, ye Mighty, and despair!"
Nothing beside remains.
—Percy Bysshe Shelley, *Ozymandias* (1817)

The binary `%` operator is said to yield the remainder of its operands from an implied division; the left-hand operand is the dividend and the right-hand operand is the divisor.

In C and C++, the remainder operator accepts only integral operands, but in Java, it also accepts floating-point operands.

The remainder operation for operands that are integers after binary numeric promotion (§5.6.2) produces a result value such that `(a/b)*b+(a%b)` is equal to `a`. This identity holds even in the special case that the dividend is the negative integer of largest possible magnitude for its type and the divisor is `-1` (the remainder is `0`). It follows from this rule that the result of the remainder operation can be negative only if the dividend is negative, and can be positive only if the dividend is positive; moreover, the magnitude of the result is always less than the magnitude of the divisor. If the value of the divisor for an integer remainder operator is `0`, then an `ArithmeticException` is thrown.

Examples:

```
5%3 produces 2              (note that 5/3 produces 1)
5%(-3) produces 2           (note that 5/(-3) produces -1)
(-5)%3 produces -2          (note that (-5)/3 produces -1)
(-5)%(-3) produces -2       (note that (-5)/(-3) produces 1)
```

The result of a floating-point remainder operation as computed by the `%` operator is *not* the same as that produced by the remainder operation defined by IEEE 754. The IEEE 754 remainder operation computes the remainder from a rounding division, not a truncating division, and so its behavior is *not* analogous to that of the usual integer remainder operator. Instead, the Java language defines `%` on floating-point operations to behave in a manner analogous to that of the Java integer remainder operator; this may be compared with the C library function `fmod`. The IEEE 754 remainder operation may be computed by the Java library routine `Math.IEEEremainder` (§20.11.14).

The result of a Java floating-point remainder operation is determined by the rules of IEEE arithmetic:

- If either operand is NaN, the result is NaN.
- If the result is not NaN, the sign of the result equals the sign of the dividend.
- If the dividend is an infinity, or the divisor is a zero, or both, the result is NaN.
- If the dividend is finite and the divisor is an infinity, the result equals the dividend.
- If the dividend is a zero and the divisor is finite, the result equals the dividend.
- In the remaining cases, where neither an infinity, nor a zero, nor NaN is involved, the floating-point remainder r from the division of a dividend n by a divisor d is defined by the mathematical relation $r = n - (d \cdot q)$ where q is an integer that is negative only if n/d is negative and positive only if n/d is positive, and whose magnitude is as large as possible without exceeding the magnitude of the true mathematical quotient of n and d.

Evaluation of a floating-point remainder operator `%` never throws a run-time exception, even if the right-hand operand is zero. Overflow, underflow, or loss of precision cannot occur.

Examples:

```
5.0%3.0 produces 2.0
5.0%(-3.0) produces 2.0
(-5.0)%3.0 produces -2.0
(-5.0)%(-3.0) produces -2.0
```

15.17 Additive Operators

The operators + and - are called the *additive operators*. They have the same precedence and are syntactically left-associative (they group left-to-right).

AdditiveExpression:
  MultiplicativeExpression
  AdditiveExpression + *MultiplicativeExpression*
  AdditiveExpression - *MultiplicativeExpression*

If the type of either operand of a + operator is `String`, then the operation is string concatenation.

Otherwise, the type of each of the operands of the + operator must be a primitive numeric type, or a compile-time error occurs.

In every case, the type of each of the operands of the binary - operator must be a primitive numeric type, or a compile-time error occurs.

15.17.1 String Concatenation Operator +

If only one operand expression is of type `String`, then string conversion is performed on the other operand to produce a string at run time. The result is a reference to a newly created `String` object that is the concatenation of the two operand strings. The characters of the left-hand operand precede the characters of the right-hand operand in the newly created string.

15.17.1.1 *String Conversion*

Any type may be converted to type `String` by *string conversion.*

A value *x* of primitive type *T* is first converted to a reference value as if by giving it as an argument to an appropriate class instance creation expression:

- If *T* is `boolean`, then use `new Boolean(x)` (§20.4).
- If *T* is `char`, then use `new Character(x)` (§20.5).
- If *T* is `byte`, `short`, or `int`, then use `new Integer(x)` (§20.7).
- If *T* is `long`, then use `new Long(x)` (§20.8).
- If *T* is `float`, then use `new Float(x)` (§20.9).
- If *T* is `double`, then use `new Double(x)` (§20.10).

This reference value is then converted to type `String` by string conversion.

Now only reference values need to be considered. If the reference is `null`, it is converted to the string `"null"` (four ASCII characters `n`, `u`, `l`, `l`). Otherwise, the conversion is performed as if by an invocation of the `toString` method of the referenced object with no arguments; but if the result of invoking the `toString` method is `null`, then the string `"null"` is used instead. The `toString` method (§20.1.2) is defined by the primordial class `Object` (§20.1); many classes override it, notably `Boolean`, `Character`, `Integer`, `Long`, `Float`, `Double`, and `String`.

15.17.1.2 *Optimization of String Concatenation*

An implementation may choose to perform conversion and concatenation in one step to avoid creating and then discarding an intermediate `String` object. To increase the performance of repeated string concatenation, a Java compiler may use the `StringBuffer` class (§20.13) or a similar technique to reduce the number of intermediate `String` objects that are created by evaluation of an expression.

For primitive objects, an implementation may also optimize away the creation of a wrapper object by converting directly from a primitive type to a string.

15.17.1.3 *Examples of String Concatenation*

The example expression:

```
"The square root of 2 is " + Math.sqrt(2)
```

produces the result:

```
"The square root of 2 is 1.4142135623730952"
```

The + operator is syntactically left-associative, no matter whether it is later determined by type analysis to represent string concatenation or addition. In some cases care is required to get the desired result. For example, the expression:

```
a + b + c
```

is always regarded as meaning:

```
(a + b) + c
```

Therefore the result of the expression:

```
1 + 2 + " fiddlers"
```

is:

```
"3 fiddlers"
```

but the result of:

```
"fiddlers " + 1 + 2
```

is:

```
"fiddlers 12"
```

In this jocular little example:

```
class Bottles {

    static void printSong(Object stuff, int n) {
        String plural = "s";
        loop: while (true) {
            System.out.println(n + " bottle" + plural
                + " of " + stuff + " on the wall,");
            System.out.println(n + " bottle" + plural
                + " of " + stuff + ";");
            System.out.println("You take one down "
                + "and pass it around:");
            --n;
            plural = (n == 1) ? "" : "s";
            if (n == 0)
                break loop;
            System.out.println(n + " bottle" + plural
                + " of " + stuff + " on the wall!");
            System.out.println();
        }
        System.out.println("No bottles of " +
                            stuff + " on the wall!");
    }

}
```

the method `printSong` will print a version of a children's song. Popular values for stuff include `"pop"` and `"beer"`; the most popular value for `n` is `100`. Here is the output that results from `Bottles.printSong("slime", 3)`:

```
3 bottles of slime on the wall,
3 bottles of slime;
You take one down and pass it around:
2 bottles of slime on the wall!

2 bottles of slime on the wall,
2 bottles of slime;
You take one down and pass it around:
1 bottle of slime on the wall!

1 bottle of slime on the wall,
1 bottle of slime;
You take one down and pass it around:
No bottles of slime on the wall!
```

In the code, note the careful conditional generation of the singular "`bottle`" when appropriate rather than the plural "`bottles`"; note also how the string concatenation operator was used to break the long constant string:

```
"You take one down and pass it around:"
```

into two pieces to avoid an inconveniently long line in the source code.

15.17.2 Additive Operators (+ and -) for Numeric Types

The binary + operator performs addition when applied to two operands of numeric type, producing the sum of the operands. The binary - operator performs subtraction, producing the difference of two numeric operands.

Binary numeric promotion is performed on the operands (§5.6.2). The type of an additive expression on numeric operands is the promoted type of its operands. If this promoted type is `int` or `long`, then integer arithmetic is performed; if this promoted type is `float` or `double`, then floating-point arithmetic is performed.

Addition is a commutative operation if the operand expressions have no side effects. Integer addition is associative when the operands are all of the same type, but floating-point addition is not associative.

If an integer addition overflows, then the result is the low-order bits of the mathematical sum as represented in some sufficiently large two's-complement format. If overflow occurs, then the sign of the result is not the same as the sign of the mathematical sum of the two operand values.

The result of a floating-point addition is determined using the following rules of IEEE arithmetic:

- If either operand is NaN, the result is NaN.
- The sum of two infinities of opposite sign is NaN.
- The sum of two infinities of the same sign is the infinity of that sign.
- The sum of an infinity and a finite value is equal to the infinite operand.
- The sum of two zeros of opposite sign is positive zero.
- The sum of two zeros of the same sign is the zero of that sign.
- The sum of a zero and a nonzero finite value is equal to the nonzero operand.
- The sum of two nonzero finite values of the same magnitude and opposite sign is positive zero.
- In the remaining cases, where neither an infinity, nor a zero, nor NaN is involved, and the operands have the same sign or have different magnitudes, the sum is computed. If the magnitude of the sum is too large to represent, we

say the operation overflows; the result is then an infinity of appropriate sign. If the magnitude is too small to represent, we say the operation underflows; the result is then a zero of appropriate sign. Otherwise, the sum is rounded to the nearest representable value using IEEE 754 round-to-nearest mode. The Java language requires support of gradual underflow as defined by IEEE 754 (§4.2.4).

The binary `-` operator performs subtraction when applied to two operands of numeric type producing the difference of its operands; the left-hand operand is the minuend and the right-hand operand is the subtrahend. For both integer and floating-point subtraction, it is always the case that `a-b` produces the same result as `a+(-b)`. Note that, for integer values, subtraction from zero is the same as negation. However, for floating-point operands, subtraction from zero is *not* the same as negation, because if `x` is `+0.0`, then `0.0-x` equals `+0.0`, but `-x` equals `-0.0`.

Despite the fact that overflow, underflow, or loss of information may occur, evaluation of a numeric additive operator never throws a run-time exception.

15.18 Shift Operators

What, I say, is to become of those wretches?
. . . What more can you say to them than "shift for yourselves?"
—Thomas Paine, *The American Crisis* (1780)

The *shift operators* include left shift <<, signed right shift >>, and unsigned right shift >>>; they are syntactically left-associative (they group left-to-right). The left-hand operand of a shift operator is the value to be shifted; the right-hand operand specifies the shift distance.

ShiftExpression:
    AdditiveExpression
    ShiftExpression << *AdditiveExpression*
    ShiftExpression >> *AdditiveExpression*
    ShiftExpression >>> *AdditiveExpression*

The type of each of the operands of a shift operator must be a primitive integral type, or a compile-time error occurs. Binary numeric promotion (§5.6.2) is *not* performed on the operands; rather, unary numeric promotion (§5.6.1) is performed on each operand separately. The type of the shift expression is the promoted type of the left-hand operand.

If the promoted type of the left-hand operand is `int`, only the five lowest-order bits of the right-hand operand are used as the shift distance. It is as if the right-hand operand were subjected to a bitwise logical AND operator `&` (§15.21.1) with the mask value `0x1f`. The shift distance actually used is therefore always in the range 0 to 31, inclusive.

If the promoted type of the left-hand operand is `long`, then only the six lowest-order bits of the right-hand operand are used as the shift distance. It is as if the right-hand operand were subjected to a bitwise logical AND operator `&` (§15.21.1) with the mask value `0x3f`. The shift distance actually used is therefore always in the range 0 to 63, inclusive.

At run time, shift operations are performed on the two's complement integer representation of the value of the left operand.

The value of `n<<s` is `n` left-shifted `s` bit positions; this is equivalent (even if overflow occurs) to multiplication by two to the power `s`.

The value of `n>>s` is `n` right-shifted `s` bit positions with sign-extension. The resulting value is $\lfloor n/2^s \rfloor$. For nonnegative values of `n`, this is equivalent to truncating integer division, as computed by the integer division operator `/`, by two to the power `s`.

The value of `n>>>s` is `n` right-shifted `s` bit positions with zero-extension. If `n` is positive, then the result is the same as that of `n>>s`; if `n` is negative, the result is equal to that of the expression `(n>>s)+(2<<~s)` if the type of the left-hand operand is `int`, and to the result of the expression `(n>>s)+(2L<<~s)` if the type of the left-hand operand is `long`. The added term `(2<<~s)` or `(2L<<~s)` cancels out the propagated sign bit. (Note that, because of the implicit masking of the right-hand operand of a shift operator, `~s` as a shift distance is equivalent to `31-s` when shifting an `int` value and to `63-s` when shifting a `long` value.)

15.19 Relational Operators

The *relational operators* are syntactically left-associative (they group left-to-right), but this fact is not useful; for example, `a<b<c` parses as `(a<b)<c`, which is always a compile-time error, because the type of `a<b` is always `boolean` and `<` is not an operator on `boolean` values.

RelationalExpression:
  ShiftExpression
  RelationalExpression `<` *ShiftExpression*
  RelationalExpression `>` *ShiftExpression*
  RelationalExpression `<=` *ShiftExpression*
  RelationalExpression `>=` *ShiftExpression*
  RelationalExpression `instanceof` *ReferenceType*

The type of a relational expression is always `boolean`.

15.19.1 Numerical Comparison Operators <, <=, >, and >=

The type of each of the operands of a numerical comparison operator must be a primitive numeric type, or a compile-time error occurs. Binary numeric promotion is performed on the operands (§5.6.2). If the promoted type of the operands is `int` or `long`, then signed integer comparison is performed; if this promoted type is `float` or `double`, then floating-point comparison is performed.

The result of a floating-point comparison, as determined by the specification of the IEEE 754 standard, is:

- If either operand is NaN, then the result is `false`.
- All values other than NaN are ordered, with negative infinity less than all finite values, and positive infinity greater than all finite values.
- Positive zero and negative zero are considered equal. Therefore, `-0.0<0.0` is `false`, for example, but `-0.0<=0.0` is `true`. (Note, however, that the methods `Math.min` (§20.11.27, §20.11.28) and `Math.max` (§20.11.31, §20.11.32) treat negative zero as being strictly smaller than positive zero.)

Subject to these considerations for floating-point numbers, the following rules then hold for integer operands or for floating-point operands other than NaN:

- The value produced by the < operator is `true` if the value of the left-hand operand is less than the value of the right-hand operand, and otherwise is `false`.
- The value produced by the <= operator is `true` if the value of the left-hand operand is less than or equal to the value of the right-hand operand, and otherwise is `false`.
- The value produced by the > operator is `true` if the value of the left-hand operand is greater than the value of the right-hand operand, and otherwise is `false`.
- The value produced by the >= operator is `true` if the value of the left-hand operand is greater than or equal to the value of the right-hand operand, and otherwise is `false`.

15.19.2 Type Comparison Operator `instanceof`

The type of a *RelationalExpression* operand of the `instanceof` operator must be a reference type or the null type; otherwise, a compile-time error occurs. The *ReferenceType* mentioned after the `instanceof` operator must denote a reference type; otherwise, a compile-time error occurs.

At run time, the result of the `instanceof` operator is `true` if the value of the *RelationalExpression* is not `null` and the reference could be cast (§15.15) to the *ReferenceType* without raising a `ClassCastException`. Otherwise the result is `false`.

If a cast of the *RelationalExpression* to the *ReferenceType* would be rejected as a compile-time error, then the `instanceof` relational expression likewise produces a compile-time error. In such a situation, the result of the `instanceof` expression could never be `true`.

Consider the example program:

```
class Point { int x, y; }

class Element { int atomicNumber; }

class Test {
    public static void main(String[] args) {
        Point p = new Point();
        Element e = new Element();
        if (e instanceof Point) {           // compile-time error
            System.out.println("I get your point!");
            p = (Point)e;                   // compile-time error
        }
    }
}
```

This example results in two compile-time errors. The cast `(Point)e` is incorrect because no instance of `Element` or any of its possible subclasses (none are shown here) could possibly be an instance of any subclass of `Point`. The `instanceof` expression is incorrect for exactly the same reason. If, on the other hand, the class `Point` were a subclass of `Element` (an admittedly strange notion in this example):

```
class Point extends Element { int x, y; }
```

then the cast would be possible, though it would require a run-time check, and the `instanceof` expression would then be sensible and valid. The cast `(Point)e` would never raise an exception because it would not be executed if the value of `e` could not correctly be cast to type `Point`.

15.20 Equality Operators

The equality operators are syntactically left-associative (they group left-to-right), but this fact is essentially never useful; for example, `a==b==c` parses as `(a==b)==c`. The result type of `a==b` is always `boolean`, and `c` must therefore be of type `boolean` or a compile-time error occurs. Thus, `a==b==c` does *not* test to see whether `a`, `b`, and `c` are all equal.

EqualityExpression:
  RelationalExpression
  EqualityExpression == *RelationalExpression*
  EqualityExpression != *RelationalExpression*

The == (equal to) and the != (not equal to) operators are analogous to the relational operators except for their lower precedence. Thus, `a<b==c<d` is `true` whenever `a<b` and `c<d` have the same truth value.

The equality operators may be used to compare two operands of numeric type, or two operands of type `boolean`, or two operands that are each of either reference type or the null type. All other cases result in a compile-time error. The type of an equality expression is always `boolean`.

In all cases, `a!=b` produces the same result as `!(a==b)`. The equality operators are commutative if the operand expressions have no side effects.

15.20.1 Numerical Equality Operators == and !=

If the operands of an equality operator are both of primitive numeric type, binary numeric promotion is performed on the operands (§5.6.2). If the promoted type of the operands is `int` or `long`, then an integer equality test is performed; if the promoted type is `float` or `double`, then a floating-point equality test is performed.

Floating-point equality testing is performed in accordance with the rules of the IEEE 754 standard:

- If either operand is NaN, then the result of == is `false` but the result of != is `true`. Indeed, the test `x!=x` is true if and only if the value of `x` is NaN. (The methods `Float.isNaN` (§20.9.19) and `Double.isNaN` (§20.10.17) may also be used to test whether a value is NaN.)
- Positive zero and negative zero are considered equal. Therefore, `-0.0==0.0` is `true`, for example.
- Otherwise, two distinct floating-point values are considered unequal by the equality operators. In particular, there is one value representing positive infinity and one value representing negative infinity; each compares equal only to itself, and each compares unequal to all other values.

Subject to these considerations for floating-point numbers, the following rules then hold for integer operands or for floating-point operands other than NaN:

- The value produced by the == operator is `true` if the value of the left-hand operand is equal to the value of the right-hand operand; otherwise, the result is `false`.
- The value produced by the != operator is `true` if the value of the left-hand operand is not equal to the value of the right-hand operand; otherwise, the result is `false`.

15.20.2 Boolean Equality Operators == and !=

If the operands of an equality operator are both of type `boolean`, then the operation is boolean equality. The `boolean` equality operators are associative.

The result of == is `true` if the operands are both `true` or both `false`; otherwise, the result is `false`.

The result of != is `false` if the operands are both `true` or both `false`; otherwise, the result is `true`. Thus != behaves the same as ^ (§15.21.2) when applied to boolean operands.

15.20.3 Reference Equality Operators == and !=

Things are more like they are now than they ever were before.
—Dwight D. Eisenhower

If the operands of an equality operator are both of either reference type or the null type, then the operation is object equality.

A compile-time error occurs if it is impossible to convert the type of either operand to the type of the other by a casting conversion (§5.4). The run-time values of the two operands would necessarily be unequal.

At run time, the result of == is `true` if the operand values are both `null` or both refer to the same object or array; otherwise, the result is `false`.

The result of != is `false` if the operand values are both `null` or both refer to the same object or array; otherwise, the result is `true`.

While == may be used to compare references of type `String`, such an equality test determines whether or not the two operands refer to the same `String` object. The result is `false` if the operands are distinct `String` objects, even if they contain the same sequence of characters. The contents of two strings `s` and `t` can be tested for equality by the method invocation `s.equals(t)` (§20.12.9). See also §3.10.5 and §20.12.47.

15.21 Bitwise and Logical Operators

The *bitwise operators* and *logical operators* include the AND operator &, exclusive OR operator ^, and inclusive OR operator |. These operators have different precedence, with & having the highest precedence and | the lowest precedence. Each of these operators is syntactically left-associative (each groups left-to-right). Each operator is commutative if the operand expressions have no side effects. Each operator is associative.

AndExpression:
  EqualityExpression
  AndExpression & *EqualityExpression*

ExclusiveOrExpression:
  AndExpression
  ExclusiveOrExpression ^ *AndExpression*

InclusiveOrExpression:
  ExclusiveOrExpression
  InclusiveOrExpression | *ExclusiveOrExpression*

The bitwise and logical operators may be used to compare two operands of numeric type or two operands of type `boolean`. All other cases result in a compile-time error.

15.21.1 Integer Bitwise Operators &, ^, and |

When both operands of an operator &, ^, or | are of primitive integral type, binary numeric promotion is first performed on the operands (§5.6.2). The type of the bitwise operator expression is the promoted type of the operands.

For &, the result value is the bitwise AND of the operand values.

For ^, the result value is the bitwise exclusive OR of the operand values.

For |, the result value is the bitwise inclusive OR of the operand values.

For example, the result of the expression `0xff00 & 0xf0f0` is `0xf000`. The result of `0xff00 ^ 0xf0f0` is `0x0ff0`.The result of `0xff00 | 0xf0f0` is `0xfff0`.

15.21.2 Boolean Logical Operators &, ^, and |

When both operands of a &, ^, or | operator are of type `boolean`, then the type of the bitwise operator expression is `boolean`.

For &, the result value is `true` if both operand values are `true`; otherwise, the result is `false`.

For `^`, the result value is `true` if the operand values are different; otherwise, the result is `false`.

For `|`, the result value is `false` if both operand values are `false`; otherwise, the result is `true`.

15.22 Conditional-And Operator &&

The && operator is like & (§15.21.2), but evaluates its right-hand operand only if the value of its left-hand operand is `true`. It is syntactically left-associative (it groups left-to-right). It is fully associative with respect to both side effects and result value; that is, for any expressions *a*, *b*, and *c*, evaluation of the expression `((`*a*`)&&(`*b*`))&&(`*c*`)` produces the same result, with the same side effects occurring in the same order, as evaluation of the expression `(`*a*`)&&((`*b*`)&&(`*c*`))`.

ConditionalAndExpression:
  InclusiveOrExpression
  ConditionalAndExpression && *InclusiveOrExpression*

Each operand of && must be of type `boolean`, or a compile-time error occurs. The type of a conditional-and expression is always `boolean`.

At run time, the left-hand operand expression is evaluated first; if its value is `false`, the value of the conditional-and expression is `false` and the right-hand operand expression is not evaluated. If the value of the left-hand operand is `true`, then the right-hand expression is evaluated and its value becomes the value of the conditional-and expression. Thus, && computes the same result as & on `boolean` operands. It differs only in that the right-hand operand expression is evaluated conditionally rather than always.

15.23 Conditional-Or Operator ||

The `||` operator is like `|` (§15.21.2), but evaluates its right-hand operand only if the value of its left-hand operand is `false`. It is syntactically left-associative (it groups left-to-right). It is fully associative with respect to both side effects and result value; that is, for any expressions *a*, *b*, and *c*, evaluation of the expression `((`*a*`)||(`*b*`))||(`*c*`)` produces the same result, with the same side effects occurring in the same order, as evaluation of the expression `(`*a*`)||((`*b*`)||(`*c*`))`.

ConditionalOrExpression:
  ConditionalAndExpression
  ConditionalOrExpression `||` *ConditionalAndExpression*

Each operand of `||` must be of type `boolean`, or a compile-time error occurs. The type of a conditional-or expression is always `boolean`.

At run time, the left-hand operand expression is evaluated first; if its value is `true`, the value of the conditional-or expression is `true` and the right-hand operand expression is not evaluated. If the value of the left-hand operand is `false`, then the right-hand expression is evaluated and its value becomes the value of the conditional-or expression. Thus, `||` computes the same result as `|` on `boolean` operands. It differs only in that the right-hand operand expression is evaluated conditionally rather than always.

15.24 Conditional Operator `? :`

The conditional operator `? :` uses the boolean value of one expression to decide which of two other expressions should be evaluated.

The conditional operator is syntactically right-associative (it groups right-to-left), so that `a?b:c?d:e?f:g` means the same as `a?b:(c?d:(e?f:g))`.

ConditionalExpression:
  ConditionalOrExpression
  ConditionalOrExpression `?` *Expression* `:` *ConditionalExpression*

The conditional operator has three operand expressions; `?` appears between the first and second expressions, and `:` appears between the second and third expressions.

The first expression must be of type `boolean`, or a compile-time error occurs.

The conditional operator may be used to choose between second and third operands of numeric type, or second and third operands of type `boolean`, or second and third operands that are each of either reference type or the null type. All other cases result in a compile-time error.

Note that it is not permitted for either the second or the third operand expression to be an invocation of a `void` method. In fact, it is not permitted for a conditional expression to appear in any context where an invocation of a `void` method could appear (§14.7).

The type of a conditional expression is determined as follows:

- If the second and third operands have the same type (which may be the null type), then that is the type of the conditional expression.
- Otherwise, if the second and third operands have numeric type, then there are several cases:
  - If one of the operands is of type `byte` and the other is of type `short`, then the type of the conditional expression is `short`.
  - If one of the operands is of type *T* where *T* is `byte`, `short`, or `char`, and the other operand is a constant expression of type `int` whose value is representable in type *T*, then the type of the conditional expression is *T*.
  - Otherwise, binary numeric promotion (§5.6.2) is applied to the operand types, and the type of the conditional expression is the promoted type of the second and third operands.
- If one of the second and third operands is of the null type and the type of the other is a reference type, then the type of the conditional expression is that reference type.
- If the second and third operands are of different reference types, then it must be possible to convert one of the types to the other type (call this latter type *T*) by assignment conversion (§5.2); the type of the conditional expression is *T*. It is a compile-time error if neither type is assignment compatible with the other type.

At run time, the first operand expression of the conditional expression is evaluated first; its `boolean` value is then used to choose either the second or the third operand expression:

- If the value of the first operand is `true`, then the second operand expression is chosen.
- If the value of the first operand is `false`, then the third operand expression is chosen.

The chosen operand expression is then evaluated and the resulting value is converted to the type of the conditional expression as determined by the rules stated above. The operand expression not chosen is not evaluated for that particular evaluation of the conditional expression.

15.25 Assignment Operators

There are 12 *assignment operators*; all are syntactically right-associative (they group right-to-left). Thus, `a=b=c` means `a=(b=c)`, which assigns the value of `c` to `b` and then assigns the value of `b` to `a`.

AssignmentExpression:
  ConditionalExpression
  Assignment

Assignment:
  LeftHandSide AssignmentOperator AssignmentExpression

LeftHandSide:
  ExpressionName
  FieldAccess
  ArrayAccess

AssignmentOperator: one of
  `=  *=  /=  %=  +=  -=  <<=  >>=  >>>=  &=  ^=  |=`

The result of the first operand of an assignment operator must be a variable, or a compile-time error occurs. This operand may be a named variable, such as a local variable or a field of the current object or class, or it may be a computed variable, as can result from a field access (§15.10) or an array access (§15.12). The type of the assignment expression is the type of the variable.

At run time, the result of the assignment expression is the value of the variable after the assignment has occurred. The result of an assignment expression is not itself a variable.

A variable that is declared `final` cannot be assigned to, because when an access of a `final` variable is used as an expression, the result is a value, not a variable, and so it cannot be used as the operand of an assignment operator.

15.25.1 Simple Assignment Operator =

A compile-time error occurs if the type of the right-hand operand cannot be converted to the type of the variable by assignment conversion (§5.2).

At run time, the expression is evaluated in one of two ways. If the left-hand operand expression is not an array access expression, then three steps are required:

- First, the left-hand operand is evaluated to produce a variable. If this evaluation completes abruptly, then the assignment expression completes abruptly for the same reason; the right-hand operand is not evaluated and no assignment occurs.

- Otherwise, the right-hand operand is evaluated. If this evaluation completes abruptly, then the assignment expression completes abruptly for the same reason and no assignment occurs.
- Otherwise, the value of the right-hand operand is converted to the type of the left-hand variable and the result of the conversion is stored into the variable.

If the left-hand operand expression is an array access expression (§15.12), then many steps are required:

- First, the array reference subexpression of the left-hand operand array access expression is evaluated. If this evaluation completes abruptly, then the assignment expression completes abruptly for the same reason; the index subexpression (of the left-hand operand array access expression) and the right-hand operand are not evaluated and no assignment occurs.
- Otherwise, the index subexpression of the left-hand operand array access expression is evaluated. If this evaluation completes abruptly, then the assignment expression completes abruptly for the same reason and the right-hand operand is not evaluated and no assignment occurs.
- Otherwise, the right-hand operand is evaluated. If this evaluation completes abruptly, then the assignment expression completes abruptly for the same reason and no assignment occurs.
- Otherwise, if the value of the array reference subexpression is `null`, then no assignment occurs and a `NullPointerException` is thrown.
- Otherwise, the value of the array reference subexpression indeed refers to an array. If the value of the index subexpression is less than zero, or greater than or equal to the length of the array, then no assignment occurs and an `IndexOutOfBoundsException` is thrown.
- Otherwise, the value of the index subexpression is used to select a component of the array referred to by the value of the array reference subexpression. This component is a variable; call its type *SC*. Also, let *TC* be the type of the left-hand operand of the assignment operator as determined at compile time.
    - If *TC* is a primitive type, then *SC* is necessarily the same as *TC*. The value of the right-hand operand is converted to a value of type *TC* and stored into the selected array component.

- If *T* is a reference type, then *SC* may not be the same as *T*, but rather a type that extends or implements *TC*. Let *RC* be the class of the object referred to by the value of the right-hand operand at run time.

  The compiler may be able to prove at compile time that the array component will be of type *TC* exactly (for example, *TC* might be `final`). But if the compiler cannot prove at compile time that the array component will be of type *TC* exactly, then a check must be performed at run time to ensure that the class *RC* is assignment compatible (§5.2) with the actual type *SC* of the array component. This check is similar to a narrowing cast (§5.4, §15.15), except that if the check fails, an `ArrayStoreException` is thrown rather than a `ClassCastException`. Therefore:

  - If class *RC* is not assignable to type *SC*, then no assignment occurs and an `ArrayStoreException` is thrown.
  - Otherwise, the reference value of the right-hand operand is stored into the selected array component.

The rules for assignment to an array component are illustrated by the following example program:

```
class ArrayReferenceThrow extends RuntimeException { }

class IndexThrow extends RuntimeException { }

class RightHandSideThrow extends RuntimeException { }

class IllustrateSimpleArrayAssignment {

    static Object[] objects = { new Object(), new Object() };

    static Thread[] threads = { new Thread(), new Thread() };

    static Object[] arrayThrow() {
        throw new ArrayReferenceThrow();
    }

    static int indexThrow() { throw new IndexThrow(); }

    static Thread rightThrow() {
        throw new RightHandSideThrow();
    }

    static String name(Object q) {
        String sq = q.getClass().getName();
        int k = sq.lastIndexOf('.');
        return (k < 0) ? sq : sq.substring(k+1);
    }

    static void testFour(Object[] x, int j, Object y) {
        String sx = x == null ? "null" : name(x[0]) + "s";
        String sy = name(y);
```

```
        System.out.println();
        try {
            System.out.print(sx + "[throw]=throw => ");
            x[indexThrow()] = rightThrow();
            System.out.println("Okay!");
        } catch (Throwable e) { System.out.println(name(e)); }
        try {
            System.out.print(sx + "[throw]=" + sy + " => ");
            x[indexThrow()] = y;
            System.out.println("Okay!");
        } catch (Throwable e) { System.out.println(name(e)); }
        try {
            System.out.print(sx + "[" + j + "]=throw => ");
            x[j] = rightThrow();
            System.out.println("Okay!");
        } catch (Throwable e) { System.out.println(name(e)); }
        try {
            System.out.print(sx + "[" + j + "]=" + sy + " => ");
            x[j] = y;
            System.out.println("Okay!");
        } catch (Throwable e) { System.out.println(name(e)); }
    }

    public static void main(String[] args) {
        try {
            System.out.print("throw[throw]=throw => ");
            arrayThrow()[indexThrow()] = rightThrow();
            System.out.println("Okay!");
        } catch (Throwable e) { System.out.println(name(e)); }
        try {
            System.out.print("throw[throw]=Thread => ");
            arrayThrow()[indexThrow()] = new Thread();
            System.out.println("Okay!");
        } catch (Throwable e) { System.out.println(name(e)); }
        try {
            System.out.print("throw[1]=throw => ");
            arrayThrow()[1] = rightThrow();
            System.out.println("Okay!");
        } catch (Throwable e) { System.out.println(name(e)); }
        try {
            System.out.print("throw[1]=Thread => ");
            arrayThrow()[1] = new Thread();
            System.out.println("Okay!");
        } catch (Throwable e) { System.out.println(name(e)); }

        testFour(null, 1, new StringBuffer());
        testFour(null, 1, new StringBuffer());
        testFour(null, 9, new Thread());
        testFour(null, 9, new Thread());
        testFour(objects, 1, new StringBuffer());
        testFour(objects, 1, new Thread());
        testFour(objects, 9, new StringBuffer());
```

```
        testFour(objects, 9, new Thread());
        testFour(threads, 1, new StringBuffer());
        testFour(threads, 1, new Thread());
        testFour(threads, 9, new StringBuffer());
        testFour(threads, 9, new Thread());
    }
}
```

This program prints:

```
throw[throw]=throw => ArrayReferenceThrow
throw[throw]=Thread => ArrayReferenceThrow
throw[1]=throw => ArrayReferenceThrow
throw[1]=Thread => ArrayReferenceThrow

null[throw]=throw => IndexThrow
null[throw]=StringBuffer => IndexThrow
null[1]=throw => RightHandSideThrow
null[1]=StringBuffer => NullPointerException

null[throw]=throw => IndexThrow
null[throw]=StringBuffer => IndexThrow
null[1]=throw => RightHandSideThrow
null[1]=StringBuffer => NullPointerException

null[throw]=throw => IndexThrow
null[throw]=Thread => IndexThrow
null[9]=throw => RightHandSideThrow
null[9]=Thread => NullPointerException

null[throw]=throw => IndexThrow
null[throw]=Thread => IndexThrow
null[9]=throw => RightHandSideThrow
null[9]=Thread => NullPointerException

Objects[throw]=throw => IndexThrow
Objects[throw]=StringBuffer => IndexThrow
Objects[1]=throw => RightHandSideThrow
Objects[1]=StringBuffer => Okay!

Objects[throw]=throw => IndexThrow
Objects[throw]=Thread => IndexThrow
Objects[1]=throw => RightHandSideThrow
Objects[1]=Thread => Okay!

Objects[throw]=throw => IndexThrow
Objects[throw]=StringBuffer => IndexThrow
Objects[9]=throw => RightHandSideThrow
Objects[9]=StringBuffer => IndexOutOfBoundsException

Objects[throw]=throw => IndexThrow
Objects[throw]=Thread => IndexThrow
Objects[9]=throw => RightHandSideThrow
Objects[9]=Thread => IndexOutOfBoundsException
```

```
Threads[throw]=throw => IndexThrow
Threads[throw]=StringBuffer => IndexThrow
Threads[1]=throw => RightHandSideThrow
Threads[1]=StringBuffer => ArrayStoreException

Threads[throw]=throw => IndexThrow
Threads[throw]=Thread => IndexThrow
Threads[1]=throw => RightHandSideThrow
Threads[1]=Thread => Okay!

Threads[throw]=throw => IndexThrow
Threads[throw]=StringBuffer => IndexThrow
Threads[9]=throw => RightHandSideThrow
Threads[9]=StringBuffer => IndexOutOfBoundsException

Threads[throw]=throw => IndexThrow
Threads[throw]=Thread => IndexThrow
Threads[9]=throw => RightHandSideThrow
Threads[9]=Thread => IndexOutOfBoundsException
```

The most interesting case of the lot is the one thirteenth from the end:

```
Threads[1]=StringBuffer => ArrayStoreException
```

which indicates that the attempt to store a reference to a `StringBuffer` into an array whose components are of type `Thread` throws an `ArrayStoreException`. The code is type-correct at compile time: the assignment has a left-hand side of type `Object[]` and a right-hand side of type `Object`. At run time, the first actual argument to method `testFour` is a reference to an instance of "array of `Thread`" and the third actual argument is a reference to an instance of class `StringBuffer`.

15.25.2 Compound Assignment Operators

All compound assignment operators require both operands to be of primitive type, except for +=, which allows the right-hand operand to be of any type if the left-hand operand is of type `String`.

A compound assignment expression of the form *`E1 op= E2`* is equivalent to *`E1 = (T)((E1) op (E2))`*, where *`T`* is the type of *`E1`*, except that *`E1`* is evaluated only once. Note that the implied cast to type *`T`* may be either an identity conversion (§5.1.1) or a narrowing primitive conversion (§5.1.3). For example, the following code is correct:

```
short x = 3;
x += 4.6;
```

and results in `x` having the value `7` because it is equivalent to:

```
short x = 3;
x = (short)(x + 4.6);
```

At run time, the expression is evaluated in one of two ways. If the left-hand operand expression is not an array access expression, then four steps are required:

- First, the left-hand operand is evaluated to produce a variable. If this evaluation completes abruptly, then the assignment expression completes abruptly for the same reason; the right-hand operand is not evaluated and no assignment occurs.
- Otherwise, the value of the left-hand operand is saved and then the right-hand operand is evaluated. If this evaluation completes abruptly, then the assignment expression completes abruptly for the same reason and no assignment occurs.
- Otherwise, the saved value of the left-hand variable and the value of the right-hand operand are used to perform the binary operation indicated by the compound assignment operator. If this operation completes abruptly (the only possibility is an integer division by zero—see §15.16.2), then the assignment expression completes abruptly for the same reason and no assignment occurs.
- Otherwise, the result of the binary operation is converted to the type of the left-hand variable and the result of the conversion is stored into the variable.

If the left-hand operand expression is an array access expression (§15.12), then many steps are required:

- First, the array reference subexpression of the left-hand operand array access expression is evaluated. If this evaluation completes abruptly, then the assignment expression completes abruptly for the same reason; the index subexpression (of the left-hand operand array access expression) and the right-hand operand are not evaluated and no assignment occurs.
- Otherwise, the index subexpression of the left-hand operand array access expression is evaluated. If this evaluation completes abruptly, then the assignment expression completes abruptly for the same reason and the right-hand operand is not evaluated and no assignment occurs.
- Otherwise, if the value of the array reference subexpression is `null`, then no assignment occurs and a `NullPointerException` is thrown.
- Otherwise, the value of the array reference subexpression indeed refers to an array. If the value of the index subexpression is less than zero, or greater than or equal to the length of the array, then no assignment occurs and an `IndexOutOfBoundsException` is thrown.
- Otherwise, the value of the index subexpression is used to select a component of the array referred to by the value of the array reference subexpression. The

value of this component is saved and then the right-hand operand is evaluated. If this evaluation completes abruptly, then the assignment expression completes abruptly for the same reason and no assignment occurs. (For a simple assignment operator, the evaluation of the right-hand operand occurs before the checks of the array reference subexpression and the index subexpression, but for a compound assignment operator, the evaluation of the right-hand operand occurs after these checks.)

- Otherwise, consider the array component selected in the previous step, whose value was saved. This component is a variable; call its type *S*. Also, let *T* be the type of the left-hand operand of the assignment operator as determined at compile time.
  - If *T* is a primitive type, then *S* is necessarily the same as *T*.
    - The saved value of the array component and the value of the right-hand operand are used to perform the binary operation indicated by the compound assignment operator. If this operation completes abruptly (the only possibility is an integer division by zero—see §15.16.2), then the assignment expression completes abruptly for the same reason and no assignment occurs.
    - Otherwise, the result of the binary operation is converted to the type of the array component and the result of the conversion is stored into the array component.
  - If *T* is a reference type, then it must be `String`. Because class `String` is a `final` class, *S* must also be `String`. Therefore the run-time check that is sometimes required for the simple assignment operator is never required for a compound assignment operator.
    - The saved value of the array component and the value of the right-hand operand are used to perform the binary operation (string concatenation) indicated by the compound assignment operator (which is necessarily +=). If this operation completes abruptly, then the assignment expression completes abruptly for the same reason and no assignment occurs.
    - Otherwise, the `String` result of the binary operation is stored into the array component.

The rules for compound assignment to an array component are illustrated by the following example program:

```
class ArrayReferenceThrow extends RuntimeException { }
class IndexThrow extends RuntimeException { }
```

```
class RightHandSideThrow extends RuntimeException { }

class IllustrateCompoundArrayAssignment {

   static String[] strings = { "Simon", "Garfunkel" };

   static double[] doubles = { Math.E, Math.PI };

   static String[] stringsThrow() {
      throw new ArrayReferenceThrow();
   }

   static double[] doublesThrow() {
      throw new ArrayReferenceThrow();
   }

   static int indexThrow() { throw new IndexThrow(); }

   static String stringThrow() {
      throw new RightHandSideThrow();
   }

   static double doubleThrow() {
      throw new RightHandSideThrow();
   }

   static String name(Object q) {
      String sq = q.getClass().getName();
      int k = sq.lastIndexOf('.');
      return (k < 0) ? sq : sq.substring(k+1);
   }

   static void testEight(String[] x, double[] z, int j) {
      String sx = (x == null) ? "null" : "Strings";
      String sz = (z == null) ? "null" : "doubles";
      System.out.println();
      try {
         System.out.print(sx + "[throw]+=throw => ");
         x[indexThrow()] += stringThrow();
         System.out.println("Okay!");
      } catch (Throwable e) { System.out.println(name(e)); }
      try {
         System.out.print(sz + "[throw]+=throw => ");
         z[indexThrow()] += doubleThrow();
         System.out.println("Okay!");
      } catch (Throwable e) { System.out.println(name(e)); }

      try {
         System.out.print(sx + "[throw]+=\"heh\" => ");
         x[indexThrow()] += "heh";
         System.out.println("Okay!");
      } catch (Throwable e) { System.out.println(name(e)); }
      try {
         System.out.print(sz + "[throw]+=12345 => ");
         z[indexThrow()] += 12345;
         System.out.println("Okay!");
```

```
        } catch (Throwable e) { System.out.println(name(e)); }
        try {
            System.out.print(sx + "[" + j + "]+=throw => ");
            x[j] += stringThrow();
            System.out.println("Okay!");
        } catch (Throwable e) { System.out.println(name(e)); }
        try {
            System.out.print(sz + "[" + j + "]+=throw => ");
            z[j] += doubleThrow();
            System.out.println("Okay!");
        } catch (Throwable e) { System.out.println(name(e)); }
        try {
            System.out.print(sx + "[" + j + "]+=\"heh\" => ");
            x[j] += "heh";
            System.out.println("Okay!");
        } catch (Throwable e) { System.out.println(name(e)); }
        try {
            System.out.print(sz + "[" + j + "]+=12345 => ");
            z[j] += 12345;
            System.out.println("Okay!");
        } catch (Throwable e) { System.out.println(name(e)); }
    }

    public static void main(String[] args) {
        try {
            System.out.print("throw[throw]+=throw => ");
            stringsThrow()[indexThrow()] += stringThrow();
            System.out.println("Okay!");
        } catch (Throwable e) { System.out.println(name(e)); }
        try {
            System.out.print("throw[throw]+=throw => ");
            doublesThrow()[indexThrow()] += doubleThrow();
            System.out.println("Okay!");
        } catch (Throwable e) { System.out.println(name(e)); }
        try {
            System.out.print("throw[throw]+=\"heh\" => ");
            stringsThrow()[indexThrow()] += "heh";
            System.out.println("Okay!");
        } catch (Throwable e) { System.out.println(name(e)); }

        try {
            System.out.print("throw[throw]+=12345 => ");
            doublesThrow()[indexThrow()] += 12345;
            System.out.println("Okay!");
        } catch (Throwable e) { System.out.println(name(e)); }
        try {
            System.out.print("throw[1]+=throw => ");
            stringsThrow()[1] += stringThrow();
            System.out.println("Okay!");
        } catch (Throwable e) { System.out.println(name(e)); }
        try {
            System.out.print("throw[1]+=throw => ");
```

```
            doublesThrow()[1] += doubleThrow();
            System.out.println("Okay!");
        } catch (Throwable e) { System.out.println(name(e)); }
        try {
            System.out.print("throw[1]+=\"heh\" => ");
            stringsThrow()[1] += "heh";
            System.out.println("Okay!");
        } catch (Throwable e) { System.out.println(name(e)); }
        try {
            System.out.print("throw[1]+=12345 => ");
            doublesThrow()[1] += 12345;
            System.out.println("Okay!");
        } catch (Throwable e) { System.out.println(name(e)); }

        testEight(null, null, 1);
        testEight(null, null, 9);
        testEight(strings, doubles, 1);
        testEight(strings, doubles, 9);
    }
}
```

This program prints:

```
throw[throw]+=throw => ArrayReferenceThrow
throw[throw]+=throw => ArrayReferenceThrow
throw[throw]+="heh" => ArrayReferenceThrow
throw[throw]+=12345 => ArrayReferenceThrow
throw[1]+=throw => ArrayReferenceThrow
throw[1]+=throw => ArrayReferenceThrow
throw[1]+="heh" => ArrayReferenceThrow
throw[1]+=12345 => ArrayReferenceThrow

null[throw]+=throw => IndexThrow
null[throw]+=throw => IndexThrow
null[throw]+="heh" => IndexThrow
null[throw]+=12345 => IndexThrow
null[1]+=throw => NullPointerException
null[1]+=throw => NullPointerException
null[1]+="heh" => NullPointerException
null[1]+=12345 => NullPointerException

null[throw]+=throw => IndexThrow
null[throw]+=throw => IndexThrow
null[throw]+="heh" => IndexThrow
null[throw]+=12345 => IndexThrow
null[9]+=throw => NullPointerException
null[9]+=throw => NullPointerException
null[9]+="heh" => NullPointerException
null[9]+=12345 => NullPointerException

Strings[throw]+=throw => IndexThrow
doubles[throw]+=throw => IndexThrow
Strings[throw]+="heh" => IndexThrow
```

```
doubles[throw]+=12345 => IndexThrow
Strings[1]+=throw => RightHandSideThrow
doubles[1]+=throw => RightHandSideThrow
Strings[1]+="heh" => Okay!
doubles[1]+=12345 => Okay!

Strings[throw]+=throw => IndexThrow
doubles[throw]+=throw => IndexThrow
Strings[throw]+="heh" => IndexThrow
doubles[throw]+=12345 => IndexThrow
Strings[9]+=throw => IndexOutOfBoundsException
doubles[9]+=throw => IndexOutOfBoundsException
Strings[9]+="heh" => IndexOutOfBoundsException
doubles[9]+=12345 => IndexOutOfBoundsException
```

The most interesting cases of the lot are tenth and eleventh from the end:

```
Strings[1]+=throw => RightHandSideThrow
doubles[1]+=throw => RightHandSideThrow
```

They are the cases where a right-hand side that throws an exception actually gets to throw the exception; moreover, they are the only such cases in the lot. This demonstrates that the evaluation of the right-hand operand indeed occurs after the checks for a null array reference value and an out-of-bounds index value.

The following program illustrates the fact that the value of the left-hand side of a compound assignment is saved before the right-hand side is evaluated:

```
class Test {
    public static void main(String[] args) {
        int k = 1;
        int[] a = { 1 };
        k += (k = 4) * (k + 2);
        a[0] += (a[0] = 4) * (a[0] + 2);
        System.out.println("k==" + k + " and a[0]==" + a[0]);
    }
}
```

This program prints:

```
k==25 and a[0]==25
```

The value `1` of `k` is saved by the compound assignment operator `+=` before its right-hand operand `(k = 4) * (k + 2)` is evaluated. Evaluation of this right-hand operand then assigns `4` to `k`, calculates the value `6` for `k + 2`, and then multiplies `4` by `6` to get `24`. This is added to the saved value `1` to get `25`, which is then stored into `k` by the `+=` operator. An identical analysis applies to the case that uses `a[0]`. In short, the statements

```
k += (k = 4) * (k + 2);
a[0] += (a[0] = 4) * (a[0] + 2);
```

behave in exactly the same manner as the statements:

```
k = k + (k = 4) * (k + 2);
a[0] = a[0] + (a[0] = 4) * (a[0] + 2);
```

15.26 Expression

An *Expression* is any assignment expression:

Expression:
    AssignmentExpression

Unlike C and C++, the Java language has no comma operator.

15.27 Constant Expression

ConstantExpression:
    Expression

A compile-time *constant expression* is an expression denoting a value of primitive type or a `String` that is composed using only the following:

- Literals of primitive type and literals of type `String`
- Casts to primitive types and casts to type `String`
- The unary operators +, -, ~, and ! (but not ++ or --)
- The multiplicative operators *, /, and %
- The additive operators + and -
- The shift operators <<, >>, and >>>
- The relational operators <, <=, >, and >= (but not `instanceof`)
- The equality operators == and !=
- The bitwise and logical operators &, ^, and |
- The conditional-and operator && and the conditional-or operator ||
- The ternary conditional operator ? :
- Simple names that refer to `final` variables whose initializers are constant expressions

- Qualified names of the form *TypeName* . *Identifier* that refer to `final` variables whose initializers are constant expressions

Compile-time constant expressions are used in `case` labels in `switch` statements (§14.9) and have a special significance for assignment conversion (§5.2).

Examples of constant expressions:

```
true

(short)(1*2*3*4*5*6)

Integer.MAX_VALUE / 2

2.0 * Math.PI

"The integer " + Long.MAX_VALUE + " is mighty big."
```

. . . when faces of the throng turned toward him and ambiguous eyes stared into his, he assumed the most romantic of expressions . . .
—F. Scott Fitzgerald, *This Side of Paradise* (1920)

CHAPTER 16

Definite Assignment

All the evolution we know of proceeds from the vague to the definite.
—Charles Peirce

EACH local variable must have a *definitely assigned* value when any access of its value occurs. An access to its value consists of the simple name of the variable occurring anywhere in an expression except as the left-hand operand of the simple assignment operator =.

A Java compiler must carry out a specific conservative flow analysis to make sure that, for every access of a local variable, the local variable is definitely assigned before the access; otherwise a compile-time error must occur.

The remainder of this chapter is devoted to a precise explanation of the words "definitely assigned before". The idea is that an assignment to the local variable must occur on every possible execution path to the access from the beginning of the constructor, method, or static initializer that contains the access. The analysis takes into account the structure of statements and expressions; it also provides a special treatment of the expression operators `!`, `&&`, `||`, and `? :`, the operators `&`, `|`, `^`, `==`, and `!=` with `boolean` operands, and boolean-valued constant expressions. For example, a Java compiler recognizes that `k` is definitely assigned before its access (as an argument of a method invocation) in the code:

```
{
    int k;
    if (v > 0 && (k = System.in.read()) >= 0)
        System.out.println(k);
}
```

because the access occurs only if the value of the expression:

```
v > 0 && (k = System.in.read()) >= 0
```

is true, and the value can be `true` only if the assignment to `k` is executed (more properly, evaluated). Similarly, a Java compiler will recognize that in the code:

```
{
    int k;
    while (true) {
        k = n;
        if (k >= 5) break;
        n = 6;
    }
    System.out.println(k);
}
```

the variable k is definitely assigned by the while statement because the condition expression true never has the value false, so only the break statement can cause the while statement to complete normally, and k is definitely assigned before the break statement.

Except for the special treatment of certain boolean operators and of boolean-valued constant expressions, the values of expressions are not taken into account in the flow analysis. For example, a Java compiler must produce a compile-time error for the code:

```
{
    int k;
    int n = 5;
    if (n > 2)
        k = 3;
    System.out.println(k);// k is not "definitely assigned" before this
}
```

even though the value of n is known at compile time, and in principle it can be known at compile time that the assignment to k will always be executed (more properly, evaluated). A Java compiler must operate according to the rules laid out in this section. The rules recognize only constant expressions; in this example, the expression n > 2 is not a constant expression as defined in §15.27.

As another example, a Java compiler will accept the code:

```
void flow(boolean flag) {
    int k;
    if (flag)
        k = 3;
    else
        k = 4;
    System.out.println(k);
}
```

as far as definite assignment of k is concerned, because the rules outlined in this section allow it to tell that k is assigned no matter whether the flag is true or false. But the rules do not accept the variation:

```
void flow(boolean flag) {
    int k;
    if (flag)
        k = 3;
    if (!flag)
        k = 4;
    System.out.println(k); // k is not "definitely assigned" before here
}
```

and so compiling this program must cause a compile-time error to occur.

In order to precisely specify all the cases of definite assignment, the rules in this section define two technical terms:

- whether a local variable is *definitely assigned before* a statement or expression, and
- whether a local variable is *definitely assigned after* a statement or expression.

In order to specify boolean-valued expressions, the latter notion is refined into two cases:

- whether a local variable is *definitely assigned after* the expression *when true*, and
- whether a local variable is *definitely assigned after* the expression *when false*.

Here *when true* and *when false* refer to the value of the expression. For example, the local variable k is definitely assigned a value after evaluation of the expression

```
a && ((k=m) > 5)
```

when the expression is `true` but not when the expression is `false` (because if `a` is `false`, then the assignment to `k` is not executed (more properly, evaluated)).

The statement "*V* is definitely assigned after *X*" (where *V* is a local variable and *X* is a statement or expression) means "*V* is definitely assigned after *X* if *X* completes normally". If *X* completes abruptly, the assignment may not have occurred, and the rules stated here take this into account. A peculiar consequence of this definition is that "*V* is definitely assigned after `break;`" is always true! Because a `break` statement never completes normally, it is vacuously true that *V* has been assigned a value if the `break` statement completes normally.

To shorten the rules, the customary abbreviation "iff" is used to mean "if and only if".

Let *V* be a local variable. Let *a*, *b*, *c*, and *e* be expressions. Let *S* and *T* be statements.

16.1 Definite Assignment and Expressions

Driftwood: The party of the first part shall be known in this contract as the party of the first part.
—Groucho Marx, *A Night at the Opera* (1935)

16.1.1 Boolean Constant Expressions

V is definitely assigned after any constant expression whose value is `true` when false. *V* is definitely assigned after any constant expression whose value is `false` when true.

A constant expression whose value is `true` never has the value `false`, and a constant expression whose value is `false` never has the value `true`, these definitions are vacuously satisfied. They are helpful in analyzing expressions involving the boolean operators &&, `||`, and `!` (§16.1.3, §16.1.4, §16.1.5).

16.1.2 Boolean-valued Expressions

For every boolean-valued expression:

- If the expression has no subexpressions, *V* is definitely assigned after the expression iff *V* is definitely assigned before the expression. This case applies to literals and simple names.
- Otherwise, *V* is definitely assigned after the expression iff *V* is definitely assigned after the expression when true and *V* is definitely assigned after the expression when false.

16.1.3 The Boolean Operator &&

- *V* is definitely assigned after *a* && *b* when true iff *V* is definitely assigned after *a* when true or *V* is definitely assigned after *b* when true.
- *V* is definitely assigned after *a* && *b* when false iff *V* is definitely assigned after *a* when false and *V* is definitely assigned after *b* when false.
- *V* is definitely assigned before *a* iff *V* is definitely assigned before *a* && *b*.
- *V* is definitely assigned before *b* iff *V* is definitely assigned after *a* when true.

16.1.4 The Boolean Operator ||

- *V* is definitely assigned after *a* || *b* when true iff *V* is definitely assigned after *a* when true and *V* is definitely assigned after *b* when true.
- *V* is definitely assigned after *a* || *b* when false iff *V* is definitely assigned after *a* when false or *V* is definitely assigned after *b* when false.
- *V* is definitely assigned before *a* iff *V* is definitely assigned before *a* || *b*.
- *V* is definitely assigned before *b* iff *V* is definitely assigned after *a* when false.

16.1.5 The Boolean Operator !

- *V* is definitely assigned after !*a* when true iff *V* is definitely assigned after *a* when false.
- *V* is definitely assigned after !*a* when false iff *V* is definitely assigned after *a* when true.
- *V* is definitely assigned before *a* iff *V* is definitely assigned before !*a*.

16.1.6 The Boolean Operator &

- *V* is definitely assigned after *a* & *b* when true iff *V* is definitely assigned after *a* when true or *V* is definitely assigned after *b* when true.
- *V* is definitely assigned after *a* & *b* when false iff at least one of the following is true:
  - *V* is definitely assigned after *b*. (Note that if *V* is definitely assigned after *a*, it follows that *V* is definitely assigned after *b*.)
  - *V* is definitely assigned after *a* when false and *V* is definitely assigned after *b* when false.
- *V* is definitely assigned before *a* iff *V* is definitely assigned before *a* & *b*.
- *V* is definitely assigned before *b* iff *V* is definitely assigned after *a*.

16.1.7 The Boolean Operator |

- V is definitely assigned after *a* | *b* when true iff at least one of the following is true:
  - V is definitely assigned after *b*. (Note that if V is definitely assigned after *a*, it follows that V is definitely assigned after *b*.)
  - V is definitely assigned after *a* when true and V is definitely assigned after *b* when true.
- V is definitely assigned after *a* | *b* when false iff V is definitely assigned after *a* when false or V is definitely assigned after *b* when false.
- V is definitely assigned before *a* iff V is definitely assigned before *a* | *b*.
- V is definitely assigned before *b* iff V is definitely assigned after *a*.

16.1.8 The Boolean Operator ^

Driftwood: Would you like to hear it once more?
Fiorello: Just the first part.
Driftwood: What do you mean? The party of the first part?
Fiorello: No, the first part of the party of the first part.

—Groucho Marx and Chico Marx,
A Night at the Opera (1935)

- V is definitely assigned after *a* ^ *b* when true iff at least one of the following is true:
  - V is definitely assigned after *b*.
  - V is definitely assigned after *a* when true and V is definitely assigned after *b* when true.
  - V is definitely assigned after *a* when false and V is definitely assigned after *b* when false.
- V is definitely assigned after *a* ^ *b* when false iff at least one of the following is true:
  - V is definitely assigned after *b*.
  - V is definitely assigned after *a* when true and V is definitely assigned after *b* when false.

  - *V* is definitely assigned after *a* when false and *V* is definitely assigned after *b* when true.
- *V* is definitely assigned before *a* iff *V* is definitely assigned before *a* ^ *b*.
- *V* is definitely assigned before *b* iff *V* is definitely assigned after *a*.

16.1.9 The Boolean Operator ==

- *V* is definitely assigned after *a* == *b* when true iff at least one of the following is true:
  - *V* is definitely assigned after *b*.
  - *V* is definitely assigned after *a* when true and *V* is definitely assigned after *b* when false.
  - *V* is definitely assigned after *a* when false and *V* is definitely assigned after *b* when true.
- *V* is definitely assigned after *a* == *b* when false iff at least one of the following is true:
  - *V* is definitely assigned after *b*.
  - *V* is definitely assigned after *a* when true and *V* is definitely assigned after *b* when true.
  - *V* is definitely assigned after *a* when false and *V* is definitely assigned after *b* when false.
- *V* is definitely assigned before *a* iff *V* is definitely assigned before *a* == *b*.
- *V* is definitely assigned before *b* iff *V* is definitely assigned after *a*.

16.1.10 The Boolean Operator !=

The rules for *a* != *b* are identical to the rules for *a* ^ *b* (§16.1.8).

16.1.11 The Boolean Operator ? :

Suppose that *b* and *c* are boolean-valued expressions.

- *V* is definitely assigned after *a* ? *b* : *c* when true iff both of the following are true:
  - *V* is definitely assigned before *b* or *V* is definitely assigned after *b* when true.

  - *V* is definitely assigned before *c* or *V* is definitely assigned after *c* when true.
- *V* is definitely assigned after *a* ? *b* : *c* when false iff both of the following are true:
  - *V* is definitely assigned before *b* or *V* is definitely assigned after *b* when false.
  - *V* is definitely assigned before *c* or *V* is definitely assigned after *c* when false.
- *V* is definitely assigned before *a* iff *V* is definitely assigned before *a* ? *b* : *c*.
- *V* is definitely assigned before *b* iff *V* is definitely assigned after *a* when true.
- *V* is definitely assigned before *c* iff *V* is definitely assigned after *a* when false.

16.1.12 The Conditional Operator ? :

Suppose that *b* and *c* are expressions that are not boolean-valued.

- *V* is definitely assigned after *a* ? *b* : *c* iff both of the following are true:
  - *V* is definitely assigned after *b*.
  - *V* is definitely assigned after *c*.
- *V* is definitely assigned before *a* iff *V* is definitely assigned before *a* ? *b* : *c*.
- *V* is definitely assigned before *b* iff *V* is definitely assigned after *a* when true.
- *V* is definitely assigned before *c* iff *V* is definitely assigned after *a* when false.

16.1.13 Boolean Assignment Expressions

Driftwood: All right. It says the, uh, the first part of the party of the first part, should be known in this contract as the first part of the party of the first part, should be known in this contract . . .

—Groucho Marx, *A Night at the Opera* (1935)

Suppose that an assignment expression *a* = *b*, *a* &= *b*, *a* |= *b*, or *a* ^= *b* is boolean-valued.

- *V* is definitely assigned before *a* iff *V* is definitely assigned before the assignment expression.
- *V* is definitely assigned before *b* iff *V* is definitely assigned after *a*.
- *V* is definitely assigned after *a* = *b* when true iff either *a* is *V* or *V* is definitely assigned after the right-hand operand expression when true.
- *V* is definitely assigned after *a* = *b* when false iff either *a* is *V* or *V* is definitely assigned after the right-hand operand expression when false.
- *V* is definitely assigned after *a* &= *b* when true iff either *a* is *V* or *V* would be definitely assigned after *a* & *b* (in the same context) when true.
- *V* is definitely assigned after *a* &= *b* when false iff either *a* is *V* or *V* would be definitely assigned after *a* & *b* (in the same context) when false.
- *V* is definitely assigned after *a* |= *b* when true iff either *a* is *V* or *V* would be definitely assigned after *a* | *b* (in the same context) when true.
- *V* is definitely assigned after *a* |= *b* when false iff either *a* is *V* or *V* would be definitely assigned after *a* | *b* (in the same context) when false.
- *V* is definitely assigned after *a* ^= *b* when true iff either *a* is *V* or *V* would be definitely assigned after *a* ^ *b* (in the same context) when true.
- *V* is definitely assigned after *a* ^= *b* when false iff either *a* is *V* or *V* would be definitely assigned after *a* ^ *b* (in the same context) when false.

Note that if *a* is *V* and *V* is not definitely assigned before a compound assignment such as *a* &= *b*, then a compile-time error will necessarily occur. The rules stated above include the disjunct "*a* is *V*" so that *V* will be considered to have been definitely assigned at later points in the code. Including the disjunct "*a* is *V*" does not affect the binary decision as to whether a program is acceptable or will result in a compile-time error, but it affects *how many* different points in the code may be regarded as erroneous, and so in practice it can improve the quality of error reporting.

16.1.14 Other Assignment Expressions

Suppose that an assignment expression *a* = *b*, *a* += *b*, *a* -= *b*, *a* *= *b*, *a* /= *b*, *a* %= *b*, *a* <<= *b*, *a* >>= *b*, *a* >>>= *b*, *a* &= *b*, *a* |= *b*, or *a* ^= *b* is not boolean-valued.

- *V* is definitely assigned after the assignment expression iff either *a* is *V* or *V* is definitely assigned after *b*.
- *V* is definitely assigned before *a* iff *V* is definitely assigned before the assignment expression.
- *V* is definitely assigned before *b* iff *V* is definitely assigned after *a*.

16.1.15 Operators ++ and --

- *V* is definitely assigned after a preincrement, predecrement, postincrement, or postdecrement expression iff either the operand expression is *V* or *V* is definitely assigned after the operand expression.
- *V* is definitely assigned before the operand expression iff *V* is definitely assigned before the preincrement, predecrement, postincrement, or postdecrement expression.

16.1.16 Other Expressions

If an expression is not boolean-valued and is not a conditional-operator expression or assignment expression, the following rules apply:

- If the expression has no subexpressions, *V* is definitely assigned after the expression iff *V* is definitely assigned before the expression. This case applies to literals, simple names, `this`, `super`, and `null`.
- If the expression has subexpressions, *V* is definitely assigned after the expression iff *V* is definitely assigned after its rightmost immediate subexpression.

For any immediate subexpression *y* of an expression *x*, *V* is definitely assigned before *y* iff *V* is definitely assigned before *x* or one of the following situations is true:

- *y* is the right-hand operand of a binary operator and *V* is definitely assigned after the left-hand operand.
- *x* is an array reference, *y* is the subexpression within the brackets, and *V* is definitely assigned after the subexpression before the brackets.
- *x* is a method invocation expression for an object; *y* is the first argument expression in the method invocation expression; there is a subexpression whose value is an object to the left of the dot, method name, and left parenthesis of the method invocation expression; and *V* is definitely assigned after this subexpression.

- x is a method invocation expression or class instance creation expression; y is an argument expression, but not the first; and *V* is definitely assigned after the argument expression to the left of y.
- x is an class instance creation expression; y is a dimension expression, but not the first; and *V* is definitely assigned after the dimension expression to the left of y.

16.2 Definite Assignment and Statements

> *Driftwood: The party of the second part shall be known in this contract as the party of the second part.*
> —Groucho Marx, *A Night at the Opera* (1935)

16.2.1 Empty Statements

- *V* is definitely assigned after an empty statement iff it is definitely assigned before the empty statement.

16.2.2 Blocks

- *V* is definitely assigned after an empty block iff it is definitely assigned before the empty block.
- *V* is definitely assigned after a nonempty block iff it is definitely assigned after the last statement in the block.
- *V* is definitely assigned before the first statement of the block iff it is definitely assigned before the block.
- *V* is definitely assigned before any other statement *S* of the block iff it is definitely assigned after the statement immediately preceding *S* in the block.

16.2.3 Local Variable Declaration Statements

- *V* is definitely assigned after a local variable declaration statement that contains no initializers iff it is definitely assigned before the local variable declaration statement.
- *V* is definitely assigned after a local variable declaration statement that contains initializers iff either it is definitely assigned after the last initializer

expression in the local variable declaration statement or the last initializer expression in the declaration is in the declarator that declares *V*.

- *V* is definitely assigned before the first initializer expression iff it is definitely assigned before the local variable declaration statement.
- *V* is definitely assigned before any other initializer expression *e* iff either it is definitely assigned after the initializer expression immediately preceding *e* in the local variable declaration statement or the initializer expression immediately preceding *e* in the local variable declaration statement is in the declarator that declares *V*.

16.2.4 Labeled Statements

- *V* is definitely assigned after a labeled statement *L*`:`*S* (where *L* is a label) iff *V* is definitely assigned after *S* and *V* is definitely assigned before every `break` statement that may exit the labeled statement *L*`:`*S*.
- *V* is definitely assigned before *S* iff *V* is definitely assigned before *L*`:`*S*.

16.2.5 Expression Statements

- *V* is definitely assigned after an expression statement *e*`;` iff it is definitely assigned after *e*.
- *V* is definitely assigned before *e* iff it is definitely assigned before *e*`;`.

16.2.6 `if` Statements

- *V* is definitely assigned after `if (`*e*`)` *S* iff *V* is definitely assigned after *S* and *V* is definitely assigned after *e* when false.
- *V* is definitely assigned before *e* iff *V* is definitely assigned before `if (`*e*`)` *S*. *V* is definitely assigned before *S* iff *V* is definitely assigned after *e* when true.
- *V* is definitely assigned after `if (`*e*`)` *S* `else` *T* iff *V* is definitely assigned after *S* and *V* is definitely assigned after *T*.
- *V* is definitely assigned before *e* iff *V* is definitely assigned before `if (`*e*`)` *S* `else` *T*. *V* is definitely assigned before *S* iff *V* is definitely assigned after *e* when true. *V* is definitely assigned before *T* iff *V* is definitely assigned after *e* when false.

16.2.7 `switch` Statements

- *V* is definitely assigned after a `switch` statement iff both of the following are true:
  - Either the `switch` block is empty or *V* is definitely assigned after the last statement of the `switch` block.
  - *V* is definitely assigned before every `break` statement that may exit the `switch` statement.
- *V* is definitely assigned before the switch expression iff *V* is definitely assigned before the `switch` statement.
- *V* is definitely assigned before a statement or local variable declaration statement *S* in the switch block iff at least one of the following is true:
  - *V* is definitely assigned after the switch expression.
  - *S* is not labeled by a `case` or `default` label and *V* is definitely assigned after the preceding statement.

16.2.8 `while` Statements

- *V* is definitely assigned after `while (`*e*`)` *S* iff *V* is definitely assigned after *e* when false and *V* is definitely assigned before every `break` statement that may exit the `while` statement.
- *V* is definitely assigned before *e* iff *V* is definitely assigned before the `while` statement.
- *V* is definitely assigned before *S* iff *V* is definitely assigned after *e* when true.

16.2.9 do Statements

- *V* is definitely assigned after do *S* `while (`*e*`);` iff *V* is definitely assigned after *e* when false and *V* is definitely assigned before every `break` statement that may exit the do statement.
- *V* is definitely assigned before *S* iff *V* is definitely assigned before the do statement.
- *V* is definitely assigned before *e* iff *V* is definitely assigned after *S* and *V* is definitely assigned before every `continue` statement that may exit the body of the do statement.

16.2.10 `for` Statements

- *V* is definitely assigned after a `for` statement iff both of the following are true:
  - Either a condition expression is not present or *V* is definitely assigned after the condition expression when false.
  - *V* is definitely assigned before every `break` statement that may exit the `for` statement.
- *V* is definitely assigned before the initialization part of the `for` statement iff *V* is definitely assigned before the `for` statement.
- *V* is definitely assigned before the condition part of the `for` statement iff *V* is definitely assigned after the initialization part of the `for` statement.
- *V* is definitely assigned before the contained statement iff either of the following is true:
  - A condition expression is present and *V* is definitely assigned after the condition expression when true.
  - No condition expression is present and *V* is definitely assigned after the initialization part of the `for` statement.
- *V* is definitely assigned before the incrementation part of the `for` statement iff *V* is definitely assigned after the contained statement and *V* is definitely assigned before every `continue` statement that may exit the body of the `for` statement.

16.2.10.1 *Initialization Part*

- If the initialization part of the `for` statement is a local variable declaration statement, the rules of §16.2.3 apply.
- Otherwise, if the initialization part is empty, then *V* is definitely assigned after the initialization part iff *V* is definitely assigned before the initialization part.
- Otherwise, three rules apply:
  - *V* is definitely assigned after the initialization part iff *V* is definitely assigned after the last expression statement in the initialization part.
  - *V* is definitely assigned before the first expression statement in the initialization part iff *V* is definitely assigned before the initialization part.
  - *V* is definitely assigned before an expression statement *E* other than the first in the initialization part iff *V* is definitely assigned after the expression statement immediately preceding *E*.

16.2.10.2 *Incrementation Part*

- If the incrementation part of the `for` statement is empty, then *V* is definitely assigned after the incrementation part iff *V* is definitely assigned before the incrementation part.
- Otherwise, three rules apply:
  - *V* is definitely assigned after the incrementation part iff *V* is definitely assigned after the last expression statement in the incrementation part.
  - *V* is definitely assigned before the first expression statement in the incrementation part iff *V* is definitely assigned before the incrementation part.
  - *V* is definitely assigned before an expression statement *E* other than the first in the incrementation part iff *V* is definitely assigned after the expression statement immediately preceding *E*.

16.2.11 `break`, `continue`, `return`, and `throw` Statements

> *Fiorello:* *Hey, look! Why can't the first part of the second party be the second part of the first party? Then you've got something!*
>
> —Chico Marx, *A Night at the Opera* (1935)

- By convention, we say that *V* is definitely assigned after any `break`, `continue`, `return`, or `throw` statement. The notion that a variable is "definitely assigned after" a statement or expression really means "is definitely assigned after the statement or expression completes normally". Because a `break`, `continue`, `return`, or `throw` statement never completes normally, it vacuously satisfies this notion.
- In a `return` statement with an expression or a `throw` statement, *V* is definitely assigned before the expression iff *V* is definitely assigned before the `return` or `throw` statement.

16.2.12 `synchronized` Statements

- *V* is definitely assigned after `synchronized (`*e*`)` *S* iff *V* is definitely assigned after *S*.
- *V* is definitely assigned before *e* iff *V* is definitely assigned before the statement `synchronized (`*e*`)` *S*.
- *V* is definitely assigned before *S* iff *V* is definitely assigned after *e*.

16.2.13 `try` Statements

- *V* is definitely assigned after a `try` statement iff one of the following is true:
  - *V* is definitely assigned after the try block and *V* is definitely assigned after every catch block in the try statement.
  - The `try` statement has a `finally` block and *V* is definitely assigned after the `finally` block.
- *V* is definitely assigned before the `try` block iff *V* is definitely assigned before the `try` statement.
- *V* is definitely assigned before a `catch` block iff *V* is definitely assigned before the `try` statement.

V is definitely assigned before a `finally` block iff *V* is definitely assigned before the `try` statement.

I resolved to assign Bartleby a corner by the folding-doors . . .
—Herman Melville, *Bartleby, the Scrivener* (1853)

It does not strike me that there is any thing definite about that.
—Herman Melville, *Bartleby, the Scrivener* (1853)

CHAPTER 17

Threads and Locks

And oft-times in the most forbidding den
Of solitude, with love of science strong,
How patiently the yoke of thought they bear;
How subtly glide its finest threads along!
—William Wordsworth, *Monks and Schoolmen,*
in *Ecclesiastical Sonnets* (1822)

WHILE most of the discussion in the preceding chapters is concerned only with the behavior of Java code as executed a single statement or expression at a time, that is, by a single *thread*, each Java Virtual Machine can support many threads of execution at once. These threads independently execute Java code that operates on Java values and objects residing in a shared main memory. Threads may be supported by having many hardware processors, by time-slicing a single hardware processor, or by time-slicing many hardware processors.

Java supports the coding of programs that, though concurrent, still exhibit deterministic behavior, by providing mechanisms for *synchronizing* the concurrent activity of threads. To synchronize threads, Java uses *monitors*, which are a high-level mechanism for allowing only one thread at a time to execute a region of code protected by the monitor. The behavior of monitors is explained in terms of *locks*; there is a lock associated with each object.

The `synchronized` statement (§14.17) performs two special actions relevant only to multithreaded operation: (1) after computing a reference to an object but before executing its body, it *locks* a lock associated with the object, and (2) after execution of the body has completed, either normally or abruptly, it *unlocks* that same lock. As a convenience, a method may be declared `synchronized`; such a method behaves as if its body were contained in a `synchronized` statement.

The methods `wait` (§20.1.6, §20.1.7, §20.1.8), `notify` (§20.1.9), and `notifyAll` (§20.1.10) of class `Object` support an efficient transfer of control from one thread to another. Rather than simply "spinning" (repeatedly locking and unlocking an object to see whether some internal state has changed), which consumes computational effort, a thread can suspend itself using `wait` until such time as another thread awakens it using `notify`. This is especially appropriate in situations where threads have a producer-consumer relationship (actively cooperating on a common goal) rather than a mutual exclusion relationship (trying to avoid conflicts while sharing a common resource).

As a thread executes code, it carries out a sequence of actions. A thread may *use* the value of a variable or *assign* it a new value. (Other actions include arithmetic operations, conditional tests, and method invocations, but these do not involves variables directly.) If two or more concurrent threads act on a shared variable, there is a possibility that the actions on the variable will produce timing-dependent results. This dependence on timing is inherent in concurrent programming, producing one of the few places in Java where the result of executing a program is not determined solely by this specification.

Each thread has a working memory, in which it may keep copies of the values of variables from the main memory that is shared between all threads. To access a shared variable, a thread usually first obtains a lock and flushes its working memory. This guarantees that shared values will be thereafter be loaded from the shared main memory to the threads working memory. When a thread unlocks a lock it guarantees the values it holds in its working memory will be written back to the main memory.

This chapter explains the interaction of threads with the main memory, and thus with each other, in terms of certain low-level actions. There are rules about the order in which these actions may occur. These rules impose constraints on any implementation of Java, and a Java programmer may rely on the rules to predict the possible behaviors of a concurrent Java program. The rules do, however, intentionally give the implementor certain freedoms; the intent is to permit certain standard hardware and software techniques that can greatly improve the speed and efficiency of concurrent code.

Briefly put, these are the important consequences of the rules:

- Proper use of synchronization constructs will allow reliable transmission of values or sets of values from one thread to another through shared variables.
- When a thread uses the value of a variable, the value it obtains is in fact a value stored into the variable by that thread or by some other thread. This is true even if the program does not contain code for proper synchronization. For example, if two threads store references to different objects into the same reference value, the variable will subsequently contain a reference to one object or the other, not a reference to some other object or a corrupted reference value. (There is a special exception for `long` and `double` values; see §17.4.)

- In the absence of explicit synchronization, a Java implementation is free to update the main memory in an order that may be surprising. Therefore the programmer who prefers to avoid surprises should use explicit synchronization.

17.1 Terminology and Framework

A *variable* is any location within a Java program that may be stored into. This includes not only class variables and instance variables but also components of arrays. Variables are kept in a *main memory* that is shared by all threads. Because it is impossible for one thread to access parameters or local variables of another thread, it doesn't matter whether parameters and local variables are thought of as residing in the shared main memory or in the working memory of the thread that owns them.

Every thread has a *working memory* in which it keeps its own *working copy* of variables that it must use or assign. As the thread executes a Java program, it operates on these working copies. The main memory contains the *master copy* of every variable. There are rules about when a thread is permitted or required to transfer the contents of its working copy of a variable into the master copy or vice versa

The main memory also contains *locks*; there is one lock associated with each object. Threads may compete to acquire a lock.

For the purposes of this chapter, the verbs *use*, *assign*, *load*, *store*, *lock*, and *unlock* name *actions* that a thread can perform. The verbs *read*, *write*, *lock*, and *unlock* name actions that the main memory subsystem can perform. Each of these actions is *atomic* (indivisible).

A *use* or *assign* action is a tightly coupled interaction between a thread's execution engine and the thread's working memory. A *lock* or *unlock* action is a tightly coupled interaction between a thread's execution engine and the main memory. But the transfer of data between the main memory and a thread's working memory is loosely coupled. When data is copied from the main memory to a working memory, two actions must occur: a *read* action performed by the main memory followed some time later by a corresponding *load* action performed by the working memory. When data is copied from a working memory to the main memory, two actions must occur: a *store* action performed by the working memory followed some time later by a corresponding *write* action performed by the main memory. There may be some transit time between main memory and a working memory, and the transit time may be different for each transaction; thus actions initiated by a thread on different variables may viewed by another thread as occurring in a different order. For each variable, however, the actions in main memory on behalf of any one thread are performed in the same order as the corresponding actions by that thread. (This is explained in greater detail below.)

A single Java thread issues a stream of *use*, *assign*, *lock*, and *unlock* actions as dictated by the semantics of the Java program it is executing. The underlying Java implementation is then required additionally to perform appropriate *load*, *store*, *read*, and *write* actions so as to obey a certain set of constraints, explained below. If the Java implementation correctly follows these rules and the Java application programmer follows certain other rules of programming, then data can be reliably transferred between threads through shared variables. The rules are designed to be "tight" enough to make this possible but "loose" enough to allow hardware and software designers considerable freedom to improve speed and throughput through such mechanisms as registers, queues, and caches.

Here are the detailed definitions of each of the actions:

- A *use* action (by a thread) transfers the contents of the thread's working copy of a variable to the thread's execution engine. This action is performed whenever a thread executes a virtual machine instruction that uses the value of a variable.
- An *assign* action (by a thread) transfers a value from the thread's execution engine into the thread's working copy of a variable. This action is performed whenever a thread executes a virtual machine instruction that assigns to a variable.
- A *read* action (by the main memory) transmits the contents of the master copy of a variable to a thread's working memory for use by a later *load* action.
- A *load* action (by a thread) puts a value transmitted from main memory by a *read* action into the thread's working copy of a variable.
- A *store* action (by a thread) transmits the contents of the thread's working copy of a variable to main memory for use by a later *write* action.
- A *write* action (by the main memory) puts a value transmitted from the thread's working memory by a *store* action into the master copy of a variable in main memory.
- A *lock* action (by a thread tightly synchronized with main memory) causes a thread to acquire one claim on a particular lock.
- An *unlock* action (by a thread tightly synchronized with main memory) causes a thread to release one claim on a particular lock.

Thus the interaction of a thread with a variable over time consists of a sequence of *use*, *assign*, *load*, and *store* actions. Main memory performs a *read* action for every *load* and a *write* action for every *store*. A thread's interactions with a lock over time consists of a sequence of *lock* and *unlock* actions. All the globally visible behavior of a thread thus comprises all the thread's actions on variables and locks.

17.2 Execution Order

The rules of execution order constrain the order in which certain events may occur. There are four general constraints on the relationships among actions:

- The actions performed by any one thread are totally ordered; that is, for any two actions performed by a thread, one action precedes the other.
- The actions performed by the main memory for any one variable are totally ordered; that is, for any two actions performed by the main memory on the same variable, one action precedes the other.
- The actions performed by the main memory for any one lock are totally ordered; that is, for any two actions performed by the main memory on the same lock, one action precedes the other.
- It is not permitted for an action to follow itself.

The last rule may seem trivial, but it does need to be stated separately and explicitly for completeness. Without it, it would be possible to propose a set of actions by two or more threads and precedence relationships among the actions that would satisfy all the other rules but would require an action to follow itself.

Threads do not interact directly; they communicate only through the shared main memory. The relationships between the actions of a thread and the actions of main memory are constrained in three ways:

- Each *lock* or *unlock* action is performed jointly by some thread and the main memory.
- Each *load* action by a thread is uniquely paired with a *read* action by the main memory such that the *load* action follows the *read* action.
- Each *store* action by a thread is uniquely paired with a *write* action by the main memory such that the *write* action follows the *store* action.

Most of the rules in the following sections further constrain the order in which certain actions take place. A rule may state that one action must precede or follow some other action. Note that this relationship is transitive: if action *A* must precede action *B*, and *B* must precede *C*, then *A* must precede *C*. The programmer must remember that these rules are the *only* constraints on the ordering of actions; if no rule or combination of rules implies that action *A* must precede action *B*, then a Java implementation is free to perform action *B* before action *A*, or to perform action *B* concurrently with action *A*. This freedom can be the key to good performance. Conversely, an implementation is not required to take advantage of all the freedoms given it.

In the rules that follow, the phrasing "*B* must intervene between *A* and *C*" means that action *B* must follow action *A* and precede action *C*.

17.3 Rules about Variables

Let *T* be a thread and *V* be a variable. There are certain constraints on the actions performed by *T* with respect to *V*:

- An *use* or *assign* by *T* of *V* is permitted only when dictated by execution by *T* of the Java program according to the standard Java execution model. For example, an occurrence of *V* as an operand of the + operator requires that a single *use* action occur on *V*; an occurrence of *V* as the left-hand operand of the assignment operator = requires that a single *assign* action occur. All *use* and *assign* actions by a given thread must occur in the order specified by the program being executed by the thread. If the following rules forbid *T* to perform a required *use* as its next action, it may be necessary for *T* to perform a *load* first in order to make progress.
- A *store* action by *T* on *V* must intervene between an *assign* by *T* of *V* and a subsequent *load* by *T* of *V*. (Less formally: a thread is not permitted to lose its most recent assign.)
- An *assign* action by *T* on *V* must intervene between a *load* or *store* by *T* of *V* and a subsequent *store* by *T* of *V*. (Less formally: a thread is not permitted to write data from its working memory back to main memory for no reason.)
- After a thread is created, it must perform an *assign* or *load* action on a variable before performing a *use* or *store* action on that variable. (Less formally: a new thread starts with an empty working memory.)

- After a variable is created, every thread must perform an *assign* or *load* action on that variable before performing a *use* or *store* action on that variable. (Less formally: a new variable is created only in main memory and is not initially in any thread's working memory.)

Provided that all the constraints above and below are obeyed, a *load* or *store* action may be issued at any time by any thread on any variable, at the whim of the implementation.

There are also certain constraints on the *read* and *write* actions performed by main memory:

- For every *load* action performed by any thread `T` on its working copy of a variable `V`, there must be a corresponding preceding *read* action by the main memory on the master copy of `V`, and the *load* action must put into the working copy the data transmitted by the corresponding *read* action.
- For every *store* action performed by any thread `T` on its working copy of a variable `V`, there must be a corresponding following *write* action by the main memory on the master copy of `V`, and the *write* action must put into the master copy the data transmitted by the corresponding *store* action.
- Let action `A` be a *load* or *store* by thread `T` on variable `V`, and let action `P` be the corresponding *read* or *write* by the main memory on variable `V`. Similarly, let action `B` be some other *load* or *store* by thread `T` on that same variable `V`, and let action `Q` be the corresponding *read* or *write* by the main memory on variable `V`. If `A` precedes `B`, then `P` must precede `Q`. (Less formally: actions on the master copy of any given variable on behalf of a thread are performed by the main memory in exactly the order that the thread requested.)

Note that this last rule applies *only* to actions by a thread on the *same* variable. However, there is a more stringent rule for `volatile` variables (§17.7).

17.4 Nonatomic Treatment of `double` and `long`

If a `double` or `long` variable is not declared `volatile`, then for the purposes of *load*, *store*, *read*, and *write* actions they are treated as if they were two variables of 32 bits each: wherever the rules require one of these actions, two such actions are performed, one for each 32-bit half. The manner in which the 64 bits of a `double` or `long` variable are encoded into two 32-bit quantities is implementation-dependent.

This matters only because a *read* or *write* of a `double` or `long` variable may be handled by an actual main memory as two 32-bit *read* or *write* actions that may be separated in time, with other actions coming between them. Consequently, if two threads concurrently assign distinct values to the same shared non-`volatile` `double` or `long` variable, a subsequent use of that variable may obtain a value that is not equal to either of the assigned values, but some implementation-dependent mixture of the two values.

An implementation is free to implement *load*, *store*, *read*, and *write* actions for `double` and `long` values as atomic 64-bit actions; in fact, this is strongly encouraged. The model divides them into 32-bit halves for the sake of several currently popular microprocessors that fail to provide efficient atomic memory transactions on 64-bit quantities. It would have been simpler for Java to define all memory transactions on single variables as atomic; this more complex definition is a pragmatic concession to current hardware practice. In the future this concession may be eliminated. Meanwhile, programmers are cautioned always to explicitly synchronize access to shared `double` and `long` variables.

17.5 Rules about Locks

By the pricking of my thumbs,
Something wicked this way comes.
Open, locks,
Whoever knocks!
—William Shakespeare, *Macbeth*, Act IV, scene i

Let *T* be a thread and *L* be a lock. There are certain constraints on the actions performed by *T* with respect to *L*:

- A *lock* action by *T* on *L* may occur only if, for every thread *S* other than *T*, the number of preceding *unlock* actions by *S* on *L* equals the number of preceding *lock* actions by *S* on *L*. (Less formally: only one thread at a time is permitted to lay claim to a lock, and moreover a thread may acquire the same lock multiple times and doesn't relinquish ownership of it until a matching number of *unlock* actions have been performed.)
- An *unlock* action by thread *T* on lock *L* may occur only if the number of preceding *unlock* actions by *T* on *L* is strictly less than the number of preceding *lock* actions by *T* on *L*. (Less formally: a thread is not permitted to unlock a lock it doesn't own.)

With respect to a lock, the *lock* and *unlock* actions performed by all the threads are performed in some total sequential order. This total order must be consistent with the total order on the actions of each thread.

17.6 Rules about the Interaction of Locks and Variables

Let *T* be any thread, let *V* be any variable, and let *L* be any lock. There are certain constraints on the actions performed by *T* with respect to *V* and *L*:

- Between an *assign* action by *T* on *V* and a subsequent *unlock* action by *T* on *L*, a *store* action by *T* on *V* must intervene; moreover, the *write* action corresponding to that *store* must precede the *unlock* action, as seen by main memory. (Less formally: if a thread is to perform an *unlock* action on *any* lock, it must first copy *all* assigned values in its working memory back out to main memory.)
- Between a *lock* action by *T* on *L* and a subsequent *use* or *store* action by *T* on a variable *V*, an *assign* or *load* action on *V* must intervene; moreover, if it is a *load* action, then the *read* action corresponding to that *load* must follow the *lock* action, as seen by main memory. (Less formally: a *lock* action acts as if it flushes *all* variables from the thread's working memory; before use they must be assigned or loaded from main memory.)

17.7 Rules for Volatile Variables

If a variable is declared `volatile`, then additional constraints apply to the actions of each thread. Let *T* be a thread and let *V* and *W* be volatile variables.

- An *use* action by *T* on *V* is permitted only if the previous action by *T* on *V* was *load*, and a *load* action by *T* on *V* is permitted only if the next action by *T* on *V* is *use*. The *use* action is said to be "associated" with the *read* action that corresponds to the *load*.
- A *store* action by *T* on *V* is permitted only if the previous action by *T* on *V* was *assign*, and an *assign* action by *T* on *V* is permitted only if the next action by *T* on *V* is *store*. The *assign* action is said to be "associated" with the *write* action that corresponds to the *store*.
- Let action *A* be a *use* or *assign* by thread *T* on variable *V*, let action *F* be the *load* or *store* associated with *A*, and let action *P* be the *read* or *write* of *V* that corresponds to *F*. Similarly, let action *B* be a *use* or *assign* by thread *T* on variable *W*, let action *G* be the *load* or *store* associated with *B*, and let action *Q* be the *read* or *write* of *V* that corresponds to *G*. If *A* precedes *B*, then *P* must precede *Q*. (Less formally: actions on the master copies of volatile variables on behalf of a thread are performed by the main memory in exactly the order that the thread requested.)

17.8 Prescient Store Actions

If a variable is not declared `volatile`, then the rules in the previous sections are relaxed slightly to allow *store* actions to occur earlier than would otherwise be permitted. The purpose of this relaxation is to allow optimizing Java compilers to perform certain kinds of code rearrangement that preserve the semantics of properly synchronized programs but might be caught in the act of performing memory actions out of order by programs that are not properly synchronized.

Suppose that a *store* by *T* of *V* would follow a particular *assign* by *T* of *V* according to the rules of the previous sections, with no intervening *load* or *assign* by *T* of *V*. Then that *store* action would send to the main memory the value that the *assign* action put into the working memory of thread *T*. The special rule allows the *store* action to instead occur before the *assign* action, if the following restrictions are obeyed:

- If the *store* action occurs, the *assign* is bound to occur. (Remember, these are restrictions on what actually happens, not on what a thread plans to do. No fair performing a *store* and then throwing an exception before the *assign* occurs!)
- No *lock* action intervenes between the relocated *store* and the *assign*.
- No *load* of *V* intervenes between the relocated *store* and the *assign*.
- No other *store* of *V* intervenes between the relocated *store* and the *assign*.
- The *store* action sends to the main memory the value that the *assign* action will put into the working memory of thread *T*.

This last property inspires us to call such an early *store* action *prescient*: it has to know ahead of time, somehow, what value will be stored by the *assign* that it should have followed. In practice, optimized compiled code will compute such values early (which is permitted if, for example, the computation has no side effects and throws no exceptions), store them early (before entering a loop, for example), and keep them in working registers for later use within the loop.

17.9 Discussion

Any association between locks and variables is purely conventional. Locking any lock conceptually flushes *all* variables from a thread's working memory, and unlocking any lock forces the writing out to main memory of *all* variables that the thread has assigned. That a lock may be associated with a particular object or a class is purely a convention. In some applications, it may be appropriate always to lock an object before accessing any of its instance variables, for example; synchronized methods are a convenient way to follow this convention. In other applications, it may suffice to use a single lock to synchronize access to a large collection of objects.

If a thread uses a particular shared variable only after locking a particular lock and before the corresponding unlocking of that same lock, then the thread will read the shared value of that variable from main memory after the *lock* action, if necessary, and will copy back to main memory the value most recently assigned to that variable before the *unlock* action. This, in conjunction with the mutual exclusion rules for locks, suffices to guarantee that values are correctly transmitted from one thread to another through shared variables.

The rules for `volatile` variables effectively require that main memory be touched exactly once for each *use* or *assign* of a `volatile` variable by a thread, and that main memory be touched in exactly the order dictated by the thread execution semantics. However, such memory actions are not ordered with respect to *read* and *write* actions on nonvolatile variables.

17.10 Example: Possible Swap

Consider a class that has class variables `a` and `b` and methods `hither` and `yon`:

```
class Sample {
    int a = 1, b = 2;
    void hither() {
        a = b;
    }
    void yon() {
        b = a;
    }
}
```

Now suppose that two threads are created, and that one thread calls `hither` while the other thread calls `yon`. What is the required set of actions and what are the ordering constraints?

Let us consider the thread that calls `hither`. According to the rules, this thread must perform an *use* of `b` followed by an *assign* of `a`. That is the bare minimum required to execute a call to the method `hither`.

Now, the first action on variable `b` by the thread cannot be *use*. But it may be *assign* or *load*. An *assign* to `b` cannot occur because the program text does not call for such an *assign* action, so a *load* of `b` is required. This *load* action by the thread in turn requires a preceding *read* action for `b` by the main memory.

The thread may optionally *store* the value of a after the *assign* has occurred. If it does, then the *store* action in turn requires a following *write* action for a by the main memory.

The situation for the thread that calls yon is similar, but with the roles of a and b exchanged.

The total set of actions may be pictured as follows:

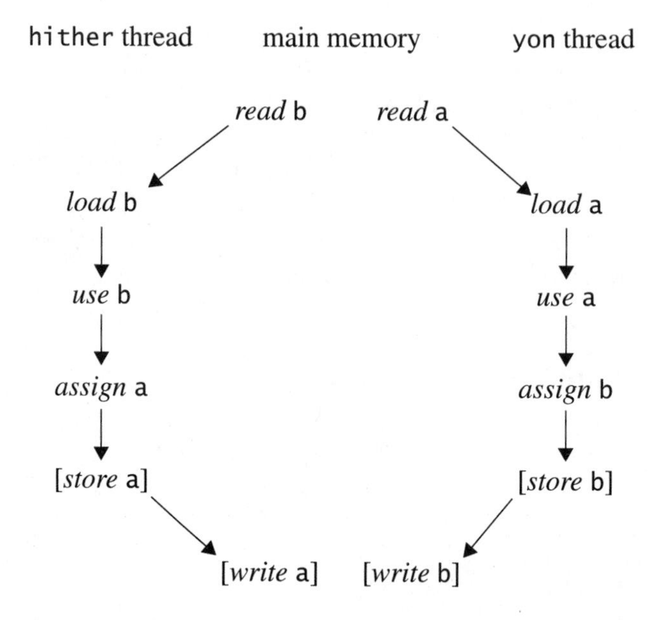

Here an arrow from action *A* to action *B* indicates that *A* must precede *B*.

In what order may the actions by the main memory occur? The only constraint is that it is not possible both for the *write* of a to precede the *read* of a and for the *write* of b to precede the *read* of b, because the causality arrows in the diagram would form a loop so that an action would have to precede itself, which is not allowed. Assuming that the optional *store* and *write* actions are to occur, there are three possible orderings in which the main memory might legitimately perform its actions. Let ha and hb be the working copies of a and b for the hither thread, let ya and yb be the working copies for the yon thread, and let ma and mb be the master copies in main memory. Initially ma=1 and mb=2. Then the three possible orderings of actions and the resulting states are as follows:

- *write* a→*read* a, *read* b→*write* b (then ha=2, hb=2, ma=2, mb=2, ya=2, yb=2)
- *read* a→*write* a, *write* b→*read* b (then ha=1, hb=1, ma=1, mb=1, ya=1, yb=1)
- *read* a→*write* a, *read* b→*write* b (then ha=2, hb=2, ma=2, mb=1, ya=1, yb=1)

Thus the net result might be that, in main memory, b is copied into a, a is copied into b, or the values of a and b are swapped; moreover, the working copies of the variables might or might not agree. It would be incorrect, of course, to assume that any one of these outcomes is more likely than another. This is one place in which the behavior of a Java program is necessarily timing-dependent.

Of course, an implementation might also choose not to perform the *store* and *write* actions, or only one of the two pairs, leading to yet other possible results.

Now suppose that we modify the example to use synchronized methods:

```
class SynchSample {
    int a = 1, b = 2;
    synchronized void hither() {
        a = b;
    }
    synchronized void yon() {
        b = a;
    }
}
```

Let us again consider the thread that calls hither. According to the rules, this thread must perform a *lock* action (on the class object for class SynchSample) before the body of method hither is executed. This is followed by a *use* of b and then an *assign* of a. Finally, an *unlock* action on the class object must be performed after the body of method hither completes. That is the bare minimum required to execute a call to the method hither.

As before, a *load* of b is required, which in turn requires a preceding *read* action for b by the main memory. Because the *load* follows the *lock* action, the corresponding *read* must also follow the *lock* action.

Because an *unlock* action follows the *assign* of a, a *store* action on a is mandatory, which in turn requires a following *write* action for a by the main memory. The *write* must precede the *unlock* action.

The situation for the thread that calls yon is similar, but with the roles of a and b exchanged.

The total set of actions may be pictured as follows:

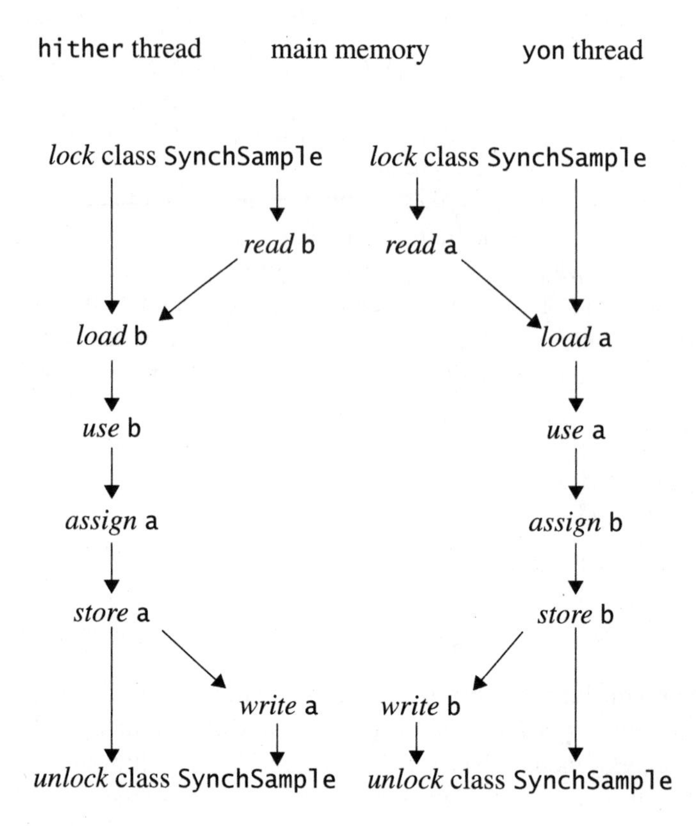

The *lock* and *unlock* actions provide further constraints on the order of actions by the main memory; the *lock* action by one thread cannot occur between the *lock* and *unlock* actions of the other thread. Moreover, the *unlock* actions require that the *store* and *write* actions occur. It follows that only two sequences are possible:

- *write* a→*read* a, *read* b→*write* b (then ha=2, hb=2, ma=2, mb=2, ya=2, yb=2)
- *read* a→*write* a, *write* b→*read* b (then ha=1, hb=1, ma=1, mb=1, ya=1, yb=1)

While the resulting state is timing-dependent, it can be seen that the two threads will necessarily agree on the values of a and b.

17.11 Example: Out-of-Order Writes

This example is similar to that in the preceding section, except that one method assigns to both variables and the other method reads both variables. Consider a class that has class variables `a` and `b` and methods `to` and `fro`:

```
class Simple {
    int a = 1, b = 2;
    void to() {
        a = 3;
        b = 4;
    }
    void fro() {
        System.out.println("a= " + a + ", b=" + b);
    }
}
```

Now suppose that two threads are created, and that one thread calls `to` while the other thread calls `fro`. What is the required set of actions and what are the ordering constraints?

Let us consider the thread that calls `to`. According to the rules, this thread must perform an *assign* of `a` followed by an *assign* of `b`. That is the bare minimum required to execute a call to the method `to`. Because there is no synchronization, it is at the option of the implementation whether or not to *store* the assigned values back to main memory! Therefore the thread that calls `fro` may obtain either `1` or `3` for the value of `a`, and independently may obtain either `2` or `4` for the value of `b`.

Now suppose that `to` is `synchronized` but `fro` is not:

```
class SynchSimple {
    int a = 1, b = 2;
    synchronized void to() {
        a = 3;
        b = 4;
    }
    void fro() {
        System.out.println("a= " + a + ", b=" + b);
    }
}
```

In this case the method `to` will be forced to *store* the assigned values back to main memory before the *unlock* action at the end of the method. The method `fro` must, of course, use `a` and `b` (in that order) and so must *load* values for `a` and `b` from main memory.

The total set of actions may be pictured as follows:

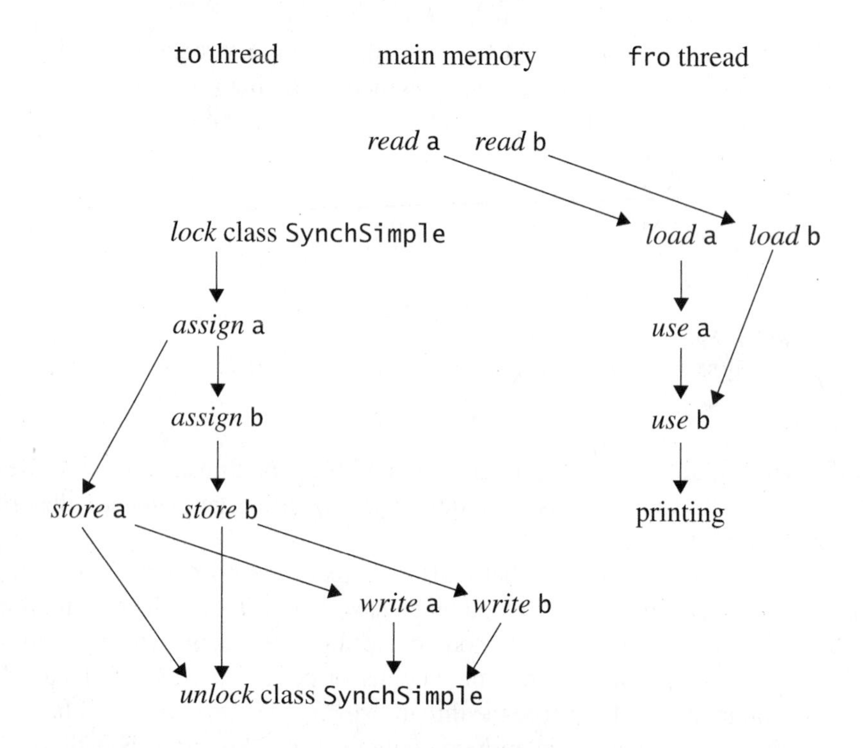

Here an arrow from action *A* to action *B* indicates that *A* must precede *B*.

In what order may the actions by the main memory occur? Note that the rules do not require that *write* a occur before *write* b; neither do they require that *read* a occur before *read* b. Also, even though method `to` is `synchronized`, method `fro` is not `synchronized`, so there is nothing to prevent the *read* actions from occurring between the *lock* and *unlock* actions. (The point is that declaring one method `synchronized` does not of itself make that method behave as if it were atomic.)

As a result, the method `fro` could still obtain either `1` or `3` for the value of `a`, and independently could obtain either `2` or `4` for the value of `b`. In particular, `fro` might observe the value `1` for `a` and `4` for `b`. Thus, even though `to` does an *assign* to `a` and then an *assign* to `b`, the *write* actions to main memory may be observed by another thread to occur as if in the opposite order.

Finally, suppose that `to` and `fro` are both `synchronized`:

```
class SynchSynchSimple {
    int a = 1, b = 2;
    synchronized void to() {
        a = 3;
        b = 4;
    }
    synchronized void fro() {
        System.out.println("a= " + a + ", b=" + b);
    }
}
```

In this case, the actions of method `fro` cannot be interleaved with the actions of method `to`, and so `fro` will print either "`a=1, b=2`" or "`a=3, b=4`".

17.12 Threads

They plant dead trees for living, and the dead
They string together with a living thread . . .
But in no hush they string it . . . With a laugh, . . .
They bring the telephone and telegraph.

—Robert Frost, *The Line-gang* (1920)

Threads are created and managed by the built-in classes `Thread` (§20.20) and `ThreadGroup` (§20.21). Creating a `Thread` object creates a thread and that is the only way to create a thread. When the thread is created, it is not yet active; it begins to run when its `start` method (§20.20.14) is called.

Every thread has a *priority*. When there is competition for processing resources, threads with higher priority are generally executed in preference to threads with lower priority. Such preference is not, however, a guarantee that the highest priority thread will always be running, and thread priorities cannot be used to reliably implement mutual exclusion.

17.13 Locks and Synchronization

There is a lock associated with every object. The Java language does not provide a way to perform separate *lock* and *unlock* actions; instead, they are implicitly performed by high-level constructs that arrange always to pair such actions correctly. (We note, however, that the Java Virtual Machine provides separate *monitorenter* and *monitorexit* instructions that implement the *lock* and *unlock* actions.)

The `synchronized` statement (§14.17) computes a reference to an object; it then attempts to perform a *lock* action on that object and does not proceed further until the *lock* action has successfully completed. (A *lock* action may be delayed because the rules about locks can prevent the main memory from participating until some other thread is ready to perform one or more *unlock* actions.) After the lock action has been performed, the body of the `synchronized` statement is executed. If execution of the body is ever completed, either normally or abruptly, an *unlock* action is automatically performed on that same lock.

A `synchronized` method (§8.4.3.5) automatically performs a *lock* action when it is invoked; its body is not executed until the *lock* action has successfully completed. If the method is an instance method, it locks the lock associated with the instance for which it was invoked (that is, the object that will be known as `this` during execution of the body of the method). If the method is `static`, it locks the lock associated with the `Class` object that represents the class in which the method is defined. If execution of the method's body is ever completed, either normally or abruptly, an *unlock* action is automatically performed on that same lock.

Best practice is that if a variable is ever to be assigned by one thread and used or assigned by another, then all accesses to that variable should be enclosed in `synchronized` methods or `synchronized` statements.

Java does not prevent, nor require detection of, deadlock conditions. Programs where threads hold (directly or indirectly) locks on multiple objects should use conventional techniques for deadlock avoidance, creating higher-level locking primitives that don't deadlock, if necessary.

17.14 Wait Sets and Notification

Every object, in addition to having an associated lock, has an associated *wait set*, which is a set of threads. When an object is first created, its wait set is empty.

Wait sets are used by the methods `wait` (§20.1.6, §20.1.7, §20.1.8), `notify` (§20.1.9), and `notifyAll` (§20.1.10) of class `Object`. These methods also interact with the scheduling mechanism for threads (§20.20).

The method `wait` should be called for an object only when the current thread (call it *T*) has already locked the object's lock. Suppose that thread *T* has in fact performed *N lock* actions that have not been matched by *unlock* actions. The `wait` method then adds the current thread to the wait set for the object, disables the current thread for thread scheduling purposes, and performs *N unlock* actions to relinquish the lock. The thread *T* then lies dormant until one of three things happens:

- Some other thread invokes the `notify` method for that object and thread *T* happens to be the one arbitrarily chosen as the one to notify.
- Some other thread invokes the `notifyAll` method for that object.
- If the call by thread *T* to the wait method specified a timeout interval, the specified amount of real time has elapsed.

The thread *T* is then removed from the wait set and re-enabled for thread scheduling. It then locks the object again (which may involve competing in the usual manner with other threads); once it has gained control of the lock, it performs $N-1$ additional *lock* actions and then returns from the invocation of the `wait` method. Thus, on return from the `wait` method, the state of the object's lock is exactly as it was when the `wait` method was invoked.

The `notify` method should be called for an object only when the current thread has already locked the object's lock. If the wait set for the object is not empty, then some arbitrarily chosen thread is removed from the wait set and re-enabled for thread scheduling. (Of course, that thread will not be able to proceed until the current thread relinquishes the object's lock.)

The `notifyAll` method should be called for an object only when the current thread has already locked the object's lock. Every thread in the wait set for the object is removed from the wait set and re-enabled for thread scheduling. (Of course, those threads will not be able to proceed until the current thread relinquishes the object's lock.)

These pearls of thought in Persian gulfs were bred,
Each softly lucent as a rounded moon;
The diver Omar plucked them from their bed,
Fitzgerald strung them on an English thread.

—James Russell Lowell,
in a copy of Omar Khayyam

CHAPTER 18

Documentation Comments

The view that documentation is something that is added to a program after it has been commissioned seems to be wrong in principle, and counterproductive in practice. Instead, documentation must be regarded as an integral part of the process of design and coding.
—C. A. R. Hoare,
Hints on Programming Language Design (1973)

JAVA programs can include documentation in their source code, in special documentation comments (§3.7). Such comments can appear before each class or interface declaration and before each method, constructor, or field declaration. Hypertext web pages can then be produced automatically from the source code of the program and these documentation comments.

This chapter gives an informal description of documentation comments. A complete formal specification would require a detailed description of those parts of the Hypertext Markup Language (HTML) that can be used within the documentation comments, which is beyond the scope of this specification.

18.1 The Text of a Documentation Comment

The text of a documentation comment consists of the characters between the /** that begins the comment and the */ that ends it. The text is divided into one or more lines. On each of these lines, leading * characters are ignored; for lines other than the first, blanks and tabs preceding the initial * characters are also discarded.

So, for example, in the comment:

```
/**XYZ
 ** Initialize to pre-trial defaults.
 123*/
```

the text of the comment has three lines. The first line consists of the text "XYZ"; the second line consists of the text " Initialize to pre-trial defaults." and the third line consists of the text "123"

18.2 HTML in a Documentation Comment

Text in a documentation comment may use HTML markers for formatting, with the exception that the specific markers <H1>, <H2>, <H3>, <H4>, <H5>, <H6>, and <HR> are reserved for use by the documentation generator and should not be used in the text. A complete description of HTML is available from the web site http://www.w3.org and also through the Internet documentation database at http://www.internic.net, where the document "Hypertext Markup Language —Version 2.0" by T. Berners-Lee and D. Connolly may be found as RFC1866.

18.3 Summary Sentence and General Description

The first sentence of each documentation comment should be a summary sentence, containing a concise but complete description of the declared entity. This sentence ends at the first period that is followed by a blank, tab, or line terminator, or at the first tagline (as defined below). This simple rule means that a first sentence such as:

```
This is a simulation of Prof. Knuth's MIX computer.
```

will not work properly, because the period after the abbreviation "Prof" ends the first sentence, as far as the Java documentation comment processor is concerned. Take care to avoid such difficulties.

Sentences following the summary sentence but preceding the first tagged paragraph (if any) form the general description part of the documentation comment.

18.4 Tagged Paragraphs

A line of a documentation comment that begins with the character @ followed by one of a few special keywords starts a *tagged paragraph*. The tagged paragraph also includes any following lines up to, but not including, either the first line of the next tagged paragraph or the end of the documentation comment.

Tagged paragraphs identify certain information that has a routine structure, such as the intended purpose of each parameter of a method, in a form that the documentation comment processor can easily marshal into standard typographical formats for purposes of presentation and cross-reference.

Different kinds of tagged paragraphs are available for class and interface declarations and for method, field, and constructor declarations.

18.4.1 The @see Tag

The following are examples of @see paragraphs, which may be used in any documentation comment to indicate a cross-reference to a class, interface, method, constructor, field, or URL:

```
@see java.lang.String
@see String
@see java.io.InputStream;
@see String#equals
@see java.lang.Object#wait(int)
@see java.io.RandomAccessFile#RandomAccessFile(File, String)
@see Character#MAX_RADIX
@see <a href="spec.html">Java Spec</a>
```

The character # separates the name of a class from the name of one of its fields, methods, or constructors. One of several overloaded methods or constructors may be selected by including a parenthesized list of argument types after the method or constructor name.

A documentation comment may contain more than one @see tag.

18.4.2 The @author Tag

The following are examples of @author taglines, which may be used in documentation comments for class and interface declarations:

```
@author Mary Wollstonecraft
@author Hildegard von Bingen
@author Dorothy Parker
```

The information in an @author paragraph has no special internal structure.

A documentation comment may contain more than one @author tag. Alternatively, a single @author paragraph may mention several authors:

```
@author Jack Kent, Peggy Parish, Crockett Johnson,
   James Marshall, Marjorie Weinman Sharmat,
   Robert McCloskey, and Madeleine L'Engle
```

However, we recommend specifying one author per @author paragraph, which allows the documentation processing tool to provide the correct punctuation in all circumstances.

18.4.3 The @version Tag

The following is an example of a @version paragraph, which may be used in documentation comments for class and interface declarations:

```
@version 493.0.1beta
```

The information in a @version paragraph has no special internal structure.
A documentation comment may contain at most one @version tag.

18.4.4 The @param Tag

The following are examples of @param paragraphs, which may be used in documentation comments for method and constructor declarations:

```
@param file the file to be searched
@param pattern
   the pattern to be matched during the search
@param count  the number of lines to print for each match
```

The information in a @param paragraph should consist of the name of the parameter followed by a short description.

A documentation comment may contain more than one @param tag. The usual convention is that if any @param paragraphs are present in a documentation comment, then there should be one @param paragraph for each parameter of the method or constructor, and the @param paragraphs should appear in the order in which the parameters are declared.

18.4.5 The @return Tag

The following is an example of a @return paragraph, which may be used in documentation comments for declarations of methods whose result type is not void:

```
@return the number of widgets that pass the quality test
```

The information in a @return paragraph has no special internal structure. The usual convention is that it consists of a short description of the returned value.

A documentation comment may contain at most one @return tag.

18.4.6 The @exception Tag

The following is an example of an @exception paragraph, which may be used in documentation comments for method and constructor declarations:

```
@exception IndexOutOfBoundsException
            the matrix is too large
@exception UnflangedWidgetException the widget does not
            have a flange, or its flange has size zero
@exception java.io.FileNotFoundException the file
            does not exist
```

The information in an `@exception` paragraph should consist of the name of an exception class (which may be a simple name or a qualified name) followed by a short description of the circumstances that cause the exception to be thrown.

A documentation comment may contain more than one `@exception` tag.

18.5 Example

Here, as an example, is a version of the source code for the class `Object` of the package `java.lang`, including its documentation comments.

```
/*
 * @(#)Object.java 1.37 96/06/26
 *
 * Copyright (c) 1994, 1995, 1996 Sun Microsystems, Inc.
 * All Rights Reserved.
 *
 * Permission to use, copy, modify, and distribute this
 * software and its documentation for NON-COMMERCIAL purposes
 * and without fee is hereby granted provided that this
 * copyright notice appears in all copies. Please refer to
 * the file "copyright.html" for further important copyright
 * and licensing information.
 *
 * SUN MAKES NO REPRESENTATIONS OR WARRANTIES ABOUT THE
 * SUITABILITY OF THE SOFTWARE, EITHER EXPRESS OR IMPLIED,
 * INCLUDING BUT NOT LIMITED TO THE IMPLIED WARRANTIES OF
 * MERCHANTABILITY, FITNESS FOR A PARTICULAR PURPOSE, OR
 * NON-INFRINGEMENT. SUN SHALL NOT BE LIABLE FOR ANY DAMAGES
 * SUFFERED BY LICENSEE AS A RESULT OF USING, MODIFYING OR
 * DISTRIBUTING THIS SOFTWARE OR ITS DERIVATIVES.
 */

package java.lang;

/**
 * The root of the Class hierarchy.  Every Class in the
 * system has Object as its ultimate parent.  Every variable
 * and method defined here is available in every Object.
 * @see     Class
 * @version 1.37, 26 Jun 1996
 */
```

```
public class Object {
    /**
     * Returns the Class of this Object. Java has a runtime
     * representation for classes--a descriptor of type Class
     * --which the method getClass() returns for any Object.
     */
    public final native Class getClass();

    /**
     * Returns a hashcode for this Object.
     * Each Object in the Java system has a hashcode.
     * The hashcode is a number that is usually different
     * for different Objects. It is used when storing Objects
     * in hashtables.
     * Note: hashcodes can be negative as well as positive.
     * @see      java.util.Hashtable
     */
    public native int hashCode();

    /**
     * Compares two Objects for equality.
     * Returns a boolean that indicates whether this Object
     * is equivalent to the specified Object. This method is
     * used when an Object is stored in a hashtable.
     * @param    obj       the Object to compare with
     * @return   true if these Objects are equal;
     *              false otherwise.
     * @see      java.util.Hashtable
     */
    public boolean equals(Object obj) {
        return (this == obj);
    }

    /**
     * Creates a clone of the object. A new instance is
     * allocated and a bitwise clone of the current object
     * is placed in the new object.
     * @return   a clone of this Object.
     * @exception   OutOfMemoryError If there is not enough
     *                 memory.
     * @exception   CloneNotSupportedException Object
     *                 explicitly does not want to be
     *                 cloned, or it does not support
     *                 the Cloneable interface.
     */
    protected native Object clone()
        throws CloneNotSupportedException;
```

```
/**
 * Returns a String that represents this Object.
 * It is recommended that all subclasses override
 * this method.
 */
public String toString() {
   return getClass().getName() + "@" +
      Integer.toHexString(hashCode());
}

/**
 * Notifies a single waiting thread on a change in
 * condition of another thread. The thread effecting
 * the change notifies the waiting thread using notify().
 * Threads that want to wait for a condition to change
 * before proceeding can call wait(). <p>
 * <em>The method notify() can be called only by the
 * thread that is the owner of the current object's
 * monitor lock.</em>
 *
 * @exception   IllegalMonitorStateException If the
 *                 current thread is not the owner
 *                 of the Object's monitor lock.
 * @see      Object#wait
 * @see      Object#notifyAll
 */
public final native void notify();

/**
 * Notifies all the threads waiting for a condition to
 * change. Threads that are waiting are generally waiting
 * for another thread to change some condition. Thus, the
 * thread effecting a change that more than one thread is
 * waiting for notifies all the waiting threads using
 * the method notifyAll(). Threads that want to wait for
 * a condition to change before proceeding can call
 * wait(). <p>
 * <em>The method notifyAll() can be called only by the
 * thread that is the owner of the current object's
 * monitor lock.</em>
 *
 * @exception   IllegalMonitorStateException If the
 *                 current thread is not the owner
 *                 of the Object's monitor lock.
 * @see      Object#wait
 * @see      Object#notify
 */
public final native void notifyAll();
```

```
/**
 * Causes a thread to wait until it is notified or the
 * specified timeout expires. <p>
 * <em>The method wait(millis) can be called only by
 * the thread that is the owner of the current object's
 * monitor lock.</em>
 *
 * @param    millis    the maximum time to wait,
 *                         in milliseconds
 * @exception   IllegalMonitorStateException If the
 *                 current thread is not the owner
 *                 of the Object's monitor lock.
 * @exception   InterruptedException Another thread has
 *                 interrupted this thread.
 */
public final native void wait(long millis)
    throws InterruptedException;

/**
 * More accurate wait.
 * <em>The method wait(millis, nanos) can be called only
 * by the thread that is the owner of the current
 * object's monitor lock.</em>
 *
 * @param millis    the maximum time to wait,
 *                      in milliseconds
 * @param nano      additional time to wait,
 *                      in nanoseconds
 *                      (range 0-999999)
 * @exception   IllegalMonitorStateException If the
 *                 current thread is not the owner
 *                 of the Object's monitor lock.
 * @exception   InterruptedException Another thread has
 *                 interrupted this thread.
 */
public final void wait(long millis, int nanos)
    throws InterruptedException
{
    if (nanos >= 500000 || (nanos != 0 && millis==0))
        timeout++;
    wait(timeout);
}

/**
 * Causes a thread to wait forever until it is notified.
 * <p>
 * <em>The method wait() can be called only by the
 * thread that is the owner of the current object's
 * monitor lock.</em>
 *
```

```
     * @exception   IllegalMonitorStateException If the
     *                  current thread is not the owner
     *                  of the Object's monitor lock.
     * @exception   InterruptedException Another thread has
     *                  interrupted this thread.
     */
    public final void wait() throws InterruptedException {
       wait(0);
    }

    /**
     * Code to perform when this object is garbage collected.
     * The default is that nothing needs to be performed.
     *
     * Any exception thrown by a finalize method causes the
     * finalization to halt.  But otherwise, it is ignored.
     */
    protected void finalize() throws Throwable { }
}
```

From this source code, the javadoc tool produced the following HTML file, which is available for browsing at http://java.sun.com/Series, our Java Series web site:

```
<!--NewPage-->
<html>
<head>
<!-- Generated by javadoc on Wed Jun 26 11:40:38 EDT 1996 -->
<a name="_top_"></a>
<title>
  Class java.lang.Object
</title>
</head>
<body>
<pre>
<a href="packages.html">All Packages</a>  <a href="tree.html">Class Hierarchy¬
</a>  <a href="Package-java.lang.html">This Package</a>  <a href="java.lang.N¬
umber.html#_top_">Previous</a>  <a href="java.lang.OutOfMemoryError.html#_top¬
_">Next</a>  <a href="AllNames.html">Index</a></pre>
<hr>
<h1>
  Class java.lang.Object
</h1>
<pre>
java.lang.Object
</pre>
<hr>
<dl>
  <dt> public class <b>Object</b>
</dl>
The root of the Class hierarchy.  Every Class in the
system has Object as its ultimate parent.  Every variable
and method defined here is available in every Object.
<dl>
  <dt> <b>Version:</b>
  <dd> 1.37, 26 Jun 1996
    <dt> <b>See Also:</b>
    <dd> <a href="java.lang.Class.html#_top_">Class</a>
</dl>
<hr>
<a name="index"></a>
```

```
<h2>
  <img src="images/constructor-index.gif" width=275 height=38 alt="Constructo¬
r Index">
</h2>
<dl>
  <dt> <img src="images/yellow-ball-small.gif" width=6 height=6 alt=" o ">
    <a href="#Object()"><b>Object</b></a>()
  <dd>
</dl>
<h2>
  <img src="images/method-index.gif" width=207 height=38 alt="Method Index">
</h2>
<dl>
  <dt> <img src="images/red-ball-small.gif" width=6 height=6 alt=" o ">
    <a href="#clone()"><b>clone</b></a>()
  <dd> Creates a clone of the object.
  <dt> <img src="images/red-ball-small.gif" width=6 height=6 alt=" o ">
    <a href="#equals(java.lang.Object)"><b>equals</b></a>(Object)
  <dd> Compares two Objects for equality.
  <dt> <img src="images/red-ball-small.gif" width=6 height=6 alt=" o ">
    <a href="#finalize()"><b>finalize</b></a>()
  <dd> Code to perform when this object is garbage collected.
  <dt> <img src="images/red-ball-small.gif" width=6 height=6 alt=" o ">
    <a href="#getClass()"><b>getClass</b></a>()
  <dd> Returns the Class of this Object.
  <dt> <img src="images/red-ball-small.gif" width=6 height=6 alt=" o ">
    <a href="#hashCode()"><b>hashCode</b></a>()
  <dd> Returns a hashcode for this Object.
  <dt> <img src="images/red-ball-small.gif" width=6 height=6 alt=" o ">
    <a href="#notify()"><b>notify</b></a>()
  <dd> Notifies a single waiting thread on a change in
condition of another thread.
  <dt> <img src="images/red-ball-small.gif" width=6 height=6 alt=" o ">
    <a href="#notifyAll()"><b>notifyAll</b></a>()
  <dd> Notifies all the threads waiting for a condition to
change.
  <dt> <img src="images/red-ball-small.gif" width=6 height=6 alt=" o ">
    <a href="#toString()"><b>toString</b></a>()
  <dd> Returns a String that represents this Object.
  <dt> <img src="images/red-ball-small.gif" width=6 height=6 alt=" o ">
    <a href="#wait()"><b>wait</b></a>()
  <dd> Causes a thread to wait forever until it is notified.
  <dt> <img src="images/red-ball-small.gif" width=6 height=6 alt=" o ">
    <a href="#wait(long)"><b>wait</b></a>(long)
  <dd> Causes a thread to wait until it is notified or the
specified timeout expires.
  <dt> <img src="images/red-ball-small.gif" width=6 height=6 alt=" o ">
    <a href="#wait(long, int)"><b>wait</b></a>(long, int)
  <dd> More accurate wait.
</dl>
<a name="constructors"></a>
<h2>
  <img src="images/constructors.gif" width=231 height=38 alt="Constructors">
</h2>
<a name="Object"></a>
<a name="Object()"><img src="images/yellow-ball.gif" width=12 height=12 alt="¬
o "></a>
<b>Object</b>
<pre>
  public Object()
</pre>
<a name="methods"></a>
<h2>
  <img src="images/methods.gif" width=151 height=38 alt="Methods">
</h2>
<a name="getClass()"><img src="images/red-ball.gif" width=12 height=12 alt=" ¬
o "></a>
<a name="getClass"><b>getClass</b></a>
<pre>
  public final <a href="java.lang.Class.html#_top_">Class</a> getClass()
</pre>
```

```
<dl>
  <dd> Returns the Class of this Object. Java has a runtime
representation for classes--a descriptor of type Class
--which the method getClass() returns for any Object.
</dl>
<a name="hashCode()"><img src="images/red-ball.gif" width=12 height=12 alt=" ¬
o "></a>
<a name="hashCode"><b>hashCode</b></a>
<pre>
  public int hashCode()
</pre>
<dl>
  <dd> Returns a hashcode for this Object.
Each Object in the Java system has a hashcode.
The hashcode is a number that is usually different
for different Objects. It is used when storing Objects
in hashtables.
Note: hashcodes can be negative as well as positive.
  <dl>
    <dt> <b>See Also:</b>
    <dd> <a href="java.util.Hashtable.html#_top_">Hashtable</a>
  </dl>
</dl>
<a name="equals(java.lang.Object)"><img src="images/red-ball.gif" width=12 he¬
ight=12 alt=" o "></a>
<a name="equals"><b>equals</b></a>
<pre>
  public boolean equals(<a href="#_top_">Object</a> obj)
</pre>
<dl>
  <dd> Compares two Objects for equality.
Returns a boolean that indicates whether this Object
is equivalent to the specified Object. This method is
used when an Object is stored in a hashtable.
  <dl>
    <dt> <b>Parameters:</b>
    <dd> obj - the Object to compare with
    <dt> <b>Returns:</b>
    <dd> true if these Objects are equal;
           false otherwise.
    <dt> <b>See Also:</b>
    <dd> <a href="java.util.Hashtable.html#_top_">Hashtable</a>
  </dl>
</dl>
<a name="clone()"><img src="images/red-ball.gif" width=12 height=12 alt=" o "¬
></a>
<a name="clone"><b>clone</b></a>
<pre>
  protected <a href="#_top_">Object</a> clone() throws <a href="java.lang.Clo¬
neNotSupportedException.html#_top_">CloneNotSupportedException</a>
</pre>
<dl>
  <dd> Creates a clone of the object. A new instance is
allocated and a bitwise clone of the current object
is placed in the new object.
  <dl>
    <dt> <b>Returns:</b>
    <dd> a clone of this Object.
    <dt> <b>Throws:</b> <a href="java.lang.OutOfMemoryError.html#_top_">OutOf¬
MemoryError</a>
    <dd> If there is not enough
            memory.
    <dt> <b>Throws:</b> <a href="java.lang.CloneNotSupportedException.html#_t¬
op_">CloneNotSupportedException</a>
    <dd> Object
            explicitly does not want to be
            cloned, or it does not support
            the Cloneable interface.
  </dl>
</dl>
```

```
<a name="toString()"><img src="images/red-ball.gif" width=12 height=12 alt=" ¬
o "></a>
<a name="toString"><b>toString</b></a>
<pre>
  public <a href="java.lang.String.html#_top_">String</a> toString()
</pre>
<dl>
  <dd> Returns a String that represents this Object.
It is recommended that all subclasses override
this method.
</dl>
<a name="notify()"><img src="images/red-ball.gif" width=12 height=12 alt=" o ¬
"></a>
<a name="notify"><b>notify</b></a>
<pre>
  public final void notify()
</pre>
<dl>
  <dd> Notifies a single waiting thread on a change in
condition of another thread. The thread effecting
the change notifies the waiting thread using notify().
Threads that want to wait for a condition to change
before proceeding can call wait(). <p>
<em>The method notify() can be called only by the
thread that is the owner of the current object's
monitor lock.</em>
  <dl>
    <dt> <b>Throws:</b> <a href="java.lang.IllegalMonitorStateException.html#¬
_top_">IllegalMonitorStateException</a>
    <dd> If the
           current thread is not the owner
           of the Object's monitor lock.
    <dt> <b>See Also:</b>
    <dd> <a href="#wait">wait</a>, <a href="#notifyAll">notifyAll</a>
  </dl>
</dl>
<a name="notifyAll()"><img src="images/red-ball.gif" width=12 height=12 alt="¬
o "></a>
<a name="notifyAll"><b>notifyAll</b></a>
<pre>
  public final void notifyAll()
</pre>
<dl>
  <dd> Notifies all the threads waiting for a condition to
change. Threads that are waiting are generally waiting
for another thread to change some condition. Thus, the
thread effecting a change that more than one thread is
waiting for notifies all the waiting threads using
the method notifyAll(). Threads that want to wait for
a condition to change before proceeding can call
wait(). <p>
<em>The method notifyAll() can be called only by the
thread that is the owner of the current object's
monitor lock.</em>
  <dl>
    <dt> <b>Throws:</b> <a href="java.lang.IllegalMonitorStateException.html#¬
_top_">IllegalMonitorStateException</a>
    <dd> If the
           current thread is not the owner
           of the Object's monitor lock.
    <dt> <b>See Also:</b>
    <dd> <a href="#wait">wait</a>, <a href="#notify">notify</a>
  </dl>
</dl>
<a name="wait(long)"><img src="images/red-ball.gif" width=12 height=12 alt=" ¬
o "></a>
<a name="wait"><b>wait</b></a>
<pre>
  public final void wait(long millis) throws <a href="java.lang.InterruptedEx¬
ception.html#_top_">InterruptedException</a>
</pre>
```

```
<dl>
  <dd> Causes a thread to wait until it is notified or the
specified timeout expires. <p>
<em>The method wait(millis) can be called only by
the thread that is the owner of the current object's
monitor lock.</em>
  <dl>
    <dt> <b>Parameters:</b>
    <dd> millis - the maximum time to wait,
             in milliseconds
    <dt> <b>Throws:</b> <a href="java.lang.IllegalMonitorStateException.html#¬
_top_">IllegalMonitorStateException</a>
    <dd> If the
           current thread is not the owner
           of the Object's monitor lock.
    <dt> <b>Throws:</b> <a href="java.lang.InterruptedException.html#_top_">I¬
nterruptedException</a>
    <dd> Another thread has
           interrupted this thread.
  </dl>
</dl>
<a name="wait(long, int)"><img src="images/red-ball.gif" width=12 height=12 a¬
lt=" o "></a>
<a name="wait"><b>wait</b></a>
<pre>
  public final void wait(long millis,
                         int nanos) throws <a href="java.lang.InterruptedExce¬
ption.html#_top_">InterruptedException</a>
</pre>
<dl>
  <dd> More accurate wait.
<em>The method wait(millis, nanos) can be called only
by the thread that is the owner of the current
object's monitor lock.</em>
  <dl>
    <dt> <b>Parameters:</b>
    <dd> millis - the maximum time to wait,
             in milliseconds
    <dd> nano - additional time to wait,
             in nanoseconds
             (range 0-999999)
    <dt> <b>Throws:</b> <a href="java.lang.IllegalMonitorStateException.html#¬
_top_">IllegalMonitorStateException</a>
    <dd> If the
           current thread is not the owner
           of the Object's monitor lock.
    <dt> <b>Throws:</b> <a href="java.lang.InterruptedException.html#_top_">I¬
nterruptedException</a>
    <dd> Another thread has
           interrupted this thread.
  </dl>
</dl>
<a name="wait()"><img src="images/red-ball.gif" width=12 height=12 alt=" o ">¬
</a>
<a name="wait"><b>wait</b></a>
<pre>
  public final void wait() throws <a href="java.lang.InterruptedException.htm¬
l#_top_">InterruptedException</a>
</pre>
<dl>
  <dd> Causes a thread to wait forever until it is notified.
<p>
<em>The method wait() can be called only by the
thread that is the owner of the current object's
monitor lock.</em>
  <dl>
    <dt> <b>Throws:</b> <a href="java.lang.IllegalMonitorStateException.html#¬
_top_">IllegalMonitorStateException</a>
    <dd> If the
           current thread is not the owner
           of the Object's monitor lock.
```

```
    <dt> <b>Throws:</b> <a href="java.lang.InterruptedException.html#_top_">I¬
nterruptedException</a>
    <dd> Another thread has
           interrupted this thread.
  </dl>
</dl>
<a name="finalize()"><img src="images/red-ball.gif" width=12 height=12 alt=" ¬
o "></a>
<a name="finalize"><b>finalize</b></a>
<pre>
  protected void finalize() throws <a href="java.lang.Throwable.html#_top_">T¬
hrowable</a>
</pre>
<dl>
  <dd> Code to perform when this object is garbage collected.
The default is that nothing needs to be performed.
Any exception thrown by a finalize method causes the
finalization to halt.  But otherwise, it is ignored.
</dl>
<hr>
<pre>
<a href="packages.html">All Packages</a>  <a href="tree.html">Class Hierarchy¬
</a>  <a href="Package-java.lang.html">This Package</a>  <a href="java.lang.N¬
umber.html#_top_">Previous</a>  <a href="java.lang.OutOfMemoryError.html#_top¬
_">Next</a>  <a href="AllNames.html">Index</a></pre>
</body>
</html>
```

Many of the lines in this HTML file are far too long to fit onto these pages. We have used the character "¬" at the end of a line to indicate that the following line of text on the page is part of the same line in the generated file.

This generated HTML file is meant only as an example, not as a specification of the behavior of the `javadoc` tool, which may be changed over time to improve the HTML presentation of the documentation information.

Very few facts are able to tell their own story,
without comments to bring out their meaning.
—John Stuart Mill, *On Liberty* (1869)

CHAPTER 19

LALR(1) Grammar

Is there grammar in a title. There is grammar in a title. Thank you.
—Gertrude Stein, *Arthur a Grammar,* in *How to Write* (1931)

THIS chapter presents a grammar for Java. The grammar has been mechanically checked to insure that it is LALR(1).

The grammar for Java presented piecemeal in the preceding chapters is much better for exposition, but it cannot be parsed left-to-right with one token of lookahead because of certain syntactic peculiarities, some of them inherited from C and C++. These problems and the solutions adopted for the LALR(1) grammar are presented below, followed by the grammar itself.

19.1 Grammatical Difficulties

There are five problems with the grammar presented in preceding chapters.

19.1.1 Problem #1: Names Too Specific

Consider the two groups of productions:

PackageName:
    Identifier
    PackageName . *Identifier*

TypeName:
    Identifier
    PackageName . *Identifier*

and:

MethodName:
  Identifier
  AmbiguousName . *Identifier*

AmbiguousName:
  Identifier
  AmbiguousName . *Identifier*

Now consider the partial input:

```
class Problem1 { int m() { hayden.
```

When the parser is considering the token `hayden`, with one-token lookahead to symbol ".", it cannot yet tell whether `hayden` should be a *PackageName* that qualifies a type name, as in:

```
hayden.Dinosaur rex = new hayden.Dinosaur(2);
```

or an *AmbiguousName* that qualifies a method name, as in:

```
hayden.print("Dinosaur Rex!");
```

Therefore, the productions shown above result in a grammar that is not LALR(1). There are also other problems with drawing distinctions among different kinds of names in the grammar.

The solution is to eliminate the nonterminals *PackageName*, *TypeName*, *ExpressionName*, *MethodName*, and *AmbiguousName*, replacing them all with a single nonterminal *Name*:

Name:
  SimpleName
  QualifiedName

SimpleName:
  Identifier

QualifiedName:
  Name . *Identifier*

A later stage of compiler analysis then sorts out the precise role of each name or name qualifier.

For related reasons, these productions in §4.3:

ClassOrInterfaceType:
  ClassType
  InterfaceType

ClassType:
    TypeName

InterfaceType:
    TypeName

were changed to:

ClassOrInterfaceType:
    Name

ClassType:
    ClassOrInterfaceType

InterfaceType:
    ClassOrInterfaceType

19.1.2 Problem #2: Modifiers Too Specific

Consider the two groups of productions:

FieldDeclaration:
    FieldModifiers$_{opt}$ *Type VariableDeclarators* ;

FieldModifiers:
    FieldModifier
    FieldModifiers FieldModifier

FieldModifier: one of
```
public protected private
final static transient volatile
```

and:

MethodHeader:
    MethodModifiers$_{opt}$ *ResultType MethodDeclarator Throws*$_{opt}$

MethodModifiers:
    MethodModifier
    MethodModifiers MethodModifier

MethodModifier: one of
```
public protected private
static
abstract final native synchronized
```

Now consider the partial input:

```
class Problem2 { public static int
```

When the parser is considering the token `static`, with one-token lookahead to symbol `int`—or, worse yet, considering the token `public` with lookahead to `static`—it cannot yet tell whether this will be a field declaration such as:

```
public static int maddie = 0;
```

or a method declaration such as:

```
public static int maddie(String art) { return art.length(); }
```

Therefore, the parser cannot tell with only one-token lookahead whether `static` (or, similarly, `public`) should be reduced to *FieldModifier* or *MethodModifier*. Therefore, the productions shown above result in a grammar that is not LALR(1). There are also other problems with drawing distinctions among different kinds of modifiers in the grammar.

While not all contexts provoke the problem, the simplest solution is to combine all contexts in which such modifiers are used, eliminating all six of the nonterminals *ClassModifiers* (§8.1.2), *FieldModifiers* (§8.3.1), *MethodModifiers* (§8.4.3), *ConstructorModifiers* (§8.6.3), *InterfaceModifiers* (§9.1.2), and *ConstantModifiers* (§9.3) from the grammar, replacing them all with a single nonterminal *Modifiers*:

Modifiers:
  Modifier
  Modifiers Modifier

Modifier: one of
  `public protected private`
  `static`
  `abstract final native synchronized transient volatile`

A later stage of compiler analysis then sorts out the precise role of each modifier and whether it is permitted in a given context.

19.1.3 Problem #3: Field Declaration versus Method Declaration

Consider the two productions (shown after problem #2 has been corrected):

FieldDeclaration:
  Modifiers$_{opt}$ *Type VariableDeclarators* ;

and:

MethodHeader:
  Modifiers$_{opt}$ *ResultType MethodDeclarator Throws*$_{opt}$

where *ResultType* is defined as:

ResultType:
  Type
  `void`

Now consider the partial input:

```
class Problem3 { int julie
```

Note that, in this simple example, no *Modifiers* are present. When the parser is considering the token `int`, with one-token lookahead to symbol `julie`, it cannot yet tell whether this will be a field declaration such as:

```
int julie = 14;
```

or a method declaration such as:

```
int julie(String art) { return art.length(); }
```

Therefore, after the parser reduces `int` to the nonterminal *Type*, it cannot tell with only one-token lookahead whether *Type* should be further reduced to *ResultType* (for a method declaration) or left alone (for a field declaration). Therefore, the productions shown above result in a grammar that is not LALR(1).

The solution is to eliminate the *ResultType* production and to have separate alternatives for *MethodHeader*:

MethodHeader:
  Modifiers$_{opt}$ *Type MethodDeclarator Throws*$_{opt}$
  Modifiers$_{opt}$ `void` *MethodDeclarator Throws*$_{opt}$

This allows the parser to reduce `int` to *Type* and then leave it as is, delaying the decision as to whether a field declaration or method declaration is in progress.

19.1.4 Problem #4: Array Type versus Array Access

Consider the productions (shown after problem #1 has been corrected):

ArrayType:
    Type `[ ]`

and:

ArrayAccess:
    Name `[` *Expression* `]`
    PrimaryNoNewArray `[` *Expression* `]`

Now consider the partial input:

```
class Problem4 { Problem4() { peter[
```

When the parser is considering the token `peter`, with one-token lookahead to symbol `[`, it cannot yet tell whether `peter` will be part of a type name, as in:

```
peter[] team;
```

or part of an array access, as in:

```
peter[3] = 12;
```

Therefore, after the parser reduces `peter` to the nonterminal *Name*, it cannot tell with only one-token lookahead whether *Name* should be reduced ultimately to *Type* (for an array type) or left alone (for an array access). Therefore, the productions shown above result in a grammar that is not LALR(1).

The solution is to have separate alternatives for *ArrayType*:

ArrayType:
    PrimitiveType `[ ]`
    Name `[ ]`
    ArrayType `[ ]`

This allows the parser to reduce `peter` to *Name* and then leave it as is, delaying the decision as to whether an array type or array access is in progress.

19.1.5 Problem #5: Cast versus Parenthesized Expression

Consider the production:

CastExpression:
    `(` *PrimitiveType* `)` *UnaryExpression*
    `(` *ReferenceType* `)` *UnaryExpressionNotPlusMinus*

Now consider the partial input:

```
class Problem5 { Problem5() { super((matthew)
```

When the parser is considering the token `matthew`, with one-token lookahead to symbol `)`, it cannot yet tell whether `(matthew)` will be a parenthesized expression, as in:

```
super((matthew), 9);
```

or a cast, as in:

```
super((matthew)baz, 9);
```

Therefore, after the parser reduces `matthew` to the nonterminal *Name*, it cannot tell with only one-token lookahead whether *Name* should be further reduced to *PostfixExpression* and ultimately to *Expression* (for a parenthesized expression) or to *ClassOrInterfaceType* and then to *ReferenceType* (for a cast). Therefore, the productions shown above result in a grammar that is not LALR(1).

The solution is to eliminate the use of the nonterminal *ReferenceType* in the definition of *CastExpression*, which requires some reworking of both alternatives to avoid other ambiguities:

CastExpression:
(*PrimitiveType* $Dims_{opt}$) *UnaryExpression*
(*Expression*) *UnaryExpressionNotPlusMinus*
(*Name Dims*) *UnaryExpressionNotPlusMinus*

This allows the parser to reduce `matthew` to *Expression* and then leave it there, delaying the decision as to whether a parenthesized expression or a cast is in progress. Inappropriate variants such as:

```
(int[])+3
```

and:

```
(matthew+1)baz
```

must then be weeded out and rejected by a later stage of compiler analysis.

The remaining sections of this chapter constitute a LALR(1) grammar for Java syntax, in which the five problems described above have been solved.

19.2 Productions from §2.3: The Syntactic Grammar

Grammar is mistaken at times for burnt ivy with a piece of glass.
—Gertrude Stein, *Arthur a Grammar*, in *How to Write* (1931)

Goal:
CompilationUnit

19.3 Productions from §3: Lexical Structure

The question is if you have a vocabulary have you any need of grammar . . .
—Gertrude Stein, *Arthur a Grammar*, in *How to Write* (1931)

Literal:
IntegerLiteral
FloatingPointLiteral
BooleanLiteral
CharacterLiteral
StringLiteral
NullLiteral

19.4 Productions from §4: Types, Values, and Variables

Type:
PrimitiveType
ReferenceType

PrimitiveType:
NumericType
`boolean`

NumericType:
IntegralType
FloatingPointType

IntegralType: one of
`byte short int long char`

FloatingPointType: one of
`float double`

ReferenceType:
ClassOrInterfaceType
ArrayType

ClassOrInterfaceType:
Name

ClassType:
ClassOrInterfaceType

InterfaceType:
ClassOrInterfaceType

ArrayType:
PrimitiveType `[ ]`
Name `[ ]`
ArrayType `[ ]`

19.5 Productions from §6: Names

Grammar refers to names as very pretty names.
—Gertrude Stein, *Arthur a Grammar*, in *How to Write* (1931)

Name:
SimpleName
QualifiedName

SimpleName:
Identifier

QualifiedName:
Name `.` *Identifier*

19.6 Productions from §7: Packages

CompilationUnit:
  PackageDeclaration$_{opt}$ ImportDeclarations$_{opt}$ TypeDeclarations$_{opt}$

ImportDeclarations:
  ImportDeclaration
  ImportDeclarations ImportDeclaration

TypeDeclarations:
  TypeDeclaration
  TypeDeclarations TypeDeclaration

PackageDeclaration:
  `package` *Name* `;`

ImportDeclaration:
  SingleTypeImportDeclaration
  TypeImportOnDemandDeclaration

SingleTypeImportDeclaration:
  `import` *Name* `;`

TypeImportOnDemandDeclaration:
  `import` *Name* `. * ;`

TypeDeclaration:
  ClassDeclaration
  InterfaceDeclaration
  `;`

19.7 Productions Used Only in the LALR(1) Grammar

Modifiers:
  Modifier
  Modifiers Modifier

Modifier: one of
```
public protected private
static
abstract final native synchronized transient volatile
```

19.8 Productions from §8: Classes

19.8.1 Productions from §8.1: Class Declaration

ClassDeclaration:
  Modifiers$_{opt}$ `class` *Identifier Super*$_{opt}$ *Interfaces*$_{opt}$ *ClassBody*

Super:
  `extends` *ClassType*

Interfaces:
  `implements` *InterfaceTypeList*

InterfaceTypeList:
  InterfaceType
  InterfaceTypeList `,` *InterfaceType*

ClassBody:
  `{` *ClassBodyDeclarations*$_{opt}$ `}`

ClassBodyDeclarations:
  ClassBodyDeclaration
  ClassBodyDeclarations ClassBodyDeclaration

ClassBodyDeclaration:
  ClassMemberDeclaration
  StaticInitializer
  ConstructorDeclaration

ClassMemberDeclaration:
  FieldDeclaration
  MethodDeclaration

19.8.2 Productions from §8.3: Field Declarations

FieldDeclaration:
  Modifiers$_{opt}$ *Type VariableDeclarators* `;`

VariableDeclarators:
  VariableDeclarator
  VariableDeclarators `,` *VariableDeclarator*

VariableDeclarator:
  VariableDeclaratorId
  VariableDeclaratorId `=` *VariableInitializer*

VariableDeclaratorId:
  Identifier
  VariableDeclaratorId `[ ]`

VariableInitializer:
  Expression
  ArrayInitializer

19.8.3 Productions from §8.4: Method Declarations

MethodDeclaration:
  MethodHeader MethodBody

MethodHeader:
  Modifiers$_{opt}$ *Type MethodDeclarator Throws*$_{opt}$
  Modifiers$_{opt}$ `void` *MethodDeclarator Throws*$_{opt}$

MethodDeclarator:
  Identifier `(` *FormalParameterList*$_{opt}$ `)`
  MethodDeclarator `[ ]`

FormalParameterList:
  FormalParameter
  FormalParameterList `,` *FormalParameter*

FormalParameter:
  Type VariableDeclaratorId

Throws:
  `throws` *ClassTypeList*

ClassTypeList:
  ClassType
  ClassTypeList `,` *ClassType*

MethodBody:
  Block
  `;`

19.8.4 Productions from §8.5: Static Initializers

StaticInitializer:
  `static` *Block*

19.8.5 Productions from §8.6: Constructor Declarations

ConstructorDeclaration:
  Modifiers$_{opt}$ ConstructorDeclarator Throws$_{opt}$ ConstructorBody

ConstructorDeclarator:
  SimpleName `(` *FormalParameterList$_{opt}$* `)`

ConstructorBody:
  `{` *ExplicitConstructorInvocation$_{opt}$ BlockStatements$_{opt}$* `}`

ExplicitConstructorInvocation:
  `this (` *ArgumentList$_{opt}$* `) ;`
  `super (` *ArgumentList$_{opt}$* `) ;`

19.9 Productions from §9: Interfaces

Grammar is useless because there is nothing to say.
—Gertrude Stein, *Arthur a Grammar*, in *How to Write* (1931)

19.9.1 Productions from §9.1: Interface Declarations

InterfaceDeclaration:
  Modifiers$_{opt}$ `interface` *Identifier ExtendsInterfaces$_{opt}$ InterfaceBody*

ExtendsInterfaces:
  `extends` *InterfaceType*
  ExtendsInterfaces `,` *InterfaceType*

InterfaceBody:
  `{` *InterfaceMemberDeclarations$_{opt}$* `}`

InterfaceMemberDeclarations:
  InterfaceMemberDeclaration
  InterfaceMemberDeclarations InterfaceMemberDeclaration

InterfaceMemberDeclaration:
  ConstantDeclaration
  AbstractMethodDeclaration

ConstantDeclaration:
  FieldDeclaration

AbstractMethodDeclaration:
  MethodHeader `;`

19.10 Productions from §10: Arrays

ArrayInitializer:
  { *VariableInitializers*$_{opt}$,$_{opt}$ }

VariableInitializers:
  VariableInitializer
  VariableInitializers , *VariableInitializer*

19.11 Productions from §14: Blocks and Statements

Successions of words are so agreeable.
—Gertrude Stein, *Arthur a Grammar*, in *How to Write* (1931)

Block:
  { *BlockStatements*$_{opt}$ }

BlockStatements:
  BlockStatement
  BlockStatements BlockStatement

BlockStatement:
  LocalVariableDeclarationStatement
  Statement

LocalVariableDeclarationStatement:
  LocalVariableDeclaration ;

LocalVariableDeclaration:
  Type VariableDeclarators

Statement:
  StatementWithoutTrailingSubstatement
  LabeledStatement
  IfThenStatement
  IfThenElseStatement
  WhileStatement
  ForStatement

StatementNoShortIf:
  StatementWithoutTrailingSubstatement
  LabeledStatementNoShortIf
  IfThenElseStatementNoShortIf
  WhileStatementNoShortIf
  ForStatementNoShortIf

StatementWithoutTrailingSubstatement:
  Block
  EmptyStatement
  ExpressionStatement
  SwitchStatement
  DoStatement
  BreakStatement
  ContinueStatement
  ReturnStatement
  SynchronizedStatement
  ThrowStatement
  TryStatement

EmptyStatement:
  ;

LabeledStatement:
  Identifier : *Statement*

LabeledStatementNoShortIf:
  Identifier : *StatementNoShortIf*

ExpressionStatement:
  StatementExpression ;

StatementExpression:
  Assignment
  PreIncrementExpression
  PreDecrementExpression
  PostIncrementExpression
  PostDecrementExpression
  MethodInvocation
  ClassInstanceCreationExpression

IfThenStatement:
  `if ( ` *Expression* ` ) ` *Statement*

IfThenElseStatement:
  `if ( ` *Expression* ` ) ` *StatementNoShortIf* ` else ` *Statement*

IfThenElseStatementNoShortIf:
  `if ( ` *Expression* ` ) ` *StatementNoShortIf* ` else ` *StatementNoShortIf*

SwitchStatement:
  `switch ( ` *Expression* ` ) ` *SwitchBlock*

SwitchBlock:
  `{ ` $SwitchBlockStatementGroups_{opt}$ $SwitchLabels_{opt}$ ` }`

SwitchBlockStatementGroups:
  SwitchBlockStatementGroup
  SwitchBlockStatementGroups SwitchBlockStatementGroup

SwitchBlockStatementGroup:
  SwitchLabels BlockStatements

SwitchLabels:
  SwitchLabel
  SwitchLabels SwitchLabel

SwitchLabel:
  `case ` *ConstantExpression* ` :`
  `default :`

WhileStatement:
  `while ( ` *Expression* ` ) ` *Statement*

WhileStatementNoShortIf:
  `while ( ` *Expression* ` ) ` *StatementNoShortIf*

DoStatement:
  `do ` *Statement* ` while ( ` *Expression* ` ) ;`

ForStatement:
  `for ( `*ForInit*$_{opt}$` ; `*Expression*$_{opt}$` ; `*ForUpdate*$_{opt}$` )`
    Statement

ForStatementNoShortIf:
  `for ( `*ForInit*$_{opt}$` ; `*Expression*$_{opt}$` ; `*ForUpdate*$_{opt}$` )`
    StatementNoShortIf

ForInit:
  StatementExpressionList
  LocalVariableDeclaration

ForUpdate:
  StatementExpressionList

StatementExpressionList:
  StatementExpression
  StatementExpressionList `,` *StatementExpression*

BreakStatement:
  `break` *Identifier*$_{opt}$ `;`

ContinueStatement:
  `continue` *Identifier*$_{opt}$ `;`

ReturnStatement:
  `return` *Expression*$_{opt}$ `;`

ThrowStatement:
  `throw` *Expression* `;`

SynchronizedStatement:
  `synchronized (` *Expression* `)` *Block*

TryStatement:
  `try` *Block Catches*
  `try` *Block Catches*$_{opt}$ *Finally*

Catches:
  CatchClause
  Catches CatchClause

CatchClause:
  `catch (` *FormalParameter* `)` *Block*

Finally:
  `finally` *Block*

19.12 Productions from §15: Expressions

Grammar does mean arithmetic.
They act quickly.
Grammar matters if they add quickly.
—Gertrude Stein, *Arthur a Grammar*, in *How to Write* (1931)

Primary:
    PrimaryNoNewArray
    ArrayCreationExpression

PrimaryNoNewArray:
    Literal
    `this`
    `(` *Expression* `)`
    ClassInstanceCreationExpression
    FieldAccess
    MethodInvocation
    ArrayAccess

ClassInstanceCreationExpression:
    `new` *ClassType* `(` $ArgumentList_{opt}$ `)`

ArgumentList:
    Expression
    ArgumentList `,` *Expression*

ArrayCreationExpression:
    `new` *PrimitiveType DimExprs* $Dims_{opt}$
    `new` *ClassOrInterfaceType DimExprs* $Dims_{opt}$

DimExprs:
    DimExpr
    DimExprs DimExpr

DimExpr:
    `[` *Expression* `]`

Dims:
    `[ ]`
    Dims `[ ]`

FieldAccess:
    Primary `.` *Identifier*
    `super` `.` *Identifier*

MethodInvocation:
    Name `(` *ArgumentList*$_{opt}$ `)`
    Primary `.` *Identifier* `(` *ArgumentList*$_{opt}$ `)`
    `super` `.` *Identifier* `(` *ArgumentList*$_{opt}$ `)`

ArrayAccess:
    Name `[` *Expression* `]`
    PrimaryNoNewArray `[` *Expression* `]`

PostfixExpression:
    Primary
    Name
    PostIncrementExpression
    PostDecrementExpression

PostIncrementExpression:
    PostfixExpression `++`

PostDecrementExpression:
    PostfixExpression `--`

UnaryExpression:
    PreIncrementExpression
    PreDecrementExpression
    `+` *UnaryExpression*
    `-` *UnaryExpression*
    UnaryExpressionNotPlusMinus

PreIncrementExpression:
    `++` *UnaryExpression*

PreDecrementExpression:
    `--` *UnaryExpression*

UnaryExpressionNotPlusMinus:
    PostfixExpression
    `~` *UnaryExpression*
    `!` *UnaryExpression*
    CastExpression

CastExpression:
    `(` *PrimitiveType Dims*$_{opt}$ `)` *UnaryExpression*
    `(` *Expression* `)` *UnaryExpressionNotPlusMinus*
    `(` *Name Dims* `)` *UnaryExpressionNotPlusMinus*

MultiplicativeExpression:
UnaryExpression
MultiplicativeExpression * *UnaryExpression*
MultiplicativeExpression / *UnaryExpression*
MultiplicativeExpression % *UnaryExpression*

AdditiveExpression:
MultiplicativeExpression
AdditiveExpression + *MultiplicativeExpression*
AdditiveExpression - *MultiplicativeExpression*

ShiftExpression:
AdditiveExpression
ShiftExpression << *AdditiveExpression*
ShiftExpression >> *AdditiveExpression*
ShiftExpression >>> *AdditiveExpression*

RelationalExpression:
ShiftExpression
RelationalExpression < *ShiftExpression*
RelationalExpression > *ShiftExpression*
RelationalExpression <= *ShiftExpression*
RelationalExpression >= *ShiftExpression*
RelationalExpression `instanceof` *ReferenceType*

EqualityExpression:
RelationalExpression
EqualityExpression == *RelationalExpression*
EqualityExpression != *RelationalExpression*

AndExpression:
EqualityExpression
AndExpression & *EqualityExpression*

ExclusiveOrExpression:
AndExpression
ExclusiveOrExpression ^ *AndExpression*

InclusiveOrExpression:
ExclusiveOrExpression
InclusiveOrExpression | *ExclusiveOrExpression*

ConditionalAndExpression:
InclusiveOrExpression
ConditionalAndExpression && *InclusiveOrExpression*

ConditionalOrExpression:
  ConditionalAndExpression
  ConditionalOrExpression || *ConditionalAndExpression*

ConditionalExpression:
  ConditionalOrExpression
  ConditionalOrExpression ? *Expression* : *ConditionalExpression*

AssignmentExpression:
  ConditionalExpression
  Assignment

Assignment:
  LeftHandSide AssignmentOperator AssignmentExpression

LeftHandSide:
  Name
  FieldAccess
  ArrayAccess

AssignmentOperator: one of
  = *= /= %= += -= <<= >>= >>>= &= ^= |=

Expression:
  AssignmentExpression

ConstantExpression:
  Expression

Grammar is not a matter of seasons or of finishing early.
—Gertrude Stein, *Arthur a Grammar*, in *How to Write* (1931)

CHAPTER 20

The Package `java.lang`

THE `java.lang` package contains classes that are fundamental to the design of the Java language. The most important classes are `Object`, which is the root of the class hierarchy, and `Class`, instances of which represent classes at run time.

Frequently it is necessary to represent a value of primitive type as if it were an object. The wrapper classes `Boolean`, `Character`, `Integer`, `Long`, `Float`, and `Double` serve this purpose. An object of type `Double`, for example, contains a field whose type is `double`, representing that value in such a way that a reference to it can be stored in a variable of reference type. These classes also provide a number of methods for converting among primitive values, as well as supporting such standard methods as `equals` and `hashCode`.

The class `Math` provides commonly used mathematical functions such as sine, cosine, and square root. The classes `String` and `StringBuffer` similarly provide commonly used operations on character strings.

Classes `ClassLoader`, `Process`, `Runtime`, `SecurityManager`, and `System` provide "system operations" that manage the dynamic loading of classes, creation of external processes, host environment inquiries such as the time of day, and enforcement of security policies.

Class `Throwable` encompasses objects that may be thrown by the `throw` statement (§14.16). Subclasses of `Throwable` represent errors and exceptions.

The hierarchy of classes defined in package `java.lang` is as follows.

```
Object                              §20.1
    interface Cloneable                 §20.2
    Class                               §20.3
    Boolean                             §20.4
    Character                           §20.5
    Number                              §20.6
        Integer                             §20.7
        Long                                §20.8
        Float                               §20.9
        Double                              §20.10
    Math                                §20.11
    String                              §20.12
```

```
StringBuffer                                   §20.13
ClassLoader                                    §20.14
Process                                        §20.15
Runtime                                        §20.16
SecurityManager                                §20.17
System                                         §20.18
interface Runnable                             §20.19
Thread                                         §20.20
ThreadGroup                                    §20.21
Throwable                                      §20.22
   Error
      LinkageError
         ClassCircularityError
         ClassFormatError
         ExceptionInInitializerError
         IncompatibleClassChangeError
            AbstractMethodError
            IllegalAccessError
            InstantiationError
            NoSuchFieldError
            NoSuchMethodError
         NoClassDefFoundError
         UnsatisfiedLinkError
         VerifyError
      VirtualMachineError
         InternalError
         OutOfMemoryError
         StackOverflowError
         UnknownError
      ThreadDeath
   Exception
      ClassNotFoundException
      CloneNotSupportedException
      IllegalAccessException
      InstantiationException
      InterruptedException
      RuntimeException
         ArithmeticException
         ArrayStoreException
         ClassCastException
         IllegalArgumentException
            IllegalThreadStateException
            NumberFormatException
         IllegalMonitorStateException
```

```
IndexOutOfBoundsException
NegativeArraySizeException
NullPointerException
SecurityException
```

20.1 The Class java.lang.Object

The class Object is the single root of the class hierarchy. All objects, including arrays, implement the methods of this class.

```
public class Object {
    public final Class getClass();
    public String toString();
    public boolean equals(Object obj);
    public int hashCode();
    protected Object clone()
        throws CloneNotSupportedException;
    public final void wait()
        throws IllegalMonitorStateException,
            InterruptedException;
    public final void wait(long millis)
        throws IllegalMonitorStateException,
            InterruptedException;
    public final void wait(long millis, int nanos)
        throws IllegalMonitorStateException,
            InterruptedException;
    public final void notify()
        throws IllegalMonitorStateException;
    public final void notifyAll()
        throws IllegalMonitorStateException;
    protected void finalize()
        throws Throwable;
}
```

20.1.1 public final Class getClass()

This method returns a reference to the unique object of type Class (§20.3) that represents the class of this object. That Class object is the object that is locked by static synchronized methods of the represented class.

20.1.2 public String toString()

The general contract of toString is that it returns a string that "textually represents" this object. The idea is to provide a concise but informative representation that will be useful to a person reading it.

The toString method defined by class Object returns a string consisting of the name of the class of which the object is an instance, a commercial at character

'@', and the unsigned hexadecimal representation of the hashcode of the object. In other words, this method returns a string equal to the value of:

```
getClass().getName() + '@' + Integer.toHexString(hashCode())
```

Overridden by `Class` (§20.3), `Boolean` (§20.4), `Character` (§20.5), `Integer` (§20.7), `Long` (§20.8), `Float` (§20.9), `Double` (§20.10), `String` (§20.12), `StringBuffer` (§20.13), `Thread` (§20.20), `ThreadGroup` (§20.21), `Throwable` (§20.22.4), and `Bitset` (§21.2).

20.1.3 `public boolean` **`equals`**`(Object obj)`

This method indicates whether some other object is "equal to" this one.

The general contract of `equals` is that it implements an equivalence relation:

- It is *reflexive*: for any reference value `x`, `x.equals(x)` should return `true`.
- It is *symmetric*: for any reference values `x` and `y`, `x.equals(y)` should return `true` if and only if `y.equals(x)` returns `true`.
- It is *transitive*: for any reference values `x`, `y`, and `z`, if `x.equals(y)` returns `true` and `y.equals(z)` returns `true`, then `x.equals(z)` should return `true`.
- It is *consistent*: for any reference values `x` and `y`, multiple invocations of `x.equals(y)` consistently return `true` or consistently return `false`, provided no information used by `x` and `y` in `equals` comparisons is modified.
- For any non-null reference value `x`, `x.equals(null)` should return `false`.

The `equals` method defined by class `Object` implements the most discriminating possible equivalence relation on objects; that is, for any reference values `x` and `y`, `((Object)x).equals(y)` returns `true` if and only if `x` and `y` refer to the same object.

Overridden by `Boolean` (§20.4), `Character` (§20.5), `Integer` (§20.7), `Long` (§20.8), `Float` (§20.9), `Double` (§20.10), `String` (§20.12), and `Bitset` (§21.2).

20.1.4 `public int` **`hashCode`**`()`

This method is supported principally for the benefit of hash tables such as those provided by the Java library class `java.util.Hashtable` (§21.5).

The general contract of `hashCode` is as follows:

- Whenever it is invoked on the same object more than once during an execution of a Java application, `hashCode` must consistently return the same integer. The integer may be positive, negative, or zero. This integer does not, however, have to remain consistent from one Java application to another, or from one execution of an application to another execution of the same application.

- If two objects are equal according to the `equals` method (§20.1.3), then calling the `hashCode` method on each of the two objects must produce the same integer result.

- It is *not* required that if two objects are unequal according to the `equals` method (§20.1.3), then calling the `hashCode` method on each of the two objects must produce distinct integer results. However, the programmer should be aware that producing distinct integer results for unequal objects may improve the performance of hashtables.

As much as is reasonably practical, the `hashCode` method defined by class `Object` does return distinct integers for distinct objects. (This is typically implemented by converting the internal address of the object into an integer, but this implementation technique is not required by the Java language.)

Overridden by `Boolean` (§20.4), `Character` (§20.5), `Integer` (§20.7), `Long` (§20.8), `Float` (§20.9), `Double` (§20.10), `String` (§20.12), and `Bitset` (§21.2).

20.1.5 `protected Object clone() throws CloneNotSupportedException`

The general contract of clone is that it creates and returns a copy of this object. The precise meaning of "copy" may depend on the class of the object. The general intent is that, for any object `x`, the expression:

```
x.clone() != x
```

will be `true`, and that the expression:

```
x.clone.getClass() == x.getClass()
```

will be `true`, but these are not absolute requirements. While it is typically the case that:

```
x.clone.equals(x)
```

will be `true`, this is not an absolute requirement. Copying an object will typically entail creating a new instance of its class, but it also may require copying of internal data structures as well.

The method `clone` for class `Object` performs a specific cloning operation. First, if the class of this object does not implement the interface `Cloneable`, then a `CloneNotSupportedException` is thrown. Note that all arrays are considered to implement the interface `Cloneable`. Otherwise, this method creates a new instance of the class of this object and initializes all its fields with exactly the contents of the corresponding fields of this object, as if by assignment; the contents of the fields are not themselves cloned. Thus, this method performs a "shallow copy" of this object, not a "deep copy" operation.

The class `Object` does *not* itself implement the interface `Cloneable`, so calling the `clone` method on an object whose class is `Object` will result in throwing an exception at run time. The `clone` method is implemented by the class `Object` as a convenient, general utility for subclasses that implement the interface `Cloneable`, possibly also overriding the `clone` method, in which case the overriding definition can refer to this utility definition by the call:

```
super.clone()
```

20.1.6 `public final void wait() throws IllegalMonitorStateException, InterruptedException`

This method causes the current thread to wait until some other thread invokes the `notify` method (§20.1.9) or the `notifyAll` method (§20.1.10) for this object.

In other words, this method behaves exactly as if it simply performs the call `wait(0)` (§20.1.7).

20.1.7 `public final void wait(long millis) throws IllegalMonitorStateException, InterruptedException`

This method causes the current thread to wait until either some other thread invokes the `notify` method (§20.1.9) or the `notifyAll` method (§20.1.10) for this object, or a certain amount of real time has elapsed.

This method may be called only when the current thread is already synchronized on this object. If the current thread does not own the lock on this object, an `IllegalMonitorStateException` is thrown.

This method causes the current thread (call it *T*) to place itself in the wait set (§17.14) for this object and then to relinquish any and all synchronization claims on this object. Thread *T* becomes disabled for thread scheduling purposes and lies dormant until one of four things happens:

- Some other thread invokes the `notify` method for this object and thread *T* happens to be arbitrarily chosen as the thread to be awakened.
- Some other thread invokes the `notifyAll` method for this object.
- Some other thread interrupts (§20.20.31) thread *T*.
- The specified amount of real time has elapsed, more or less. The amount of real time, measured in milliseconds, is given by `millis`. If `millis` is zero, however, then real time is not taken into consideration and the thread simply waits until notified.

The thread *T* is then removed from the wait set for this object and re-enabled for thread scheduling. It then competes in the usual manner with other threads for the right to synchronize on the object; once it has gained control of the object, all its synchronization claims on the object are restored to the status quo ante—that is, to the situation as of the time that the `wait` method was invoked. Thread *T* then returns from the invocation of the `wait` method. Thus, on return from the `wait` method, the synchronization state of the object and of thread *T* is exactly as it was when the `wait` method was invoked.

If the current thread is interrupted (§20.20.31) by another thread while it is waiting, then an `InterruptedException` is thrown. This exception is not thrown until the lock status of this object has been restored as described above.

Note that the `wait` method, as it places the current thread into the wait set for this object, unlocks only this object; any other objects on which the current thread may be synchronized remain locked while the thread waits.

20.1.8 `public final void wait(long millis, int nanos) throws IllegalMonitorStateException, InterruptedException`

```
public final void wait(long millis, int nanos)
        throws IllegalMonitorStateException,
            InterruptedException
```

This method causes the current thread to wait until either some other thread invokes the `notify` method (§20.1.9) or the `notifyAll` method (§20.1.10) for this object, or some other thread interrupts the current thread, or a certain amount of real time has elapsed.

The amount of real time, measured in nanoseconds, is given by:

```
1000000*millis+nanos
```

In all other respects, this method does the same thing as the method `wait` of one argument (§20.1.7). In particular, `wait(0, 0)` means the same thing as `wait(0)`.

20.1.9 `public final void notify() throws IllegalMonitorStateException`

If any threads are waiting (§20.1.7) on this object, one of them is chosen to be awakened. The choice is arbitrary and at the discretion of the implementation.

The `notify` method may be called only when the current thread is already synchronized on this object. If the current thread does not own the lock on this object, an `IllegalMonitorStateException` is thrown.

The awakened thread will not be able to proceed until the current thread relinquishes the lock on this object. The awakened thread will compete in the usual manner with any other threads that might be actively competing to synchronize on this object; for example, the awakened thread enjoys no reliable privilege or disadvantage in being the next thread to lock this object.

20.1.10 `public final void notifyAll() throws IllegalMonitorStateException`

All the threads waiting (§20.1.7) on this object are awakened.

The `notifyAll` method may be called only when the current thread is already synchronized on this object. If the current thread does not own the lock on this object, an `IllegalMonitorStateException` is thrown.

The awakened threads will not be able to proceed until the current thread relinquishes the lock on this object. The awakened threads will compete in the usual manner with any other threads that might be actively competing to synchronize on this object; for example, the awakened threads enjoy no reliable privilege or disadvantage in being the next thread to lock this object.

20.1.11 `protected void finalize() throws Throwable`

The general contract of `finalize` is that it is invoked if and when the Java Virtual Machine has determined that there is no longer any means by which this object can be accessed by any thread that has not yet died (§12.7), except as a result of an action taken by the finalization of some other object or class which is ready to be finalized. The `finalize` method may take any action, including making this object available again to other threads; the usual purpose of `finalize`, however, is to perform cleanup actions before the object is irrevocably discarded. For example, the `finalize` method for an object that represents an input/output connection might perform explicit I/O transactions to break the connection before the object is permanently discarded.

The `finalize` method of class `Object` performs no special action; it simply returns normally. Subclasses of `Object` may override this definition.

Java does not guarantee which thread will invoke the `finalize` method for any given object. It is guaranteed, however, that the thread that invokes `finalize` will not be holding any user-visible synchronization locks when `finalize` is invoked. If an uncaught exception is thrown by the `finalize` method, the exception is ignored and finalization of that object terminates.

After the `finalize` method has been invoked for an object, no further action is taken until the Java Virtual Machine has again determined that there is no longer any means by which this object can be accessed by any thread that has not yet died, including possible actions by other objects or classes which are ready to be finalized, at which point the object may be discarded.

The `finalize` method is never invoked more than once by a Java Virtual Machine for any given object.

20.2 The Interface java.lang.Cloneable

The Cloneable interface should be implemented by any class that is intended to support or override the method clone (§20.1.5).

```
public interface Cloneable { }
```

The interface Cloneable declares no methods.

I am disappointed in Japp. He has no method!
—Agatha Christie, *The Mysterious Affair at Styles* (1920), Chapter 8

20.3 The Class `java.lang.Class`

Instances of the class `Class` represent classes and interfaces in a way that can be manipulated by a running Java program. Every array also belongs to a class represented by a `Class` object that is shared among all arrays with the same element type and number of dimensions.

There is no public constructor for the class `Class`. The Java Virtual Machine automatically constructs `Class` objects as classes are loaded; such objects cannot be created by user programs.

```
public final class Class {
    public String toString();
    public String getName();
    public boolean isInterface();
    public Class getSuperclass();
    public Class[] getInterfaces();
    public Object newInstance()
        throws InstantiationException, IllegalAccessException;
    public ClassLoader getClassLoader();
    public static Class forName(String className)
        throws ClassNotFoundException;
}
```

20.3.1 `public String toString()`

If this `Class` object represents a class (which may be a declared class or an array class), a string is returned consisting of the word `class`, a space, and the name of the class as returned by the `getName` method (§20.3.2). If this `Class` object represents an interface, a string is returned consisting of the word `interface`, a space, and the name of the interface as returned by the `getName` method.

In other words, this method returns a string equal to the value of:

```
(isInterface() ? "interface " : "class ") + getName()
```

Overrides the `toString` method of `Object` (§20.1.2).

20.3.2 `public String getName()`

The fully qualified name (except for arrays, see below) of the class or interface represented by this `Class` object is returned as a `String`. For example:

```
new Object().getClass().getName()
```

returns `"java.lang.Object"`.

If this class object represents a class of arrays, then the internal form of the name consists of the name of the element type in Java signature format, preceded by one or more "[" characters representing the depth of array nesting. Thus:

```
(new Object[3]).getClass().getName()
```

returns "[Ljava.lang.Object;" and:

```
(new int[3][4][5][6][7][8][9]).getClass().getName()
```

returns "[[[[[[[I". The encoding of element type names is as follows:

```
B            byte
C            char
D            double
F            float
I            int
J            long
Lclassname;  class or interface
S            short
Z            boolean
```

A class or interface name *classname* is given in fully qualified form as shown in the example above. For a full description of type descriptors see the chapter on the format of class files in the *Java Virtual Machine Specification*.

20.3.3 public boolean **isInterface**()

If this Class object represents an interface, true is returned. If this Class object represents a class, false is returned.

20.3.4 public Class **getSuperclass**()

If this Class object represents any class other than the class Object, then the Class that represents the superclass of that class is returned. If this Class object is the one that represents the class Object, or if it represents an interface, null is returned. If this Class object represents an array class, then the Class that represents class Object is returned.

20.3.5 public Class[] **getInterfaces**()

This method returns an array of objects that represent interfaces. The array may be empty.

If this Class object represents a class, the array contains objects representing all interfaces directly implemented by the class. The order of the interface objects in the array corresponds to the order of the interface names in the `implements` clause of the declaration of the class represented by this `Class` object. For example, given the class declaration:

```
class Shimmer implements FloorWax, DessertTopping { ... }
```

suppose the value of `s` is an instance of `Shimmer`; the value of the expression:

```
s.getClass().getInterfaces()[0]
```

is the `Class` object that represents interface `FloorWax`; and the value of:

```
s.getClass().getInterfaces()[1]
```

is the `Class` object that represents interface `DessertTopping`.

If this `Class` object represents an interface, the array contains objects representing all interfaces directly extended by the interface—that is, the immediate superinterfaces of the interface. The order of the interface objects in the array corresponds to the order of the interface names in the `extends` clause of the declaration of the interface represented by this `Class` object.

20.3.6 `public Object` **`newInstance`**`()`
`throws InstantiationException, IllegalAccessException`

This method creates and returns a new instance of the class represented by this `Class` object. This is done exactly as if by a class instance creation expression (§15.8) with an empty argument list; for example, if `t` is the `Class` object that represents class `Thread`, then `t.newInstance()` does exactly the same thing as `new Thread()`. If evaluation of such a class instance creation expression would complete abruptly, then the call to the `newInstance` method will complete abruptly for the same reason. See also §11.5.1.2 for more on `InstantiationException`.

20.3.7 `public ClassLoader` **`getClassLoader`**`()`

This method returns a reference to the class loader (§20.14) that loaded this class. If this class has no class loader, then `null` is returned.

20.3.8 `public static Class` **`forName`**`(String className)`
`throws ClassNotFoundException`

Given the name of a class á la `getName` (§20.3.2), this method attempts to locate, load, and link the class (§12.2). If it succeeds, then a reference to the `Class` object for the class is returned. If it fails, then a `ClassNotFoundException` is thrown.

20.4 The Class `java.lang.Boolean`

Objects of type `Boolean` represent primitive values of type `boolean`.

```
public final class Boolean {
    public static final Boolean TRUE = new Boolean(true);
    public static final Boolean FALSE = new Boolean(false);
    public Boolean(boolean value);
    public Boolean(String s);
    public String toString();
    public boolean equals(Object obj);
    public int hashCode();
    public boolean booleanValue();
    public static Boolean valueOf(String s);
    public static boolean getBoolean(String name);
}
```

20.4.1 `public static final Boolean TRUE = new Boolean(true);`

The constant value of this field is a `Boolean` object corresponding to the primitive value `true`.

20.4.2 `public static final Boolean FALSE = new Boolean(false);`

The constant value of this field is a `Boolean` object corresponding to the primitive value `false`.

20.4.3 `public Boolean(boolean value)`

This constructor initializes a newly created `Boolean` object so that it represents the primitive value that is the argument.

20.4.4 `public Boolean(String s)`

This constructor initializes a newly created `Boolean` object so that it represents `true` if and only if the argument is not `null` and is equal, ignoring case, to the string `"true"`.

Examples:

`new Boolean("True")` produces a `Boolean` object that represents `true`.
`new Boolean("yes")` produces a `Boolean` object that represents `false`.

20.4.5 public String **toString**()

If this Boolean object represents true, a string equal to "true" is returned. If this Boolean object represents false, a string equal to "false" is returned.

Overrides the toString method of Object (§20.1.2).

20.4.6 public boolean **equals**(Object obj)

The result is true if and only if the argument is not null and is a Boolean object that represents the same boolean value as this Boolean object.

Overrides the equals method of Object (§20.1.3).

20.4.7 public int **hashCode**()

If this Boolean object represents true, the integer 1231 is returned. If this Boolean object represents false, the integer 1237 is returned.

Overrides the hashCode method of Object (§20.1.4).

20.4.8 public boolean **booleanValue**()

The primitive boolean value represented by this Boolean object is returned.

20.4.9 public static boolean **valueOf**(String s)

The result is true if and only if the argument is not null and is equal, ignoring case, to the string "true".

Example: Boolean.valueOf("True") returns true.

Example: Boolean.valueOf("yes") returns false.

20.4.10 public static boolean **getBoolean**(String name)

The result is true if and only if the value of the system property (§20.18.9) named by the argument is equal, ignoring case, to the string "true".

This above all: to thine ownself be true,
And it must follow, as the night the day,
Thou canst not then be false to any man.
—William Shakespeare, *Hamlet*, Act I, scene iii

20.5 The Class java.lang.Character

Here is the whole set! a character dead at every word.
—Richard Brinsley Sheridan, *The School for Scandal*, Act 2, scene 2

Objects of type Character represent primitive values of type char.

```
public final class Character {
    public static final char MIN_VALUE = '\u0000';
    public static final char MAX_VALUE = '\uffff';
    public static final int MIN_RADIX = 2;
    public static final int MAX_RADIX = 36;
    public Character(char value);
    public String toString();
    public boolean equals(Object obj);
    public int hashCode();
    public char charValue();
    public static boolean isDefined(char ch);
    public static boolean isLowerCase(char ch);
    public static boolean isUpperCase(char ch);
    public static boolean isTitleCase(char ch);
    public static boolean isDigit(char ch);
    public static boolean isLetter(char ch);
    public static boolean isLetterOrDigit(char ch);
    public static boolean isJavaLetter(char ch);
    public static boolean isJavaLetterOrDigit(char ch);
    public static boolean isSpace(char ch);
    public static char toLowerCase(char ch);
    public static char toUpperCase(char ch);
    public static char toTitleCase(char ch);
    public static int digit(char ch, int radix);
    public static char forDigit(int digit, int radix);
}
```

Many of the methods of class Character are defined in terms of a "Unicode attribute table" that specifies a name for every defined Unicode character as well as other possible attributes, such as a decimal value, an uppercase equivalent, a lowercase equivalent, and/or a titlecase equivalent. Prior to Java 1.1, these methods were internal to the Java compiler and based on Unicode 1.1.5, as described here. The most recent versions of these methods should be used in Java compilers that are to run on Java systems that do not yet include these methods.

The Unicode 1.1.5 attribute table is available on the World Wide Web as:

```
ftp://unicode.org/pub/MappingTables/UnicodeData-1.1.5.txt
```

However, this file contains a few errors. The term "Unicode attribute table" in the following sections refers to the contents of this file after the following corrections have been applied:

- The following entries should have titlecase mappings as shown here:

```
03D0;GREEK BETA SYMBOL;Ll;0;L;;;;;N;GREEK SMALL LETTER CURLED BETA;;0392;;0392
03D1;GREEK THETA SYMBOL;Ll;0;L;;;;;N;GREEK SMALL LETTER SCRIPT THETA;;0398;;0398
03D5;GREEK PHI SYMBOL;Ll;0;L;;;;;N;GREEK SMALL LETTER SCRIPT PHI;;03A6;;03A6
03D6;GREEK PI SYMBOL;Ll;0;L;;;;;N;GREEK SMALL LETTER OMEGA PI;;03A0;;03A0
03F0;GREEK KAPPA SYMBOL;Ll;0;L;;;;;N;GREEK SMALL LETTER SCRIPT KAPPA;;039A;;039A
03F1;GREEK RHO SYMBOL;Ll;0;L;;;;;N;GREEK SMALL LETTER TAILED RHO;;03A1;;03A1
```

- The following entries should have numeric values as shown here:

```
FF10;FULLWIDTH DIGIT ZERO;Nd;0;EN;0030;0;0;0;N;;;;;
FF11;FULLWIDTH DIGIT ONE;Nd;0;EN;0031;1;1;1;N;;;;;
FF12;FULLWIDTH DIGIT TWO;Nd;0;EN;0032;2;2;2;N;;;;;
FF13;FULLWIDTH DIGIT THREE;Nd;0;EN;0033;3;3;3;N;;;;;
FF14;FULLWIDTH DIGIT FOUR;Nd;0;EN;0034;4;4;4;N;;;;;
FF15;FULLWIDTH DIGIT FIVE;Nd;0;EN;0035;5;5;5;N;;;;;
FF16;FULLWIDTH DIGIT SIX;Nd;0;EN;0036;6;6;6;N;;;;;
FF17;FULLWIDTH DIGIT SEVEN;Nd;0;EN;0037;7;7;7;N;;;;;
FF18;FULLWIDTH DIGIT EIGHT;Nd;0;EN;0038;8;8;8;N;;;;;
FF19;FULLWIDTH DIGIT NINE;Nd;0;EN;0039;9;9;9;N;;;;;
```

- The following entries should have no lowercase equivalents:

```
03DA;GREEK LETTER STIGMA;Lu;0;L;;;;;N;GREEK CAPITAL LETTER STIGMA;;;;
03DC;GREEK LETTER DIGAMMA;Lu;0;L;;;;;N;GREEK CAPITAL LETTER DIGAMMA;;;;
03DE;GREEK LETTER KOPPA;Lu;0;L;;;;;N;GREEK CAPITAL LETTER KOPPA;;;;
03E0;GREEK LETTER SAMPI;Lu;0;L;;;;;N;GREEK CAPITAL LETTER SAMPI;;;;
```

- This entry should have uppercase and titlecase equivalents as shown here:

```
03C2;GREEK SMALL LETTER FINAL SIGMA;Ll;0;L;;;;;N;;;03A3;;03A3
```

It is anticipated that these problems will be corrected for Unicode version 2.0.

Java 1.1 will include the methods defined here, either based on Unicode 1.1.5 or, we hope, updated versions of the methods that use the newer Unicode 2.0. The character attribute table for Unicode 2.0 is currently available on the World Wide Web as the file:

```
ftp://unicode.org/pub/MappingTables/UnicodeData-2.0.12.txt
```

If you are implementing a Java compiler or system, please refer to the page:

```
http://java.sun.com/Series
```

which will be updated with information about the Unicode-dependent methods.

The biggest change in Unicode 2.0 is a complete rearrangement of the Korean Hangul characters. There are numerous smaller improvements as well.

It is our intention that Java will track Unicode as it evolves over time. Given that full Unicode support is just emerging in the marketplace, and that changes in Unicode are in areas which are not yet widely used, this should cause minimal problems and further Java's goal of worldwide language support.

20.5.1 `public static final char` **`MIN_VALUE`** `= '\u0000';`

The constant value of this field is the smallest value of type `char`.

[This field is scheduled for introduction in Java version 1.1.]

20.5.2 `public static final char` **`MAX_VALUE`** `= '\uffff';`

The constant value of this field is the smallest value of type `char`.

[This field is scheduled for introduction in Java version 1.1.]

20.5.3 `public static final int` **`MIN_RADIX`** `= 2;`

The constant value of this field is the smallest value permitted for the radix argument in radix-conversion methods such as the `digit` method (§20.5.23), the `forDigit` method (§20.5.24), and the `toString` method of class `Integer` (§20.7).

20.5.4 `public static final int` **`MAX_RADIX`** `= 36;`

The constant value of this field is the largest value permitted for the radix argument in radix-conversion methods such as the `digit` method (§20.5.23), the `forDigit` method (§20.5.24), and the `toString` method of class `Integer` (§20.7).

20.5.5 `public` **`Character`**`(char value)`

This constructor initializes a newly created `Character` object so that it represents the primitive value that is the argument.

20.5.6 `public String` **`toString`**`()`

The result is a `String` whose length is `1` and whose sole component is the primitive `char` value represented by this `Character` object.

Overrides the `toString` method of `Object` (§20.1.2).

20.5.7 `public boolean` **`equals`**`(Object obj)`

The result is `true` if and only if the argument is not `null` and is a `Character` object that represents the same `char` value as this `Character` object.

Overrides the `equals` method of `Object` (§20.1.3).

20.5.8 public int **hashCode**()

The result is the primitive char value represented by this Character object, cast to type int.

Overrides the hashCode method of Object (§20.1.4).

20.5.9 public char **charValue**()

The primitive char value represented by this Character object is returned.

20.5.10 public static boolean **isDefined**(char ch)

The result is true if and only if the character argument is a defined Unicode character.

A character is a defined Unicode character if and only if at least one of the following is true:

- It has an entry in the Unicode attribute table.
- It is not less than \u3040 and not greater than \u9FA5.
- It is not less than \uF900 and not greater than \uFA2D.

It follows, then, that for Unicode 1.1.5 as corrected above, the defined Unicode characters are exactly those with codes in the following list, which contains both single codes and inclusive ranges: 0000-01F5, 01FA-0217, 0250-02A8, 02B0-02DE, 02E0-02E9, 0300-0345, 0360-0361, 0374-0375, 037A, 037E, 0384-038A, 038C, 038E-03A1, 03A3-03CE, 03D0-03D6, 03DA, 03DC, 03DE, 03E0, 03E2-03F3, 0401-040C, 040E-044F, 0451-045C, 045E-0486, 0490-04C4, 04C7-04C8, 04CB-04CC, 04D0-04EB, 04EE-04F5, 04F8-04F9, 0531-0556, 0559-055F, 0561-0587, 0589, 05B0-05B9, 05BB-05C3, 05D0-05EA, 05F0-05F4, 060C, 061B, 061F, 0621-063A, 0640-0652, 0660-066D, 0670-06B7, 06BA-06BE, 06C0-06CE, 06D0-06ED, 06F0-06F9, 0901-0903, 0905-0939, 093C-094D, 0950-0954, 0958-0970, 0981-0983, 0985-098C, 098F-0990, 0993-09A8, 09AA-09B0, 09B2, 09B6-09B9, 09BC, 09BE-09C4, 09C7-09C8, 09CB-09CD, 09D7, 09DC-09DD, 09DF-09E3, 09E6-09FA, 0A02, 0A05-0A0A, 0A0F-0A10, 0A13-0A28, 0A2A-0A30, 0A32-0A33, 0A35-0A36, 0A38-0A39, 0A3C, 0A3E-0A42, 0A47-0A48, 0A4B-0A4D, 0A59-0A5C, 0A5E, 0A66-0A74, 0A81-0A83, 0A85-0A8B, 0A8D, 0A8F-0A91, 0A93-0AA8, 0AAA-0AB0, 0AB2-0AB3, 0AB5-0AB9, 0ABC-0AC5, 0AC7-0AC9, 0ACB-0ACD, 0AD0, 0AE0, 0AE6-0AEF, 0B01-0B03, 0B05-0B0C, 0B0F-0B10,

0B13-0B28, 0B2A-0B30, 0B32-0B33, 0B36-0B39, 0B3C-0B43, 0B47-0B48, 0B4B-0B4D, 0B56-0B57, 0B5C-0B5D, 0B5F-0B61, 0B66-0B70, 0B82-0B83, 0B85-0B8A, 0B8E-0B90, 0B92-0B95, 0B99-0B9A, 0B9C, 0B9E-0B9F, 0BA3-0BA4, 0BA8-0BAA, 0BAE-0BB5, 0BB7-0BB9, 0BBE-0BC2, 0BC6-0BC8, 0BCA-0BCD, 0BD7, 0BE7-0BF2, 0C01-0C03, 0C05-0C0C, 0C0E-0C10, 0C12-0C28, 0C2A-0C33, 0C35-0C39, 0C3E-0C44, 0C46-0C48, 0C4A-0C4D, 0C55-0C56, 0C60-0C61, 0C66-0C6F, 0C82-0C83, 0C85-0C8C, 0C8E-0C90, 0C92-0CA8, 0CAA-0CB3, 0CB5-0CB9, 0CBE-0CC4, 0CC6-0CC8, 0CCA-0CCD, 0CD5-0CD6, 0CDE, 0CE0-0CE1, 0CE6-0CEF, 0D02-0D03, 0D05-0D0C, 0D0E-0D10, 0D12-0D28, 0D2A-0D39, 0D3E-0D43, 0D46-0D48, 0D4A-0D4D, 0D57, 0D60-0D61, 0D66-0D6F, 0E01-0E3A, 0E3F-0E5B, 0E81-0E82, 0E84, 0E87-0E88, 0E8A, 0E8D, 0E94-0E97, 0E99-0E9F, 0EA1-0EA3, 0EA5, 0EA7, 0EAA-0EAB, 0EAD-0EB9, 0EBB-0EBD, 0EC0-0EC4, 0EC6, 0EC8-0ECD, 0ED0-0ED9, 0EDC-0EDD, 10A0-10C5, 10D0-10F6, 10FB, 1100-1159, 115F-11A2, 11A8-11F9, 1E00-1E9A, 1EA0-1EF9, 1F00-1F15, 1F18-1F1D, 1F20-1F45, 1F48-1F4D, 1F50-1F57, 1F59, 1F5B, 1F5D, 1F5F-1F7D, 1F80-1FB4, 1FB6-1FC4, 1FC6-1FD3, 1FD6-1FDB, 1FDD-1FEF, 1FF2-1FF4, 1FF6-1FFE, 2000-202E, 2030-2046, 206A-2070, 2074-208E, 20A0-20AA, 20D0-20E1, 2100-2138, 2153-2182, 2190-21EA, 2200-22F1, 2300, 2302-237A, 2400-2424, 2440-244A, 2460-24EA, 2500-2595, 25A0-25EF, 2600-2613, 261A-266F, 2701-2704, 2706-2709, 270C-2727, 2729-274B, 274D, 274F-2752, 2756, 2758-275E, 2761-2767, 2776-2794, 2798-27AF, 27B1-27BE, 3000-3037, 303F, 3041-3094, 3099-309E, 30A1-30FE, 3105-312C, 3131-318E, 3190-319F, 3200-321C, 3220-3243, 3260-327B, 327F-32B0, 32C0-32CB, 32D0-32FE, 3300-3376, 337B-33DD, 33E0-33FE, 3400-9FA5, F900-FA2D, FB00-FB06, FB13-FB17, FB1E-FB36, FB38-FB3C, FB3E, FB40-FB41, FB43-FB44, FB46-FBB1, FBD3-FD3F, FD50-FD8F, FD92-FDC7, FDF0-FDFB, FE20-FE23, FE30-FE44, FE49-FE52, FE54-FE66, FE68-FE6B, FE70-FE72, FE74, FE76-FEFC, FEFF, FF01-FF5E, FF61-FFBE, FFC2-FFC7, FFCA-FFCF, FFD2-FFD7, FFDA-FFDC, FFE0-FFE6, FFE8-FFEE, FFFD.

[This method is scheduled for introduction in Java version 1.1, either as defined here, or updated for Unicode 2.0; see §20.5.]

20.5.11 public static boolean **isLowerCase**(char ch)

The result is true if and only if the character argument is a lowercase character.

A character is considered to be lowercase if and only if all of the following are true:

- The character ch is not in the range \u2000 through \u2FFF.
- The Unicode attribute table does not specify a mapping to lowercase for this character (the purpose of this requirement is to exclude titlecase characters).
- At least one of the following is true:
  - The Unicode attribute table specifies a mapping to uppercase for this character.
  - The name for the character in the Unicode attribute table contains the words SMALL LETTER or the words SMALL LIGATURE.

It follows, then, that for Unicode 1.1.5 as corrected above, the lowercase Unicode characters are exactly those with codes in the following list, which contains both single codes and inclusive ranges: 0061–007A, 00DF–00F6, 00F8–00FF, 0101–0137 (odds only), 0138–0148 (evens only), 0149–0177 (odds only), 017A–017E (evens only), 017F–0180, 0183, 0185, 0188, 018C–018D, 0192, 0195, 0199–019B, 019E, 01A1–01A5 (odds only), 01A8, 01AB, 01AD, 01B0, 01B4, 01B6, 01B9–01BA, 01BD, 01C6, 01C9, 01CC–01DC (evens only), 01DD–01EF (odds only), 01F0, 01F3, 01F5, 01FB–0217 (odds only), 0250–0261, 0263–0269, 026B–0273, 0275, 0277–027F, 0282–028E, 0290–0293, 029A, 029D–029E, 02A0, 02A3–02A8, 0390, 03AC–03CE, 03D0–03D1, 03D5–03D6, 03E3–03EF (odds only), 03F0–03F1, 0430–044F, 0451–045C, 045E–045F, 0461–0481 (odds only), 0491–04BF (odds only), 04C2, 04C4, 04C8, 04CC, 04D1–04EB (odds only), 04EF–04F5 (odds only), 04F9, 0561–0587, 1E01–1E95 (odds only), 1E96–1E9A, 1EA1–1EF9 (odds only), 1F00–1F07, 1F10–1F15, 1F20–1F27, 1F30–1F37, 1F40–1F45, 1F50–1F57, 1F60–1F67, 1F70–1F7D, 1F80–1F87, 1F90–1F97, 1FA0–1FA7, 1FB0–1FB4, 1FB6–1FB7, 1FC2–1FC4, 1FC6–1FC7, 1FD0–1FD3, 1FD6–1FD7, 1FE0–1FE7, 1FF2–1FF4, 1FF6–1FF7, FB00–FB06, FB13–FB17, FF41–FF5A.

Of the first 128 Unicode characters, exactly 26 are considered to be lowercase:

```
abcdefghijklmnopqrstuvwxyz
```

[This specification for the method isLowerCase is scheduled for introduction in Java version 1.1, either as defined here, or updated for Unicode 2.0; see §20.5. In previous versions of Java, this method returns false for all arguments larger than \u00FF.]

20.5.12 `public static boolean isUpperCase(char ch)`

The result is `true` if and only if the character argument is an uppercase character.

A character is considered to be uppercase if and only if all of the following are true:

- The character `ch` is not in the range `\u2000` through `\u2FFF`.
- The Unicode attribute table does not specify a mapping to uppercase for this character (the purpose of this requirement is to exclude titlecase characters).
- At least one of the following is true:
  - The Unicode attribute table specifies a mapping to lowercase for this character.
  - The name for the character in the Unicode attribute table contains the words `CAPITAL LETTER` or the words `CAPITAL LIGATURE`.

It follows, then, that for Unicode 1.1.5 as corrected above, the uppercase Unicode characters are exactly those with codes in the following list, which contains both single codes and inclusive ranges: `0041–005A`, `00C0–00D6`, `00D8–00DE`, `0100–0136` (evens only), `0139–0147` (odds only), `014A–0178` (evens only), `0179–017D` (odds only), `0181–0182`, `0184`, `0186`, `0187`, `0189–018B`, `018E–0191`, `0193–0194`, `0196–0198`, `019C–019D`, `019F–01A0`, `01A2`, `01A4`, `01A7`, `01A9`, `01AC`, `01AE`, `01AF`, `01B1–01B3`, `01B5`, `01B7`, `01B8`, `01BC`, `01C4`, `01C7`, `01CA`, `01CD–01DB` (odds only), `01DE–01EE` (evens only), `01F1`, `01F4`, `01FA–0216` (evens only), `0386`, `0388–038A`, `038C`, `038E`, `038F`, `0391–03A1`, `03A3–03AB`, `03E2–03EE` (evens only), `0401–040C`, `040E–042F`, `0460–0480` (evens only), `0490–04BE` (evens only), `04C1`, `04C3`, `04C7`, `04CB`, `04D0–04EA` (evens only), `04EE–04F4` (evens only), `04F8`, `0531–0556`, `10A0–10C5`, `1E00–1E94` (evens only), `1EA0–1EF8` (evens only), `1F08–1F0F`, `1F18–1F1D`, `1F28–1F2F`, `1F38–1F3F`, `1F48–1F4D`, `1F59–1F5F` (odds only), `1F68–1F6F`, `1F88–1F8F`, `1F98–1F9F`, `1FA8–1FAF`, `1FB8–1FBC`, `1FC8–1FCC`, `1FD8–1FDB`, `1FE8–1FEC`, `1FF8–1FFC`, `FF21–FF3A`.

Of the first 128 Unicode characters, exactly 26 are considered to be uppercase:

```
ABCDEFGHIJKLMNOPQRSTUVWXYZ
```

[This specification for the method `isUpperCase` is scheduled for introduction in Java version 1.1, either as defined here, or updated for Unicode 2.0; see §20.5. In previous versions of Java, this method returns `false` for all arguments larger than `\u00FF`.]

20.5.13 public static boolean **isTitleCase**(char ch)

The result is `true` if and only if the character argument is a titlecase character.

The notion of "titlecase" was introduced into Unicode to handle a peculiar situation: there are single Unicode characters whose appearance in each case looks exactly like two ordinary Latin letters. For example, there is a single Unicode character 'LJ' (`\u01C7`) that looks just like the characters 'L' and 'J' put together. There is a corresponding lowercase letter 'lj' (`\u01C9`) as well. These characters are present in Unicode primarily to allow one-to-one translations from the Cyrillic alphabet, as used in Serbia, for example, to the Latin alphabet. Now suppose the word "LJUBINJE" (which has *six* characters, not eight, because two of them are the single Unicode characters 'LJ' and 'NJ', perhaps produced by one-to-one translation from the Cyrillic) is to be written as part of a book title, in capitals and lowercase. The strategy of making the first letter uppercase and the rest lowercase results in "LJubinje"—most unfortunate. The solution is that there must be a third form, called a *titlecase* form. The titlecase form of 'LJ' is 'Lj' (`\u01C8`) and the titlecase form of 'NJ' is 'Nj'. A word for a book title is then best rendered by converting the first letter to titlecase if possible, otherwise to uppercase; the remaining letters are then converted to lowercase.

A character is considered to be titlecase if and only if both of the following are true:

- The character `ch` is not in the range `\u2000` through `\u2FFF`.
- The Unicode attribute table specifies a mapping to uppercase *and* a mapping to lowercase for this character.

There are exactly four Unicode 1.1.5 characters for which `isTitleCase` returns `true`:

```
\u01C5  LATIN CAPITAL LETTER D WITH SMALL LETTER Z WITH CARON
\u01C8  LATIN CAPITAL LETTER L WITH SMALL LETTER J
\u01CB  LATIN CAPITAL LETTER N WITH SMALL LETTER J
\u01F2  LATIN CAPITAL LETTER D WITH SMALL LETTER Z
```

[This method is scheduled for introduction in Java version 1.1, either as defined here, or updated for Unicode 2.0; see §20.5.]

20.5.14 public static boolean **isDigit**(char ch)

The result is `true` if and only if the character argument is a digit.

A character is considered to be a digit if and only if both of the following are true:

- The character `ch` is not in the range `\u2000` through `\u2FFF`.
- The name for the character in the Unicode attribute table contains the word `DIGIT`.

The digits are those characters with the following codes:

0030–0039	ISO-Latin-1 (and ASCII) digits ('0'–'9')
0660–0669	Arabic-Indic digits
06F0–06F9	Eastern Arabic-Indic digits
0966–096F	Devanagari digits
09E6–09EF	Bengali digits
0A66–0A6F	Gurmukhi digits
0AE6–0AEF	Gujarati digits
0B66–0B6F	Oriya digits
0BE7–0BEF	Tamil digits (there are only nine of these—no zero digit)
0C66–0C6F	Telugu digits
0CE6–0CEF	Kannada digits
0D66–0D6F	Malayalam digits
0E50–0E59	Thai digits
0ED0–0ED9	Lao digits
FF10–FF19	Fullwidth digits

Of the first 128 Unicode characters, exactly 10 are considered to be digits:

```
0123456789
```

[This specification for the method `isDigit` is scheduled for introduction in Java version 1.1, either as defined here, or updated for Unicode 2.0; see §20.5. In previous versions of Java, this method returns `false` for all arguments larger than `\u00FF`.]

20.5.15 `public static boolean isLetter(char ch)`

The result is `true` if and only if the character argument is a letter.

A character is considered to be a letter if and only if it is a letter or digit (§20.5.16) but is not a digit (§20.5.14).

[This method is scheduled for introduction in Java version 1.1, either as defined here, or updated for Unicode 2.0; see §20.5.]

20.5.16 `public static boolean isLetterOrDigit(char ch)`

The result is `true` if and only if the character argument is a letter-or-digit.

A character is considered to be a letter-or-digit if and only if it is a defined Unicode character (§20.5.10) and its code lies in one of the following ranges:

`0030–0039`	ISO-Latin-1 (and ASCII) digits (`'0'–'9'`)
`0041–005A`	ISO-Latin-1 (and ASCII) uppercase Latin letters (`'A'-'Z'`)
`0061–007A`	ISO-Latin-1 (and ASCII) lowercase Latin letters (`'a'-'z'`)
`00C0–00D6`	ISO-Latin-1 supplementary letters
`00D8–00F6`	ISO-Latin-1 supplementary letters
`00F8–00FF`	ISO-Latin-1 supplementary letters
`0100–1FFF`	Latin extended-A, Latin extended-B, IPA extensions, spacing modifier letters, combining diacritical marks, basic Greek, Greek symbols and Coptic, Cyrillic, Armenian, Hebrew extended-A, Basic Hebrew, Hebrew extended-B, Basic Arabic, Arabic extended, Devanagari, Bengali, Gurmukhi, Gujarati, Oriya, Tamil, Telugu, Kannada, Malayalam, Thai, Lao, Basic Georgian, Georgian extended, Hanguljamo, Latin extended additional, Greek extended
`3040–9FFF`	Hiragana, Katakana, Bopomofo, Hangul compatibility Jamo, CJK miscellaneous, enclosed CJK characters and months, CJK compatibility, Hangul, Hangul supplementary-A, Hangul supplementary-B, CJK unified ideographs
`F900–FDFF`	CJK compatibility ideographs, alphabetic presentation forms, Arabic presentation forms-A
`FE70–FEFE`	Arabic presentation forms-B
`FF10–FF19`	Fullwidth digits
`FF21–FF3A`	Fullwidth Latin uppercase
`FF41–FF5A`	Fullwidth Latin lowercase
`FF66–FFDC`	Halfwidth Katakana and Hangul

It follows, then, that for Unicode 1.1.5 as corrected above, the Unicode letters and digits are exactly those with codes in the following list, which contains both single codes and inclusive ranges: `0030–0039`, `0041–005A`, `0061–007A`, `00C0–00D6`, `00D8–00F6`, `00F8–01F5`, `01FA–0217`, `0250–02A8`, `02B0–02DE`, `02E0–02E9`, `0300–0345`, `0360–0361`, `0374–0375`, `037A`, `037E`, `0384–038A`, `038C`, `038E`, `038F–03A1`, `03A3–03CE`, `03D0–03D6`, `03DA–03E2`, `03DA`, `03DC`, `03DE`, `03E0`, `03E2–03F3`, `0401–040C`, `040E–044F`, `0451–045C`, `045E–0486`, `0490–04C4`, `04C7–04C8`, `04CB–04CC`, `04D0–04EB`, `04EE–04F5`, `04F8–04F9`, `0531–0556`, `0559–055F`, `0561–0587`, `0589`, `05B0–05B9`, `05BB–05C3`, `05D0–05EA`, `05F0–05F4`,

060C, 061B, 061F, 0621, 0622–063A, 0640–0652, 0660–066D, 0670–06B7, 06BA–06BE, 06C0–06CE, 06D0–06ED, 06F0–06F9, 0901–0903, 0905–0939, 093C–094D, 0950–0954, 0958–0970, 0981–0983, 0985–098C, 098F–0990, 0993–09A8, 09AA–09B0, 09B2, 09B6–09B9, 09BC, 09BE, 09BF–09C4, 09C7–09C8, 09CB–09CD, 09D7, 09DC–09DD, 09DF–09E3, 09E6–09FA, 0A02, 0A05–0A0A, 0A0F–0A10, 0A13–0A28, 0A2A–0A30, 0A32–0A33, 0A35–0A36, 0A38–0A39, 0A3C, 0A3E, 0A3F–0A42, 0A47–0A48, 0A4B–0A4D, 0A59–0A5C, 0A5E, 0A66–0A74, 0A81–0A83, 0A85–0A8B, 0A8D, 0A8F, 0A90–0A91, 0A93–0AA8, 0AAA–0AB0, 0AB2–0AB3, 0AB5–0AB9, 0ABC–0AC5, 0AC7–0AC9, 0ACB–0ACD, 0AD0, 0AE0, 0AE6–0AEF, 0B01–0B03, 0B05–0B0C, 0B0F–0B10, 0B13–0B28, 0B2A–0B30, 0B32–0B33, 0B36–0B39, 0B3C–0B43, 0B47–0B48, 0B4B–0B4D, 0B56–0B57, 0B5C–0B5D, 0B5F–0B61, 0B66–0B70, 0B82–0B83, 0B85–0B8A, 0B8E–0B90, 0B92–0B95, 0B99–0B9A, 0B9C, 0B9E, 0B9F, 0BA3–0BA4, 0BA8–0BAA, 0BAE–0BB5, 0BB7–0BB9, 0BBE–0BC2, 0BC6–0BC8, 0BCA–0BCD, 0BD7, 0BE7–0BF2, 0C01–0C03, 0C05–0C0C, 0C0E–0C10, 0C12–0C28, 0C2A–0C33, 0C35–0C39, 0C3E–0C44, 0C46–0C48, 0C4A–0C4D, 0C55–0C56, 0C60–0C61, 0C66–0C6F, 0C82–0C83, 0C85–0C8C, 0C8E–0C90, 0C92–0CA8, 0CAA–0CB3, 0CB5–0CB9, 0CBE–0CC4, 0CC6–0CC8, 0CCA–0CCD, 0CD5–0CD6, 0CDE, 0CE0, 0CE1, 0CE6–0CEF, 0D02–0D03, 0D05–0D0C, 0D0E–0D10, 0D12–0D28, 0D2A–0D39, 0D3E–0D43, 0D46–0D48, 0D4A–0D4D, 0D57, 0D60–0D61, 0D66–0D6F, 0E01–0E3A, 0E3F–0E5B, 0E81–0E82, 0E84, 0E87–0E88, 0E8A, 0E8D, 0E94–0E97, 0E99–0E9F, 0EA1–0EA3, 0EA5, 0EA7, 0EAA–0EAB, 0EAD–0EB9, 0EBB–0EBD, 0EC0–0EC4, 0EC6, 0EC8, 0EC9–0ECD, 0ED0–0ED9, 0EDC–0EDD, 10A0–10C5, 10D0–10F6, 10FB, 1100–1159, 115F–11A2, 11A8–11F9, 1E00–1E9A, 1EA0–1EF9, 1F00–1F15, 1F18–1F1D, 1F20–1F45, 1F48–1F4D, 1F50–1F57, 1F59, 1F5B, 1F5D, 1F5F–1F7D, 1F80–1FB4, 1FB6–1FC4, 1FC6–1FD3, 1FD6–1FDB, 1FDD–1FEF, 1FF2–1FF4, 1FF6–1FFE, 3041–3094, 3099–309E, 30A1–30FE, 3105–312C, 3131–318E, 3190–319F, 3200–321C, 3220–3243, 3260–327B, 327F–32B0, 32C0–32CB, 32D0–32FE, 3300–3376, 337B–33DD, 33E0–33FE, 3400–9FA5, F900–FA2D, FB00–FB06, FB13–FB17, FB1E–FB36, FB38–FB3C, FB3E, FB40, FB41, FB43, FB44, FB46, FB47–FBB1, FBD3–FD3F, FD50–FD8F, FD92–FDC7, FDF0–FDFB, FE70–FE72, FE74, FE76, FE77–FEFC, FF10–FF19, FF21–FF3A, FF41–FF5A, FF66–FFBE, FFC2–FFC7, FFCA–FFCF, FFD2–FFD7, FFDA–FFDC.

[This method is scheduled for introduction in Java version 1.1, either as defined here, or updated for Unicode 2.0; see §20.5.]

20.5.17 `public static boolean isJavaLetter(char ch)`

The result is true if and only if the character argument is a character that can begin a Java identifier.

A character is considered to be a Java letter if and only if it is a letter (§20.5.15) or is the dollar sign character `'$'` (`\u0024`) or the underscore ("low line") character `'_'` (`\u005F`).

[This method is scheduled for introduction in Java version 1.1, either as defined here, or updated for Unicode 2.0; see §20.5.]

20.5.18 `public static boolean isJavaLetterOrDigit(char ch)`

The result is true if and only if the character argument is a character that can occur in a Java identifier after the first character.

A character is considered to be a Java letter-or-digit if and only if it is a letter-or-digit (§20.5.16) or is the dollar sign character `'$'` (`\u0024`) or the underscore ("low line") character `'_'` (`\u005F`).

[This method is scheduled for introduction in Java version 1.1, either as defined here, or updated for Unicode 2.0; see §20.5.]

20.5.19 `public static boolean isSpace(char ch)`

The result is `true` if the argument `ch` is one of the following characters:

`'\t'`	`\u0009`	HT	HORIZONTAL TABULATION
`'\n'`	`\u000A`	LF	LINE FEED (also known as NEW LINE)
`'\f'`	`\u000C`	FF	FORM FEED
`'\r'`	`\u000D`	CR	CARRIAGE RETURN
`' '`	`\u0020`	SP	SPACE

Otherwise, the result is `false`.

20.5.20 `public static char toLowerCase(char ch)`

If the character `ch` has a lowercase equivalent specified in the Unicode attribute table, then that lowercase equivalent character is returned. Otherwise, the argument `ch` is returned.

The lowercase equivalents specified in the Unicode attribute table, for Unicode 1.1.5 as corrected above, are as follows, where character codes to the right of arrows are the lowercase equivalents of character codes to the left of arrows: 0041–005A⇒0061–007A, 00C0–00D6⇒00E0–00F6, 00D8–00DE⇒00F8–00FE, 0100–012E⇒0101–012F (evens to odds), 0132–0136⇒0133–0137 (evens to odds), 0139–0147⇒013A–0148 (odds to evens), 014A–0176⇒014B–0177 (evens to odds), 0178⇒00FF, 0179–017D⇒017A–017E (odds to evens), 0181⇒0253, 0182⇒0183, 0184⇒0185, 0186⇒0254, 0187⇒0188, 018A⇒0257, 018B⇒018C, 018E⇒0258, 018F⇒0259, 0190⇒025B, 0191⇒0192, 0193⇒0260, 0194⇒0263, 0196⇒0269, 0197⇒0268, 0198⇒0199, 019C⇒026F, 019D⇒0272, 01A0–01A4⇒01A1–01A5 (evens to odds), 01A7⇒01A8, 01A9⇒0283, 01AC⇒01AD, 01AE⇒0288, 01AF⇒01B0, 01B1⇒028A, 01B2⇒028B, 01B3⇒01B4, 01B5⇒01B6, 01B7⇒0292, 01B8⇒01B9, 01BC⇒01BD, 01C4⇒01C6, 01C5⇒01C6, 01C7⇒01C9, 01C8⇒01C9, 01CA⇒01CC, 01CB–01DB⇒01CC–01DC (odds to evens), 01DE–01EE⇒01DF–01EF (evens to odds), 01F1⇒01F3, 01F2⇒01F3, 01F4⇒01F5, 01FA–0216⇒01FB–0217 (evens to odds), 0386⇒03AC, 0388–038A⇒03AD–03AF, 038C⇒03CC, 038E⇒03CD, 038F⇒03CE, 0391–03A1⇒03B1–03C1, 03A3–03AB⇒03C3–03CB, 03E2–03EE⇒03E3–03EF (evens to odds), 0401–040C⇒0451–045C, 040E⇒045E, 040F⇒045F, 0410–042F⇒0430–044F, 0460–0480⇒0461–0481 (evens to odds), 0490–04BE⇒0491–04BF (evens to odds), 04C1⇒04C2, 04C3⇒04C4, 04C7⇒04C8, 04CB⇒04CC, 04D0–04EA⇒04D1–04EB (evens to odds), 04EE–04F4⇒04EF–04F5 (evens to odds), 04F8⇒04F9, 0531–0556⇒0561–0586, 10A0–10C5⇒10D0–10F5, 1E00–1E94⇒1E01–1E95 (evens to odds), 1EA0–1EF8⇒1EA1–1EF9 (evens to odds), 1F08–1F0F⇒1F00–1F07, 1F18–1F1D⇒1F10–1F15, 1F28–1F2F⇒1F20–1F27, 1F38–1F3F⇒1F30–1F37, 1F48–1F4D⇒1F40–1F45, 1F59⇒1F51, 1F5B⇒1F53, 1F5D⇒1F55, 1F5F⇒1F57, 1F68–1F6F⇒1F60–1F67, 1F88–1F8F⇒1F80–1F87, 1F98–1F9F⇒1F90–1F97, 1FA8–1FAF⇒1FA0–1FA7, 1FB8⇒1FB0, 1FB9⇒1FB1, 1FBA⇒1F70, 1FBB⇒1F71, 1FBC⇒1FB3, 1FC8–1FCB⇒1F72–1F75, 1FCC⇒1FC3, 1FD8⇒1FD0, 1FD9⇒1FD1, 1FDA⇒1F76, 1FDB⇒1F77, 1FE8⇒1FE0, 1FE9⇒1FE1, 1FEA⇒1F7A, 1FEB⇒1F7B, 1FEC⇒1FE5, 1FF8⇒1F78, 1FF9⇒1F79, 1FFA⇒1F7C, 1FFB⇒1F7D, 1FFC⇒1FF3, 2160–216F⇒2170–217F, 24B6–24CF⇒24D0–24E9, FF21–FF3A⇒FF41–FF5A.

Note that the method `isLowerCase` (§20.5.11) will not necessarily return `true` when given the result of the `toLowerCase` method.

[This specification for the method `toLowerCase` is scheduled for introduction in Java version 1.1, either as defined here, or updated for Unicode 2.0; see §20.5. In previous versions of Java, this method returns its argument for all arguments larger than \u00FF.]

20.5.21 `public static char toUpperCase(char ch)`

If the character `ch` has an uppercase equivalent specified in the Unicode attribute table, then that uppercase equivalent character is returned. Otherwise, the argument `ch` is returned.

The uppercase equivalents specified in the Unicode attribute table for Unicode 1.1.5 as corrected above, are as follows, where character codes to the right of arrows are the uppercase equivalents of character codes to the left of arrows: 0061–007A⇒0041–005A, 00E0–00F6⇒00C0–00D6, 00F8–00FE⇒00D8–00DE, 00FF⇒0178, 0101–012F⇒0100–012E (odds to evens), 0133–0137⇒0132–0136 (odds to evens), 013A–0148⇒0139–0147 (evens to odds), 014B–0177⇒014A–0176 (odds to evens), 017A–017E⇒0179–017D (evens to odds), 017F⇒0053, 0183–0185⇒0182–0184 (odds to evens), 0188⇒0187, 018C⇒018B, 0192⇒0191, 0199⇒0198, 01A1–01A5⇒01A0–01A4 (odds to evens), 01A8⇒01A7, 01AD⇒01AC, 01B0⇒01AF, 01B4⇒01B3, 01B6⇒01B5, 01B9⇒01B8, 01BD⇒01BC, 01C5⇒01C4, 01C6⇒01C4, 01C8⇒01C7, 01C9⇒01C7, 01CB⇒01CA, 01CC⇒01CA, 01CE–01DC⇒01CD–01DB (evens to odds), 01DF–01EF⇒01DE–01EE (odds to evens), 01F2⇒01F1, 01F3⇒01F1, 01F5⇒01F4, 01FB–0217⇒01FA–0216 (odds to evens), 0253⇒0181, 0254⇒0186, 0257⇒018A, 0258⇒018E, 0259⇒018F, 025B⇒0190, 0260⇒0193, 0263⇒0194, 0268⇒0197, 0269⇒0196, 026F⇒019C, 0272⇒019D, 0283⇒01A9, 0288⇒01AE, 028A⇒01B1, 028B⇒01B2, 0292⇒01B7, 03AC⇒0386, 03AD–03AF⇒0388–038A, 03B1–03C1⇒0391–03A1, 03C2⇒03A3, 03C3–03CB⇒03A3–03AB, 03CC⇒038C, 03CD⇒038E, 03CE⇒038F, 03D0⇒0392, 03D1⇒0398, 03D5⇒03A6, 03D6⇒03A0, 03E3–03EF⇒03E2–03EE (odds to evens), 03F0⇒039A, 03F1⇒03A1, 0430–044F⇒0410–042F, 0451–045C⇒0401–040C, 045E⇒040E, 045F⇒040F, 0461–0481⇒0460–0480 (odds to evens), 0491–04BF⇒0490–04BE (odds to evens), 04C2⇒04C1, 04C4⇒04C3, 04C8⇒04C7, 04CC⇒04CB, 04D1–04EB⇒04D0–04EA (odds to evens), 04EF–04F5⇒04EE–04F4 (odds to evens), 04F9⇒04F8, 0561–0586⇒0531–0556, 1E01–1E95⇒1E00–1E94 (odds to evens), 1EA1–1EF9⇒1EA0–1EF8 (odds to evens), 1F00–1F07⇒1F08–1F0F, 1F10–1F15⇒1F18–1F1D, 1F20–1F27⇒1F28–1F2F, 1F30–1F37⇒1F38–1F3F, 1F40–1F45⇒1F48–1F4D, 1F51⇒1F59, 1F53⇒1F5B, 1F55⇒1F5D, 1F57⇒1F5F, 1F60–1F67⇒1F68–1F6F, 1F70⇒1FBA, 1F71⇒1FBB, 1F72–1F75⇒1FC8–1FCB, 1F76⇒1FDA, 1F77⇒1FDB, 1F78⇒1FF8, 1F79⇒1FF9, 1F7A⇒1FEA, 1F7B⇒1FEB, 1F7C⇒1FFA, 1F7D⇒1FFB, 1F80–1F87⇒1F88–1F8F, 1F90–1F97⇒1F98–1F9F, 1FA0–1FA7⇒1FA8–1FAF, 1FB0⇒1FB8, 1FB1⇒1FB9, 1FB3⇒1FBC, 1FC3⇒1FCC, 1FD0⇒1FD8, 1FD1⇒1FD9, 1FE0⇒1FE8, 1FE1⇒1FE9, 1FE5⇒1FEC, 1FF3⇒1FFC, 2170–217F⇒2160–216F, 24D0–24E9⇒24B6–24CF, FF41–FF5A⇒FF21–FF3A.

Note that the method `isUpperCase` (§20.5.12) will not necessarily return `true` when given the result of the `toUpperCase` method.

[This specification for the method toUpperCase is scheduled for introduction in Java version 1.1, either as defined here, or updated for Unicode 2.0; see §20.5. In previous versions of Java, this method returns its argument for all arguments larger than \u00FE. Note that although \u00FF is a lowercase character, its uppercase equivalent is \u0178; toUpperCase in versions of Java prior to version 1.1 simply do not consistently handle or use Unicode character codes above \u00FF.]

20.5.22 public static char **toTitleCase**(char ch)

If the character ch has a titlecase equivalent specified in the Unicode attribute table, then that titlecase equivalent character is returned; otherwise, the argument ch is returned.

Note that the method isTitleCase (§20.5.13) will not necessarily return true when given the result of the toTitleCase method. The Unicode attribute table always has the titlecase attribute equal to the uppercase attribute for characters that have uppercase equivalents but no separate titlecase form.

Example: Character.toTitleCase('a') returns 'A'

Example: Character.toTitleCase('Q') returns 'Q'

Example: Character.toTitleCase('lj') returns 'Lj' where 'lj' is the Unicode character \u01C9 and 'Lj' is its titlecase equivalent character \u01C8.

[This method is scheduled for introduction in Java version 1.1.]

20.5.23 public static int **digit**(char ch, int radix)

Returns the numeric value of the character ch considered as a digit in the specified radix. If the value of radix is not a valid radix, or the character ch is not a valid digit in the specified radix, then -1 is returned.

A radix is valid if and only if its value is not less than Character.MIN_RADIX (§20.5.3) and not greater than Character.MAX_RADIX (§20.5.4).

A character is a valid digit if and only if one of the following is true:

- The method isDigit returns true for the character, and the decimal digit value of the character, as specified in the Unicode attribute table, is less than the specified radix. In this case, the decimal digit value is returned.
- The character is one of the uppercase Latin letters 'A'–'Z' (\u0041–\u005A) and its code is less than radix+'A'-10. In this case ch-'A'+10 is returned.
- The character is one of the lowercase Latin letters 'a'–'z' (\u0061–\u007A) and its code is less than radix+'a'-10. In this case ch-'a'+10 is returned.

[This specification for the method `digit` is scheduled for introduction in Java version 1.1, either as defined here, or updated for Unicode 2.0; see §20.5. In previous versions of Java, this method returns `-1` for all character codes larger than `\u00FF`.]

20.5.24 `public static char` **`forDigit`**`(int digit, int radix)`

Returns a character that represents the given digit in the specified radix. If the value of `radix` is not a valid radix, or the value of `digit` is not a valid digit in the specified radix, the null character `'\u0000'` is returned.

A radix is valid if and only if its value is not less than `Character.MIN_RADIX` (§20.5.3) and not greater than `Character.MAX_RADIX` (§20.5.4).

A digit is valid if and only if it is nonnegative and less than the `radix`.

If the digit is less than `10`, then the character value `'0'+digit` is returned; otherwise, `'a'+digit-10` is returned. Thus, the digits produced by `forDigit`, in increasing order of value, are the ASCII characters:

```
0123456789abcdefghijklmnopqrstuvwxyz
```

(these are `'\u0030'` through `'\u0039'` and `'\u0061'` through `'\u007a'`). If uppercase letters are desired, the `toUpperCase` method may be called on the result:

```
Character.toUpperCase(Character.forDigit(digit, radix))
```

20.6 The Class `java.lang.Number`

The abstract class `Number` has subclasses `Integer`, `Long`, `Float`, and `Double` which wrap primitive types, defining abstract methods to convert the represented numeric value to `int`, `long`, `float`, and `double`.

```
public abstract class Number {
    public abstract int intValue();
    public abstract long longValue();
    public abstract float floatValue();
    public abstract double doubleValue();
}
```

20.6.1 `public abstract int intValue()`

The general contract of the `intValue` method is that it returns the numeric value represented by this `Number` object after converting it to type `int`.

Overridden by `Integer` (§20.7.8), `Long` (§20.8.8), `Float` (§20.9.12), and `Double` (§20.10.11).

20.6.2 `public abstract long longValue()`

The general contract of the `longValue` method is that it returns the numeric value represented by this `Number` object after converting it to type `long`.

Overridden by `Integer` (§20.7.9), `Long` (§20.8.9), `Float` (§20.9.13), and `Double` (§20.10.12).

20.6.3 `public abstract float floatValue()`

The general contract of the `floatValue` method is that it returns the numeric value represented by this `Number` object after converting it to type `float`.

Overridden by `Integer` (§20.7.10), `Long` (§20.8.10), `Float` (§20.9.14), and `Double` (§20.10.13).

20.6.4 `public abstract double doubleValue()`

The general contract of the `doubleValue` method is that it returns the numeric value represented by this `Number` object after converting it to type `double`.

Overridden by `Integer` (§20.7.11), `Long` (§20.8.11), `Float` (§20.9.15), and `Double` (§20.10.14).

20.7 The Class java.lang.Integer

```
public final class Integer extends Number {
   public static final int MIN_VALUE = 0x80000000;
   public static final int MAX_VALUE = 0x7fffffff;
   public Integer(int value);
   public Integer(String s)
      throws NumberFormatException;
   public String toString();
   public boolean equals(Object obj);
   public int hashCode();
   public int intValue();
   public long longValue();
   public float floatValue();
   public double doubleValue();
   public static String toString(int i);
   public static String toString(int i, int radix);
   public static String toHexString(long i);
   public static String toOctalString(long i);
   public static String toBinaryString(long i);
   public static int parseInt(String s)
      throws NumberFormatException;
   public static int parseInt(String s, int radix)
      throws NumberFormatException;
   public static Integer valueOf(String s)
      throws NumberFormatException;
   public static Integer valueOf(String s, int radix)
      throws NumberFormatException;
   public static Integer getInteger(String nm);
   public static Integer getInteger(String nm, int val);
   public static Integer getInteger(String nm, Integer val);
}
```

20.7.1 `public static final int MIN_VALUE = 0x80000000;`

The constant value of this field is `-2147483648`, the lowest value of type `int`.

20.7.2 `public static final int MAX_VALUE = 0x7fffffff;`

The constant value of this field is `2147483647`, the highest value of type `int`.

20.7.3 public **Integer**(int value)

This constructor initializes a newly created Integer object so that it represents the primitive value that is the argument.

20.7.4 public **Integer**(String s) throws NumberFormatException

This constructor initializes a newly created Integer object so that it represents the integer represented by the string in decimal form. The string is converted to an int in exactly the manner used by the parseInt method (§20.7.18) for radix 10.

20.7.5 public String **toString**()

The integer value represented by this Integer object is converted to signed decimal representation and returned as a string, exactly as if the integer value were given as an argument to the toString method that takes one argument (§20.7.12).

Overrides the toString method of Object (§20.1.2).

20.7.6 public boolean **equals**(Object obj)

The result is true if and only if the argument is not null and is an Integer object that represents the same int value as this Integer object.

Overrides the equals method of Object (§20.1.3).

20.7.7 public int **hashCode**()

The result is the primitive int value represented by this Integer object.

Overrides the hashCode method of Object (§20.1.4).

20.7.8 public int **intValue**()

The int value represented by this Integer object is returned.

Overrides the intValue method of Number (§20.6.1).

20.7.9 public long **longValue**()

The int value represented by this Integer object is converted (§5.1.2) to type long and the result of the conversion is returned.

Overrides the longValue method of Number (§20.6.2).

20.7.10 public float **floatValue**()

The `int` value represented by this `Integer` object is converted (§5.1.2) to type `float` and the result of the conversion is returned.

Overrides the `floatValue` method of `Number` (§20.6.3).

20.7.11 public double **doubleValue**()

The `int` value represented by this `Integer` object is converted (§5.1.2) to type `double` and the result of the conversion is returned.

Overrides the `doubleValue` method of `Number` (§20.6.4).

20.7.12 public static String **toString**(int i)

The argument is converted to signed decimal representation and returned as a string, exactly as if the argument and the radix `10` were given as arguments to the `toString` method that takes two arguments (§20.7.13).

20.7.13 public static String **toString**(int i, int radix)

The first argument is converted to a signed representation in the radix specified by the second argument; this representation is returned as a string.

If the `radix` is smaller than `Character.MIN_RADIX` (§20.5.3) or larger than `Character.MAX_RADIX` (§20.5.4), then the value `10` is used instead.

If the first argument is negative, the first character of the result will be the character `'-'` (`'\u002d'`). If the first argument is not negative, no sign character appears in the result.

The remaining characters of the result represent the magnitude of the first argument. If the magnitude is zero, it is represented by a single zero character `'0'` (`'\u0030'`); otherwise, the first character of the representation of the magnitude will not be the zero character.The following ASCII characters are used as digits:

```
0123456789abcdefghijklmnopqrstuvwxyz
```

These are `'\u0030'` through `'\u0039'` and `'\u0061'` through `'\u007a'`. If the `radix` is *N*, then the first *N* of these characters are used as radix-*N* digits in the order shown. Thus, the digits for hexadecimal (radix 16) are `0123456789abcdef`. If uppercase letters are desired, the `toUpperCase` method (§20.12.36) of class `String` may be called on the result:

```
Integer.toString(n, 16).toUpperCase()
```

20.7.14 `public static String toHexString(int i)`

The argument is converted to an unsigned representation in hexadecimal radix (base 16); this representation is returned as a string.

The result represents the unsigned magnitude of the argument. This equals the argument plus 2^{32} if the argument is negative; otherwise, it equals the argument.

If the unsigned magnitude is zero, it is represented by a single zero character `'0'` (`'\u0030'`); otherwise, the first character of the representation of the unsigned magnitude will not be the zero character. The following characters are used as hexadecimal digits:

```
0123456789abcdef
```

These are the characters `'\u0030'` through `'\u0039'` and `'\u0061'` through `'\u0066'`. If uppercase letters are desired, the `toUpperCase` method (§20.12.36) of class `String` may be called on the result:

```
Long.toHexString(n).toUpperCase()
```

20.7.15 `public static String toOctalString(int i)`

The argument is converted to an unsigned representation in octal radix (base 8); this representation is returned as a string.

The result represents the unsigned magnitude of the argument. This equals the argument plus 2^{32} if the argument is negative; otherwise, it equals the argument.

If the unsigned magnitude is zero, it is represented by a single zero character `'0'` (`'\u0030'`); otherwise, the first character of the representation of the unsigned magnitude will not be the zero character. The octal digits are:

```
01234567
```

These are the characters `'\u0030'` through `'\u0037'`.

20.7.16 `public static String toBinaryString(int i)`

The argument is converted to an unsigned representation in binary radix (base 2); this representation is returned as a string.

The result represents the unsigned magnitude of the argument. This equals the argument plus 2^{32} if the argument is negative; otherwise, it equals the argument.

If the unsigned magnitude is zero, it is represented by a single zero character `'0'` (`'\u0030'`); otherwise, the first character of the representation of the unsigned magnitude will not be the zero character. The characters `'0'` (`'\u0030'`) and `'1'` (`'\u0031'`) are used as binary digits.

20.7.17 `public static int` **`parseInt`**`(String s) throws NumberFormatException`

The argument is interpreted as representing a signed decimal integer. The components of the string must all be decimal digits, except that the first character may be `'-'` (`'\u002d'`) to indicate a negative value. The resulting integer value is returned, exactly as if the argument and the radix `10` were given as arguments to the `parseInt` method that takes two arguments (§20.7.18).

20.7.18 `public static int` **`parseInt`**`(String s, int radix) throws NumberFormatException`

The first argument is interpreted as representing a signed integer in the radix specified by the second argument. The components of the string must all be digits of the specified radix (as determined by whether `Character.digit` (§20.5.23) returns a nonnegative value), except that the first character may be `'-'` (`'\u002d'`) to indicate a negative value. The resulting integer value is returned.

An exception of type `NumberFormatException` is thrown if any of the following situations occurs:

- The first argument is `null` or is a string of length zero.
- The `radix` is either smaller than `Character.MIN_RADIX` (§20.5.3) or larger than `Character.MAX_RADIX` (§20.5.4).
- Any character of the string is not a digit of the specified `radix`, except that the first character may be a minus sign `'-'` (`'\u002d'`) provided that the string is longer than length 1.
- The integer value represented by the string is not a value of type `int`.

Examples:

```
parseInt("0", 10) returns 0
parseInt("473", 10) returns 473
parseInt("-0", 10) returns 0
parseInt("-FF", 16) returns -255
parseInt("1100110", 2) returns 102
parseInt("2147483647", 10) returns 2147483647
parseInt("-2147483648", 10) returns -2147483648
parseInt("2147483648", 10) throws a NumberFormatException
parseInt("99", 8) throws a NumberFormatException
parseInt("Kona", 10) throws a NumberFormatException
parseInt("Kona", 27) returns 411787
```

20.7.19 `public static Integer` **`valueOf`**`(String s)`
`throws NumberFormatException`

The argument is interpreted as representing a signed decimal integer, exactly as if the argument were given to the `parseInt` method that takes one argument (§20.7.17). The result is an `Integer` object that represents the integer value specified by the string.

In other words, this method returns an `Integer` object equal to the value of:

```
new Integer(Integer.parseInt(s))
```

20.7.20 `public static Integer` **`valueOf`**`(String s, int radix)`
`throws NumberFormatException`

The first argument is interpreted as representing a signed integer in the radix specified by the second argument, exactly as if the arguments were given to the `parseInt` method that takes two arguments (§20.7.18). The result is an `Integer` object that represents the integer value specified by the string.

In other words, this method returns an `Integer` object equal to the value of:

```
new Integer(Integer.parseInt(s, radix))
```

20.7.21 `public static Integer` **`getInteger`**`(String nm)`

The first argument is treated as the name of a system property to be obtained as if by the method `System.getProperty` (§20.18.9). The string value of this property is then interpreted as an integer value and an `Integer` object representing this value is returned. If there is no property of the specified name, or if the property does not have the correct numeric format, then `null` is returned.

In other words, this method returns an `Integer` object equal to the value of:

```
getInteger(nm, null)
```

20.7.22 `public static Integer` **`getInteger`**`(String nm, int val)`

The first argument is treated as the name of a system property to be obtained as if by the method `System.getProperty` (§20.18.9). The string value of this property is then interpreted as an integer value and an `Integer` object representing this value is returned. If the property does not have the correct numeric format, then an `Integer` object that represents the value of the second argument is returned.

In other words, this method returns an Integer object equal to the value of:

```
getInteger(nm, new Integer(val))
```

but in practice it may be implemented in a manner such as:

```
Integer result = getInteger(nm, null);
return (result == null) ? new Integer(val) : result;
```

to avoid the unnecessary allocation of an Integer object when the default value is not needed.

20.7.23 public static Integer **getInteger**(String nm, Integer val)

The first argument is treated as the name of a system property to be obtained as if by the method System.getProperty (§20.18.9). The string value of this property is then interpreted as an integer value and an Integer object representing this value is returned.

- If the property value begins with the two ASCII characters 0x or the ASCII character #, not followed by a minus sign, then the rest of it is parsed as a hexadecimal integer exactly as for the method Integer.valueOf (§20.7.20) with radix 16.
- If the property value begins with the ASCII character 0 followed by another character, it is parsed as an octal integer exactly as for the method Integer.valueOf (§20.7.20) with radix 8.
- Otherwise, the property value is parsed as a decimal integer exactly as for the method Integer.valueOf (§20.7.20) with radix 10.

The second argument serves as a default value. If there is no property of the specified name, or if the property does not have the correct numeric format, then the second argument is returned.

20.8 The Class java.lang.Long

```
public final class Long extends Number {
    public static final long MIN_VALUE = 0x8000000000000000L;
    public static final long MAX_VALUE = 0x7fffffffffffffffL;
    public Long(long value);
    public Long(String s)
        throws NumberFormatException;
    public String toString();
    public boolean equals(Object obj);
    public int hashCode();
    public int intValue();
    public long longValue();
    public float floatValue();
    public double doubleValue();
    public static String toString(long i);
    public static String toString(long i, int radix);
    public static String toHexString(long i);
    public static String toOctalString(long i);
    public static String toBinaryString(long i);
    public static long parseLong(String s)
        throws NumberFormatException;
    public static long parseLong(String s, int radix)
        throws NumberFormatException;
    public static Long valueOf(String s)
        throws NumberFormatException;
    public static Long valueOf(String s, int radix)
        throws NumberFormatException;
    public static Long getLong(String nm);
    public static Long getLong(String nm, long val);
    public static Long getLong(String nm, Long val);
}
```

20.8.1 `public static final long MIN_VALUE = 0x8000000000000000L;`

The constant value of this field is the lowest value of type `long`.

20.8.2 `public static final long MAX_VALUE = 0x7fffffffffffffffL;`

The constant value of this field is the highest value of type `long`.

20.8.3 public **Long**(long value)

This constructor initializes a newly created Long object so that it represents the primitive value that is the argument.

20.8.4 public **Long**(String s) throws NumberFormatException

This constructor initializes a newly created Long object so that it represents the integer represented by the string in decimal form. The string is converted to a long value in exactly the manner used by the parseLong method (§20.8.17) for radix 10.

20.8.5 public String **toString**()

The long integer value represented by this Long object is converted to signed decimal representation and returned as a string, exactly as if the integer value were given as an argument to the toString method that takes one argument (§20.7.12).

Overrides the toString method of Object (§20.1.2).

20.8.6 public boolean **equals**(Object obj)

The result is true if and only if the argument is not null and is a Long object that represents the same long value as this Long object.

Overrides the equals method of Object (§20.1.3).

20.8.7 public int **hashCode**()

The result is the exclusive OR of the two halves of the primitive long value represented by this Long object. That is, the hashcode is the value of the expression:

```
(int)(this.longValue()^(this.longValue()>>>32))
```

Overrides the hashCode method of Object (§20.1.4).

20.8.8 public int **intValue**()

The long value represented by this Long object is converted (§5.1.3) to type int and the result of the conversion is returned.

Overrides the intValue method of Number (§20.6.1).

20.8.9 `public long longValue()`

The `long` value represented by this `Long` object is returned.

Overrides the `longValue` method of `Number` (§20.6.2).

20.8.10 `public float floatValue()`

The `long` value represented by this `Long` object is converted (§5.1.2) to type `float` and the result of the conversion is returned.

Overrides the `floatValue` method of `Number` (§20.6.3).

20.8.11 `public double doubleValue()`

The `long` value represented by this `Long` object is converted (§5.1.2) to type `double` and the result of the conversion is returned.

Overrides the `doubleValue` method of `Number` (§20.6.4).

20.8.12 `public static String toString(long i)`

The argument is converted to signed decimal representation and returned as a string, exactly as if the argument and the radix `10` were given as arguments to the `toString` method that takes two arguments (§20.8.13).

20.8.13 `public static String toString(long i, int radix)`

The first argument is converted to a signed representation in the radix specified by the second argument; this representation is returned as a string.

If the `radix` is smaller than `Character.MIN_RADIX` (§20.5.3) or larger than `Character.MAX_RADIX` (§20.5.4), then the value `10` is used instead.

If the first argument is negative, the first character of the result will be the character `'-'` (`'\u002d'`). If the first argument is not negative, no sign character appears in the result.

The remaining characters of the result represent the magnitude of the first argument. If the magnitude is zero, it is represented by a single zero character `'0'` (`'\u0030'`); otherwise, the first character of the representation of the magnitude will not be the zero character. The following ASCII characters are used as digits:

```
0123456789abcdefghijklmnopqrstuvwxyz
```

These are `'\u0030'` through `'\u0039'` and `'\u0061'` through `'\u007a'`. If the `radix` is *N*, then the first *N* of these characters are used as radix-*N* digits in the order shown. Thus, the digits for hexadecimal (radix 16) are `0123456789abcdef`. If uppercase letters are desired, the `toUpperCase` method (§20.12.36) of class `String` may be called on the result:

```
Long.toString(n, 16).toUpperCase()
```

20.8.14 `public static String` **`toHexString`**`(long i)`

The argument is converted to an unsigned representation in hexadecimal radix (base 16); this representation is returned as a string.

The result represents the unsigned magnitude of the argument. This equals the argument plus 2^{64} if the argument is negative; otherwise, it equals the argument.

If the unsigned magnitude is zero, it is represented by a single zero character `'0'` (`'\u0030'`); otherwise, the first character of the representation of the unsigned magnitude will not be the zero character. The following characters are used as hexadecimal digits:

```
0123456789abcdef
```

These are the characters `'\u0030'` through `'\u0039'` and `'\u0061'` through `'\u0066'`. If uppercase letters are desired, the `toUpperCase` method (§20.12.36) of class `String` may be called on the result:

```
Long.toHexString(n).toUpperCase()
```

20.8.15 `public static String` **`toOctalString`**`(long i)`

The argument is converted to an unsigned representation in octal radix (base 8); this representation is returned as a string.

The result represents the unsigned magnitude of the argument. This equals the argument plus 2^{64} if the argument is negative; otherwise, it equals the argument.

If the unsigned magnitude is zero, it is represented by a single zero character `'0'` (`'\u0030'`); otherwise, the first character of the representation of the unsigned magnitude will not be the zero character. The following characters are used as octal digits:

```
01234567
```

These are the characters `'\u0030'` through `'\u0037'`.

20.8.16 `public static String` **`toBinaryString`**`(long i)`

The argument is converted to an unsigned representation in binary radix (base 2); this representation is returned as a string.

The result represents the unsigned magnitude of the argument. This equals the argument plus 2^{64} if the argument is negative; otherwise, it equals the argument.

If the unsigned magnitude is zero, it is represented by a single zero character `'0'` (`'\u0030'`); otherwise, the first character of the representation of the unsigned magnitude will not be the zero character. The characters `'0'` (`'\u0030'`) and `'1'` (`'\u0031'`) are used as binary digits.

20.8.17 `public static long` **`parseLong`**`(String s)`
`throws NumberFormatException`

The argument is interpreted as representing a signed decimal integer. The components of the string must all be decimal digits, except that the first character may be `'-'` (`'\u002d'`) to indicate a negative value. The resulting `long` value is returned, exactly as if the argument and the radix `10` were given as arguments to the `parseLong` method that takes two arguments (§20.8.18).

Note that neither `L` nor `l` is permitted to appear at the end of the string as a type indicator, as would be permitted in Java source code (§3.10.1).

20.8.18 `public static long` **`parseLong`**`(String s, int radix)`
`throws NumberFormatException`

The first argument is interpreted as representing a signed integer in the radix specified by the second argument. The components of the string must all be digits of the specified radix (as determined by whether `Character.digit` (§20.5.23) returns a nonnegative value), except that the first character may be `'-'` (`'\u002d'`) to indicate a negative value. The resulting `long` value is returned.

Note that neither `L` nor `l` is permitted to appear at the end of the string as a type indicator, as would be permitted in Java source code (§3.10.1)—except that either `L` or `l` may appear as a digit for a radix greater than `22`.

An exception of type `NumberFormatException` is thrown if any of the following situations occurs:

- The first argument is `null` or is a string of length zero.
- The `radix` is either smaller than `Character.MIN_RADIX` (§20.5.3) or larger than `Character.MAX_RADIX` (§20.5.4).

- The first character of the string is not a digit of the specified `radix` and is not a minus sign `'-'` (`'\u002d'`).
- The first character of the string is a minus sign and the string is of length 1.
- Any character of the string after the first is not a digit of the specified `radix`.
- The integer value represented by the string cannot be represented as a value of type `long`.

Examples:

```
parseLong("0", 10) returns 0L
parseLong("473", 10) returns 473L
parseLong("-0", 10) returns 0L
parseLong("-FF", 16) returns -255L
parseLong("1100110", 2) returns 102L
parseLong("99", 8) throws a NumberFormatException
parseLong("Hazelnut", 10) throws a NumberFormatException
parseLong("Hazelnut", 36) returns 1356099454469L
```

20.8.19 `public static Long` **`valueOf`**`(String s)`
`throws NumberFormatException`

The argument is interpreted as representing a signed decimal integer, exactly as if the argument were given to the `parseLong` method that takes one argument (§20.8.17). The result is a `Long` object that represents the integer value specified by the string.

In other words, this method returns a `Long` object equal to the value of:

```
new Long(Long.parseLong(s))
```

20.8.20 `public static Long` **`valueOf`**`(String s, int radix)`
`throws NumberFormatException`

The first argument is interpreted as representing a signed integer in the radix specified by the second argument, exactly as if the arguments were given to the `parseLong` method that takes two arguments (§20.8.18). The result is a `Long` object that represents the integer value specified by the string.

In other words, this method returns a `Long` object equal to the value of:

```
new Long(Long.parseLong(s, radix))
```

20.8.21 `public static Long getLong(String nm)`

The first argument is treated as the name of a system property to be obtained as if by the method `System.getProperty` (§20.18.9). The string value of this property is then interpreted as an integer value and a `Long` object representing this value is returned. If there is no property of the specified name, or if the property does not have the correct numeric format, then `null` is returned.

In other words, this method returns a `Long` object equal to the value of:

```
getLong(nm, null)
```

20.8.22 `public static Long getLong(String nm, long val)`

The first argument is treated as the name of a system property to be obtained as if by the method `System.getProperty` (§20.18.9). The string value of this property is then interpreted as an integer value and a `Long` object representing this value is returned. If there is no property of the specified name, or if the property does not have the correct numeric format, then a `Long` object that represents the value of the second argument is returned.

In other words, this method returns a `Long` object equal to the value of:

```
getLong(nm, new Long(val))
```

but in practice it may be implemented in a manner such as:

```
Long result = getLong(nm, null);
return (result == null) ? new Long(val) : result;
```

to avoid the unnecessary allocation of a `Long` object when the default value is not needed.

20.8.23 `public static Long getLong(String nm, Long val)`

The first argument is treated as the name of a system property to be obtained as if by the method `System.getProperty` (§20.18.9). The string value of this property is then interpreted as an integer value and a `Long` object representing this value is returned.

- If the property value begins with the two ASCII characters `0x` or the ASCII character `#`, not followed by a minus sign, then the rest of it is parsed as a hexadecimal integer exactly as for the method `Long.valueOf` (§20.7.20) with radix `16`.

- If the property value begins with the character `0` followed by another character, it is parsed as an octal integer exactly as for the method `Long.valueOf` (§20.7.20) with radix `8`.
- Otherwise the property value is parsed as a decimal integer exactly as for the method `Long.valueOf` (§20.7.20) with radix `10`.

Note that, in every case, neither `L` nor `l` is permitted to appear at the end of the property value as a type indicator, as would be permitted in Java source code (§3.10.1).

The second argument serves as a default value. If there is no property of the specified name, or if the property does not have the correct numeric format, then the second argument is returned.

20.9 The Class java.lang.Float

```
public final class Float extends Number {
    public static final float MIN_VALUE = 1.4e-45f;
    public static final float MAX_VALUE = 3.4028235e+38f;
    public static final float NEGATIVE_INFINITY = -1.0f/0.0f;
    public static final float POSITIVE_INFINITY = 1.0f/0.0f;
    public static final float NaN = 0.0f/0.0f;
    public Float(float value);
    public Float(double value);
    public Float(String s)
        throws NumberFormatException;
    public String toString();
    public boolean equals(Object obj);
    public int hashCode();
    public int intValue();
    public long longValue();
    public float floatValue();
    public double doubleValue();
    public static String toString(float f);
    public static Float valueOf(String s)
        throws NullPointerException, NumberFormatException;
    public boolean isNaN();
    public static boolean isNaN(float v);
    public boolean isInfinite();
    public static boolean isInfinite(float v);
    public static int floatToIntBits(float value);
    public static float intBitsToFloat(int bits);
}
```

20.9.1 public static final float **MIN_VALUE** = 1.4e-45f;

The constant value of this field is the smallest positive nonzero value of type `float`. It is equal to the value returned by `Float.intBitsToFloat(0x1)`.

20.9.2 public static final float **MAX_VALUE** = 3.4028235e+38f;

The constant value of this field is the largest positive finite value of type `float`. It is equal to the value returned by `Float.intBitsToFloat(0x7f7fffff)`.

20.9.3 `public static final float` **`NEGATIVE_INFINITY`** `= -1.0f/0.0f;`

The constant value of this field is the negative infinity of type `float`. It is equal to the value returned by `Float.intBitsToFloat(0xff800000)`.

20.9.4 `public static final float` **`POSITIVE_INFINITY`** `= 1.0f/0.0f;`

The constant value of this field is the positive infinity of type `float`. It is equal to the value returned by `Float.intBitsToFloat(0x7f800000)`.

20.9.5 `public static final float` **`NaN`** `= 0.0f/0.0f;`

The constant value of this field is the Not-a-Number value of type `float`. It is equal to the value returned by `Float.intBitsToFloat(0x7fc00000)`.

20.9.6 `public` **`Float`**`(float value)`

This constructor initializes a newly created `Float` object so that it represents the primitive value that is the argument.

20.9.7 `public` **`Float`**`(double value)`

This constructor initializes a newly created `Float` object so that it represents the result of narrowing (§5.1.3) the argument from type `double` to type `float`.

20.9.8 `public` **`Float`**`(String s) throws NumberFormatException`

This constructor initializes a newly created `Float` object so that it represents the floating-point value of type `float` represented by the string. The string is converted to a `float` value in exactly the manner used by the `valueOf` method (§20.9.17).

20.9.9 `public String` **`toString`**`()`

The primitive `float` value represented by this `Float` object is converted to a string exactly as if by the method `toString` of one argument (§20.9.16).

Overrides the `toString` method of `Object` (§20.1.2).

20.9.10 `public boolean` **`equals`**`(Object obj)`

The result is `true` if and only if the argument is not `null` and is a `Float` object that represents the same `float` value as this `Float` object. For this purpose, two `float` values are considered to be the same if and only if the method `floatToIntBits` (§20.9.22) returns the same `int` value when applied to each. Note that even though the == operator returns `false` if both operands are NaN, this `equals` method will return `true` if this `Float` object and the argument are both `Float` objects that represent NaN. On the other hand, even though the == operator returns `true` if one operand is positive zero and the other is negative zero, this `equals` method will return `false` if this `Float` object and the argument represent zeroes of different sign. This definition allows hashtables to operate properly.

Overrides the `equals` method of `Object` (§20.1.3).

20.9.11 `public int` **`hashCode`**`()`

The result is the integer bit representation, exactly as produced by the method `floatToIntBits` (§20.9.22), of the primitive `float` value represented by this `Float` object.

Overrides the `hashCode` method of `Object` (§20.1.4).

20.9.12 `public int` **`intValue`**`()`

The `float` value represented by this `Float` object is converted (§5.1.3) to type `int` and the result of the conversion is returned.

Overrides the `intValue` method of `Number` (§20.6.1).

20.9.13 `public long` **`longValue`**`()`

The `float` value represented by this `Float` object is converted (§5.1.3) to type `long` and the result of the conversion is returned.

Overrides the `longValue` method of `Number` (§20.6.2).

20.9.14 `public float` **`floatValue`**`()`

The `float` value represented by this `Float` object is returned.

Overrides the `floatValue` method of `Number` (§20.6.3).

20.9.15 public double **doubleValue**()

The `float` value represented by this `Float` object is converted (§5.1.2) to type `double` and the result of the conversion is returned.

Overrides the `doubleValue` method of `Number` (§20.6.4).

20.9.16 public static String **toString**(float f)

The argument is converted to a readable string format as follows. All characters and characters in strings mentioned below are ASCII characters.

- If the argument is NaN, the result is the string `"NaN"`.
- Otherwise, the result is a string that represents the sign and magnitude (absolute value) of the argument. If the sign is negative, the first character of the result is `'-'` (`'\u002d'`); if the sign is positive, no sign character appears in the result. As for the magnitude *m*:
  - If *m* is infinity, it is represented by the characters "`Infinity`"; thus, positive infinity produces the result `"Infinity"` and negative infinity produces the result `"-Infinity"`.
  - If *m* is zero, it is represented by the characters `"0.0"`; thus, negative zero produces the result `"-0.0"` and positive zero produces the result `"0.0"`.
  - If *m* is greater than or equal to 10^{-3} but less than 10^7, then it is represented as the integer part of *m*, in decimal form with no leading zeroes, followed by `'.'` (`\u002E`), followed by one or more decimal digits representing the fractional part of *m*.
  - If *m* is less than 10^{-3} or not less than 10^7, then it is represented in so-called "computerized scientific notation." Let *n* be the unique integer such that $10^n \le m < 10^{n+1}$; then let *a* be the mathematically exact quotient of *m* and 10^n so that $1 \le a < 10$. The magnitude is then represented as the integer part of *a*, as a single decimal digit, followed by `'.'` (`\u002E`), followed by decimal digits representing the fractional part of *a*, followed by the letter `'E'` (`\u0045`), followed by a representation of *n* as a decimal integer, as produced by the method `Integer.toString` of one argument (§20.7.12).

How many digits must be printed for the fractional part of *m* or *a*? There must be at least one digit to represent the fractional part, and beyond that as many, but only as many, more digits as are needed to uniquely distinguish the argument value from adjacent values of type `float`. That is, suppose that *x* is the exact mathematical value represented by the decimal representation produced by this method for a finite nonzero argument *f*. Then *f* must be the `float` value nearest to *x*; or, if two `float` values are equally close to *x*, then *f* must be one of them and the least significant bit of the significand of *f* must be `0`.

[This specification for the method `toString` is scheduled for introduction in Java version 1.1. In previous versions of Java, this method produces `Inf` instead of `Infinity` for infinite values. Also, it renders finite values in the same form as the `%g` format of the `printf` function in the C programming language, which can lose precision because it produces at most six digits after the decimal point.]

20.9.17 `public static Float valueOf(String s) throws NullPointerException, NumberFormatException`

The string `s` is interpreted as the representation of a floating-point value and a `Float` object representing that value is created and returned.

If `s` is `null`, then a `NullPointerException` is thrown.

Leading and trailing whitespace (§20.5.19) characters in `s` are ignored. The rest of `s` should constitute a *FloatValue* as described by the lexical syntax rules:

FloatValue:
  $Sign_{opt}$ *Digits* `.` $Digits_{opt}$ $ExponentPart_{opt}$
  $Sign_{opt}$ `.` *Digits* $ExponentPart_{opt}$

where *Sign*, *Digits*, and *ExponentPart* are as defined in §3.10.2. If it does not have the form of a *FloatValue*, then a `NumberFormatException` is thrown. Otherwise, it is regarded as representing an exact decimal value in the usual "computerized scientific notation"; this exact decimal value is then conceptually converted to an "infinitely precise" binary value that is then rounded to type `float` by the usual round-to-nearest rule of IEEE 754 floating-point arithmetic. Finally, a new object of class `Float` is created to represent this `float` value.

Note that neither `F` nor `f` is permitted to appear in `s` as a type indicator, as would be permitted in Java source code (§3.10.1).

20.9.18 `public boolean isNaN()`

The result is `true` if and only if the value represented by this `Float` object is NaN.

20.9.19 `public static boolean isNaN(float v)`

The result is `true` if and only if the value of the argument is NaN.

20.9.20 `public boolean isInfinite()`

The result is `true` if and only if the value represented by this `Float` object is positive infinity or negative infinity.

20.9.21 `public static boolean isInfinite(float v)`

The result is `true` if and only if the value of the argument is positive infinity or negative infinity.

20.9.22 `public static int floatToIntBits(float value)`

The result is a representation of the floating-point argument according to the IEEE 754 floating-point "single format" bit layout:

- Bit 31 (the bit that is selected by the mask `0x80000000`) represents the sign of the floating-point number.
- Bits 30–23 (the bits that are selected by the mask `0x7f800000`) represent the exponent.
- Bits 22–0 (the bits that are selected by the mask `0x007fffff`) represent the significand (sometimes called the mantissa) of the floating-point number.
- If the argument is positive infinity, the result will be `0x7f800000`.
- If the argument is negative infinity, the result will be `0xff800000`.
- If the argument is NaN, the result will be `0x7fc00000`.

In all cases, the result is an integer that, when given to the `intBitsToFloat` method (§20.9.23), will produce a floating-point value equal to the argument to `floatToIntBits`.

20.9.23 `public static float intBitsToFloat(int bits)`

The argument is considered to be a representation of a floating-point value according to the IEEE 754 floating-point "single format" bit layout. That floating-point value is returned as the result.

- If the argument is `0x7f800000`, the result will be positive infinity.
- If the argument is `0xff800000`, the result will be negative infinity.

- If the argument is any value in the range `0x7f800001` through `0x7fffffff` or in the range `0xff800001` through `0xffffffff`, the result will be NaN. (All IEEE 754 NaN values are, in effect, lumped together by the Java language into a single value called NaN.)
- In all other cases, let *s*, *e*, and *m* be three values that can be computed from the argument:

```
int s = ((bits >> 31) == 0) ? 1 : -1;
int e = ((bits >> 23) & 0xff);
int m = (e == 0) ?
        (bits & 0x7fffff) << 1 :
        (bits & 0x7fffff) | 0x800000;
```

Then the floating-point result equals the value of the mathematical expression $s \cdot m \cdot 2^{e-150}$.

I'm floating in a most peculiar way.
—David Bowie, *Space Oddity* (1969)

20.10 The Class java.lang.Double

```
public final class Double extends Number {
    public static final double MIN_VALUE =
          5e-324;
    public static final double MAX_VALUE =
          1.7976931348623157e+308;
    public static final double NEGATIVE_INFINITY = -1.0/0.0;
    public static final double POSITIVE_INFINITY = 1.0/0.0;
    public static final double NaN = 0.0/0.0;
    public Double(double value);
    public Double(String s)
       throws NumberFormatException;
    public String toString();
    public boolean equals(Object obj);
    public int hashCode();
    public int intValue();
    public long longValue();
    public float floatValue();
    public double doubleValue();
    public static String toString(double d);
    public static Double valueOf(String s)
       throws NullPointerException, NumberFormatException;
    public boolean isNaN();
    public static boolean isNaN(double v);
    public boolean isInfinite();
    public static boolean isInfinite(double v);
    public static long doubleToLongBits(double value);
    public static double longBitsToDouble(long bits);
}
```

20.10.1 `public static final double MIN_VALUE = 5e-324;`

The constant value of this field is the smallest positive nonzero value of type `double`. It is equal to the value returned by `Double.longBitsToDouble(0x1L)`.

20.10.2 `public static final double MAX_VALUE =`
`1.7976931348623157e+308;`

The constant value of this field is the largest positive finite value of type `double`. It is equal to the returned by:

```
Double.longBitsToDouble(0x7fefffffffffffffL)
```

20.10.3 `public static final double` **`NEGATIVE_INFINITY`** `= -1.0/0.0;`

The constant value of this field is the negative infinity of type `double`. It is equal to the value returned by `Double.longBitsToDouble(0xfff0000000000000L)`.

20.10.4 `public static final double` **`POSITIVE_INFINITY`** `= 1.0/0.0;`

The constant value of this field is the positive infinity of type `double`. It is equal to the value returned by `Double.longBitsToDouble(0x7ff0000000000000L)`.

20.10.5 `public static final double` **`NaN`** `= 0.0/0.0;`

The constant value of this field is the Not-a-Number of type `double`. It is equal to the value returned by `Double.longBitsToDouble(0x7ff8000000000000L)`.

20.10.6 `public` **`Double`**`(double value)`

This constructor initializes a newly created `Double` object so that it represents the primitive value that is the argument.

20.10.7 `public` **`Double`**`(String s)`
`        throws NumberFormatException`

This constructor initializes a newly created `Double` object so that it represents the floating-point value of type `double` represented by the string. The string is converted to a `double` value in exactly the manner used by the `valueOf` method (§20.9.17).

20.10.8 `public String` **`toString`**`()`

The primitive `double` value represented by this `Double` object is converted to a string exactly as if by the method `toString` of one argument (§20.10.15).

Overrides the `toString` method of `Object` (§20.1.2).

20.10.9 public boolean **equals**(Object obj)

The result is true if and only if the argument is not null and is a Double object that represents the same double value as this Double object. For this purpose, two double values are considered to be the same if and only if the method doubleToLongBits (§20.10.21) returns the same long value when applied to each. Note that even though the == operator returns false if both operands are NaN, this equals method will return true if this Double object and the argument are both Double objects that represent NaN. On the other hand, even though the == operator returns true if one operand is positive zero and the other is negative zero, this equals method will return false if this Double object and the argument represent zeroes of different sign. This allows hashtables to operate properly.

Overrides the equals method of Object (§20.1.3).

20.10.10 public int **hashCode**()

The result is the exclusive OR of the two halves of the long integer bit representation, exactly as produced by the method doubleToLongBits (§20.10.21), of the primitive double value represented by this Double object. That is, the hashcode is the value of the expression:

```
(int)(v^(v>>>32))
```

where v is defined by:

```
long v = Double.doubleToLongBits(this.longValue());
```

Overrides the hashCode method of Object (§20.1.4).

20.10.11 public int **intValue**()

The double value represented by this Double object is converted (§5.1.3) to type int and the result of the conversion is returned.

Overrides the intValue method of Number (§20.6.1).

20.10.12 public long **longValue**()

The double value represented by this Double object is converted (§5.1.3) to type long and the result of the conversion is returned.

Overrides the longValue method of Number (§20.6.2).

20.10.13 public float **floatValue**()

The double value represented by this Double object is converted (§5.1.3) to type float and the result of the conversion is returned.

Overrides the floatValue method of Number (§20.6.3).

20.10.14 public double **doubleValue**()

The double value represented by this Double object is returned.

Overrides the doubleValue method of Number (§20.6.4).

20.10.15 public static String **toString**(double d)

The argument is converted to a readable string format as follows. All characters mentioned below are ASCII characters.

- If the argument is NaN, the result is the string "NaN".
- Otherwise, the result is a string that represents the sign and magnitude (absolute value) of the argument. If the sign is negative, the first character of the result is '-' ('\u002d'); if the sign is positive, no sign character appears in the result. As for the magnitude *m*:
  - If *m* is infinity, it is represented by the characters "Infinity"; thus, positive infinity produces the result "Infinity" and negative infinity produces the result "-Infinity".
  - If *m* is zero, it is represented by the characters "0.0"; thus, negative zero produces the result "-0.0" and positive zero produces the result "0.0".
  - If *m* is greater than or equal to 10^{-3} but less than 10^7, then it is represented as the integer part of *m*, in decimal form with no leading zeroes, followed by '.' (\u002E), followed by one or more decimal digits representing the fractional part of *m*.
  - If *m* is less than 10^{-3} or not less than 10^7, then it is represented in so-called "computerized scientific notation." Let *n* be the unique integer such that $10^n \le m < 10^{n+1}$; then let *a* be the mathematically exact quotient of *m* and 10^n so that $1 \le a < 10$. The magnitude is then represented as the integer part of *a*, as a single decimal digit, followed by '.' (\u002E), followed by decimal digits representing the fractional part of *a*, followed by the letter 'E' (\u0045), followed by a representation of *n* as a decimal integer, as produced by the method Integer.toString of one argument (§20.7.12).

How many digits must be printed for the fractional part of *m* or *a*? There must be at least one digit to represent the fractional part, and beyond that as many, but only as many, more digits as are needed to uniquely distinguish the argument value from adjacent values of type `double`. That is, suppose that *x* is the exact mathematical value represented by the decimal representation produced by this method for a finite nonzero argument *d*. Then *d* must be the `double` value nearest to *x*; or if two `double` values are equally close to *x*, then *d* must be one of them and the least significant bit of the significand of *d* must be `0`.

[This specification for the method `toString` is scheduled for introduction in Java version 1.1. In previous versions of Java, this method produces `Inf` instead of `Infinity` for infinite values. Also, it rendered finite values in the same form as the `%g` format of the `printf` function in the C programming language, which can lose information because it produces at most six digits after the decimal point.]

20.10.16 `public static Double valueOf(String s) throws NullPointerException, NumberFormatException`

The string `s` is interpreted as the representation of a floating-point value and a `Double` object representing that value is created and returned.

If `s` is `null`, then a `NullPointerException` is thrown.

Leading and trailing whitespace (§20.5.19) characters in `s` are ignored. The rest of `s` should constitute a *FloatValue* as described by the lexical syntax rule:

FloatValue:
  $Sign_{opt}$ *Digits* `.` $Digits_{opt}$ $ExponentPart_{opt}$
  $Sign_{opt}$ `.` *Digits* $ExponentPart_{opt}$

where *Sign*, *Digits*, and *ExponentPart* are as defined in §3.10.2. If it does not have the form of a *FloatValue*, then a `NumberFormatException` is thrown. Otherwise, it is regarded as representing an exact decimal value in the usual "computerized scientific notation"; this exact decimal value is then conceptually converted to an "infinitely precise" binary value that is then rounded to type `double` by the usual round-to-nearest rule of IEEE 754 floating-point arithmetic. Finally, a new object of class `Double` is created to represent the `double` value.

Note that neither `D` nor `d` is permitted to appear in `s` as a type indicator, as would be permitted in Java source code (§3.10.1).

20.10.17 `public boolean isNaN()`

The result is `true` if and only if the value represented by this `Double` object is NaN.

20.10.18 public static boolean **isNaN**(double v)

The result is `true` if and only if the value of the argument is NaN.

20.10.19 public boolean **isInfinite**()

The result is `true` if and only if the value represented by this `Double` object is positive infinity or negative infinity.

20.10.20 public static boolean **isInfinite**(double v)

The result is `true` if and only if the value of the argument is positive infinity or negative infinity.

20.10.21 public static long **doubleToLongBits**(double value)

The result is a representation of the floating-point argument according to the IEEE 754 floating-point "double format" bit layout:

- Bit 63 (the bit that is selected by the mask `0x8000000000000000L`) represents the sign of the floating-point number.
- Bits 62–52 (the bits that are selected by the mask `0x7ff0000000000000L`) represent the exponent.
- Bits 51–0 (the bits that are selected by the mask `0x000fffffffffffffL`) represent the significand (sometimes called the mantissa) of the floating-point number.
- If the argument is positive infinity, the result will be `0x7ff0000000000000L`.
- If the argument is negative infinity, the result will be `0xfff0000000000000L`.
- If the argument is NaN, the result will be `0x7ff8000000000000L`.

In all cases, the result is a `long` integer that, when given to the `longBitsToDouble` method (§20.10.22), will produce a floating-point value equal to the argument to `doubleToLongBits`.

20.10.22 `public static double` **`longBitsToDouble`**`(long bits)`

The argument is considered to be a representation of a floating-point value according to the IEEE 754 floating-point "double format" bit layout. That floating-point value is returned as the result.

- If the argument is `0x7f80000000000000L`, the result will be positive infinity.
- If the argument is `0xff80000000000000L`, the result will be negative infinity.
- If the argument is any value in the range `0x7ff0000000000001L` through `0x7fffffffffffffffL` or in the range `0xfff0000000000001L` through `0xffffffffffffffffL`, the result will be NaN. (All IEEE 754 NaN values are, in effect, lumped together by the Java language into a single value called NaN.)
- In all other cases, let *s*, *e*, and *m* be three values that can be computed from the argument:

```
int s = ((bits >> 63) == 0) ? 1 : -1;
int e = (int)((bits >> 52) & 0x7ffL);
long m = (e == 0) ?
        (bits & 0xfffffffffffffL) << 1 :
        (bits & 0xfffffffffffffL) | 0x10000000000000L;
```

Then the floating-point result equals the value of the mathematical expression $s \cdot m \cdot 2^{e-1075}$.

Let beeves and home-bred kine partake
The sweets of Burn-mill meadow;
The swan on still St. Mary's Lake
Float double, swan and shadow!
—William Wordsworth, *Yarrow Unvisited* (1803)

20.11 The Class `java.lang.Math`

Oh, back to the days that were free from care in the 'Ology 'varsity shop,
With nothing to do but analyse air in an anemometrical top,
Or the differentiation of the trigonometrical pow'rs
Of the constant pi that made me sigh in those happy days of ours!
—I. W. Litchfield, *Take Me Back to Tech* (1885)

The class `Math` contains useful basic numerical constants and methods.

```
public final class Math {
    public static final double E = 2.7182818284590452354;
    public static final double PI = 3.14159265358979323846;
    public static double sin(double a);
    public static double cos(double a);
    public static double tan(double a);
    public static double asin(double a);
    public static double acos(double a);
    public static double atan(double a);
    public static double atan2(double a, double b);
    public static double exp(double a);
    public static double log(double a);
    public static double sqrt(double a);
    public static double pow(double a, double b);
    public static double IEEEremainder(double f1, double f2);
    public static double ceil(double a);
    public static double floor(double a);
    public static double rint(double a);
    public static int round(float a);
    public static long round(double a);
    public static double random();
    public static int abs(int a);
    public static long abs(long a);
    public static float abs(float a);
    public static double abs(double a);
    public static int min(int a, int b);
    public static long min(long a, long b);
    public static float min(float a, float b);
    public static double min(double a, double b);
    public static int max(int a, int b);
    public static long max(long a, long b);
    public static float max(float a, float b);
    public static double max(double a, double b);
}
```

To ensure portability of Java programs, the specifications of many of the numerical functions in this package require that they produce the same results as certain published algorithms. These algorithms are available from the well-known network library `netlib` as the package `fdlibm` ("Freely Distributable Math Library"). These algorithms, which are written in the C programming language, are to be understood as if executed in Java execution order with all floating-point operations following the rules of Java floating-point arithmetic.

The network library may be found at `http://netlib.att.com` on the World Wide Web; then perform a keyword search for `fdlibm`. The library may also be retrieved by E-mail; to begin the process, send a message containing the line:

```
send index from fdlibm
```

to `netlib@research.att.com`. The Java math library is defined with respect to the version of `fdlibm` dated 95/01/04. Where `fdlibm` provides more than one definition for a function (such as `acos`), the "IEEE754 core function" version is to be used (residing in a file whose name begins with the letter `e`).

A complete and self-contained description of the algorithms to be used for these functions will be provided in a future version of this specification. It is also anticipated that the algorithms will be coded in Java to provide a reference implementation that is not tied to `fdlibm`.

20.11.1 `public static final double E = 2.7182818284590452354;`

The constant value of this field is the `double` value that is closer than any other to e, the base of the natural logarithms.

20.11.2 `public static final double PI = 3.14159265358979323846;`

The constant value of this field is the `double` value that is closer than any other to π, the ratio of the circumference of a circle to its diameter.

20.11.3 `public static double sin(double a)`

This method computes an approximation to the sine of the argument, using the `sin` algorithm as published in `fdlibm` (see the introduction to this section).

Special cases:

- If the argument is NaN or an infinity, then the result is NaN.
- If the argument is positive zero, then the result is positive zero; if the argument is negative zero, then the result is negative zero.

20.11.4 `public static double cos(double a)`

This method computes an approximation to the cosine of the argument, using the `cos` algorithm as published in `fdlibm` (see the introduction to this section).

Special case:

- If the argument is NaN or an infinity, then the result is NaN.

20.11.5 `public static double tan(double a)`

This method computes an approximation to the tangent of the argument, using the `tan` algorithm as published in `fdlibm` (see the introduction to this section).

Special cases:

- If the argument is NaN or an infinity, then the result is NaN.
- If the argument is positive zero, then the result is positive zero; if the argument is negative zero, then the result is negative zero.

20.11.6 `public static double asin(double a)`

This method computes an approximation to the arc sine of the argument, using the `asin` algorithm as published in `fdlibm` (see the introduction to this section).

Special cases:

- If the argument is NaN or its absolute value is greater than 1, then the result is NaN.
- If the argument is positive zero, then the result is positive zero; if the argument is negative zero, then the result is negative zero.

20.11.7 `public static double acos(double a)`

This method computes an approximation to the arc cosine of the argument, using the `acos` algorithm as published in `fdlibm` (see the introduction to this section).

Special case:

- If the argument is NaN or its absolute value is greater than 1, then the result is NaN.

20.11.8 `public static double atan(double a)`

This method computes an approximation to the arc tangent of the argument, using the `atan` algorithm as published in `fdlibm` (see the introduction to this section).

Special cases:

- If the argument is NaN, then the result is NaN.
- If the argument is positive zero, then the result is positive zero; if the argument is negative zero, then the result is negative zero.

20.11.9 `public static double atan2(double y, double x)`

This method computes an approximation to the arc tangent of the quotient y/x of the arguments, using the `atan2` algorithm as published in `fdlibm` (see the introduction to this section).

Special cases:

- If either argument is NaN, then the result is NaN.
- If the first argument is positive zero and the second argument is positive, or the first argument is positive and finite and the second argument is positive infinity, then the result is positive zero.
- If the first argument is negative zero and the second argument is positive, or the first argument is negative and finite and the second argument is positive infinity, then the result is negative zero.
- If the first argument is positive zero and the second argument is negative, or the first argument is positive and finite and the second argument is negative infinity, then the result is the `double` value closest to π.
- If the first argument is negative zero and the second argument is negative, or the first argument is negative and finite and the second argument is negative infinity, then the result is the `double` value closest to $-\pi$.
- If the first argument is positive and the second argument is positive zero or negative zero, or the first argument is positive infinity and the second argument is finite, then the result is the `double` value closest to $\pi/2$.
- If the first argument is negative and the second argument is positive zero or negative zero, or the first argument is negative infinity and the second argument is finite, then the result is the `double` value closest to $-\pi/2$.
- If both arguments are positive infinity, then the result is the `double` value closest to $\pi/4$.

- If the first argument is positive infinity and the second argument is negative infinity, then the result is the `double` value closest to $3\pi/4$.
- If the first argument is negative infinity and the second argument is positive infinity, then the result is the `double` value closest to $-\pi/4$.
- If both arguments are negative infinity, then the result is the `double` value closest to $-3\pi/4$.

20.11.10 `public static double exp(double a)`

This method computes an approximation to the exponential function of the argument (*e* raised to the power of the argument, where *e* is the base of the natural logarithms (§20.11.1)), using the `exp` algorithm as published in `fdlibm` (see the introduction to this section).

Special cases:

- If the argument is NaN, then the result is NaN.
- If the argument is positive infinity, then the result is positive infinity.
- If the argument is negative infinity, then the result is positive zero.

20.11.11 `public static double log(double a)`

This method computes an approximation to the natural logarithm of the argument, using the `log` algorithm as published in `fdlibm` (see the introduction to this section).

Special cases:

- If the argument is NaN or less than zero, then the result is NaN.
- If the argument is positive infinity, then the result is positive infinity.
- If the argument is positive zero or negative zero, then the result is negative infinity.

20.11.12 `public static double sqrt(double a)`

Whanne that April with his shoures sote
The droughte of March hath perced to the rote . . .

—Geoffrey Chaucer (1328–1400),
The Canterbury Tales, Prologue

This method computes an approximation to the square root of the argument.
Special cases:

- If the argument is NaN or less than zero, then the result is NaN.
- If the argument is positive infinity, then the result is positive infinity.
- If the argument is positive zero or negative zero, then the result is the same as the argument.

Otherwise, the result is the `double` value closest to the true mathematical square root of the argument value.

20.11.13 `public static double pow(double a, double b)`

This method computes an approximation to the mathematical operation of raising the first argument to the power of the second argument, using the `pow` algorithm as published in `fdlibm` (see the introduction to this section).
Special cases:

- If the second argument is positive or negative zero, then the result is `1.0`.
- If the second argument is `1.0`, then the result is the same as the first argument.
- If the second argument is NaN, then the result is NaN.
- If the first argument is NaN and the second argument is nonzero, then the result is NaN.
- If the absolute value of the first argument is greater than 1 and the second argument is positive infinity, or the absolute value of the first argument is less than 1 and the second argument is negative infinity, then the result is positive infinity.
- If the absolute value of the first argument is greater than 1 and the second argument is negative infinity, or the absolute value of the first argument is less than 1 and the second argument is positive infinity, then the result is positive zero.
- If the absolute value of the first argument equals 1 and the second argument is infinite, then the result is NaN.
- If the first argument is positive zero and the second argument is greater than zero, or the first argument is positive infinity and the second argument is less than zero, then the result is positive zero.

- If the first argument is positive zero and the second argument is less than zero, or the first argument is positive infinity and the second argument is greater than zero, then the result is positive infinity.
- If the first argument is negative zero and the second argument is greater than zero but not a finite odd integer, or the first argument is negative infinity and the second argument is less than zero but not a finite odd integer, then the result is positive zero.
- If the first argument is negative zero and the second argument is a positive finite odd integer, or the first argument is negative infinity and the second argument is a negative finite odd integer, then the result is negative zero.
- If the first argument is negative zero and the second argument is less than zero but not a finite odd integer, or the first argument is negative infinity and the second argument is greater than zero but not a finite odd integer, then the result is positive infinity.
- If the first argument is negative zero and the second argument is a negative finite odd integer, or the first argument is negative infinity and the second argument is a positive finite odd integer, then the result is negative infinity.
- If the first argument is less than zero and the second argument is a finite even integer, then the result is equal to the result of raising the absolute value of the first argument to the power of the second argument.
- If the first argument is less than zero and the second argument is a finite odd integer, then the result is equal to the negative of the result of raising the absolute value of the first argument to the power of the second argument.
- If the first argument is finite and less than zero and the second argument is finite and not an integer, then the result is NaN.
- If both arguments are integers, then the result is exactly equal to the mathematical result of raising the first argument to the power of the second argument if that result can in fact be represented exactly as a `double` value.

(In the foregoing descriptions, a floating-point value is considered to be an integer if and only if it is a fixed point of the method `ceil` (§20.11.15) or, which is the same thing, a fixed point of the method `floor` (§20.11.16). A value is a fixed point of a one-argument method if and only if the result of applying the method to the value is equal to the value.)

20.11.14 `public static double IEEEremainder(double x, double y)`

This method computes the remainder operation on two arguments as prescribed by the IEEE 754 standard: the remainder value is mathematically equal to $x - y \times n$ where n is the mathematical integer closest to the exact mathematical value of the quotient x/y; if two mathematical integers are equally close to x/y then n is the integer that is even. If the remainder is zero, its sign is the same as the sign of the first argument.

Special cases:

- If either argument is NaN, or the first argument is infinite, or the second argument is positive zero or negative zero, then the result is NaN.
- If the first argument is finite and the second argument is infinite, then the result is the same as the first argument.

20.11.15 `public static double ceil(double a)`

The result is the smallest (closest to negative infinity) `double` value that is not less than the argument and is equal to a mathematical integer.

Special cases:

- If the argument value is already equal to a mathematical integer, then the result is the same as the argument.
- If the argument is NaN or an infinity or positive zero or negative zero, then the result is the same as the argument.
- If the argument value is less than zero but greater than `-1.0`, then the result is negative zero.

Note that the value of `Math.ceil(x)` is exactly the value of `-Math.floor(-x)`.

20.11.16 `public static double floor(double a)`

The result is the largest (closest to positive infinity) `double` value that is not greater than the argument and is equal to a mathematical integer.

Special cases:

- If the argument value is already equal to a mathematical integer, then the result is the same as the argument.
- If the argument is NaN or an infinity or positive zero or negative zero, then the result is the same as the argument.

20.11.17 `public static double **rint**(double a)`

The result is the `double` value that is closest in value to the argument and is equal to a mathematical integer. If two `double` values that are mathematical integers are equally close to the value of the argument, the result is the integer value that is even.

Special cases:

- If the argument value is already equal to a mathematical integer, then the result is the same as the argument.
- If the argument is NaN or an infinity or positive zero or negative zero, then the result is the same as the argument.

20.11.18 `public static int **round**(float a)`

Round numbers are always false.
—Samuel Johnson (1709–1784)

The result is rounded to an integer by adding `1/2`, taking the floor of the result, and casting the result to type `int`.

In other words, the result is equal to the value of the expression:

```
(int)Math.floor(a + 0.5f)
```

Special cases:

- If the argument is NaN, the result is `0`.
- If the argument is negative infinity, or indeed any value less than or equal to the value of `Integer.MIN_VALUE` (§20.7.1), the result is equal to the value of `Integer.MIN_VALUE`.
- If the argument is positive infinity, or indeed any value greater than or equal to the value of `Integer.MAX_VALUE` (§20.7.2), the result is equal to the value of `Integer.MAX_VALUE`.

20.11.19 `public static long **round**(double a)`

The result is rounded to an integer by adding `1/2`, taking the floor of the result, and casting the result to type `long`.

In other words, the result is equal to the value of the expression:

```
(long)Math.floor(a + 0.5d)
```

Special cases:

- If the argument is NaN, the result is `0`.
- If the argument is negative infinity, or indeed any value less than or equal to the value of `Long.MIN_VALUE` (§20.7.1), the result is equal to the value of `Long.MIN_VALUE`.
- If the argument is positive infinity, or indeed any value greater than or equal to the value of `Long.MAX_VALUE` (§20.7.2), the result is equal to the value of `Long.MAX_VALUE`.

20.11.20 `public static double` **`random`**`()`

The result is a double value with positive sign, greater than or equal to zero but less than `1.0`, chosen pseudorandomly with (approximately) uniform distribution from that range.

When this method is first called, it creates a single new pseudorandom-number generator, exactly as if by the expression

```
new java.util.Random()
```

This new pseudorandom-number generator is used thereafter for all calls to this method and is used nowhere else.

This method is properly synchronized to allow correct use by more than one thread. However, if many threads need to generate pseudorandom numbers at a great rate, it may reduce contention for each thread to have its own pseudorandom number generator.

20.11.21 `public static int` **`abs`**`(int a)`

The result is the absolute value of the argument, if possible.

If the argument is not negative, the argument is returned.

If the argument is negative, the negation of the argument is returned. Note that if the argument is equal to the value of `Integer.MIN_VALUE` (§20.7.1), the most negative representable `int` value, the result will be that same negative value.

20.11.22 `public static long` **`abs`**`(long a)`

The result is the absolute value of the argument, if possible.

If the argument is not negative, the argument is returned.

If the argument is negative, the negation of the argument is returned. Note that if the argument is equal to the value of `Long.MIN_VALUE` (§20.8.1), the most negative representable `long` value, the result will be that same negative value.

20.11.23 `public static float abs(float a)`

The argument is returned with its sign changed to be positive.

Special cases:

- If the argument is positive zero or negative zero, the result is positive zero.
- If the argument is infinite, the result is positive infinity.
- If the argument is NaN, the result is NaN.

In other words, the result is equal to the value of the expression:

```
Float.intBitsToFloat(0x7fffffff & Float.floatToIntBits(a))
```

[This specification for the method `abs` is scheduled for introduction in Java version 1.1. In previous versions of Java, `abs(-0.0f)` returns `-0.0f`, which is not correct.]

20.11.24 `public static double abs(double a)`

The argument is returned with its sign changed to be positive.

Special cases:

- If the argument is positive zero or negative zero, the result is positive zero.
- If the argument is infinite, the result is positive infinity.
- If the argument is NaN, the result is NaN.

In other words, the result is equal to the value of the expression:

```
Double.longBitsToDouble((Double.doubleToLongBits(a)<<1)>>>1)
```

[This specification for the method `abs` is scheduled for introduction in Java version 1.1. In previous versions of Java, `abs(-0.0d)` returns `-0.0d`, which is not correct.]

20.11.25 `public static int min(int a, int b)`

E duobus malis minimum eligendum.
—Marcus Tullius Cicero (106–43 B. C.), *De officiis*, iii

The result is the smaller of the two arguments—that is, the one closer to the value of `Integer.MIN_VALUE` (§20.7.1). If the arguments have the same value, the result is that same value.

20.11.26 `public static long min(long a, long b)`

Of harmes two the lesse is for to cheese.
—Geoffrey Chaucer (1328–1400),
Troilus and Creseide, Book ii

The result is the smaller of the two arguments—that is, the one closer to the value of `Long.MIN_VALUE` (§20.8.1). If the arguments have the same value, the result is that same value.

20.11.27 `public static float min(float a, float b)`

Of two evils, the less is always to be chosen.
—Thomas à Kempis (1380–1471),
Imitation of Christ, Book iii, chapter 12

The result is the smaller of the two arguments—that is, the one closer to negative infinity. If the arguments have the same value, the result is that same value.

Special cases:

- If one argument is positive zero and the other is negative zero, the result is negative zero.
- If either argument is NaN, the result is NaN.

[This specification for the method `min` is scheduled for introduction in Java version 1.1. In previous versions of Java, `min(0.0f, -0.0f)` returns `0.0f`, which is not correct.]

20.11.28 `public static double min(double a, double b)`

Of two evils I have chose the least.
—Matthew Prior (1664–1721),
Imitation of Horace

The result is the smaller of the two arguments—that is, the one closer to negative infinity. If the arguments have the same value, the result is that same value.

Special cases:

- If one argument is positive zero and the other is negative zero, the result is negative zero.
- If either argument is NaN, the result is NaN.

[This specification for the method `min` is scheduled for introduction in Java version 1.1. In previous versions of Java, `min(0.0d, -0.0d)` returns `0.0d`, which is not correct.]

20.11.29 `public static int max(int a, int b)`

The result is the larger of the two arguments—that is, the one closer to the value of `Integer.MAX_VALUE` (§20.7.2). If the arguments have the same value, the result is that same value.

20.11.30 `public static long max(long a, long b)`

The result is the larger of the two arguments—that is, the one closer to the value of `Long.MAX_VALUE` (§20.8.2). If the arguments have the same value, the result is that same value.

20.11.31 `public static float max(float a, float b)`

The result is the larger of the two arguments—that is, the one closer to positive infinity. If the arguments have the same value, the result is that same value.

Special cases:

- If one argument is positive zero and the other is negative zero, the result is positive zero.
- If either argument is NaN, the result is NaN.

[This specification for the method `max` is scheduled for introduction in Java version 1.1. In previous versions of Java, `max(-0.0f, 0.0f)` returns `-0.0f`, which is not correct.]

20.11.32 `public static double max(double a, double b)`

The result is the larger of the two arguments—that is, the one closer to positive infinity. If the arguments have the same value, the result is that same value.

Special cases:

- If one argument is positive zero and the other is negative zero, the result is positive zero.
- If either argument is NaN, the result is NaN.

[This specification for the method `max` is scheduled for introduction in Java version 1.1. In previous versions of Java, `max(-0.0d, 0.0d)` returns `-0.0d`, which is not correct.].

In mathematics he was greater
Than Tycho Brahe or Erra Pater
For he, by geometric scale,
Could take the size of pots of ale;
Resolve, by sines and tangents straight
Whether bread or butter wanted weight;
And wisely tell what hour o' the day
The clock does strike, by algebra.

—Samuel Butler, *Hudibras*, Part I, canto i

20.12 The Class java.lang.String

An object of type String, once created, is immutable. It represents a fixed-length sequence of characters. Compare this to the class StringBuffer (§20.13), which represents a modifiable, variable-length sequence of characters.

The class String has methods for examining individual characters of the sequence, for comparing strings, for searching strings, for extracting substrings, for creating a copy of a string with all characters translated to uppercase or to lowercase, and so on.

```
public final class String {
    public String();
    public String(String value)
        throws NullPointerException;
    public String(StringBuffer buffer)
        throws NullPointerException;
    public String(char[] value)
        throws NullPointerException;
    public String(char[] value, int offset, int count)
        throws NullPointerException, IndexOutOfBoundsException;
    public String(byte[] ascii, int hibyte)
        throws NullPointerException;
    public String(byte[] ascii, int hibyte,
            int offset, int count)
        throws NullPointerException, IndexOutOfBoundsException;
    public String toString();
    public boolean equals(Object anObject);
    public int hashCode();
    public int length();
    public char charAt(int index);
    public void getChars(int srcBegin, int srcEnd,
            char dst[], int dstBegin)
        throws NullPointerException, IndexOutOfBoundsException;
    public void getBytes(int srcBegin, int srcEnd,
            byte dst[], int dstBegin)
        throws NullPointerException, IndexOutOfBoundsException;
    public char[] toCharArray();
    public boolean equalsIgnoreCase(String anotherString);
    public int compareTo(String anotherString)
        throws NullPointerException;
    public boolean regionMatches(int toffset, String other,
            int ooffset, int len)
        throws NullPointerException;
```

```
    public boolean regionMatches(boolean ignoreCase, int toffset,
            String other, int ooffset, int len)
        throws NullPointerException;
    public boolean startsWith(String prefix)
        throws NullPointerException;
    public boolean startsWith(String prefix, int toffset)
        throws NullPointerException;
    public boolean endsWith(String suffix)
        throws NullPointerException;
    public int indexOf(int ch);
    public int indexOf(int ch, int fromIndex);
    public int indexOf(String str)
        throws NullPointerException;
    public int indexOf(String str, int fromIndex)
        throws NullPointerException;
    public int lastIndexOf(int ch);
    public int lastIndexOf(int ch, int fromIndex);
    public int lastIndexOf(String str)
        throws NullPointerException;
    public int lastIndexOf(String str, int fromIndex)
        throws NullPointerException;
    public String substring(int beginIndex);
    public String substring(int beginIndex, int endIndex);
    public String concat(String str)
        throws NullPointerException;
    public String replace(char oldChar, char newChar);
    public String toLowerCase();
    public String toUpperCase();
    public String trim();
    public static String valueOf(Object obj);
    public static String valueOf(char[] data)
        throws NullPointerException;
    public static String valueOf(char[] data,
            int offset, int count)
        throws NullPointerException, IndexOutOfBoundsException;
    public static String valueOf(boolean b);
    public static String valueOf(char c);
    public static String valueOf(int i);
    public static String valueOf(long l);
    public static String valueOf(float f);
    public static String valueOf(double d);
    public String intern();
}
```

20.12.1 `public String()`

This constructor initializes a newly created `String` object so that it represents an empty character sequence.

20.12.2 `public String(String value)`

This constructor initializes a newly created `String` object so that it represents the same sequence of characters as the argument; in other words, the newly created string is a copy of the argument string.

20.12.3
```
public String(StringBuffer buffer)
        throws NullPointerException
```

This constructor initializes a newly created `String` object so that it represents the sequence of characters that is currently contained in the `StringBuffer` argument (§20.13). The contents of the string buffer are copied; subsequent modification of the string buffer does not affect the newly created string.

If `buffer` is `null`, then a `NullPointerException` is thrown.

20.12.4
```
public String(char[] data)
        throws NullPointerException
```

This constructor initializes a newly created `String` object so that it represents the sequence of characters currently contained in the character array argument. The contents of the character array are copied; subsequent modification of the character array does not affect the newly created string.

If `data` is `null`, then a `NullPointerException` is thrown.

20.12.5
```
public String(char[] data, int offset, int count)
        throws NullPointerException,
            IndexOutOfBoundsException
```

This constructor initializes a newly created `String` object so that it represents the sequence of characters currently contained in a subarray of the character array argument. The `offset` argument is the index of the first character of the subarray and the `count` argument specifies the length of the subarray. The contents of the subarray are copied; subsequent modification of the character array does not affect the newly created string.

If data is null, then a NullPointerException is thrown.

If offset is negative, or count is negative, or offset+count is larger than data.length, then an IndexOutOfBoundsException is thrown.

20.12.6 `public String(byte[] ascii, int hibyte) throws NullPointerException`

This constructor initializes a newly created String object so that it represents a sequence of characters constructed from an array of 8-bit integer values. Each character c in the result string is constructed from the corresponding element b of the byte array in such a way that:

```
c == ((hibyte & 0xff) << 8) | (b & 0xff)
```

If ascii is null, then a NullPointerException is thrown.

20.12.7 `public String(byte[] ascii, int hibyte, int offset, int count) throws NullPointerException, IndexOutOfBoundsException`

This constructor initializes a newly created String object so that it represents the sequence of characters constructed from a subarray of an array of 8-bit integer values. The offset argument is the index of the first byte of the subarray and the count argument specifies the length of the subarray. Each character c in the result string is constructed from the corresponding element b of the byte subarray in such a way that:

```
c == ((hibyte & 0xff) << 8) | (b & 0xff)
```

If ascii is null, then a NullPointerException is thrown.

If offset is negative, or count is negative, or offset+count is larger than ascii.length, then an IndexOutOfBoundsException is thrown.

20.12.8 `public String toString()`

A reference to this object (which is, after all, already a String) is returned.

Overrides the toString method of Object (§20.1.2).

20.12.9 `public boolean equals(Object anObject)`

The result is `true` if and only if the argument is not `null` and is a `String` object that represents the same sequence of characters as this `String` object.

Overrides the `equals` method of `Object` (§20.1.3).

See also the methods `equalsIgnoreCase` (§20.12.16) and `compareTo` (§20.12.17).

20.12.10 `public int hashCode()`

The hashcode for a `String` object is computed in one of two ways, depending on its length. Let n be the length (§20.12.11) of the character sequence and let c_i mean the character with index i.

- If $n \leq 15$, then the hashcode is computed as

$$\sum_{i=0}^{n-1} c_i \cdot 37^i$$

using `int` arithmetic.

- If $n > 15$, then the hashcode is computed as

$$\sum_{i=0}^{m} c_{i \cdot k} \cdot 39^i$$

using `int` arithmetic, where $k = \left\lfloor \frac{n}{8} \right\rfloor$ and $m = \left\lceil \frac{n}{k} \right\rceil$, sampling only eight or nine characters of the string.

Overrides the `hashCode` method of `Object` (§20.1.4).

20.12.11 `public int length()`

The length of the sequence of characters represented by this `String` object is returned.

20.12.12 `public char charAt(int index) throws IndexOutOfBoundsException`

This method returns the character indicated by the `index` argument within the sequence of characters represented by this `String`. The first character of the sequence is at index `0`, the next at index `1`, and so on, as for array indexing. If the `index` argument is negative or not less than the length (§20.12.11) of this string, then an `IndexOutOfBoundsException` is thrown.

20.12.13 `public void getChars(int srcBegin, int srcEnd, char dst[], int dstBegin) throws NullPointerException, IndexOutOfBoundsException`

Characters are copied from this `String` object into the destination character array `dst`. The first character to be copied is at index `srcBegin`; the last character to be copied is at index `srcEnd-1` (thus the total number of characters to be copied is `srcEnd-srcBegin`). The characters are copied into the subarray of `dst` starting at index `dstBegin` and ending at index `dstbegin+(srcEnd-srcBegin)-1`.

If `dst` is `null`, then a `NullPointerException` is thrown.

An `IndexOutOfBoundsException` is thrown if any of the following is true:

- `srcBegin` is negative
- `srcBegin` is greater than `srcEnd`
- `srcEnd` is greater than the length of this String
- `dstBegin` is negative
- `dstBegin+(srcEnd-srcBegin)` is larger than `dst.length`

20.12.14 `public void getBytes(int srcBegin, int srcEnd, byte dst[], int dstBegin) throws NullPointerException, IndexOutOfBoundsException`

Characters are copied from this `String` object into the destination byte array `dst`. Each byte receives only the eight low-order bits of the corresponding character. The eight high-order bits of each character are not copied and do not participate in the transfer in any way. The first character to be copied is at index `srcBegin`; the last character to be copied is at index `srcEnd-1` (thus the total number of characters to be copied is `srcEnd-srcBegin`). The characters, converted to bytes, are copied into the subarray of `dst` starting at index `dstBegin` and ending at index `dstbegin+(srcEnd-srcBegin)-1`.

If `dst` is `null`, then a `NullPointerException` is thrown.

An `IndexOutOfBoundsException` is thrown if any of the following is true:

- `srcBegin` is negative
- `srcBegin` is greater than `srcEnd`
- `srcEnd` is greater than the length of this *String*
- `dstBegin` is negative
- `dstBegin+(srcEnd-srcBegin)` is larger than `dst.length`

20.12.15 `public char[] toCharArray()`

A new character array is created and returned. The length of the array is equal to the length (§20.12.11) of this `String` object. The array is initialized to contain the character sequence represented by this `String` object.

20.12.16 `public boolean equalsIgnoreCase(String anotherString)`

The result is `true` if and only if the argument is not `null` and is a `String` object that represents the same sequence of characters as this `String` object, where case is ignored.

Two characters are considered the same, ignoring case, if at least one of the following is true:

- The two characters are the same (as compared by the == operator).
- Applying the method `Character.toUppercase` (§20.5.21) to each character produces the same result.
- Applying the method `Character.toLowercase` (§20.5.20) to each character produces the same result.

Two sequences of characters are the same, ignoring case, if the sequences have the same length and corresponding characters are the same, ignoring case.

See also the method `equals` (§20.12.9).

20.12.17 `public int` **`compareTo`**`(String anotherString)`
`throws NullPointerException`

The character sequence represented by this `String` object is compared lexicographically to the character sequence represented by the argument string. The result is a negative integer if this `String` object lexicographically precedes the argument string. The result is a positive integer if this `String` object lexicographically follows the argument string. The result is zero if the strings are equal; `compareTo` returns 0 exactly when the `equals` method (§20.12.9) would return `true`.

If `anotherString` is `null`, then a `NullPointerException` is thrown.

This is the definition of lexicographic ordering. If two strings are different, then either they have different characters at some index that is a valid index for both strings, or their lengths are different, or both. If they have different characters at one or more index positions, let *k* be the smallest such index; then the string whose character at position *k* has the smaller value, as determined by using the < operator, lexicographically precedes the other string. In this case, `compareTo` returns the difference of the two character values at position *k* in the two strings—that is, the value:

```
this.charAt(k)-anotherString.charAt(k)
```

If there is no index position at which they differ, then the shorter string lexicographically precedes the longer string. In this case, `compareTo` returns the difference of the lengths of the strings—that is, the value:

```
this.length()-anotherString.length()
```

20.12.18 `public boolean` **`regionMatches`**`(int toffset,`
`String other, int ooffset, int len)`
`throws NullPointerException`

A substring of this `String` object is compared to a substring of the argument `other`. The result is `true` if these substrings represent identical character sequences. The substring of this `String` object to be compared begins at index `toffset` and has length `len`. The substring of `other` to be compared begins at index `ooffset` and has length `len`. The result is `false` if and only if at least one of the following is true:

- `toffset` is negative.
- `ooffset` is negative.
- `toffset+len` is greater than the length of this `String` object.

- `ooffset+len` is greater than the length of the `other` argument.
- There is some nonnegative integer *k* less than `len` such that:

  `this.charAt(toffset+k) != other.charAt(ooffset+k)`

If `other` is `null`, then a `NullPointerException` is thrown.

20.12.19 `public boolean` **`regionMatches`**`(boolean ignoreCase, int toffset, String other, int ooffset, int len) throws NullPointerException`

A substring of this `String` object is compared to a substring of the argument `other`. The result is `true` if these substrings represent character sequences that are the same, ignoring case if and only if `ignoreCase` is true. The substring of this `String` object to be compared begins at index `toffset` and has length `len`. The substring of `other` to be compared begins at index `ooffset` and has length `len`. The result is `false` if and only if at least one of the following is true:

- `toffset` is negative.
- `ooffset` is negative.
- `toffset+len` is greater than the length of this `String` object.
- `ooffset+len` is greater than the length of the `other` argument.
- There is some nonnegative integer *k* less than `len` such that:

  `this.charAt(toffset+k) != other.charAt(ooffset+k)`

- `ignoreCase` is `true` and there is some nonnegative integer *k* less than `len` such that:

  ```
  Character.toLowerCase(this.charAt(toffset+k)) !=
     Character.toLowerCase(other.charAt(ooffset+k))
  ```

  and:

  ```
  Character.toUpperCase(this.charAt(toffset+k)) !=
     Character.toUpperCase(other.charAt(ooffset+k))
  ```

If `other` is `null`, then a `NullPointerException` is thrown.

20.12.20 `public boolean` **`startsWith`**`(String prefix)`
`throws NullPointerException`

The result is `true` if and only if the character sequence represented by the argument is a prefix of the character sequence represented by this `String` object.

If `prefix` is `null`, a `NullPointerException` is thrown.

Note that the result will be `true` if the argument is an empty string or is equal to this `String` object as determined by the `equals` method (§20.12.9).

20.12.21 `public boolean` **`startsWith`**`(String prefix, int toffset)`
`throws NullPointerException`

The result is `true` if and only if the character sequence represented by the argument is a prefix of the substring of this `String` object starting at index `toffset`.

If `prefix` is `null`, then a `NullPointerException` is thrown.

The result is `false` if `toffset` is negative or greater than the length of this `String` object; otherwise, the result is the same as the result of the expression

```
this.subString(toffset).startsWith(prefix)
```

20.12.22 `public boolean` **`endsWith`**`(String suffix)`
`throws NullPointerException`

The result is `true` if and only if the character sequence represented by the argument is a suffix of the character sequence represented by this `String` object.

If `suffix` is `null`, then a `NullPointerException` is thrown.

Note that the result will be `true` if the argument is an empty string or is equal to this `String` object as determined by the `equals` method (§20.12.9).

20.12.23 `public int` **`indexOf`**`(int ch)`

If a character with value `ch` occurs in the character sequence represented by this `String` object, then the index of the first such occurrence is returned—that is, the smallest value *k* such that:

```
this.charAt(k) == ch
```

is `true`. If no such character occurs in this string, then `-1` is returned.

20.12.24 `public int indexOf(int ch, int fromIndex)`

If a character with value `ch` occurs in the character sequence represented by this `String` object at an index no smaller than `fromIndex`, then the index of the first such occurrence is returned—that is, the smallest value *k* such that:

```
(this.charAt(k) == ch) && (k >= fromIndex)
```

is `true`. If no such character occurs in this string at or after position `fromIndex`, then `-1` is returned.

There is no restriction on the value of `fromIndex`. If it is negative, it has the same effect as if it were zero: this entire string may be searched. If it is greater than the length of this string, it has the same effect as if it were equal to the length of this string: `-1` is returned.

20.12.25 `public int indexOf(String str) throws NullPointerException`

If the string `str` occurs as a substring of this `String` object, then the index of the first character of the first such substring is returned—that is, the smallest value *k* such that:

```
this.startsWith(str, k)
```

is `true`. If `str` does not occur as a substring of this string, then `-1` is returned.

If `str` is `null`, a `NullPointerException` is thrown.

20.12.26 `public int indexOf(String str, int fromIndex) throws NullPointerException`

If the string `str` occurs as a substring of this `String` object starting at an index no smaller than `fromIndex`, then the index of the first character of the first such substring is returned—that is, the smallest value *k* such that:

```
this.startsWith(str, k) && (k >= fromIndex)
```

is `true`. If `str` does not occur as a substring of this string at or after position `fromIndex`, then `-1` is returned.

There is no restriction on the value of `fromIndex`. If it is negative, it has the same effect as if it were zero: this entire string may be searched. If it is greater than the length of this string, it has the same effect as if it were equal to the length of this string: `-1` is returned.

If `str` is `null`, a `NullPointerException` is thrown.

20.12.27 `public int lastIndexOf(int ch)`

If a character with value `ch` occurs in the character sequence represented by this `String` object, then the index of the last such occurrence is returned—that is, the largest value *k* such that:

```
this.charAt(k) == ch
```

is true. If no such character occurs in this string, then `-1` is returned.

20.12.28 `public int lastIndexOf(int ch, int fromIndex)`

If a character with value `ch` occurs in the character sequence represented by this `String` object at an index no larger than `fromIndex`, then the index of the last such occurrence is returned—that is, the largest value *k* such that:

```
(this.charAt(k) == ch) && (k <= fromIndex)
```

is true. If no such character occurs in this string at or before position `fromIndex`, then `-1` is returned.

There is no restriction on the value of `fromIndex`. If it is greater than or equal to the length of this string, it has the same effect as if it were equal to one less than the length of this string: this entire string may be searched. If it is negative, it has the same effect as if it were `-1`: `-1` is returned.

20.12.29 `public int lastIndexOf(String str)`
`throws NullPointerException`

If the string `str` occurs as a substring of this `String` object, then the index of the first character of the last such substring is returned—that is, the largest value *k* such that:

```
this.startsWith(str, k)
```

is true. If `str` does not occur as a substring of this string, then `-1` is returned.

If `str` is `null`, a `NullPointerException` is thrown.

20.12.30 `public int lastIndexOf(String str, int fromIndex)`
`throws NullPointerException`

If the string `str` occurs as a substring of this `String` object starting at an index no larger than `fromIndex`, then the index of the first character of the last such substring is returned—that is, the largest value *k* such that:

```
this.startsWith(str, k) && (k <= fromIndex)
```

is `true`. If `str` does not occur as a substring of this string at or before position `fromIndex`, then `-1` is returned.

There is no restriction on the value of `fromIndex`. If it is greater than the length of this string, it has the same effect as if it were equal to the length of this string: this entire string may be searched. If it is negative, it has the same effect as if it were `-1`: `-1` is returned.

If `str` is `null`, a `NullPointerException` is thrown.

20.12.31 `public String` **`substring`**`(int beginIndex)`
`throws IndexOutOfBoundsException`

The result is a newly created `String` object that represents a subsequence of the character sequence represented by this `String` object; this subsequence begins with the character at position `beginIndex` and extends to the end of the character sequence.

If `beginIndex` is negative or larger than the length of this `String` object, then an `IndexOutOfBoundsException` is thrown.

Examples:

`"unhappy".substring(2)` returns `"happy"`

`"Harbison".substring(3)` returns `"bison"`

`"emptiness".substring(9)` returns `""` (an empty string)

20.12.32 `public String` **`substring`**`(int beginIndex, int endIndex)`
`throws IndexOutOfBoundsException`

The result is a newly created `String` object that represents a subsequence of the character sequence represented by this `String` object; this subsequence begins with the character at position `beginIndex` and ends with the character at position `endIndex-1`. Thus, the length of the subsequence is `endIndex-beginIndex`.

If `beginIndex` is negative, or `endIndex` is larger than the length of this `String` object, or `beginIndex` is larger than `endIndex`, then this method throws an `IndexOutOfBoundsException`.

Examples:

`"hamburger".substring(4, 8)` returns `"urge"`

`"smiles".substring(1, 5)` returns `"mile"`

20.12.33 public String **concat**(String str) throws NullPointerException

If the length of the argument string is zero, then a reference to this `String` object is returned. Otherwise, a new `String` object is created, representing a character sequence that is the concatenation of the character sequence represented by this `String` object and the character sequence represented by the argument string.

Examples:

```
"cares".concat("s") returns "caress"
"to".concat("get").concat("her") returns "together"
```

If `str` is `null`, a `NullPointerException` is thrown.

20.12.34 public String **replace**(char oldChar, char newChar)

If the character `oldChar` does not occur in the character sequence represented by this `String` object, then a reference to this `String` object is returned. Otherwise, a new `String` object is created that represents a character sequence identical to the character sequence represented by this `String` object, except that every occurrence of `oldChar` is replaced by an occurrence of `newChar`.

Examples:

```
"mesquite in your cellar".replace('e', 'o')
                returns "mosquito in your collar"
"the war of baronets".replace('r', 'y')
                returns "the way of bayonets"
"sparring with a purple porpoise".replace('p', 't')
                returns "starring with a turtle tortoise"
"JonL".replace('q', 'x') returns "JonL" (no change)
```

20.12.35 public String **toLowerCase**()

If this `String` object does not contain any character that is mapped to a different character by the method `Character.toLowerCase` (§20.5.20), then a reference to this `String` object is returned. Otherwise, this method creates a new `String` object that represents a character sequence identical in length to the character sequence represented by this `String` object, with every character equal to the result of applying the method `Character.toLowerCase` to the corresponding character of this `String` object.

Examples:

```
"French Fries".toLowerCase() returns "french fries"
"ΙΧΘΥΣ".toLowerCase() returns "ιχθυς"
```

20.12.36 `public String` **`toUpperCase`**`()`

If this `String` object does not contain any character that is mapped to a different character by the method `Character.toUpperCase` (§20.5.21), then a reference to this `String` object is returned. Otherwise, this method creates a new `String` object representing a character sequence identical in length to the character sequence represented by this `String` object and with every character equal to the result of applying the method `Character.toUpperCase` to the corresponding character of this `String` object.

Examples:

`"Fahrvergnügen".toUpperCase()` returns `"FAHRVERGNÜGEN"`

`"Visit Ljubinje!".toUpperCase()` returns `"VISIT LJUBINJE!"`

20.12.37 `public String` **`trim`**`()`

If this `String` object represents an empty character sequence, or the first and last characters of character sequence represented by this `String` object both have codes greater than `\u0020` (the space character), then a reference to this `String` object is returned.

Otherwise, if there is no character with a code greater than `\u0020` in the string, then a new `String` object representing an empty string is created and returned.

Otherwise, let *k* be the index of the first character in the string whose code is greater than `\u0020`, and let *m* be the index of the last character in the string whose code is greater than `\u0020`. A new `String` object is created, representing the substring of this string that begins with the character at index *k* and ends with the character at index *m*—that is, the result of `this.substring(`*k*`, `*m*`+1)`.

This method may be used to trim whitespace (§20.5.19) from the beginning and end of a string; in fact, it trims all ASCII control characters as well.

20.12.38 `public static String` **`valueOf`**`(Object obj)`

If the argument is `null`, then a string equal to `"null"` is returned. Otherwise, the value of `obj.toString()` is returned. See the `toString` method (§20.1.2).

20.12.39 `public static String` **`valueOf`**`(char[] data)`
`throws NullPointerException`

A string is created and returned. The string represents the sequence of characters currently contained in the character array argument. The contents of the character array are copied; subsequent modification of the character array does not affect the newly created string.

20.12.40 `public static String` **`valueOf`**`(char[] data,`
`int offset, int count)`
`throws NullPointerException,`
`IndexOutOfBoundsException`

A string is created and returned. The string represents the sequence of characters currently contained in a subarray of the character array argument. The `offset` argument is the index of the first character of the subarray and the `count` argument specifies the length of the subarray. The contents of the subarray are copied; subsequent modification of the character array does not affect the newly created string.

If `data` is `null`, then a `NullPointerException` is thrown.

If `offset` is negative, or `count` is negative, or `offset+count` is larger than `data.length`, then an `IndexOutOfBoundsException` is thrown.

20.12.41 `public static String` **`valueOf`**`(boolean b)`

A string representation of `b` is returned.

If the argument is `true`, the string `"true"` is returned.

If the argument is `false`, the string `"false"` is returned.

20.12.42 `public static String` **`valueOf`**`(char c)`

A string is created and returned. The string contains one character, equal to `c`.

20.12.43 `public static String` **`valueOf`**`(int i)`

A string is created and returned. The string is computed exactly as if by the method `Integer.toString` of one argument (§20.7.12).

20.12.44 public static String **valueOf**(long l)

A string is created and returned. The string is computed exactly as if by the method Long.toString of one argument (§20.8.12).

20.12.45 public static String **valueOf**(float f)

A string is created and returned. The string is computed exactly as if by the method Float.toString of one argument (§20.9.16).

20.12.46 public static String **valueOf**(double d)

A string is created and returned. The string is computed exactly as if by the method Double.toString of one argument (§20.10.15).

20.12.47 public String **intern**()

A pool of strings, initially empty, is maintained privately by the class String.

When the intern method is invoked, if the pool already contains a string equal to this String object as determined by the equals method (§20.12.9), then the string from the pool is returned. Otherwise, this String object is added to the pool and a reference to this String object is returned.

It follows that for any two strings s and t, s.intern() == t.intern() is true if and only if s.equals(t) is true.

All literal strings and string-valued constant expressions are interned (§3.10.5).

20.13 The Class java.lang.StringBuffer

A string buffer is like a String (§20.12), but can be modified. At any point in time it contains some particular sequence of characters, but the length and content of the sequence can be changed through certain method calls.

```
public class StringBuffer {
   public StringBuffer();
   public StringBuffer(int length)
      throws NegativeArraySizeException;
   public StringBuffer(String str);
   public String toString();
   public int length();
   public void setLength(int newLength)
      throws IndexOutOfBoundsException;
   public int capacity();
   public void ensureCapacity(int minimumCapacity);
   public char charAt(int index)
      throws IndexOutOfBoundsException;
   public void setCharAt(int index, char ch)
      throws IndexOutOfBoundsException;
   public void getChars(int srcBegin, int srcEnd,
         char[] dst, int dstBegin)
      throws NullPointerException, IndexOutOfBoundsException;
   public StringBuffer append(Object obj);
   public StringBuffer append(String str);
   public StringBuffer append(char[] str)
      throws NullPointerException;
   public StringBuffer append(char[] str, int offset, int len)
      throws NullPointerException, IndexOutOfBoundsException;
   public StringBuffer append(boolean b);
   public StringBuffer append(char c);
   public StringBuffer append(int i);
   public StringBuffer append(long l);
   public StringBuffer append(float f);
   public StringBuffer append(double d);
   public StringBuffer insert(int offset, Object obj)
      throws IndexOutOfBoundsException;
   public StringBuffer insert(int offset, String str)
      throws IndexOutOfBoundsException;
   public StringBuffer insert(int offset, char[] str)
      throws NullPointerException, IndexOutOfBoundsException;
   public StringBuffer insert(int offset, boolean b)
      throws IndexOutOfBoundsException;
```

```
    public StringBuffer insert(int offset, char c)
        throws IndexOutOfBoundsException;
    public StringBuffer insert(int offset, int i)
        throws IndexOutOfBoundsException;
    public StringBuffer insert(int offset, long l)
        throws IndexOutOfBoundsException;
    public StringBuffer insert(int offset, float f)
        throws IndexOutOfBoundsException;
    public StringBuffer insert(int offset, double d)
        throws IndexOutOfBoundsException;
    public StringBuffer reverse();
}
```

A string buffer has a *capacity*. As long as the length of the character sequence contained in the string buffer does not exceed the capacity, it is not necessary to create a new internal buffer array.

String buffers are safe for use by multiple threads. The methods are synchronized where necessary so that all the operations on any particular instance behave as if they occur in some serial order that is consistent with the order of the method calls made by each of the individual threads involved.

String buffers can be used by a compiler to implement the binary string concatenation operator + (§15.17.1). For example, suppose `k` has type `int` and `a` has type `Object`. Then the expression:

```
k + "/" + a
```

can be compiled as if it were the expression:

```
new StringBuffer().append(k).append("/").
                                append(a).toString()
```

which creates a new string buffer (initially empty), appends the string representation of each operand to the string buffer in turn, and then converts the contents of the string buffer to a string. Overall, this avoids creating many temporary strings.

The principal operations on a `StringBuffer` are the `append` and `insert` methods, which are overloaded so as to accept data of any type. Each effectively converts a given datum to a string and then adds the characters of that string to the contents of the string buffer. The `append` method always adds these characters at the end of the buffer; the `insert` method adds the characters at a specified point.

For example, if `z` refers to a string buffer object whose current contents are the characters "`start`", then the method call `z.append("le")` would alter the string buffer to contain the characters "`startle`", but `z.insert(4, "le")` would alter the string buffer to contain the characters "`starlet`".

In general, if `sb` refers to an instance of a `StringBuffer`, then `sb.append(x)` has the same effect as `sb.insert(sb.length(), x)`.

20.13.1 public **StringBuffer**()

This constructor initializes a newly created StringBuffer object so that it initially represents an empty character sequence and has capacity 16.

20.13.2 public **StringBuffer**(int length) throws NegativeArraySizeException

This constructor initializes a newly created StringBuffer object so that it initially represents an empty character sequence, but has the capacity specified by the argument.

If the argument is negative, a NegativeArraySizeException is thrown.

20.13.3 public **StringBuffer**(String str)

This constructor initializes a newly created StringBuffer object so that it represents the same sequence of characters as the argument; in other words, the initial contents of the string buffer is a copy of the argument string. The initial capacity of the string buffer is 16 plus the length of the argument string.

20.13.4 public String **toString**()

A new String object is created and initialized to contain the character sequence currently represented by the string buffer; the new String is then returned. Any subsequent changes to the string buffer do not affect the contents of the returned string.

Implementation advice: This method can be coded so as to create a new String object without allocating new memory to hold a copy of the character sequence. Instead, the string can share the memory used by the string buffer. Any subsequent operation that alters the content or capacity of the string buffer must then make a copy of the internal buffer at that time. This strategy is effective for reducing the amount of memory allocated by a string concatenation operation (§15.17.1) when it is implemented using a string buffer.

Overrides the toString method of Object (§20.1.2).

20.13.5 public int **length**()

This method returns the length of the sequence of characters currently represented by this StringBuffer object.

20.13.6 `public int capacity()`

The current capacity of this `StringBuffer` object is returned.

20.13.7 `public void ensureCapacity(int minimumCapacity)`

If the current capacity of this `StringBuffer` object is less than the argument, then a new internal buffer is created with greater capacity. The new capacity will be the larger of:

- the `minimumCapacity` argument
- twice the old capacity, plus `2`

If the `minimumCapacity` argument is nonpositive, this method takes no action and simply returns.

20.13.8 `public void setLength(int newLength) throws IndexOutOfBoundsException`

This string buffer is altered to represent a new character sequence whose length is specified by the argument. For every nonnegative index *k* less than `newLength`, the character at index *k* in the new character sequence is the same as the character at index *k* in the old sequence if *k* is less than the length of the old character sequence; otherwise, it is the null character `'\u0000'`. This method also calls the `ensureCapacity` method (§20.13.7) with argument `newLength`.

If the argument is negative, an `IndexOutOfBoundsException` is thrown.

20.13.9 `public char charAt(int index) throws IndexOutOfBoundsException`

The specified character of the sequence currently represented by the string buffer, as indicated by the `index` argument, is returned. The first character of the sequence is at index `0`, the next at index `1`, and so on, as for array indexing.

If the `index` argument is negative or not less than the current length (§20.13.5) of the string buffer, an `IndexOutOfBoundsException` is thrown.

20.13.10 `public void` **`setCharAt`**`(int index, char ch)`
`throws IndexOutOfBoundsException`

The string buffer is altered to represent a new character sequence that is identical to the old character sequence, except that it contains the character `ch` at position `index`.

If the `index` argument is negative or not less than the current length (§20.13.5) of the string buffer, an `IndexOutOfBoundsException` is thrown.

20.13.11 `public void` **`getChars`**`(int srcBegin, int srcEnd, char[] dst, int dstBegin)`
`throws NullPointerException, IndexOutOfBoundsException`

Characters are copied from this `StringBuffer` object into the destination array `dst`. The first character to be copied is at index `srcBegin`; the last character to be copied is at index `srcEnd-1` (thus, the total number of characters to be copied is `srcEnd-srcBegin`). The characters are copied into the subarray of `dst` starting at index `dstBegin` and ending at index `dstbegin+(srcEnd-srcBegin)-1`.

If `dst` is `null`, then a `NullPointerException` is thrown.

Otherwise, if any of the following is true, an `IndexOutOfBoundsException` is thrown and the destination is not modified:

- The `srcBegin` argument is negative.
- The `srcBegin` argument is greater than the `srcEnd` argument.
- `srcEnd` is greater than `this.length()`, the current length of this string buffer.
- `dstBegin+srcEnd-srcBegin` is greater than `dst.length`.

20.13.12 `public StringBuffer` **`append`**`(Object obj)`

The argument is converted to a string as if by the method `String.valueOf` (§20.12.38) and the characters of that string are then appended (§20.13.13) to this `StringBuffer` object. A reference to this `StringBuffer` object is returned.

20.13.13 `public StringBuffer` **`append`**`(String str)`

The characters of the `String` argument are appended, in order, to the contents of this string buffer, increasing the length of this string buffer by the length of the argument. If `str` is `null`, then the four characters "`null`" are appended to this string buffer. The method `ensureCapacity` (§20.13.7) is first called with this new string buffer length as its argument. A reference to this `StringBuffer` object is returned.

Let n be the length of the old character sequence, the one contained in the string buffer just prior to execution of the `append` method. Then the character at index k in the new character sequence is equal to the character at index k in the old character sequence, if k is less than n; otherwise, it is equal to the character at index $k-n$ in the argument `str`.

20.13.14 `public StringBuffer` **`append`**`(char[] str)`

```
        throws NullPointerException
```

The characters of the array argument are appended, in order, to the contents of this string buffer, increasing the length of this string buffer by the length of the argument. The method `ensureCapacity` (§20.13.7) is first called with this new string buffer length as its argument. A reference to this `StringBuffer` object is returned.

The overall effect is exactly as if the argument were converted to a string by the method `String.valueOf` (§20.12.39) and the characters of that string were then appended (§20.13.13) to this `StringBuffer` object.

20.13.15 `public StringBuffer` **`append`**`(char[] str,`

```
            int offset, int len)
        throws NullPointerException,
            IndexOutOfBoundsException
```

Characters of the character array `str`, starting at index `offset`, are appended, in order, to the contents of this string buffer, increasing the length of this string buffer by `len`. The method `ensureCapacity` (§20.13.7) is first called with this new string buffer length as its argument. A reference to this `StringBuffer` object is returned.

The overall effect is exactly as if the arguments were converted to a string by the method `String.valueOf` of three arguments (§20.12.40) and the characters of that string were then appended (§20.13.13) to this `StringBuffer` object.

20.13.16 `public StringBuffer append(boolean b)`

The argument is converted to a string as if by the method `String.valueOf` (§20.12.41) and the characters of that string are then appended (§20.13.13) to this `StringBuffer` object. A reference to this `StringBuffer` object is returned.

20.13.17 `public StringBuffer append(char c)`

The argument is appended to the contents of this string buffer, increasing the length of this string buffer by `1`. The method `ensureCapacity` (§20.13.7) is first called with this new string buffer length as its argument. A reference to this `StringBuffer` object is returned.

The overall effect is exactly as if the argument were converted to a string by the method `String.valueOf` (§20.12.42) and the character in that string were then appended (§20.13.13) to this `StringBuffer` object.

20.13.18 `public StringBuffer append(int i)`

The argument is converted to a string as if by the method `String.valueOf` (§20.12.43) and the characters of that string are then appended (§20.13.13) to this `StringBuffer` object. A reference to this `StringBuffer` object is returned.

20.13.19 `public StringBuffer append(long l)`

The argument is converted to a string as if by the method `String.valueOf` (§20.12.44) and the characters of that string are then appended (§20.13.13) to this `StringBuffer` object. A reference to this `StringBuffer` object is returned.

20.13.20 `public StringBuffer append(float f)`

The argument is converted to a string as if by the method `String.valueOf` (§20.12.45) and the characters of that string are then appended (§20.13.13) to this `StringBuffer` object. A reference to this `StringBuffer` object is returned.

20.13.21 `public StringBuffer append(double d)`

The argument is converted to a string as if by the method `String.valueOf` (§20.12.46) and the characters of that string are then appended (§20.13.13) to this `StringBuffer` object. A reference to this `StringBuffer` object is returned.

20.13.22 `public StringBuffer insert(int offset, Object obj)`
`throws IndexOutOfBoundsException`

The argument is converted to a string as if by the method `String.valueOf` (§20.12.38) and the characters of that string are then inserted (§20.13.23) into this `StringBuffer` object at the position indicated by `offset`. A reference to this `StringBuffer` object is returned.

20.13.23 `public StringBuffer insert(int offset, String str)`
`throws IndexOutOfBoundsException`

The characters of the `String` argument are inserted, in order, into the string buffer at the position indicated by `offset`, moving up any characters originally above that position and increasing the length of the string buffer by the length of the argument. If `str` is `null`, then the four characters "`null`" are inserted into this string buffer. The method `ensureCapacity` (§20.13.7) is first called with this new string buffer length as its argument. A reference to this `StringBuffer` object is returned.

The character at index *k* in the new character sequence is equal to:

- the character at index *k* in the old character sequence, if *k* is less than `offset`
- the character at index *k*`-offset` in the argument `str`, if *k* is not less than `offset` but is less than `offset+str.length()`
- the character at index *k*`-str.length()` in the old character sequence, if *k* is not less than `offset+str.length()`

20.13.24 `public StringBuffer insert(int offset, char[] str)`
`throws NullPointerException,`
`IndexOutOfBoundsException`

The characters of the array argument, taken in order, are inserted into this string buffer, increasing the length of the string buffer by the length of the argument. The method `ensureCapacity` (§20.13.7) is first called with this new string buffer length as its argument. A reference to this `StringBuffer` object is returned.

The overall effect is exactly as if the argument were converted to a string by the method `String.valueOf` (§20.12.39) and the characters of that string were then inserted (§20.13.23) into this `StringBuffer` object at the position indicated by `offset`.

Note that while the `StringBuffer` class provides an `append` method that takes an offset, a character array, and two other arguments (§20.13.15), it does not currently provide an `insert` method that takes an offset, a character array, and two other arguments.

20.13.25 `public StringBuffer insert(int offset, boolean b) throws IndexOutOfBoundsException`

The argument is converted to a string as if by the method `String.valueOf` (§20.12.41) and the characters of that string are then inserted (§20.13.23) into this `StringBuffer` object at the position indicated by `offset`. A reference to this `StringBuffer` object is returned.

20.13.26 `public StringBuffer insert(int offset, char c) throws IndexOutOfBoundsException`

The argument is inserted into the contents of this string buffer at the position indicated by `offset`, increasing the length of this string buffer by `1`. The method `ensureCapacity` (§20.13.7) is first called with this new string buffer length as its argument. A reference to this `StringBuffer` object is returned.

The overall effect is exactly as if the argument were converted to a string by the method `String.valueOf` (§20.12.42) and the character in that string were then inserted (§20.13.23) into this `StringBuffer` object at the position indicated by `offset`.

20.13.27 `public StringBuffer insert(int offset, int i) throws IndexOutOfBoundsException`

The argument is converted to a string as if by the method `String.valueOf` (§20.12.43) and the characters of that string are then inserted (§20.13.23) into this `StringBuffer` object at the position indicated by `offset`. A reference to this `StringBuffer` object is returned.

20.13.28 `public StringBuffer insert(int offset, long l) throws IndexOutOfBoundsException`

The argument is converted to a string as if by the method `String.valueOf` (§20.12.44) and the characters of that string are inserted (§20.13.23) into this

StringBuffer object at the position indicated by offset. A reference to this StringBuffer object is returned.

20.13.29 `public StringBuffer insert(int offset, float f) throws IndexOutOfBoundsException`

The argument is converted to a string as if by the method String.valueOf (§20.12.45) and the characters of that string are then inserted (§20.13.23) into this StringBuffer object at the position indicated by offset. A reference to this StringBuffer object is returned.

20.13.30 `public StringBuffer insert(int offset, double d) throws IndexOutOfBoundsException`

The argument is converted to a string as if by the method String.valueOf (§20.12.46) and the characters of that string are then inserted (§20.13.23) into this StringBuffer object at the position indicated by offset. A reference to this StringBuffer object is returned.

20.13.31 `public StringBuffer reverse()`

The character sequence contained in this StringBuffer object is replaced by the reverse of that sequence. A reference to this StringBuffer object is returned.

Let *n* be the length of the old character sequence, the one contained in the string buffer just prior to execution of the reverse method. Then the character at index *k* in the new character sequence is equal to the character at index *n*-*k*-1 in the old character sequence.

20.14 The Class java.lang.ClassLoader

A class loader is an object that is responsible for loading classes. Given the name of a class, it should attempt to locate or generate data that constitutes a definition for the class. A typical strategy is to transform the name into a file name and then read a "class file" of that name from a file system.

Every Class object contains a reference to the ClassLoader that defined it (§20.3.7). Whenever executable Java code needs to use a class that has not yet been loaded, the loadClass method is invoked for the class loader of the class containing the code in question.

Class objects for array classes are not created by class loaders, but are created automatically as required by the Java runtime. The class loader for an array class, as returned by the getClassLoader method of class Class (§20.3.7), is the same as the class loader for its element type; if the element type is a primitive type, then the array class has no class loader.

Class loaders may typically be used by security managers (§20.17) to indicate security domains: two classes may considered to be "friendly" or "related" to each other only if they were defined by the same class loader.

```
public abstract class ClassLoader {
    protected ClassLoader() throws SecurityException;
    protected abstract Class loadClass(String name,
            boolean resolve)
        throws ClassNotFoundException;
    protected final Class defineClass(byte data[],
            int offset, int length)
        throws NullPointerException, IndexOutOfBoundsException,
            ClassFormatError;
    protected final void resolveClass(Class c)
        throws NullPointerException;
    protected final Class findSystemClass(String name)
        throws ClassNotFoundException;
}
```

20.14.1 protected **ClassLoader**() throws SecurityException

This constructor is invoked for every newly created class loader. Because the class ClassLoader is abstract, it is not possible to create a new instance of the class ClassLoader itself; however, every constructor for a subclass of ClassLoader necessarily invokes this constructor, explicitly or implicitly, directly or indirectly.

All this constructor does is to enforce a security check: if there is a security manager, its checkCreateClassLoader method (§20.17.10) is called.

20.14.2 `protected abstract Class loadClass(String name, boolean link) throws ClassNotFoundException`

```
protected abstract Class loadClass(String name,
        boolean link)
    throws ClassNotFoundException
```

Every subclass of `ClassLoader` that is not itself abstract must provide an implementation of the method `loadClass`.

The general contract of `loadClass` is that, given the `name` of a class, it either returns the `Class` object for the class or throws a `ClassNotFoundException`.

If a `Class` object is to be returned and `link` is `true`, then the `Class` object should be linked (§12.3, §20.14.4) before it is returned.

In most cases, it is wise for a subclass of `ClassLoader` (§20.14) to implement the `loadClass` method as a `synchronized` method.

20.14.3

```
protected final Class defineClass(byte data[],
        int offset, int length)
    throws NullPointerException,
        IndexOutOfBoundsException, ClassFormatError
```

This method may be used by a class loader to define a new class.

The bytes in the array `data` in positions `offset` through `offset+length-1` should have the format of a valid class file as defined by the *Java Virtual Machine Specification*.

If `data` is `null`, then a `NullPointerException` is thrown.

An `IndexOutOfBoundsException` is thrown if any of the following are true:

- `offset` is negative
- `length` is negative
- `offset+length` is greater than `data.length`

If the indicated bytes of `data` do not constitute a valid class definition, then a `ClassFormatError` is thrown. Otherwise, this method creates and returns a `Class` object as described by the data bytes

20.14.4 `protected final void` **`resolveClass`**`(Class c)`
`throws NullPointerException`

This (misleadingly named) method may be used by a class loader to link (§12.3, §20.14.4) a class.

If `c` is `null`, then a `NullPointerException` is thrown.

If the `Class` object `c` has already been linked, then this method simply returns.

Otherwise, the class is linked as described in §12.3.

20.14.5 `protected final Class` **`findSystemClass`**`(String name)`
`throws ClassNotFoundException`

This method may be used by a class loader to locate a class that has no class loader. This includes built-in classes such as `java.lang.Object`, as well as classes that the host implementation may keep in, for example, a local file system.

Given the `name` of a class, this method, like the `loadClass` method, either returns the `Class` object for the class or throws a `ClassNotFoundException`.

20.15 The Class `java.lang.Process`

The method `exec` (§20.16.3) of class `Runtime` returns a reference to a `Process` object. The class `Process` provides methods for performing input from the process, performing output to the process, waiting for the process to complete, checking the exit status of the process, and destroying (killing) the process.

Dropping the last reference to a `Process` instance, thus allowing the `Process` object to be reclaimed, does *not* automatically kill the associated process.

There is no requirement that a process represented by a `Process` object execute asynchronously or concurrently with respect to the Java process that owns the `Process` object.

```
public abstract class Process {
    public abstract OutputStream getOutputStream();
    public abstract InputStream getInputStream();
    public abstract InputStream getErrorStream();
    public abstract int waitFor()
        throws InterruptedException;
    public abstract int exitValue()
        throws IllegalThreadStateException;
    public abstract void destroy();
}
```

20.15.1 `public abstract OutputStream getOutputStream()`

This method returns an `OutputStream`. Output to the stream is piped into the standard input stream of the process represented by this `Process` object.

Implementation note: It is a good idea for the output stream to be buffered.

20.15.2 `public abstract InputStream getInputStream()`

This method returns an `InputStream`. The stream obtains data piped from the standard output stream of the process represented by this `Process` object.

Implementation note: It is a good idea for the input stream to be buffered.

20.15.3 `public abstract InputStream getErrorStream()`

This method returns an `InputStream`. The stream obtains data piped from the error output stream of the process represented by this `Process` object.

Implementation note: It is a good idea for the input stream to be buffered.

20.15.4 `public abstract int` **`waitFor()`**
`throws InterruptedException`

This method causes the current thread to wait, if necessary, until the process represented by this `Process` object has terminated. Then the exit value of the process is returned. By convention, the value `0` indicates normal termination.

If the current thread is interrupted (§20.20.31) by another thread while it is waiting, then the wait is ended and an `InterruptedException` is thrown.

20.15.5 `public abstract int` **`exitValue()`**
`throws IllegalThreadStateException`

If the process represented by this `Process` object has not yet terminated, then an `IllegalThreadStateException` is thrown. Otherwise, the exit value of the process is returned. By convention, the value `0` indicates normal termination.

20.15.6 `public abstract void` **`destroy()`**

The process represented by this `Process` object is forcibly terminated.

It was my hint to speak—such was the process.
—William Shakespeare, *Othello*, Act I, scene iii

20.16 The Class java.lang.Runtime

```
public class Runtime {
   public static Runtime getRuntime();
   public void exit(int status) throws SecurityException;
   public Process exec(String command) throws
      IOException, SecurityException, IndexOutOfBoundsException;
   public Process exec(String command, String envp[]) throws
      IOException, SecurityException, IndexOutOfBoundsException;
   public Process exec(String cmdarray[]) throws
      IOException, SecurityException, IndexOutOfBoundsException;
   public Process exec(String cmdarray[], String envp[]) throws
      IOException, SecurityException, IndexOutOfBoundsException;
   public long totalMemory();
   public long freeMemory();
   public void gc();
   public void runFinalization();
   public void traceInstructions(boolean on);
   public void traceMethodCalls(boolean on);
   public void load(String filename)
      throws SecurityException, UnsatisfiedLinkError;
   public void loadLibrary(String libname)
      throws SecurityException, UnsatisfiedLinkError;
   public InputStream getLocalizedInputStream(InputStream in);
   public OutputStream
      getLocalizedOutputStream(OutputStream out);
}
```

20.16.1 `public static Runtime getRuntime()`

This method returns the current `Runtime` object. Most of the methods of class `Runtime` are instance methods and must be invoked with respect to the current runtime object.

20.16.2 `public void exit(int status) throws SecurityException`

First, if there is a security manager, its `checkExit` method (§20.17.13) is called with the `status` value as its argument.

This method terminates the currently running Java Virtual Machine. The argument serves as a status code; by convention, a nonzero status code indicates abnormal termination.

This method never returns normally.

See also the method exit (§20.18.11) of class System, which is the conventional and convenient means of invoking this method.

20.16.3 public Process exec(String command) throws IOException, SecurityException, IndexOutOfBoundsException

```
20.16.3 public Process exec(String command)
            throws IOException, SecurityException,
               IndexOutOfBoundsException
```

The command argument is parsed into tokens and then executed as a command in a separate process. The token parsing is done by a StringTokenizer (§21.10) created by the call:

```
new StringTokenizer(command)
```

with no further modification of the character categories.

This method behaves exactly as if it performs the call:

```
exec(command, null)
```

See §20.16.4.

20.16.4 public Process exec(String command, String envp[]) throws IOException, SecurityException, IndexOutOfBoundsException

```
20.16.4 public Process exec(String command, String envp[])
            throws IOException, SecurityException,
                IndexOutOfBoundsException
```

The command argument is parsed into tokens and then executed as a command in a separate process with an environment specified by envp. The token parsing is done by a StringTokenizer (§21.10) created by the call:

```
new StringTokenizer(command)
```

with no further modification of the character categories.

This method breaks the command string into tokens and creates a new array cmdarray containing the tokens in the order that they were produced by the string tokenizer; it then behaves exactly as if it performs the call:

```
exec(cmdarray, envp)
```

See §20.16.6.

20.16.5 `public Process exec(String cmdarray[])`
```
        throws IOException, SecurityException,
            NullPointerException, IndexOutOfBoundsException
```

The command specified by the tokens in `cmdarray` is executed as a command in a separate process.

This method behaves exactly as if it performs the call:

```
exec(cmdarray, null)
```

See §20.16.6.

20.16.6 `public Process exec(String cmdarray[], String envp[])`
```
        throws IOException, SecurityException,
            NullPointerException, IndexOutOfBoundsException
```

First, if there is a security manager, its `checkExec` method (§20.17.14) is called with the first component of the array `cmdarray` as its argument.

If `cmdarray` is `null`, a `NullPointerException` is thrown. If `cmdarray` is an empty array (has length `0`), an `IndexOutOfBoundsException` is thrown.

Given an array of strings `cmdarray`, representing the tokens of a command line, and an array of strings `envp`, representing an "environment" that defines system properties, this method creates a new process in which to execute the specified command and returns a `Process` object (§20.15) representing the new process.

20.16.7 `public long totalMemory()`

The total amount of memory currently available for current and future created objects, measured in bytes, is returned. The value returned by this method may vary over time, depending on the host environment.

Note that the amount of memory required to hold an object of any given type may be implementation-dependent.

20.16.8 `public long freeMemory()`

An approximation to the total amount of memory currently available for future created objects, measured in bytes, is returned. This value is always less than the current value returned by the `totalMemory` method. Calling the `gc` method may increase the value returned by `freeMemory`.

20.16.9 public void **gc**()

Calling this method suggests that the Java Virtual Machine expend effort toward recycling discarded objects in order to make the memory they currently occupy available for quick reuse. When control returns from the method call, the Java Virtual Machine has made a best effort to recycle all discarded objects. (The name `gc` stands for "garbage collector.")

The Java runtime system will perform this recycling process automatically as needed, in a separate thread, if the `gc` method is not invoked explicitly.

See also the method `gc` (§20.18.12) of class `System`, which is the conventional and convenient means of invoking this method.

20.16.10 public void **runFinalization**()

Calling this method suggests that the Java Virtual Machine expend effort toward running the `finalize` methods of objects that have been found to be discarded but whose `finalize` methods have not yet been run. When control returns from the method call, the Java Virtual Machine has made a best effort to complete all outstanding finalizations.

The Java runtime system will perform the finalization process automatically as needed, in a separate thread, if the `runFinalization` method is not invoked explicitly.

See also the method `runFinalization` (§20.18.13) of class `System`, which is the conventional and convenient means of invoking this method.

20.16.11 public void **traceInstructions**(boolean on)

Calling this method with argument `true` suggests that the Java Virtual Machine emit debugging information for every instruction it executes. The format of this information, and the file or other output stream to which it is emitted, depends on the host environment.

Calling this method with argument `false` suggests that the Java Virtual Machine cease emitting per-instruction debugging information.

20.16.12 public void **traceMethodCalls**(boolean on)

Calling this method with argument `true` suggests that the Java Virtual Machine emit debugging information for every method call it executes. The format of this information, and the file or other output stream to which it is emitted, depends on the host environment.

Calling this method with argument `false` suggests that the Java Virtual Machine cease emitting per-call debugging information.

20.16.13 public void **load**(String filename)

First, if there is a security manager, its `checkLink` method (§20.17.17) is called with the `filename` as its argument.

This is similar to the method `loadLibrary` (§20.16.14), but accepts a general file name as an argument rather than just a library name, allowing any file of native code to be loaded.

See also the method `load` (§20.18.14) of class `System`, which is the conventional and convenient means of invoking this method.

20.16.14 public void **loadLibrary**(String libname)

First, if there is a security manager, its `checkLink` method (§20.17.17) is called with the `libname` as its argument.

A file containing native code is loaded from the local file system from a place where library files are conventionally obtained. The details of this process are implementation-dependent.

See also the method `loadLibrary` (§20.18.15) of class `System`, which is the conventional and convenient means of invoking this method. If `native` methods are to be used in the implementation of a class, a standard strategy is to put the native code in a library file (call it `LibFile`) and then to put a static initializer:

```
static { System.loadLibrary("LibFile"); }
```

within the class declaration. When the class is loaded and initialized (§12.4), the necessary native code implementation for the `native` methods will then be loaded as well.

20.16.15 public InputStream **getLocalizedInputStream**(InputStream in)

This method takes an `InputStream` (§22.3) and returns an `InputStream` equivalent to the argument in all respects except that it is localized: as data is read from the stream, it is automatically converted from the local format to Unicode. If the argument is already a localized stream, then it will be returned as the result.

20.16.16 `public OutputStream`
`**getLocalizedOutputStream**(OutputStream out)`

This method takes an `OutputStream` (§22.15) and returns an `OutputStream` equivalent to the argument in all respects except that it is localized: as data is written to the stream, it is automatically converted from Unicode to the local format. If the argument is already a localized stream, then it will be returned as the result.

20.17 The Class java.lang.SecurityManager

```
public abstract class SecurityManager {
   protected boolean inCheck;
   protected SecurityManager()
      throws SecurityException;
   protected Class[] getClassContext();
   protected int classDepth(String name);
   protected boolean inClass(String name);
   protected ClassLoader currentClassLoader();
   protected int classLoaderDepth();
   protected boolean inClassLoader();
   public boolean getInCheck();
   public void checkCreateClassLoader()
      throws SecurityException;
   public void checkAccess(Thread t)
      throws SecurityException;
   public void checkAccess(ThreadGroup g)
      throws SecurityException;
   public void checkExit(int status)
      throws SecurityException;
   public void checkExec(String cmd)
      throws SecurityException;
   public void checkPropertiesAccess()
      throws SecurityException;
   public void checkPropertyAccess(String key)
      throws SecurityException;
   public void checkLink(String libname)
      throws SecurityException;
   public void checkRead(int fd)
      throws SecurityException;
   public void checkRead(String file)
      throws SecurityException;
   public void checkWrite(int fd)
      throws SecurityException;
   public void checkWrite(String file)
      throws SecurityException;
   public void checkDelete(String file)
      throws SecurityException;
   public void checkConnect(String host, int port)
      throws SecurityException;
   public void checkListen(int port)
      throws SecurityException;
```

```
    public void checkAccept(String host, int port)
        throws SecurityException;
    public void checkSetFactory()
        throws SecurityException;
    public boolean checkTopLevelWindow()
        throws SecurityException;
    public void checkPackageAccess(String packageName)
        throws SecurityException;
    public void checkPackageDefinition(String packageName)
        throws SecurityException;
}
```

A running Java program may have a security manager, which is an instance of class `SecurityManager`. The current security manager is the one returned by the method invocation `System.getSecurityManager()` (§20.18.4).

The `SecurityManager` class contains a large number of methods whose names begin with "`check`". They are called by various methods throughout the Java libraries before those methods perform certain sensitive operations. The invocation of such a check method typically looks like this:

```
SecurityManager security = System.getSecurityManager();
if (security != null) {
    security.checkXXX(arguments);
}
```

The security manager is thereby given an opportunity to prevent completion of the operation by throwing an exception. The usual convention is that a security manager checking routine simply returns if the operation is permitted, or throws a `SecurityException` if the operation is not permitted. In one case, namely `checkTopLevelWindow` (§20.17.27), the checking routine must return a `boolean` value to indicate one of two levels of permission.

20.17.1 `protected boolean inCheck = false;`

By convention, this field should be assigned the value `true` whenever a security check is in progress. This matters when one of the checking routines needs to call outside code to do its work. Outside code can then use the method `getInCheck` (§20.17.9) to test the status of this flag.

20.17.2 protected **SecurityManager**() throws SecurityException

This constructor checks to see whether a security manager has already been installed (§20.18.5); if so, creation of another security manager is not permitted, and so a SecurityException is thrown.

20.17.3 protected Class[] **getClassContext**()

This utility method for security managers scans the execution stack for the current thread and returns an array with one component for each stack frame. The component at position 0 corresponds to the top of the stack. If a component is a Class object, then the corresponding stack frame is for an invocation of a method of the class represented by that Class object.

20.17.4 protected int **classDepth**(String name)

This utility method for security managers searches the execution stack for the current thread to find the most recently invoked method whose execution has not yet completed and whose class has name as its fully qualified name. If such a method is found, its distance from the top of the stack is returned as a nonnegative integer; otherwise, -1 is returned.

20.17.5 protected boolean **inClass**(String name)

This utility method for security managers searches the execution stack for the current thread to find the most recently invoked method whose execution has not yet completed and whose class has name as its fully qualified name. If such a method is found, true is returned; otherwise, false is returned.

20.17.6 protected ClassLoader **currentClassLoader**()

This utility method for security managers searches the execution stack for the current thread to find the most recently invoked method whose execution has not yet completed and whose class was created by a class loader (§20.14). If such a method is found, a reference to the ClassLoader object for its class is returned; otherwise, null is returned.

20.17.7 protected int **classLoaderDepth**()

This utility method for security managers searches the execution stack for the current thread to find the most recently invoked method whose execution has not yet completed and whose class was created by a class loader (§20.14). If such a method is found, its distance from the top of the stack is returned as a nonnegative integer; otherwise, `-1` is returned.

20.17.8 protected boolean **inClassLoader**()

This utility method for security managers searches the execution stack for the current thread to find the most recently invoked method whose execution has not yet completed and whose class was created by a class loader (§20.14). If such a method is found, `true` is returned; otherwise `false` is returned.

20.17.9 public boolean **getInCheck**()

The value of the `inCheck` field (§20.17.1) is returned.

20.17.10 public void **checkCreateClassLoader**() throws SecurityException

The general contract of this method is that it should throw a `SecurityException` if creation of a class loader is not permitted.

This method is invoked for the current security manager (§20.18.4) by the constructor for class `ClassLoader` (§20.14.1).

The `checkCreateClassLoader` method defined by class `SecurityManager` always throws a `SecurityException`. A subclass must override this method if a class loader creation operation is to be permitted with a security manager installed.

20.17.11 public void **checkAccess**(Thread t) throws SecurityException

The general contract of this method is that it should throw a `SecurityException` if an operation that would modify the thread `t` is not permitted.

This method is invoked for the current security manager (§20.18.4) by method `checkAccess` (§20.20.12) of class `Thread`.

The `checkAccess` method defined by class `SecurityManager` always throws a `SecurityException`. A subclass must override this method if a thread modification operation is to be permitted with a security manager installed.

20.17.12 `public void` **`checkAccess`**`(ThreadGroup g) throws SecurityException`

The general contract of this method is that it should throw a `SecurityException` if an operation that would modify the thread group `g` is not permitted.

This method is invoked for the current security manager (§20.18.4) by method `checkAccess` (§20.21.4) of class `ThreadGroup`.

The `checkAccess` method defined by class `SecurityManager` always throws a `SecurityException`. A subclass must override this method if a thread group modification operation is to be permitted with a security manager installed.

20.17.13 `public void` **`checkExit`**`(int status) throws SecurityException`

The general contract of this method is that it should throw a `SecurityException` if an exit operation that would terminate the running Java Virtual Machine is not permitted.

This method is invoked for the current security manager (§20.18.4) by method `exit` (§20.16.2) of class `Runtime`.

The `checkExit` method defined by class `SecurityManager` always throws a `SecurityException`. A subclass must override this method if the exit operation is to be permitted with a security manager installed.

20.17.14 `public void` **`checkExec`**`(String cmd) throws SecurityException`

The general contract of this method is that it should throw a `SecurityException` if a command `exec` operation is not permitted. The argument `cmd` is the name of the command to be executed.

This method is invoked for the current security manager (§20.18.4) by method `exec` (§20.16.6) of class `Runtime`.

The `checkExec` method defined by class `SecurityManager` always throws a `SecurityException`. A subclass must override this method if a command `exec` operation is to be permitted with a security manager installed.

20.17.15 `public void checkPropertiesAccess() throws SecurityException`

The general contract of this method is that it should throw a SecurityException if getting or setting the system properties data structure is not permitted.

This method is invoked for the current security manager (§20.18.4) by the methods getProperties (§20.18.7) and setProperties (§20.18.8) of class System.

The checkPropertiesAccess method defined by class SecurityManager always throws a SecurityException. A subclass must override this method if a properties access operation is to be permitted with a security manager installed.

20.17.16 `public void checkPropertyAccess(String key) throws SecurityException`

The general contract of this method is that it should throw a SecurityException if getting the value of the system property named by the key is not permitted.

This method is invoked for the current security manager (§20.18.4) by the methods getProperty of one argument (§20.18.9) and getProperty of two arguments (§20.18.10) of class System.

The checkPropertyAccess method defined by class SecurityManager always throws a SecurityException. A subclass must override this method if accessing the value of a system property is to be permitted with a security manager installed.

20.17.17 `public void checkLink(String libname) throws SecurityException`

The general contract of this method is that it should throw a SecurityException if dynamic linking of the specified library code file is not permitted. The argument may be a simple library name or a complete file name.

This method is invoked for the current security manager (§20.18.4) by methods load (§20.16.13) and loadLibrary (§20.16.14) of class Runtime.

The checkLink method defined by class SecurityManager always throws a SecurityException. A subclass must override this method if a dynamic code linking operation is to be permitted with a security manager installed.

20.17.18 `public void checkRead(int fd) throws SecurityException`

The general contract of this method is that it should throw a `SecurityException` if creating an input stream using the specified file descriptor is not permitted.

This method is invoked for the current security manager (§20.18.4) by one constructor for `java.io.FileInputStream` (§22.4.3).

The `checkRead` method defined by class `SecurityManager` always throws a `SecurityException`. A subclass must override this method if creating an input stream from an existing file descriptor is to be permitted with a security manager installed.

20.17.19 `public void checkRead(String file) throws SecurityException`

The general contract of this method is that it should throw a `SecurityException` if reading the specified file or directory, or examining associated file-system information, or testing for its existence, is not permitted.

This method is invoked for the current security manager (§20.18.4) by two constructors for `java.io.FileInputStream` (§22.4.1, §22.4.2); by two constructors for `java.io.RandomAccessFile` (§22.23.1, §22.23.2); and by methods `exists` (§22.24.16), `canRead` (§22.24.17), `isFile` (§22.24.19), `isDirectory` (§22.24.20), `lastModified` (§22.24.21), `length` (§22.24.22), `list` with no arguments (§22.24.25), and `list` with one argument (§22.24.26) of the class `java.io.File`.

The `checkRead` method defined by class `SecurityManager` always throws a `SecurityException`. A subclass must override this method if read access to a file is to be permitted with a security manager installed.

20.17.20 `public void checkWrite(int fd) throws SecurityException`

The general contract of this method is that it should throw a `SecurityException` if creating an output stream using the specified file descriptor is not permitted.

This method is invoked for the current security manager (§20.18.4) by one constructor for `java.io.FileOutputStream` (§22.16.3).

The `checkWrite` method defined by class `SecurityManager` always throws a `SecurityException`. A subclass must override this method if creating an output stream from an existing file descriptor is to be permitted with a security manager installed.

20.17.21 `public void checkWrite(String file) throws SecurityException`

The general contract of this method is that it should throw a `SecurityException` if writing, modifying, creating (for output), or renaming the specified file or directory is not permitted.

This method is invoked for the current security manager (§20.18.4) by two constructors for `java.io.FileOutputStream` (§22.16.1, §22.16.2); by two constructors for `java.io.RandomAccessFile` (§22.23.1, §22.23.2); and by methods `canWrite` (§22.24.18), `mkdir` (§22.24.23), and `renameTo` (§22.24.27) of class `java.io.File`.

The `checkWrite` method defined by class `SecurityManager` always throws a `SecurityException`. A subclass must override this method if write access to a file is to be permitted with a security manager installed.

20.17.22 `public void checkDelete(String file) throws SecurityException`

The general contract of this method is that it should throw a `SecurityException` if deleting the specified file is not permitted.

This method is invoked for the current security manager (§20.18.4) by method `delete` (§22.24.28) of class `java.io.File`.

The `checkDelete` method defined by class `SecurityManager` always throws a `SecurityException`. A subclass must override this method if a file deletion operation is to be permitted with a security manager installed.

20.17.23 `public void checkConnect(String host, int port) throws SecurityException`

The general contract of this method is that it should throw a `SecurityException` if connecting to the indicated `port` of the indicated network `host` is not permitted.

This method is invoked for the current security manager (§20.18.4) by two constructors for class `java.net.Socket`, methods `send` and `receive` of class `java.net.DatagramSocket`, and methods `getByName` and `getAllByName` of class `java.net.InetAddress`. (These classes are not documented in this specification. See *The Java Application Programming Interface*.)

The `checkConnect` method defined by class `SecurityManager` always throws a `SecurityException`. A subclass must override this method if a network connection is to be permitted with a security manager installed.

20.17.24 `public void` **`checkListen`**`(int port)`
`throws SecurityException`

The general contract of this method is that it should throw a `SecurityException` if listening to the specified local network `port` is not permitted.

This method is invoked for the current security manager (§20.18.4) by the constructor of one argument for class `java.net.DatagramSocket` and by the constructors for class `java.net.ServerSocket`. (These classes are not documented in this specification. See *The Java Application Programming Interface*.)

The `checkListen` method defined by class `SecurityManager` always throws a `SecurityException`. A subclass must override this method if listening to a local network port is to be permitted with a security manager installed.

20.17.25 `public void` **`checkAccept`**`(String host, int port)`
`throws SecurityException`

The general contract of this method is that it should throw a `SecurityException` if accepting a connection from the indicated `port` of the indicated network `host` is not permitted.

This method is invoked for the current security manager (§20.18.4) by method `accept` of class `java.net.ServerSocket`. (This class is not documented in this specification. See *The Java Application Programming Interface*.)

The `checkAccept` method defined by class `SecurityManager` always throws a `SecurityException`. A subclass must override this method if accepting a network connection is to be permitted with a security manager installed.

20.17.26 `public void` **`checkSetFactory`**`()`
`throws SecurityException`

The general contract of this method is that it should throw a `SecurityException` if installing a "factory" for a socket, server socket, URL, or URL connection is not permitted.

This method is invoked for the current security manager (§20.18.4) by:

method `setSocketFactory` of class `java.net.ServerSocket`
method `setSocketImplFactory` of class `java.net.Socket`
method `setURLStreamHandlerFactory` of class `java.net.URL`
method `setContentHandlerFactory` of class `java.net.URLConnection`

(These classes are not documented in this specification. See *The Java Application Programming Interface*.)

The `checkSetFactory` method defined by class `SecurityManager` always throws a `SecurityException`. A subclass must override this method if a factory installation operation is to be permitted with a security manager installed.

20.17.27 `public boolean` **`checkTopLevelWindow`**`()`
`throws SecurityException`

The general contract of this method is that it should throw a `SecurityException` if creation of a top-level window is not permitted. If creation of a top-level window is permitted, then this method should return `false` if the window ought to bear a clear warning that it is a window for an executable applet. A returned value of `true` means that the security manager places no restriction on window creation.

This method is invoked for the current security manager (§20.18.4) by the constructors for class `java.awt.Window`. (This class is not documented in this specification. See *The Java Application Programming Interface*.)

The `checkTopLevelWindow` method defined by class `SecurityManager` always returns `false`. A subclass must override this method if a window creation operation is to be unrestricted or forbidden with a security manager installed.

20.17.28 `public void` **`checkPackageAccess`**`(String packageName)`
`throws SecurityException`

The general contract of this method is that it should throw a `SecurityException` if the current applet is not permitted to access the package named by the argument. This method is intended for use by Java-capable web browsers.

The `checkPackageAccess` method defined by class `SecurityManager` always throws a `SecurityException`. A subclass must override this method if package access by an applet is to be permitted with a security manager installed.

20.17.29 `public void` **`checkPackageDefinition`**`(String packageName)`
`throws SecurityException`

The general contract of this method is that it should throw a `SecurityException` if the current applet is not permitted to define a class (or interface) in the package named by the argument. This method is intended for use by Java-capable web browsers.

The `checkPackageAccess` method defined by class `SecurityManager` always throws a `SecurityException`. A subclass must override this method if class definition by an applet is to be permitted with a security manager installed.

20.18 The Class `java.lang.System`

The `System` class contains a number of useful class variables and class methods. It cannot be instantiated. Among the facilities provided by the `System` class are standard input, output, and error output streams; access to externally defined "properties"; a means of loading files and libraries; and a utility method for quickly copying a portion of an array.

```
public final class System {
   public static InputStream in;
   public static PrintStream out;
   public static PrintStream err;
   public static SecurityManager getSecurityManager();
   public static void setSecurityManager(SecurityManager s)
      throws SecurityException;
   public static long currentTimeMillis();
   public static Properties getProperties()
      throws SecurityException;
   public static void setProperties(Properties props)
      throws SecurityException;
   public static String getProperty(String key)
      throws SecurityException;
   public static String getProperty(String key, String defaults)
      throws SecurityException;
   public static void exit(int status) throws SecurityException;
   public static void gc();
   public static void runFinalization();
   public static void load(String filename)
      throws SecurityException, UnsatisfiedLinkError;
   public static void loadLibrary(String libname)
      throws SecurityException, UnsatisfiedLinkError;
   public static void arraycopy(Object src, int srcOffset,
         Object dst, int dstOffset, int length)
      throws NullPointerException,
         ArrayStoreException, IndexOutOfBoundsException;
}
```

20.18.1 `public static InputStream in;`

The initial value of this variable is a "standard" input stream, already open and ready to supply input data. Typically, this corresponds to keyboard input or another input source specified by the host environment or user. Note that this field is not `final`, so its value may be updated if necessary.

20.18.2 `public static PrintStream out;`

The initial value of this variable is a "standard" output stream, already open and ready to accept output data. Typically, this corresponds to display output or another output destination specified by the host environment or user. Note that this field is not `final`, so its value may be updated if necessary.

For simple Java applications, a typical way to write a line of output data is:

```
System.out.println(data)
```

See the `println` method of class `PrintStream` (§22.22).

20.18.3 `public static PrintStream err;`

The initial value of this variable is a "standard" error output stream, already open and ready to accept output data. Typically, this corresponds to display output or another output destination specified by the host environment or user. By convention, this output stream is used to display error messages or other information that should come to the immediate attention of a user even if the principal output stream, the value of the variable `out`, has been redirected to a file or other destination that is typically not continuously monitored. Note that this field is not `final`, so its value may be updated if necessary.

20.18.4 `public static SecurityManager getSecurityManager()`

If a security manager has already been established for the currently running Java system, a reference to that security manager is returned. Otherwise, `null` is returned.

20.18.5 `public static void setSecurityManager(SecurityManager s) throws SecurityException`

If a security manager has already been established for the currently running Java system, a `SecurityException` is thrown. Otherwise, the argument is established as the current security manager. If the argument is `null` and no security manager has been established, then no action is taken and the method simply returns normally.

20.18.6 `public static long` **`currentTimeMillis`**`()`

Returns the difference, measured in milliseconds, between the current time and the standard base time known as "the epoch," 00:00:00 GMT on January 1, 1970. See the description of the class `Date` (§21.3) for a discussion of slight discrepancies that may arise between "computer time" and UTC (Coordinated Universal Time).

20.18.7 `public static Properties` **`getProperties`**`() throws SecurityException`

First, if there is a security manager, its `checkPropertiesAccess` method (§20.17.15) is called with no arguments.

The current set of system properties for use by the `getProperty` method is returned as a Properties object (§21.6). If there is no current set of system properties, a set of system properties is first created and initialized. This set of system properties always includes values for the following keys:

Key	*Description of associated value*
`java.version`	Java version number
`java.vendor`	Java-vendor–specific string
`java.vendor.url`	Java vendor URL
`java.home`	Java installation directory
`java.class.version`	Java class format version number
`java.class.path`	Java classpath
`os.name`	Operating system name
`os.arch`	Operating system architecture
`os.version`	Operating system version
`file.separator`	File separator (/ on UNIX)
`path.separator`	Path separator (`:` on UNIX)
`line.separator`	Line separator (`\n` on UNIX)
`user.name`	User account name
`user.home`	User home directory
`user.dir`	User's current working directory

Note that even if the security manager does not permit the `getProperties` operation, it may choose to permit the `getProperty` operation (§20.18.9).

20.18.8 `public static void` **`setProperties`**`(Properties props)`
`throws SecurityException`

First, if there is a security manager, its `checkPropertiesAccess` method (§20.17.15) is called with no arguments.

The argument becomes the current set of system properties for use by the `getProperty` method. See the class `Properties` (§21.6). If the argument is `null`, then the current set of system properties is forgotten.

20.18.9 `public static String` **`getProperty`**`(String key)`
`throws SecurityException`

First, if there is a security manager, its `checkPropertyAccess` method (§20.17.16) is called with the `key` as its argument.

If there is no current set of system properties, a set of system properties is first created and initialized in the same manner as for the `getProperties` method (§20.18.7).

The system property value associated with the specified `key` string is returned. If there is no property with that key, then `null` is returned.

20.18.10 `public static String` **`getProperty`**`(String key,`
`String defaults)`
`throws SecurityException`

First, if there is a security manager, its `checkPropertyAccess` method (§20.17.16) is called with the `key` as its argument.

If there is no current set of system properties, a set of system properties is first created and initialized in the same manner as for the `getProperties` method (§20.18.7).

The system property value associated with the specified `key` string is returned. If there is no property with that key, then the argument `defaults` is returned.

20.18.11 `public static void` **`exit`**`(int status)`
`throws SecurityException`

This method terminates the currently running Java Virtual Machine. The argument serves as a status code; by convention, a nonzero status code indicates abnormal termination.

This method never returns normally.

The call `System.exit(n)` is effectively equivalent to the call:

```
Runtime.getRuntime().exit(n)
```

For a more complete description, see the `exit` method of class `Runtime` (§20.16.2).

20.18.12 `public static void gc()`

Calling this method suggests that the Java Virtual Machine expend effort toward recycling discarded objects in order to make the memory they currently occupy available for quick reuse. When control returns from the method call, the Java Virtual Machine has made a best effort to recycle all discarded objects.

The call `System.gc()` is effectively equivalent to the call:

```
Runtime.getRuntime().gc()
```

For a more complete description, see the `gc` method of class `Runtime` (§20.16.9).

20.18.13 `public static void runFinalization()`

Calling this method suggests that the Java Virtual Machine expend effort toward running the finalization methods of objects that have been found to be discarded but whose finalization methods have not yet been run. When control returns from the method call, the Java Virtual Machine has made a best effort to complete all outstanding finalizations.

The call `System.runFinalization()` is effectively equivalent to the call:

```
Runtime.getRuntime().runFinalization()
```

For a more complete description, see the `runFinalization` method of class `Runtime` (§20.16.10).

20.18.14 `public static void load(String filename) throws SecurityException, UnsatisfiedLinkError`

This method loads a code file with the specified file name from the local file system.

The call `System.load(name)` is effectively equivalent to the call:

```
Runtime.getRuntime().load(name)
```

For a more complete description, see the `load` method of class `Runtime` (§20.16.13).

20.18.15 `public static void loadLibrary(String libname) throws SecurityException, UnsatisfiedLinkError`

This method loads a library code file with the specified library name from the local file system.

The call `System.loadLibrary(name)` is effectively equivalent to the call

```
Runtime.getRuntime().loadLibrary(name)
```

For a more complete description, see the `loadLibrary` method of class `Runtime` (§20.16.14).

20.18.16 `public static void arraycopy(Object src, int srcOffset, Object dst, int dstOffset, int length) throws NullPointerException, ArrayStoreException, IndexOutOfBoundsException`

A subsequence of array components is copied from the source array referenced by `src` to the destination array referenced by `dst`. The number of components copied is equal to the `length` argument. The components at the positions `srcOffset` through `srcOffset+length-1` in the source array are copied into the positions `dstOffset` through `dstOffset+length-1`, respectively, of the destination array.

If the `src` and `dst` arguments refer to the same array object, then copying is performed as if the components of the source array at positions `srcOffset` through `srcOffset+length-1` were first copied to a temporary array of length `length` and then the contents of the temporary array were copied into positions `dstOffset` through `dstOffset+length-1` of the destination array.

If `dst` is `null`, then a `NullPointerException` is thrown.

If `src` is `null`, then a `NullPointerException` is thrown and the destination array is not modified.

Otherwise, if any of the following is true, then an `ArrayStoreException` is thrown and the destination is not modified:

- The `src` argument refers to an object that is not an array.
- The `dst` argument refers to an object that is not an array.
- The `src` argument and `dst` argument refer to arrays whose component types are different primitive types.
- The `src` argument refers to an array of primitive component type and the `dst` argument refers to an array of reference component type.

- The `src` argument refers to an array of reference component type and the `dst` argument refers to an array of primitive component type.

Otherwise, if any of the following is true, an `IndexOutOfBoundsException` is thrown and the destination is not modified:

- The `srcOffset` argument is negative.
- The `dstOffset` argument is negative.
- The `length` argument is negative.
- `srcOffset+length` is greater than `src.length`, the length of the `src` array.
- `dstOffset+length` is greater than `dst.length`, the length of the `dst` array.

Otherwise, if the actual value of any component of the source array from position `srcOffset` through `srcOffset+length-1` cannot be converted to the component type of the destination array by assignment conversion, then an `ArrayStoreException` is thrown. In this case, let *k* be the smallest nonnegative integer less than length such that `src[srcOffset+`*k*`]` cannot be converted to the component type of the destination array. When the exception is thrown, the source array components from positions `srcOffset` through `srcOffset+`*k*`-1` have been copied to destination array positions `dstOffset` through `dstOffset+`*k*`-1` and no other positions of the destination array will have been modified. (Because of the restrictions already itemized, this paragraph effectively applies only to the situation where both arrays have component types that are reference types.)

20.19 The Interface java.lang.Runnable

The Runnable interface should be implemented by any class whose instances are intended to be executed by a new thread. All that is required of such a class is that it implement a method of no arguments called run.

```
public interface Runnable {
    public abstract void run();
}
```

20.19.1 public abstract void run()

The general contract of the method run is that it may take any action whatsoever.

If an object implementing interface Runnable is used to create a thread (§20.20), then starting the thread will (normally) lead to the invocation of the object's run method in that separately executing thread.

20.20 The Class java.lang.Thread

A thread is a single sequential flow of control. Thread objects allow multithreaded Java programming; a single Java Virtual Machine can execute many threads in an interleaved or concurrent manner.

In the method descriptions that follow, it is very important to distinguish among "the current thread" (the thread executing the method), "this Thread" (the object for which the method was invoked), and "this thread" (the thread that is represented by the Thread object for which the method was invoked).

```
public class Thread implements Runnable {
   public final static int MIN_PRIORITY = 1;
   public final static int MAX_PRIORITY = 10;
   public final static int NORM_PRIORITY = 5;
   public Thread();
   public Thread(String name);
   public Thread(Runnable runObject);
   public Thread(Runnable runObject, String name);
   public Thread(ThreadGroup group, String name)
      throws SecurityException, IllegalThreadStateException;
   public Thread(ThreadGroup group, Runnable runObject)
      throws SecurityException, IllegalThreadStateException;
   public Thread(ThreadGroup group, Runnable runObject,
         String name)
      throws SecurityException, IllegalThreadStateException;
   public String toString();
   public void checkAccess() throws SecurityException;
   public void run();
   public void start()
      throws IllegalThreadStateException;
   public final void stop()
      throws SecurityException;
   public final void stop(Throwable thr)
      throws SecurityException, NullPointerException;
   public final void suspend()
      throws SecurityException;
   public final void resume()
      throws SecurityException;
   public final String getName();
   public final void setName(String name)
      throws SecurityException;
   public final ThreadGroup getThreadGroup();
   public final int getPriority();
```

```
    public final void setPriority(int newPriority)
        throws SecurityException, IllegalArgumentException;
    public final boolean isDaemon();
    public final void setDaemon(boolean on)
        throws SecurityException, IllegalThreadStateException;
    public final boolean isAlive();
    public int countStackFrames();
    public final void join()
        throws InterruptedException;
    public final void join(long millis)
        throws InterruptedException;
    public final void join(long millis, int nanos)
        throws InterruptedException;
    public void interrupt();
    public boolean isInterrupted();
    public static boolean interrupted();
    public static Thread currentThread();
    public static int activeCount();                  // deprecated
    public static int enumerate(Thread tarray[]);     // deprecated
    public static void dumpStack();
    public static void yield();
    public static void sleep(long millis)
        throws InterruptedException;
    public static void sleep(long millis, int nanos)
        throws InterruptedException;
    public void destroy();
}
```

When a new `Thread` object is created, the thread it represents is not yet active. It is activated when some other thread calls the `start` method (§20.20.14) of the `Thread` object. This causes the thread represented by the `Thread` object to invoke the `run` method (§20.20.13) of the `Thread` object. The newly activated thread then remains alive until it stops because one of five things occurs:

- The initial invocation of the `run` method by the newly activated thread completes normally through a normal return from the `run` method.
- The initial invocation of the `run` method by the newly activated thread completes abruptly because an exception was thrown.
- The thread invokes the `stop` method (§20.20.15) of the `Thread` object (and the security manager (§20.17.11) approves execution of the `stop` operation).
- Some other thread invokes the `stop` method of the `Thread` object (and the security manager (§20.17.11) approves execution of the `stop` operation).

- Some thread invokes the `exit` method (§20.16.2) of class `Runtime` (and the security manager (§20.17.13) approves execution of the `exit` operation); this stops every thread being run by the Java Virtual Machine that is running the thread that invokes the `exit` method.

As a thread dies, the `notifyAll` method (§20.1.10) is invoked for the `Thread` object that represents it; this fact is important for the proper operation of the `join` methods (§20.20.28, §20.20.29, §20.20.30). A thread is also removed from its thread group as it dies. Once a thread has been stopped, it is no longer alive and it cannot be restarted.

A thread that is alive can be *suspended* and *resumed*. A suspended thread is considered to be alive, but it performs no work, makes no progress, executes no virtual machine instructions. Resumption restores a thread to the state of active execution. A thread is suspended when it or another thread calls the `suspend` method (§20.20.17) of the `Thread` object that represents it (and the security manager (§20.17.11) approves execution of the `suspend` operation). A thread is resumed when another thread calls the `resume` method (§20.20.18) of the `Thread` object that represents it (and the security manager (§20.17.11) approves execution of the `resume` operation).

Every thread has a *priority*. When there is competition for processing resources, threads with higher priority are generally executed in preference to threads with lower priority. Such preference is not, however, a guarantee that the highest priority thread will always be running, and thread priorities cannot be used to implement mutual exclusion. When code running in some thread creates a new `Thread` object, the newly created thread has its priority initially set equal to the priority of the creating thread. But the priority of a thread *T* may be changed at any time if some thread invokes the `setPriority` method of the `Thread` object that represents *T* (and the security manager (§20.17.11) approves execution of the `setPriority` operation).

Each thread may or may not be marked as a *daemon*. When code running in some thread creates a new `Thread` object, the newly created thread is a daemon thread if and only if the creating thread is a daemon. But the daemonhood of a thread *T* may be changed before it is activated if some other thread invokes the `setDaemon` method of the `Thread` object that represents *T* (and the security manager (§20.17.11) approves execution of the `setDaemon` operation).

When a Java Virtual Machine starts up, there is usually a single non-daemon thread, which typically begins by invoking the method `main` of some designated class. The Java Virtual Machine continues to execute threads according to the thread execution model until all threads that are not daemon threads have stopped.

There are two ways to create a new thread of execution. One is to declare some class to be a subclass of `Thread`; this subclass should override the `run` method of class `Thread`. An instance of the subclass can then be created and started. For example, consider code for a thread whose job is to compute primes larger than a stated value:

```
class PrimeThread extends Thread {
    long minPrime;
    PrimeThread(long minPrime) {
        this.minPrime = minPrime;
    }
    public void run() {
        // compute primes larger than minPrime
        ...
    }
}
```

The following code would then create a thread and start it running:

```
PrimeThread p = new PrimeThread(143);
p.start();
```

The other way to create a thread is to is to declare some class to implement the `Runnable` interface, which also requires that the class implement the `run` method. An instance of the class can then be created, used to create a `Thread`, and started. The same example in this other style looks like this:

```
class PrimeRun implements Runnable {
    long minPrime;
    PrimeRun(long minPrime) {
        this.minPrime = minPrime;
    }
    public void run() {
        // compute primes larger than minPrime
        ...
    }
}
```

The following code would then create a thread and start it running:

```
PrimeRun p = new PrimeRun(143);
new Thread(p).start();
```

Every thread has a name, which is a `String`, for identification purposes. More than one thread may have the same name. If a name is not specified when a thread is created, a new name is generated for it.

Every thread that has not yet been stopped belongs to a thread group (§20.21). A thread can always create a new thread in its own thread group. To create a thread in some other thread group requires the approval of the `checkAccess` method (§20.21.4) of that thread group, which forwards the decision to the security manager (§20.17.11).

20.20.1 `public final static int` **`MIN_PRIORITY`** `= 1;`

The constant value of this field is `1`, the smallest allowed priority for a thread.

20.20.2 `public final static int` **`MAX_PRIORITY`** `= 10;`

The constant value of this field is `10`, the largest allowed priority value for a thread.

20.20.3 `public final static int` **`NORM_PRIORITY`** `= 5;`

The constant value of this field is `5`, the normal priority for a thread that is not a daemon.

20.20.4 `public` **`Thread()`**

This constructor initializes a newly created `Thread` object so that it has no separate run object, has a newly generated name, and belongs to the same thread group as the thread that is creating the new thread.

This constructor has exactly the same effect as the explicit constructor call `this(null, null, `*`gname`*`)` (§20.20.10), where *`gname`* is a newly generated name. Automatically generated names are of the form `"Thread-"+`*`n`*, where *`n`* is an integer.

20.20.5 `public` **`Thread`**`(String name)`

This constructor initializes a newly created `Thread` object so that it has no separate run object, has the specified `name` as its name, and belongs to the same thread group as the thread that is creating the new thread.

This constructor has exactly the same effect as the explicit constructor call `this(null, null, name)` (§20.20.10).

20.20.6 `public` **`Thread`**`(Runnable runObject)`

This constructor initializes a newly created `Thread` object so that it has the given `runObject` as its separate run object, has a newly generated name, and belongs to the same thread group as the thread that is creating the new thread.

This constructor has exactly the same effect as the explicit constructor call `this(null, runObject,` *`gname`*`)` (§20.20.10) where *`gname`* is a newly generated name. Automatically generated names are of the form `"Thread-"+`*`n`* where *`n`* is an integer.

20.20.7 `public` **`Thread`**`(Runnable runObject, String name)`

This constructor initializes a newly created `Thread` object so that it has the given `runObject` as its separate run object, has the specified `name` as its name, and belongs to the same thread group as the thread that is creating the new thread.

This constructor has exactly the same effect as the explicit constructor call `this(null, runObject, name)` (§20.20.10).

20.20.8 `public` **`Thread`**`(ThreadGroup group, String name)`
`throws SecurityException, IllegalThreadStateException`

First, if group is not `null`, the `checkAccess` method (§20.21.4) of that thread group is called with no arguments.

This constructor initializes a newly created `Thread` object so that it has no separate run object, has the specified `name` as its name, and belongs to the thread group referred to by `group` (but if `group` is `null`, then the new thread will belong to the same thread group as the thread that is creating the new thread).

If `group` is a `ThreadGroup` that has been destroyed by method `destroy` (§20.21.11), then an `IllegalThreadStateException` is thrown.

This constructor has exactly the same effect as the explicit constructor call `Thread(group, null, name)` (§20.20.10).

20.20.9 `public Thread(ThreadGroup group, Runnable runObject) throws SecurityException, IllegalThreadStateException`

First, if group is not `null`, the `checkAccess` method (§20.21.4) of that thread group is called with no arguments.

This constructor initializes a newly created `Thread` object so that it has the given `runObject` as its separate run object, has a newly generated name, and belongs to the thread group referred to by `group` (but if `group` is `null`, then the new thread will belong to the same thread group as the thread that is creating the new thread).

If `group` is a `ThreadGroup` that has been destroyed by method `destroy` (§20.21.11), then an `IllegalThreadStateException` is thrown.

This constructor has exactly the same effect as the explicit constructor call `this(group, runObject, gname)` (§20.20.10) where *gname* is a newly generated name. Automatically generated names are of the form `"Thread-"+n` where *n* is an integer.

20.20.10 `public Thread(ThreadGroup group, Runnable runObject, String name) throws SecurityException, IllegalThreadStateException`

First, if group is not `null`, the `checkAccess` method (§20.21.4) of that thread group is called with no arguments; this may result in a `SecurityException` being thrown.

This constructor initializes a newly created `Thread` object so that it has the given `runObject` as its separate run object, has the specified `name` as its name, and belongs to the thread group referred to by `group` (but if `group` is `null`, then the new thread will belong to the same thread group as the thread that is creating the new thread).

If `group` is a `ThreadGroup` that has been destroyed by method `destroy` (§20.21.11), then an `IllegalThreadStateException` is thrown.

The priority of the newly created thread is set equal to the priority of the creating thread—that is, the currently running thread. The method `setPriority` (§20.20.23) may be used to change the priority to a new value.

The newly created thread is initially marked as being a daemon thread if and only if the thread creating it is a daemon thread. The method `setDaemon` (§20.20.25) may be used to change whether or not a thread is a daemon.

20.20.11 `public String toString()`

The returned value is a concatenation of the following seven strings:

- `"Thread["`
- The current name of the thread (§20.20.19)
- `","`
- The current priority of the thread (§20.20.22), as a decimal numeral
- `","`
- The name (§20.21.5) of the thread group (§20.20.21) that contains this thread
- `"]"`

All literal characters mentioned above are from the ACSII subset of Unicode.
Overrides the `toString` method of `Object` (§20.1.3).

20.20.12 `public void checkAccess() throws SecurityException`

If there is a security manager, its `checkAccess` method (§20.17.11) is called with this `Thread` object as its argument. This may result in a `SecurityException` being thrown in the current thread,.

This method is called by methods `stop` of no arguments (§20.20.15), `stop` of one argument (§20.20.16), `suspend` (§20.20.17), `resume` (§20.20.18), `setName` (§20.20.20), `setPriority` (§20.20.23), and `setDaemon` (§20.20.25).

20.20.13 `public void run()`

The general contract of this method is that it should perform the intended action of the thread.

The `run` method of class `Thread` simply calls the `run` method of the separate run object, if there is one; otherwise, it does nothing.

20.20.14 `public void start() throws IllegalThreadStateException`

Invoking this method causes this thread to begin execution; this thread calls the `run` method of this `Thread` object. The result is that two threads are running concurrently: the current thread (which returns from the call to the `start` method) and the thread represented by this `Thread` object (which executes its `run` method).

20.20.15 `public final void stop() throws SecurityException`

Creole babies with flashing eyes
Softly whisper with tender sighs,
"Stop! Oh, won't you give your lady fair a little smile?"
Stop! You bet your life you'll linger there a little while!
—Henry Creamer and Turner Layton, *Way Down Yonder in New Orleans* (1922)

First, the `checkAccess` method (§20.20.12) of this `Thread` object is called with no arguments. This may result in throwing a `SecurityException` (in the current thread).

This thread is forced to complete abnormally whatever it was doing and to throw a `ThreadDeath` object as an exception. For this purpose, this thread is resumed if it had been suspended, and is awakened if it had been asleep.

It is permitted to stop a thread that has not yet been started. If the thread is eventually started, it will immediately terminate.

User code should not normally try to catch `ThreadDeath` unless some extraordinary cleanup operation is necessary (note that the process of throwing a `ThreadDeath` exception *will* cause `finally` clauses of `try` statements to be executed before the thread officially dies). If a `catch` clause does catch a `ThreadDeath` object, it is important to rethrow the object so that the thread will actually die. The top-level error handler that reacts to otherwise uncaught exceptions will not print a message or otherwise signal or notify the user if the uncaught exception is an instance of `ThreadDeath`.

20.20.16 `public final void stop(Throwable thr) throws SecurityException, NullPointerException`

First, the `checkAccess` method (§20.20.12) of this `Thread` object is called with no arguments. This may result in throwing a `SecurityException` (in the current thread).

If the argument `thr` is null, then a `NullPointerException` is thrown (in the current thread).

This thread is forced to complete abnormally whatever it was doing and to throw the `Throwable` object `thr` as an exception. For this purpose, this thread is resumed if it had been suspended, and is awakened if it had been asleep. This is an unusual action to take; normally, the `stop` method that takes no arguments (§20.20.15) should be used.

It is permitted to stop a thread that has not yet been started. If the thread is eventually started, it will immediately terminate.

20.20.17 `public final void suspend() throws SecurityException`

First, the `checkAccess` method (§20.20.12) of this `Thread` object is called with no arguments. This may result in throwing a `SecurityException` (in the current thread).

If this thread is alive (§20.20.26), it is suspended and makes no further progress unless and until it is resumed. It is permitted to suspend a thread that is already in a suspended state; it remains suspended. Suspensions are not tallied; even if a thread is suspended more than once, only one call to `resume` is required to resume it.

20.20.18 `public final void resume() throws SecurityException`

First, the `checkAccess` method (§20.20.12) of this `Thread` object is called with no arguments. This may result in throwing a `SecurityException` (in the current thread).

If this thread is alive (§20.20.26) but suspended, it is resumed and is permitted to make progress in its execution. It is permitted to resume a thread that has never been suspended or has already been resumed; it continues to make progress in its execution. Resumptions are not tallied; even if a thread is resumed more than once, only one call to `suspend` is required to suspend it.

20.20.19 `public final String getName()`

The current name of this `Thread` object is returned as a `String`.

20.20.20 `public final void setName(String name) throws SecurityException`

First, the `checkAccess` method (§20.20.12) of this `Thread` object is called with no arguments. This may result in throwing a `SecurityException` (in the current thread).

The name of this `Thread` object is changed to be equal to the argument `name`.

20.20.21 `public final ThreadGroup` **`getThreadGroup`**`()`

If this thread is alive, this method returns a reference to the `ThreadGroup` object that represents the thread group to which this thread belongs. If this thread has died (has been stopped), this method returns `null`.

20.20.22 `public final int` **`getPriority`**`()`

The current priority of this `Thread` object is returned.

20.20.23 `public final void` **`setPriority`**`(int newPriority) throws SecurityException, IllegalArgumentException`

First, the `checkAccess` method (§20.20.12) of this `Thread` object is called with no arguments. This may result in throwing a `SecurityException` (in the current thread).

If the `newPriority` argument is less than `MIN_PRIORITY` (§20.20.1) or greater than `MAX_PRIORITY` (§20.20.2), then an `IllegalArgumentException` is thrown.

Otherwise, the priority of this `Thread` object is set to the smaller of the specified `newPriority` and the maximum permitted priority (§20.21.12) of the thread's thread group (§20.20.21).

20.20.24 `public final boolean` **`isDaemon`**`()`

The result is `true` if and only if this thread is marked as a daemon thread.

20.20.25 `public final void` **`setDaemon`**`(boolean on) throws SecurityException, IllegalThreadStateException`

First, the `checkAccess` method (§20.20.12) of this `Thread` object is called with no arguments. This may result in throwing a `SecurityException` (in the current thread).

If this thread is alive, an `IllegalThreadStateException` is thrown. Otherwise, this thread is marked as being a daemon thread if the argument is `true`, and as not being a daemon thread if the argument is `false`.

20.20.26 `public final boolean` **`isAlive`**`()`

The result is `true` if and only if this thread is alive (it has been started and has not yet died).

20.20.27 `public int` **`countStackFrames`**`()`

This method returns the number of Java Virtual Machine stack frames currently active for this thread.

20.20.28 `public final void` **`join`**`() throws InterruptedException`

This method causes the current thread to wait (using the `wait` method (§20.1.6) of class `Object`) until this thread is no longer alive.

If the current thread is interrupted (§20.20.31) by another thread while it is waiting, then the wait is ended and an `InterruptedException` is thrown.

20.20.29 `public final void` **`join`**`(long millis) throws InterruptedException`

This method causes the current thread to wait (using the `wait` method (§20.1.7) of class `Object`) until either this thread is no longer alive or a certain amount of real time has elapsed, more or less.

The amount of real time, measured in milliseconds, is given by `millis`. If `millis` is zero, however, then real time is not taken into consideration and this method simply waits until this thread is no longer alive.

If the current thread is interrupted (§20.20.31) by another thread while it is waiting, then the wait is ended and an `InterruptedException` is thrown.

20.20.30 `public final void` **`join`**`(long millis, int nanos) throws InterruptedException`

This method causes the current thread to wait (using the `wait` method (§20.1.8) of class `Object`) until either this thread is no longer alive or a certain amount of real time has elapsed, more or less.

The amount of real time, measured in nanoseconds, is given by:

```
1000000*millis+nanos
```

In all other respects, this method does the same thing as the method `join` of one argument (§20.20.29). In particular, `join(0, 0)` means the same thing as `join(0)`.

If the current thread is interrupted (§20.20.31) by another thread while it is waiting, then the wait is ended and an `InterruptedException` is thrown.

20.20.31 `public void` **`interrupt()`**

An interrupt request is posted for this thread. This thread does not necessarily react immediately to the interrupt, however. If this thread is waiting, it is awakened and it then throws an `InterruptedException`.

[This method is scheduled for introduction in Java version 1.1.]

20.20.32 `public boolean` **`isInterrupted()`**

The result is `true` if and only if an interrupt request has been posted for this thread.

[This method is scheduled for introduction in Java version 1.1.]

20.20.33 `public static boolean` **`interrupted()`**

The result is `true` if and only if an interrupt request has been posted for the current thread.

[This method is scheduled for introduction in Java version 1.1.]

20.20.34 `public static Thread` **`currentThread()`**

The `Thread` object that represents the current thread is returned.

20.20.35 `public static int` **`activeCount()`**

This method returns the number of active threads in the thread group to which the current thread belongs. This count includes threads in subgroups of that thread group. This is the same as the value of the expression:

```
Threads.currentThread().getThreadGroup().activeCount()
```

[This method is deprecated for use in new code after Java version 1.1 becomes available. Instead, an expression equivalent to:

```
Threads.currentThread().getThreadGroup().allThreadsCount()
```

should be used. See the method `allThreadsCount` of class `ThreadGroup`.]

20.20.36 `public static int` **`enumerate`**`(Thread tarray[])`

The active threads in the thread group to which the current thread belongs, including threads in subgroups of that thread group, are enumerated and their Thread objects are put into the array `tarray`. The number of threads actually put into the array is returned. Call this value *n*; then the threads have been put into elements `0` through *n*`-1` of `tarray`. If the number of threads exceeds the length of `tarray`, then some of the threads, `tarray.length` of them, are chosen arbitrarily and used to fill the array `tarray`.

[This method is deprecated for use in new code after Java version 1.1 becomes available. Instead, an expression equivalent to:

```
Threads.currentThread().getThreadGroup().allThreads()
```

should be used. See the method `allThreads` of class `ThreadGroup`.]

20.20.37 `public static void` **`dumpStack`**`()`

This is a utility method that makes it easy to print a stack dump for the current thread. It is equivalent in effect to:

```
new Exception("Stack trace").printStackTrace()
```

See the `printStackTrace` method (§20.22.6) of class `Throwable`.

20.20.38 `public static void` **`yield`**`()`

This method causes the current thread to yield, allowing the thread scheduler to choose another runnable thread for execution.

20.20.39 `public static void` **`sleep`**`(long millis)`
`throws InterruptedException`

This method causes the current thread to yield and not to be scheduled for further execution until a certain amount of real time has elapsed, more or less.

The amount of real time, measured in milliseconds, is given by `millis`.

If the current thread is interrupted (§20.20.31) by another thread while it is waiting, then the sleep is ended and an `InterruptedException` is thrown.

20.20.40 `public static void` **`sleep`**`(long millis, int nanos)`
`throws InterruptedException`

This method causes the current thread to yield and not to be scheduled for further execution until a certain amount of real time has elapsed, more or less.

The amount of real time, measured in nanoseconds, is given by:

```
1000000*millis+nanos
```

In all other respects, this method does the same thing as the method `sleep` of one argument (§20.20.39). In particular, `sleep(0, 0)` means the same thing as `sleep(0)`.

If the current thread is interrupted (§20.20.31) by another thread while it is waiting, then the sleep is ended and an `InterruptedException` is thrown.

20.20.41 `public void` **`destroy`**`()`
`throws SecurityException`

First, the `checkAccess` method (§20.20.12) of this `Thread` object is called with no arguments. This may result in throwing a `SecurityException` (in the current thread).

Then destroys this thread, without any cleanup. Any monitors the thread has locked remain locked.

[This method is not implemented in early versions of Java, through 1.1.]

20.21 The Class **java.lang.ThreadGroup**

A thread group is a set of threads and thread groups. Every thread belongs to exactly one thread group, and every thread group but one (called the "system thread group") belongs to some other thread group. Thus thread groups form a tree with the system thread group at the root.

Thread groups provide a way to manage threads and to impose security boundaries; for example, a thread may always create a new thread within its own thread group, but creating a thread in another thread group requires the approval of the security manager (§20.17), as does the creation of a new thread group.

```
public class ThreadGroup {
    public ThreadGroup(String name)
        throws SecurityException;
    public ThreadGroup(ThreadGroup parent, String name)
        throws NullPointerExpression, SecurityException,
            IllegalThreadStateException;
    public String toString();
    public final void checkAccess();
    public final String getName();
    public final ThreadGroup getParent();
    public final boolean parentOf(ThreadGroup g);
    public final void stop()
        throws SecurityException;
    public final void suspend()
        throws SecurityException;
    public final void resume()
        throws SecurityException;
    public final void destroy()
        throws SecurityException, IllegalThreadStateException;
    public final int getMaxPriority();
    public final void setMaxPriority(int newMaxPriority)
        throws SecurityException, IllegalArgumentException;
    public final boolean isDaemon();
    public final void setDaemon(boolean daemon)
        throws SecurityException;
    public int threadsCount();
    public int allThreadsCount();
    public int groupsCount();
    public int allGroupsCount();
    public Thread[] threads();
    public Thread[] allThreads();
    public ThreadGroup[] groups();
    public ThreadGroup[] allGroups();
```

```
    public int activeCount();                          // deprecated
    public int activeGroupCount();                     // deprecated
    public int enumerate(Thread list[]);               // deprecated
    public int enumerate(Thread list[],                // deprecated
            boolean recurse);
    public int enumerate(ThreadGroup list[]);          // deprecated
    public int enumerate(ThreadGroup list[],           // deprecated
            boolean recurse);
    public void list();
    public void uncaughtException(Thread t, Throwable e);
}
```

Every thread group has a *maximum priority*. The priority of a thread cannot be set (§20.20.23) higher than the maximum priority of its thread group.

Each thread group may or may not be marked as a *daemon*. When a new `ThreadGroup` object is created, the newly created thread group is marked as a daemon thread group if and only if the thread group to which it belongs is currently a daemon thread group. But the daemonhood of a thread group *G* may be changed at any time by calling the `setDaemon` method of the `ThreadGroup` object that represents *G* (provided that the security manager (§20.17.12) approves execution of the `setDaemon` operation).

Every thread group has a name, which is a `String`, for identification purposes. More than one thread group may have the same name.

Creation of a thread group requires the approval of the `checkAccess` method (§20.21.4) of its proposed parent thread group, which forwards the decision to the security manager (§20.17.11).

20.21.1 `public ThreadGroup(String name) throws SecurityException`

First, the `checkAccess` method (§20.21.4) of the thread group to which the current thread belongs is called with no arguments.

This constructor initializes a newly created `ThreadGroup` object so that it has the specified `name` as its name and belongs to the same thread group as the thread that is creating the new thread group.

This constructor has exactly the same effect as the explicit constructor call `this(Thread.currentThread().getThreadGroup(), name)` (§20.21.2).

20.21.2 public **ThreadGroup**(ThreadGroup parent, String name) throws NullPointerExpression, SecurityException, IllegalThreadStateException

First, the checkAccess method (§20.21.4) of the parent thread group is called with no arguments.

If parent is null, then a NullPointerExpression is thrown. If parent is a ThreadGroup that has been destroyed by method destroy (§20.21.11), then an IllegalThreadStateException is thrown.

This constructor initializes a newly created ThreadGroup object so that it has the specified name as its name and belongs to the thread group represented by parent.

The maximum priority for the newly created thread group is set equal to the maximum priority of parent. The method setMaxPriority (§20.21.13) may be used to change the maximum priority to a lower value.

The newly created thread group is initially marked as being a daemon thread group if and only parent is a daemon thread group. The method setDaemon (§20.21.15) may be used to change whether or not a thread group is a daemon thread group.

20.21.3 public String **toString**()

The returned value is a concatenation of the following six strings:

- The name of the class of this thread group object
- "[name="
- The name (§20.21.5) of this thread group
- ",maxpri="
- The current maximum priority (§20.21.12) for this thread group, as a decimal numeral
- "]"

All literal characters mentioned above are from the ASCII subset of Unicode.

Overrides the toString method of Object (§20.1.3).

20.21.4 public final void **checkAccess**()

If there is a security manager, its checkAccess method (§20.17.12) is called with this ThreadGroup object as its argument. This may result in throwing, in the current thread, a SecurityException.

This method is called by methods stop (§20.21.8), suspend (§20.21.9), resume (§20.21.10), destroy (§20.21.11), setMaxPriority (§20.21.13), and setDaemon (§20.21.15).

20.21.5 public final String **getName**()

The current name of this ThreadGroup object is returned as a String.

20.21.6 public final ThreadGroup **getParent**()

This method returns the ThreadGroup object that represents the thread group to which this thread group belongs. If this thread group is the system thread group, which is at the root of the thread group hierarchy, then null is returned.

20.21.7 public final boolean **parentOf**(ThreadGroup g)

This method returns true if and only if either this thread group is g or this method is true when applied to the parent of g. In other words, this method says whether this thread group is an ancestor of g or perhaps g itself.

(This method arguably is misnamed; a more accurate, if clumsy and abstruse, name would be parentOfReflexiveTransitiveClosure.)

20.21.8 public final void **stop**() throws SecurityException

First, the checkAccess method (§20.21.4) of this ThreadGroup object is called with no arguments. This may result in a SecurityException being thrown (in the current thread).

Every thread in this thread group or any of its subgroups is stopped. More precisely, the method stop is called for every ThreadGroup and every Thread (§20.20.15) that belongs to this ThreadGroup.

20.21.9 `public final void suspend() throws SecurityException`

Suspended under a twilight canopy,
We'll search the clouds for a star to guide us.
—Jimmy Webb, *Up, Up and Away* (1967)

First, the checkAccess method (§20.21.4) of this ThreadGroup object is called with no arguments. This may result in a SecurityException being thrown (in the current thread).

Every thread in this thread group or any of its subgroups is suspended. More precisely, the method suspend is called for every ThreadGroup and every Thread (§20.20.17) that belongs to this ThreadGroup.

20.21.10 `public final void resume() throws SecurityException`

First, the checkAccess method (§20.21.4) of this ThreadGroup object is called with no arguments. This may result in a SecurityException being thrown (in the current thread).

Every thread in this thread group or any of its subgroups is resumed. More precisely, the method resume is called for every ThreadGroup and every Thread (§20.20.18) that belongs to this ThreadGroup.

20.21.11 `public final void destroy() throws SecurityException, IllegalThreadStateException`

First, the checkAccess method (§20.21.4) of this ThreadGroup object is called with no arguments. This may result in a SecurityException being thrown (in the current thread).

This thread group is destroyed. If it has already been destroyed, or if any threads belong to it directly, then an IllegalThreadStateException is thrown. Otherwise, this method is called recursively for every thread group that belongs to this thread group, and this thread group is removed from its parent thread group.

A thread group that is currently marked as a daemon thread group is destroyed automatically if both of the following conditions are true:

- A thread or thread group has just been removed from it (because the thread has died or the thread group has been destroyed).
- The thread group now contains no more threads or thread groups.

20.21.12 `public final int` **`getMaxPriority`**`()`

The current maximum priority of this `ThreadGroup` object is returned.

20.21.13 `public final void` **`setMaxPriority`**`(int newMaxPriority)`
`throws SecurityException, IllegalArgumentException`

First, the `checkAccess` method (§20.21.4) of this `ThreadGroup` object is called with no arguments. This may result in a `SecurityException` being thrown (in the current thread).

If the `newMaxPriority` argument is less than `MIN_PRIORITY` (§20.20.1) or greater than `MAX_PRIORITY` (§20.20.2), then an `IllegalArgumentException` is thrown.

Otherwise, the priority of this `ThreadGroup` object is set to the smaller of the specified `newMaxPriority` and the maximum permitted priority (§20.21.12) of the parent of this thread group (§20.21.12). (If this thread group is the system thread group, which has no parent, then its maximum priority is simply set to `newMaxPriority`.) Then this method is called recursively, with `newMaxPriority` as its argument, for every thread group that belongs to this thread group.

20.21.14 `public final boolean` **`isDaemon`**`()`

The result is `true` if and only if this thread group is currently marked as a daemon thread group.

20.21.15 `public final void` **`setDaemon`**`(boolean daemon)`
`throws SecurityException`

First, the `checkAccess` method (§20.21.4) of this `ThreadGroup` object is called with no arguments. This may result in a `SecurityException` being thrown (in the current thread).

This thread group is marked as being a daemon thread group if the argument is `true`, and as not being a daemon thread group if the argument is `false`.

20.21.16 `public int` **`threadsCount`**`()`

This method returns the number of threads that directly belong to this thread group.

20.21.17 `public int` **`allThreadsCount()`**

This method returns the number of threads that belong to this thread group or to any of its subgroups.

20.21.18 `public int` **`groupsCount()`**

This method returns the number of thread groups that directly belong to this thread group.

20.21.19 `public int` **`allGroupsCount()`**

This method returns the number of thread groups that belong to this thread group or to any of its subgroups.

20.21.20 `public Thread[]` **`threads()`**

This method returns a newly created array containing the `Thread` objects for all threads that directly belong to this thread group.

20.21.21 `public Thread[]` **`allThreads()`**

This method returns a newly created array containing the `Thread` objects for all threads that belong to this thread group or to any of its subgroups.

20.21.22 `public ThreadGroup[]` **`groups()`**

This method returns a newly created array containing the `ThreadGroup` objects for all thread groups that directly belong to this thread group.

20.21.23 `public ThreadGroup[]` **`allGroups()`**

This method returns a newly created array containing the `ThreadGroup` objects for all thread groups that belong to this thread group or to any of its subgroups.

20.21.24 `public int` **`activeCount`**`()`

[This method is deprecated for use in new code after Java version 1.1 becomes available. Use the equivalent method `allThreadsCount` instead.]

20.21.25 `public int` **`activeGroupCount`**`()`

[This method is deprecated for use in new code after Java version 1.1 becomes available. Use the equivalent method `allGroupsCount` instead.]

20.21.26 `public int` **`enumerate`**`(Thread list[])`

[This method is deprecated for use in new code after Java version 1.1 becomes available. Use the method `allThreads` instead.]

20.21.27 `public int` **`enumerate`**`(Thread list[], boolean recurse)`

[This method is deprecated for use in new code after Java version 1.1 becomes available. Use the method `threads` or `allThreads` instead.]

20.21.28 `public int` **`enumerate`**`(ThreadGroup list[])`

[This method is deprecated for use in new code after Java version 1.1 becomes available. Use the method `allGroups` instead.]

20.21.29 `public int` **`enumerate`**`(ThreadGroup list[], boolean recurse)`

[This method is deprecated for use in new code after Java version 1.1 becomes available. Use the method `groups` or `allGroups` instead.]

20.21.30 `public void` **`list`**`()`

This method prints a detailed description of this thread group to the output stream `System.out` (§20.18.2). It is intended as a convenient utility for debugging.

The output is a series of lines; each line contains some space characters (for indentation) followed by the `toString` representation of one thread (§20.20.11) or one thread group (§20.21.3).

The first line gives the `toString` representation for this thread group, with no indentation spaces. Following lines are then generated by a recursive rule: whenever a line is printed for a thread group `G` with n leading spaces, it is immediately followed by one line for each thread that directly belongs to `G`, with $n + 4$ spaces of indentation; then one line is printed for each thread group that directly belongs to `G`, with $n + 4$ spaces of indentation, using the recursive case.

20.21.31 `public void uncaughtException(Thread t, Throwable e)`

If you fall, I will catch you, I'll be waiting
—Cyndi Lauper and Rob Hyman, *Time after Time* (1983)

The general contract of `uncaughtException` is that it is called whenever a thread that belongs directly to this thread group dies because an exception was thrown in that thread and not caught. The arguments are the `Thread` object for the thread in question and the `Throwable` object that was thrown. The `uncaughtException` method may then take any appropriate action.

The call to `uncaughtException` is performed by the thread that failed to catch the exception, so `t` is the current thread. The call to `uncaughtException` is the last action of the thread before it dies. If the call to `uncaughtException` itself results in an (uncaught) exception, this fact is ignored and the thread merely goes on to die.

The method `uncaughtException` defined by class `ThreadGroup` takes one of two actions. If this thread group has a parent thread group, then this method is invoked for that parent thread group, with the same arguments. If this thread group is the system thread group (which has no parent), then if the exception `e` is not an instance of `ThreadDeath` (§20.22), a stack trace (§20.22.6) for `e` is printed on the error output stream that is the value of the field `System.err` (§20.18.3).

Subclasses of `ThreadGroup` may override the `uncaughtException` method.

20.22 The Class java.lang.Throwable and its Subclasses

The throw statement (§14.16) is permitted to throw only instances of the class Throwable and its subclasses. Instances of two subclasses, Error and Exception, are conventionally used to indicate that exceptional situations have occurred. Typically, these instances are freshly created in the context of the exceptional situation so as to include relevant information (such as stack trace data).

The following list shows the hierarchical relationships of all the exception classes predefined in package java.lang by the Java language:

```
Throwable
    Error
        LinkageError
            ClassCircularityError
            ClassFormatError
            ExceptionInInitializerError
            IncompatibleClassChangeError
                AbstractMethodError
                IllegalAccessError
                InstantiationError
                NoSuchFieldError
                NoSuchMethodError
            NoClassDefFoundError
            UnsatisfiedLinkError
            VerifyError
        VirtualMachineError
            InternalError
            OutOfMemoryError
            StackOverflowError
            UnknownError
        ThreadDeath
    Exception
        ClassNotFoundException
        CloneNotSupportedException
        IllegalAccessException
        InstantiationException
        InterruptedException
        RuntimeException
            ArithmeticException
            ArrayStoreException
            ClassCastException
            IllegalArgumentException
                IllegalThreadStateException
                NumberFormatException
            IllegalMonitorStateException
            IndexOutOfBoundsException
            NegativeArraySizeException
            NullPointerException
            SecurityException
```

By convention, class Throwable and all its subclasses have two constructors, one that takes no arguments and one that takes a String argument that can be used to produce an error message. This is true of all the classes shown above, with one exception: ExceptionInInitializerError. These predefined classes otherwise have no new content; they merely inherit methods from class Throwable.

```
public class Throwable {
   public Throwable();
   public Throwable(String message);
   public String toString();
   public String getMessage();
   public Throwable fillInStackTrace();
   public void printStackTrace();
   public void printStackTrace(java.io.PrintStream s);
}
```

20.22.1 public Throwable()

This constructor initializes a newly created Throwable object with null as its error message string. Also, the method fillInStackTrace (§20.22.5) is called for this object.

20.22.2 public Throwable(String message)

This constructor initializes a newly created Throwable object by saving a reference to the error message string s for later retrieval by the getMessage method (§20.22.3). Also, the method fillInStackTrace (§20.22.5) is called for this object.

20.22.3 public String getMessage()

If this Throwable object was created with an error message string (§20.22.2), then a reference to that string is returned.

If this Throwable object was created with no error message string (§20.22.1), then null is returned.

20.22.4 public String toString()

If this Throwable object was created with an error message string (§20.22.2), then the result is the concatenation of three strings:

- The name of the actual class of this object
- `": "` (a colon and a space)
- The result of the `getMessage` method (§20.22.3) for this object

If this `Throwable` object was created with no error message string (§20.22.1), then the name of the actual class of this object is returned.

20.22.5 `public Throwable` **`fillInStackTrace`**`()`

This method records within this `Throwable` object information about the current state of the stack frames for the current thread.

20.22.6 `public void` **`printStackTrace`**`()`

This method prints a stack trace for this `Throwable` object on the error output stream that is the value of the field `System.err` (§20.18.3). The first line of output contains the result of the `toString` method (§20.22.4) for this object. Remaining lines represent data previously recorded by the method `fillInStackTrace` (§20.22.5). The format of this information depends on the implementation, but the following example may be regarded as typical:

```
java.lang.NullPointerException
   at MyClass.mash(MyClass.java:9)
   at MyClass.crunch(MyClass.java:6)
   at MyClass.main(MyClass.java:3)
```

This example was produced by running the program:

```
class MyClass {

   public static void main(String[] argv) {
      crunch(null);
   }

   static void crunch(int[] a) {
      mash(a);
   }

   static void mash(int[] b) {
      System.out.println(b[0]);
   }
```

20.23 The Class java.lang.ExceptionInInitializerError

An ExceptionInInitializerError is thrown to indicate that an exception occurred during evaluation of a static initializer or the initializer for a static variable (§12.4.2).

```
public class ExceptionInInitializerError
      extends RuntimeException {
   public ExceptionInInitializerError();
   public ExceptionInInitializerError(String s);
   public ExceptionInInitializerError(Throwable thrown);
   public Throwable getException();
}
```

20.23.1 public ExceptionInInitializerError()

This constructor initializes a newly created ExceptionInInitializerError with null as its error message string and with a no saved throwable object.

20.23.2 public ExceptionInInitializerError(String s)

This constructor initializes a newly created ExceptionInInitializerError by saving a reference to the error message string s for later retrieval by the getMessage method (§20.22.3). There is no saved throwable object.

20.23.3 public ExceptionInInitializerError(Throwable thrown)

This constructor initializes a newly created ExceptionInInitializerError by saving a reference to the Throwable object thrown for later retrieval by the getException method (§20.22.3). The error message string is set to null.

20.23.4 public Throwable getException(Throwable thrown)

The saved throwable object of this ExceptionInInitializerError is returned; null is returned if this ExceptionInInitializerError has no saved throwable object.

CHAPTER 21

The Package `java.util`

THE `java.util` package contains various utility classes and interfaces.

Notable among these utilities is the `Enumeration` interface. An object that implements this interface will generate a series of items, delivering them on demand, one by one. Container classes such as `Dictionary` and `Vector` provide one or more methods that return an `Enumeration`.

A `BitSet` contains an indexed collection of bits that may be used to represent a set of nonnegative integers.

The class `Date` provides a convenient way to represent and manipulate time and date information. Dates may be constructed from a year, month, day of month, hour, minute, and second, and those six components, as well as the day of the week, may be extracted from a date. Time zones and daylight saving time are properly accounted for.

The `abstract` class `Dictionary` represents a collection of key–value pairs and allows a value to be fetched given the key. The class `Hashtable` is one concrete implementation of `Dictionary`. The class `Properties` extends `Hashtable` by allowing one table to provide default values for another and by providing standard means for reading entries from files and writing entries to files.

The class `Observable` provides a mechanism for notifying other objects, called "observers," whenever an `Observable` object is changed. An observer object may be any object that implements the `Observer` interface. (This notification mechanism is distinct from that provided by the `wait` and `notify` methods of class `Object` (§20.1) and is not connected with the thread scheduling mechanism.)

The class `Random` provides an extensive set of methods for pseudorandomly generating numeric values of various primitive types and with various distributions. Each instance of class `Random` is an independent pseudorandom generator.

A `StringTokenizer` provides an easy way to divide strings into tokens. The set of characters that delimit tokens is programmable. The tokenizing method is much simpler than the one used by the class `java.io.StreamTokenizer`. For example, a `StringTokenizer` does not distinguish among identifiers, numbers, and quoted strings; moreover, it does not recognize and skip comments.

The classes `Vector` and `Stack` are simple container classes that provide extensions to the capabilities of Java arrays. A `Vector`, unlike a Java array, can change its size, and many convenient methods are provided for adding, removing, and searching for items. A `Stack` is a `Vector` with additional operations such as `push` and `pop`.

The hierarchy of classes defined in package `java.util` is as follows. (Classes whose names are shown here in **`boldface`** are in package `java.util`; the others are in package `java.lang` and are shown here to clarify subclass relationships.)

```
Object                                          §20.1
    interface Enumeration                           §21.1
    BitSet                                          §21.2
    Date                                            §21.3
    Dictionary                                      §21.4
        Hashtable                                       §21.5
            Properties                                      §21.6
    Observable                                      §21.7
    interface Observer                              §21.8
    Random                                          §21.9
    StringTokenizer                                 §21.10
    Vector                                          §21.11
        Stack                                           §21.12
    Throwable                                       §20.22
        Exception
            RuntimeException
                EmptyStackException                             §21.13
                NoSuchElementException                          §21.14
```

21.1 The Interface `java.util.Enumeration`

An object that implements the `Enumeration` interface will generate a series of elements, one at a time. Successive calls to the `nextElement` method will return successive elements of the series.

```
public interface Enumeration {
    public boolean hasMoreElements();
    public Object nextElement() throws NoSuchElementException;
}
```

21.1.1 `public boolean hasMoreElements()`

The result is `true` if and only if this enumeration object has at least one more element to provide.

21.1.2 `public Object nextElement() throws NoSuchElementException`

If this enumeration object has at least one more element to provide, such an element is returned; otherwise, a `NoSuchElementException` is thrown.

As an example, the following code prints every key in the hashtable `ht` and its length. The method `keys` returns an enumeration that will deliver all the keys, and we suppose that the keys are, in this case, known to be strings:

```
Enumeration e = ht.keys();
while (e.hasMoreElements()) {
    String key = (String)e.nextElement();
    System.out.println(key + " " + key.length());
}
```

21.2 The Class java.util.BitSet

'T is an old maxim in the schools,
That flattery's the food of fools;
Yet now and then your men of wit
Will condescend to take a bit.
—Jonathan Swift, *Cadenus and Vanessa*

A BitSet object is a set of bits that grows as needed. The bits of a BitSet are indexed by nonnegative integers. Each bit can be individually examined, set, or cleared. One BitSet may be used to modify the contents of another BitSet through logical AND, logical inclusive OR, and logical exclusive OR operations.

```
public final class BitSet implements Cloneable {
    public BitSet();
    public BitSet(int nbits);
    public String toString();
    public boolean equals(Object obj)
    public int hashCode();
    public Object clone();
    public boolean get(int bitIndex);
    public void set(int bitIndex);
    public void clear(int bitIndex);
    public void and(BitSet set);
    public void or(BitSet set);
    public void xor(BitSet set);
    public int size();
}
```

21.2.1 public BitSet()

This constructor initializes a newly created BitSet so that all bits are clear.

21.2.2 public BitSet(int nbits)

This constructor initializes a newly created BitSet so that all bits are clear. Enough space is reserved to explicitly represent bits with indices in the range 0 through nbits-1.

21.2.3 public String **toString**()

For every index for which this BitSet contains a bit in the set state, the decimal representation of that index is included in the result. Such indices are listed in order from lowest to highest, separated by ", " (a comma and a space) and surrounded by braces, resulting in the usual mathematical notation for a set of integers.

Overrides the toString method of Object (§20.1.2).

Example:

```
BitSet drPepper = new BitSet();
```

Now drPepper.toString() returns "{}".

```
drPepper.set(2);
```

Now drPepper.toString() returns "{2}".

```
drPepper.set(4);
drPepper.set(10);
```

Now drPepper.toString() returns "{2, 4, 10}".

21.2.4 public boolean **equals**(Object obj)

The result is true if and only if the argument is not null and is a BitSet object such that, for every nonnegative int index k:

```
((BitSet)obj).get(k) == this.get(k)
```

Overrides the equals method of Object (§20.1.3).

21.2.5 public int **hashCode**()

The hash code depends only on which bits have been set within this BitSet. The algorithm used to compute it may be described as follows.

Suppose the bits in the BitSet were to be stored in an array of long integers called, say, bits, in such a manner that bit k is set in the BitSet (for nonnegative values of k) if and only if the expression:

```
((k>>6) < bits.length) &&
            ((bits[k>>6] & (1L << (bit & 0x3F))) != 0)
```

is true. Then the following definition of the hashCode method would be a correct implementation of the actual algorithm:

```
public synchronized int hashCode() {
    long h = 1234;
    for (int i = bits.length; --i >= 0; ) {
        h ^= bits[i] * (i + 1);
    }
    return (int)((h >> 32) ^ h);
}
```

Note that the hash code value changes if the set of bits is altered.

Overrides the `hashCode` method of `Object` (§20.1.4).

21.2.6 `public Object clone()`

Cloning this `BitSet` produces a new `BitSet` that is equal to it.

Overrides the `clone` method of `Object` (§20.1.5).

21.2.7 `public boolean get(int bitIndex)`

The result is `true` if the bit with index `bitIndex` is currently set in this `BitSet`; otherwise, the result is `false`.

If `bitIndex` is negative, an `IndexOutOfBoundsException` is thrown.

21.2.8 `public void set(int bitIndex)`

The bit with index `bitIndex` in this `BitSet` is changed to the "set" (`true`) state.

If `bitIndex` is negative, an `IndexOutOfBoundsException` is thrown.

If `bitIndex` is not smaller than the value that would be returned by the `size` method (§21.2.13), then the size of this `BitSet` is increased to be larger than `bitIndex`.

21.2.9 `public void clear(int bitIndex)`

The bit with index `bitIndex` in this `BitSet` is changed to the "clear" (`false`) state.

If `bitIndex` is negative, an `IndexOutOfBoundsException` is thrown.

If `bitIndex` is not smaller than the value that would be returned by the `size` method (§21.2.13), then the size of this `BitSet` is increased to be larger than `bitIndex`.

21.2.10 `public void and(BitSet set)`

This `BitSet` may be modified by clearing some of its bits. For every nonnegative `int` index `k`, bit `k` of this `BitSet` is cleared if bit `k` of `set` is clear.

21.2.11 `public void or(BitSet set)`

This `BitSet` may be modified by setting some of its bits. For every nonnegative `int` index `k`, bit `k` of this `BitSet` is set if bit `k` of `set` is set.

21.2.12 `public void xor(BitSet set)`

This `BitSet` may be modified by inverting some of its bits. For every nonnegative `int` index `k`, bit `k` of this `BitSet` is inverted if bit `k` of `set` is set.

21.2.13 `public int size()`

This method returns the number of bits of space actually in use by this `BitSet` to represent bit values.

At Mooneen he had leaped a place
So perilous that half the astonished meet
Had shut their eyes, and where was it
He rode a race without a bit?

—William Butler Yeats,
In Memory of Major Robert Gregory (1919)

21.3 The Class `java.util.Date`

The class `Date` provides a system-independent abstraction of dates and times, to a millisecond precision. Dates may be constructed from a year, month, date (day of month), hour, minute, and second; those six components and the day of the week, may be extracted; and dates may be compared and converted to a readable string.

```
public class Date {
   public Date();
   public Date(long time);
   public Date(int year, int month, int date);
   public Date(int year, int month, int date,
         int hours, int minutes);
   public Date(int year, int month, int date,
         int hours, int minutes, int seconds);
   public Date(String s) throws IllegalArgumentException;
   public String toString();
   public boolean equals(Object obj);
   public int hashCode();
   public int getYear();
   public void setYear(int year);
   public int getMonth();
   public void setMonth(int month);
   public int getDate();
   public void setDate(int date);
   public int getDay();
   public int getHours();
   public void setHours(int hours);
   public int getMinutes();
   public void setMinutes(int minutes);
   public int getSeconds();
   public void setSeconds(int seconds);
   public long getTime();
   public void setTime(long time);
   public boolean before(Date when);
   public boolean after(Date when);
   public String toLocaleString();
   public String toGMTString();
   public int getTimezoneOffset();
   public static long UTC(int year, int month, int date,
         int hours, int minutes, int seconds);
   public static long parse(String s)
      throws IllegalArgumentException;
}
```

Examples:

- To print today's date:

```
System.out.println("today = " + new Date());
```

- To find out the day of the week for some particular date, for example, January 16, 1963:

```
new Date(63, 0, 16).getDay()
```

While the `Date` class is intended to reflect UTC (Coordinated Universal Time), it may not do so exactly, depending on the host environment of the Java system. Nearly all modern operating systems assume that 1 day = $24 \times 60 \times 60$ = 86400 seconds in all cases. In UTC, however, about once every year or two there is an extra second, called a "leap second." The leap second is always added as the last second of the day, and nearly always on December 31 or June 30. For example, the last minute of the year 1995 was 61 seconds long, thanks to an added leap second.

Most computer clocks are currently not accurate enough to be able to reflect the leap-second distinction. Some computer standards are defined in terms of GMT (Greenwich Mean Time), which is equivalent to UT (Universal Time). GMT is the "civil" name for the standard; UT is the "scientific" name for the same standard. The distinction between UTC and UT is that UTC is based on an atomic clock and UT is based on astronomical observations, which for all practical purposes is an invisibly fine hair to split. Because the earth's rotation is not uniform—it slows down and speeds up in complicated ways—UT does not always flow uniformly. Leap seconds are introduced as needed into UTC so as to keep UTC within 0.9 seconds of UT1, which is a version of UT with certain corrections applied. There are other time and date systems as well; for example, the time scale used by GPS (the satellite-based Global Positioning System) is synchronized to UTC but is *not* adjusted for leap seconds. An interesting source of further information is the U. S. Naval Observatory, particularly the Directorate of Time at:

```
http://tycho.usno.navy.mil
```

and their definitions of "Systems of Time" at:

```
http://tycho.usno.navy.mil/systime.html
```

In all methods of class `Date` that accept or return year, month, day of month, hours, minutes, and seconds values, the following representations are used:

- A year y is represented by the integer $y - 1900$.
- A month is represented by an integer form 0 to 11; 0 is January, 1 is February, and so on; thus 11 is December.

- A date (day of month) is represented by an integer from 1 to 31 in the usual manner.
- An hour is represented by an integer from 0 to 23. Thus the hour from midnight to 1 AM is hour 0, and the hour from noon to 1 PM is hour 12.
- A minute is represented by an integer from 0 to 59 in the usual manner.
- A second is represented by an integer from 0 to 61. The values 60 and 61 will occur only for leap seconds, and even then only in Java implementations that actually track leap seconds correctly. Because of the manner in which leap seconds are currently introduced, it is extremely unlikely that two leap seconds will occur in the same minute, but this specification follows the date and time conventions for ISO C.

In all cases, arguments given to methods for these purposes need not fall within the indicated ranges; for example, a date may be specified as January 32 and will be interpreted as meaning February 1.

21.3.1 `public Date()`

This constructor initializes a newly created `Date` object so that it represents the instant of time that it was created, measured to the nearest millisecond.

21.3.2 `public Date(long time)`

This constructor initializes a newly created `Date` object so that it represents the instant of time that is `time` milliseconds after the standard base time known as "the epoch," namely 00:00:00 GMT on January 1, 1970. See also the method `currentTimeMillis` (§20.18.6) of class `System`.

21.3.3 `public Date(int year, int month, int date)`

This constructor initializes a newly created `Date` object so that it represents midnight at the beginning of the day specified by the `year`, `month`, and `date` arguments, in the local time zone. Thus, it has the same effect as the constructor call (§21.3.5):

```
Date(year, month, date, 0, 0, 0)
```

21.3.4 `public` **`Date`**`(int year, int month, int date,`
`int hours, int minutes)`

This constructor initializes a newly created `Date` object so that it represents the instant at the start of the minute specified by the `year`, `month`, `date`, `hours`, and `minutes` arguments, in the local time zone. Thus, it has the same effect as the constructor call (§21.3.5):

```
Date(year, month, date, hours, minutes, 0)
```

21.3.5 `public` **`Date`**`(int year, int month, int date,`
`int hours, int minutes, int seconds)`

This constructor initializes a newly created `Date` object so that it represents the instant at the start of the second specified by the `year`, `month`, `date`, `hours`, `minutes`, and `seconds` arguments, in the local time zone.

21.3.6 `public` **`Date`**`(String s)`
`throws IllegalArgumentException`

This constructor initializes a newly created `Date` object so that it represents the date and time indicated by the string s, which is interpreted as if by the `parse` method (§21.3.31).

21.3.7 `public String` **`toString`**`()`

This `Date` object is converted to a `String` of the form:

```
"dow mon dd hh:mm:ss zzz yyyy"
```

where:

- `dow` is the day of the week (`Sun`, `Mon`, `Tue`, `Wed`, `Thu`, `Fri`, `Sat`).
- `mon` is the month (`Jan`, `Feb`, `Mar`, `Apr`, `May`, `Jun`, `Jul`, `Aug`, `Sep`, `Oct`, `Nov`, `Dec`).
- `dd` is the day of the month (`01` through `31`), as two decimal digits.
- `hh` is the hour of the day (`00` through `23`), as two decimal digits.
- `mm` is the minute within the hour (`00` through `59`), as two decimal digits.
- `ss` is the second within the minute (`00` through `61`), as two decimal digits.

- zzz is the time zone (and may reflect daylight saving time). Standard time zone abbreviations include those recognized by the method parse (§21.3.31). If time zone information is not available, then zzz is empty—that is, it consists of no characters at all.
- yyyy is the year, as four decimal digits.

See also methods toLocaleString (§21.3.27) and toGMTString (§21.3.28). Overrides the toString method of Object (§20.1.2).

21.3.8 public boolean **equals**(Object obj)

The result is true if and only if the argument is not null and is a Date object that represents the same point in time, to the millisecond, as this Date object. Thus two Date objects are equal if and only if the getTime method (§21.3.23) returns the same long value from both.

Overrides the equals method of Object (§20.1.3).

21.3.9 public int **hashCode**()

The result is the exclusive OR of the two halves of the primitive long value returned by the getTime method (§21.3.23). That is, the hash code is the value of the expression:

```
(int)(this.getTime()^(this.getTime()>>>32))
```

Overrides the hashCode method of Object (§20.1.4).

21.3.10 public int **getYear**()

The returned value is the result of subtracting 1900 from the year that contains or begins with the instant in time represented by this Date object, as interpreted in the local time zone.

21.3.11 public void **setYear**(int year)

This Date object is modified so that it represents a point in time within the specified year, with the month, date, hour, minute, and second the same as before, as interpreted in the local time zone. (Of course, if the date was February 29, for example, and the year is set to a non–leap year, then the new date will be treated as if it were on March 1.)

21.3.12 `public int getMonth()`

The returned value is a number (`0` through `11`) representing the month that contains or begins with the instant in time represented by this `Date` object, as interpreted in the local time zone.

21.3.13 `public void setMonth(int month)`

This `Date` object is modified so that it represents a point in time within the specified month, with the year, date, hour, minute, and second the same as before, as interpreted in the local time zone. If the date was October 31, for example, and the month is set to June, then the new date will be treated as if it were on July 1, because June has only 30 days.

21.3.14 `public int getDate()`

The returned value is a number (`1` through `31`) representing day of the month that contains or begins with the instant in time represented by this `Date` object, as interpreted in the local time zone.

21.3.15 `public void setDate(int date)`

This `Date` object is modified so that it represents a point in time within the specified day of the month, with the year, month, hour, minute, and second the same as before, as interpreted in the local time zone.If the date was April 30, for example, and the date is set to 31, then it will be treated as if it were on May 1, because April has only 30 days.

21.3.16 `public int getDay()`

The returned value (`0` = Sunday, `1` = Monday, `2` = Tuesday, `3` = Wednesday, `4` = Thursday, `5` = Friday, `6` = Saturday) represents the day of the week that contains or begins with the instant in time represented by this `Date` object, as interpreted in the local time zone.

21.3.17 `public int getHours()`

The returned value is a number (`0` through `23`) representing the hour within the day that contains or begins with the instant in time represented by this `Date` object, as interpreted in the local time zone.

21.3.18 `public void setHours(int hours)`

This `Date` object is modified so that it represents a point in time within the specified hour of the day, with the year, month, date, minute, and second the same as before, as interpreted in the local time zone.

21.3.19 `public int getMinutes()`

The returned value is a number (`0` through `59`) representing the minute within the hour that contains or begins with the instant in time represented by this `Date` object, as interpreted in the local time zone.

21.3.20 `public void setMinutes(int minutes)`

This `Date` object is modified so that it represents a point in time within the specified minute of the hour, with the year, month, date, hour, and second the same as before, as interpreted in the local time zone.

21.3.21 `public int getSeconds()`

The returned value is a number (`0` through `61`) representing the second within the minute that contains or begins with the instant in time represented by this `Date` object, as interpreted in the local time zone.

21.3.22 `public void setSeconds(int seconds)`

This `Date` object is modified so that it represents a point in time within the specified second of the minute, with the year, month, date, hour, and minute the same as before, as interpreted in the local time zone.

21.3.23 public long **getTime**()

This method returns the time represented by this Date object, represented as the distance, measured in milliseconds, of that time from the epoch (00:00:00 GMT on January 1, 1970).

21.3.24 public void **setTime**(long time)

This Date object is modified so that it represents a point in time that is time milliseconds after the epoch (00:00:00 GMT on January 1, 1970).

21.3.25 public boolean **before**(Date when)

The result is true if and only if the instant represented by this Date object is strictly earlier than the instant represented by when.

21.3.26 public boolean **after**(Date when)

The result is true if and only if the instant represented by this Date object is strictly later than the instant represented by when.

21.3.27 public String **toLocaleString**()

This Date object is converted to a String of an implementation-dependent form. The general intent is that the form should be familiar to the user of the Java application, wherever it may happen to be running. The intent is comparable to that of the %c format supported by the strftime function of ISO C.

See also methods toString (§21.3.7) and toGMTString (§21.3.28).

21.3.28 public String **toGMTString**()

This Date object is converted to a String of length 23 or 24 of the form:

"*d mon yyyy hh*:*mm*:*ss GMT*"

where:

- *d* is the day of the month (1 through 31), as one or two decimal digits.
- *mon* is the month (Jan, Feb, Mar, Apr, May, Jun, Jul, Aug, Sep, Oct, Nov, Dec).

- *yyyy* is the year, as four decimal digits.
- *hh* is the hour of the day (00 through 23), as two decimal digits.
- *mm* is the minute within the hour (00 through 59), as two decimal digits.
- *ss* is the second within the minute (00 through 61), as two decimal digits.
- *GMT* is exactly the ASCII letters "GMT" to indicate Greenwich Mean Time.

The result does not depend on the local time zone.
See also methods `toString` (§21.3.7) and `toLocaleString` (§21.3.27).

21.3.29 `public int` **`getTimezoneOffset`**`()`

This method returns the offset, measured in minutes, for the local time zone relative to UTC that is appropriate for the time represented by this `Date` object.

For example, in Massachusetts, five time zones west of Greenwich:

`new Date(96, 1, 14).getTimezoneOffset()` returns `300`

because on February 14, 1996, standard time (Eastern Standard Time) is in use, which is offset five hours from UTC; but:

`new Date(96, 5, 1).getTimezoneOffset()` returns `240`

because on May 1, 1996, daylight saving time (Eastern Daylight Time) is in use, which is offset only four hours from UTC.

This method produces the same result as if it computed:

```
(this.getTime() - UTC(this.getYear(),
                      this.getMonth(),
                      this.getDate(),
                      this.getHours(),
                      this.getMinutes(),
                      this.getSeconds())) / (60 * 1000)
```

21.3.30 `public static long` **`UTC`**`(int year, int month, int date, int hours, int minutes, int seconds)`

The arguments are interpreted as a year, month, day of the month, hour of the day, minute within the hour, and second within the minute, exactly as for the `Date` constructor of six arguments (§21.3.5), except that the arguments are interpreted relative to UTC rather than to the local time zone. The time indicated is returned represented as the distance, measured in milliseconds, of that time from the epoch (00:00:00 GMT on January 1, 1970).

21.3.31 `public static long` **`parse`**`(String s)`
`throws IllegalArgumentException`

An attempt is made to interpret the string `s` as a representation of a date and time. If the attempt is successful, the time indicated is returned represented as the distance, measured in milliseconds, of that time from the epoch (00:00:00 GMT on January 1, 1970). If the attempt fails, an `IllegalArgumentException` is thrown.

The string `s` is processed from left to right, looking for data of interest.

Any material in `s` that is within the ASCII parenthesis characters `(` and `)` is ignored. Parentheses may be nested. Otherwise, the only characters permitted within `s` are these ASCII characters:

```
abcdefghijklmnopqrstuvwxyz
ABCDEFGHIJKLMNOPQRSTUVWXYZ
0123456789,+-:/
```

and whitespace characters (§20.5.19).

A consecutive sequence of decimal digits is treated as a decimal number:

- If a number is preceded by `+` or `-` and a year has already been recognized, then the number is a time-zone offset. If the number is less than 24, it is an offset measured in hours. Otherwise, it is regarded as an offset in minutes, expressed in 24-hour time format without punctuation. A preceding `+` means an eastward offset and a preceding `-` means a westward offset. Time zone offsets are always relative to UTC (Greenwich). Thus, for example, `-5` occurring in the string would mean "five hours west of Greenwich" and `+0430` would mean "four hours and thirty minutes east of Greenwich." It is permitted for the string to specify `GMT`, `UT`, or `UTC` redundantly—for example, `GMT-5` or `utc+0430`.

- If a number is greater than 70, it is regarded as a year number. It must be followed by a space, comma, slash, or end of string. If it is greater than 1900, then 1900 is subtracted from it.

- If the number is followed by a colon, it is regarded as an hour, unless an hour has already been recognized, in which case it is regarded as a minute.

- If the number is followed by a slash, it is regarded as a month (it is decreased by `1` to produce a number in the range `0` to `11`), unless a month has already been recognized, in which case it is regarded as a day of the month.

- If the number is followed by whitespace, a comma, a hyphen, or end of string, then if an hour has been recognized but not a minute, it is regarded as a minute; otherwise, if a minute has been recognized but not a second, it is regarded as a second; otherwise, it is regarded as a day of the month.

A consecutive sequence of letters is regarded as a word and treated as follows:

- A word that matches AM, ignoring case, is ignored (but the parse fails if an hour has not been recognized or is less than 1 or greater than 12).
- A word that matches PM, ignoring case, adds 12 to the hour (but the parse fails if an hour has not been recognized or is less than 1 or greater than 12).
- Any word that matches any prefix of SUNDAY, MONDAY, TUESDAY, WEDNESDAY, THURSDAY, FRIDAY, or SATURDAY, ignoring case, is ignored. For example, sat, Friday, TUE, and Thurs are ignored.
- Otherwise, any word that matches any prefix of JANUARY, FEBRUARY, MARCH, APRIL, MAY, JUNE, JULY, AUGUST, SEPTEMBER, OCTOBER, NOVEMBER, or DECEMBER, ignoring case, and considering them in the order given here, is recognized as specifying a month and is converted to a number (0 to 11). For example, aug, Sept, april, and NOV are recognized as months. So is Ma, which is recognized as MARCH, not MAY.
- Any word that matches GMT, UT, or UTC, ignoring case, is treated as referring to UTC.
- Any word that matches EST, CST, MST, or PST, ignoring case, is recognized as referring to the time zone in North America that is five, six, seven, or eight hours west of Greenwich, respectively. Any word that matches EDT, CDT, MDT, or PDT, ignoring case, is recognized as referring to the same time zone, respectively, during daylight saving time. (In the future, this method may be upgraded to recognize other time zone designations.)

Once the entire string s has been scanned, it is converted to a time result in one of two ways. If a time zone or time-zone offset has been recognized, then the year, month, day of month, hour, minute, and second are interpreted in UTC (§21.3.30) and then the time-zone offset is applied. Otherwise, the year, month, day of month, hour, minute, and second are interpreted in the local time zone.

21.4 The Class java.util.Dictionary

A Dictionary is an object that associates *elements* with *keys*. Every key and every element is an object. In any one Dictionary, every key is associated at most one element. Given a Dictionary and a key, the associated element can be looked up.

```
public abstract class Dictionary {
    abstract public int size();
    abstract public boolean isEmpty();
    abstract public Object get(Object key)
        throws NullPointerException;
    abstract public Object put(Object key, Object element)
        throws NullPointerException;
    abstract public Object remove(Object key)
        throws NullPointerException;
    abstract public Enumeration keys();
    abstract public Enumeration elements();
}
```

As a rule, the equals method (§20.1.3) should be used by implementations of the class Dictionary to decide whether two keys are the same.

21.4.1 abstract public int size()

The general contract for the size method is that it returns the number of entries (distinct keys) in this dictionary.

21.4.2 abstract public boolean isEmpty()

The general contract for the isEmpty method is that the result is true if and only if this dictionary contains no entries.

21.4.3 abstract public Object get(Object key) throws NullPointerException

The general contract for the isEmpty method is that if this dictionary contains an entry for the specified key, the associated element is returned; otherwise, null is returned.

If the key is null, a NullPointerException is thrown.

21.4.4 `abstract public Object` **`put`**`(Object key, Object element)`
`throws NullPointerException`

The general contract for the `put` method is that it adds an entry to this dictionary.

If this dictionary already contains an entry for the specified `key`, the element already in this dictionary for that `key` is returned, after modifying the entry to contain the new `element`.

If this dictionary does not already have an entry for the specified `key`, an entry is created for the specified `key` and `element`, and `null` is returned.

If the `key` or the `element` is `null`, a `NullPointerException` is thrown.

21.4.5 `abstract public Object` **`remove`**`(Object key)`
`throws NullPointerException`

The general contract for the `remove` method is that it removes an entry from this dictionary.

If this dictionary contains an entry for the specified `key`, the element in this dictionary for that `key` is returned, after removing the entry from this dictionary.

If this dictionary does not already have an entry for the specified `key`, `null` is returned.

If the `key` is `null`, a `NullPointerException` is thrown.

21.4.6 `abstract public Enumeration` **`keys`**`()`

The general contract for the `keys` method is that an `Enumeration` (§21.1) is returned that will generate all the keys for which this dictionary contains entries.

21.4.7 `abstract public Enumeration` **`elements`**`()`

The general contract for the `elements` method is that an `Enumeration` (§21.1) is returned that will generate all the elements contained in entries in this dictionary.

21.5 The Class `java.util.Hashtable`

. . . never did they seem to have new experiences in common . . . and the things they had for dissection—college, contemporary personality, and the like—they had hashed and rehashed for many a frugal conversational meal.

—F. Scott Fitzgerald, *This Side of Paradise* (1920)

The class `Hashtable` implements the abstract class `Dictionary` (§21.4), with some additional functionality.

```
public class Hashtable extends Dictionary implements Cloneable {
    public Hashtable(int initialCapacity, float loadFactor);
    public Hashtable(int initialCapacity);
    public Hashtable();
    public String toString();
    public Object clone();
    public int size();
    public boolean isEmpty();
    public Object get(Object key)
        throws NullPointerException;
    public Object put(Object key, Object value)
        throws NullPointerException;
    public Object remove(Object key)
        throws NullPointerException;
    public Enumeration keys();
    public Enumeration elements();
    public boolean contains(Object value);
    public boolean containsKey(Object key);
    protected void rehash();
    public void clear();
}
```

A `Hashtable` has two parameters that affect its efficiency: its *capacity* and its *load factor.* The load factor should be between `0.0` and `1.0`. When the number of entries in the hashtable exceeds the product of the load factor and the current capacity, the capacity is increased, using the `rehash` method. Larger load factors use memory more efficiently at the expense of larger expected time per lookup. If many entries are to be made in a `Hashtable`, creating it with a sufficiently large capacity may allow the entries to be inserted more efficiently than letting it perform automatic rehashing as needed to grow the table.

21.5.1 public **Hashtable**(int initialCapacity, float loadFactor)

This constructor initializes a newly created Hashtable object so that its capacity is initialCapacity and its load factor is loadFactor. Initially, there are no entries in the table.

21.5.2 public **Hashtable**(int initialCapacity)

This constructor initializes a newly created Hashtable object so that its capacity is initialCapacity and its load factor is 0.75. Initially, there are no entries in the table.

21.5.3 public **Hashtable**()

This constructor initializes a newly created Hashtable object so that its load factor is 0.75. Initially, there are no entries in the table.

21.5.4 public String **toString**()

This Hashtable is represented in string form as a set of entries, enclosed in braces and separated by the ASCII characters ", " (comma and space). Each entry is rendered as the key, an equals sign =, and the associated element, where the toString method is used to convert the key and element to strings.

Overrides the toString method of Object (§21.2.3).

21.5.5 public Object **clone**()

A copy of this Hashtable is constructed and returned. All the structure of the hashtable itself is copied, but the keys and elements are not cloned.

Overrides the clone method of Object (§21.2.6).

21.5.6 public int **size**()

Implements the size method of Dictionary (§21.4.1).

21.5.7 public boolean **isEmpty**()

Implements the isEmpty method of Dictionary (§21.4.2).

21.5.8 `public Object` **`get`**`(Object key)`

Implements the `get` method of `Dictionary` (§21.4.3).

21.5.9 `public Object` **`put`**`(Object key, Object value)`

Implements the `put` method of `Dictionary` (§21.4.4).

21.5.10 `public Object` **`remove`**`(Object key)`

Implements the `remove` method of `Dictionary` (§21.4.5).

21.5.11 `public Enumeration` **`keys`**`()`

Implements the `keys` method of `Dictionary` (§21.4.6).

21.5.12 `public Enumeration` **`elements`**`()`

Implements the `elements` method of `Dictionary` (§21.4.7).

21.5.13 `public boolean` **`contains`**`(Object value)`

The result is `true` if and only if this `Hashtable` contains at least one entry for which the element is equal to `value`, as determined by the `equals` method (§20.1.3).

21.5.14 `public boolean` **`containsKey`**`(Object key)`

The result is `true` if and only if this `Hashtable` contains an entry for which the key is equal to `key`, as determined by the `equals` method (§20.1.3). In other words, this method produces the same result as the expression:

```
get(key) != null
```

21.5.15 `protected void` **`rehash`**`()`

This `Hashtable` is increased in capacity and reorganized internally, in order to accommodate and access its entries more efficiently.

21.5.16 `public void clear()`

The `clear` method removes all entries from this `Hashtable`.

Twelve sphered tables, by silk seats insphered,
High as the level of a man's breast rear'd
On libbard's paws, upheld the heavy gold
Of cups and goblets, and the store thrice told
Of Ceres' horn, and, in huge vessels, wine
Came from the gloomy tun with merry shine.
Thus loaded with a feast the tables stood . . .

—John Keats, *Lamia*, Part II

21.6 The Class java.util.Properties

A Properties table is a kind of Hashtable with two functionality extensions and with the restriction that keys and elements must be strings. First, there are methods for reading entries into the table from an input stream and writing all the entries in the table to an output stream. Second, a Properties table may refer to another Properties table that provides default values. The getProperty method is much like the get method (§21.4.3), but if an entry is not found in this table, then the defaults table is searched (and that defaults table may itself refer to another defaults table, and so on, recursively).

```
public class Properties extends Hashtable {
    protected Properties defaults;
    public Properties();
    public Properties(Properties defaults);
    public String getProperty(String key);
    public String getProperty(String key, String defaultValue);
    public Enumeration propertyNames();
    public void load(InputStream in) throws IOException;
    public void save(OutputStream out, String header);
    public void list(PrintStream out);
}
```

21.6.1 protected Properties defaults;

If the defaults field is not null, it is another Properties table that provides default values for this Properties table.

21.6.2 public Properties()

This constructor initializes a newly created Properties table so that it has no defaults table. Initially, there are no entries in the newly created table.

21.6.3 public Properties(Properties defaults)

This constructor initializes a newly created Properties table so its defaults table is defaults. The argument defaults may be null, in which case the newly created Properties table will not have a defaults table. Initially, there are no entries in the newly created table.

21.6.4 `public String` **`getProperty`**`(String key)`

If there is an entry in this `Properties` table with `key` as its key, the associated element is returned. Otherwise, if this `Properties` table has a defaults table, then whatever its `getProperty` method returns is returned. Otherwise, `null` is returned.

21.6.5 `public String` **`getProperty`**`(String key, String defaultValue)`

If there is an entry in this `Properties` table with `key` as its key, the associated element is returned. Otherwise, if this `Properties` table has a defaults table, then whatever its `getProperty` method returns is returned. Otherwise, `defaultValue` is returned.

21.6.6 `public Enumeration` **`propertyNames`**`()`

An `Enumeration` (§21.1) is returned that will generate all the keys for which this `Properties` table could supply an associated element. If this `Properties` table has a defaults table (§21.6.1), then keys for which the defaults table has entries are also supplied by the `Enumeration`, and so on, recursively; but no key is supplied by the `Enumeration` more than once.

21.6.7 `public void` **`load`**`(InputStream in) throws IOException`

Properties (key and element pairs) are read from the input stream:

```
Runtime.getRuntime().getLocalizedInputStream(in)
```

and added to this `Properties` table. See the `getLocalizedInputStream` method of `Runtime` (§20.16.14).

Every property occupies one line of the input stream. Each line is terminated by a line terminator (`\n` or `\r` or `\r\n`). Lines from the input stream are processed until end of file is reached on the input stream.

A line that contains only whitespace (§20.5.19) or whose first non-whitespace character is an ASCII `#` or `!` is ignored (thus, `#` or `!` indicate comment lines).

Every line other than a blank line or a comment line describes one property to be added to the table (except that if a line ends with \, then the following line is treated as a continuation line, as described below). The key consists of all the characters in the line starting with the first non-whitespace character and up to, but not including, the first ASCII `=`, `:`, or whitespace character. Any whitespace after the key is skipped; if the first non-whitespace character after the key is = or `:`, then it is ignored and any whitespace characters after it are also skipped. All remaining characters on the line become part of the associated element string. Within the element string (but not the key), the ASCII escape sequences `\t`, `\n`, `\r`, `\\`, `\"`, `\'`, `\ ` (a backslash and a space), and `\u`*xxxx* are recognized and converted to single characters. Moreover, if the last character on the line is `\`, then the next line is treated as a continuation of the current line; the `\` and line terminator are simply discarded, and any leading whitespace characters on the continuation line are also discarded and are not part of the element string.

As an example, each of the following four lines specifies the key `"Truth"` and the associated element value `"Beauty"`:

```
Truth Beauty
Truth = Beauty
    Truth:Beauty
Truth       :Beauty
```

As another example, the following three lines specify a single property:

```
fruits          apple, banana, pear, \
                cantaloupe, watermelon, \
                kiwi, mango
```

The key is `"fruit"` and the associated element is:

```
"apple, banana, pear, cantaloupe, watermelon, kiwi, mango"
```

Note that a space appears before each `\` so that a space will appear after each comma in the final result; the `\`, line terminator, and leading whitespace on the continuation line are merely discarded and are *not* replaced by one or more other characters.

As a third example, the line:

```
cheeses
```

specifies that the key is `"cheeses"` and the associated element is the empty string.

21.6.8 `public void` **`save`**`(OutputStream out, String header)`

All the properties (key and element pairs) in this `Properties` table are written to the output stream:

```
Runtime.getRuntime().getLocalizedOutputStream(out)
```

in a format suitable for loading into a `Properties` table using the `load` method (§21.6.7). See the `getLocalizedOutputStream` method of `Runtime` (§20.16.16).

Properties from the defaults table of this `Properties` table (if any) are *not* written out by this method.

If the header argument is not null, then an ASCII # character, the header string, and a newline are first written to the output stream. Thus, the `header` can serve as an identifying comment.

Next, a comment line is always written, consisting of an ASCII # character, the current date and time (as if produced by the `toString` method of `Date` (§21.3.7) for the current time), and a newline.

Then every entry in this `Properties` table is written out, one per line. For each entry the key string is written, then an ASCII =, then the associated element string. Each character of the element string is examined to see whether it should be rendered as an escape sequence. The ASCII characters \, tab, newline, and carriage return are written as `\\`, `\t`, `\n`, and `\r`, respectively. Characters less than `\u0020` and characters greater than `\u007E` (if necessary, depending on the needs of the localized output stream) are written as `\u`*`xxxx`* for the appropriate hexadecimal value *`xxxx`*. Leading space characters, but not embedded or trailing space characters, are written with a preceding \.

21.6.9 `public void list(PrintStream out)`

Properties (key and element pairs) in this `Properties` table are written to the output stream `out` in a possibly abbreviated form that may be more convenient for use in debugging than the output of the `save` method. No header is written, and element values longer than 40 character are truncated to the first 37 characters, to which the characters "`...`" are appended. Thus, if the names of the keys are not too long, there is a fighting chance that each property will fit into the space of one line of a physical output device.

21.7 The Class java.util.Observable

Each instance of class Observable maintains a set of "observers" that are notified whenever the Observable object changes in some significant way. An observer may be any object that implements interface Observer (§21.8).

Note that this notification mechanism is has nothing to do with threads (§20.20) and is completely separate from the wait and notify mechanism of class Object (§20.1).

```
public class Observable {
    public void addObserver(Observer o);
    public void deleteObserver(Observer o);
    public void deleteObservers();
    public int countObservers();
    public void notifyObservers();
    public void notifyObservers(Object arg);
    protected void setChanged();
    protected void clearChanged();
    public boolean hasChanged();
}
```

When an observable object is newly created, its set of observers is empty.

Two observers are considered the same if and only if the equals method (§20.1.3) returns true for them.

21.7.1 public void addObserver(Observer o)

The observer o is added to this Observable object's set of observers, provided that it is not the same as some observer already in the set.

21.7.2 public void deleteObserver(Observer o)

The observer o is removed from this Observable object's set of observers.

21.7.3 public void deleteObservers()

All observers are removed from this Observable object's set of observers.

21.7.4 public int countObservers()

The number of observers in this Observable object's set of observers is returned.

21.7.5 public void **notifyObservers**()

If this Observable object has been marked as changed, this method causes all observers to be notified with null as the second argument; in other words, this method is equivalent to:

```
notifyObservers(null)
```

21.7.6 public void **notifyObservers**(Object arg)

If this Observable object has been marked as changed (§21.7.9), this method causes all observers to be notified with arg as the second argument. An observer is notified by calling its update method (§21.8.1) on two arguments: this Observable object and arg. The mark on this object is then cleared (§21.7.8).

21.7.7 protected void **setChanged**()

This Observable object is marked as having been changed; the hasChanged method will now return true.

21.7.8 protected void **clearChanged**()

This Observable object is marked as not having been changed; the hasChanged method will now return false.

21.7.9 public boolean **hasChanged**()

The result is true if and only if the setChanged method has been called for this Observable object more recently than either the clearChanged method or the notifyObservers method.

21.8 The Interface java.util.Observer

A class should implement the Observer interface if it is to be notified whenever an Observable object has been changed. See the Observable class (§21.7) for a discussion of how Observer objects are notified.

```
public interface Observer {
   public void update(Observable o, Object arg);
}
```

21.8.1 public void update(Observable o, Object arg)

When an Observable object has been changed and its notifyObservers method (§21.7.6) is called, every Observer object in its set of observers is notified by invoking its update method, passing it two arguments: the Observable object and another argument specified by the call to the notifyObservers method.

21.9 The Class `java.util.Random`

Oh, many a shaft at random sent
Finds mark the archer little meant!
And many a word at random spoken
May soothe, or wound, a heart that's broken!
—Sir Walter Scott, *The Lady of the Lake*, Canto V, stanza 18

Each instance of class `Random` serves as a separate, independent pseudorandom generator of primitive values.

```
public class Random {
    protected long seed;
    protected double nextNextGaussian;
    protected boolean haveNextNextGaussian = false;
    public Random();
    public Random(long seed);
    public void setSeed(long seed);
    protected int next(int bits);
    public int nextInt();
    public long nextLong();
    public float nextFloat();
    public double nextDouble();
    public double nextGaussian();
}
```

If two `Random` objects are created with the same seed and the same sequence of method calls is made for each, they will generate and return identical sequences of numbers in all Java implementations. In order to guarantee this property, particular algorithms are specified for the class `Random`. Java implementations must use all the algorithms shown here for the class `Random`, for the sake of absolute portability of Java code. However, subclasses of class `Random` are permitted use other algorithms, so long as they adhere to the general contracts for all the methods.

The algorithms implemented by class `Random` use three state variables, which are `protected`. They also use a `protected` utility method that on each invocation can supply up to up to 32 pseudorandomly generated bits.

21.9.1 `protected long seed;`

A variable used by method `next` (§21.9.7) to hold the state of the pseudorandom number generator.

21.9.2 `protected double` **`nextNextGaussian;`**

A variable used by method `nextGaussian` (§21.9.12) to hold a precomputed value to be delivered by that method the next time it is called.

21.9.3 `protected boolean` **`haveNextNextGaussian`** `= false;`

A variable used by method `nextGaussian` (§21.9.12) to keep track of whether it has precomputed and stashed away the next value to be delivered by that method.

21.9.4 `public` **`Random`**`()`

This constructor initializes a newly created `Random` number generator by using the current time of day (§20.18.6) as a seed.

```
public Random() { this(System.currentTimeMillis()); }
```

21.9.5 `public` **`Random`**`(long seed)`

This constructor initializes a newly created `Random` number generator by using the argument `seed` as a seed.

```
public Random(long seed) { setSeed(seed); }
```

21.9.6 `public void` **`setSeed`**`(long seed)`

The general contract of `setSeed` is that it alters the state of this random number generator object so as to be in exactly the same state as if it had just been created with the argument `seed` as a seed.

The method `setSeed` is implemented by class `Random` as follows:

```
synchronized public void setSeed(long seed) {
    this.seed = (seed ^ 0x5DEECE66DL) & ((1L << 48) - 1);
    haveNextNextGaussian = false;
}
```

The implementation of `setSeed` by class `Random` happens to use only 48 bits of the given seed. In general, however, an overriding method may use all 64 bits of the long argument as a seed value.

[In certain early versions of Java, the `setSeed` method failed to reset the value of `haveNextNextGaussian` to `false`; this flaw could lead to failure to produce repeatable behavior.]

21.9.7 protected int **next**(int bits)

The general contract of next is that it returns an int value and if the argument bits is between 1 and 32 (inclusive), then that many low-order bits of the returned value will be (approximately) independently chosen bit values, each of which is (approximately) equally likely to be 0 or 1.

The method next is implemented by class Random as follows:

```
synchronized protected int next(int bits) {
    seed = (seed * 0x5DEECE66DL + 0xBL) & ((1L << 48) - 1);
    return (int)(seed >>> (48 - bits));
}
```

This is a linear congruential pseudorandom number generator, as defined by D. H. Lehmer and described by Donald E. Knuth in *The Art of Computer Programming*, Volume 2: *Seminumerical Algorithms*, section 3.2.1.

21.9.8 public int **nextInt**()

The general contract of nextInt is that one int value is pseudorandomly generated and returned. All 2^{32} possible int values are produced with (approximately) equal probability.

The method setSeed is implemented by class Random as follows:

```
public int nextInt() {  return next(32); }
```

21.9.9 public long **nextLong**()

The general contract of nextLong is that one long value is pseudorandomly generated and returned. All 2^{64} possible long values are produced with (approximately) equal probability.

The method setSeed is implemented by class Random as follows:

```
public long nextLong() {
    return ((long)next(32) << 32) + next(32);
}
```

21.9.10 public float **nextFloat**()

The general contract of nextFloat is that one float value, chosen (approximately) uniformly from the range 0.0f (inclusive) to 1.0f (exclusive), is pseudorandomly generated and returned. All 2^{24} possible float values of the form $m \cdot 2^{-24}$, where m is a positive integer less than 2^{24}, are produced with (approximately) equal probability.

The method setSeed is implemented by class Random as follows:

```
public float nextFloat() {
    return next(24) / ((float)(1 << 24));
}
```

The hedge "approximately" is used in the foregoing description only because the next method is only approximately an unbiased source of independently chosen bits. If it were a perfect source or randomly chosen bits, then the algorithm shown would choose float values from the stated range with perfect uniformity.

[In early versions of Java, the result was incorrectly calculated as:

```
    return next(30) / ((float)(1 << 30));
```

This might seem to be equivalent, if not better, but in fact it introduced a slight nonuniformity because of the bias in the rounding of floating-point numbers: it was slightly more likely that the low-order bit of the significand would be 0 than that it would be 1.]

21.9.11 public double **nextDouble**()

The general contract of nextDouble is that one double value, chosen (approximately) uniformly from the range 0.0d (inclusive) to 1.0d (exclusive), is pseudorandomly generated and returned. All 2^{53} possible float values of the form $m \cdot 2^{-53}$, where m is a positive integer less than 2^{53}, are produced with (approximately) equal probability.

The method setSeed is implemented by class Random as follows:

```
public double nextDouble() {
    return (((long)next(26) << 27) + next(27))
                / (double)(1L << 53);
}
```

The hedge "approximately" is used in the foregoing description only because the next method is only approximately an unbiased source of independently chosen bits. If it were a perfect source or randomly chosen bits, then the algorithm shown would choose double values from the stated range with perfect uniformity.

[In early versions of Java, the result was incorrectly calculated as:

```
return (((long)next(27) << 27) + next(27))
        / (double)(1L << 54);
```

This might seem to be equivalent, if not better, but in fact it introduced a large nonuniformity because of the bias in the rounding of floating-point numbers: it was three times as likely that the low-order bit of the significand would be 0 than that it would be 1! This nonuniformity probably doesn't matter much in practice, but we strive for perfection.]

21.9.12 public double **nextGaussian**()

The general contract of nextGaussian is that one double value, chosen from (approximately) the usual normal distribution with mean 0.0 and standard deviation 1.0, is pseudorandomly generated and returned.

The method setSeed is implemented by class Random as follows:

```
synchronized public double nextGaussian() {
    if (haveNextNextGaussian) {
        haveNextNextGaussian = false;
        return nextNextGaussian;
    } else {
        double v1, v2, s;
        do {
            v1 = 2 * nextDouble() - 1; // between -1.0 and 1.0
            v2 = 2 * nextDouble() - 1; // between -1.0 and 1.0
            s = v1 * v1 + v2 * v2;
        } while (s >= 1);
        double norm = Math.sqrt(-2 * Math.log(s)/s);
        nextNextGaussian = v2 * norm;
        haveNextNextGaussian = true;
        return v1 * norm;
    }
}
```

This uses the *polar method* of G. E. P. Box, M. E. Muller, and G. Marsaglia, as described by Donald E. Knuth in *The Art of Computer Programming*, Volume 2: *Seminumerical Algorithms*, section 3.4.1, subsection C, algorithm P. Note that it generates two independent values at the cost of only one call to Math.log and one call to Math.sqrt.

. . . who can tell what may be the event? . . .
The mind of the multitude is left at random . . .
—Thomas Paine, *Common Sense* (1776), Appendix A

21.10 The Class java.util.StringTokenizer

The StringTokenizer class provides a way to break a String into tokens. The tokenizing method used by this class is much simpler than the one used by the class java.io.StreamTokenizer. For example, a StringTokenizer does not distinguish among identifiers, numbers, and quoted strings; moreover, it does not recognize and skip comments.

A StringTokenizer can serve as an Enumeration (§21.1).

```
public class StringTokenizer implements Enumeration {
    public StringTokenizer(String str, String delim,
        boolean returnTokens);
    public StringTokenizer(String str, String delim);
    public StringTokenizer(String str);
    public boolean hasMoreTokens();
    public String nextToken();
    public String nextToken(String delim);
    public boolean hasMoreElements();
    public Object nextElement();
    public int countTokens();
}
```

A StringTokenizer simply divides characters into classes: delimiters and other characters. The tokenizer behaves in one of two ways, depending on whether it was created with returnTokens having the value true or false.

If returnTokens is false, delimiter characters merely serve to separate tokens of interest. A token is thus a maximal sequence of consecutive characters that are not delimiters.

If returnTokens is true, delimiter characters are themselves considered to be tokens of interest. A token is thus either one delimiter character or a maximal sequence of consecutive characters that are not delimiters.

A StringTokenizer internally maintains a current position within the String to be tokenized. Some operations advance this current position past the characters processed.

A token is returned by taking a substring (§20.12.32) of the string that was used to create the StringTokenizer.

21.10.1 public **StringTokenizer**(String str, String delim, boolean returnTokens)

This constructor initializes a newly created `StringTokenizer` so that it will recognize tokens within the given string `str`. All characters in the string `delim` will be considered delimiters. The argument `returnTokens` specifies whether delimiter characters themselves are to be considered tokens.

21.10.2 public **StringTokenizer**(String str, String delim)

This constructor initializes a newly created `StringTokenizer` so that it will recognize tokens within the given string `str`. All characters in the string `delim` will be considered delimiters. Delimiter characters themselves will not be treated as tokens.

21.10.3 public **StringTokenizer**(String str)

This constructor initializes a newly created `StringTokenizer` so that it will recognize tokens within the given string `str`. All whitespace characters (§20.5.19) will be considered delimiters. Delimiter characters themselves will not be treated as tokens.

21.10.4 public boolean **hasMoreTokens**()

The result is `true` if and only if there is at least one token in the string after the current position. If this method returns `true`, then a subsequent call to `nextToken` with no argument will successfully return a token.

21.10.5 public String **nextToken**()

The next token in the string after the current position is returned. The current position is advanced beyond the recognized token.

21.10.6 public String **nextToken**(String delim)

First, the set of characters considered to be delimiters by this `StringTokenizer` is changed to be the characters in the string `delim`. Then the next token in the string after the current position is returned. The current position is advanced beyond the recognized token.

21.10.7 public boolean **hasMoreElements**()

This method has exactly the same behavior as hasMoreTokens (§21.10.4). It is provided so that a StringTokenizer can serve as an Enumeration (§21.1).

21.10.8 public Object **nextElement**()

This method has exactly the same behavior as nextToken (§21.10.5). It is provided so that a StringTokenizer can serve as an Enumeration (§21.1).

21.10.9 public int **countTokens**()

The result is the number of tokens in the string after the current position, using the current set of delimiter characters. The current position is not advanced.

21.11 The Class `java.util.Vector`

A `Vector`, like an array, contains items that can be accessed using an integer index. However, the size of a `Vector` can grow and shrink as needed to accommodate adding and removing items after the `Vector` has been created.

```
public class Vector implements Cloneable {
   protected Object[] elementData;
   protected int elementCount;
   protected int capacityIncrement;
   public Vector(int initialCapacity, int capacityIncrement);
   public Vector(int initialCapacity);
   public Vector();
   public final String toString();
   public Object clone();
   public final Object elementAt(int index)
      throws IndexOutOfBoundsException;
   public final void setElementAt(Object obj, int index)
      throws IndexOutOfBoundsException;
   public final Object firstElement()
      throws NoSuchElementException;
   public final Object lastElement()
      throws NoSuchElementException;
   public final void addElement(Object obj);
   public final void insertElementAt(Object obj, int index)
      throws IndexOutOfBoundsException;
   public final boolean removeElement(Object obj);
   public final void removeElementAt(int index)
      throws IndexOutOfBoundsException;
   public final void removeAllElements();
   public final boolean isEmpty();
   public final int size();
   public final void setSize(int newSize);
   public final int capacity();
   public final void ensureCapacity(int minCapacity);
   public final void trimToSize();
   public final void copyInto(Object anArray[])
      throws IndexOutOfBoundsException;
   public final Enumeration elements();
   public final boolean contains(Object elem);
   public final int indexOf(Object elem);
   public final int indexOf(Object elem, int index)
      throws IndexOutOfBoundsException;
   public final int lastIndexOf(Object elem);
```

```
    public final int lastIndexOf(Object elem, int index)
        throws IndexOutOfBoundsException;
}
```

21.11.1 `protected Object[] elementData;`

Internally, a `Vector` keeps its elements in an array that is at least large enough to contain all the elements.

21.11.2 `protected int elementCount;`

This field holds the number of items currently in this `Vector` object. Components `elementData[0]` through `elementData[elementCount-1]` are the actual items.

21.11.3 `protected int capacityIncrement;`

When the method `ensureCapacity` (§21.11.22) must increase the size of the data array in the field `elementData` (by creating a new array), it increases the size by at least the amount in `capacityIncrement`; but if `capacityIncrement` is zero, then it at least doubles the size of the data array.

21.11.4 `public Vector(int initialCapacity, int capacityIncrement)`

This constructor initializes a newly created `Vector` so that its internal data array has size `initialCapacity` and its standard capacity increment is the value of `capacityIncrement`. Initially, the `Vector` contains no items.

21.11.5 `public Vector(int initialCapacity)`

This constructor initializes a newly created `Vector` so that its internal data array has size `initialCapacity` and its standard capacity increment is zero. Initially, the `Vector` contains no items.

21.11.6 `public Vector()`

This constructor initializes a newly created `Vector` so that its internal data array has size `10` and its standard capacity increment is zero. Initially the `Vector` contains no items.

21.11.7 `public final String toString()`

This `Vector` is represented in string form as a list of its items, enclosed in ASCII square brackets and separated by the ASCII characters ", " (comma and space). The `toString` method is used to convert the items to strings; a null reference is rendered as the string "`null`".

The example fragment:

```
Vector v = new Vector();
v.addElement("Canberra");
v.addElement("Cancun");
v.addElement("Canandaigua");
System.out.println(v.toString());
```

produces the output:

```
[Canberra, Cancun, Canandaigua]
```

Overrides the `toString` method of `Object` (§20.1.2).

21.11.8 `public Object clone()`

A copy of this `Vector` is constructed and returned. The copy will contains a reference to a clone of the internal data array, not a reference to the original internal data array of this `Vector`.

Overrides the `clone` method of `Object` (§20.1.5).

21.11.9 `public final Object elementAt(int index) throws IndexOutOfBoundsException`

The item of this `Vector` with the specified `index` is returned.

If the `index` is negative or not less than the current size of this `Vector`, an `IndexOutOfBoundsException` is thrown.

21.11.10 `public final void setElementAt(Object obj, int index) throws IndexOutOfBoundsException`

The item of this `Vector` with the specified `index` is replaced with `obj`, so that `obj` is now the item at the specified `index` within this `Vector`.

If the `index` is negative or not less than the current size of this `Vector`, an `IndexOutOfBoundsException` is thrown.

21.11.11 `public final Object` **`firstElement`**`()`
`throws NoSuchElementException`

If this `Vector` is empty, a `NoSuchElementException` is thrown. Otherwise, the first item (the item at index 0) is returned.

21.11.12 `public final Object` **`lastElement`**`()`
`throws NoSuchElementException`

If this `Vector` is empty, a `NoSuchElementException` is thrown. Otherwise, the last item (the item at index `size()-1`) is returned.

21.11.13 `public final void` **`addElement`**`(Object obj)`

The size of this `Vector` is increased by `1` and `obj` becomes the new last item.

21.11.14 `public final void` **`insertElementAt`**`(Object obj, int index)`
`throws IndexOutOfBoundsException`

The size of this `Vector` is increased by `1` and `obj` becomes the new item at the specified `index`. Any item in this `Vector` that was previously at index `k` is first moved to index `k+1` if and only if `k` is not less than `index`.

21.11.15 `public final boolean` **`removeElement`**`(Object obj)`

If this `Vector` contains an occurrence of `obj`, then the first (lowest-indexed) such occurrence is removed, as if by the method `removeElementAt` (§21.11.16), and `true` is returned. If this `Vector` contains no occurrence of `obj`, this `Vector` is not modified and `false` is returned.

21.11.16 `public final void` **`removeElementAt`**`(int index)`
`throws IndexOutOfBoundsException`

The size of this `Vector` is decreased by `1` and the item at the specified `index` is removed from this `Vector`. Any item in this `Vector` that was previously at index `k` is first moved to index `k-1` if and only if `k` is greater than `index`.

21.11.17 `public final void` **`removeAllElements`**`()`

All elements are removed from this `Vector`, making it empty.

21.11.18 `public final boolean` **`isEmpty`**`()`

The result is `true` if and only if this `Vector` is empty, that is, its size is zero.

21.11.19 `public final int` **`size`**`()`

The size of this `Vector` (the number of items it currently contains) is returned.

21.11.20 `public final void` **`setSize`**`(int newSize)`

The size of this `Vector` is changed to `newSize`. If the new size is smaller than the old size, then items are removed from the end and discarded. If the new size is larger than the old size, then the new items are set to `null`.

21.11.21 `public final int` **`capacity`**`()`

The current capacity of this `Vector` (the length of its internal data array, kept in the field `elementData`) is returned.

21.11.22 `public final void` **`ensureCapacity`**`(int minCapacity)`

If the current capacity of this `Vector` is less than `minCapacity`, then its capacity is increased by replacing its internal data array, kept in the field `elementData` (§21.11.1), with a larger one. The size of the new data array will be the old size plus `capacityIncrement` (§21.11.3), unless the value of `capacityIncrement` is nonpositive, in which case the new capacity will be twice the old capacity; but if this new size is still smaller than `minCapacity`, then the new capacity will be `minCapacity`.

21.11.23 `public final void` **`trimToSize`**`()`

If the capacity of this `Vector` is larger than its current `size` (§21.11.19), then the capacity is changed to equal the size by replacing its internal data array, kept in the field `elementData`, with a smaller one.

21.11.24 `public final void` **`copyInto`**`(Object anArray[]) throws IndexOutOfBoundsException`

All the items in this `Vector` are copied into the array `anArray`. The item at index `k` in this `Vector` is copied into component `k` of `anArray`. If the length of `anArray` is smaller than the size of this `Vector`, an `IndexOutOfBoundsException` is thrown.

21.11.25 `public final Enumeration` **`elements`**`()`

An `Enumeration` (§21.1) is returned that will generate all items in this `Vector`. The first item generated is the item at index `0`, then the item at index `1`, and so on.

21.11.26 `public final boolean` **`contains`**`(Object elem)`

The result is `true` if and only if some item in this `Vector` is the same as `elem`, as determined by the `equals` method (§20.1.3).

21.11.27 `public final int` **`indexOf`**`(Object elem)`

If an item equal to `elem` is in this `Vector`, then the index of the first such occurrence is returned, that is, the smallest value `k` such that:

```
elem.equals(elementData[k])
```

is `true`. If no such item occurs in this `Vector`, then `-1` is returned.

21.11.28 `public final int` **`indexOf`**`(Object elem, int index) throws IndexOutOfBoundsException`

If an item equal to `elem` is in this `Vector` at position `k` or higher, then the index of the first such occurrence is returned, that is, the smallest value `k` such that:

```
elem.equals(elementData[k]) && (k >= index)
```

is `true`. If no such item occurs in this `Vector`, then `-1` is returned.

21.11.29 `public final int` **`lastIndexOf`**`(Object elem)`

If an item equal to `elem` is in this `Vector`, then the index of the last such occurrence is returned, that is, the largest value `k` such that:

```
elem.equals(elementData[k])
```

is `true`. If no such item occurs in this `Vector`, then `-1` is returned.

21.11.30 `public final int` **`lastIndexOf`**`(Object elem, int index)`
`throws IndexOutOfBoundsException`

If an item equal to `elem` is in this `Vector` at position `k` or lower, then the index of the last such occurrence is returned, that is, the largest value `k` such that:

```
elem.equals(elementData[k]) && (k <= index)
```

is `true`. If no such item occurs in this `Vector`, then `-1` is returned.

21.12 The Class java.util.Stack

. . . and from the stack a thin blue wreath of smoke
Curled through the air across the ripening oats . . .
—Oscar Wilde, *Charmides* (1881)

The class Stack extends Vector with five operations that allow a vector to be treated as a stack. The usual push and pop operations are provided, as well as a method to peek at the top item on the stack, a method to test for whether the stack is empty, and a method to search the stack for an item and discover how far it is from the top.

```
public class Stack extends Vector {
    public Object push(Object item);
    public Object pop() throws EmptyStackException;
    public Object peek() throws EmptyStackException;
    public boolean empty();
    public int search(Object o);
}
```

When a stack is first created, it contains no items.

21.12.1 public Object push(Object item)

The item is pushed onto the top of this stack. This has exactly the same effect as:

```
addElement(item)
```

See method addElement of Vector (§21.11.13).

21.12.2 public Object pop() throws EmptyStackException

If the stack is empty, an EmptyStackException is thrown. Otherwise, the topmost item (last item of the Vector) is removed and returned.

21.12.3 public Object peek() throws EmptyStackException

If the stack is empty, an EmptyStackException is thrown. Otherwise, the topmost item (last item of the Vector) is returned but not removed.

21.12.4 `public boolean empty()`

The result is `true` if and only if the stack contains no items.

21.12.5 `public int search(Object o)`

If the object `o` occurs as an item in this `Stack`, this method returns the distance from the top of the stack of the occurrence nearest the top of the stack; the topmost item on the stack is considered to be at distance `1`. The `equals` method (§20.1.3) is used to compare `o` to the items in this `Stack`.

. . . And overhead in circling listlessness
The cawing rooks whirl round the frosted stacks . . .
—Oscar Wilde, *Humanitad* (1881)

21.13 The Class java.util.EmptyStackException

A EmptyStackException is thrown to indicate an attempt to pop (§21.12.2) or peek (§21.12.3) an empty Stack object.

```
public class EmptyStackException extends RuntimeException {
    public EmptyStackException();
}
```

21.13.1 public EmptyStackException()

This constructor initializes a newly created EmptyStackException with null as its error message string.

21.14 The Class `java.util.NoSuchElementException`

A `NoSuchElementException` is thrown to indicate that another element was requested from an `Enumeration` object that has no more elements to supply. See method `nextElement` of interface `Enumeration` (§21.1.2).

```
public class NoSuchElementException extends RuntimeException {
    public NoSuchElementException();
    public NoSuchElementException(String s);
}
```

21.14.1 `public NoSuchElementException()`

This constructor initializes a newly created `NoSuchElementException` with `null` as its error message string.

21.14.2 `public NoSuchElementException(String s)`

This constructor initializes a newly created `NoSuchElementException` by saving a reference to the error message string `s` for later retrieval by the `getMessage` method (§20.22.3).

CHAPTER 22

The Package `java.io`

INPUT and output in Java is organized around the concept of streams. A stream is a sequence of items, usually 8-bit bytes, read or written over the course of time.

In the `java.io` package, all input is done through subclasses of the abstract class `InputStream`, and all output is done through subclasses of the abstract class `OutputStream`. The one exception to this rule is the class `RandomAccessFile`, which handles files that allow random access and perhaps intermixed reading and writing of the file.

For an input stream, the source of data might be a file, a `String`, an array of bytes, or bytes written to an output stream (typically by another thread). There are also "filter input streams" that take data from another input stream and transform or augment the data before delivering it as input. For example, a `LineNumberInputStream` passes bytes through verbatim but counts line terminators as they are read.

For an output stream, the sink of data might be a file, an array of bytes, or a buffer to be read as an input stream (typically by another thread). There are also "filter output streams" that transform or augment data before writing it to some other output stream.

An instance of class `File` represents a path name (a string) that might identify a particular file within a file system. Certain operations on the file system, such as renaming and deleting files, are done by this class rather than through streams.

An instance of class `FileDescriptor` represents an abstract indication of a particular file within a file system; such file descriptors are created internally by the Java I/O system.

There are two interfaces, `DataInput` and `DataOutput`, that support the transfer of data other than bytes or characters, such as long integers, floating-point numbers and strings. The class `DataInputStream` implements `DataInput`; the class `DataOutputStream` implements `DataOutput`; and `RandomAccessFile` implements both `DataInput` and `DataOutput`.

The class `StreamTokenizer` provides some simple support for parsing bytes or characters from an input stream into tokens such as identifiers, numbers, and strings, optionally ignoring comments and optionally recognizing or ignoring line terminators.

The hierarchy of classes defined in package `java.io` is as follows. (Classes whose names are shown here in **boldface** are in package `java.io`; the others are in package `java.lang` and are shown here to clarify subclass relationships.)

```
Object                                  §20.1
    interface DataInput                     §22.1
    interface DataOutput                    §22.2
    InputStream                             §22.3
        FileInputStream                         §22.4
        PipedInputStream                        §22.5
        ByteArrayInputStream                    §22.6
        StringBufferInputStream                 §22.7
        SequenceInputStream                     §22.8
        FilterInputStream                       §22.9
            BufferedInputStream                     §22.10
            DataInputStream                         §22.11
            LineNumberInputStream                   §22.12
            PushBackInputStream                     §22.13
    StreamTokenizer                         §22.14
    OutputStream                            §22.15
        FileOutputStream                        §22.16
        PipedOutputStream                       §22.17
        ByteArrayOutputStream                   §22.18
        FilterOutputStream                      §22.19
            BufferedOutputStream                    §22.20
            DataOutputStream                        §22.21
            PrintStream                             §22.22
    RandomAccessFile                        §22.23
    File                                    §22.24
    interface FileNameFilter                §22.25
    FileDescriptor                          §22.26
    Throwable                               §20.22
        Exception                               §20.22
            IOException                             §22.27
                EOFException                            §22.28
                FileNotFoundException                   §22.29
                InterruptedIOException                  §22.30
                UTFDataFormatException                  §22.31
```

22.1 The Interface java.io.DataInput

The DataInput interface provides for reading bytes from a binary stream and reconstructing from them data in any of the Java primitive types. There is also a facility for reconstructing a String from data in Java modified UTF-8 format.

The DataOutput interface (§22.2) supports the creation of binary output data suitable for reading back in through the DataInput interface.

The DataInput interface is implemented by classes DataInputStream (§22.11) and RandomAccessFile (§22.23).

```
public interface DataInput {
    public void readFully(byte[] b)
        throws IOException, NullPointerException;
    public void readFully(byte[] b, int off, int len)
        throws IOException, NullPointerException,
            IndexOutOfBoundsException;
    public int skipBytes(int n) throws IOException;
    public boolean readBoolean() throws IOException;
    public byte readByte() throws IOException;
    public int readUnsignedByte() throws IOException;
    public short readShort() throws IOException;
    public int readUnsignedShort() throws IOException;
    public char readChar() throws IOException;
    public int readInt() throws IOException;
    public long readLong() throws IOException;
    public float readFloat() throws IOException;
    public double readDouble() throws IOException;
    public String readLine() throws IOException;
    public String readUTF() throws IOException;
}
```

It is generally true of all the reading routines in this interface that if end of file is reached before the desired number of bytes has been read, an EOFException (which is a kind of IOException) is thrown. If any byte cannot be read for any reason other than end of file, an IOException other than EOFException is thrown. In particular, an IOException may be thrown if the input stream has been closed (§22.3.6).

22.1.1 `public void readFully(byte[] b) throws IOException, NullPointerException;`

The general contract of `readFully(b)` is that it reads some bytes from an input stream and stores them into the buffer array `b`. The number of bytes read is equal to the length of `b`.

This method blocks until one of the following conditions occurs:

- `b.length` bytes of input data are available, in which case a normal return is made.
- End of file is detected, in which case an `EOFException` is thrown.
- An I/O error occurs, in which case an `IOException` other than `EOFException` is thrown.

If `b` is `null`, a `NullPointerException` is thrown.

If `b.length` is zero, then no bytes are read. Otherwise, the first byte read is stored into element `b[0]`, the next one into `b[1]`, and so on.

If an exception is thrown from this method, then it may be that some but not all bytes of `b` have been updated with data from the input stream.

22.1.2 `public void readFully(byte[] b, int off, int len) throws IOException, NullPointerException, IndexOutOfBoundsException`

The general contract of `readFully(b, off, len)` is that it reads `len` bytes from an input stream.

This method blocks until one of the following conditions occurs:

- `len` bytes of input data are available, in which case a normal return is made.
- End of file is detected, in which case an `EOFException` is thrown.
- An I/O error occurs, in which case an `IOException` other than `EOFException` is thrown.

If `b` is `null`, a `NullPointerException` is thrown.

If `off` is negative, or `len` is negative, or `off+len` is greater than the length of the array `b`, then an `IndexOutOfBoundsException` is thrown.

If `len` is zero, then no bytes are read. Otherwise, the first byte read is stored into element `b[off]`, the next one into `b[off+1]`, and so on. The number of bytes read is, at most, equal to `len`.

If an exception is thrown from this method, then it may be that some but not all bytes of `b` in positions `off` through `off+len-1` have been updated with data from the input stream.

22.1.3 `public int` **`skipBytes`**`(int n) throws IOException`

The general contract of `skipBytes` is that it makes an attempt to skip over `n` bytes of data from the input stream, discarding the skipped bytes. However, it may skip over some smaller number of bytes, possibly zero. This may result from any of a number of conditions; reaching end of file before `n` bytes have been skipped is only one possibility. This method never throws an `EOFException`. The actual number of bytes skipped is returned.

22.1.4 `public boolean` **`readBoolean`**`() throws IOException;`

The general contract of `readBoolean` is that it reads one input byte and returns `true` if that byte is nonzero, `false` if that byte is zero.

This method is suitable for reading the byte written by the `writeBoolean` method of interface `DataOutput` (§22.2.4).

22.1.5 `public byte` **`readByte`**`() throws IOException`

The general contract of `readByte` is that it reads and returns one input byte. The byte is treated as a signed value in the range `-128` through `127`, inclusive.

This method is suitable for reading the byte written by the `writeByte` method of interface `DataOutput` (§22.2.5).

22.1.6 `public int` **`readUnsignedByte`**`() throws IOException`

The general contract of `readUnsignedByte` is that it reads one input byte, zero-extends it to type `int`, and returns the result, which is therefore in the range `0` through `255`.

This method is suitable for reading the byte written by the `writeByte` method of interface `DataOutput` (§22.2.5) if the argument to `writeByte` was intended to be a value in the range `0` through `255`.

22.1.7 `public short readShort() throws IOException`

The general contract of `readShort` is that it reads two input bytes and returns a `short` value. Let `a` be the first byte read and `b` be the second byte. The value returned is:

```
(short)((a << 8) | (b & 0xff))
```

This method is suitable for reading the bytes written by the `writeShort` method of interface `DataOutput` (§22.2.6).

22.1.8 `public int readUnsignedShort() throws IOException`

The general contract of `readUnsignedShort` is that it reads two input bytes and returns an `int` value in the range `0` through `65535`. Let `a` be the first byte read and `b` be the second byte. The value returned is:

```
(((a & 0xff) << 8) | (b & 0xff))
```

This method is suitable for reading the bytes written by the `writeShort` method of interface `DataOutput` (§22.2.6) if the argument to `writeShort` was intended to be a value in the range `0` through `65535`.

22.1.9 `public char readChar() throws IOException`

The general contract of `readChar` is that it reads two input bytes and returns a `char` value. Let `a` be the first byte read and `b` be the second byte. The value returned is:

```
(char)((a << 8) | (b & 0xff))
```

This method is suitable for reading bytes written by the `writeChar` method of interface `DataOutput` (§22.2.7).

22.1.10 `public int readInt() throws IOException`

The general contract of `readInt` is that it reads four input bytes and returns an `int` value. Let `a` be the first byte read, `b` be the second byte, `c` be the third byte, and `d` be the fourth byte. The value returned is:

```
(((a & 0xff) << 24) | ((b & 0xff) << 16) |
 ((c & 0xff) <<  8) | (d & 0xff))
```

This method is suitable for reading bytes written by the `writeInt` method of interface `DataOutput` (§22.2.8).

22.1.11 `public long readLong() throws IOException`

The general contract of `readLong` is that it reads eight input bytes and returns a `long` value. Let `a` be the first byte read, `b` be the second byte, `c` be the third byte, `d` be the fourth byte, `e` be the fifth byte, `f` be the sixth byte, `g` be the seventh byte, and `h` be the eighth byte. The value returned is:

```
(((long)(a & 0xff) << 56) |
 ((long)(b & 0xff) << 48) |
 ((long)(c & 0xff) << 40) |
 ((long)(d & 0xff) << 32) |
 ((long)(e & 0xff) << 24) |
 ((long)(f & 0xff) << 16) |
 ((long)(g & 0xff) <<  8) |
 ((long)(h & 0xff)))
```

This method is suitable for reading bytes written by the `writeLong` method of interface `DataOutput` (§22.2.9).

22.1.12 `public float readFloat() throws IOException`

The general contract of `readFloat` is that it reads four input bytes and returns a `float` value. It does this by first constructing an `int` value in exactly the manner of the `readInt` method (§22.1.10), then converting this `int` value to a `float` in exactly the manner of the method `Float.intBitsToFloat` (§20.9.23).

This method is suitable for reading bytes written by the `writeFloat` method of interface `DataOutput` (§22.2.10).

22.1.13 `public double readDouble() throws IOException`

The general contract of `readDouble` is that it reads eight input bytes and returns a `double` value. It does this by first constructing a `long` value in exactly the manner of the `readlong` method (§22.1.11), then converting this `long` value to a `double` in exactly the manner of the method `Double.longBitsToDouble` (§20.10.22).

This method is suitable for reading bytes written by the `writeDouble` method of interface `DataOutput` (§22.2.11).

22.1.14 `public String readLine() throws IOException`

The general contract of `readLine` is that it reads successive bytes, converting each byte separately into a character, until it encounters a line terminator or end of file; the characters read are then returned as a `String`. Note that because this method processes bytes, it does not support input of the full Unicode character set.

If end of file is encountered before even one byte can be read, then `null` is returned. Otherwise, each byte that is read is converted to type `char` by zero-extension. If the character `'\n'` is encountered, it is discarded and reading ceases. If the character `'\r'` is encountered, it is discarded and, if the following byte converts to the character `'\n'`, then that is discarded also; reading then ceases. If end of file is encountered before either of the characters `'\n'` and `'\r'` is encountered, reading ceases. Once reading has ceased, a `String` is returned that contains all the characters read and not discarded, taken in order. Note that every character in this string will have a value less than `\u0100`, that is, `(char)256`.

22.1.15 `public String readUTF() throws IOException`

The general contract of `readUTF` is that it reads a representation of a Unicode character string encoded in Java modified UTF-8 format; this string of characters is then returned as a `String`.

First, two bytes are read and used to construct an unsigned 16-bit integer in exactly the manner of the `readUnsignedShort` method (§22.1.8). This integer value is called the *UTF length* and specifies the number of additional bytes to be read. These bytes are then converted to characters by considering them in groups. The length of each group is computed from the value of the first byte of the group. The byte following a group, if any, is the first byte of the next group.

If the first byte of a group matches the bit pattern `0xxxxxxx` (where `x` means "may be `0` or `1`"), then the group consists of just that byte. The byte is zero-extended to form a character.

If the first byte of a group matches the bit pattern `110xxxxx`, then the group consists of that byte `a` and a second byte `b`. If there is no byte `b` (because byte `a` was the last of the bytes to be read), or if byte `b` does not match the bit pattern `10xxxxxx`, then a `UTFDataFormatException` is thrown. Otherwise, the group is converted to the character:

```
(char)(((a & 0x1F) << 6) | (b & 0x3F))
```

If the first byte of a group matches the bit pattern `1110xxxx`, then the group consists of that byte `a` and two more bytes `b` and `c`. If there is no byte `c` (because byte `a` was one of the last two of the bytes to be read), or either byte `b` or byte `c` does not match the bit pattern `10xxxxxx`, then a `UTFDataFormatException` is thrown. Otherwise, the group is converted to the character:

```
(char)(((a & 0x0F) << 12) | ((b & 0x3F) << 6) | (c & 0x3F))
```

If the first byte of a group matches the pattern `1111xxxx` or the pattern `10xxxxxx`, then a `UTFDataFormatException` is thrown.

If end of file is encountered at any time during this entire process, then an `EOFException` is thrown.

After every group has been converted to a character by this process, the characters are gathered, in the same order in which their corresponding groups were read from the input stream, to form a `String`, which is returned.

The `writeUTF` method of interface `DataOutput` (§22.2.14) may be used to write data that is suitable for reading by this method.

22.2 The Interface java.io.DataOutput

The DataOutput interface provides for converting data from any of the Java primitive types to a series of bytes and writing these bytes to a binary stream. There is also a facility for converting a String into Java modified UTF-8 format and writing the resulting series of bytes.

The DataInput interface (§22.1) can be used to read in and reconstruct Java data from the binary output data produced by the DataOutput interface.

The DataOutput interface is implemented by classes DataOutputStream (§22.21) and RandomAccessFile (§22.23).

```
public interface DataOutput {
   public void write(int b) throws IOException;
   public void write(byte[] b)
      throws IOException, NullPointerException;
   public void write(byte[] b, int off, int len)
      throws IOException, NullPointerException,
         IndexOutOfBoundsException;
   public void writeBoolean(boolean v) throws IOException;
   public void writeByte(int v) throws IOException;
   public void writeShort(int v) throws IOException;
   public void writeChar(int v) throws IOException;
   public void writeInt(int v) throws IOException;
   public void writeLong(long v) throws IOException;
   public void writeFloat(float v) throws IOException;
   public void writeDouble(double v) throws IOException;
   public void writeBytes(String s)
      throws IOException, NullPointerException;
   public void writeChars(String s)
      throws IOException, NullPointerException;
   public void writeUTF(String s)
      throws IOException, NullPointerException;
}
```

For all the methods in this interface that write bytes, it is generally true that if a byte cannot be written for any reason, an IOException is thrown.

22.2.1 public void write(int b) throws IOException

The general contract for write is that one byte is written to the output stream. The byte to be written is the eight low-order bits of the argument b. The 24 high-order bits of b are ignored.

22.2.2 `public void write(byte[] b)`
`throws IOException, NullPointerException`

The general contract for `write` is that all the bytes in array `b` are written, in order, to the output stream.

If `b` is `null`, a `NullPointerException` is thrown.

If `b.length` is zero, then no bytes are written. Otherwise, the byte `b[0]` is written first, then `b[1]`, and so on; the last byte written is `b[b.length-1]`.

22.2.3 `public void write(byte[] b, int off, int len)`
`throws IOException, NullPointerException,`
`IndexOutOfBoundsException`

The general contract for `write` is that `len` bytes from array `b` are written, in order, to the output stream.

If `b` is `null`, a `NullPointerException` is thrown.

If `off` is negative, or `len` is negative, or `off+len` is greater than the length of the array `b`, then an `IndexOutOfBoundsException` is thrown.

If `len` is zero, then no bytes are written. Otherwise, the byte `b[off]` is written first, then `b[off+1]`, and so on; the last byte written is `b[off+len-1]`.

22.2.4 `public void writeBoolean(boolean v) throws IOException`

The general contract for `writeBoolean` is that one byte is written to the output stream. If the argument `v` is `true`, the value `(byte)1` is written; if `v` is `false`, the value `(byte)0` is written.

The byte written by this method may be read by the `readBoolean` method of interface `DataInput` (§22.1.4), which will then return a `boolean` equal to `v`.

22.2.5 `public void writeByte(int v) throws IOException`

The general contract for `writeByte` is that one byte is written to the output stream to represent the value of the argument. The byte to be written is the eight low-order bits of the argument `b`. The 24 high-order bits of `b` are ignored. (This means that `writeByte` does exactly the same thing as `write` for an integer argument.)

The byte written by this method may be read by the `readByte` method of interface `DataInput` (§22.1.5), which will then return a `byte` equal to `(byte)v`.

22.2.6 public void **writeShort**(int v) throws IOException

The general contract for `writeShort` is that two bytes are written to the output stream to represent the value of the argument. The byte values to be written, in the order shown, are:

```
(byte)(0xff & (v >> 8))
(byte)(0xff & v)
```

The bytes written by this method may be read by the `readShort` method of interface `DataInput` (§22.1.7), which will then return a `short` equal to `(short)v`.

22.2.7 public void **writeChar**(int v) throws IOException

The general contract for `writeChar` is that two bytes are written to the output stream to represent the value of the argument. The byte values to be written, in the order shown, are:

```
(byte)(0xff & (v >> 8))
(byte)(0xff & v)
```

The bytes written by this method may be read by the `readChar` method of interface `DataInput` (§22.1.9), which will then return a `char` equal to `(char)v`.

22.2.8 public void **writeInt**(int v) throws IOException

The general contract for `writeInt` is that four bytes are written to the output stream to represent the value of the argument. The byte values to be written, in the order shown, are:

```
(byte)(0xff & (v >> 24))
(byte)(0xff & (v >> 16))
(byte)(0xff & (v >>  8))
(byte)(0xff & v)
```

The bytes written by this method may be read by the `readInt` method of interface `DataInput` (§22.1.10), which will then return an `int` equal to `v`.

22.2.9 public void **writeLong**(long v) throws IOException

The general contract for `writeLong` is that four bytes are written to the output stream to represent the value of the argument. The byte values to be written, in the order shown, are:

```
(byte)(0xff & (v >> 56))
(byte)(0xff & (v >> 48))
(byte)(0xff & (v >> 40))
(byte)(0xff & (v >> 32))
(byte)(0xff & (v >> 24))
(byte)(0xff & (v >> 16))
(byte)(0xff & (v >>  8))
(byte)(0xff & v)
```

The bytes written by this method may be read by the `readLong` method of interface `DataInput` (§22.1.11), which will then return a `long` equal to `v`.

22.2.10 `public void` **`writeFloat`**`(float v) throws IOException`

The general contract for `writeFloat` is that four bytes are written to the output stream to represent the value of the argument. It does this as if it first converts this `float` value to an `int` in exactly the manner of the `Float.floatToIntBits` method (§20.9.22) and then writes the `int` value in exactly the manner of the `writeInt` method (§22.2.8).

The bytes written by this method may be read by the `readFloat` method of interface `DataInput` (§22.1.12), which will then return a `float` equal to `v`.

22.2.11 `public void` **`writeDouble`**`(double v) throws IOException`

The general contract for `writeDouble` is that eight bytes are written to the output stream to represent the value of the argument. It does this as if it first converts this `double` value to a `long` in exactly the manner of the `Double.doubleToLongBits` method (§20.10.21) and then writes the `long` value in exactly the manner of the `writeLong` method (§22.2.9).

The bytes written by this method may be read by the `readDouble` method of interface `DataInput` (§22.1.13), which will then return a `double` equal to `v`.

22.2.12 `public void` **`writeBytes`**`(String s)`
`        throws IOException, NullPointerException`

The general contract for `writeBytes` is that for every character in the string `s`, taken in order, one byte is written to the output stream.

If `s` is `null`, a `NullPointerException` is thrown.

If `s.length` is zero, then no bytes are written. Otherwise, the character `s[0]` is written first, then `s[1]`, and so on; the last character written is `s[s.length-1]`. For each character, one byte is written, the low-order byte, in exactly the manner of the writeByte method (§22.2.5). The high-order eight bits of each character in the string are ignored.

22.2.13 public void **writeChars**(String s) throws IOException, NullPointerException

The general contract for writeChars is that every character in the string s is written, in order, to the output stream, two bytes per character.

If s is null, a NullPointerException is thrown.

If s.length is zero, then no characters are written. Otherwise, the character s[0] is written first, then s[1], and so on; the last character written is s[s.length-1]. For each character, two bytes are actually written, high-order byte first, in exactly the manner of the writeChar method (§22.2.7).

22.2.14 public void **writeUTF**(String s) throws IOException, NullPointerException

The general contract for writeUTF is that two bytes of length information are written to the output stream, followed by the Java modified UTF representation of every character in the string s.

If s is null, a NullPointerException is thrown.

Each character in the string s is converted to a group of one, two, or three bytes, depending on the value of the character.

If a character c is in the range '\u0001' through '\u007f', it is represented by one byte:

```
(byte)c
```

If a character c is '\u0000' or is in the range '\u0080' through '\u07ff', then it is represented by two bytes, to be written in the order shown:

```
(byte)(0xc0 | (0x1f & (c >> 6)))
(byte)(0x80 | (0x3f & c))
```

If a character c is in the range '\u0800' through '\uffff', then it is represented by three bytes, to be written in the order shown:

```
(byte)(0xc0 | (0x0f & (c >> 12)))
(byte)(0x80 | (0x3f & (c >>  6)))
(byte)(0x80 | (0x3f & c))
```

First, the total number of bytes needed to represent all the characters of s is calculated. If this number is larger than 65535, then a UTFDataFormatError is thrown. Otherwise, this length is written to the output stream in exactly the manner of the `writeShort` method (§22.2.6); after this, the one-, two-, or three-byte representation of each character in the string `s` is written.

The bytes written by this method may be read by the `readUTF` method of interface `DataInput` (§22.1.15), which will then return a `String` equal to `s`.

22.3 The Class `java.io.InputStream`

An input stream makes input bytes available from some source.

```
public abstract class InputStream {
   public abstract int read() throws IOException;
   public int read(byte[] b)
   throws IOException, NullPointerException;
   public int read(byte[] b, int off, int len)
      throws IOException, NullPointerException,
         IndexOutOfBoundsException;
   public long skip(long n) throws IOException;
   public int available() throws IOException;
   public void close() throws IOException;
   public void mark(int readlimit);
   public void reset() throws IOException;
   public boolean markSupported();
}
```

22.3.1 `public abstract int read() throws IOException`

The general contract of `read` is that it reads one byte from the input stream. The byte is returned as an integer in the range `0` to `255` (`0x00`–`0xff`). If no byte is available because the stream is at end of file, the value `-1` is returned.

This method blocks until input data is available, end of file is detected, or an exception is thrown.

If the byte cannot be read for any reason other than end of file, an `IOException` is thrown. In particular, an `IOException` is thrown if the input stream has been closed (§22.3.6).

22.3.2 `public int read(byte[] b) throws IOException, NullPointerException`

The general contract of `read(b)` is that it reads some number of bytes from the input stream and stores them into the buffer array `b`. The number of bytes actually read is returned as an integer.

This method blocks until input data is available, end of file is detected, or an exception is thrown.

If `b` is `null`, a `NullPointerException` is thrown.

If the length of `b` is zero, then no bytes are read and `0` is returned; otherwise, there is an attempt to read at least one byte. If no byte is available because the stream is at end of file, the value -1 is returned; otherwise, at least one byte is read and stored into b.

The first byte read is stored into element b[0], the next one into b[1], and so on. The number of bytes read is, at most, equal to the length of b. Let *k* be the number of bytes actually read; these bytes will be stored in elements b[0] through b[*k*-1], leaving elements b[*k*] through b[b.length-1] unaffected.

If the first byte cannot be read for any reason other than end of file, then an IOException is thrown. In particular, an IOException is thrown if the input stream has been closed (§22.15.5).

The read(b) method for class InputStream has the same effect as:

```
read(b, 0, b.length)
```

22.3.3 public int **read**(byte[] b, int off, int len) throws IOException, NullPointerException, IndexOutOfBoundsException

The general contract of read(b, off, len) is that it reads some number of bytes from the input stream and stores them into the buffer array b. An attempt is made to read as many as len bytes, but a smaller number may be read, possibly zero. The number of bytes actually read is returned as an integer.

This method blocks until input data is available, end of file is detected, or an exception is thrown.

If b is null, a NullPointerException is thrown.

If off is negative, or len is negative, or off+len is greater than the length of the array b, then an IndexOutOfBoundsException is thrown.

If len is zero, then no bytes are read and 0 is returned; otherwise, there is an attempt to read at least one byte. If no byte is available because the stream is at end of file, the value -1 is returned; otherwise, at least one byte is read and stored into b.

The first byte read is stored into element b[off], the next one into b[off+1], and so on. The number of bytes read is, at most, equal to len. Let *k* be the number of bytes actually read; these bytes will be stored in elements b[off] through b[off+*k*-1], leaving elements b[off+*k*] through b[off+len-1] unaffected.

In every case, elements b[0] through b[off] and elements b[off+len] through b[b.length-1] are unaffected.

If the first byte cannot be read for any reason other than end of file, then an IOException is thrown. In particular, an IOException is thrown if the input stream has been closed (§22.15.5).

The read(b, off, len) method for class InputStream simple calls the method read() repeatedly. If the first such call results in an IOException, that exception is returned from the call to the `read(b, off, len)` method. If any subsequent call to `read()` results in a `IOException`, the exception is caught and treated as if it were end of file; the bytes read up to that point are stored into `b` and the number of bytes read before the exception occurred is returned.

22.3.4 `public long skip(long n) throws IOException`

The general contract of `skip` is that it makes an attempt to skip over `n` bytes of data from the input stream, discarding the skipped bytes. However, it may skip over some smaller number of bytes, possibly zero. This may result from any of a number of conditions; reaching end of file before `n` bytes have been skipped is only one possibility. The actual number of bytes skipped is returned.

22.3.5 `public int available() throws IOException`

The general contract of `available` is that it returns an integer `k`; the next caller of a method for this input stream, which might be the same thread or another thread, can then expect to be able to read or skip up to `k` bytes without blocking (waiting for input data to arrive).

The `available` method for class `InputStream` always returns `0`.

22.3.6 `public int close() throws IOException`

The general contract of `close` is that it closes the input stream. A closed stream cannot perform input operations and cannot be reopened.

The `close` method for class `InputStream` does nothing and simply returns.

22.3.7 `public void mark(int readlimit)`

The general contract of `mark` is that, if the method `markSupported` returns `true`, the stream somehow remembers all the bytes read after the call to `mark` and stands ready to supply those same bytes again if and whenever the method `reset` is called. However, the stream is not required to remember any data at all if more than `readlimit` bytes are read from the stream before `reset` is called.

The `mark` method for class `InputStream` does nothing.

22.3.8 `public void reset() throws IOException`

The general contract of `reset` is:

- If the method `markSupported` returns `true`, then:
  - If the method `mark` has not been called since the stream was created, or the number of bytes read from the stream since `mark` was last called is larger than the argument to `mark` at that last call, then an `IOException` might be thrown.
  - If such an `IOException` is not thrown, then the stream is reset to a state such that all the bytes read since the most recent call to `mark` (or since the start of the file, if `mark` has not been called) will be resupplied to subsequent callers of the `read` method, followed by any bytes that otherwise would have been the next input data as of the time of the call to `reset`.
- If the method `markSupported` returns `false`, then:
  - The call to `reset` may throw an `IOException`.
  - If an `IOException` is not thrown, then the stream is reset to a fixed state that depends on the particular type of the input stream and how it was created. The bytes that will be supplied to subsequent callers of the `read` method depend on the particular type of the input stream.

The method `reset` for class `InputStream` always throws an `IOException`.

22.3.9 `public boolean markSupported()`

The general contract of `markSupported` is that if it returns `true`, then the stream supports the `mark` (§22.3.7) and `reset` (§22.3.8) operations. For any given instance of `InputStream`, this method should consistently return the same truth value whenever it is called.

The `markSupported` method for class `InputStream` returns `false`.

22.4 The Class java.io.FileInputStream

A file input stream obtains input bytes from a file in a file system. What files are available depends on the host environment.

```
public class FileInputStream extends InputStream {
    public FileInputStream(String path)
        throws SecurityException, FileNotFoundException;
    public FileInputStream(File file)
        throws SecurityException, FileNotFoundException;
    public FileInputStream(FileDescriptor fdObj)
        throws SecurityException;
    public native int read() throws IOException;
    public int read(byte[] b)
        throws IOException, NullPointerException;
    public int read(byte[] b, int off, int len)
        throws IOException, NullPointerException,
            IndexOutOfBoundsException;
    public native long skip(long n) throws IOException;
    public native int available() throws IOException;
    public native void close() throws IOException;
    public final FileDescriptor getFD() throws IOException;
    protected void finalize() throws IOException;
}
```

22.4.1 public FileInputStream(String path) throws SecurityException, FileNotFoundException

This constructor initializes a newly created `FileInputStream` by opening a connection to an actual file, the file named by the path name `path` in the file system. A new `FileDescriptor` object is created to represent this file connection.

First, if there is a security manager, its `checkRead` method (§20.17.19) is called with the `path` argument as its argument.

If the actual file cannot be opened, a `FileNotFoundException` is thrown.

22.4.2 public FileInputStream(File file) throws SecurityException, FileNotFoundException

This constructor initializes a newly created `FileInputStream` by opening a connection to an actual file, the file named by the `File` object `file` in the file system. A new `FileDescriptor` object is created to represent this file connection.

First, if there is a security manager, its `checkRead` method (§20.17.19) is called with the path represented by the `file` argument as its argument.

If the actual file cannot be opened, a `FileNotFoundException` is thrown.

22.4.3 `public FileInputStream(FileDescriptor fdObj) throws SecurityException`

This constructor initializes a newly created `FileInputStream` by using the file descriptor `fdObj`, which represents an existing connection to an actual file in the file system.

First, if there is a security manager, its `checkRead` method (§20.17.18) is called with the file descriptor `fdObj` as its argument.

22.4.4 `public final FileDescriptor getFD() throws IOException`

This method returns the `FileDescriptor` object (§22.26) that represents the connection to the actual file in the file system being used by this `FileInputStream`.

22.4.5 `public int read() throws IOException;`

The byte for this operation is read from the actual file with which this file input stream is connected.

Implements the `read` method of `InputStream` (§22.3.1).

22.4.6 `public int read(byte[] b) throws IOException, NullPointerException`

Bytes for this operation are read from the actual file with which this file input stream is connected.

Overrides the `read` method of `InputStream` (§22.3.2).

22.4.7 `public int read(byte[] b, int off, int len) throws IOException, NullPointerException, IndexOutOfBoundsException`

Bytes for this operation are read from the actual file with which this file input stream is connected.

Overrides the `read` method of `InputStream` (§22.3.3).

22.4.8 `public long skip(long n) throws IOException`

Bytes for this operation are read from the actual file with which this file input stream is connected.

Overrides the `skip` method of `InputStream` (§22.3.4).

22.4.9 `public int available() throws IOException`

Overrides the `available` method of `InputStream` (§22.3.5).

22.4.10 `public void close() throws IOException`

This file input stream is closed and may no longer be used for reading bytes.

Overrides the `close` method of `InputStream` (§22.3.6).

22.4.11 `protected void finalize() throws IOException`

A `FileInputStream` uses finalization to clean up the connection to the actual file.

22.5 The Class java.io.PipedInputStream

A piped input stream should be connected to a piped output stream; the piped input stream then provides whatever data bytes are written to the piped output stream. Typically, data is read from a PipedInputStream object by one thread and data is written to the corresponding PipedOutputStream (§22.17) by some other thread. Attempting to use both objects from a single thread is not recommended, as it may deadlock the thread. The piped input stream contains a buffer, decoupling read operations from write operations, within limits.

```
public class PipedInputStream extends InputStream {
   public PipedInputStream(PipedOutputStream src)
      throws IOException;
   public PipedInputStream();
   public void connect(PipedOutputStream src)
      throws IOException;
   public int read() throws IOException;
   public int read(byte[] b, int off, int len)
      throws IOException, NullPointerException,
         IndexOutOfBoundsException;
   public void close() throws IOException;
}
```

22.5.1 public PipedInputStream(PipedOutputStream src) throws IOException

This constructor initializes a newly created PipedInputStream so that it is connected to the piped output stream src. Data bytes written to src will then be available as input from this stream.

22.5.2 public PipedInputStream()

This constructor initializes a newly created PipedInputStream so that it is not yet connected. It must be connected to a PipedOutputStream before being used.

22.5.3 public void connect(PipedOutputStream src) throws IOException

The connect method causes this piped input stream to be connected to the piped output stream src. If this object is already connected to some other piped output stream, an IOException is thrown.

If `src` is an unconnected piped output stream and `snk` is an unconnected piped input stream, they may be connected by either the call:

```
snk.connect(src)
```

or the call:

```
src.connect(snk)
```

The two calls have the same effect.

22.5.4 `public int read() throws IOException`

If a thread was providing data bytes to the connected piped output stream, but the thread is no longer alive, then an `IOException` is thrown.

Implements the `read` method of `InputStream` (§22.3.1).

22.5.5 `public int read(byte[] b, int off, int len) throws IOException, NullPointerException, IndexOutOfBoundsException`

If a thread was providing data bytes to the connected piped output stream, but the thread is no longer alive, then an `IOException` is thrown.

Overrides the `read` method of `InputStream` (§22.3.3).

22.5.6 `public void close() throws IOException`

This piped input stream is closed and may no longer be used for reading bytes.

Overrides the `close` method of `InputStream` (§22.3.6).

22.6 The Class java.io.ByteArrayInputStream

A ByteArrayInputStream contains an internal buffer that contains bytes that may be read from the stream. An internal counter keeps track of the next byte to be supplied by the read method. See also StringBufferInputStream (§22.7).

```
public class ByteArrayInputStream extends InputStream {
   protected byte[] buf;
   protected int pos;
   protected int count;
   public ByteArrayInputStream(byte[] buf);
   public ByteArrayInputStream(byte[] buf,
         int offset, int length);
   public int read()
      throws NullPointerException, IndexOutOfBoundsException;
   public int read(byte[] b, int off, int len)
      throws NullPointerException, IndexOutOfBoundsException;
   public long skip(long n);
   public int available();
   public void reset();
}
```

22.6.1 protected byte[] buf;

An array of bytes that was provided by the creator of the stream. Elements buf[0] through buf[count-1] are the only bytes that can ever be read from the stream; element buf[pos] is the next byte to be read.

22.6.2 protected int pos;

This value should always be nonnegative and not larger than the value of count. The next byte to be read from this stream will be buf[pos].

22.6.3 protected int count;

This value should always be nonnegative and not larger than the length of buf. It is one greater than the position of the last byte within buf that can ever be read from this stream.

22.6.4 `public ByteArrayInputStream(byte[] buf)`

This constructor initializes a newly created ByteArrayInputStream so that it uses buf as its buffer array. The initial value of pos is 0 and the initial value of count is the length of buf.

22.6.5 `public ByteArrayInputStream(byte[] buf, int offset, int length)`

```
public ByteArrayInputStream(byte[] buf,
        int offset, int length)
```

This constructor initializes a newly created ByteArrayInputStream so that it uses buf as its buffer array. The initial value of pos is offset and the initial value of count is offset+len.

Note that if bytes are simply read from the resulting input stream, elements buf[pos] through buf[pos+len-1] will be read; however, if a reset operation (§22.6.10) is performed, then bytes buf[0] through buf[pos-1] will then become available for input.

22.6.6 `public int read()`

```
public int read()
        throws NullPointerException,
           IndexOutOfBoundsException
```

If pos equals count, then -1 is returned to indicate end of file. Otherwise, the value buf[pos]&0xff is returned; just before the return, pos is incremented by 1.

Implements the read method of InputStream (§22.3.1).

22.6.7 `public int read(byte[] b, int off, int len)`

```
public int read(byte[] b, int off, int len)
        throws NullPointerException,
           IndexOutOfBoundsException
```

If pos equals count, then -1 is returned to indicate end of file. Otherwise, the number k of bytes read is equal to the smaller of len and count-pos. If k is positive, then bytes buf[pos] through buf[pos+k-1] are copied into b[off] through b[off+k-1] in the manner performed by System.arraycopy (§20.18.16). The value k is added into pos and k is returned.

Overrides the read method of InputStream (§22.3.3).

22.6.8 `public long skip(long n)`

The actual number `k` of bytes to be skipped is equal to the smaller of `n` and `count-pos`. The value `k` is added into `pos` and `k` is returned.

Overrides the `skip` method of `InputStream` (§22.3.4).

22.6.9 `public int available()`

The quantity `count-pos` is returned.

Overrides the `available` method of `InputStream` (§22.3.5).

22.6.10 `public void reset()`

The value of `pos` is set to `0`.

Overrides the `reset` method of `InputStream` (§22.3.8).

22.7 The Class java.io.StringBufferInputStream

A StringBufferInputStream contains an internal buffer that contains bytes that may be read from the stream. An internal counter keeps track of the next byte to be supplied by the read method. See also ByteArrayInputStream (§22.6).

```
public class StringBufferInputStream extends InputStream {
    protected String buffer;
    protected int pos;
    protected int count;
    public StringBufferInputStream(String s)
        throws NullPointerException;
    public int read();
    public int read(byte[] b, int off, int len)
        throws NullPointerException, IndexOutOfBoundsException;
    public long skip(long n);
    public int available();
    public void reset();
}
```

Note that bytes read from a StringBufferInputStream are the low-order eight bits of each character in the string; the high-order eight bits of each character are ignored.

22.7.1 protected String buffer;

A String that was provided by the creator of the stream. Elements buffer[0] through buffer[count-1] are the only bytes that can ever be read from this stream; element buffer[pos] is the next byte to be read.

22.7.2 protected int pos;

This value should always be nonnegative and not larger than the value of count. The next byte to be read from this stream will be buffer[pos].

22.7.3 protected int count;

This value equals the length of buffer. It is the number of bytes of data in buffer that can ever be read from this stream.

22.7.4 `public` **`StringBufferInputStream`**`(String s)`
`throws NullPointerException`

This constructor initializes a newly created `StringBufferInputStream` so that it uses `s` as its buffer array. The initial value of `pos` is `0` and the initial value of `count` is the length of `buffer`.

22.7.5 `public int` **`read`**`()`

If `pos` equals `count`, then `-1` is returned to indicate end of file. Otherwise, the value `buffer[pos]&0xff` is returned; just before the return, `1` is added to `pos`.

Implements the `read` method of `InputStream` (§22.3.1).

22.7.6 `public int` **`read`**`(byte[] b, int off, int len)`
`throws NullPointerException,`
`IndexOutOfBoundsException`

If `pos` equals `count`, then `-1` is returned to indicate end of file. Otherwise, the number `k` of bytes read is equal to the smaller of `len` and `count-pos`. If `k` is positive, then bytes `buffer[pos]` through `buffer[pos+k-1]` are copied into `b[off]` through `b[off+k-1]` in the manner performed by `System.arraycopy` (§20.18.16). The value `k` is added into `pos` and `k` is returned.

Overrides the `read` method of `InputStream` (§22.3.3).

22.7.7 `public long` **`skip`**`(long n)`

The actual number `k` of bytes to be skipped is equal to the smaller of `n` and `count-pos`. The value `k` is added into `pos` and `k` is returned.

Overrides the `skip` method of `InputStream` (§22.3.4).

22.7.8 `public int` **`available`**`()`

The quantity `count-pos` is returned.

Overrides the `available` method of `InputStream` (§22.3.5).

22.7.9 `public void` **`reset`**`()`

The value of `pos` is set to `0`.

Overrides the `reset` method of `InputStream` (§22.3.8).

22.8 The Class `java.io.SequenceInputStream`

A SequenceInputStream represents the logical concatenation of other input streams. It starts out with an ordered collection of input streams and reads from the first one until end of file is reached, whereupon it reads from the second one, and so on, until end of file is reached on the last of the contained input streams.

```
public class SequenceInputStream extends InputStream {
   public SequenceInputStream(Enumeration e);
   public SequenceInputStream(InputStream s1, InputStream s2);
   public int read() throws IOException;
   public int read(byte[] buf, int pos, int len)
      throws IOException, NullPointerException,
         IndexOutOfBoundsException;
   public void close() throws IOException;
}
```

22.8.1 `public SequenceInputStream(Enumeration e)`

This constructor initializes a newly created SequenceInputStream by remembering the argument, which must be an Enumeration (§21.1) that produces objects whose run-time type is InputStream (§22.3). The input streams that are produced by the enumeration will be read, in order, to provide the bytes to be read from this SequenceInputStream. After each input stream from the enumeration is exhausted, it is closed by calling its close method.

22.8.2 `public SequenceInputStream(InputStream s1, InputStream s2)`

This constructor initializes a newly created SequenceInputStream by remembering the two arguments, which will be read in order, first s1 and then s2, to provide the bytes to be read from this SequenceInputStream.

22.8.3 `public int read() throws IOException`

Implements the read method of InputStream (§22.3.1).

22.8.4 `public int` **`read`**`(byte[] buf, int pos, int len)`
`throws IOException, NullPointerException,`
`IndexOutOfBoundsException`

Overrides the `read` method of `InputStream` (§22.3.3).

22.8.5 `public void` **`close`**`() throws IOException`

This `SequenceInputStream` is closed. A closed `SequenceInputStream` cannot perform input operations and cannot be reopened.

If this stream was created from an enumeration, all remaining elements are requested from the enumeration and closed before the `close` method returns.

Overrides the `close` method of `InputStream` (§22.3.6).

22.9 The Class java.io.FilterInputStream

A FilterInputStream contains some other input stream, which it uses as its basic source of data, possibly transforming the data along the way or providing additional functionality. The class FilterInputStream itself simply overrides all methods of InputStream with versions that pass all requests to the contained input stream. Subclasses of FilterInputStream may further override some of these methods and may also provide additional methods and fields.

```
public class FilterInputStream extends InputStream {
    protected InputStream in;
    protected FilterInputStream(InputStream in);
    public int read() throws IOException;
    public int read(byte[] b)
        throws IOException, NullPointerException;
    public int read(byte[] b, int off, int len)
        throws IOException, NullPointerException,
            IndexOutOfBoundsException;
    public long skip(long n) throws IOException;
    public int available() throws IOException;
    public void close() throws IOException;
    public void mark(int readlimit);
    public void reset() throws IOException;
    public boolean markSupported();
}
```

22.9.1 protected InputStream in;

The input stream to be filtered.

22.9.2 protected FilterInputStream(InputStream in)

This constructor initializes a newly created FilterInputStream by assigning the argument in to the field this.in so as to remember it for later use.

22.9.3 public int read() throws IOException

This method simply performs in.read() and returns the result.

Implements the read method of InputStream (§22.3.1).

22.9.4 `public int read(byte[] b) throws IOException, NullPointerException`

This method simply performs the call `read(b, 0, b.length)` and returns the result. It is important that it does *not* do `in.read(b)` instead; certain subclasses of `FilterInputStream` depend on the implementation strategy actually used.

Overrides the `read` method of `InputStream` (§22.3.2).

22.9.5 `public int read(byte[] b, int off, int len) throws IOException, NullPointerException, IndexOutOfBoundsException`

This method simply performs `in.read(b, off, len)` and returns the result.

Overrides the `read` method of `InputStream` (§22.3.3).

22.9.6 `public long skip(long n) throws IOException`

This method simply performs `in.skip()` and returns the result.

Overrides the `skip` method of `InputStream` (§22.3.4).

22.9.7 `public int available() throws IOException`

This method simply performs `in.available()` and returns the result.

Overrides the `available` method of `InputStream` (§22.3.5).

22.9.8 `public void close() throws IOException`

This method simply performs `in.close()`.

Overrides the `close` method of `InputStream` (§22.3.6).

22.9.9 `public void mark(int readlimit)`

This method simply performs `in.mark()`.

Overrides the `mark` method of `InputStream` (§22.3.7).

22.9.10 `public void reset() throws IOException`

This method simply performs `in.reset()`.

Overrides the `reset` method of `InputStream` (§22.3.8).

22.9.11 `public boolean markSupported()`

This method simply performs `in.markSupported()` and returns whatever value is returned from that invocation.

Overrides the `markSupported` method of `InputStream` (§22.3.9).

22.10 The Class `java.io.BufferedInputStream`

A `BufferedInputStream` adds functionality to another input stream—namely, the ability to buffer the input and to support the `mark` and `reset` methods. When the `BufferedInputStream` is created, an internal buffer array is created. As bytes from the stream are read or skipped, the internal buffer is refilled as necessary from the contained input stream, many bytes at a time. The `mark` operation remembers a point in the input stream and the `reset` operation causes all the bytes read since the most recent `mark` operation to be reread before new bytes are taken from the contained input stream.

```
public class BufferedInputStream extends FilterInputStream {
    protected byte[] buf;
    protected int count = 0;
    protected int pos = 0;
    protected int markpos = -1;
    protected int marklimit = 0;
    public BufferedInputStream(InputStream in);
    public BufferedInputStream(InputStream in, int size);
    public int read() throws IOException;
    public int read(byte[] b)
        throws IOException, NullPointerException;
    public int read(byte[] b, int off, int len)
        throws IOException, NullPointerException,
            IndexOutOfBoundsException;
    public long skip(long n) throws IOException;
    public int available() throws IOException;
    public void mark(int readlimit);
    public void reset() throws IOException;
    public boolean markSupported();
}
```

22.10.1 `protected byte[] buf;`

The internal buffer array. When necessary, it may be replaced by another array of a different size.

22.10.2 `protected int count = 0;`

This value is always in the range `0` through `buf.length`; elements `buf[0]` through `buf[count-1]` contain buffered input data obtained from the underlying input stream.

22.10.3 `protected int` **`pos`** `= 0;`

This value is always in the range `0` through `count`. If it is less than `count`, then `buf[pos]` is the next byte to be supplied as input; if it is equal to `count`, then the next `read` or `skip` operation will require more bytes to be read from the contained input stream.

22.10.4 `protected int` **`markpos`** `= -1;`

This value is always in the range `-1` through `pos`. If there is no marked position in the input stream, this field is `-1`. If there is a marked position in the input stream, then `buf[markpos]` is the first byte to be supplied as input after a `reset` operation. If `markpos` is not `-1`, then all bytes from positions `buf[markpos]` through `buf[pos-1]` must remain in the buffer array (though they may be moved to another place in the buffer array, with suitable adjustments to the values of `count`, `pos`, and `markpos`); they may not be discarded unless and until the difference between `pos` and `markpos` exceeds `marklimit`.

22.10.5 `protected int` **`marklimit`**`;`

Whenever the difference between `pos` and `markpos` exceeds `marklimit`, then the mark may be dropped by setting `markpos` to `-1`.

22.10.6 `public` **`BufferedInputStream`**`(InputStream in)`

This constructor initializes a newly created `BufferedInputStream` by saving its argument, the input stream `in`, for later use. An internal buffer array is created and stored in `buf`.

22.10.7 `public` **`BufferedInputStream`**`(InputStream in, int size)`

This constructor initializes a newly created `BufferedInputStream` by saving its argument, the input stream `in`, for later use. An internal buffer array of length `size` is created and stored in `buf`.

22.10.8 `public int` **`read`**`() throws IOException`

See the general contract of the `read` method of `InputStream` (§22.3.1).

Overrides the `read` method of `FilterInputStream` (§22.9.3).

22.10.9 `public int read(byte[] b) throws IOException, NullPointerException`

See the general contract of the read method of InputStream (§22.3.2).

Overrides the read method of FilterInputStream (§22.9.4).

22.10.10 `public int read(byte[] b, int off, int len) throws IOException, NullPointerException, IndexOutOfBoundsException`

See the general contract of the read method of InputStream (§22.3.3).

Overrides the read method of FilterInputStream (§22.9.5).

22.10.11 `public long skip(long n) throws IOException`

See the general contract of the skip method of InputStream (§22.3.4).

Overrides the skip method of FilterInputStream (§22.9.6).

22.10.12 `public int available() throws IOException`

See the general contract of the available method of InputStream (§22.3.5).

Overrides the available method of FilterInputStream (§22.9.7).

22.10.13 `public void mark(int readlimit)`

The field marklimit is set equal to the argument and markpos is set equal to pos

Overrides the mark method of FilterInputStream (§22.9.9).

22.10.14 `public void reset() throws IOException`

See the general contract of the reset method of InputStream (§22.3.8).

If markpos is -1 (no mark has been set or the mark has been invalidated), an IOException is thrown. Otherwise, pos is set equal to markpos.

Overrides the reset method of FilterInputStream (§22.9.10).

22.10.15 `public boolean markSupported()`

This method returns `true` (a `BufferedInputStream` always supports `mark`).

Overrides the `markSupported` method of `FilterInputStream` (§22.9.11).

22.11 The Class java.io.DataInputStream

A data input stream provides facilities for reading bytes from an input source and interpreting specific character sequences as representing data of diverse types.

```
public class DataInputStream extends FilterInputStream
      implements DataInput {
   public DataInputStream(InputStream in);
   public final void readFully(byte[] b)
      throws IOException, NullPointerException;
   public final void readFully(byte[] b, int off, int len)
      throws IOException, NullPointerException,
         IndexOutOfBoundsException;
   public final int skipBytes(int n) throws IOException;
   public final boolean readBoolean() throws IOException;
   public final byte readByte() throws IOException;
   public final int readUnsignedByte() throws IOException;
   public final short readShort() throws IOException;
   public final int readUnsignedShort() throws IOException;
   public final char readChar() throws IOException;
   public final int readInt() throws IOException;
   public final long readLong() throws IOException;
   public final float readFloat() throws IOException;
   public final double readDouble() throws IOException;
   public final String readLine() throws IOException;
   public final String readUTF() throws IOException;
   public final static String readUTF(DataInput in)
      throws IOException;
}
```

22.11.1 public **DataInputStream**(InputStream in)

This constructor initializes a newly created DataInputStream by saving its argument, the input stream in, for later use.

22.11.2 public final void **readFully**(byte[] b) throws IOException, NullPointerException

See the general contract of the readFully method of DataInput (§22.1.1).

Bytes for this operation are read from the contained input stream.

22.11.3 `public final void` **`readFully`**`(byte[] b, int off, int len)`
`throws IOException, NullPointerException,`
`IndexOutOfBoundsException`

See the general contract of the `readFully` method of `DataInput` (§22.1.2).
Bytes for this operation are read from the contained input stream.

22.11.4 `public final int` **`skipBytes`**`(int n) throws IOException`

See the general contract of the `skipBytes` method of `DataInput` (§22.1.3).
Bytes for this operation are read from the contained input stream.

22.11.5 `public final boolean` **`readBoolean`**`() throws IOException`

See the general contract of the `readBoolean` method of `DataInput` (§22.1.4).
The byte for this operation is read from the contained input stream.

22.11.6 `public final byte` **`readByte`**`() throws IOException`

See the general contract of the `readByte` method of `DataInput` (§22.1.5).
The byte for this operation is read from the contained input stream.

22.11.7 `public final int` **`readUnsignedByte`**`() throws IOException`

See the general contract of the `readUnsignedByte` method of `DataInput` (§22.1.6).
The byte for this operation is read from the contained input stream.

22.11.8 `public final short` **`readShort`**`() throws IOException`

See the general contract of the `readShort` method of `DataInput` (§22.1.7).
Bytes for this operation are read from the contained input stream.

22.11.9 `public final int` **`readUnsignedShort`**`() throws IOException`

See the general contract of the `readUnsignedShort` method of `DataInput` (§22.1.8).
Bytes for this operation are read from the contained input stream.

22.11.10 `public final char` **`readChar`**`() throws IOException`

See the general contract of the `readChar` method of `DataInput` (§22.1.9).
Bytes for this operation are read from the contained input stream.

22.11.11 `public final int` **`readInt`**`() throws IOException`

See the general contract of the `readInt` method of `DataInput` (§22.1.10).
Bytes for this operation are read from the contained input stream.

22.11.12 `public final long` **`readLong`**`() throws IOException`

See the general contract of the `readLong` method of `DataInput` (§22.1.11).
Bytes for this operation are read from the contained input stream.

22.11.13 `public final float` **`readFloat`**`() throws IOException`

See the general contract of the `readFloat` method of `DataInput` (§22.1.12).
Bytes for this operation are read from the contained input stream.

22.11.14 `public final double` **`readDouble`**`() throws IOException`

See the general contract of the `readDouble` method of `DataInput` (§22.1.13).
Bytes for this operation are read from the contained input stream.

22.11.15 `public final String` **`readLine`**`() throws IOException`

See the general contract of the `readLine` method of `DataInput` (§22.1.14).
Bytes for this operation are read from the contained input stream.

22.11.16 `public final String` **`readUTF`**`() throws IOException`

See the general contract of the `readUTF` method of `DataInput` (§22.1.15).
Bytes for this operation are read from the contained input stream.

22.11.17 `public final static String` **`readUTF`**`(DataInput in)`
`throws IOException`

The `readUTF` method reads from the stream `in` a representation of a Unicode character string encoded in Java modified UTF-8 format; this string of characters is then returned as a `String`. The details of the modified UTF-8 representation are exactly the same as for the `readUTF` method of `DataInput` (§22.1.15).

22.12 The Class java.io.LineNumberInputStream

A LineNumberInputStream adds functionality to another input stream, namely the ability to count lines. When the LineNumberInputStream is created, the line number counter is set to zero. As bytes from the stream are read or skipped, the counter is incremented whenever a line terminator (\n, \r, or \r\n) is encountered. Such line terminators are also converted to a single '\n' character. The method getLineNumber returns the current value of the counter, and the method setLineNumber sets the counter to a given integer value. If the contained input stream supports the mark operation, then so does the LineNumberInputStream; the mark operation remembers the line number counter and the reset operation sets the counter to the value remembered by the mark operation.

```
public class LineNumberInputStream extends FilterInputStream {
    public LineNumberInputStream(InputStream in);
    public int read() throws IOException;
    public int read(byte[] b)
        throws IOException, NullPointerException;
    public int read(byte[] b, int off, int len)
        throws IOException, NullPointerException,
            IndexOutOfBoundsException;
    public long skip(long n) throws IOException;
    public int available() throws IOException;
    public void mark(int readlimit);
    public void reset() throws IOException;
    public int getLineNumber();
    public void setLineNumber(int lineNumber);
}
```

22.12.1 public LineNumberInputStream(InputStream in)

This constructor initializes a newly created LineNumberInputStream by saving its argument, the input stream in, for later use.

22.12.2 public int read() throws IOException

See the general contract of the read method of InputStream (§22.3.1).

As bytes are read from the contained input stream, line terminators are recognized and counted. For each line terminator recognized in the contained input stream, a single character '\n' is returned.

Overrides the read method of FilterInputStream (§22.9.3).

22.12.3 `public int read(byte[] b) throws IOException, NullPointerException`

See the general contract of the `read` method of `InputStream` (§22.3.2).

As bytes are read from the contained input stream, line terminators are recognized and counted. For each line terminator recognized in the contained input stream, a single character `'\n'` is returned.

Overrides the `read` method of `FilterInputStream` (§22.9.4).

22.12.4 `public int read(byte[] b, int off, int len) throws IOException, NullPointerException, IndexOutOfBoundsException`

See the general contract of the `read` method of `InputStream` (§22.3.3).

As bytes are read from the contained input stream, line terminators are recognized and counted. For each line terminator recognized in the contained input stream, a single character `'\n'` is returned.

Overrides the `read` method of `FilterInputStream` (§22.9.5).

22.12.5 `public long skip(long n) throws IOException`

See the general contract of the `skip` method of `InputStream` (§22.3.4).

As bytes are read from the contained input stream, line terminators are recognized and counted. Each line terminator recognized in the contained input stream is considered to be a single byte skipped, even if it is the sequence `\r\n`.

Overrides the `skip` method of `FilterInputStream` (§22.9.6).

22.12.6 `public int available() throws IOException`

See the general contract of the `available` method of `InputStream` (§22.3.5).

Note that if the contained input stream is able to supply k input characters without blocking, the `LineNumberInputStream` can guarantee only to provide $k/2$ characters without blocking, because the k characters from the contained input stream might consist of $k/2$ `\r\n` pairs, which will be converted to just $k/2$ `'\n'` characters.

Overrides the `available` method of `FilterInputStream` (§22.9.7).

22.12.7 `public void mark(int readlimit)`

See the general contract of the `mark` method of `InputStream` (§22.3.7).

Marking a point in the input stream remembers the current line number as it would be returned by `getLineNumber` (§22.12.9).

Overrides the `mark` method of `FilterInputStream` (§22.9.9).

22.12.8 `public void reset() throws IOException`

See the general contract of the `reset` method of `InputStream` (§22.3.8).

Resetting the input stream to a previous point also resets the line number to the value it had at the marked point.

Overrides the `reset` method of `FilterInputStream` (§22.9.10).

22.12.9 `public int getLineNumber()`

The current line number is returned. This quantity depends on k, the number of line terminators encountered since the most recent occurrence of one of the following three kinds of events:

- If a call to the `setLineNumber` method was most recent, let n be the argument that was given to `setLineNumber`; then the current line number is $n + k$.
- If a call to the `reset` method was most recent, let m be the line number that had been remembered by `mark`; then the current line number is $m + k$.
- If creation of the `LineNumberInputStream` was most recent (that is, neither of the other kinds of event have occurred), then the current line number is k.

These rules imply that the current line number is `0` as the characters of the first line are read, and becomes `1` after the line terminator for the first line has been read.

22.12.10 `public void setLineNumber(int lineNumber)`

The current line number is set equal to the argument.

22.13 The Class java.io.PushbackInputStream

A PushbackInputStream adds functionality to another input stream, namely the ability to "push back" or "unread" one byte. This is useful in situations where it is convenient for a fragment of code to read an indefinite number of data bytes that are delimited by a particular byte value; after reading the terminating byte, the code fragment can "unread" it, so that the next read operation on the input stream will reread the byte that was pushed back. For example, bytes representing the characters constituting an identifier might be terminated by a byte representing an operator character; a method whose job is to read just an identifier can read until it sees the operator and then push the operator back to be re-read.

```
public class PushbackInputStream extends FilterInputStream {
    protected int pushBack = -1;
    public PushbackInputStream(InputStream in);
    public int read() throws IOException;
    public int read(byte[] bytes, int offset, int length)
        throws IOException, NullPointerException,
            IndexOutOfBoundsException;
    public void unread(int ch) throws IOException;
    public int available() throws IOException;
    public boolean markSupported();
}
```

22.13.1 protected int pushBack = -1;

If this field has a nonnegative value, it is a byte that was pushed back. If this field is -1, there is currently no pushed-back byte.

22.13.2 public PushbackInputStream(InputStream in)

This constructor initializes a newly created PushbackInputStream by saving its argument, the input stream in, for later use. Initially, there is no pushed-back byte (the field pushBack is initialized to -1).

22.13.3 public int read() throws IOException

See the general contract of the read method of InputStream (§22.3.1).

If pushBack is not -1, the value of pushBack is returned and pushBack is set to -1. Otherwise, a byte is obtained from the contained input stream.

Overrides the read method of FilterInputStream (§22.9.3).

22.13.4 `public int read(byte[] bytes, int offset, int length) throws IOException, NullPointerException, IndexOutOfBoundsException`

See the general contract of the read method of InputStream (§22.3.3).

If pushBack is not -1, it is used as an input byte (and pushBack is set to -1) before any bytes are read from the contained input stream.

Overrides the read method of FilterInputStream (§22.9.5).

22.13.5 `public void unread(int b) throws IOException`

If pushBack is not -1, an IOException is thrown (it is not permitted to push back more than one byte). Otherwise, the byte value b is pushed back by assigning b to pushBack.

22.13.6 `public int available() throws IOException`

See the general contract of the available method of InputStream (§22.3.1).

This method first calls the available method of the contained input stream. If pushBack is -1, the result is returned; otherwise, the result plus 1 is returned.

Overrides the available method of FilterInputStream (§22.9.7).

22.13.7 `public boolean markSupported()`

This method returns false (a PushbackInputStream does not support mark).

22.14 The Class java.io.StreamTokenizer

A StreamTokenizer takes an input stream and parses it into "tokens," allowing the tokens to be read one at a time. The parsing process is controlled by a table and a number of flags that can be set to various states, allowing recognition of identifiers, numbers, quoted strings, and comments in a standard style.

```
public class StreamTokenizer {
    public static final int TT_EOF = -1;
    public static final int TT_EOL = '\n';
    public static final int TT_NUMBER = -2;
    public static final int TT_WORD = -3;
    public int ttype;
    public String sval;
    public double nval;
    public StreamTokenizer(InputStream in);
    public void resetSyntax();
    public void wordChars(int low, int hi);
    public void whitespaceChars(int low, int hi);
    public void ordinaryChars(int low, int hi);
    public void ordinaryChar(int ch);
    public void commentChar(int ch);
    public void quoteChar(int ch);
    public void parseNumbers();
    public void eolIsSignificant(boolean flag);
    public void slashStarComments(boolean flag);
    public void slashSlashComments(boolean flag);
    public void lowerCaseMode(boolean flag);
    public int nextToken() throws IOException;
    public void pushBack();
    public int lineno();
    public String toString();
}
```

Each byte read from the input stream is regarded as a character in the range '\u0000' through '\u00FF'. The character value is used to look up five possible attributes of the character: whitespace, alphabetic, numeric, string quote, and comment character (a character may have more than one of these attributes, or none at all). In addition, there are three flags controlling whether line terminators are to be recognized as tokens, whether Java-style end-of-line comments that start with // should be recognized and skipped, and whether Java-style "traditional" comments delimited by /* and */ should be recognized and skipped. One more flag controls whether all the characters of identifiers are converted to lowercase.

Here is a simple example of the use of a StreamTokenizer. The following code merely reads all the tokens in the standard input stream and prints an identification of each one. Changes in the line number are also noted.

```
import java.io.StreamTokenizer;

import java.io.IOException;

class Tok {
   public static void main(String[] args) {
      StreamTokenizer st = new StreamTokenizer(System.in);
      st.ordinaryChar('/');
      int lineNum = -1;
      try {
         for (int tokenType = st.nextToken();
               tokenType != StreamTokenizer.TT_EOF;
               tokenType = st.nextToken()) {
            int newLineNum = st.lineno();
            if (newLineNum != lineNum) {
               System.out.println("[line " + newLineNum
                                 + "]");
               lineNum = newLineNum;
            }
            switch(tokenType) {
            case StreamTokenizer.TT_NUMBER:
               System.out.println("the number " + st.nval);
               break;
            case StreamTokenizer.TT_WORD:
               System.out.println("identifier " + st.sval);
               break;
            default:
               System.out.println("  operator "
                                 + (char)tokenType);
            }
         }
      } catch (IOException e) {
         System.out.println("I/O failure");
      }
   }
}
```

If the input stream contains this data:

```
10 LET A = 4.5
20 LET B = A*A
30 PRINT A, B
```

then the resulting output is:

```
[line 1]
the number 10.0
identifier LET
```

```
identifier A
  operator =
the number 4.5
[line 2]
the number 20.0
identifier LET
identifier B
  operator =
identifier A
  operator *
identifier A
[line 3]
the number 30.0
identifier PRINT
identifier A
  operator ,
identifier B
```

22.14.1 `public static final int` **`TT_EOF`** `= -1;`

A constant that indicates end of file was reached.

22.14.2 `public static final int` **`TT_EOL`** `= '\n';`

A constant that indicates that a line terminator was recognized.

22.14.3 `public static final int` **`TT_NUMBER`** `= -2;`

A constant that indicates that a number was recognized.

22.14.4 `public static final int` **`TT_WORD`** `= -3;`

A constant that indicates that a word (identifier) was recognized.

22.14.5 `public int` **`ttype`**`;`

The type of the token that was last recognized by this `StreamTokenizer`. This will be `TT_EOF`, `TT_EOL`, `TT_NUMBER`, `TT_WORD`, or a nonnegative byte value that was the first byte of the token (for example, if the token is a string token, then `ttype` has the quote character that started the string).

22.14.6 `public String sval;`

If the value of `ttype` is `TT_WORD` or a string quote character, then the value of `sval` is a `String` that contains the characters of the identifier or of the string (without the delimiting string quotes). For all other types of tokens recognized, the value of `sval` is `null`.

22.14.7 `public double nval;`

If the value of `ttype` is `TT_NUMBER`, then the value of `nval` is the numerical value of the number.

22.14.8 `public StreamTokenizer(InputStream in)`

This constructor initializes a newly created `StreamTokenizer` by saving its argument, the input stream `in`, for later use. The `StreamTokenizer` is also initialized to the following default state:

- All byte values `'A'` through `'Z'`, `'a'` through `'z'`, and `0xA0` through `0xFF` are considered to be alphabetic.
- All byte values `0x00` through `0x20` are considered to be whitespace.
- `'/'` is a comment character.
- Single quote `'\''` and double quote `'"'` are string quote characters.
- Numbers are parsed.
- End of line is not significant.
- `//` comments and `/*` comments are not recognized.

22.14.9 `public void resetSyntax()`

The syntax table for this `StreamTokenizer` is reset so that every byte value is "ordinary"; thus, no character is recognized as being a whitespace, alphabetic, numeric, string quote, or comment character. Calling this method is therefore equivalent to:

```
ordinaryChars(0x00, 0xff)
```

The three flags controlling recognition of line terminators, `//` comments, and `/*` comments are unaffected.

22.14.10 public void **wordChars**(int low, int hi)

The syntax table for this StreamTokenizer is modified so that every character in the range low through hi has the "alphabetic" attribute.

22.14.11 public void **whitespaceChars**(int low, int hi)

The syntax table for this StreamTokenizer is modified so that every character in the range low through hi has the "whitespace" attribute.

22.14.12 public void **ordinaryChars**(int low, int hi)

The syntax table for this StreamTokenizer is modified so that every character in the range low through hi has no attributes.

22.14.13 public void **ordinaryChar**(int ch)

The syntax table for this StreamTokenizer is modified so that the character ch has no attributes.

22.14.14 public void **commentChar**(int ch)

The syntax table for this StreamTokenizer is modified so that the character ch has the "comment character" attribute.

22.14.15 public void **quoteChar**(int ch)

The syntax table for this StreamTokenizer is modified so that the character ch has the "string quote" attribute.

22.14.16 public void **parseNumbers**()

The syntax table for this StreamTokenizer is modified so that each of the twelve characters

```
0 1 2 3 4 5 6 7 8 9 . -
```

has the "numeric" attribute.

22.14.17 public void **eolIsSignificant**(boolean flag)

This StreamTokenizer henceforth recognizes line terminators as tokens if and only if the flag argument is true.

22.14.18 public void **slashStarComments**(boolean flag)

This StreamTokenizer henceforth recognizes and skips Java-style "traditional" comments, which are delimited by /* and */ and do not nest, if and only if the flag argument is true.

22.14.19 public void **slashSlashComments**(boolean flag)

This StreamTokenizer henceforth recognizes and skips Java-style end-of-line comments that start with // if and only if the flag argument is true.

22.14.20 public void **lowerCaseMode**(boolean flag)

This StreamTokenizer henceforth converts all the characters in identifiers to lowercase if and only if the flag argument is true.

22.14.21 public int **nextToken**() throws IOException

If the previous token was pushed back (§22.14.22), then the value of ttype is returned, effectively causing that same token to be reread.

Otherwise, this method parses the next token in the contained input stream. The type of the token is returned; this same value is also made available in the ttype field, and related data may be made available in the sval and nval fields.

First, whitespace characters are skipped, except that if a line terminator is encountered and this StreamTokenizer is currently recognizing line terminators, then the type of the token is TT_EOL.

If a numeric character is encountered, then an attempt is made to recognize a number. If the first character is '-' and the next character is not numeric, then the '-' is considered to be an ordinary character and is recognized as a token in its own right. Otherwise, a number is parsed, stopping before the next occurrence of '-', the second occurrence of '.', the first nonnumeric character encountered, or end of file, whichever comes first. The type of the token is TT_NUMBER and its value is made available in the field nval.

If an alphabetic character is encountered, then an identifier is recognized, consisting of that character and all following characters up to, but not including, the first character that is neither alphabetic nor numeric, or up to end of file, whichever comes first. The characters of the identifier may be converted to lowercase if this `StreamTokenizer` is in lowercase mode.

If a comment character is encountered, then all subsequent characters are skipped and ignored, up to but not including the next line terminator or end of file. Then another attempt is made to recognize a token. If this `StreamTokenizer` is currently recognizing line terminators, then a line terminator that ends a comment will be recognized as a token in the same manner as any other line terminator in the contained input stream.

If a string quote character is encountered, then a string is recognized, consisting of all characters after (but not including) the string quote character, up to (but not including) the next occurrence of that same string quote character, or a line terminator, or end of file. The usual escape sequences (§3.10.6) such as `\n` and `\t` are recognized and converted to single characters as the string is parsed.

If `//` is encountered and this `StreamTokenizer` is currently recognizing `//` comments, then all subsequent characters are skipped and ignored, up to but not including the next line terminator or end of file. Then another attempt is made to recognize a token. (If this `StreamTokenizer` is currently recognizing line terminators, then a line terminator that ends a comment will be recognized as a token in the same manner as any other line terminator in the contained input stream.)

If `/*` is encountered and this `StreamTokenizer` is currently recognizing `/*` comments, then all subsequent characters are skipped and ignored, up to and including the next occurrence of `*/` or end of file. Then another attempt is made to recognize a token.

If none of the cases listed above applies, then the only other possibility is that the first non-whitespace character encountered is an ordinary character. That character is considered to be a token and is stored in the `ttype` field and returned.

22.14.22 `public void` **`pushBack()`**

Calling this method "pushes back" the current token; that is, it causes the next call to `nextToken` to return the same token that it just provided. Note that this method does *not* restore the line number to its previous value, so if the method `lineno` is called after a call to `pushBack` but before the next call to `nextToken`, an incorrect line number may be returned.

22.14.23 `public int lineno()`

The number of the line on which the current token appeared is returned. The first token in the input stream, if not a line terminator, is considered to appear on line `1`. A line terminator token is considered to appear on the line that it precedes, not on the line it terminates; thus, the first line terminator in the input stream is considered to be on line `2`.

22.14.24 `public String toString()`

The current token and the current line number are converted to a string of the form:

```
"Token[x], line m"
```

where *m* is the current line number in decimal form and *x* depends on the type of the current token:

- If the token type is `TT_EOF`, then *x* is "`EOF`".
- If the token type is `TT_EOL`, then *x* is "`EOL`".
- If the token type is `TT_WORD`, then *x* is the current value of `sval` (§22.14.6).
- If the token type is `TT_NUMBER`, then *x* is "`n=`" followed by the result of converting the current value of `nval` (§22.14.7) to a string (§20.10.15).

Overrides the `toString` method of `Object` (§20.1.2).

22.15 The Class java.io.OutputStream

An output stream accepts output bytes and sends them to some sink.

```
public abstract class OutputStream {
    public abstract void write(int b) throws IOException;
    public void write(byte[] b)
        throws IOException, NullPointerException;
    public void write(byte[] b, int off, int len)
        throws IOException, NullPointerException,
            IndexOutOfBoundsException;
    public void flush() throws IOException;
    public void close() throws IOException;
}
```

22.15.1 public abstract void write(int b) throws IOException

The general contract for write is that one byte is written to the output stream. The byte to be written is the eight low-order bits of the argument b. The 24 high-order bits of b are ignored.

If the byte cannot be written for any reason, an IOException is thrown. In particular, an IOException may be thrown if the output stream has been closed (§22.15.5).

22.15.2 public void write(byte[] b) throws IOException, NullPointerException

The general contract for write(b) is that it should have exactly the same effect as the call write(b, 0, b.length) (§22.15.3).

The write(b) method for class OutputStream in fact makes such a call.

22.15.3 public void write(byte[] b, int off, int len) throws IOException, NullPointerException, IndexOutOfBoundsException

The general contract for write(b, off, len) is that some of the bytes in the array b are written to the output stream as if one at a time, in order; element b[off] is the first byte written and b[off+len-1] is the last byte written by this operation.

If b is null, a NullPointerException is thrown.

If `off` is negative, or `len` is negative, or `off+len` is greater than the length of the array `b`, then an `IndexOutOfBoundsException` is thrown.

If the byte cannot be written for any reason, an `IOException` is thrown. In particular, an `IOException` is thrown if the output stream has been closed (§22.15.5).

The `write(b, off, len)` method for class `OutputStream` simply calls the method `write` (§22.15.1) repeatedly, once for each byte in `b` to be written.

22.15.4 `public void flush() throws IOException`

The general contract of `flush` is that calling it is an indication that, if any bytes previously written have been buffered by the implementation of the output stream, such bytes should immediately be written to their intended destination.

The `flush` method for class `OutputStream` does nothing and simply returns.

22.15.5 `public void close() throws IOException`

The general contract of `close` is that it closes the output stream. A closed stream cannot perform output operations and cannot be reopened.

The `close` method for class `OutputStream` does nothing and simply returns.

22.16 The Class java.io.FileOutputStream

A file output stream writes output bytes to a file in a file system. What files are available or may be created depends on the host environment.

```
public class FileOutputStream extends OutputStream {
    public FileOutputStream(String path)
        throws SecurityException, FileNotFoundException;
    public FileOutputStream(File file)
        throws SecurityException, FileNotFoundException;
    public FileOutputStream(FileDescriptor fdObj)
        throws SecurityException;
    public final FileDescriptor getFD() throws IOException;
    public void write(int b) throws IOException;
    public void write(byte[] b)
        throws IOException, NullPointerException;
    public void write(byte[] b, int off, int len)
        throws IOException, NullPointerException,
            IndexOutOfBoundsException;
    public void close() throws IOException;
    protected void finalize() throws IOException;
}
```

22.16.1 public FileOutputStream(String path) throws SecurityException, FileNotFoundException

This constructor initializes a newly created `FileOutputStream` by opening a connection to an actual file, the file named by the path name `path` in the file system. A new `FileDescriptor` object is created to represent this file connection.

First, if there is a security manager, its `checkWrite` method (§20.17.21) is called with the `path` argument as its argument.

If the actual file cannot be opened, a `FileNotFoundException` is thrown.

22.16.2 public FileOutputStream(File file) throws SecurityException, FileNotFoundException

This constructor initializes a newly created `FileOutputStream` by opening a connection to an actual file, the file named by `file` in the file system. A new `FileDescriptor` object is created to represent this file connection.

First, if there is a security manager, its `checkWrite` method (§20.17.21) is called with the path represented by the `file` argument as its argument.

If the actual file cannot be opened, a `FileNotFoundException` is thrown.

22.16.3 `public FileOutputStream(FileDescriptor fdObj) throws SecurityException`

This constructor initializes a newly created `FileOutputStream` by using the file descriptor `fdObj`, which represents an existing connection to an actual file in the file system.

First, if there is a security manager, its `checkWrite` method (§20.17.20) is called with the file descriptor `fdObj` argument as its argument.

22.16.4 `public final FileDescriptor getFD() throws IOException`

This method returns the `FileDescriptor` object (§22.26) that represents the connection to the actual file in the file system being used by this `FileOutputStream`.

22.16.5 `public void write(int b) throws IOException`

The byte for this operation is written to the actual file to which this file output stream is connected.

Implements the `write` method of `OutputStream` (§22.15.1).

22.16.6 `public void write(byte[] b) throws IOException, NullPointerException`

Bytes for this operation are written to the actual file to which this file output stream is connected.

Overrides the `write` method of `OutputStream` (§22.15.2).

22.16.7 `public void write(byte[] b, int off, int len) throws IOException, NullPointerException, IndexOutOfBoundsException`

Bytes for this operation are written to the actual file to which this file output stream is connected.

Overrides the `write` method of `OutputStream` (§22.15.3).

22.16.8 `public void close() throws IOException`

This file output stream is closed and may no longer be used for writing bytes.

Overrides the `close` method of `OutputStream` (§22.15.5).

22.16.9 `protected void finalize() throws IOException`

A `FileOutputStream` uses finalization to clean up the connection to the actual file.

22.17 The Class java.io.PipedOutputStream

A piped output stream should be connected to a piped input stream; the piped input stream then provides whatever data bytes are written to the piped output stream. Typically, data is written to a PipeOutputStream object by one thread and data is read from the corresponding PipedInputStream (§22.5) by some other thread. Attempting to use both objects from a single thread is not recommended, as it may deadlock the thread.

```
public class PipedOutputStream extends OutputStream {
    public PipedOutputStream(PipedInputStream snk)
        throws IOException;
    public PipedOutputStream();
    public void connect(PipedInputStream snk)
        throws IOException;
    public void write(int b) throws IOException;
    public void write(byte[] b, int off, int len)
        throws IOException, NullPointerException,
            IndexOutOfBoundsException;
    public void close() throws IOException;
}
```

22.17.1 public PipedOutputStream(PipedInputStream snk) throws IOException

This constructor initializes a newly created PipedOutputStream so that it is connected to the piped input stream snk. Data bytes written to this stream will then be available as input from snk.

22.17.2 public PipedOutputStream()

This constructor initializes a newly created PipedOutputStream so that it is not yet connected. It must be connected to a PipedInputStream before being used.

22.17.3 public void connect(PipedInputStream snk) throws IOException

The connect method causes this piped output stream to be connected to the piped input stream snk. If this object is already connected to some other piped input stream, an IOException is thrown.

If snk is an unconnected piped input stream and src is an unconnected piped output stream, they may be connected by either the call:

```
src.connect(snk)
```

or the call:

```
snk.connect(src)
```

The two calls have the same effect.

22.17.4 public void **write**(int b) throws IOException

If a thread was reading data bytes from the connected piped input stream, but the thread is no longer alive, then an IOException is thrown.

Implements the write method of OutputStream (§22.15.1).

22.17.5 public void **write**(byte[] b, int off, int len) throws IOException, NullPointerException, IndexOutOfBoundsException

If a thread was reading data bytes from the connected piped input stream, but the thread is no longer alive, then an IOException is thrown.

Overrides the write method of OutputStream (§22.15.3).

22.17.6 public void **close**() throws IOException

This piped output stream is closed and may no longer be used for writing bytes.

Overrides the close method of OutputStream (§22.15.5).

22.18 The Class java.io.ByteArrayOutputStream

A ByteArrayOutputStream contains an internal buffer that accumulates all the bytes written to the stream since its creation or the most recent call to the **reset** method. At any point, the bytes written to the stream so far may be retrieved in the form of an array of bytes or a String. The bytes written so far may also be copied to some other output stream. The size method returns the number of characters written so far.

```
public class ByteArrayOutputStream extends OutputStream {
    protected byte[] buf;
    protected int count;
    public ByteArrayOutputStream();
    public ByteArrayOutputStream(int size);
    public void write(int b);
    public void write(byte[] b, int off, int len)
        throws NullPointerException, IndexOutOfBoundsException;
    public int size();
    public void reset();
    public byte[] toByteArray();
    public String toString();
    public String toString(int hibyte);
    public void writeTo(OutputStream out) throws IOException;
}
```

22.18.1 protected byte[] **buf**;

An internal array of bytes. Elements buf[0] through buf[count-1] are the bytes that have been written to the stream since its creation or the last reset (§22.18.8) operation.

22.18.2 protected int **count**;

This value should always be nonnegative. It is the number of bytes that have been written to the stream since its creation or the last reset (§22.18.8) operation.

22.18.3 public **ByteArrayOutputStream**()

This constructor initializes a newly created ByteArrayOutputStream so that its internal buffer array has length 32.

22.18.4 public **ByteArrayOutputStream**(int size)

This constructor initializes a newly created ByteArrayOutputStream so that its internal buffer array has length size. This matters only for reasons of efficiency; the buffer array is replaced by a larger one whenever necessary to accommodate additional bytes written to the stream.

22.18.5 public void **write**(int b)

One byte is added on the internal buffer. The byte to be added is the eight low-order bits of the argument n. The 24 high-order bits of n are ignored.

Implements the write method of OutputStream (§22.15.1).

22.18.6 public void **write**(byte[] b, int off, int len)

```
throws NullPointerException,
    IndexOutOfBoundsException
```

Elements b[off] through b[off+len-1] are appended to the internal buffer.

If b is null, a NullPointerException is thrown.

If off is negative, or len is negative, or off+len is greater than the length of the array b, then an IndexOutOfBoundsException is thrown.

Overrides the write method of OutputStream (§22.15.3).

22.18.7 public int **size**()

The current value of count is returned.

22.18.8 public void **reset**()

The internal variable count is reset to zero, thereby logically discarding all bytes written to the stream so far. However, the internal buffer array, which may be quite large, remains as it is.

22.18.9 public byte[] **toByteArray**()

A new array of bytes is created and returned. Its length is equal to the current value of count. Its initial contents are copies of the bytes written to the stream so far—that is, elements 0 through count-1 of buf.

22.18.10 `public String toString()`

A new `String` is created and returned. Its length is equal to the current value of `count`. Its initial contents are copies of the bytes written to the stream so far—that is, elements `0` through `count-1` of `buf`, zero-extended to produce characters. Thus, `tostring()` has the same effect as `toString(0)` (§22.18.11).

Overrides the `toString` method of `Object` (§20.1.2).

22.18.11 `public String toString(int hibyte)`

A new array of bytes is created and returned. Its length is equal to the current value of `count`. Its initial contents are copies of the bytes written to the stream so far—that is, elements `0` through `count-1` of `buf`—with `hibyte` supplying the high-order eight bits of each character. Thus, character `k` of the result is equal to:

```
((hibyte & 0xff) << 8) | (buf[k] & 0xff)
```

See the `String` constructor that accepts a `hibyte` argument (§20.12.6).

22.18.12 `public void writeTo(OutputStream out) throws IOException`

The current contents of the internal buffer are written to the output stream `out` by the call:

```
out.write(buf, 0, count)
```

Note that if `out` is the same as `this`, the effect is simply to append to the buffer a copy of its current contents, thereby doubling the number of buffered bytes. This may not be a particularly useful effect; the point is merely that the operation does terminate, having had a sensible effect, rather than running off into an endless loop.

22.19 The Class java.io.FilterOutputStream

A FilterOutputStream contains some other output stream, which it uses as its basic sink of data, possibly transforming the data along the way or providing additional functionality. The class FilterOutputStream itself simply overrides all methods of OutputStream with versions that pass all requests to the contained output stream. Subclasses of FilterOutputStream may further override some of these methods and may also provide additional methods and fields.

```
public class FilterOutputStream extends OutputStream {
    protected OutputStream out;
    public FilterOutputStream(OutputStream out);
    public void write(int b) throws IOException;
    public void write(byte[] b)
        throws IOException, NullPointerException;
    public void write(byte[] b, int off, int len)
        throws IOException, NullPointerException,
            IndexOutOfBoundsException;
    public void flush() throws IOException;
    public void close() throws IOException;
}
```

22.19.1 protected OutputStream **out**;

The output stream to be filtered.

22.19.2 public **FilterOutputStream**(OutputStream out)

This constructor initializes a newly created FilterInputStream by assigning the argument out to the field this.out so as to remember it for later use.

22.19.3 public void **write**(int b) throws IOException

This method simply performs out.write(b).

Implements the abstract write method of OutputStream (§22.15.1).

22.19.4 public void **write**(byte[] b) throws IOException, NullPointerException

This method simply performs out.write(b).

Overrides the write method of OutputStream (§22.15.2).

22.19.5 `public void **write**(byte[] b, int off, int len) throws IOException, NullPointerException, IndexOutOfBoundsException`

This method simply performs `out.write(b, off, len)`.

Overrides the `write` method of `OutputStream` (§22.15.3).

22.19.6 `public void **flush**() throws IOException`

This method simply performs `out.flush()`.

Overrides the `flush` method of `OutputStream` (§22.15.4).

22.19.7 `public void **close**() throws IOException`

This method simply performs `out.close()`.

Overrides the `close` method of `OutputStream` (§22.15.5).

22.20 The Class java.io.BufferedOutputStream

A BufferedOutputStream adds functionality to another output stream, namely the ability to buffer the output. When the BufferedOutputStream is created, an internal buffer array is created. As bytes are written to the stream, they are stored in the internal buffer, which is flushed as necessary, thereby performing output to the contained output stream in large blocks rather than a byte at a time.

```
public class BufferedOutputStream extends FilterOutputStream {
    protected byte[] buf;
    protected int count;
    public BufferedOutputStream(OutputStream out);
    public BufferedOutputStream(OutputStream out, int size);
    public void write(int b) throws IOException;
    public void write(byte[] b)
        throws IOException, NullPointerException;
    public void write(byte[] b, int off, int len)
        throws IOException, NullPointerException,
            IndexOutOfBoundsException;
    public void flush() throws IOException;
}
```

22.20.1 protected byte[] **buf**;

The internal buffer array.

22.20.2 protected int **count**;

This value is always in the range 0 through buf.length; elements buf[0] through buf[count-1] contain valid byte data.

22.20.3 public **BufferedOutputStream**(OutputStream out)

This constructor initializes a newly created BufferedOutputStream by saving its argument, the input stream out, for later use. An internal buffer array is created and stored in buf.

22.20.4 `public` **`BufferedOutputStream`**`(OutputStream out, int size)`

This constructor initializes a newly created `BufferedOutputStream` by saving its argument, the input stream `out`, for later use. An internal buffer array of length `size` is created and stored in `buf`.

22.20.5 `public void` **`write`**`(int b) throws IOException`

See the general contract of the `write` method of `OutputStream` (§22.15.1).
Overrides the `write` method of `FilterOutputStream` (§22.19.3).

22.20.6 `public void` **`write`**`(byte[] b)`
`throws IOException, NullPointerException`

See the general contract of the `write` method of `OutputStream` (§22.15.2).
Overrides the `write` method of `FilterOutputStream` (§22.19.4).

22.20.7 `public void` **`write`**`(byte[] b, int off, int len)`
`throws IOException, NullPointerException,`
`IndexOutOfBoundsException`

See the general contract of the `write` method of `OutputStream` (§22.15.3).
Overrides the `write` method of `FilterOutputStream` (§22.19.5).

22.20.8 `public void` **`flush`**`() throws IOException`

See the general contract of the `flush` method of `OutputStream` (§22.15.4).
Overrides the `flush` method of `FilterOutputStream` (§22.19.6).

22.21 The Class java.io.DataOutputStream

A data output stream provides facilities for converting data of diverse types into character sequence of specific formats that are then sent to some output stream.

```
public class DataOutputStream extends FilterOutputStream
      implements DataOutput {
   protected int written;
   public DataOutputStream(OutputStream out);
   public void write(int b) throws IOException;
   public void write(byte[] b, int off, int len)
      throws IOException, NullPointerException,
         IndexOutOfBoundsException;
   public void flush() throws IOException;
   public final void writeBoolean(boolean v) throws IOException;
   public final void writeByte(int v) throws IOException;
   public final void writeShort(int v) throws IOException;
   public final void writeChar(int v) throws IOException;
   public final void writeInt(int v) throws IOException;
   public final void writeLong(long v) throws IOException;
   public final void writeFloat(float v) throws IOException;
   public final void writeDouble(double v) throws IOException;
   public final void writeBytes(String s)
      throws IOException, NullPointerException;
   public final void writeChars(String s)
      throws IOException, NullPointerException;
   public final void writeUTF(String str)
      throws IOException, NullPointerException;
   public final int size();
}
```

22.21.1 protected int **written**;

This field contains the number of bytes written to the stream so far.

22.21.2 public **DataOutputStream**(OutputStream out)

This constructor initializes a newly created `DataOutputStream` by saving its argument, the output stream `out`, for later use. The counter `written` is set to zero.

22.21.3 `public void write(int b) throws IOException`

The byte for this operation (the low eight bits of the argument b) is written to the contained output stream. If no exception is thrown, the counter written is incremented by 1.

Implements the write method of OutputStream (§22.15.1).

22.21.4 `public void write(byte[] b, int off, int len) throws IOException, NullPointerException, IndexOutOfBoundsException`

Bytes for this operation are written to the contained output stream. If no exception is thrown, the counter written is incremented by len.

Overrides the write method of OutputStream (§22.15.3).

22.21.5 `public void flush() throws IOException`

The contained output stream is flushed.

Overrides the flush method of OutputStream (§22.15.4).

22.21.6 `public final void writeBoolean(boolean v) throws IOException`

See the general contract of the writeBoolean method of DataOutput (§22.2.4).

The byte for this operation is written to the contained output stream. If no exception is thrown, the counter written is incremented by 1.

22.21.7 `public final void writeByte(int v) throws IOException`

See the general contract of the writeByte method of DataOutput (§22.2.5).

The byte for this operation is written to the contained output stream. If no exception is thrown, the counter written is incremented by 1.

22.21.8 `public final void writeShort(int v) throws IOException`

See the general contract of the writeShort method of DataOutput (§22.2.6).

Bytes for this operation are written to the contained output stream. If no exception is thrown, the counter written is incremented by 2.

22.21.9 `public final void writeChar(int v) throws IOException`

See the general contract of the `writeChar` method of `DataOutput` (§22.2.7).

Bytes for this operation are written to the contained output stream. If no exception is thrown, the counter `written` is incremented by `2`.

22.21.10 `public final void writeInt(int v) throws IOException`

See the general contract of the `writeInt` method of `DataOutput` (§22.2.8).

Bytes for this operation are written to the contained output stream. If no exception is thrown, the counter `written` is incremented by `4`.

22.21.11 `public final void writeLong(long v) throws IOException`

See the general contract of the `writeLong` method of `DataOutput` (§22.2.9).

Bytes for this operation are written to the contained output stream. If no exception is thrown, the counter `written` is incremented by `8`.

22.21.12 `public final void writeFloat(float v) throws IOException`

See the general contract of the `writeFloat` method of `DataOutput` (§22.2.10).

Bytes for this operation are written to the contained output stream. If no exception is thrown, the counter `written` is incremented by `4`.

22.21.13 `public final void writeDouble(double v) throws IOException`

See the general contract of the `writeDouble` method of `DataOutput` (§22.2.11).

Bytes for this operation are written to the contained output stream. If no exception is thrown, the counter `written` is incremented by `8`.

22.21.14 `public final void writeBytes(String s) throws IOException, NullPointerException, IndexOutOfBoundsException`

See the general contract of the `writeBytes` method of `DataOutput` (§22.2.12).

Bytes for this operation are written to the contained output stream. If no exception is thrown, the counter `written` is incremented by the length of `s`.

22.21.15 `public final void` **`writeChars`**`(String s)`
```
        throws IOException, NullPointerException,
            IndexOutOfBoundsException
```

See the general contract of the `writeChars` method of `DataOutput` (§22.2.13).

Bytes for this operation are written to the contained output stream. If no exception is thrown, the counter `written` is incremented by twice the length of `s`.

22.21.16 `public final void` **`writeUTF`**`(String str)`
```
        throws IOException, NullPointerException,
            IndexOutOfBoundsException
```

See the general contract of the `writeUTF` method of `DataOutput` (§22.2.14).

Bytes for this operation are written to the contained output stream. If no exception is thrown, the counter `written` is incremented by the total number of bytes written to the output stream. This will be at least two plus the length of `s`, and at most two plus thrice the length of `s`.

22.21.17 `public final int` **`size`**`()`

The `size` method returns the current value of the counter `written`, the number of bytes written to the stream so far.

22.22 The Class java.io.PrintStream

A PrintStream adds functionality to another output stream—namely, the ability to print representations of various data values conveniently. Two other features are provided as well. Unlike other output streams, a PrintStream never throws an IOException; instead, exceptional situations merely set an internal flag that can be tested by the checkError method. Optionally, a PrintStream can be created so as to "autoflush"; this means that after an array of bytes is written, or after a single byte equal to '\n' is written, the flush method is automatically invoked.

```
public class PrintStream extends FilterOutputStream {
    public PrintStream(OutputStream out);
    public PrintStream(OutputStream out, boolean autoflush);
    public void write(int b);
    public void write(byte[] b, int off, int len)
        throws NullPointerException, IndexOutOfBoundsException;
    public void flush();
    public void close();
    public boolean checkError();
    public void print(Object obj);
    public void print(String s);
    public void print(char[] s) throws NullPointerException;
    public void print(boolean b);
    public void print(char c);
    public void print(int i);
    public void print(long l);
    public void print(float f);
    public void print(double d);
    public void println();
    public void println(Object obj);
    public void println(String s);
    public void println(char[] s) throws NullPointerException;
    public void println(boolean b);
    public void println(char c);
    public void println(int i);
    public void println(long l);
    public void println(float f);
    public void println(double d);
}
```

22.22.1 `public PrintStream(OutputStream out)`

This constructor initializes a newly created `PrintStream` by saving its argument, the output stream `out`, for later use. This stream will not autoflush.

22.22.2 `public PrintStream(OutputStream out, boolean autoflush)`

This constructor initializes a newly created `PrintStream` by saving its argument, the output stream `out`, for later use. This stream will autoflush if and only if `autoflush` is `true`.

22.22.3 `public void write(int b)`

See the general contract of the `write` method of `OutputStream` (§22.15.1).

Overrides the `write` method of `FilterOutputStream` (§22.19.3).

22.22.4 `public void write(byte[] b, int off, int len)`

```
        throws NullPointerException,
            IndexOutOfBoundsException
```

See the general contract of the `write` method of `OutputStream` (§22.15.3).

Overrides the `write` method of `FilterOutputStream` (§22.19.5).

22.22.5 `public void flush()`

See the general contract of the `flush` method of `OutputStream` (§22.15.4).

Overrides the `flush` method of `FilterOutputStream` (§22.19.6).

22.22.6 `public void close()`

See the general contract of the `close` method of `OutputStream` (§22.15.5).

Overrides the `close` method of `FilterOutputStream` (§22.19.7).

22.22.7 `public boolean checkError()`

The result is `true` if and only if this output stream has ever encountered any kind of trouble—that is, if any operation on the contained output stream has ever resulted in an `IOException` other than an `InterruptedIOException`. If an operation on the contained output stream throws an `InterruptedIOException`, then the `PrintStream` class converts the exception back to an interrupt by doing:

```
Thread.currentThread().interrupt();
```

or the equivalent.

22.22.8 public void **print**(Object obj)

The low-order bytes of the characters in the `String` that would be produced by `String.valueOf(obj)` (§20.12.38) are written, in order, to the contained output stream in exactly the manner of the `write` method (§22.22.3).

22.22.9 public void **print**(String s)

The low-order bytes of the characters in the string `s` are written, in order, to the contained output stream in exactly the manner of the `write` method (§22.22.3). If `s` is `null`, then the low-order bytes of the four characters `n`, `u`, `l`, `l` are written to the contained output stream.

22.22.10 public void **print**(char[] s) throws NullPointerException

The low-order bytes of the characters in the character array `s` are written, in order, to the contained output stream in exactly the manner of the `write` method (§22.22.3).

If `s` is `null`, a `NullPointerException` is thrown.

22.22.11 public void **print**(boolean b)

The low-order bytes of the characters in the `String` that would be produced by `String.valueOf(b)` (§20.12.41) as a string are written, in order, to the contained output stream in exactly the manner of the `write` method (§22.22.3).

22.22.12 public void **print**(char c)

The low-order byte of the character `c` is written to the contained output stream in exactly the manner of the `write` method (§22.22.3).

22.22.13 public void **print**(int i)

The low-order bytes of the characters in the `String` that would be produced by `String.valueOf(i)` (§20.12.43) as a string are written, in order, to the contained output stream in exactly the manner of the `write` method (§22.22.3).

22.22.14 public void **print**(long l)

The low-order bytes of the characters in the `String` that would be produced by `String.valueOf(l)` (§20.12.44) as a string are written, in order, to the contained output stream in exactly the manner of the `write` method (§22.22.3).

22.22.15 public void **print**(float f)

The low-order bytes of the characters in the `String` that would be produced by `String.valueOf(f)` (§20.12.45) as a string are written, in order, to the contained output stream in exactly the manner of the `write` method (§22.22.3).

22.22.16 public void **print**(double d)

The low-order bytes of the characters in the `String` that would be produced by `String.valueOf(d)` (§20.12.46) as a string are written, in order, to the contained output stream in exactly the manner of the `write` method (§22.22.3).

22.22.17 public void **println**()

The low-order byte of the newline character `'\n'` is written to the contained output stream in exactly the manner of the `write` method (§22.22.3).

22.22.18 public void **println**(Object obj)

This is exactly the same as `print(obj)` (§22.22.8) followed by writing the low-order byte of the newline character `'\n'` to the contained output stream.

22.22.19 public void **println**(String s)

This is exactly the same as `print(s)` (§22.22.9) followed by writing the low-order byte of the newline character `'\n'` to the contained output stream.

22.22.20 `public void` **`println`**`(char[] s) throws NullPointerException`

This is exactly the same as `print(s)` (§22.22.10) followed by writing the low-order byte of the newline character `'\n'` to the contained output stream.

If `s` is `null`, a `NullPointerException` is thrown.

22.22.21 `public void` **`println`**`(boolean b)`

This is exactly the same as `print(b)` (§22.22.11) followed by writing the low-order byte of the newline character `'\n'` to the contained output stream.

22.22.22 `public void` **`println`**`(char c)`

This is exactly the same as `print(c)` (§22.22.12) followed by writing the low-order byte of the newline character `'\n'` to the contained output stream.

22.22.23 `public void` **`println`**`(int i)`

This is exactly the same as `print(i)` (§22.22.13) followed by writing the low-order byte of the newline character `'\n'` to the contained output stream.

22.22.24 `public void` **`println`**`(long l)`

This is exactly the same as `print(l)` (§22.22.14) followed by writing the low-order byte of the newline character `'\n'` to the contained output stream.

22.22.25 `public void` **`println`**`(float f)`

This is exactly the same as `print(f)` (§22.22.15) followed by writing the low-order byte of the newline character `'\n'` to the contained output stream.

22.22.26 `public void` **`println`**`(double d)`

This is exactly the same as `print(d)` (§22.22.16) followed by writing the low-order byte of the newline character `'\n'` to the contained output stream.

22.23 The Class java.io.RandomAccessFile

A random access file behaves like a large array of bytes stored in the file system. There is a kind of cursor, or index into the implied array, called the *file pointer*; input operations read bytes starting at the file pointer and advance the file pointer past the bytes read. If the random access file is created in read/write mode, then output operations are also available; output operations write bytes starting at the file pointer and advance the file pointer past the bytes written. Output operations that write past the current end of the implied array cause the array to be extended. The file pointer can be read by the getFilePointer method and set by the seek method.

```
public class RandomAccessFile implements DataOutput, DataInput {
    public RandomAccessFile(String path, String mode)
        throws SecurityException, IOException,
            IllegalArgumentException;
    public RandomAccessFile(File file, String mode)
        throws SecurityException, IOException,
            IllegalArgumentException;
    public final FileDescriptor getFD() throws IOException;
    public native long getFilePointer() throws IOException;
    public native void seek(long pos) throws IOException;
    public native long length() throws IOException;
    public native void close() throws IOException;
    public native int read() throws IOException;
    public int read(byte[] b)
        throws IOException, NullPointerException;
    public int read(byte[] b, int off, int len)
        throws IOException, NullPointerException,
            IndexOutOfBoundsException;
    // The methods that implement interface DataInput:
    public final void readFully(byte[] b)
        throws IOException, NullPointerException;
    public final void readFully(byte[] b, int off, int len)
        throws IOException, NullPointerException,
            IndexOutOfBoundsException;
    public int skipBytes(int n) throws IOException;
    public final boolean readBoolean() throws IOException;
    public final byte readByte() throws IOException;
    public final int readUnsignedByte() throws IOException;
    public final short readShort() throws IOException;
    public final int readUnsignedShort() throws IOException;
    public final char readChar() throws IOException;
    public final int readInt() throws IOException;
```

```
    public final long readLong() throws IOException;
    public final float readFloat() throws IOException;
    public final double readDouble() throws IOException;
    public final String readLine() throws IOException;
    public final String readUTF() throws IOException;
    // The methods that implement interface DataOutput:
    public native void write(int b) throws IOException;
    public void write(byte[] b)
        throws IOException, NullPointerException;
    public void write(byte[] b, int off, int len)
        throws IOException, NullPointerException,
            IndexOutOfBoundsException;
    public final void writeBoolean(boolean v) throws IOException;
    public final void writeByte(int v) throws IOException;
    public final void writeShort(int v) throws IOException;
    public final void writeChar(int v) throws IOException;
    public final void writeInt(int v) throws IOException;
    public final void writeLong(long v) throws IOException;
    public final void writeFloat(float v) throws IOException;
    public final void writeDouble(double v) throws IOException;
    public final void writeBytes(String s) throws IOException;
    public final void writeChars(String s) throws IOException;
    public final void writeUTF(String str) throws IOException;
}
```

It is generally true of all the reading routines in this class that if end of file is reached before the desired number of bytes has been read, an EOFException (which is a kind of IOException) is thrown. If any byte cannot be read for any reason other than end of file, an IOException other than EOFException is thrown. In particular, an IOException may be thrown if the stream has been closed (§22.23.7).

22.23.1 public RandomAccessFile(String path, String mode) throws SecurityException, IOException, IllegalArgumentException

This constructor initializes a newly created RandomAccessFile by opening a connection to an actual file, the file named by the path name path in the file system. A new FileDescriptor object is created to represent this file connection.

First, if there is a security manager, its checkRead method (§20.17.19) is called with the path argument as its argument.

Next, if mode is "rw" and there is a security manager, its checkWrite method (§20.17.21) is called with the path argument as its argument.

If mode is "rw", then the file may be both read and written. If mode is "r", then the file may be read but may not be written (every write method for this object will simply throw an IOException). If mode is not "r" or "rw", then this constructor throws an IllegalArgumentException.

22.23.2 `public RandomAccessFile(File file, String mode) throws SecurityException, IOException, IllegalArgumentException`

This constructor initializes a newly created RandomAccessFile by opening a connection to an actual file, the file named by file in the file system. A new FileDescriptor object is created to represent this file connection.

First, if there is a security manager, its checkRead method (§20.17.19) is called with the path represented by the file argument as its argument.

Next, if mode is "rw" and there is a security manager, its checkWrite method (§20.17.21) is called with the path represented by the file argument as its argument.

If mode is "rw", then the file may be both read and written. If mode is "r", then the file may be read but may not be written (every write method for this object will simply throw an IOException). If mode is not "r" or "rw", then this constructor throws an IllegalArgumentException.

22.23.3 `public final FileDescriptor getFD() throws IOException`

This method returns the FileDescriptor object (§22.26) that represents the connection to the actual file in the file system being used by this RandomAccessFile.

22.23.4 `public long getFilePointer() throws IOException`

The current file pointer for this random access file is returned. An IOException is thrown if the file pointer cannot be read for any reason.

22.23.5 `public void seek(long pos) throws IOException`

The file pointer for this random access file is set to pos, which is a position within the file, measured in bytes. Position 0 is the start of the file. An IOException is thrown if pos is less than zero or greater than the length of the file, or if the file pointer cannot be set for any other reason.

22.23.6 `public long length() throws IOException`

The length of this random access file, measured in bytes, is returned.

An `IOException` is thrown if the length cannot be read for any reason.

22.23.7 `public void close() throws IOException`

This random access file is closed. A closed random access file cannot perform input or output operations and cannot be reopened.

22.23.8 `public int read() throws IOException`

This method reads one byte from the random access file. The byte is returned as an integer in the range 0 to 255 (`0x00`–`0xff`). If no byte is available because the file pointer is at end of file, the value `-1` is returned.

If the byte cannot be read for any reason other than end of file, an `IOException` is thrown. In particular, an `IOException` is thrown if the input stream has been closed (§22.23.7).

Although `RandomAccessFile` is not a subclass of `InputStream`, this method behaves in exactly the same way as the `read` method of `InputStream` (§22.3.1).

22.23.9 `public int read(byte[] b) throws IOException, NullPointerException`

Although `RandomAccessFile` is not a subclass of `InputStream`, this method behaves in exactly the same way as the `read` method of `InputStream` (§22.3.2).

22.23.10 `public int read(byte[] b, int off, int len) throws IOException, NullPointerException, IndexOutOfBoundsException`

Although `RandomAccessFile` is not a subclass of `InputStream`, this method behaves in exactly the same way as the `read` method of `InputStream` (§22.3.3).

22.23.11 `public final void readFully(byte[] b) throws IOException, NullPointerException`

See the general contract of the `readFully` method of `DataInput` (§22.1.1).

Bytes for this operation are read from the random access file, starting at the current file pointer.

22.23.12 `public final void **readFully**(byte[] b, int off, int len) throws IOException, NullPointerException, IndexOutOfBoundsException`

See the general contract of the `readFully` method of `DataInput` (§22.1.2).

Bytes for this operation are read from the random access file, starting at the current file pointer.

22.23.13 `public int **skipBytes**(int n) throws IOException`

See the general contract of the `skipBytes` method of `DataInput` (§22.1.3).

Bytes for this operation are read from the random access file, starting at the current file pointer.

22.23.14 `public final boolean **readBoolean**() throws IOException`

See the general contract of the `readBoolean` method of `DataInput` (§22.1.4).

The byte for this operation is read from the random access file, starting at the current file pointer.

22.23.15 `public final byte **readByte**() throws IOException`

See the general contract of the `readByte` method of `DataInput` (§22.1.5).

The byte for this operation is read from the random access file, starting at the current file pointer.

22.23.16 `public final int **readUnsignedByte**() throws IOException`

See the general contract of the `readUnsignedByte` method of `DataInput` (§22.1.6).

The byte for this operation is read from the random access file, starting at the current file pointer.

22.23.17 `public final short` **`readShort`**`() throws IOException`

See the general contract of the `readShort` method of `DataInput` (§22.1.7).

Bytes for this operation are read from the random access file, starting at the current file pointer.

22.23.18 `public final int` **`readUnsignedShort`**`() throws IOException`

See the general contract of the `readUnsignedShort` method of `DataInput` (§22.1.8).

Bytes for this operation are read from the random access file, starting at the current file pointer.

22.23.19 `public final char` **`readChar`**`() throws IOException`

See the general contract of the `readChar` method of `DataInput` (§22.1.9).

Bytes for this operation are read from the random access file, starting at the current file pointer.

22.23.20 `public final int` **`readInt`**`() throws IOException`

See the general contract of the `readInt` method of `DataInput` (§22.1.10).

Bytes for this operation are read from the random access file, starting at the current file pointer.

22.23.21 `public final long` **`readLong`**`() throws IOException`

See the general contract of the `readLong` method of `DataInput` (§22.1.11).

Bytes for this operation are read from the random access file, starting at the current file pointer.

22.23.22 `public final float` **`readFloat`**`() throws IOException`

See the general contract of the `readFloat` method of `DataInput` (§22.1.12).

Bytes for this operation are read from the random access file, starting at the current file pointer.

22.23.23 `public final double readDouble() throws IOException`

See the general contract of the `readDouble` method of `DataInput` (§22.1.13).

Bytes for this operation are read from the random access file, starting at the current file pointer.

22.23.24 `public final String readLine() throws IOException`

See the general contract of the `readLine` method of `DataInput` (§22.1.14).

Bytes for this operation are read from the random access file, starting at the current file pointer.

22.23.25 `public final String readUTF() throws IOException`

See the general contract of the `readUTF` method of `DataInput` (§22.1.15).

Bytes for this operation are read from the random access file, starting at the current file pointer.

22.23.26 `public void write(int b) throws IOException;`

See the general contract of the `write` method of `DataOutput` (§22.2.1).

The byte for this operation is written to the random access file, starting at the current file pointer.

22.23.27
```
public void write(byte[] b)
    throws IOException, NullPointerException
```

See the general contract of the `write` method of `DataOutput` (§22.2.2).

Bytes for this operation are written to the random access file, starting at the current file pointer.

22.23.28
```
public void write(byte[] b, int off, int len)
    throws IOException, NullPointerException,
        IndexOutOfBoundsException
```

See the general contract of the `write` method of `DataOutput` (§22.2.3).

Bytes for this operation are written to the random access file, starting at the current file pointer.

22.23.29 `public final void writeBoolean(boolean v) throws IOException`

See the general contract of the `writeBoolean` method of `DataOutput` (§22.2.4).

The byte for this operation is written to the random access file, starting at the current file pointer.

22.23.30 `public final void writeByte(int v) throws IOException`

See the general contract of the `writeByte` method of `DataOutput` (§22.2.5).

The byte for this operation is written to the random access file, starting at the current file pointer.

22.23.31 `public final void writeShort(int v) throws IOException`

See the general contract of the `writeShort` method of `DataOutput` (§22.2.6).

Bytes for this operation are written to the random access file, starting at the current file pointer.

22.23.32 `public final void writeChar(int v) throws IOException`

See the general contract of the `writeChar` method of `DataOutput` (§22.2.7).

Bytes for this operation are written to the random access file, starting at the current file pointer.

22.23.33 `public final void writeInt(int v) throws IOException`

See the general contract of the `writeInt` method of `DataOutput` (§22.2.8).

Bytes for this operation are written to the random access file, starting at the current file pointer.

22.23.34 `public final void writeLong(long v) throws IOException`

See the general contract of the `writeLong` method of `DataOutput` (§22.2.9).

Bytes for this operation are written to the random access file, starting at the current file pointer.

22.23.35 `public final void writeFloat(float v) throws IOException`

See the general contract of the `writeFloat` method of `DataOutput` (§22.2.10).

Bytes for this operation are written to the random access file, starting at the current file pointer.

22.23.36 `public final void writeDouble(double v)`
`throws IOException`

See the general contract of the `writeDouble` method of `DataOutput` (§22.2.11).

Bytes for this operation are written to the random access file, starting at the current file pointer.

22.23.37 `public final void writeBytes(String s) throws IOException`

See the general contract of the `writeBytes` method of `DataOutput` (§22.2.12).

Bytes for this operation are written to the random access file, starting at the current file pointer.

22.23.38 `public final void writeChars(String s) throws IOException`

See the general contract of the `writeChars` method of `DataOutput` (§22.2.13).

Bytes for this operation are written to the random access file, starting at the current file pointer.

22.23.39 `public final void writeUTF(String str) throws IOException`

See the general contract of the `writeUTF` method of `DataOutput` (§22.2.14).

Bytes for this operation are written to the random access file, starting at the current file pointer.

22.24 The Class `java.io.File`

A `File` object contains a *path*, which is a character string that can be used to identify a file within a file system. A path is assumed to consist of two parts, the *directory* and the *file name*, separated by the last occurrence within the path of a particular character known as the *separator character*. Some methods provide access to parts of the path string; other methods operate on the file that is identified by the path string. The details of such operations on files are to some extent dependent on the implementation of the host file system. The `File` class is designed to provide a set of abstract operations that are reasonably portable across otherwise incompatible file systems.

```
public class File {
    public static final String separator =
        System.getProperty("file.separator");
    public static final char separatorChar =
        separator.charAt(0);
    public static final String pathSeparator =
        System.getProperty("path.separator");
    public static final char pathSeparatorChar =
        pathSeparator.charAt(0);
    public File(String path) throws NullPointerException;
    public File(String dirname, String name)
        throws NullPointerException
    public File(File dir, String name)
        throws NullPointerException
    public String toString();
    public boolean equals(Object obj);
    public int hashCode();
    public String getName();
    public String getPath();
    public String getAbsolutePath();
    public String getParent();
    public native boolean isAbsolute();
    public boolean exists() throws SecurityException;
    public boolean canRead() throws SecurityException;
    public boolean canWrite() throws SecurityException;
    public boolean isFile() throws SecurityException;
    public boolean isDirectory() throws SecurityException;
    public long lastModified() throws SecurityException;
    public long length() throws SecurityException;
    public boolean mkdir() throws SecurityException;
    public boolean mkdirs() throws SecurityException;
    public String[] list() throws SecurityException;
```

```
    public String[] list(FilenameFilter filter)
        throws SecurityException;
    public boolean renameTo(File dest) throws SecurityException;
    public boolean delete() throws SecurityException;
}
```

22.24.1 `public static final String separator =
System.getProperty("file.separator");`

This string should consist of a single character, whose value is also available in the field separatorChar; the string is provided merely for convenience.

22.24.2 `public static final char separatorChar =
separator.charAt(0);`

The last occurrence of this character in a path string is assumed to separate the directory part of the path from the file name part of the path. On UNIX systems this character is typically '/'.

22.24.3 `public static final String pathSeparator =
System.getProperty("path.separator");`

This string should consist of a single character, whose value is also available in the field pathSeparatorChar; the string is provided merely for convenience.

22.24.4 `public static final char pathSeparatorChar =
pathSeparator.charAt(0);`

The first occurrence of this character in a string is sometimes assumed to separate a host name from a path name. On UNIX systems this character is typically ':'.

22.24.5 `public File(String path) throws NullPointerException`

This constructor initializes a newly created File so that it represents the path indicated by the argument path.

If the path is null, a NullPointerException is thrown.

22.24.6 `public File(String dirname, String name) throws NullPointerException`

This constructor initializes a newly created `File` so that it represents the path whose directory part is specified by the argument `dirname` and whose file name part is specified by the argument `name`. If the `dirname` argument is `null`, the `name` is used as the path; otherwise the concatenation of `dirname`, the `separatorChar` (§22.24.2), and the `name` is used as the path.

If the `name` is `null`, a `NullPointerException` is thrown.

22.24.7 `public File(File dir, String name) throws NullPointerException`

This constructor initializes a newly created `File` so that it represents the path whose directory part is specified by the `File` object `dir` and whose file name part is specified by the argument `name`.

If the `name` is `null`, a `NullPointerException` is thrown.

22.24.8 `public String toString()`

The result is a `String` equal to the path represented by this `File` object.

Overrides the `toString` method of `Object` (§20.1.2).

22.24.9 `public boolean equals(Object obj)`

The result is `true` if and only if the argument is not `null` and is a `File` object that represents the same path as this `File` object. In other words, two `File` objects are equal if and only if the strings returned by the `getPath` method (§22.24.12) are equal.

Overrides the `equals` method of `Object` (§20.1.3).

22.24.10 `public int hashCode()`

The hash code of this `File` object is equal to the exclusive OR of the hash code of its path string and the decimal value `1234321`:

```
this.getPath().hashcode() ^ 1234321
```

Overrides the `hashCode` method of `Object` (§20.1.4).

22.24.11 `public String getName()`

If the path string contains the `separatorChar` character (§22.24.2), this method returns the substring of the path that follows the last occurrence of the separator character; otherwise, the entire path string is returned.

22.24.12 `public String getPath()`

The result is a `String` equal to the path represented by this `File` object.

22.24.13 `public String getAbsolutePath()`

The result is a `String` equal to the result of converting to "absolute form" the path represented by this `File` object.

22.24.14 `public String getParent()`

If the path has a parent directory, a `String` representing the path of that parent directory is returned; otherwise, `null` is returned.

22.24.15 `public boolean isAbsolute()`

The result is `true` if and only if the path represented by the File object is in absolute form, indicating a complete name that starts from the root of the directory hierarchy, rather than a name relative to some implied directory.

22.24.16 `public boolean exists() throws SecurityException`

First, if there is a security manager, its `checkRead` method (§20.17.19) is called with the path represented by this `File` object as its argument.

The result is `true` if and only if the file system actually contains a file that is specified by the path of the `File` object.

22.24.17 `public boolean canRead() throws SecurityException`

First, if there is a security manager, its `checkRead` method (§20.17.19) is called with the path represented by this `File` object as its argument.

The result is `true` if and only if both of the following are true:

- The file system actually contains a file specified by the path of the `File` object.
- The file so specified can be read.

22.24.18 `public boolean canWrite() throws SecurityException`

First, if there is a security manager, its `checkWrite` method (§20.17.21) is called with the path represented by this `File` object as its argument.

The result is `true` if and only if both of the following are true:

- The file system actually contains a file specified by the path of the `File` object.
- The file so specified can be written.

22.24.19 `public boolean isFile() throws SecurityException`

First, if there is a security manager, its `checkRead` method (§20.17.19) is called with the path represented by this `File` object as its argument.

The result is `true` if and only if both of the following are true:

- The file system actually contains a file specified by the path of the `File` object.
- The file so specified is a data file rather than a directory.

22.24.20 `public boolean isDirectory() throws SecurityException`

First, if there is a security manager, its `checkRead` method (§20.17.19) is called with the path represented by this `File` object as its argument.

The result is `true` if and only if both of the following are true:

- The file system actually contains a file specified by the path of the `File` object.
- The file so specified is a directory rather than a data file.

22.24.21 `public long lastModified() throws SecurityException`

First, if there is a security manager, its `checkRead` method (§20.17.19) is called with the path represented by this `File` object as its argument.

An abstract modification time is returned. If two values returned by this method are compared, whether for the same file or for two different files, the smaller value represents an earlier modification time. Abstract modification times do not necessarily bear any relationship, even monotonicity, to times returned by the method `System.currentTimeMillis` (§20.18.6).

22.24.22 `public long length() throws SecurityException`

First, if there is a security manager, its `checkRead` method (§20.17.19) is called with the path represented by this `File` object as its argument.

The length of the file, measured in bytes, is returned.

22.24.23 `public boolean mkdir() throws SecurityException`

First, if there is a security manager, its `checkWrite` method (§20.17.21) is called with the path represented by this `File` object as its argument.

An attempt is made to create the directory specified by the path represented by this `File` object; the result is true if and only if the creation operation succeeds.

22.24.24 `public boolean mkdirs() throws SecurityException`

First, if there is a security manager, its `checkRead` method (§20.17.19) is called with the path represented by this `File` object as its argument.

If the directory name represented by this `File` object has a parent directory name (§22.24.14), an attempt is first made to create the parent directory; if this attempt fails, the result is `false`. Otherwise, once the parent directory has been determined to exist, or if the path has no parent, an attempt is made to create the directory specified by this `File` object. The result is `true` if and only if the creation operation succeeds.

22.24.25 `public String[] list() throws SecurityException`

First, if there is a security manager, its `checkRead` method (§20.17.19) is called with the path represented by this `File` object as its argument.

If the path represented by this `File` object does not correspond to a directory in the file system, then `null` is returned. Otherwise, an array of strings is returned, one for each file in the directory (on UNIX systems, the names "`.`" and "`..`" are not included). Each string is a file name, not a complete path. There is no guarantee that the strings will appear in any particular order within the array; for example, they are not guaranteed to appear in alphabetical order.

22.24.26 `public String[] list(FilenameFilter filter) throws SecurityException`

First, if there is a security manager, its `checkRead` method (§20.17.19) is called with the path represented by this `File` object as its argument.

If the path represented by this `File` object does not correspond to a directory in the file system, then `null` is returned. Otherwise, an array of strings is returned, one for each file in the directory (on UNIX systems, the names "`.`" and "`..`" are not included) whose name satisfies the given `filter`. Each string is a file name, not a complete path. There is no guarantee that the strings will appear in any particular order within the array; for example, they are not guaranteed to appear in alphabetical order. A file name satisfies the filter if and only if the value `true` results when the `accept` method (§22.25.1) of the filter is called with this `File` object and the name as arguments.

22.24.27 `public boolean renameTo(File dest) throws SecurityException`

First, if there is a security manager, its `checkWrite` method (§20.17.21) is called twice, first with the path represented by this `File` object as its argument and again with the path of `dest` as its argument.

An attempt is made to rename the file specified by the path represented by this `File` object to the name specified by `dest`; the result is `true` if and only if the renaming operation succeeds.

22.24.28 `public boolean delete() throws SecurityException`

First, if there is a security manager, its `checkDelete` method (§20.17.22) is called with the path represented by this `File` object as its argument.

An attempt is made to delete the file specified by the path represented by this `File` object; the result is `true` if and only if the deletion operation succeeds.

22.25 The Interface `java.io.FilenameFilter`

The `list` method (§22.24.26) of class `File` requires, as an argument, an object that implements the `FilenameFilter` interface. The only purpose of such an object is to provide a method `accept` that decides which files should appear in the generated directory listing.

```
public interface FilenameFilter {
   public boolean accept(File dir, String name);
}
```

22.25.1 `public boolean accept(File dir, String name)`

This method should return `true` if and only if the given file named `name` in the directory `dir` is to appear in the final list of files generated by the `list` method (§22.24.26) of class `File`.

22.26 The Class java.io.FileDescriptor

A FileDescriptor is an opaque representation of a connection to an actual file in a file system, or to a network socket, or to another source or sink of bytes. The main practical use for a file descriptor is to create a FileInputStream (§22.4.3) or FileOutputStream (§22.16.3) to contain it.

```
public final class FileDescriptor {
    public static final FileDescriptor in = ...;
    public static final FileDescriptor out = ...;
    public static final FileDescriptor err = ...;
    public boolean valid();
}
```

22.26.1 public static final FileDescriptor in = ...

A file descriptor for the standard input stream. Usually, this file descriptor is not used directly, but rather the input stream known as System.in (§20.18.1).

22.26.2 public static final FileDescriptor out = ...

A file descriptor for the standard output stream. Usually, this file descriptor is not used directly, but rather the output stream known as System.out (§20.18.2).

22.26.3 public static final FileDescriptor err = ...

A file descriptor for the standard error output stream. Usually, this file descriptor is not used directly, but rather the output stream known as System.err (§20.18.3).

22.26.4 public boolean valid()

If this FileDescriptor is valid (represents an active connection to a file or other active I/O connection), then the result is true. Otherwise, the result is false.

22.27 The Class `java.io.IOException`

The class `IOException` is the general class of exceptions produced by failed or interrupted input/output operations. Subclasses of `IOException` include:

```
EOFException
FileNotFoundException
InterruptedIOException
UTFDataFormatException
```

```
public class IOException extends Exception {
    public IOException();
    public IOException(String s);
}
```

22.27.1 `public IOException()`

This constructor initializes a newly created `IOException` with `null` as its error message string.

22.27.2 `public IOException(String s)`

This constructor initializes a newly created `IOException` by saving a reference to the error message string `s` for later retrieval by the `getMessage` method (§20.22.3).

22.28 The Class `java.io.EOFException`

An `EOFException` is thrown to indicate that an input operation has encountered end of file. Note that some Java input operations react to end of file by returning a distinguished value (such as `-1`) rather than by throwing an exception.

```
public class EOFException extends IOException {
    public EOFException();
    public EOFException(String s);
}
```

22.28.1 `public EOFException()`

This constructor initializes a newly created `EOFException` with `null` as its error message string.

22.28.2 `public EOFException(String s)`

This constructor initializes a newly created `EOFException` by saving a reference to the error message string `s` for later retrieval by the `getMessage` method (§20.22.3).

22.29 The Class `java.io.FileNotFoundException`

A `FileNotFoundException` is thrown to indicate that no actual file could be opened for a specified path name. See constructors `FileInputStream` (§22.4.1, §22.4.2) and `FileOutputStream` (§22.16.1, §22.16.2).

```
public class FileNotFoundException extends IOException {
    public FileNotFoundException();
    public FileNotFoundException(String s);
}
```

22.29.1 `public FileNotFoundException()`

This constructor initializes a newly created `FileNotFoundException` with `null` as its error message string.

22.29.2 `public FileNotFoundException(String s)`

This constructor initializes a newly created `FileNotFoundException` by saving a reference to the error message string `s` for later retrieval by the `getMessage` method (§20.22.3).

22.30 The Class java.io.InterruptedIOException

An InterruptedIOException is thrown to indicate that an input or output transfer has been terminated because the thread performing it was interrupted. The field bytesTransferred indicates how many bytes were successfully transferred before the interruption occurred.

```
public class InterruptedIOException extends IOException {
    public int bytesTransferred = 0;
    public InterruptedIOException();
    public InterruptedIOException(String s);
}
```

22.30.1 public int bytesTransferred = 0;

The number of bytes that had been transferred by the I/O operation before the operation was interrupted.

22.30.2 public InterruptedIOException()

This constructor initializes a newly created InterruptedIOException with null as its error message string.

22.30.3 public InterruptedIOException(String s)

This constructor initializes a newly created InterruptedIOException by saving a reference to the error message string s for later retrieval by the getMessage method (§20.22.3).

22.31 The Class `java.io.UTFDataFormatException`

A `UTFDataFormatException` is thrown to indicate that a problem occurred in converting data from Java modified UTF-8 format. See method `readUTF` of `DataInput` (§22.1.15).

```
public class UTFDataFormatException extends IOException {
   public UTFDataFormatException();
   public UTFDataFormatException(String s);
}
```

22.31.1 `public UTFDataFormatException()`

This constructor initializes a newly created `UTFDataFormatException` with `null` as its error message string.

22.31.2 `public UTFDataFormatException(String s)`

This constructor initializes a newly created `UTFDataFormatException` by saving a reference to the error message string `s` for later retrieval by the `getMessage` method (§20.22.3).

Index

B

C

H

I

J

U

Credits

THE following organizations and copyright holders granted permission for quotations used in this book.

Colophon

CAMERA-READY electronic copy for this book was prepared by the authors using FrameMaker (release 5) on Sun workstations.

The body type is Times, set 11 on 13. Chapter titles, section titles, quotations, and running heads are also in Times, in various sizes, weights, and styles. The index is set 9 on 10.

Some of the bullets used in bulleted lists are taken from Zapf Dingbats. Greek and mathematical symbols are taken from the Symbol typeface.

The monospace typeface used for program code in both displays and running text is Lucida Sans Typewriter; for code fragments in chapter titles, section titles, and first-level index entries, Lucida Sans Typewriter Bold is used. In every case it is set at 85% of the nominal size of the surrounding Times text; for example, in the body it is 85% of 11 point.

This book was printed by Maple-Vail Book Manufacturing Group at their York, Pennsylvania, facility on 45# Restorecote.

Learning hath gained most by those books by which the printers have lost.
—Thomas Fuller (1608–1661), *Of Books*

Some said, "John, print it"; others said, "Not so."
Some said, "It might do good"; others said, "No."
—John Bunyan (1628–1688), *Pilgrim's Progress—Apology for his Book*

'T is pleasant, sure, to see one's name in print;
A book's a book, although there's nothing in 't.
—Lord Byron (1788–1824)